GENDER, SEXUALITY AND CONSTITUTIONALISM IN ASIA

This book analyses the equal citizenship claims of women and sexual and gender diverse people across several Asian jurisdictions. The volume examines the rich diversity of constitutional responses to sex, gender and sexuality in the region from a comparative perspective. Leading comparative constitutional law scholars identify 'opportunity structures' to explain the uneven advancement of gender equality through constitutional litigation and consider a combination of variables which shape the diverging trajectories of the jurisdictions in this study.

The authors also embed the relevant constitutional and legal developments in their historical, political and social contexts. This deep contextual understanding of the relationship between sex, gender, sexuality and constitutionalism greatly enriches the analysis. The case studies reflect a variety of constitutional structures, institutional designs and contextual dynamics which may advance or impede developments with respect to sex, gender and sexuality. As a whole, the chapters further an understanding of the constitutional domain as a fruitful site for advancing gender equality and the rights of sexual and gender diverse people.

The jurisdictions covered represent all Asian sub-regions including: East Asia (Japan, Taiwan, Hong Kong and South Korea), Southeast Asia (Malaysia, Singapore, Philippines and Indonesia), and South Asia (India, Nepal, Pakistan and Sri Lanka). The introductory framework chapter situates these insights from the region within the broader global context of the evolution of gender constitutionalism.

Constitutionalism in Asia series

unesco

NUS National University of Singapore | Centre for Asian Legal Studies Faculty of Law

Gender, Sexuality and Constitutionalism in Asia

Edited by
Wen-Chen Chang
Kelley Loper
Mara Malagodi
and
Ruth Rubio-Marín

•HART•
OXFORD • LONDON • NEW YORK • NEW DELHI • SYDNEY

HART PUBLISHING

Bloomsbury Publishing Plc

Kemp House, Chawley Park, Cumnor Hill, Oxford, OX2 9PH, UK

1385 Broadway, New York, NY 10018, USA

29 Earlsfort Terrace, Dublin 2, Ireland

HART PUBLISHING, the Hart/Stag logo, BLOOMSBURY and the Diana logo are trademarks of Bloomsbury Publishing Plc

First published in Great Britain 2024

A catalogue record for this book is available from the British Library.

A catalogue record for this book is available from the Library of Congress.

Library of Congress Control Number: 2023944349

ISBN: HB: 978-1-50994-191-9
ePDF: 978-1-50994-193-3
ePub: 978-1-50994-192-6

Typeset by Compuscript Ltd, Shannon

Acknowledgements

COMPARATIVE STUDY, BY its very nature, requires collaboration and reciprocity. While putting this volume together, we have benefited much more than we ever could give back. To prepare the manuscript, we held two conferences. The first was hosted by the University of Hong Kong's Faculty of Law and Centre for Comparative and Public Law in mid-January 2019. The second was held in December 2019 in Hsinchu, Taiwan, by the School of Law, National Chiao Tung University, which became National Yang Ming Chiao Tung University in February 2021. We are extremely grateful to both institutions for their generous financial and administrative support. The first conference was designed as a scoping exercise to identify suitable case studies along various axes of contextual dynamics, constitutional architectures and cultures in which the development of constitutionalism can be assessed for its attention to gender equality. At the second conference, the authors presented and discussed their draft chapters, followed by rounds of editorial comments and revisions.

However, when the COVID-19 pandemic hit, like many people around the world, those involved in this project had a difficult time balancing work, caretaking roles and other responsibilities. Some of us have lost loved ones. As editors of a book on gender constitutionalism, we felt strongly that a gender-sensitive approach and supportive attitude were essential to the successful completion of this volume. Even though this created delays and required updates along the way, we have stood firm in our gender-friendly academic collegiality. We could not be more grateful to the authors for their patience and invaluable contributions and to our publisher for their generous support. Last but not least, we would like to give special thanks to Ms You-Jhen Huang at the National Yang Ming Chiao Tung University School of Law and Dr Pei-Jung Li at the National Taiwan University College of Law. We could not have completed this book project without their superb assistance and meticulous editorial efforts.

Contents

List of Contributors

Cristóbal ALVEAR-GARIJO is a doctoral candidate in Constitutional Law at the Universidad de Sevilla. He completed his LLM at the Universidad Pablo de Olavide, obtained a master's degree in IR from the Diplomatic School of Spain, and has been lecturer on Asian legal systems at IE Law School. He has developed his career in India, Pakistan and Malaysia, and he is currently the director of the Spain–India Observatory and a board member of AEEII. His areas of interest include the impact of intersectionality, counter-majoritarianism and the role of courts on sexual diversity and gender identity rights.

Shreya ATREY is Associate Professor in International Human Rights Law based at the Bonavero Institute of Human Rights at the University of Oxford. She is an Editor for the *Human Rights Law Review* and an Official Fellow of Kellogg College. She completed BCL with distinction and DPhil in Law on the Rhodes Scholarship from Magdalen College, University of Oxford. Her research is on discrimination law, feminist theory, poverty and disability law.

Sadaf AZIZ is the Dean and Associate Professor at the Shaikh Ahmad Hassan School of Law, LUMS. She has studied law at UBC, economic history at the LSE and has completed her PhD in Law from the University of Melbourne. She is the author of the book *The Pakistani Constitution; A Contextual Analysis*, and has published articles and chapters focused on gender and constitutionalism, constitutional foundations, and the interface of liberal and non-liberal legal orders. Her current book project is a study of the early post-Partition Pakistani state.

Gautam BHATIA is a practising lawyer based in New Delhi, India. He attained his LLB from National Law School of India University, and went on to pursue a BCL and MPhil from Balliol College, University of Oxford as a Rhodes Scholar. Subsequently, he received a LLM from Yale University, specialising in constitutional law, and attained DPhil at University of Oxford. He is presently working on a power-based analysis of the Indian Constitution.

Simon BUTT is Professor of Indonesian Law and Director of the Centre for Asian and Pacific Law, University of Sydney, Australia. He also serves on the Executive of the Sydney Southeast Asia Centre (SSEAC). Fluent in Indonesian, he has consulted on Indonesian law to the private and public sectors, and has provided advice and expert opinions about Indonesian law for litigation in the United States, United Kingdom, Hong Kong, Singapore and Australia.

Wen-Chen CHANG is Distinguished Professor of National Taiwan University College of Law and Joint-Appointment Professor at National Yang Ming Chiao Tung University School of Law. She serves in the editorial boards of the

International Journal of Constitutional Law, *Cambridge Journal of Global Constitutionalism* and *Asian Journal of Comparative Law*. She has received numerous awards for her teaching and research including most recently the Excellence in English Teaching Award from National Taiwan University in 2021 and the Outstanding Research Award by Taiwan's Ministry of Science and Technology in 2015. Her teaching and research interests lie in comparative constitutional law, international human rights, administrative laws, and law and society.

Akiko EJIMA is Professor of Constitutional Law at the School of Law, Meiji University, Japan and a member of the Executive Committee of the International Association of Constitutional Law. She attained her LLM in Law & Doctor of Law degree from Meiji University. Her areas of interest include the multilayered human rights protection system combining constitutional law and international human rights law, circulatory constitutionalism, constitution-building, judicial dialogue, AI and human rights.

Mario GOMEZ is the Executive Director at the International Centre for Ethnic Studies, an independent think-tank in Sri Lanka. He has a doctorate in law and has worked in academia, human rights and peacebuilding. He has published in the areas of public law, human rights, gender equality and transitional justice.

Kelley LOPER is Associate Professor, the Director of the LLM in Human Rights Programme, and Co-Editor-in-Chief of the *Asia-Pacific Journal on Human Rights and the Law* in the Faculty of Law at the University of Hong Kong. She also sits on the advisory board of the Berkeley Center on Comparative Equality and Anti-discrimination Law. Her work centres on comparative equality law and the implementation of international human rights law in domestic contexts, especially Hong Kong.

Mara MALAGODI is Reader in Law at the School of Law of the University of Warwick, a non-practising barrister in England and Wales, a scholar of the Honourable Society of the Middle Temple, and an award-winning documentary filmmaker. She is a leading comparative constitutional lawyer and a socio-legal scholar with a linguistically informed expertise in South Asian law and politics (in particular Nepal, India and Pakistan), human rights law, legal history, law and film, and comparative politics.

Angbeen Atif MIRZA is Assistant Professor at the Shaikh Ahmad Hassan School of Law, LUMS. She holds a BA, LLB from LUMS, and an LLM from the University of Michigan Law School. She served as the inaugural Faculty Director for the LUMS Office of Accessibility and Inclusion. She is involved in human rights work in various capacities. Her primary area of interest lies in clinical legal education, specifically street law, live client clinics and access to justice work.

Jaclyn L NEO is Associate Professor of Law at the National University of Singapore, and presently the Director of the Centre for Asian Legal Studies. A graduate of NUS Faculty of Law and the Yale Law School, she is a recipient of multiple academic scholarships from the Singapore Ministry of Education and the National University of Singapore. Her research focuses on comparative constitutional law, law and religion in Asia, as well as access to justice in Singapore.

Ruth RUBIO-MARÍN is Professor of Constitutional Law at the University of Sevilla in Spain, and head of the Gender and Governance programme of the School of Transnational Governance at the European University Institute in Florence. She is also a member of the Faculty of The Hauser Global Law School Program at New York University and Director of the UNIA UNESCO Chair in Human Rights and Interculturalism. Among the courses she has offered around the world are Gender in the Constitution; Comparative Constitutional Law; Law and Culture; Gender and Human Rights; Citizenship and Immigration; and Transitional Justice. Her research represents an attempt to understand how public law creates categories of inclusion and exclusion around different axis including gender, citizenship, nationality and ethnicity. Methodologically, she combines law and political theory. Her latest books are *Global Gender Constitutionalism and Women's Citizenship: A Struggle for Transformative Inclusion* (Cambridge University Press, 2022) and *The Cambridge Companion on Law and Gender* (with S Hennette-Vauchez, eds) (Cambridge University Press, 2023).

Dian AH SHAH is Assistant Professor of Law at the National University of Singapore. She completed her LLM and SJD degrees at Duke University Law School, and prior to that she graduated with an LLB from Warwick University. Her research interests span the fields of law and religion, comparative constitutional law and human rights. Her work focuses on the interaction of law and politics in Asia's divided societies and Asian democracies.

Yoon Jin SHIN is Associate Professor of Seoul National University School of Law, South Korea. She received her LLB, *summa cum laude*, at Seoul National University and served as a judge in South Korea before she studied at Yale Law School for her LLM and JSD degrees. Her areas of interest include human rights, transnational law, global constitutionalism, democracy and minorities' rights, and gender and law.

Bryan Dennis G TIOJANCO is Project Associate Professor at the University of Tokyo's Graduate Schools for Law and Politics. He obtained his Doctor of the Science of Law and Master of Laws degrees from Yale Law School, and his Juris Doctor degree from the University of the Philippines College of Law. He is also a member of the Integrated Bar of the Philippines. His areas of interest include comparative constitutional law and democratic theory, law and the formation of transnational East Asia, transnational law and political economy, and Philippine constitutional law.

Daryl WJ YANG is a practising lawyer in Singapore and a member of the editorial board of Berkeley Law's *Comparative Equality* blog. He obtained his LLB and BA (Liberal Arts) from the National University of Singapore and Yale–NUS College as a proud graduate of its Double Degree Programme before pursuing an LLM at the University of California, Berkeley as a Fulbright scholar. His areas of interest include feminist, queer and disability legal studies, comparative constitutional and equality law, and law and social movements.

1

Gender Constitutionalism in Asia: A Comparative Framework

RUTH RUBIO-MARÍN, WEN-CHEN CHANG,
MARA MALAGODI AND KELLEY LOPER

I. REMIT AND GOALS OF GENDER CONSTITUTIONALISM

CONSTITUTIONS ARE NOT neutral with respect to sex, gender or sexuality. The modern constitutional project is defined, rather, by a specific gender order: one premised on patriarchal and heteronormative gender roles as intrinsic to the political system it configures. Feminist constitutional law scholarship has confirmed this line of analysis, especially since the late twentieth century. In fact, such scholarship has demonstrated that to overcome deep gender bias entrenched in the practice and discipline of constitutional law, it is insufficient merely to add women and sexual and gender diverse people (SGDP) to the domain of constitutional subjectivity, for instance by expanding their rights. Rather, for constitutional law to become a transformative tool in the struggle for gender justice a more radical approach is necessary. The resulting work on gender constitutionalism has included an analysis of central concepts and assumptions underlying mainstream constitutional theories and a systematisation of evolving trends, but also of persistent textual and doctrinal differences. It has required the identification of 'opportunity structures' as crafted by constitutional moments and constitutional instruments, and as compared to other emancipatory venues. Ultimately, it has demanded forming strategic alliances and repositories of inspiration to render constitutional texts gender-responsive, as well as reflective of international best practice and transnational social movements for gender equality.

Gender constitutionalism has thus become a bourgeoning research domain within comparative constitutional law since the turn of the century.[1] At the same

[1] See, eg, B Baines and R Rubio-Marín (eds), *The Gender of Constitutional Jurisprudence* (Cambridge University Press, 2004); H Irving, *Gender and the Constitution: Equity and Agency in Comparative Constitutional Design* (Cambridge University Press, 2008); SH Williams (ed), *Constituting Equality: Gender Equality and Comparative Constitutional Law* (Cambridge University

time, recent decades have witnessed increased activism from women and SGDP, fighting for equal citizenship on the battlefield of constitutionalism broadly defined. In doing so, they have drawn inspiration from abroad and sought the high politics of constitutionalism as a venue for status recognition. And as constitutions have become a vessel for gender innovation and international normative standards, international organisations (including UN Women) have developed guidelines for advancing gender equality in the constitutional sphere.[2]

There is now also a global network of researchers working on gender constitutionalism, producing cutting-edge scholarship in this area, and encouraging a new generation of academics – many of whom are women and SGDP – to engage without the fear of disciplinary ostracism. Existing scholarship, however, especially work with comparative ambitions, has an overrepresentation of academics from (and focusing on) the Anglo-American legal world and, to a lesser extent, continental Europe. Indeed, as Rosalind Dixon and Tom Ginsburg note, there is still a tendency in the newly revitalised field of comparative constitutional law for North America and Europe to dictate the agenda.[3] With the exception of some Asian jurisdictions such as India or Japan that have garnered attention in more recent comparative literature – sometimes in a rather tokenistic way – references to Asian case studies remain rare and unsystematic. This is despite the fact that a number of these jurisdictions have produced some of the most ground-breaking decisions in key areas of gender constitutionalism. This includes, for example, Nepal on abortion, India and Pakistan on third gender, and Taiwan on constitutional recognition of same-sex marriage, among others. There have been, to date, few attempts to invite East–West discussions on this subject matter in comparative constitutional projects.[4] In this respect, this book's emphasis on Asia contributes to recent efforts in comparative constitutional law to make the field less centred on the Global North. The underlying hope is that enhancing the visibility of the relevance of Asian constitutionalism and rendering it accessible to the rest of the world might help prevent Western standards from being unduly taken to represent universal standards and that best practices are drawn from a wider pool of case studies and regions.

Press, 2009); B Baines, D Barak-Erez and T Kahana (eds), *Feminist Constitutionalism: Global Perspectives* (Cambridge University Press, 2012); H Irving (ed), *Constitutions and Gender* (Edward Elgar, 2017); R Rubio-Marín and H Irving (eds), *Women as Constitution Makers: Case Studies from the New Democratic Era* (Cambridge University Press, 2019); R Rubio-Marín, *Global Gender Constitutionalism and Women's Citizenship: A Struggle for Transformative Inclusion* (Cambridge University Press, 2022).

[2] See, eg, UN Women Global Gender Equality Constitutional Database, available at constitutions.unwomen.org/en.

[3] R Dixon and T Ginsburg, 'Introduction' in R Dixon and T Ginsburg (eds), *Comparative Constitutional Law in Asia* (Edward Elgar, 2014) 1.

[4] For some exceptions, see R Rubio-Marín and WC Chang, 'Sites of Constitutional Struggle for Women's Equality' in M Tushnet, T Fleiner and C Saunders (eds), *Routledge Handbook of Constitutional Law* (Routledge, 2013); Rubio-Marín, *Global Gender Constitutionalism and Women's Citizenship* (n 1).

Regional evolutions, and not only a desire to overcome a pattern of neglect, certainly justify this emphasis. Ever since Japan adopted Asia's first national Constitution in 1889, the Asian continent has been home to vibrant constitutional discourses, as indigenous elites have sought to fuse Western institutional forms with the grand East Asian legal and political traditions. Furthermore, Asian jurisdictions have developed increasingly innovative constitutional practices in the early twenty-first century, with written constitutions being the norm and a growing number of constitutional courts spreading through the region and contributing to the major social and political questions in the field.[5] It is time for comparative constitutionalism to extend its reach to Asia where innovative lessons can be learned on the relationship between constitutional law and the contextual dynamics of gender and sexuality.

This volume aims to assess the potential of gender constitutionalism, including constitutional texts, structures and processes, to affirm and sustain the equal citizenship of women and SGDP in Asia. To do so, scholars from 12 representative jurisdictions across Asia have evaluated the manner in which the constitutional domain in its broader socio-political context has provided – or failed to provide – 'opportunity structures' to advance the claims of women and SGDP. More specifically, authors have assessed how constitutional texts, constitutional institutions and the doctrines developed by constitutional courts have helped to sustain or subvert the existing patriarchal and heteronormative gender order. These 'opportunity structures' include relevant constitutional provisions and case law concerning, but not limited to, political equality and citizenship status, gender identity and sexuality, reproductive autonomy and justice, the distribution of care roles within the family, competing notions of the family and marriage, life free of violence and socio-economic inequality.

Beyond providing a constitutional analysis of the gender architecture in their respective jurisdictions, authors have also critically examined contextual dynamics from a socio-legal perspective. Some elements of these opportunity structures are linked to broader conceptions of constitutional culture. This is for instance the case of the degree of normative force attributed to constitutional texts and the strategic relevance of the specific constitutional context in the various jurisdictions. Other elements and variables appear more strongly connected to the different gendered realities and dynamics. The variables authors have taken on board include but are not limited to women and SGDP's access to constitution-making; their representation on the bench interpreting the constitutional text; and the potential of constitutional litigation in general and *vis-à-vis* other venues for the advancement of gender equality such as the legislature, where the presence of women and SGDP varies from jurisdiction to jurisdiction. Also discussed is the relative importance of the gender architecture/framework at the constitutional level in each jurisdiction including the impact

[5] WC Chang et al, *Constitutionalism in Asia: Cases and Materials* (Hart Publishing, 2014).

of international norms and of the accommodation of religious beliefs, norms and practices.

To facilitate the comparative analysis of otherwise disparate constitutional experiences, we have organised individual contributions according to a modular format. Each chapter first analyses the constitutional framework of each jurisdiction in its appropriate historical, political and socio-economic context with respect to the cultural treatment of gender and sexuality, followed by an overview of the constitutional history, constitutional structure and salient instances of constitutional litigation in key domains of gender constitutionalism. The identification of a common set of variables that may account for the range of variation and a shared structure were intended to allow for comparisons across the board. At the same time, authors have focused on the dimensions or elements of their case study that can arguably best contribute to the shaping of a global narrative on gender and constitutionalism, be it in a positive or negative way. They do so in the last sections of their individual chapters where they refer to flagship developments.

In the rest of the introduction, we present the case studies selection and briefly discuss some of the comparative findings with reference to those variables that seem to better explain the range of variation as to the relative importance of constitutions in shaping the citizenship status of women and SGDP in the various jurisdictions analysed in the book.

II. CASE STUDIES SELECTION

This volume features 12 representative Asian jurisdictions from East Asia (Japan, Taiwan, Hong Kong, South Korea), Southeast Asia (Malaysia, Singapore, the Philippines, Indonesia), and South Asia (India, Nepal, Pakistan, Sri Lanka). Our selection of case studies aims to demonstrate jurisdictional diversity along the axes of constitutional architecture and culture, which may serve as opportunity structures for the advancement of gender equality and equal rights of women and SGDP. Thus, all the major archetypal models of executive–legislative relations, alongside the institutional arrangements and degree of accessibility to governmental bodies which substantially affect the equal rights of women and SGDP, are included: parliamentary systems (Japan, Malaysia, Singapore, India, Nepal, Pakistan), presidential systems (the Philippines, Indonesia) and semi-presidential systems (Taiwan, South Korea, Sri Lanka). Constitutional monarchies under a parliamentary system include Japan and Malaysia. The selection also features variety in terms of territorial organisation of power, with diverse forms of federal arrangements developed against the backdrop of serious religious and ethnic tensions, which frequently have gender undertones. At present, Malaysia, India and Pakistan have federal systems partly inherited from colonial times, while Nepal has adopted a federal framework under the new constitution; these federal frameworks face serious religious and ethnic tensions and have only been partially successful in managing these cleavages.[6] Federalism has also been debated in recent decades as a design solution to ethnic conflicts in the Philippines, Indonesia and Sri Lanka. Hong Kong is governed through a unique form of autonomy as a Special Administrative Region within the non-federal Chinese state.

Given the frequency with which religious norms are gendered, different models of religion and state adopted by respective jurisdictions provide a particularly interesting axis of analysis as discussed below in section VI. In particular, the 12 jurisdictions featured in this volume illustrate the challenges surrounding the fraught relationship between gender and religion in the constitutional domain. First, we observe the uneasy cohabitation of religious and secular provisions; the latter generally providing the constitutional basis for the advancement of women and SGDP's rights, as in Malaysia and Pakistan. Second, the extended principle of personal laws governing the family law framework may create an equality divide like it has in Sri Lanka. Finally, the ethno-national drive confronting many jurisdictions in Asia (and beyond) has hinged on religious majoritarianism and taken specific gendered forms like in India and Indonesia.

The experiences of recent constitution-making, or constitutional reforms, also entail another key axis of inquiry. Although Asia has displayed more constitutional stability than other regions and some observe that Asian jurisdictions have adopted more of a 'gradualist evolution', emphasising constitutional amendment over new constitution-making,[7] our case selection features constitutions as old as Indonesia's (1945) and as young as Nepal's (2015). It also includes jurisdictions that have in recent years undergone democratisation and undertaken grand or small-scale constitutional revisions such as Taiwan, South Korea, Malaysia, the Philippines, Indonesia and Sri Lanka. Additionally, Hong Kong's Constitution is subnational and supports a separate common law legal system with justiciable rights, distinct from the Chinese state's central constitutional arrangements, according to the principle of one country, two systems. While many countries in the region have viewed constitutional state-building as part of the modernisation project and proceeded in a top-down manner,[8] one could expect more recent constitution-making processes or reforms to better reflect the increasing engagement of women and SGDP groups as well as evolving legitimacy standards around inclusive constitution-making processes.

Without denying the relevance of premodern antecedents as well as socialist and communist models of constitutionalism in Asia,[9] we have decided to

[6] See S Choudhry, 'Classical and Post-Conflict Federalism: Implications for Asia' in R Dixon and T Ginsburg (eds), *Comparative Constitutional Law in Asia* (Edward Elgar, 2014); G Anderson and S Choudhry (eds), *Territory and Power in Constitutional Transitions* (Oxford University Press, 2019).

[7] Dixon and Ginsburg (n 3) 2.

[8] JR Yeh and WC Chang, 'The Emergence of East Asian Constitutionalism: Features in Comparison' (2011) 59 *American Journal of Comparative Law* 805.

[9] NS Bui, *Constitutional Change in the Contemporary Socialist World* (Oxford University Press, 2020).

focus on contemporary democratic, or at least semi-democratic, regimes. Our choice of most-similar case studies allows us to focus on and assess the emancipatory potential – but also the limits – of liberal democratic constitutionalism in advancing women's and SGDP's rights across Asia.

III. GENDER ARCHITECTURE AND CONSTITUTIONAL CHANGE

To understand the opportunity structures for the advancement of gender constitutionalism, it is pivotal to consider the historical development of constitutional frameworks and the role that constitutional actors have played in the design, upkeep and transformation of the gender architecture. The 12 Asian jurisdictions we explore in this volume offer tremendous insights into these constitutional dynamics spanning a 70-year period – from the promulgation of Indonesia's independence Constitution in 1945 to Nepal's post-conflict Constitution in 2015. A number of jurisdictions retain the constitution that they adopted as markers of independence from colonial domination (Indonesia 1945, India 1950 – although independence was acquired under the Dominion Constitution of 1947,[10] Malaysia 1957, Singapore 1965). Some others have repeatedly engaged in domestic processes of constitution-making and the constitutional frameworks analysed in this volume are based on the latest enacted constitutional documents (Pakistan 1973, Sri Lanka 1978, the Philippines 1987, Nepal 2015). A handful of our case studies feature constitutions that stemmed from fraught political transitions in which the very notion of sovereignty was in question (Taiwan 1946, Japan 1947, South Korea 1948, Hong Kong 1990). In any case, the majority of these constitutional documents have been significantly amended over the years to adapt to novel socio-political circumstances. As a result, constitutional texts often reflect a degree of constitutional sedimentation in terms of previous domestic experiences and cross-pollination derived from constitutional borrowing at the regional and international levels. Moreover, the timing and modality of constitutional amendments must be carefully considered in order to track and explain changes in the constitutional architecture of these jurisdictions over the years.

As a result, a persuasive comparative analysis of the gender architecture of the Asian jurisdictions in this volume requires a careful contextual approach. Two insights emerge with respect to the relationship between gender architecture and constitutional change, which is broadly defined to encompass constitution-making and constitutional amendment.

First, constitutions made in more recent times contain in their texts more explicit and extensive forms of constitutional recognition of gender equality.

[10] See M Malagodi, L McDonagh and T Poole, 'New Dominion Constitutionalism at the Twilight of the British Empire: An Introduction' (2019) 17 *International Journal of Constitutional Law* 1166.

On one end of the spectrum, the most recent documents like the 2015 Constitution of Nepal feature extensive sections on justiciable fundamental rights pertaining to women and SGDP, alongside far-reaching affirmative action measures, Directive Principles of State Policy, and 'pink quotas'. On the opposite end are those constitutions that did not include at the time of their promulgation any references to gender or sex, even as prohibited grounds of discrimination (Indonesia, Malaysia, Singapore). In an intermediate position, we find constitutions that recognise sex and/or gender as prohibited grounds of discrimination (Taiwan, Japan, South Korea, Hong Kong), and some that also contain modest forms of positive entitlements for women (India, Pakistan, Sri Lanka, the Philippines) alongside non-discrimination clauses.

This temporal progression from 'constitutional silence' on gender to 'constitutional recognition' of gender through extensive affirmative measures is in line with Ruth Rubio-Marín's analysis of the shift in the early 1990s to participatory gender constitutionalism with a focus on substantive gender equality.[11] This also affirms David Law's broader conclusions about constitutional archetypes with recent convergence towards a 'universalist' model harnessing the legitimacy of international norms[12] alongside forms of cross-pollination and constitution-making 'best practices'. In this respect, international organisations and NGOs involved in constitution-building exercises have increasingly promoted constitutional commitments to gender equality now seen as an essential feature of constitutional frameworks deemed rule of law-compliant. For instance, the Guidance Note of the Secretary-General on United Nations Constitutional Assistance (first issued in 2009) features in its 2020 iteration an explicit commitment to gender equality: 'the UN should also provide support in a manner that promotes a constitution that is gender sensitive and inclusive in its language, its institutions and its processes and that speaks to all the people in the country'.[13]

However, this temporal progression towards gender-inclusive constitution-building appears insufficient to determine explicit instances of gender-based discrimination at the time of constitution-making. For instance, gender-based discrimination in terms of citizenship featured both in the promulgated text of the Constitution of Singapore in 1965 and in that of Nepal in 2015. While Singapore amended the citizenship clause in 2004 to ensure gender equality, Nepali lawmakers have shown no intention to do so notwithstanding repeated calls by the Committee on the Elimination of Discrimination against Women (CEDAW Committee),[14] other international bodies and domestic actors.

[11] Rubio-Marín, *Global Gender Constitutionalism and Women's Citizenship* (n 1) 132–33.

[12] DS Law, 'Constitutional Archetypes' (2016) 95 *Texas Law Review* 153.

[13] United Nations, 'Guidance Note of the Secretary-General on United Nations Constitutional Assistance' (September 2020), available at peacemaker.un.org/sites/peacemaker.un.org/files/SG%20 Guidance%20Note%20on%20Constitutional%20Assistance_2.pdf.

[14] The CEDAW Committee is the expert United Nations body monitoring states parties' implementation of their obligations under the Convention on the Elimination of All Forms of Discrimination Against Women (CEDAW).

Similarly, the privileging in the constitutional text of certain narratives, values and institutions that impact gender equality and the treatment of women and SGDP reflect deep-rooted context-specific dynamics of constitutional identity and nation-building in each of the jurisdictions featured in this volume. For instance, the influence of the Catholic Church in the Philippines is evinced by the constitutional protection of 'the life of the unborn', which has placed an insurmountable burden on attempts to liberalise abortion. In line with the contradictions inherent in the post-World War II paradigm of gender constitutionalism elucidated by Rubio-Marín,[15] a number of Asian constitutions also refer explicitly to marriage and family life (Indonesia, Japan, South Korea) pointing to the dominant heteronormative and traditionalist view of gender relations at the time of constitution-making. This framing of gender by the dominant groups controlling the state has historically played a crucial role in how the political community of the nation has been imagined, narratively construed and institutionalised at the constitutional level. The constitutionalisation of forms of gender-based discrimination then becomes locked-in and path-dependent, ie particularly difficult to remove once included in the constitutional text.

Second, constitution-making processes that feature the inclusion of women and SGDP representatives, or that have at least taken into account the demands of civil society organisations with respect to gender equality, tend to produce more sophisticated and inclusive forms of gender architecture – at least at the textual level. This argument is also partially predicated on recent developments in constitution-making modalities and processes, which increasingly require both inclusion and participation.[16] While on a normative level the correlation between participation/inclusion in constitution-building and gender-sensitive constitutional outcomes has become the gold standard, this correlation (let alone causation) has been much harder to prove empirically, given the enormous number of context-specific variables at play.[17] The jurisdictions featured in this book include an array of constitution-making experiences ranging from 'imposed' constitutions like that of Japan,[18] to top-down constitutions initially drafted by small unelected commissions like those of Indonesia, Malaysia, Singapore and Hong Kong, to bodies with a degree of electoral and political legitimacy such as those in Taiwan, Sri Lanka and the Philippines (which saw the new Constitution ratified through a national plebiscite) and elected constituent assemblies in South Korea, India, Pakistan and Nepal.

[15] Rubio-Marín, *Global Gender Constitutionalism and Women's Citizenship* (n 1) 67–80.

[16] TA Eisenstadt and T Maboudi, 'Being There Is Half the Battle: Group Inclusion, Constitution-Writing, and Democracy' (2019) 52 *Comparative Political Studies* 2135.

[17] T Ginsburg, Z Elkins and J Blount, 'Does the Process of Constitution-Making Matter?' (2009) 5 *Annual Review of Law and Social Science* 201.

[18] A Ejima, 'Japan's Post-War Constitution: "Imposed" Constitution or Hybrid Between Global and Local Stakeholders?' in NS Bui and M Malagodi (eds), *Asian Comparative Constitutional Law, Volume 1: Constitution Making* (Hart Publishing, 2023) 7.

A comparative analysis of these constitutional experiences offers no straightforward answers. A participatory and inclusive constitution-making process undoubtedly increases the legitimacy of both the constitution-building exercise per se, and potentially of its outcome by securing a broader buy-in. However, as Silvia Suteu argues, the success in securing gender equality gains at the time of constitution-making is measured not just by percentages of women and SGDP's representation, but also by the quality of popular deliberation and the impact of women and SGDP's voices.[19] This, in turn, is often related to the degree of visibility, clarity and effective mobilisation strategies of civil society groups.[20] It may also explain the greater impact of women rather than gender and sexual minorities in pushing forward their agendas by taking advantage of constitutional moments in most jurisdictions.

Indeed, the case studies in this volume highlight the importance of the nexus between civil society actors and constitution-makers. These include, in particular, societies where grass-roots mobilisation of women – such as in India during the anticolonial struggle and other former British colonies like Pakistan and Bangladesh – resulted in the placement of gender equality on the constitution-building agenda, notwithstanding the small representation of women within the constituent assembly. Similarly in Japan, the effective campaigning of the suffragettes at the end of World War II succeeded in convincing the constitution-drafting body to grant Japanese women the right to vote. In Pakistan, women's voices were ignored during the making of the 1973 Constitution and the assembly took an ambiguous stance on the role of religion in the constitutional framework as a result of Zulfiqar Ali Bhutto's efforts to co-opt Islamist political forces to retain power and broaden his support base.

In the Philippines, while the drafting commission included a small number of women, some of whom are to be credited for its most gender progressive provisions, the presence of a majority of practicing Catholic members ultimately shaped the constitutional agenda for gender equality. However, the commitment to an 'open-ended' constitutional document – also in matters of gender – allowed for ordinary legislation to define the country's gender architecture. The most recent constitution-building experience analysed in this volume – the making of Nepal's 2015 Constitution – exemplifies these tensions. On the one hand, while the new dispensation features an impressive and cutting-edge gender architecture that directly resulted from the relatively high proportion (33 per cent) of female constituent assembly members, it also contains explicit gender-based discrimination in citizenship matters. On the other hand, Sunil Babu Pant's membership in the first Constituent Assembly as Nepal's first openly gay politician was instrumental in securing constitutional protections

[19] S Suteu, 'Women and Participatory Constitution-Making' in H Irving (ed), *Constitutions and Gender* (Edward Elgar, 2017) 41.

[20] See also R Rubio-Marín, 'Women and Participatory Constitutionalism' (2020) 18 *International Journal of Constitutional Law* 233.

for sexual and gender minorities. This experience illustrates that participation and inclusion alone cannot deliver gender equality and that many other factors are indispensable.

Civil society activism and interventions by various international bodies such as the CEDAW Committee have also influenced constitutional amendments aimed at achieving greater gender equality and improving the constitutional status of women and SGDP. In response to domestic and international pressures, in 2001, Malaysia's Federal Parliament amended the Constitution to include gender in the list of prohibited grounds of discrimination. In 2004, Singapore's Government amended the Constitution to remove forms of gender-based discrimination in accessing citizenship. These civil society pressures, however, have not always been successful. For instance, in the wake of democratisation in Taiwan, women's rights activists mobilised and published a Women's Charter in 1991 to serve as the basis of constitutional amendments; these proposals were ultimately ignored, however.

Constitutional amendments have also had an oblique impact on the advancement of gender constitutionalism by opening new avenues for the pursuit of gender equality claims. For instance, the 9th Amendment to South Korea's Constitution passed in 1987 significantly expanded the possibilities of constitutional adjudication thus creating opportunities for strategic litigation. Similarly, in Indonesia the four amendments passed between 1999 and 2002 by elected representatives during the *reformasi* period of democratisation created an extensive set of fundamental rights and established a constitutional court able to strike down legislation. While these reforms have produced some improvements in the position of women, they have had a negligible effect on SGDP rights.

Constitutional change – whether via constitution-making or amendment – has the potential to advance the gender equality agenda as it opens political space where strategic opportunities might be seized. These changes often overlap with periods of political transition and regime change, while in some instances governments receptive to social changes seek to avoid a radicalisation of political cleavages and aim to increase their political capital with strategically targeted reforms. It appears from all our case studies that civil society mobilisation capable of influencing constitutional actors – whether in parliament or in court – can yield the greatest results in terms of gender-sensitive constitutional change.

IV. CONSTITUTIONAL FRAMEWORK AND CULTURE

A comparative analysis of the 12 jurisdictions in this volume reveals that different constitutional frameworks and cultures have had a significant impact on the ways in which constitutional law and litigation serve as adequate venues to advance the rights and claims of women and SGDP across our case studies. The analysis of this unique combination of constitutional structures, praxis and culture (including, but not limited to, government power structures, legislatures, courts, political deference or judicial activism, diversity in the legal profession and on the bench, public interest litigation, democratisation, political process, etc) in each jurisdiction has produced both key comparative and single-jurisdiction findings.

A. Legislatures v Courts

Most chapters conclude that the courts have been a fairly effective institution, or at least a relatively more utilised venue, to assert equal citizenship for women and SGDP in many of the Asian case studies in this volume. Across Asia, lawyers fighting in court for the equal citizenship of women and SGDP generally base their claims on the fundamental rights enshrined in the Constitution and seek constitutional protection through judicial processes. The fact that many higher courts in Asia are empowered to review and invalidate legislation has further strengthened judicial redress as the courts can often fulfil law and policy-making functions for the benefit of women and SGDP as historically marginalised groups.[21] In South Korea, Taiwan, Hong Kong, the Philippines, India, Nepal and Pakistan, where judicial review powers are vested in the courts at all levels or, at least, in the apex court, individual or public-interest gender equality litigation has increased. In addition, constitutional architecture that affirms equal citizenship on the basis of gender and sexuality and provides for judicial review may further shape constitutional culture in which diverse identities of gender and sexuality can be openly and freely expressed and equally ensured, and such pluralistic constitutional culture may evolve as part of constitutional identity. As Gautam Bhatia and Shreya Atrey explain in their chapter on India, feminist constitutional claims in India have always been advanced before the courts and the Constitution, both in its letter and spirit, has shaped the contours of major public debates and social struggles, including those relating to women and sexual and gender minorities.

Although courts have grown in popularity as avenues for seeking equal rights of women and SGDP in most of the jurisdictions in this volume, they have not been prioritised in others. In Japan, Malaysia, Singapore, the Philippines and Indonesia, our authors have found that the judiciary has not been a particularly effective institution for advancing the equal rights of women and SGDP due to various institutional limits or contextual dynamics. This may be explained by a combination of constitutional design features aimed at preserving a certain political equilibrium (for example, Singapore's one-party domination and

[21] See Chang et al (n 5); Rubio-Marín, *Global Gender Constitutionalism and Women's Citizenship* (n 1).

Indonesia's history of authoritarianism) and a political commitment toward democratic deliberations over judicial activism (the Philippines, Sri Lanka and, to a lesser extent, Malaysia and Pakistan). Recent democratic backsliding may also limit progress through the political arena and lead activists to further prioritise advocacy before the courts, as Kelley Loper explains in her chapter on Hong Kong. Judicial procedural rules or culture such as judicial deference to elected representatives, jurisdictional limitations of courts, and standing rules that do not support public interest litigation may also lead to similar judicial constraints.

In Japan, although gender equality legislation generally has not been effectively implemented and thus its impact on the equal rights of women and SGDP is limited, litigation has not provided a feasible avenue either. According to Akiko Ejima in her chapter on Japan, this is due to the Supreme Court of Japan's considerable deference to the Diet, Japan's legislature, and the belief that judicial intervention should not affect societal changes.[22] In Malaysia, the limited role of the judiciary in asserting the rights of women and SGDP stems from the jurisdictional divide between civil and Syariah courts. According to Dian AH Shah in her chapter on Malaysia, the civil courts have a tendency to avoid adjudicating issues that raise important constitutional rights questions when such issues are deemed to overlap with Islamic law questions.[23] A few watershed cases in recent years notwithstanding, a more assertive role for the judiciary in protecting the rights of women and their constitutional status depends upon the courts' ability to carefully navigate the boundaries between civil and religious laws.

Unlike in Japan and Malaysia, where neither the legislature nor the courts have assumed an active role in asserting equal citizenship for women and SGDP, the legislatures in Singapore, the Philippines and Indonesia have fared better. The Singapore experience has demonstrated how gender equality may be achieved even when constitutional litigation is limited in a litigation-averse political culture. As Daryl WJ Yang and Jaclyn L Neo observe in their chapter on Singapore, given narrow standing rules that limit public interest litigation and the generally cautious judicial attitude, the main organisations campaigning for gender equality have instead lobbied the Government through advocacy, cooperation and consultation, rather than litigation.[24] An interesting example has been the decriminalisation of same-sex intimacy in Singapore in November 2022 by legislative intervention in the wake of repeated failures to challenge the so-called 'sodomy law' via constitutional litigation.

In the Philippines, despite a strong tradition of public interest litigation and a generally active judiciary, legislation has been the primary avenue to pursue

[22] See ch 2.
[23] See ch 6.
[24] See ch 7.

gender justice. This reflects the longstanding, widespread acceptance of the ballot as the main source of political legitimacy in the country. As Bryan Dennis G Tiojanco observes in his chapter on the Philippines, the Supreme Court of the Philippines has reinforced the democracy principle by giving Congress great leeway to resolve gender-related policy issues and by reliably upholding and robustly enforcing gender justice legislation.[25] In Indonesia, courts have not played vital roles in achieving gender equality due to judicial reluctance, lack of public support as well as the Supreme Court's unwillingness to decide concrete legal disputes despite its power to do so. In addition, the Constitutional Court can only address the constitutionality of laws and policies without any genuine enforcement power. As Simon Butt explains in his chapter on Indonesia, the Indonesian courts' judicial review powers, in place since constitutional reforms in the 2000s, are merely an opportunity structure 'on paper' that have not yet achieved any real progress toward the equal rights of women and SGDP.[26]

We should note the relative nature of the influence of constitutional frameworks and cultures as opportunity structures on gender equality since these often depend considerably on contextual dynamics in respective jurisdictions. For example, in Pakistan and Sri Lanka, the fundamental rights jurisdiction has expanded monumentally in the last four decades. Mario Gomez in his chapter on Sri Lanka, however, has noted 'the sparse jurisprudence on gender' compared with developments in other areas such as environmental law, religious rights and the right to administrative justice, where advocates have more frequently resorted to constitutional rights litigation.[27] However, 'the sparse jurisprudence on gender' in Sri Lanka may seem abundant from the perspective of other jurisdictions such as Malaysia or the Philippines.

B. Cooperation between Courts, Legislatures and Civil Society

Inter-branch relations in constitutional frameworks, architecture and cultures are not necessarily confrontational. It is not necessary to choose between legislatures and courts as avenues for pursuing and achieving gender equality for women and SGDP. In Taiwan and South Korea, for example, civil society has burgeoned with democratisation since the late 1980s, and lawyers and organisations advocating for the equal rights of women and SGDP have used both political and judicial processes.

In the chapter on South Korea, Yoon Jin Shin observes that civil society and individuals, who have been progressively empowered since the democratisation process in the late 1980s, have actively pursued gender-related constitutional

[25] See ch 8.
[26] See ch 9.
[27] See ch 13.

litigation.[28] Although civil society has found constitutional litigation more effective than targeting the legislature – a branch still filled predominantly by men and influenced by majoritarian preferences with lingering patriarchal ideology – the cooperation between the two institutions is necessary to achieve the equal rights of women and SGDP. This is because the Constitutional Court of South Korea conducts an ex post facto concrete review with the power to order immediate invalidation of laws or government actions found in violation of the Constitution but does not hold the power to conduct constitutional review against decisions of ordinary courts. The Constitutional Court's power and authority cannot be sustained without cooperation from the Government or the legislature to duly change policies or revise laws. As Shin explains, in most cases, the decisions by the Constitutional Court have been strictly observed and efficiently enforced by the legislature and other branches of government.

The dialogic process between the legislature and courts facilitated by civil society has been especially salient in Taiwan. As Wen-Chen Chang reports in her chapter on Taiwan, even during the time when Taiwan's Constitutional Court had a rather narrower jurisdiction in receiving petitions, women lawyers were able to tackle the challenge by persuading over 150 legislators, many of whom were first-time elected women legislators, to refer a constitutional question to the Constitutional Court. Perhaps equally important, Taiwan's Constitutional Court does not often strike down unconstitutional legislation but, instead, gives the legislature a certain amount of time to revise related laws. Those periods of time, as Chang concludes, have given women and SGDP a further opportunity structure in which they can dialogue with the Government, the legislature and the general public.[29] With victories occurring one after another, growing momentum for large-scale law reform furthering even greater protection of women's and SGDP's equal rights has persisted.

The dialogue between the legislature and courts is also a feature in Pakistan. As Sadaf Aziz, Angbeen Atif Mirza and Cristóbal Alvear-Garijo observe in their chapter on Pakistan, the judiciary has served as a watchdog to ensure implementation or addressed legal loopholes with guidelines or redesigned legal tools before legislation has been passed. Landmark judgments have paved the way toward legislation endorsing forward-looking rights including the recognition of self-perceived gender and the reframing of the legal framework for rape mainly due to the struggle of activists, pro bono lawyers, and public-spirited citizens.[30] Hong Kong's apex court also attempted dialogue with the legislature in a case concerning transgender marriage, by granting the government and legislature one year to respond.

[28] See ch 5.
[29] See ch 3.
[30] See ch 12.

C. Women on the Bench

Most chapters identify a growing presence of women in public offices including judicial posts. The increase is usually in the lower courts, but it also appears at the top of the judiciary. The presence of SGDP as well as attention to intersectionality is seriously lacking. A few jurisdictions have seen increases of women at the top of the judiciary. For example, Japan now has two women justices out of 15 on the Supreme Court, although this is less than the record number of three women justices in previous years. South Korea has three women out of nine justices on the Constitutional Court and four women out of 14 justices on the Supreme Court. In January 2022, Pakistan appointed the first woman justice, Justice Ayesha Malik, to its 75-year-old Supreme Court. In Hong Kong, there have been no women permanent judges on the Court of Final Appeal since it was established in 1997, although the proportion of women judges on the lower courts has gradually increased. Two women non-permanent judges were appointed to the apex court in 2018, although one declined to renew her appointment after her three-year term concluded in 2021.

The increase of women on the bench, however, has not necessarily led to more judicial decisions in favour of gender equality and better protection of the rights of women and SGDP. For example, although the growing presence of women judges is quite strong in both Taiwan and the Philippines, as mentioned above, in the Philippines, women and SGDP have more frequently sought affirmation of their rights and equal citizenship through the legislature.[31] In India, Nepal and Pakistan, among other jurisdictions with far fewer women judges, the number of progressive decisions favouring the equal rights of women and SGDP – the so-called thick feminisation of the judiciary – has increased. This is consistent with what Melissa Crouch and others have identified as the *thin* versus *thick* feminisation of the judiciary in the Asia-Pacific and more generally. As they explain, the thin feminisation of the judiciary (having more women on the bench) does not necessarily lead to the thick feminisation of the judiciary (having more judicial decisions promoting women's rights and gender equality).[32]

V. GENDER CONSTITUTIONALISM AND INTERNATIONAL NORMS

International human rights instruments, especially the Convention on the Elimination of All Forms of Discrimination Against Women (CEDAW) and its expert Committee, have also influenced gender constitutionalism and the

[31] See ch 8.

[32] M Crouch and N Naidu, 'The Feminisation of the Judiciary in the Asia-Pacific: The Challenges of Formal and Substantive Equality' in M Crouch (ed), *Women and the Judiciary in the Asia-Pacific* (Cambridge University Press, 2021) 3–4.

advancement of the rights of women and SGDP in all jurisdictions considered in this volume, although to varying degrees.[33] This influence takes multiple forms. For example, the ratification of CEDAW and other human rights instruments has generated legislative reform, impacted the text of constitutional provisions, and shaped litigation strategies and judicial decisions. Civil society has also leveraged international monitoring procedures to strengthen local advocacy. As Mara Malagodi observes in her chapter on Nepal, 'Gender constitutionalism advances the furthest when a constitutional system in line with international standards is combined with culturally consonant forms of constitutional recognition of socio-cultural diversity and is underpinned by societal consensus built through extensive public and inclusive deliberations'.[34]

At the same time, while every country in the Asian region has ratified CEDAW, many made reservations preserving discriminatory laws often based on cultural and religious traditions. For example, when acceding to CEDAW in 1994, Singapore made a reservation to Article 9(2), which obliges states to grant women equal rights with respect to the nationality of their children, arguing that 'husbands are the heads of households' in 'Asian tradition'.[35] (It amended discriminatory nationality laws in 2004.) When ratifying CEDAW in 1984, South Korea also made reservations to Article 9 and other provisions concerning marriage and family life. It eventually withdrew most of these in 1991 and 1999 and amended the Nationality Act in response to the CEDAW Committee's concerns. Malaysia also ratified CEDAW with reservations designed to preserve Syariah Law.[36]

Despite broad reservations, ratification nevertheless has sparked law reform in several jurisdictions, even as full implementation remains elusive. For example, CEDAW influenced the introduction of quotas for women's political participation and a constitutional amendment adding gender to the prohibited grounds of discrimination in Malaysia. The Japanese Diet enacted the Act on Securing, Etc of Equal Opportunity and Treatment between Men and Women in Employment (EQA) in 1985, the year Japan ratified CEDAW. In Hong Kong, the women's

[33] For discussions of CEDAW and gender constitutionalism, see, eg, C McCrudden, 'Why do National Court Judges Refer to Human Rights Treaties? A Comparative International Law Analysis of CEDAW' (2015) 109 *The American Journal of International Law* 534; F Raday, 'Gender and Democratic Citizenship: The Impact of CEDAW' (2012) 10 *International Journal of Constitutional Law* 512; J Resnik, 'Comparative (in)equalities: CEDAW, the jurisdiction of gender, and the heterogeneity of transnational law production' (2012) 10 *International Journal of Constitutional Law* 531. For a further critique of CEDAW and its limitations for achieving transformation, see D Otto, 'Women's Rights' in D Moeckli, S Shah, S Sivakumaran and D Harris (eds), *International Human Rights Law*, 4th edn (Oxford University Press, 2022) 322.

[34] See ch 11.

[35] 'Singapore's Initial Report to the UN Committee for the Convention on the Elimination of All Forms of Discrimination Against Women' (1 December 1999) UN Doc CEDAW/C/SGP/1, para 2.3.

[36] The term '*sharia*' varies according to different legal systems across Asia, but always refers to Islamic law (ie, the injunctions of the *Quran* and the *Sunnah*) in this chapter. It is used as an adjective and with further variations, *Syariah* in Malaysia, *Shari'ah* in the Philippines, *Shari'a* in Indonesia, and *Shariat* in Pakistan.

rights movement successfully lobbied the UK to extend CEDAW in 1996. The Sex Discrimination Ordinance came into force the same year. Shin observes that South Korea's ratification of CEDAW also 'provided momentum for lawmakers to amend patriarchal domestic laws without constitutional adjudication'. The Philippines' many treaty obligations have motivated the introduction of 'gender justice laws' and Indonesia also introduced laws implementing CEDAW after ratification in 1984. On the other hand, Bhatia and Atrey observe that despite India's ratification in 1980, it still has not passed comprehensive sex equality legislation.

Some jurisdictions have directly incorporated – even duplicated word-for-word – international treaty provisions into their domestic constitutional framework. For example, in Hong Kong, the constitutional right to equality copies the International Covenant on Civil and Political Rights (ICCPR) and prompted the courts to develop a nascent substantive equality doctrine which has dismantled policies discriminating against same-sex couples. Nepal's 2015 constitutional provisions are also derived in large part from international standards. Although Taiwan is not a member of the United Nations and cannot formally ratify international human rights instruments, it 'acceded' to CEDAW in 2007 and directly incorporated the treaty through an Enforcement Act in 2012. It has also invited experts to review the human rights conditions in Taiwan. Women's rights organisations have been heavily involved in this 'bottom-up' process. These international, cosmopolitan constitutional arrangements, grounded in international law, have provided strong support for domestic rights advocacy and progressive constitutional litigation.

In some cases, courts have referred to CEDAW and other international norms when declaring laws and policies unconstitutional. The Indian Supreme Court directly applied CEDAW in its landmark *Vishaka* decision, which set out guidelines on sexual harassment in the absence of legislation.[37] The Korean Constitutional Court has frequently cited CEDAW as a 'reference point' and has also cited CEDAW Committee materials.[38] A Hong Kong court relied on CEDAW when rejecting government justifications for education policies that directly discriminated against girls.[39] The Hong Kong courts have also frequently considered the jurisprudence of the European Court of Human Rights in cases involving the rights of SGDP. In Malaysia, the High Court applied CEDAW as an interpretive tool in decisions involving pregnancy discrimination.[40] In 2016, the Constitutional Court of Indonesia also referred to CEDAW and the ICCPR

[37] *Vishaka v State of Rajasthan* [AIR 1997 SC 3011].

[38] eg, Constitutional Court of Korea, 2013Hun-Ka2, 28-1 KCCR 259, 271 (31 March 2016), as discussed by Yoon Jin Shin in section III.B of ch 5.

[39] *EOC v Director of Education* [2001] HKLRD 690, as discussed by Kelley Loper in section IV.H of ch 4.

[40] eg, *Noorfadilla binti Ahmad Saikin v Chayed Basirun and Ors* [2012] 1 *Malayan Law Journal* 832 as discussed by Dian AH Shah in section IV of ch 6.

when ruling against requirements that the Sultan of a special province be male.[41] In Pakistan, CEDAW has contributed to the courts' increasingly clear substantive understanding of gender equality; justices, such as Ayesha Malik, have elaborated upon CEDAW with a view of achieving the elimination of patriarchal-based discrimination within the Pakistani legal system. In Sri Lanka, the Supreme Court explicitly referred to CEDAW when determining that sexual harassment in the workplace violated the constitutional right against sex-based discrimination.[42] Similarly in the Philippines, the Supreme Court aligned its decisions with the CEDAW Committee's views that 'rape myths' violated CEDAW in 2013 and CEDAW has influenced a judicial redefinition of rape as a consent-based crime.[43] However, a more recent decision contains regressive reasoning on what constitutes rape and seems 'to downplay the definition of rape' as noted in a dissenting opinion.[44]

Even when judicial decisions do not support rights-friendly outcomes, judges have still referred to CEDAW in obiter or in dissent. In Japan, for example, CEDAW has influenced dissenting opinions in cases where the majority upheld discriminatory laws. The Taiwan Constitutional Court upheld a rule that only men could be assigned as successors to worship guilds but still urged the Government to 'conduct a timely review and modification of the related law' especially taking into account Articles 2 and 5 of CEDAW.[45] In a case maintaining criminal laws punishing sex workers in Korea, three judges cited a CEDAW recommendation in dissent.[46] In Indonesia, Justice Maria Farida Indrati also referred to CEDAW in her dissenting opinion in a case preserving laws allowing child marriage.[47]

The chapters in this volume problematise the traditional distinction between monism and dualism. Courts in some dualist legal systems – which require incorporation of international norms in domestic legislation to be justiciable – cite international and comparative law as persuasive authority. At the same time, the judiciary in Japan, an ostensibly monist jurisdiction, has been more deferential to the legislature than in certain dualist states, such as India with its tradition of active public interest litigation. As Shin notes, while CEDAW has been influential in Korea, it has not been cited as a 'direct standard of review', although the Korean Constitution clarifies that rules of international law have

[41] Constitutional Court Decision No 88/PUU-XIV/2016, 311, as discussed by Simon Butt in section IV.B of ch 9.

[42] *Manohari v Secretary, Ministry of Education*, SC/FR/No. 76/2012, Supreme Court Minutes of 28 September 2016, as discussed by Mario Gomez in section III.A of ch 13.

[43] *People v Quintos*, 746 Phil 809, GR No 199402, 12 November 2014, as discussed by Bryan Dennis G Tiojanco in section V. B of ch 8.

[44] As discussed by Tiojanco in ch 8.

[45] JY Interpretation No 728 (2015), as discussed by Wen-Chen Chang in section IV.B.iv of ch 3.

[46] Constitutional Court of Korea, 2013Hun-Ka2, 28-1 KCCR 259, 271 (31 March 2016), as discussed by Shin in section III.B of ch 5.

[47] Constitutional Court Decision No 30-74/PUU-XII/2014, as discussed by Butt in section V.A of ch 9.

the same effect as domestic laws.[48] Shah observes that despite the Malaysian court's creative 'interpretive incorporation' doctrine, the absence of implementing legislation still weakens the treaty's transformative potential.[49]

CEDAW and other international treaties have also supported active social movements. Women and SGDP advocates have leveraged United Nations human rights monitoring processes with varying degrees of success. Although the courts in Singapore have been cautious, Yang and Neo point out that CEDAW has nevertheless been 'a focal point for gender equality reform … serving as a platform for dialogue between the government and civil society organisations, as moderated by the CEDAW Committee'.[50] Sri Lanka, the Philippines, South Korea and Nepal have ratified the Optional Protocol to CEDAW which allows individuals to submit claims of violations by the state party to the CEDAW Committee after exhausting domestic remedies.[51] This has produced significant decisions, including the CEDAW Committee's views that 'rape myths' (the Philippines) and the criminalisation of consensual same-sex sexual acts between adults of any gender (Sri Lanka) violate CEDAW. All states parties to CEDAW submit periodic reports reviewed by the Committee and activists have influenced the concluding recommendations through 'shadow' reports. In turn, the Committee's comments support advocacy at the local level.

Often, however, the courts, lawmakers and international processes have fallen short. Shah's remark that the implementation of international norms demanding gender equality is still a 'work in progress' in Malaysia,[52] and Gomez's observation that gender equality 'remains an aspiration' in Sri Lanka are generally true across the Asian jurisdictions we have included in this volume.[53]

VI. GENDER AND RELIGION

As one would expect, since Asia is the region of the world with the greatest religious diversity, this volume includes countries which exemplify the whole range of 'religion and state' models. The richness of religious diversity in the region is an expression of the fact that religion became a dominant identity marker at the constitutional level both for anticolonial purposes and to build a unique sense of nationhood, often distinct from their neighbours.

Given the deeply gendered nature of religious norms, this feature has natural implications for the constitutional status of women and gender minorities. According to Ran Hirschl the various models in the region include: i) constitutional 'secularism' alongside religious pluralism; ii) preferential constitutional

[48] See section II of ch 5.
[49] See section IV of ch 6.
[50] See section II of ch 7.
[51] Indonesia signed the Optional Protocol in February 2000 but has not yet ratified.
[52] See section I of ch 6.
[53] See section I of ch 13.

treatment of a particular religion or groups of religions, but 'without exclusive establishment of a single faith as a "state religion" or a mandatory source of legislation', often with the emphasis placed on religion as a source of national heritage and a marker a collective identity; and iii) varieties of 'Islamic constitutionalism' (meaning full endorsement of Islam as the single state religion and its establishment as 'a' or 'the' source of legislation).[54] All in all, they 'defy the Western ideal of separating religion and state along private/public lines' and show far less adherence 'to the classic separation of church and state model' dominant in other parts of the world.[55]

All the chapters in this volume may be categorised according to this typology. India has been said to best exemplify the secularist model even though violent forms of Hindu majoritarianism have been reflected in constitutional developments over the past 20 years. Conversely, Pakistan is an example of Islamic constitutionalism. However, the chapters also show that the 'religion and state' model, however described, does not comprehensively answer the question of how religious norms concretely impact gender relations and affect the constitutional status of women and SGDP.

On the one hand, the chapters consider questions about how to reconcile religious norms with otherwise protected fundamental rights (including equality norms) and, more generally, liberal reforms which may have been explicitly embraced to minimise the impact of religious norms on the lives of women and SGDP. Some constitutions confront the matter squarely. For instance, in this volume, we learn that in Pakistan, Islamic provisions cohabit with secular rights and existing liberal reforms. Pakistan's 1973 Constitution gave preferential place to Islam and provided that all existing and future laws should conform with the injunctions of Islam and the Sunnah.[56] At the same time, a number of laws included in the First Schedule to the 1973 Constitution (eg, the Muslim Family Laws Ordinance of 1961 intended to safeguard the protection of Muslim women within the Islamic family law system) were explicitly protected through exemptions from judicial review. In the end, Pakistan has adopted a harmonising rather than an oppositional approach to the coexistence of religious and secular norms through the pathway of a so-called 'Islamic human rights jurisprudence'. Gender equality has not only been promoted by the Supreme Court on the basis of the Constitution's right to equality, but also by the Federal Shariat Court as a principle enshrined in the *Quran*.

It can also go the other way, however, and regimes that may seem more religiously tolerant may end up carving out spaces of religious exceptionalism that undermine women's constitutional equality. In this volume, Gomez describes

[54] R Hirschl, 'Comparative Constitutional Law and Religion in Asia' in R Dixon and T Ginsburg (eds), *Comparative Constitutional Law in Asia* (Edward Elgar, 2014) 317.
[55] ibid.
[56] In fact, a particularly conservative form of *shariat* was adopted and a separate Federal Shariat Court created the Islamisation of the legal system under the dictatorship of General Zia. See ch 12.

how the Sri Lankan Constitution prioritises Buddhism to some extent, while assuring religious rights and freedoms to all religions. However, it also preserves the sanctity of past laws even where they conflict with fundamental rights, in a clause introduced precisely to preserve the operation and applicability of Muslim and other personal laws, even in cases where constitutional provisions conflict. In India – constitutionally committed to a secularist model but where members of different religious communities are afforded some legal recognition and jurisdictional autonomy – such a clause does not exist. However, Bhatia and Atrey describe how the 'the Indian judiciary's long-held view has been that uncodified 'personal laws' (ie, religious norms not formally codified by the state, and governing personal relations) were not subject to constitutional scrutiny', a principle upheld selectively.[57]

In addition to the general religion/state model and the articulation of fundamental rights and solutions to the possible tensions with religious norms, the religious beliefs of the majority population and of religious minorities are accommodated through federal and other jurisdictional arrangements which grant legal recognition and jurisdictional autonomy in the realm of personal status laws. Malaysia – a country which constitutionally recognises that Islam is the religion of the federation, mostly as a key marker of national and ethnic identity, even though religious freedom is also recognised – provides a good illustration. Shah demonstrates the extent to which the federal–state division of power, particularly in matters implicating Islam, and the separation of the civil and *syariah* jurisdictions – secured through a constitutional amendment in 1988 – has allowed individual states in the Federation to retain a degree of autonomy in legislating, regulating and administering Islamic law. In light of this and Islam's growing political force in the country, civil courts (although never formally giving up the supremacy of principles of administrative and constitutional law) have tended to exercise self-restraint when adjudicating issues that raise important questions pertaining to women's constitutional rights to avoid conflict with Islamic law questions.[58]

Similarly, in the chapter on Indonesia (a country with one of the largest Muslim populations in the world and which constitutionally recognises the great monotheist traditions including Buddhism, Catholicism, Hinduism, Islam, Protestantism and, as of 1998, Confucianism), Butt describes the propensity of some local governments – especially after the post-Soeharto decentralisation reforms – to issue subnational by-laws that unfairly target women. He also explains the reluctance of the Supreme Court, 'uncomfortable with intervening in the highly-fraught politics of regional government' to invalidate them. These laws include the controversial Qanun Aceh 6 of 2014 on Islamic Criminal Law

[57] See ch 10.
[58] See ch 6.

(*Hukum Jinayat*) which, among other things, prohibits *khalwat* and *ikhtilath*:[59] adultery, sodomy, lesbian sex, sexual abuse and rape. Indeed, it is particularly difficult for alleged victims to successfully pursue rape allegations, as alleged perpetrators can often escape a finding of guilt by declaring a willingness to face God's wrath if he or she is lying.[60] In the chapter on the Philippines (an overwhelmingly Catholic country constitutionally committed to religious freedom and religious non-establishment), Tiojanco describes how Muslims have the right to set up their own courts which implement the Islamic Shari'ah laws on personal, family and property law in the Bangsmoro Autonomous Region.[61]

Whether or not operationalised through the various territorial arrangements of power adopted 'against the backdrop of serious religious and ethnic tensions',[62] the application of Muslim personal law has also had implications for women in jurisdictions which, in the face of religious diversity, have otherwise embraced legal pluralism. In Indonesia, the Religious Courts Law lists the areas over which Shari'a tribunals have jurisdiction.[63] In Sri Lanka, Muslim hardliners have resisted the Reform of the Muslim Marriage and Divorce Act of 1951 for many years and Muslims are not allowed to opt out and marry under the General Marriages Registration Ordinance.[64] In the Philippines, the Code of Muslim Personal Laws of the Philippines governs family relations solemnised in accordance with it or with Muslim Law even if only the groom is Muslim.[65] In Singapore (where the administration of Muslim personal law is constitutionally provided for in Article 153, supported by Article 152(2) of the Constitution), state-funded institutions like the Islamic Religious Council and the Syariah Court of Singapore administer Islamic laws which require certain exemptions from general laws often affecting women's rights (eg the banning of polygamy). So far, as Yang and Neo note in their chapter, critics have not succeeded in making this optional, rather than compulsory, since in the context of complicated racial/religious sensitivities, it is likely that the Malay-Muslim minority would resent strong state intervention in their internal religious affairs, leaving only the door to internal reform dynamics open.[66] This is not unlike the case of India, where, in spite of the goal of a uniform civil code under Article 44 of the Constitution which might in principle seem promising for women subject to Islamic law, the Hindu ethno-nationalist impulse which has grown considerably over the last three decades makes such a prospect unlikely. This is especially true

[59] *Khalwat* is being alone in an enclosed or private place with a member of the opposite sex who is not a spouse or relative and *ikhtilath* refers to consensual intimate relations, such as flirting, touching, hugging and kissing, between an unmarried male and female in a private or public area.

[60] See ch 9.

[61] See ch 8.

[62] See Choudhry (n 6).

[63] See ch 9.

[64] See ch 13.

[65] See ch 8.

[66] See ch 7.

in light of the public uproar provoked in the Muslim community by the Supreme Court's limitation of Islamic law for the sake of women's 'secular' rights in certain cases (eg, the *Shah Bano* saga).[67]

Notably, several chapters consider how Muslim personal laws – covering a broad set of issues such as child marriage, polygamy, religious conversion, violence against women, moral policing, female dress codes, inheritance, divorce and custody – curtail the rights of women and sexual minorities in serious ways. At the same time, the chapters also provide abundant evidence that the subjection of women, sexual minorities and gender dissidents to a subordinate political status is not something exclusive to the Muslim community. Indeed, religious norms of other faiths also constrain women and SGDP's lives, either directly or by shaping the majority 'secular' norms in society. In the chapter on the Philippines, for instance, Tiojanco refers to the fact that 'women's and LGBT movements have gained good ground for gender justice', but mostly in the public rather than the private sphere which continues to be imbued by the Catholic doctrines which still shape the family, civil and penal law (eg, abortion is a crime and divorce is prohibited).[68] In Japan – where Shinto was the state-endorsed religion until the post-World War II reconstruction – an externally imposed constitutional scheme may have only gone so far in altering the conservative ethos in a country where gender equality reforms seem to proceed particularly slowly. In Nepal, where, until 2006, Hinduism was constitutionally endorsed, women's citizenship rights are still constitutionally sacrificed for the sake of nationalist concerns of an ethno-religious nature.

Most chapters in this volume observe that rights advocacy for gender and sexual minorities through legal and constitutional channels has emerged later than women's rights movements, which have been more empowered and better represented. Shin notes that in South Korea, conservative Christian church groups have been 'the most aggressive objectors to gender and sexual minorities' equality and mobilising efforts'. Their systematic anti-LGBTIQ public campaigns and vigorous lobbying activities have posed the biggest hurdles to adopting a general anti-discrimination law in South Korea. Muslim groups have also mobilised against gay rights activists and conservative religious groups have been particularly opposed to SGDP rights.[69] In Singapore, as Yang and Neo explain, 'Christian and Muslim groups mobilised their communities to sign petitions, write letters to elected representatives, and participate in religious events to express their disagreement and opposition' in response to gay activists advocating to decriminalise homosexual conduct.[70] Likewise, in the Philippines, religious leaders remain vocal against the passage of laws promoting SGDP equality and in Singapore, confrontations between gay rights activists and

[67] See ch 10.
[68] See ch 8.
[69] See ch 5.
[70] See ch 7.

conservative religious groups have been particularly intense. In some countries, for instance in Pakistan as Aziz, Mirza and Alvear-Garijo recount, the debate has been framed as a confrontation between religious-based principles and so-called Western rights. They write: 'conservative sections of society have supposedly seen international lobbying with an un-Islamic purpose behind the Aurat March – Women's March – or The Transgender Persons (Protection of Rights) Act, 2018'.[71] Unfortunately, these trends are unlikely to subside. Several chapters in the volume refer to the growing, rather than decreasing, religious conservatism in much of the region. In post-Soeharto Indonesia, as Butt describes, government support for Islam and its greater say in government policies as well as an increasing intolerance for liberalism and religious minorities go against gender-based reforms, whether constitutional or statutory. Similarly, Shah refers to a growing religious conservatism and politicisation of religion since the 1980s in Malaysia (partly spurred by the Iranian revolution), where conflicts tend to gravitate towards privileging the dominant religion and majoritarian religious sensitivities.

VII. CONCLUSION

This volume examines the vast array of approaches to gender constitutionalism crafted and deployed across 12 representative Asian jurisdictions. It also aims to showcase the significant constitutional innovations that have emerged in this area of law. Each chapter focuses on the opportunity structure that constitutional mechanisms have provided for the advancement of the equal citizenship of women and SGDP across Asia. By and large, this comparative framework reveals that the constitutional domain has been a fruitful site to imagine, reframe, and at times even improve the position of women and SGDP. Of course, there have been setbacks, and obstacles remain. However, the constitutional domain broadly defined has represented in all our case studies both a crucial political arena and a discursive legal terrain for the conceptualisation of gender and sexuality and a constant renegotiation of their role and scope.

Significantly, Asian jurisdictions impart innovative lessons on the relationship between constitutional law and the social context in which constitutions operate in matters of gender constitutionalism. A brief overview of the flagship developments identified for each jurisdiction reveals that Asia has been an incredible laboratory of constitutional innovation in matters of gender and sexuality. This volume showcases a staggering number of trailblazing developments in terms of gender constitutionalism across our Asian case studies. These include the development via constitutional litigation of SGDP rights in Hong Kong, Taiwan, India and Pakistan; the successful lobbying of the legislature

[71] See ch 12.

in Singapore with respect to criminalising marital rape; the introduction of gender-sensitive criminal law reforms in Sri Lanka; the enactment of anti-rape laws following pro-women constitutional litigation in Pakistan; and the legislated path to gender justice in the Philippines. We also see the constitutional reorganisation of traditional institutions – either via legislation or litigation (or a combination of both) – such as the inheritance system in Japan; the household head system in South Korea; inter-religious custody battles in Malaysia; children's welfare in Indonesia; temple access for menstruating women in India; Muslim personal law in Sri Lanka; the liberalisation of abortion in South Korea; and the protection of sexual and reproductive rights in Nepal via constitutional litigation. These innovations navigate the complex terrain of gender relations and their framing in legal terms between tradition and modernity, producing unique forms of constitutional identity that are both context-specific and anchored in international law and practice. It is hoped that these constitutional solutions developed in Asia become part of global conversations on gender constitutionalism and offer comparative insights to be deployed in other parts of the world.

2

Achievements and Challenges of Japan's Gender Constitutionalism: Consolidating Constitutional Law and International Human Rights Law

AKIKO EJIMA

I. INTRODUCTION

IN JAPAN, A fundamental change occurred in terms of the rights of women immediately after World War II. Women obtained the right to vote and the new constitution granted equality under the law, which was strongly related to the US occupation. The new Constitution of Japan amended the entirety of Japanese legislation, particularly the Civil Code and the Penal Code in the direction of formal gender equality. Since then, the rights of women should have continued to advance because of legal emancipation, economic flourishing and women's access to higher education. However, according to the most recent Global Gender Gap Index 2023, Japan is ranked as 125th among 146 countries in the general ranking, 123rd in the field of economic participation and opportunity and 138th in the field of political empowerment.[1] Furthermore, the gap in political empowerment has not significantly improved although the Government set the goal of the public sphere being 30 per cent women by 2020.[2] It is against this background that this chapter examines the potential of Japan's constitution in advancing gender equality, and explores how legislation and judicial decisions have contributed to tackling gender issues.

[1] World Economic Forum, 'The Global Gender Gap Report 2023' (June 2023), available at www3.weforum.org/docs/WEF_GGGR_2023.pdf.

[2] Index in the field of political empowerment in the annual reports: 103/144 (2016); 123/144 (2017); 125/149 (2018); 144/153(2020) and 147/156(2021). As to the 30% goal, see Cabinet Office, *Daigoji Danjo Kyoudou Sankaku Kihon Keikaku* [The Fifth Basic Plan for Gender Equality] (2021) 1, 18. The goal was revised as 'by 2030' in 2021.

As to legislation, the Act on Securing, Etc of Equal Opportunity and Treatment between Men and Women in Employment (EQA) adopted in 1985 is epoch-making legislation. The EQA was enacted after the ratification of the Convention on the Elimination of All Forms of Discrimination Against Women (CEDAW) in the same year. Since then, various other pieces of legislation have followed with limited impact because they generally lack enforcement tools and sanctions. Furthermore, Japan does not have any national human rights institution, nor a general anti-discrimination law, and it is currently difficult to bring claims of human rights violations by private actors.

Constitutional litigation could open another avenue for advancement. However, the Supreme Court of Japan (SCJ) is a discreet court that has mostly been deferential to the Diet (Japanese legislature) and has only very rarely declared laws to be unconstitutional, believing that society should not be changed via judicial power. That said, since the turn of the century, breaking an almost 16-year-long silence, the SCJ has again started to deliver judgments striking down parliamentary statutes.[3]

There have only been six cases since 2002 in which the SCJ has found legislation unconstitutional (only 11 statutes were held unconstitutional since 1947 when the SCJ was established). The reason why the SCJ changed its attitude needs further exploration, but the fact is that this new case law has declared two clauses of the Civil Code unconstitutional, first in 2013 and then in 2015 (see section V). Moreover, even in cases in which the SCJ has accepted the constitutionality of the legislation, it has included concurring opinions suggesting that the Diet should reconsider the law and/or dissenting opinions that admitted the legislation was unconstitutional by reference to foreign law and international human rights treaties. An increasing number of people consider the value of bringing a case to the attention of the SCJ and the international sphere to challenge legislation and practices which may discriminate against women and sexual and gender diverse people (SGDP). Indeed, it is fair to say that a third feminist wave is taking shape as a result of a combination of international and domestic influences such as the #MeToo movement, the Flower Demos and civil society activities encouraged by social media.[4] Against this background, it is important to see how constitutional law and international law can be used to establish a global human rights law which could accelerate the empowerment of women and SGDP in Japan.

After explaining Japan's constitutional background (section II) and framework (section III), this chapter explores to what extent and how constitutional

[3] As to the detail of cases, see Y Hasebe, 'The Supreme Court of Japan, One Step Forward (but only discreetly)' (2018) 16 *International Journal of Constitutional Law* 672.

[4] The Flower Demos is a protest against sexual violence that began in March 2019 in the wake of the acquittal of a series of sexual assault cases. There are currently demonstrations (online and on the street) in 47 prefectures and London to raise their voices on the 11th of every month. 'About Flower Demo', available at www.flowerdemo.org/english.

law and litigation, with the help of international human rights law, have provided or failed to provide an adequate venue to advance the rights of women and SGDP (section IV) and considers several essential judgments which represent a promising new trend (section V). In the concluding section VI, the importance of combining the constitutional system and international human rights system to accelerate the implementation of the constitutional and international norms relating to gender issues in Japan will be addressed.[5]

II. BACKGROUND INFORMATION

A. Constitutional History

The present Constitution of Japan (promulgated in 1946 and taking effect in 1947) adopted not only a general equality clause (Article 14) but also a specific equality clause that proclaimed equality between men and women (Article 24), and was the outcome of Japan's unique constitutional drafting process.[6] The Constitution itself was enacted after World War II when Japan accepted the Potsdam Declaration which required Japan to realise demilitarisation, liberalisation and democratisation. There are several important differences between the present Constitution and the previous one, the Constitution of the Empire of Japan (promulgated and taking effect in 1889), which was the first Western-style constitution in Asia. One difference is that the sovereign power which was formerly held by the emperor resides now with the Japanese people. The new Constitution also embraced the principle of pacifism by renouncing 'war as a sovereign right of the nation and the threat or use of force as means of settling international disputes' (Article 9). Moreover, it encompassed a richer set of rights and a system of judicial review to secure the protection of those rights.

The changes amounted to a drastic rupture which would have only been possible after a revolution or at least a complete regime change that Japan never experienced. In reality, a first draft of the Constitution of Japan was prepared by the Government Section of the US occupation army, after consulting several Japanese private drafts (including one written by the Constitutional Research Association and academics such as Eisaburo Takano and Yasuzo Suzuki) and comparative constitutional law.[7] General Douglas MacArthur, the Supreme

[5] Selective important judgments of the SCJ in English are available at the website of the SCJ; see Judgments of the Supreme Court, available at www.courts.go.jp/app/hanrei_en/search. There is also a database system for the English translation of major Japanese statutes; see Japanese Law Translation, available at www.japaneselawtranslation.go.jp/?re=02.

[6] The Constitution of Japan (3 November 1946). See section III of this chapter. The present Constitution may be classified in a group of the war-based model. See M Rosenfeld, 'Constitutional Identity' in M Rosenfeld and A Sajó (eds), *Oxford Handbook of Comparative Constitutional Law* (Oxford University Press, 2012).

[7] As to private drafts, see S Koseki, *The Birth of Japan's Postwar Constitution* (Westview Press, 1997) 26ff.

Commander for the Allied Powers (SCAP) had concluded that the US could not wait for a draft prepared by the Japanese Government, after learning that the draft the Government was preparing would not satisfy the conditions of the Potsdam Declaration.[8] General MacArthur needed to settle the Japanese occupation before the Far Eastern Committee intervened in order to ensure the continuation of US influence in Asia. In the end, the Japanese Government prepared another draft under US supervision by consulting the SCAP draft (often called the MacArthur Draft) and made every effort to 'Japanize' it: the Japanese legislative bureau amended the American draft (for example, the removal of the protection of foreigners) and the Diet also added social rights in the Constitution which did not exist in the US Constitution.[9] There was no formal opportunity for the public to participate in the process.

At the same time, Japanese suffragettes, building on the long-standing efforts of the pre-war suffragettes such as Fusae Ichikawa,[10] resumed their activity immediately after World War II and successfully petitioned the SCAP to realise women's right to vote by amending the electoral law allowing women over the age of 20 to vote and stand for election. In the general election of December 1945, women voted in Japan for the first time. In this sense, it can be said that the Diet, which discussed and passed the draft of the present Constitution, truly represented the Japanese people – men and women.[11] Although only 39 female members (among a total of 446 members) of the House of Representatives (HR) joined the Diet the first time as a result of the election, they would influence the legal process to abolish the feudal family system *(ie-seido)* by amending the Civil Code.[12]

B. Constitutional and Judicial Structure

Japan is a unitary state. The Constitution allocates powers according to the principle of separation of powers: the Diet has legislative power (Article 41), the Cabinet has executive/administrative power (Article 65), and the judiciary has judicial power (Article 76). The present Constitution like the previous Constitution created a parliamentary democracy.[13] The Diet consists of two houses: the House of Representatives (HR) and the House of Councillors (HC).

[8] ibid 68.

[9] ibid 111.

[10] DA Vavich, 'The Japanese Woman's Movement: Ichikawa Fusae, A Pioneer in Woman's Suffrage' (1967) 22 *Monumenta Nipponica* 402.

[11] 66.97% of women and 78.52% of men participated in the election.

[12] In the traditional family system, called *Ie-seido* (a patriarchal household) under the previous Constitution, the eldest son inherited all the household property to maintain the continuation of the household. As to the amendment of the Civil Code, see section III.A of this chapter.

[13] Formally, the Constitution of Japan was the amendment of the previous Constitution by using the amendment clause of the previous Constitution.

There are currently 48 female MPs (10.3 per cent) among 465 at the HR, and 64 female MPs (26.7 per cent) among 248 at the HC (as of 20 May 2023). Kanako Otsuji, a member of the HR, was the first MP to come out as a lesbian. The Cabinet is formed by the Prime Minister, who is usually the leader of the political party which wins the general election of the HR. There are three female Cabinet ministers (1.2 per cent) among 25. Officially the Prime Minister is selected from among the members of the Diet by a resolution of the Diet and appointed by the emperor. The Liberal Democratic Party (LDP), a conservative party, has kept the power in government since 1955 with few exceptions.[14] The fundamental factor behind the LDP's long-term hold on power can be found in the conservative nature of the majority of the Japanese people. The absence of strong opposition parties has also contributed. Additionally, the fact that the younger generation has lost interest in politics has worked in the LDP's favour. The disparity of the vote value between urban and rural areas also favours the LDP, which has a large voting base in the countryside where the population constantly decreases. Therefore, the political situation in Japan is an obstacle to improving gender issues through legislation.

The Japanese judiciary consists of the SCJ, eight high courts, 50 district courts, 50 family courts, and 438 summary courts. The district courts are the lowest courts of general jurisdiction. If the parties do not agree with the judgment of the District Court, they can appeal to the High Court. If the parties do not agree with the judgment of the High Court and fulfil the conditions prescribed by either the Code of Criminal Procedure, Article 405 or the Code of Civil Procedure, Article 312, section 1, they can appeal to the Supreme Court.[15] The Supreme Court does not have a US-style *certiorari* process allowing the judges to choose the cases they will consider.[16] The family courts deal with family and juvenile cases and the summary courts deal with small claims civil cases and petty crime cases. Decisions by family courts and summary courts can be appealed to district courts.

The SCJ consists of a Chief Judge and 14 additional judges (15 in total). There is no fixed term of office for Supreme Court judges, and the mandatory retirement age is 70. Therefore, political power cannot eliminate a judge of the SCJ except for an impeachment court consisting of members of both Houses (Articles 64 and 78). The judges, apart from the Chief Judge, are appointed by the Cabinet (Article 79). The Emperor appoints the Chief Judge of the SCJ who

[14] The exceptions were the Hosokawa coalition Government of eight political parties (August 1993–April 1994) and the Noda Government of the Democratic Party of Japan (September 2011–January 2012).

[15] Judicial System Reform Council Opinion pointed that the SCJ deals with too many and it should select and concentrate on important constitutional cases. For the details, see S Matsui, *The Constitution of Japan: A Contextual Analysis* (Hart Publishing, 2011) 121ff.

[16] Judicial System Reform Council, 'Judicial System Reform Council Opinion – the Judicial System to support Japan in the 21st Century' (2001), available at japan.kantei.go.jp/policy/sihou/singikai/990612_e.html.

was designated by the Cabinet before the appointment (Article 6). The Chief Judge must be a person of at least 40 years of age who has extensive knowledge and a background in law.[17] In practice, the Cabinet listens to the opinion of the Chief Judge of the SCJ and appoints them after considering various factors. Generally, the Supreme Court has consisted of six judges, four lawyers, two prosecutors, one university professor, one administrator and one diplomat according to the custom. When a judge with a lawyer background retires, the post is filled by a lawyer based on the recommendation of the Bar Association. Therefore, the appointment of Supreme Court judges has rarely been a problem from the viewpoint of judicial independence. However, appointments have been problematic from a gender perspective. The first female judge, Hisako Takahashi, was appointed in 1994. She was the former Director of the Women and Youth Bureau of the Ministry of Labor. The second and third female judges of the SCJ also came from the same ministry. In 2010, the SCJ accepted the fourth female judge, Kiyoko Okabe, who was a law professor with 18 years of experience as a judge of the lower court before she moved to academia. 2010 was also the first year that the SCJ had two female judges concurrently. Since then, the SCJ has twice had periods with three-female judges: 6 June 2013–15 January 2017 and 9 January 2018–6 February 2019. However, since 6 February 2019, the SCJ has only had two female judges despite the Government's proclaimed 30 per cent goal. In the whole of the judiciary, there are 795 female judges among 3881 judges (20 per cent). It is not officially known if there are judges from the SGDP community.

The judgment of the SCJ is given by one of three Petty Benches (PB) or by the Grand Bench (GB). Each PB consists of four or five judges and the GB consists of 15 judges. The PB can transfer a case to the GB when it finds that the case in question includes a possibility of unconstitutionality or change of the precedent of the SCJ. The opinion of the majority is shown as one opinion and the names of the judges who agree with the majority opinion are shown. Judges who disagree with the majority opinion or wish to complement it can write dissenting or concurring opinions.

The SCJ is the last and highest court 'to determine the constitutionality of any law, order, regulation or official act' (Article 81). However, it is understood that the lower courts also have the power of judicial review. There is no constitutional court. The parties who argue the unconstitutionality of legislation or administrative acts need to do so in a concrete case and show there is a sufficient connection to and harm from the law or action challenged. There is also no public interest litigation, although lawyers can and do collectively organise to pursue litigation to advance human rights and equality causes.[18] The SCJ has

[17] The Court Act, Act No 59 of 16 April 1947, Art 41.

[18] See, eg, the former Hansen's disease patients, Minamata disease patients, AIDS patients, asbestos patients, atomic bomb victims, labour discrimination victims, etc.

been deferential to the legislature and decides the constitutionality of legislation by considering if it is reasonable or not. Therefore, it does not apply judicial review standards although it studies foreign case law.

Japan has ratified eight core UN human rights treaties. However, it has not ratified any of the optional protocols which enable individuals to report human rights violations by the Member States to the treaty bodies because the Government argued that it needs to examine thoroughly the influence of ratification on the constitutional system. In Japan some of the ratified human rights treaties have played an important role in bringing about changes in legislation even though many of the changes have been weakly implemented. Japan also lacks a specific national human rights institution despite the many recommendations of human rights treaty bodies. Civil society has also been weak in bringing about changes even though there is a new trend in gender and SGDP issues.[19]

III. CONSTITUTIONAL FRAMING OF GENDER

This section first provides an overview of how the Constitution of Japan refers to equality and touches on the unique drafting process of Article 24, which is the main clause on gender equality.[20] Then, this section explains how, and to what extent, the Constitution, CEDAW and the EQA are implemented.

A. Constitutional Provisions

The Constitution of Japan has several articles concerning equality. Article 14 is the general equality clause providing for equality under the law. Article 24, however, goes further; it guarantees a right to equality in marriage for women and men but also equality in 'the choice of spouse, property rights, inheritance, choice of domicile, divorce and other matters pertaining to marriage and the family'.[21] Article 26 guarantees equal education and Article 44 guarantees equal rights to stand for election and vote.[22]

[19] L Dales, *Feminist Movements in Contemporary Japan* (Routledge, 2009).

[20] The Constitution of Japan.

[21] The Constitution of Japan, Art 24: Marriage shall be based only on the mutual consent of both sexes and it shall be maintained through cooperation with the equal rights of husband and wife as a basis. With regard to choice of spouse, property rights, inheritance, choice of domicile, divorce and other matters pertaining to marriage and the family, laws shall be enacted from the standpoint of individual dignity and the essential equality of the sexes.

[22] The Constitution of Japan, Art 26: All people shall have the right to receive an equal education correspondent to their ability, as provided by law. All people shall be obligated to have all boys and girls under their protection receive ordinary education as provided for by law. Such compulsory education shall be free. Art 44: The qualifications of members of both Houses and their electors shall be fixed by law. However, there shall be no discrimination because of race, creed, sex, social status, family origin, education, property or income.

The key articles are Article 14 and Article 24. These brought about major legal changes in 1947 including an overhaul of family law and inheritance law by abolishing *Ie-seido* (the feudal family system) and discriminatory clauses in the Penal Code which made adultery a crime only if committed by married women.[23] These amendments were influenced by the newly elected female Members of the Diet. However, discriminatory clauses including the unequal treatment of children born out of wedlock, restrictions on remarriage, differences in the age of marriage, and the same-surname system remained.[24]

Article 24's detailed content on the equal status of men and women in the sphere of family and inheritance is the result of the unique contribution by one of the original drafters, Beate Sirota Gordon (hereafter Sirota as her maiden name). She was born in Vienna in 1923 and at the age of five she followed her father, a famous Jewish pianist born in Ukraine and well-established in Vienna, when he was invited to become a music professor at a music university in Tokyo. After spending nearly 10 years in Tokyo, Sirota went to study in the United States and became fluent in five languages, including Japanese. When World War II broke out, she lost contact with her parents and managed to return to Tokyo after the war to work as a translator with the US army, where she was assigned to the Government Section.

Under MacArthur's order, she became a member of a subcommittee on civil rights of the drafting committee and, mostly because she was a woman, the drafting of a provision on women's rights was assigned to her. As the SCAP lacked the capacity to draft constitutions, the decision was made to collect and examine drafts prepared by scholars and institutions in their private capacity and to search for foreign constitutional sources in several libraries in Tokyo, including the Declaration of Independence, the American Constitution, the Magna Carta, the Weimar Constitution, the French Constitution, the Scandinavian Constitutions and the Soviet Constitution. In her search, Sirota was particularly attracted to the social rights in the Soviet Constitution and the Weimar Constitution, which she identified as resources for her clause on women's rights.[25] Conversely, she was disappointed by the US Constitution, which scarcely mentioned women's rights, except for female suffrage under the XIXth Amendment. More importantly, rather than emulating foreign sources, she identified the problems and difficulties faced by Japanese women based on what she had learned through conversations or observations of Japanese society. These problems and difficulties included young women being forced to marry, or to divorce due to infertility, married women having no rights to property, and women generally being marginalised in society. After identifying the problems, she connected them with existing human rights provisions in other constitutions. Her draft article

[23] Act No 124 of 26 October 1947 and Act No 222 of 22 December 1947.

[24] As to the same-surname system, see section V.E of this chapter.

[25] BS Gordon, *The Only Woman in the Room* (Kodansha, 1997) 107. For eg, see Art 122 of the Constitution of the Union of Soviet Socialist Republics 1936 and Art 109 of the Weimar Constitution.

became longer and more specific and included social welfare services such as free education, medical services, the protection of new mothers, and the rights of children born out of wedlock and their mothers.[26] However, Coronel Kades, Deputy Chief of the Government Section, ordered Sirota to curtail this provision because he deemed the content to be too detailed for a constitution. In the end, the protection clause for children born out of wedlock was deleted and her draft was shortened to one-third of its original length.[27] The outcome was Article 24. Sirota later regretted that she obeyed Kades's order when she learned that the legal discrimination towards children born out of wedlock remained in the law.[28] It would not be until 2013 that the SCJ finally ruled that discrimination against children born out of wedlock was unconstitutional.[29]

Sirota's contribution is a good example of how a woman non-jurist with a critical mind and a sense of justice and empathy can offer a prescription for resolving the legal problems other women encounter. Moreover, it is noteworthy that she did not merely rely on foreign constitutions. Instead, she used foreign constitutions as a guide. The setting of priorities and substance of her writing came from the identification of the problems of Japanese women and based on her experiences, observations and conversations.

B. The Japanese Constitution as Implemented via Legislation

The main legal instrument used to push for change in Japan is CEDAW, ratified in 1985, rather than the Constitution. Although, several legal reforms ensued after CEDAW ratification there is no general anti-discrimination law in Japan.[30] As a result of the ratification of CEDAW, the Nationality Law was also amended to make it possible for a child of a Japanese woman who marries a foreign husband to obtain Japanese nationality. Before the amendment, in the case of international marriage, only a child of a Japanese man could obtain Japanese nationality. The school curriculum, including home economics for male students, which was formerly only available to female students, was amended to comply with CEDAW. The major legal achievement, however, was the adoption of the

[26] In Japan a mother who gives birth out of wedlock is not only socially criticised but also legally discriminated against, for instance, in terms of tax deduction. A bereaved woman who has a child can claim a tax deduction but an unmarried woman who has a child cannot. Therefore, this chapter considers a case concerning a child born out of wedlock as a gender issue.

[27] Gordon (n 25) 116.

[28] Beate Sirota Gordon showed her disappointment during her speech at the House of Councillors (HC) in 2000. The HC, Conference of Research Commission on the Constitution, Record of Proceedings (2 May 2000).

[29] See section V.B of this chapter.

[30] A Ejima, 'Japan' in M Mercat-Bruns et al (eds), *Comparative Perspectives on the Enforcement and Effectiveness of Antidiscrimination Law: Challenges and Innovative Tools* (Springer, 2018).

EQA in 1985.[31] The EQA was enacted to promote the welfare of female workers by ensuring equal opportunities and treatment for men and women in the field of employment, developing and improving the vocational skills of female workers, assisting their re-employment, and promoting harmony between their professional and family lives. Simultaneously with the EQA, the restrictions on overtime work, holiday work and late-night work for female workers under the Labor Standards Act were reduced to establish equal working conditions for men and women. Also, protection for female workers was strengthened by extending the period of leave after childbirth. The expectation towards the EQA was so enormous that the female undergraduates who graduated in the same year aimed for jobs that were once secured for male undergraduates. These graduates were called the EQA generation. However, the EQA disappointed many women because it did not contain any mechanism for enforcement.

In theory, CEDAW should play a substantial role at the Japanese courts as ratified treaties in Japan have legal effect and a legal status higher than an ordinary statute. However, the Japanese courts have been very reluctant to apply international human rights treaties directly.[32] In general, after the treaty was ratified and minimal legislative measures were adopted to secure its compliance, its influence and the impact of the concluding observations on the Japanese Government have been limited. However, CEDAW has provided useful information for civil society. Non-governmental organisations (NGOs) focused on gender issues have regularly submitted shadow reports (alternative reports) to the CEDAW Committee and organised a network (Japan NGO Network for CEDAW) to make their approach to the CEDAW Committee more sophisticated.

The work of the NGOs has led to the strengthening of the EQA. In 1997, an obligation on employers to take measures against sexual harassment in the workplace was introduced. In 1999 the Government also adopted the Basic Act for a Gender Equal Society to clarify the basic principles of the formation of a gender-equal society, to set a course toward this end, and to promote efforts by the state, local governments and citizens for this purpose.[33] Since then, Basic Plans for a Gender Equal Society have been issued regularly to implement and advance these goals. They allow the Government to provide guidance and recommendations to employers even if they lack strong implementing measures like penalties or sanctions. In 2006, the EQA was amended to cover discrimination against men. In 2016, the prohibition of indirect discrimination and maternity harassment was adopted, which obliged employers to take preventative measures.

[31] The Act on Securing, Etc of Equal Opportunity and Treatment between Men and Women in Employment (EQA) was the amendment of the Act on Working Women Welfare (Act No 113 of 1 July 1972).

[32] A Ejima, 'Use of Foreign and Comparative Law by the Supreme Court of Japan' in GF Ferrari (ed), *Judicial Cosmopolitanism: The Use of Foreign Law in Contemporary Constitutional Systems* (Brill/Nijhoff, 2019).

[33] Act No 78 of 23 June 1999.

The Government adopted the Act on the Promotion of Female Participation and Career Advancement in the Workplace in 2015 to narrow the gender gap.[34] This Act intends to promote female participation and career advancement in the workplace by establishing fundamental principles for the promotion of female participation and career advancement in the workplace, clarifying the responsibilities of the national Government and local governments and employers, formulating a basic policy and plan of action for employers, and stipulating support measures. More gender equality-focused legislation was enacted in 2018, the Act on Promotion of Gender Equality in the Political Field.[35] This Act intends to promote gender equality in the political field by laying out the fundamental principles and clarifying the responsibilities of the central Government and local governments. However, the effectiveness of each of these Acts remains to be seen as, once again, they lack compulsory measures making everything conditional on voluntary efforts of employers and political parties.

In 2021 more specific content of responsibilities (setting the goals for the number of female candidates, improvement of the selection process of candidates, education and training for would-be candidates and efforts to eliminate sexual harassment) were added to the Act on Promotion of Gender Equality in the Political Field 2018 to address Japan's low ranking in the Global Gender Index. However, the changes did not tackle the weak implementation mechanisms.[36] In the end, the increase of female workers and women's access to managerial positions show the effect of the EQA, but the pace of change has been slow in comparison to other countries. This is the result of the poor representation of women and SGDP in the political field. So far, there has been no positive action to improve the poor representation of women and SGDP in the public sphere and no judicial case challenging the constitutionality of positive action measures. Similarly, no case has been brought to challenge the constitutionality of negligence of the Cabinet and Diet not to take any positive measures which 'shall not be considered discrimination as defined in CEDAW' (Article 4 of CEDAW). An argument can be made that Japan needs to implement a quota system. Constitutional academics have been cautious and warned against the quota system in general, which would violate Article 14 of the Constitution as 'reverse' discrimination.[37] However, some academics argue that it is possible to adopt the quota system voluntarily introduced by the political parties because the poor representation of women harms the precise reflection of the people's will.[38]

[34] Act No 64 of 4 September 2015. As to Global Gender Gap index, see n 1.

[35] Act No 28 of 23 May 2018.

[36] Act No 67 of 16 June 2021.

[37] N Ashibe, *Kenpo* [Constitutional Law], 7th edn (Iwanami Shoten, 2019) 136; K Sato, *Nihonkoku Kenpo-ron* [Theory on the Constitution of Japan], 2nd edn (Seibundo, 2020) 223–24; Y Hasebe, *Kenpo* [Constitutional Law], 7th edn (Shinseisha 2018).

[38] M Tsujimura, *Gender to Ho* [Gender and Law] (Iwanami Shoten 2016) 41; M Tsujimura, *Pojitivu Akushon* [Positive Action] (Iwanami Shoten, 2011) 145.

IV. CONSTITUTIONAL JURISPRUDENCE

This section provides an overview of the extent to which the Constitution and legislation which implement the Constitution have or have not been seized as opportunities to advance women and SGDP struggles by litigation, and includes reference to the relevance of constitutional provisions in interpreting legal norms binding private parties. Taking into account that the male-dominant Diet did not produce much legislation to support women and SGDP, it was important for women and SGDP as a start to bring cases to the courts in order to attract the attention of civil society. This section covers judgments not only by the SCJ but also by lower courts because they also have constitutional review power and some lower courts are more willing to use the constitutional review power to find unconstitutionality than the SCJ. The first constitutional lawsuits focused on women and SGDP started in employment as more women started to work outside the home and faced various discriminatory treatment at the workplace. However, the effect of constitutional law was limited as the Constitution was not considered directly applicable to private companies. Instead, it was understood by the SCJ and academics that constitutional law was helpful when courts interpret the general clauses of the civil code (the indirect application doctrine).[39] Additionally, constitutional clauses have not been resorted to in challenging discriminatory legislation and practice because gender analysis was marginalised in male-dominant constitutional law academia. For example, one of the most famous and widely used constitutional case law books only has a few entries discussing gender issues and only one female professor was included among about 120 contributors until 1986.[40]

A. Employment

Many working women who had faced discrimination concerning issues such as retirement, wages, family allowance, promotion, sexual harassment and maternity harassment brought cases to the judiciary. This is the area where not only litigation but also social pressure has been strong because of the support of unions and NGOs.

[39] Matsui (n 15) 162–63. Japanese academics established the private application doctrine by consulting the US state doctrine and the German *drittwirkung* doctrine. See Y Hasebe, 'The Supreme Court of Japan: A Judicial Court, Not Necessarily a Constitutional Court' in AHY Chen and A Harding (eds), *Constitutional Court in Asia: A Comparative Perspective* (Cambridge University Press, 2018) 291–94.

[40] The female author ratio decreased from 0.8% (1963) to 0.4% (1988) as the number of the cases in the case law book increased from 115 (1963) to 208 (1988) without increasing female contributors. The most current edition (7th edition) has 33 female authors among 214 (15%). See Y Hasebe et al (eds), *Kenpo Hanrei Hyakusen* [100 Selected Cases of Constitutional Law] (Yuhikaku, 2019).

Sumitomo Cement Corporation Case (1966) is the first retirement age discrimination case dealt with by a court. In this case a female employee challenged the obligation to retire either at 35 years old or when she married, according to a contract signed between her and the company. The company argued that once a female worker marries, she prioritises family and working efficiency decreases. The Tokyo District Court held that it was a violation of Article 90 (public order) of the Civil Code because discrimination was based on gender and restricted the freedom to marry.[41] The Court did not directly apply the Constitution. Instead, it ruled that forcing only women to retire after marriage is unreasonable and void because of Article 90 of the Civil Code by highlighting that marriage is protected by the Constitution which guarantees freedom to marry (Article 24) and equal treatment (Article 14).[42]

Nissan Motor Corporation Case (1981) is the first Supreme Court case in which the SCJ dealt with the gender equality question. According to company regulations, Nissan Motor Corporation expected women to retire five years earlier than men: 60 years old for men and 55 years old for women.[43] Because Nissan Motor Corporation is a private company the SCJ did not directly apply the Constitution. Instead, the Court admitted that the company regulation which treated men and women differently violated Civil Code Article 90's public order clause and referred to Article 14 of the Constitution.[44] This was understood as an example of indirect application of the constitutional principle of equality between men and women.[45]

The *Sumitomo Electric Industry Corporation Case* (2000) shows the limits of this approach. It also showcases the problems raised by the gendered two-track employment management system commonly adopted by Japanese companies which continued even after the EQA was put into effect in 1985. Under this system, *Sogoshoku* is a regular full-time position with the prospect of promotion and *Ippanshoku* is a position limited to clerical work, with limited possibilities for promotion or advancement in terms of role or salary. In the *Sumitomo Electric Industry Corporation Case* the company followed such a system. Men who graduated from high school and were hired for a clerical post could be transferred to an expert post through promotion, but women who graduated from high school and were hired for clerical posts were not given such an opportunity. The Osaka District Court held that the treatment was not compatible with the spirit of Article 14 of the Constitution but that it could not be said to infringe the public order principle of Article 90 of the Civil Code,

[41] The Civil Code (Act No 89 of 1896), Art 90: A juridical act that is against public order is void.
[42] Judgment of 20 December 1966, Tokyo District Court, 17(6) *Romin* 1406.
[43] Judgment of 24 March 1981, SCJ 35(2) *Minshu* 300.
[44] ibid.
[45] The Court held that it is reasonable to understand that it [the regulation] is invalid under the provisions of article 90 of the Civil Code because it stipulates unreasonable discrimination based only on gender (see Art 14(1) of the Constitution and Arts 1–2 of the Civil Code).

considering prevalent social morality norms in the 1960s when the two-track system was installed.[46] This conclusion was heavily criticised by practitioners and academics because the Constitution, as the highest law in Japan, could not quash the discriminatory treatment.[47] The plaintiff then submitted a shadow report to the CEDAW Committee. Following receipt of the shadow report, the CEDAW Committee, expressed concern in its concluding observations in 2003 'at the existing wage gap between women and men, stemming largely from the difference in the type of work, horizontal and vertical employment segregation as expressed by the two-track employment management system'.[48] With this, the plaintiff appealed to the Osaka High Court where the parties agreed to reach a settlement that allowed the female worker to obtain a job promotion in 2003.

The two-track employment management system was also challenged at the Tokyo District Court in the *Nomura Securities Case* (2002).[49] Under this system, male workers tended to choose the *Sogoshoku* track with the expectation of a high salary and promotion as the breadwinner in the family. The company argued that it did not discriminate against female workers who chose the *Ippanshoku* track of their own free will. However, most women chose this track because they were primarily in charge of household work based on traditional gender roles. The very existence of the dual-track system helped perpetuate these traditional gender role arrangements.

B. Citizenship

Until the early 1980s, a child could not obtain Japanese nationality if he or she had a foreign father and a Japanese mother, but could obtain Japanese nationality if the father was a Japanese national and the mother was a foreigner.[50] A child with a Japanese mother and an American father argued that Article 2 of the Nationality Act was against Article 14 of the Constitution. Moreover, she could not obtain US nationality because her parents resided in Japan and her father could not meet the US residential requirement of 10 years. The combination of both laws indeed generated stateless children born of Japanese mothers and US soldiers stationed in Okinawa who would eventually disappear or had a legal wife in the US. The Tokyo District Court refused the plaintiff's claim by

[46] Judgment of 31 July 2000, Osaka District Court, 1746 *Hanji* 94.

[47] M Miyaji, 'Danjobetu Kosusei to Zesei Gimu no Hitei: Sumitomo Denko Jiken' [The Two-course system and denial of the obligation to correct: Sumitomo Electric Industry Corporation case] (2000) 1491 *Rodo Horitsu Junpo* 30.

[48] Committee on the Elimination of Discrimination Against Women [hereinafter CEDAW Committee], 'Report of the UN Committee on the Elimination of Discrimination against Women', Twenty-eighth Session (13–31 January 2003), Twenty-ninth Session (30 June–18 July 2003) (18 August 2003) A/58/38, para 369.

[49] Judgment of 20 February 2002, Tokyo District Court, 1781 *Hanji* 34.

[50] Act No 147 of 1950.

holding that the Nationality Act was not unconstitutional because prevention of dual citizenship was the rationale behind patrilineal priority and that the child could obtain Japanese nationality by naturalisation.[51] The Tokyo High Court would later agree with this conclusion and emphasised the wide legislative discretion in the field.[52] This issue was not resolved until 1985 after the ratification of CEDAW. CEDAW helped resolve the citizenship issue, however, another problematic aspect of the Nationality Act was challenged again before the SCJ.[53]

C. Family Matters

Despite the overhaul of the family and inheritance sections of the Civil Code in 1947, some discriminatory clauses remained untouched until recently. These include those on the minimum age of marriage whereby women could marry at the age of 16 while men could only marry at the age of 18 (Article 731); the rule according to which women, but not men, have to wait for six months after divorce to remarry (Article 733); the rule on the same-surname system under which 96 per cent of women choose their husbands' surnames (Article 750) and the rule on legal inheritance allocation which differentiates between a child born in wedlock and a child born out of wedlock (Article 900). As we shall see, all these discriminatory provisions except the one concerning the marriageable age were challenged at the SCJ (section V). The constitutionality of the Civil Code and the Family Register Act which do not allow same-sex marriage was also challenged at the lower court. The Sapporo District Court admitted unconstitutionality (Article 14 of the Constitution) of the above Acts based on the criteria of reasonableness but denied state compensation by acknowledging the legislature's discretion.[54]

D. Bodies

The Penal Code punishes abortion (Articles 212–216). However, the Eugenic Protection Act (EPA) allowed abortions until 22 weeks of pregnancy. The EPA was enacted in 1948 to control the increase of the population after World War II and to maintain the pre-war eugenics policy.[55] It also enabled doctors to perform

[51] Judgment of 30 March 1981, Tokyo District Court, 996 *Hanji* 23.
[52] Judgment of 23 June 1982, Tokyo High Court, 1045 *Hanji* 78.
[53] Judgment of 4 June 2008, SCJ (GB), 62(6) *Minshu* 1367, Further details, see section V.A of this chapter.
[54] Judgment of 17 March 2021, Sapporo District Court, available at www.courts.go.jp/app/files/hanrei_jp/200/090200_hanrei.pdf.
[55] Act No 156 of 1948. Under the Act the forced abortion towards Hansen's disease patients and person with mental disabilities.

unconsented abortions and sterilisation under the guise of the interests of patients with disabilities. Some of these patients recently sued the Government. The Sapporo District Court admitted the EPA violated Articles 13 (right to the pursuit of happiness), 14 (equality under the law) and 24 (the right to marry) of the Constitution although the Court did not grant compensation since the plaintiff's right to claim compensation had expired once the exclusion period passed.[56] The Court held that the legislative purpose of the EPA was not reasonable, that unequal treatment was not based on reasonable evidence, and that the EPA is outside the limits of the reasonable legislative discretion of the Diet. The EPA was replaced by the Maternal Health Act and the eugenics policy was abolished only in 1996.[57] It is also problematic that contraception measures such as birth control pills are less accessible in comparison to other countries.

In 1969 The Tokyo District Court found a doctor who practised gender-reassignment surgery guilty under the EPA.[58] In 1998, the procedure was legalised after the Medical Society discussed and prepared the guidelines under which the surgery could be performed. In 2003, the Act on Special Provisions of Gender Identity of Persons with Gender Identity Disorder (AGID) was enacted to allow a gender change on the family register (*koseki*) based on a person's newly acquired gender. Advocates had sought the ability to change one's gender on the register for many years. However, the 2003 Act requires surgery and, as we shall see, its constitutionality was tested at the SCJ.[59]

V. FLAGSHIP CONSTITUTIONAL DEVELOPMENTS: THE DIALOGUE BETWEEN CONSTITUTIONAL, INTERNATIONAL AND COMPARATIVE LAW AS A PROMISING VENUE

In 2002 the SCJ broke its long silence by finding a piece of legislation unconstitutional.[60] The SCJ dealt with the constitutionality question of the Civil Code because the Diet had not addressed it. Three of the six decisions where the Court has found legislation unconstitutional are related to gender issues and two of them concern provisions on the family and inheritance sections of the Civil Code. Therefore, it is important to examine what has triggered this change of attitude of the SCJ in the twenty-first century. There are several possible reasons. First, the Supreme Court's very raison d'etre was questioned during the judicial

[56] Judgment of 15 January 2021, Sapporo District Court, 1481 *Hanji* 92. Other lower courts follow the judgment in different cases.

[57] Act No 105 of 2006 (Amendment of Act No 156 of 1948).

[58] Judgment of 15 February 1969, Tokyo District Court, 551 *Hanji* 26. The plaintiff appealed to the Sapporo High Court in 2021.

[59] The Act No 111 of 2003. For the details, see section V.D of this chapter.

[60] The SCJ had not produced unconstitutionality judgments since 1987. Formerly, the SCJ admitted the unconstitutionality of the statutes in five cases in the period 1973–1987.

reforms which started in 1999.[61] If the SCJ did not fulfil its role of judicial review as stipulated in the Constitution (there had only been five judicial review decisions finding legislation unconstitutional when the discussion for judicial reform started), then what is the purpose of the SCJ? Second, as time went on, the Diet's failure to consider some laws which needed to be updated according to changes in society became decreasingly acceptable and encouraged litigation to trigger change. In particular, the openly discriminatory family and inheritance sections of the Civil Code had remained unexamined since the post-war overhaul in 1949. Third, there had been an accumulation of recommendations of the human rights treaty bodies denouncing the negligence of the Diet and the Cabinet which have the obligation to implement Japan's human rights obligations. It should be emphasised that the second and third developments were achieved through the efforts of women, SGDP and civil society in general.

This section focuses on how the SCJ has started to refer to the international human rights treaties and treaty bodies' opinions in deciding that certain norms are unconstitutional, and how this incorporation of human rights standards is also assisting the SCJ in more active judicial review of legislation under constitutional provisions than it had before. The SCJ's prior neglect of international human rights law has turned into a 'dialogic' attitude which has, nevertheless, been far from consistent. First, the 2008 judgment for the first time referred directly to international human rights treaties when it found the Nationality Act unconstitutional. In 2013 the unanimous decision of the SCJ even went further to refer to the recommendations by the Committees of the International Covenant on Civil and Political Rights (ICCPR) and the Convention on the Rights of the Child (CRC) when finding the Civil Code unconstitutional. However, after two years the SCJ went back to its previous silence when it examined two clauses of the Civil Code, despite existing recommendations by the CEDAW Committee, which had urged the Japanese Government to amend the Civil Code. In 2019, a concurring opinion in an SCJ decision referred for the first time to a 2017 judgment of the European Court of Human Rights (ECtHR) when it raised doubts about the constitutionality of the AGID (see section IV.D). Moreover, in 2021, the SCJ revisited the constitutionality question of the Civil Code.

Before the analysis of each case, it is helpful to mention that, unlike other constitutional courts, such as the US Supreme Court or the German Constitutional Court, the SCJ does not clearly rely on systematic standards of judicial review (such as a strict scrutiny standard or proportionality principle). This makes its doctrinal construction hard to systematise. Rather, as Justice Katsumi Chiba once explained in his concurring opinion, 'the court handles each case flexibly, without being bound by any standard that it establishes.'[62]

[61] Judicial System Reform Council (n 16).
[62] Judgment of 7 December 2012, SCJ, 66(12) *Keishu* 1337.

A. The 2008 Nationality Act Judgment

In 2008 the SCJ found Article 14 of the Constitution was violated in the Nationality Act Case about the legal status (nationality) of a child who was born out of wedlock in Japan to a non-Japanese mother and Japanese father.[63] The Minister of Justice had refused the child's application for Japanese nationality because the mother and father were not legally married. The requirement of legal marriage existed in the Nationality Act to guarantee a close tie between the child and Japan despite the basic principle of *jus sanguinis* (principle of nationality by which citizenship is determined or acquired by the nationality of one or both parents).

The majority opinion of the 2008 Judgment of the Nationality Act Case held that the child is entitled to Japanese nationality by the constitutional interpretation of the Nationality Act and invalidated a part of the provision which required legal marriage. The SCJ judgment was based on the reasonable relevance standard, meaning that reasonable legislative purpose and reasonable connection between the purpose and discriminatory treatment are required.[64] First, the SCJ admitted the reasonable relevance between the purpose of the law and the provision that existed when the legal reform was introduced in 1984 by referring to a similar situation in other foreign countries. Then, the SCJ held that it was no longer reasonable, in relation to the legislative purpose, to factor in legitimacy as an indicator of the child's tie with Japan because of more recent changes, such as changes in views regarding family lifestyles and parent–child relationships, changes in the realities such as the increase in the number of children born out of wedlock, the increase in the number of children born to couples of Japanese citizens and foreign citizens, and the changes in the legal systems of foreign countries and international human rights treaties (the ICCPR and the CRC were cited).[65] Again, this case marked the first time the SCJ cites international human rights treaties in its case law.

However, the decision did not come without criticism. The comparison with foreign jurisdictions in the 2008 judgment of the Nationality Act Case is problematic in that it only refers to 'foreign countries' without mentioning specific countries. The dissenting opinion criticised the majority opinion by emphasising the differences in circumstances between Japan and Western countries but did not question taking into consideration the trends in these foreign states in the process of examining the constitutionality of the provision in Japan.[66]

[63] Judgment of 4 June 2008 (n 53).
[64] ibid 1371.
[65] ibid 1374.
[66] ibid 1374 and 1401.

B. The 2013 Inheritance Decision: A Game Changer?

The 2013 Inheritance Case was a breakthrough in terms of the SCJ's use of foreign law and international human rights treaties to find legislation unconstitutional.[67] In this decision, the SCJ finally admitted the unconstitutionality of the provision to Article 900(iv) of the Civil Code, which stipulates that the share of inheritance owed to a child born out of wedlock shall be one-half of the share of the inheritance owed to a child born in wedlock (hereinafter this shall be referred to as the 'Provision'). This allowed the unequal allocation of inheritance between 'legitimate' and 'illegitimate' children. This Provision was one of the clear legal distinctions between 'legitimate' and 'illegitimate' children that remained in the Civil Code after the large-scale legal reforms that took place to make statutes compatible with the newly adopted constitution.[68] This discriminatory clause affected not only children born out of wedlock but also their mothers because the social stigma on unmarried women who gave birth was reinforced by the existence of this Provision.

The SCJ precedent prior to this case was the GB decision in the Inheritance Case of 5 July 1995 (hereinafter the '1995 Inheritance Decision').[69] The 1995 Inheritance Decision held that the Constitution prohibits 'discrimination not based upon reasonable grounds'.[70] The SCJ ruled that the Provision did not go beyond the bounds of the reasonable discretion vested in the legislature and that it, therefore, could not be deemed to violate Article 14(1) of the Constitution because the Civil Code sanctioned legal marriage and the Provision balances the protection of legal marriage with the protection of 'illegitimate' children. Thereafter, the Petty Bench decisions of the SCJ in other inheritance cases followed the 1995 Inheritance Decision.[71] However, even in 1995 the decision was not unanimous. There were five dissenting opinions including by the only female judge, Takahashi. The dissenting opinions expressed jointly that the existence of the Provision encouraged people to consider children out of wedlock as inferior. They also expressed that it is beyond the bounds of reasonable discretion of the legislature because the substantial relevance between the legal purpose, the protection of legal marriage, and the legal measure, a different treatment between children born in wedlock and out of wedlock, no longer exists in today's society.

[67] Decision of 4 September 2013, SCJ (GB), 67(6) *Minshu* 1320. See A Ejima, 'Emerging Transjudicial Dialogue on Human Rights in Japan' (2014) 14 *Meiji Daigaku Houka Daigakuin Honshu* [Meiji Law School Law Review] 139.

[68] See section II.A of this chapter.

[69] Decision of 5 July 1995, SCJ (GB), 49(7) *Minshu* 1789.

[70] Judgment of 27 May 1964, SCJ (GB), 18(4) *Keishu* 676.

[71] When a petty bench of the SCJ thinks the necessity of change of precedent, it transfers the case in question to the Grand Bench (plenary court).

To understand why and how the SCJ changed its position it is necessary to compare the 1995 Inheritance Decision and the 2013 Inheritance Decision to examine on what points they differ.[72] In justifying the departure from the conclusion of the 1995 Inheritance Decision, the 2013 Inheritance Decision emphasised that the matters to be considered including tradition, social conditions and public sentiments change with time.[73] Therefore, the 2013 Inheritance Decision held that the reasonableness of the rules should be subject to constant examination and scrutiny in light of the Constitution, which provides for individual dignity and equality under the law. In examining the distinction at stake, the SCJ in the 2013 Inheritance Decision listed eight factors. Among them were the diversification of forms of marriage and family life, and people's perceptions of marriage and family resulting therefrom, the legislative trends in other countries that had influenced the adoption of the challenged norm in the past (comparative law), and the standards in international human rights treaties ratified by Japan, as well as the criticisms raised by the treaties' committees (international law).[74]

In weighing these factors, the SCJ declared that

> despite the discretionary power vested in the legislative body, the distinction in terms of the statutory share in inheritance between children born in wedlock and children born out of wedlock had lost reasonable grounds by the time when [the] appellant's inheritance commenced as of July 2001 at the latest.[75]

As for the Court's reliance on comparative law, the history of the legal transplant of Western law seems to provide part of the explanation. Thus, the 2013 Inheritance Decision at first points out that during the deliberation of the amendment of the Civil Code by the Diet in 1947, the existence of similar laws in other countries at that time had been called upon to justify the distinction in terms of the share of inheritance between children born in wedlock and children born out of wedlock and its consistency with the Constitution. 'This suggests that these foreign laws had influenced the process for introducing the Provision in the existing Civil Code in the first place.'[76] Therefore, legal changes in the United States and European countries seemed to offer more than a supporting reason to find a violation of the Constitution. Furthermore, the SCJ cleverly chose the examples of Germany and France, which still had the discriminatory norm when the SCJ handed down the 1995 Decision but had later eliminated it, noting that no Western country had retained the distinction.[77] In this regard,

[72] The 1995 Inheritance Decision referred to the Judgment of 27 May 1964, SCJ (GB), 18(4) *Keishu* 676, which was the first judgment to express the reasonable test and admitted the constitutionality of Art 200 of the Penal Code. The 2013 Inheritance Decision referred to the Judgment of 4 April 1973, SCJ (GB), 27(3) *Keishu* 265, which referred to the previous 1964 judgment and followed the same test, but held that Art 200 of the Penal Code was unconstitutional.

[73] Decision of 4 September 2013 (n 67) 1324.

[74] ibid.

[75] ibid 1331.

[76] ibid 1324.

[77] ibid 1325.

it can be safely deduced from both the 2013 Inheritance Decision and the 2008 Nationality Judgment that when foreign law influences the making or amending of Japanese law, later changes in that foreign law can provide an opportunity for the SCJ to reconsider the present Japanese law.

The SCJ had been very reluctant to rely on international law and case law. With a few exceptions, the typical attitude of the SCJ and other lower courts had been not to examine an international human rights treaty in detail, and not to find domestic law in violation of a human rights treaty. Instead, it had often expressed that it is not necessary to consider the violation of treaties when the Court considers the violation of constitutional law because constitutional law is superior to treaties. Alternatively, the SCJ simply rejected the proposition that treaties had been violated without much reasoning.[78] However, the 2008 Nationality Judgment had departed from this rule by referring to the ICCPR and the CRC, and the 2013 Inheritance Decision had made further advances by referring to these same treaties but also to recommendations made by the Human Rights Committee, the monitoring body of the ICCPR (HRC), and the Committee on the Rights of the Child (ComRC), with explicit mention to a 1993 concluding observation of the HRC and a 2010 concluding observation of the ComRC, both of which had called for the elimination of the discriminatory legislation.[79]

It should be appreciated that the SCJ takes international opinions into account, which are provided periodically by international treaty bodies and reflect changes in the international community's position. At present, the international human rights bodies have plenty of data for their opinions because the Japanese Government is obligated to submit reports to the Human Rights Council, the HRC, the Committee on Economic, Social and Cultural Rights, the ComRC, the CEDAW Committee, the Committee on Elimination of Racial Discrimination, the Committee against Torture, the Committee on Enforced Disappearance and the Committee on the Rights of Persons with Disabilities. Moreover, if Japan accepts the individual communication mechanism that some of the aforementioned committees provide, their views as an outcome of individual communications become important material for the SCJ. Based on the 2013 Inheritance Decision, the SCJ can refer to the committees' views even before Japan adopts the individual communication mechanism.

The 2013 Inheritance Decision contains an interesting interrelationship between foreign law and international case law. The legal revision of the French law, which the SCJ relies on in its reasoning in the 2013 Inheritance Decision, occurred because of judgments by the ECtHR, such as *Marckx v Belgium* and *Mazurek v France*.[80] The ECtHR's sensitivity to comparative law

[78] Judgment of 3 March 1989, SCJ, 43(2) *Minshu* 89 and Judgment of 7 September 2000, SCJ, 199 *Shumin* 283.

[79] Decision of 4 September 2013 (n 67) 1326.

[80] *Marckx v Belgium*, Judgment of 13 June 1979 (Plenary Court), Ser A, No 31 and *Mazurek v France*, Judgment of 1 February 2000, Reports of Judgments and Decisions 2000-II.

is understandable as a regional human rights court, given that the ECtHR must interpret an open-ended document that is considered a 'living instrument' by the ECtHR itself. The ECtHR case law, therefore, is potentially influential for Japanese courts. The fact that the French legal revision, which was referenced in the 2013 Inheritance Decision, was mentioned in the *Mazurek* judgment, denotes an indirect but noteworthy dialogue between the Japanese Court and the ECtHR. Apart from the judicial dialogue, an extra-judicial dialogue can be also identified. Justices of the SCJ have a regular opportunity to visit the ECtHR and vice versa.[81] On one of these occasions, former SCJ Justice Izumi visited the ECtHR and met with former ECtHR President Costa in 2008. They exchanged views on the issue of legal discrimination of the child born out of wedlock, and Justice Izumi was informed of the European situation, wherein the discriminatory legislation had existed in France, Belgium and Austria, but the national legislature had abolished it because of the judgments of the ECtHR.[82] One may recall that Justice Izumi wrote a dissenting opinion twice in the SCJ PB decisions.[83] More recently, Jean-Paul Costa, the former President of the ECtHR also visited the SCJ following retirement and met with a judge at the SCJ. During their discussion, the judge spoke about the 2013 Inheritance Decision and mentioned the *Mazurek* case.[84]

Scrutiny of the 2013 Inheritance Decision and the 2008 Nationality Judgment indicates a dialogue between a national court and an international body, and indirectly a regional court. This dialogue has the potential to create a sphere in which comparative and international considerations work together to address a specific issue, such as the protection of children born out of wedlock.

C. The 2015 Prohibition of Remarriage and Same-surname Judgments: A Setback?

In 2015 the SCJ had an opportunity to examine the constitutionality of two provisions of the Civil Code in separate cases, about which the UN human rights treaty bodies had expressed concerns and proposed recommendations.[85]

[81] Luzius Wildhaber, the then President of the ECtHR, visited the SCJ in 2003.

[82] T Izumi, 'Kongaishi Souzokubun Sabetsu Kitei no Iken Kettei to Kojin no Songen' [Unconstitutionality Decision of the Discriminatory Clause on Inheritance of the Child Born out of Wedlock and Human Dignity] (2013) 849 *Sekai* 229, 231.

[83] Judgment of 14 October 2004, SCJ, 1884 *Hanji* 40.

[84] J-P Costa, 'Kokusai Jinkenho Gakkai 30shunen ni yosete'[Dedié au 30e anniversaire de l'Association japonaise des droits internationaux des droits de l'homme] (2020) 30 *Kokusai Jinken* [Human Rights Law International] 7.

[85] The CEDAW Committee gave recommendations twice at that time, see CEDAW Committee (n 48) para 372; CEDAW Committee, 'Concluding observations of the Committee on the Elimination of Discrimination against Women' (7 August 2009) CEDAW/C/JPN/CO6, para 18; Human Rights Committee, 'Concluding observations on the sixth periodic report of Japan' (20 August 2014) CCPR/C/JPN/CO/6, para 8.

One is about Article 733(1) of the Civil Code, which prescribes a six-month period of prohibition of remarriage imposed on women only. The appellant claimed that Article 733 violated Article 14(1) and Article 24(2) of the Constitution. The majority opinion of the SCJ held that the provision prescribing the prohibition of remarriage for any period exceeding 100 days could not be justified as setting a necessary period for avoiding confusion over paternity and violated Articles 14 and 24 of the Constitution (The 2015 Prohibition of Remarriage Judgment).[86] In order to reach this conclusion, the majority opinion used similar reasoning to that in the 2008 Nationality Judgment and the 2013 Inheritance Decision. The SCJ used the reasonable test and underlined societal changes including the development of medical and scientific technology and changes in family and marital patterns. The Judgment also pointed out that when Article 733 of the Civil Code was passed there were similar laws in foreign countries that had since been abolished. The SCJ again in the meantime, relied, once again, on specific examples from German and French law. However, the majority opinion did not refer to international law or the recommendations of human rights treaty bodies this time even though the CEDAW Committee has given recommendations on the matter twice.[87] It thus seems that the SCJ judges may rely more on comparative rather than international law, arguably because of Japan's long tradition in comparative legal studies. In any event, it is interesting to note that none of the three female judges opposed the majority view. However, a male judge, Yamaura, argued in his dissenting opinion that even a period of 100 days was unconstitutional, referring to a judgment of the Constitutional Court of the Republic of Korea in 1997 which declared a similar law unconstitutional, but also alluding to a recommendation of the CEDAW Committee.[88]

The other provision examined by the SCJ in 2015 is Article 750 of the Civil Code which stipulates that a husband and wife shall adopt the surname of the husband or the wife as decided at the time of marriage, a rule that is formally neutral but which, in reality, reinforces the tradition whereby it is generally the wife who adopts her husband's surname. In reality, 96 per cent of women choose their husband's surnames. The appellant claimed that the Article violates Article 13 (the right to the pursuit of happiness, a general clause which guarantees human rights in general and may be used to create a new right such as the right to privacy), Article 14(1) (equality under the law), and Article 24(1)–(2) of the Constitution (the right to marry). However, the majority opinion held that the Article was not unconstitutional applying reasoning that resembled the 2015 Prohibition of Remarriage judgment.[89] The majority opinion's understanding of equality under the law is so formalistic that it emphasised that the law itself

[86] Judgment of 16 December 2015, SCJ (GB), 69(8) *Minshu* 2427.
[87] As to the recommendations, see n 85.
[88] Judgment of 16 December 2015 (n 86) 2466–68.
[89] ibid 2586.

does not differentiate between men and women, and the fact that 96 per cent of women choose their husband's surnames did not derive from the law itself. Thus, the majority opinion did not refer to foreign law or international law despite the fact that more jurisdictions have adopted a system allowing women to keep their maiden name as their surname after marriage. Moreover, the CEDAW Committee had twice made recommendations to Japan suggesting necessary legal reform in its concluding observations.[90] Once again, it was the dissenting opinion by Judge Yamaura which referred to foreign law and the recommendations of the CEDAW Committee. It was a clear setback or at least cherry-picking. Moreover, this time the three female judges, Sakurai, Okabe, and Onimaru, specifically opposed the argument made by the majority. The majority argued that the effects of the rule were mitigated by the nickname system whereby some companies allow their employees to use their maiden names at the office if they so request. It should be noted that all three female judges experienced the inconvenience directly as they could not even use their maiden names when they joined the SCJ – the nickname system was not adopted until 2017.

D. The 2019 Decision on Trans Persons

According to Japan's legal system, a trans person must lose fertility to be legally assigned their desired new gender under the Act on Special Provisions of Gender Identity of Persons with Gender Identity Disorder (AGID).[91] An appellant argued that the requirement violated Articles 13 (the right to the pursuit of happiness) and 14 of the Constitution (equality under the law).[92] Instead, a petty bench (four judges) of the SCJ upheld the Act on the basis that the generating confusion in society had to be avoided and did so without relying on any specific standard of review but simply appealing to the aim of the law and 'current social circumstances'.[93] Once more, the joint concurring opinion by Judge Onimaru and Judge Miura expressed strong doubts about the constitutionality of the AGID, referring not only to foreign laws but also international sources, including a specific judgment of the ECtHR. This suggests the possibility that the SCJ could consider not only international human rights treaties which Japan has ratified but also a regional human rights treaty such as the European Convention on Human Rights which Japan has not ratified nor can ratify but which, in some areas, provides the most relevant case law to date. The concurring opinion referred to the 2017 judgment of the ECtHR in *AP Garçon and Nicot v France.*[94] The global nature of the human rights case law is illustrated by this reference

[90] As to the recommendations, see n 85.
[91] The Act No 111 of 2003. See section IV.E of this chapter.
[92] The Constitution of Japan.
[93] Decision of 23 January 2019, SCJ (GB), 2421 *Hanji* 4.
[94] *AP, Garçon and Nicot v France*, nos 79885/12 and 2 others, 6 April 2017.

although the legitimacy of relying primarily on an unratified treaty should be further examined from the perspective of global human rights law which combines comparative constitutional law and international human rights law.

E. The 2021 Decision on the Same-surname

Although the 2015 Same-surname Judgment had upheld Article 750 of the Civil Code, a few years later the same lawyers who had brought that case decided to challenge it again by way of strategic litigation. Once again, in a 2021 Decision, the SCJ majority opinion (11 judges) upheld Article 750 of the Civil Code by taking the same standard and reasoning of the majority opinion of the 2015 Same-surname Judgment.[95] The majority opinion once again showed a deferential attitude towards the legislature where the LDP has been the ruling party. The LDP has opposed changing the existing same-surname system because they believed the change would break the unity of the traditional family. However, three dissenting opinions and one other opinion declared the provision unconstitutional.[96]

The dissenting opinion co-written by Judge Miyazaki and Judge Uga challenged the 2015 Same-surname Judgment that held that the freedom not to be forced to change one's family name is not a part of the right to personality guaranteed by Article 13 (the right to the pursuit of happiness). The same dissenting opinion stated that Article 24 (the right to marriage) was strengthened by Article 13 (the right to the pursuit of happiness) and Article 14 (equality under the law). Taking into account the importance of the function of names for personal identification and self-identification in the modern age, the dissenting opinion highly valued the personal interest in one's name and proposed that the restriction on the right to personality would amount to a violation unless it could be justified on the grounds of public welfare. The dissenting opinion concluded that denying marriage to the couple if the woman wants to keep her maiden name could not be justified by the rationale that the family name is significant as a name for the family consisting of parents and minor children (the rationale of the 2015 Same-surname Judgment). The nature of the family in reality is diverse. Moreover, if parents divorce and remarry new partners, the family name of the children would change. Even if the rationale of the 2015 Same-surname Judgment were to be used, it would still be a violation of Article 24 of the Constitution in light of the changes in circumstances after the 2015 Judgment.

[95] Decision of 23 June 2021, SCJ (GB), 2501 *Hanrei Jiho* 3.

[96] A Judge of the SCJ can write an opinion when he or she does not agree with the reasoning of the majority opinion but agrees with the conclusion. The difference between the dissenting opinion and the opinion is that the former admitted the acceptance of marriage registration, but the latter denied it because there quashing Art 750 would not produce a law to establish an optional system of different-surname system.

There have been several developments in terms of 'dialogue' between constitutional law and international human rights treaties worth underscoring. First, some SCJ judges no longer ignore the concluding observations of the CEDAW Committee. Even the concurring opinion which supported the constitutionality of Article 750 of the Civil Code did not ignore the existence of the 2016 concluding observation of the CEDAW Committee, which was made after the 2015 Same-surname Judgment.[97] Second, the dissenting opinions relied on this concluding observation. Judges Miyazaki and Uga not only provided a persuasive argument strongly supported by their analysis of Article 24, but also wrote a detailed dissenting opinion in which they argued that because Japan received the concluding observations from the CEDAW Committee which recommended the amendment of the same-surname system three times (2003, 2009 and 2016) the same-surname system was now beyond the discretion of the legislature.[98]

In the case of Article 900 of the Civil Code, it took 18 years to bring another similar case to the SCJ again. In the case of Article 750 of the Civil Code, it took only six years to try again. With the pace of change in Japanese society and further dialogue between the domestic and international levels, future development is to be expected. Furthermore, the most recent decision, the 2021 Same-surname Decision, shows that although the SCJ is ready to acknowledge foreign and/or international law even when doing so it is not useful or convenient for strengthening the SCJ's conclusions. On the other hand, dissenting opinions make ample use of foreign and/or international law to strengthen their opposition, and some of this opposition may become the majority opinion in later judgments, as was the case in the 2013 Inheritance Decision. Therefore, the conclusions of the 2021 Same-surname Decision and the 2019 Decision on trans persons are likely to be revisited in the near future.

VI. CONCLUSION

Japan is at a crossroads. Many factors limit the role of constitutionalism and particularly hinder the development of constitutional litigation in Japan. Many issues need to be tackled. First, the legislature seems not to take initiative in the field of gender issues by adopting effective measures because of the poor representation of women in the Diet. It is time to seriously consider the necessity of positive action in this domain. Second, the Japanese Supreme Court has been traditionally deferential to the legislature although section V shows new developments occurring at the SCJ. Third, gender equality issues have not been

[97] Decision of 23 June 2021 (n 95).

[98] ibid. As to the concluding observations of the CEDAW Committee, see CEDAW Committee (n 48) para 372; CEDAW Committee, 'Concluding observations' (n 85) para 18; CEDAW Committee, 'Concluding observations on the combined seventh and eighth period reports of Japan' (10 March 2016) CEDAW/C/JPN/CO7-8, para 13.

given serious consideration in mainstream constitutional studies even though new disciplines such as 'international human rights law' and 'law and gender' encourage tackling these issues through an interdisciplinary approach that combines various areas of legal study.[99] Lastly, the steady effort of civil society to realise gender equality and solve gender issues has played a significant role in achieving some changes. One of the great achievements is their effort to bring issues to the courts and the international level, which produced many concluding observations issued by international human rights bodies. As we see, the effect of one concluding observation is limited, but it is increasingly difficult to ignore repeated concluding observations which are expressed by different treaty bodies. It is necessary to enhance the capacity of human rights by combining the constitutional system with the international human rights system to accelerate the implementation of the constitutional and international norms relating to gender issues.

[99] The International Human Rights Law Association (www.ihrla.org) was established in 1988 and the Japan Association of Gender and Law (jagl.jp) was established in 2003.

3

Gender, Sexuality and Constitutionalism in Taiwan: A Successful Story in the Cooperation between the Women's Movement, the Constitution and International Human Rights

WEN-CHEN CHANG

I. INTRODUCTION

On 24 May 2019, Taiwan became the first Asian country to legally recognise same-sex marriage. Many same-sex couples chose to register their marriages with city or county governments on that day, and openly threw parties for celebration. Two years earlier, Taiwan's Constitutional Court (TCC) announced the judgment to constitutionally recognise an equal right to marriage for same-sex couples.[1] In that decision, TCC gave the legislature a two-year deadline to provide a legal basis on which same-sex couples could marry. Two days before the set deadline, the law implementing TCC's decision was promulgated.[2] Same-sex marriage has since been legalised, and same-sex couples can adopt each other's biological child. On 16 May 2023, the legislature passed a bill to grant same-sex couples the right to jointly adopt a child neither of them is related to, furthering marriage equality for same-sex couples.

The recognition of same-sex marriage is one milestone among the many in Taiwan's recent development in equal rights for both women and sexual and gender diverse people (SGDP). If assessed on the basis of the 2019 Gender

[1] JY Interpretation No 748 (2017).
[2] The Act for Implementation of JY Interpretation No 748.

Inequality Index (GII), Taiwan would be ranked sixth globally and first in Asia.[3] Taiwan's first female president was elected in 2016 and re-elected in 2020. The percentage of female members of the national legislature was 38.15 per cent in 2016 and 41.6 per cent in 2020, ranking 18th worldwide and first in Asia.[4] In the 2018 local election, the proportions of female mayors and county magistrates were 16.7 per cent and 37.5 per cent, with women representing 35.8 per cent of municipal and 32.1 per cent of county councillors.[5] The proportions of women Cabinet members and politically appointed officials were 7.32 per cent and 22.1 per cent in 2020.[6] As for civil servants, women accounted for 42.3 per cent of all civil servants and 37.2 per cent of all senior ranks. Although the gender ratio of political appointees and ministerial rank officers was less than one-third, the gender ratio of second-level agency chief of staff and directors of first-level units in second-level agencies has reached one-third.[7]

In the judiciary, female judges (51.4 per cent) have outnumbered male judges (48.6 per cent) for the first time in 2021.[8] Yet, the higher the judicial posts, the lower the ratio of female judges. In district courts, female judges are at the ratio of 52.4 per cent, and in high courts, that ratio is 50.2 per cent and decreases to 43.5 per cent in the Supreme Court.[9] The appointment of female chief judges saw a significant increase in 2021, reaching 39.1 per cent in district courts, 66.7 per cent in high courts, and 33.3 per cent in high administrative courts.[10] There is no female chief judgeship in the Supreme Court and the Supreme Administrative Court, nor in the Constitutional Court, which has four female justices among all 15 justices, already the record number in its history. The proportion of female judges has reflected gender parity in the legal profession, with female law graduates reaching 55 per cent in 2019,[11] and women lawyers reaching 40 per cent in 2021.[12] Similar gender parity has also been present in higher education and labour market. According to the 2018 statistics, the female

[3] The United Nations Development Programme has since 2010 compiled and issued the GII, which measures the state of gender inequality by analysing five indicators in the three dimensions of health, empowerment and the labour market. Because the GII does not include Taiwan, Taiwan's Government has published its own GII using the same measurement. In the 2019 GII global ranking, Switzerland ranked first at 0.025, followed by Denmark at 0.038, with Sweden coming in third at 0.039. According to the same measurement, Taiwan's GII in 2019 was 0.045, ranking 6th out of the 163 countries measured, and 1st in Asia. See The Executive Yuan Department of Gender Equality, '2022 Gender at a glance in R.O.C. (Taiwan)' 4, available at gec.ey.gov.tw/Page/8996A23EDB9871BE.

[4] ibid 5.

[5] ibid 6.

[6] ibid 7.

[7] ibid 7–8.

[8] The Judicial Yuan, '2021 Judicial Gender Statistic Summary', available at www.judicial.gov.tw/tw/lp-2182-1.html.

[9] ibid.

[10] ibid.

[11] Ministry of Education, 'Education Statistics 2019' 164, available at stats.moe.gov.tw/files/ebook/education_statistics/108/108edu.pdf.

[12] Ministry of Justice, 'Lawyers Statistics 2021', available at www.rjsd.moj.gov.tw/RJSDWeb/common/WebList3_Report.aspx?list_id=1529.

proportion of bachelor's degrees was 52.7 per cent, master's degrees 44.4 per cent and doctoral degrees 31.5 per cent.[13] Literacy rates of men and women are very close: 99 per cent and 97 per cent respectively. The labour market has seen gender parity in recent years, while there are still fewer women in the industry sector and far more in the service sector.[14]

The advancement of sex/gender equality has been developed under both Taiwan's Constitution and a few recently incorporated international human rights instruments. Pivotal to this strategy was the effective advocacy by women and SGDP groups during the period of democratisation and constitutional reforms since the late 1980s.[15] Taiwan's Constitution, under the name of the Republic of China (ROC) Constitution, was enacted on the Chinese Mainland in 1946 and as the result of the ROC Government losing the civil war to the Communist Party, applicable only to Taiwan after 1949. Although the Constitution was not fully implemented during the period of Martial Law Decree imposed from 1949 to 1987, local elections were still held, and the judicial system particularly the Council of Grand Justices (known as the Constitutional Court after 1993) was maintained. Beginning in the late 1980s, TCC became a key player to steer constitutional reforms and to begin ensuring the protection of fundamental rights and freedoms that had substantially been suspended during the authoritarian era.[16] As democratic reforms opened space for public participation, vital forces of civil society, including women and SGDP groups, were unleashed to utilise all available venues to achieve their own agendas.[17] Among those are powerful constitutional and legal means adopted, including partaking in constitutional reforms, pushing for new legislation, running for political offices, initiating strategic constitutional litigation and advocating for domestic incorporation of international human rights instruments, which will be discussed in more detail below.

International human rights instruments have become important tools for women and SGDP groups to advocate equality of sex, gender and sexuality. Yet, as a non-member of the United Nations (UN), Taiwan cannot officially accede to UN human rights conventions nor join any related mechanisms. In 1971, the ROC Government was expelled from its UN seat to the People's Republic of China Government and has since been barred from partaking in any UN activities. Unleashed from the authoritarian era, Taiwan's society was eager and ready to reconnect with international society. For many human rights groups, using international norms has added weight to their rights advocacy. Pressured

[13] The Executive Yuan Department of Gender Equality (n 3) 20.

[14] ibid 15.

[15] WC Chang, 'Public Interest Litigation in Taiwan: Strategy for Law and Policy Changes in Course of Democratization' in PJ Yap and H Lau (eds), *Public Interest Litigation in Asia* (Routledge, 2011).

[16] JR Yeh, The Constitution of Taiwan: A Contextual Analysis (Hart Publishing, 2016) 194–202.

[17] Chang (n 15).

by women and SGDP groups and other human rights groups,[18] the Government decided to undergo the constitutional process for accession to the Convention on the Elimination of All Forms of Discrimination Against Women (CEDAW) in 2007 and submitted it to the UN.[19] Notwithstanding the rejected accession, the Government issued the Initial State Report in 2009 and invited an international panel of independent experts, including one sitting member of the UN CEDAW Committee, to provide for reviews and recommendations.[20] Also in 2009, the Government ratified the International Covenant on Civil and Political Rights (ICCPR) and the International Covenant on Economic, Social and Cultural Rights (ICESCR). An implementation act was passed to give legal effect to the rights enshrined in the two Covenants.[21]

Together with these domestically incorporated international human rights documents, Taiwan's Constitution and constitutional jurisprudence have profoundly transformed the discourse of equality for women and SGDP groups. This chapter explores ways in which such profound constitutional transformation has been achieved, and more specifically, how the Constitution and international human rights instruments have provided for opportunity structures under which women's and SGDP's movements strategically fight for achieving equality.[22] Using same-sex marriage and the decriminalisation of adultery as flagship developments, this chapter is aimed at shedding light on constitutional functions for, and limits to, achieving equality for women and SGDP, and the lessons learned in Taiwan's experiences.

II. BACKGROUND

In Taiwan, strategic mobilisation of women and SGDP groups for fighting equality has been undertaken against background dynamics of constitution-making and constitutional revision, democratic transition and constitutional structure,

[18] They formed the Taiwan Civil League for promoting the Convention on the Elimination of All Forms of Discrimination against Women (CEDAW). For their advocacy on CEDAW accession, see WC Chang, 'An Isolated Nation with Global-minded Citizens: Bottom-up Transnational Constitutionalism in Taiwan' (2009) 4 *National Taiwan University Law Review* 203.

[19] ibid 226.

[20] The first panel has three members including Heisoo Shin from South Korea, who served on the CEDAW Committee from 2001 to 2004 and from 2005 to 2008, Schöpp-Schilling from Germany, and Anamah Tan from Singapore. More detailed information regarding the Initial State Report and the first international review is available at Gender Equality Committee of the Executive Yuan, 'CEDAW', available at gec.ey.gov.tw/en/D7DADA06318CA5F4.

[21] WC Chang, 'Taiwan's Human Rights Implementation Acts: A Model for Successful Incorporation?' in JA Cohen, WP Alford and CF Lo (eds), *Taiwan and International Human Rights: A Story of Transformation* (Springer, 2019).

[22] For explaining how laws may provide for opportunity structure for equality movement, see eg, MW McCann, *Rights at Work: Pay Equity Reform and Politics of Legal Mobilization* (University of Chicago Press, 1994); FK Zemans, 'Legal Mobilization: The Neglected Role of the Law in the Political System' (1983) 77 *American Political Science Review* 690.

TCC's judicial review and rights protection, and, last but not least, domestic incorporation of international human rights. These contextual dynamics are illustrated below.

A. Constitution-making and Constitutional Revision

Writing and rewriting constitutions may provide women and SGDP groups with a critical opportunity for rights advocacy.[23] In the making of the ROC Constitution on the Chinese Mainland in the 1940s, and half a century later, in the remaking of a new Constitution and reforming the existing ROC Constitution in Taiwan throughout the 1990s, women and SGDP groups have never shied away from such a vital opportunity, and their fights were rewarding.[24]

On the Chinese Mainland, it took decades to enact the ROC Constitution. In the first Provisional Constitution promulgated in 1912, an equality clause was included without mentioning sex or gender. Only race, class and religion were specified.[25] This prompted serious protests by women's groups, particularly those actively participating in the political process that had just opened after the republican revolution and the last Chinese Emperor's power abdication. These women took the right to petition that was written in the Provisional Constitution to advocate not only for the inclusion of the gender equality clause but also, more importantly, for women's representation in the drafting and enacting process of the new Constitution.[26] Meanwhile, as provinces were also enacting their own constitutions, these women's groups wasted no time in developing the network to ensure a gender equality clause be included in all provincial constitutions.[27]

The equality clause specifying sex classification – together with religion, race, class and party affiliation – was eventually included in the final draft of the ROC Constitution in 1946. Eighty-two women were elected to the Constituent National Assembly, consisting of 1,701 delegates (about five per cent). Having experienced first-hand challenges in gaining political power, these women – including one elected from Taiwan – insisted on having a female quota at all

[23] R Rubio-Marín and H Irving, 'Introduction' in R Rubio-Marín and H Irving (eds), *Women as Constitution-Makers: Case Studies from the New Democratic Era* (Cambridge University Press, 2019) 1–3 (explaining how the participatory turn of the recent wave in constitution-making has provided a critical opportunity for women's participation).

[24] CJ Chen, 'Rewriting a Male Constitution: Constitutional Mobilization by the Women's Movement from the Gender Equality Clause and Women's Charter to the Constitutional Litigation Movement' (2012) 52 *Taiwan Journal of Political Science* 43.

[25] In this Provisional Constitution, Art 5 states that all citizens, irrespective of race, class and religion, shall be equal before the law; see ibid 49.

[26] ibid 51.

[27] ibid 52–53.

levels of representative institutions. One radical proposal was to have one-third of women at all levels of legislatures.[28]

Strong women's advocacy in the process of constitution-making reaped the reward in the final product. Article 7 of the ROC Constitution guarantees that all citizens irrespective of sex, religion, race, class or party affiliation shall be equal before the law. In addition, Articles 26, 64 and 134[29] ensure the number of women to be elected to the National Assembly and the Legislative Yuan[30] and to all of the provincial and local legislatures to be stipulated by law. After the ROC Constitution became effective in 1947, the female quota at all levels of representative institutions was set at 25 per cent by law.[31] The women's quota for the Legislative Yuan was suspended in the 2005 constitutional amendment, replaced by a gender-parity requirement in proportional representation, one-half of the outcome required.[32] The 25 per cent women quota for city and county councillors has been maintained to this day.[33] As shown in the introduction, women's presence in all levels of representative institutions have exceeded 30 per cent. There is no doubt that the constitutional amendment of gender parity together with women's quota has functioned as the opportunity structure under which women's political representation is strengthened.

In Taiwan, a constitutional moment came in the late 1980s, when the Martial Law Decree was lifted and democratic transitions occurred. Heatedly debated was whether to make a new Constitution replacing the ROC Constitution

[28] ibid 56.

[29] Constitution of the Republic of China (Taiwan), Art 26: 'The number of delegates to be elected by women's organizations shall be prescribed by law.' [hereinafter the ROC Constitution]. The ROC Constitution, Art 64: 'The number of women to be elected under the various items enumerated in the first paragraph shall be prescribed by law.' The ROC Constitution, Art 134: 'In the various kinds of elections, the number of women to be elected shall be fixed, and measures pertaining thereto shall be prescribed by law.'

[30] The National Assembly and the Legislative Yuan, together with the Control Yuan, formed a tricameral legislature established by the ROC Constitution. Aside from the Legislative Yuan with power to make law, and the Control Yuan with supervisory function, the National Assembly had the power to elect both president and vice president and to amend the Constitution. It was, however, eventually abolished in the constitutional amendment of 2005. The power to elect president and vice president was given to the people by direct voting in the constitutional amendment of 1994, and the power to ratify constitutional amendments was also returned to the people through public referendum in the 2005 constitutional amendment. See Yeh (n 16) 94–100.

[31] R Rubio-Marín and WC Chang, 'Sites of Constitutional Struggle for Women's Equality' in M Tushnet, T Fleiner and C Saunders (eds), *Routledge Handbook of Constitutional Law* (Routledge, 2013) 308.

[32] Art 4 of the Additional Articles to the ROC Constitution prescribes that members for the seats set forth in Art 4(3) (34 out of 113 seats) shall be elected from the lists of political parties in proportion to the number of votes won by each party that obtains at least 5% of the total vote, and the number of elected female members on each party's list shall not be less than one-half of the total number.

[33] Art 33 of the Local Government Act stipulates that in the event there are a total of four special municipality councilors, county/city councilors, and township/city representatives to be elected by an electoral district, there should be one female among the elected. If the total number of those to be elected exceeds four, an additional female shall be among the elected for every additional four persons elected.

enacted on the Chinese Mainland and mainly frozen during the authoritarian era, or to retain the ROC Constitution with substantial revision to adjust to the new democracy in Taiwan, as was finally decided.[34] As civic organisations and social groups burgeoned as a result of this democratisation, women's groups, including the Awakening Foundation, the Grassroots Women Workers Centre, the Homemaker's Union and Foundation and many others, quickly formed a women alliance for constitutional reform.[35] A renowned female lawyer, Yu, Mei-Nu, who led the Awakening Foundation, quickly drafted a declaration for women's rights.[36] Based on that declaration and further broadened discussion, the civic organisations in Taiwan published the Women Charter in 1991.[37] Aimed at being added to the new constitution or serving as a basis for amending the existing constitution, the Women Charter included all civil, political, economic, social, and cultural rights for women and forbade sex and gender discrimination.

Many leaders in these women's groups competed in the election of the National Assembly in 1996 that had the exclusive power to amend the Constitution. The mobilisation of women was unparalleled. In the end, 42 women were elected to the National Assembly of 325 members, representing about 13 per cent.[38] Chen, Hsiu-Hui, the leader of the Homemaker's Union and Foundation, was elected as a member of the National Assembly; she then seized the opportunity to initiate the Women Charter as a proposal for the constitutional amendment.[39] Annette Lu, the leader of another women's organisation, who would later become the first female vice-president, advocated for gender parity of political representation and abolishing the women's quota.[40] The proposals made by women's groups received support across party lines, and yet, despite the effort within and outside the National Assembly – other than a general clause affirming the Government's duty to advance gender equality in a broad sense with no concrete duty specified, which was added into the amendment[41] – none of the above proposals were passed. This was mainly because the Government decided to focus only on restructuring government institutions, leaving amendment proposals for rights unresolved. With the hard lesson learned, women's groups turned their eyes to government institutions and powers.

[34] Yeh (n 16) 36–37.

[35] Chen (n 24) 62–63. For how women's organisations were formed and burgeoned since the lifting of the Martial Law Decree in 1987 and how they have contributed to constitutional reform and advancement of women's rights, see Chang (n 15) 138–39; LJ Lee, 'The Constitutionalization of Taiwanese Family Law' (2016) 11 *National Taiwan University Law Review* 273, 292–94.

[36] Chen (n 24) 63.

[37] ibid.

[38] ibid.

[39] ibid 66.

[40] ibid 67.

[41] Art 10(6) of the Additional Articles to the ROC Constitution stipulates that the state shall protect the dignity of women, safeguard their personal safety, eliminate sexual discrimination, and further substantive gender equality.

B. Constitutional Structure and Democratic Transition

Built upon the Five-Yuans theory,[42] the ROC Constitution enacted in 1946 and effective in 1947 had a unique design in the government structure.[43] The President was elected by the National Assembly, which also had an exclusive power to ratify constitutional amendment. The five Yuans included the Executive Yuan, the Legislative Yuan, the Judicial Yuan, the Control Yuan and the Examination Yuan. The Executive Yuan functioned like a Cabinet, accountable to the Legislative Yuan, which acted as a lower house with the Control Yuan as an upper house. The Judicial Yuan and the Examination Yuan were independent institutions. During the authoritarian era, however, no election at the national level was held, and the party-state dominated these constitutional institutions.[44]

Democratic transitions in the late 1980s brought back elections for political offices and opened up constitutional discussions on whether the institutional design of the Five-Yuans plus the President and National Assembly, which was written for the ROC government on the Chinese Mainland, suited the present situation in Taiwan.[45] What followed was seven rounds of constitutional revision in 1991, 1992, 1994, 1997, 1999, 2000 and 2005 that substantially altered the initial Five-Yuans structure of government. At present, the President and Vice President are directly elected by popular votes with a term of four years and can only be re-elected once. The Executive Yuan, whose head is the Premier, continues to be made accountable to the Legislative Yuan. Notably, however, the Premier is appointed by the President without the consent of the Legislative Yuan, which has the power to a vote of no confidence in the Premier who can, in turn, request the President to dissolve the Legislative Yuan. In other words, the government structure leans more towards a semi-presidential system. The National Assembly was abolished. The power to propose constitutional amendment is now vested with the Legislative Yuan, and the power to ratify constitutional amendment is with the people through public referendum. The Control Yuan was remade to function in the same way as ombudsmen, under which an independent national human rights commission was also created in 2020.[46]

The reopening of elections particularly at the national level gave women leaders an unparalleled opportunity to advocate for women's equal rights. For example, in 1989, when the election for the Legislative Yuan was reopened,

[42] The Five-Yuans theory rooted in the ROC Constitution, which is also known as the Five-Power Constitution. Under this framework, the Government consists of the Executive Yuan with executive power, the Legislative Yuan with lawmaking power, the Judicial Yuan with a judicial function, the Examination Yuan in charge of examination and management of all civil service personnel and the Control Yuan with supervisory function. Yeh (n 16) 53–54.

[43] ibid 53–54.

[44] ibid 34–36.

[45] ibid 36–37.

[46] ibid 94.

Madam Liu, Hsia – a woman born with serious disabilities and who founded the Eden Social Welfare Foundation in 1982[47] before becoming the first chair for the ROC (Taiwan) League for Persons with Disabilities in 1989[48] – decided to run for election. Yet, Madam Liu's candidacy was denied because she did not have a high school diploma due to her inability to receive regular education. She challenged the educational requirement before TCC, but failed.[49] Although Madam Liu did not participate in the election, her candidacy controversy made headlines and considerably raised public awareness of equal rights for both women and persons with disabilities.

The first direct presidential election in 1996 also attracted an outspoken feminist candidate: the famous writer, Madam Shih, Chi-Ching, who founded an organisation, Warm Life, to help divorced women.[50] Having no affiliated political party, however, she and her vice president running mate, also a woman, were required to make a deposit in the amount of NT$1,000,000 and to garner at least 1.5 per cent of the total number of electors in the most recent national election (about 240,000) for candidacy registration, pursuant to Article 23 of the Presidential and Vice-Presidential Election and Recall Act. Having failed on both points, Madam Shih and her running mate brought their case to TCC. Yet, the constitutionality of both requirements was sustained.[51] Four years later, the presidential candidate of the Democratic Progressive Party (DPP), Chen, Shui-bian, invited Annette Lu, a leading figure in Taiwan's feminist movement and a politician, to serve as his running mate. They were elected by a very thin margin in 2000 and re-elected again in 2004. Lu became the first, and so far, the only, woman vice president in history.[52]

It was under President Chen and Vice President Lu that gender mainstreaming became a government policy.[53] This policy was officially announced with tools including gender statistics, gender budget, gender impact assessment,

[47] For the history of the Eden Social Welfare Foundation, see Eden Social Welfare Foundation, 'Timeline of Major Achievements of Eden Social Welfare Foundation', available at eden.international/pages.php?level1_id=QD48PyomJTFAKCsjJV4r&level2_id=QD48PyomJTRAKCsjJV4r.

[48] The official website of the League, see The League for Persons with Disabilities, ROC (Taiwan), available at www.enable.org.tw.

[49] JY Interpretation No 290 (1992). This case concerns the review over the rules of the Public Service Election and Recall Law that provide restrictions on educational background and working experience of candidates for all levels of elected representatives. TCC found the restrictions not violating the Constitution, but pointed out that the restriction should be reconsidered in light of the popularity of education among people.

[50] Warm Life, available at warmlife.web66.com.tw.

[51] JY Interpretation No 468 (1998). This case concerns the review over the relevant provisions of the Presidential and Vice Presidential Election and Recall Act and other applicable laws in respect of the joint endorsement and the security deposits. TCC found out that the relevant rules are not in violation of the right of equality and remain within the legislative discretion.

[52] Office of the President, Republic of China (Taiwan), 'Presidents & vice presidents since 1947', available at english.president.gov.tw/Page/82.

[53] Gender mainstreaming was a key platform adopted in the fourth World Congress in Beijing, and a few women's organisations and feminist scholars were able to participate from Taiwan. They brought back the idea and strongly advocated for it. Chang (n 18) 224.

gender analysis, gender awareness training and a gender equality taskforce.[54] An advisory body, the Gender Equality Committee of the Executive Yuan, was set up to steer up policies, and the Department of Gender Equality was created under direct supervision of the Premier to coordinate policy implementations.[55] The Gender Equality Committee strongly pushed for the policy of gender parity in public governance. The first step was to require at least half of the members of the education committee of gender equality at all levels to be female.[56] Further steps were taken to extend this gender parity principle to committees at different levels across government, and to all non-governmental committees and corporation boards.[57] Even though gender parity was not made mandatory in all government committees, the Executive Yuan has deemed it a key component in gender statistics and tracked it annually.[58] In 2008, Tsai, Ing-wen became the DPP's party chairperson,[59] the first chairwoman of the political party in Taiwan's history, and in 2016, the first woman President.

Similar to women's groups, SGDP groups also sought to enhance their rights advocacy by competing in elections and running for political offices since democratic transitions began in the late 1980s.[60] Yet, they were not as successful as women's groups.[61] The first lesbian group, OURS, was created in 1990 and began publishing a bi-monthly magazine, *Female Friends*. In 1993, the first gay group on campus, GayChat, was born. In 1995, an open gay, Chuang, Sung-Fu, announced his candidacy in the election for the Legislative Yuan. Receiving only a few hundred votes, he was not elected. In 2009, the Taiwan Alliance to Promote Civil Partnership Rights (TAPCPR), was formed and made public participation a key strategy.[62] In 2010, facing the election for city/county majors and councillors, and again in 2012, with the upcoming election for the Legislative Yuan, Taiwan's Green Party made strong calls for SGDP to come out and compete in the elections. While a few responded to the call, none was elected.[63] It was not

[54] Gender Equality Committee of the Executive Yuan, 'Gender Mainstreaming', available at gec.ey.gov.tw/en/5BF83D33AF66B2FA.

[55] ibid.

[56] The Gender Equality Education Act, Arts 7, 8 and 9. English version available at Laws & Regulations Database of the Republic of China (Taiwan), Gender Equity Education Act: law.moj.gov.tw/ENG/LawClass/LawAll.aspx?pcode=H0080067.

[57] Gender Equality Committee of the Executive Yuan (n 54).

[58] Gender Equality Committee of the Executive Yuan, 'Database of Gender Statistics', available at www.gender.ey.gov.tw/gecdb/Stat_Statistics_DetailData.aspx?sn=i9VnBrHRVPG5qI2WtF2n%2bg%3d%3d.

[59] Wikipedia, 'List of Leaders of the Democratic Progressive Party', available at en.wikipedia.org/wiki/List_of_leaders_of_the_Democratic_Progressive_Party.

[60] W Shen, The 30-year Crusade of LGBT Rights Movements in Taiwan: Viewpoints from an Activist (Gate Books, 2021) 26–60.

[61] Youth Point, available at medium.com/youth-viewpoint.

[62] Shen (n 60) 60–67. Further information about TAPCPR is available at Taiwan Alliance to Promote Civil Partnership Rights, 'Introduction of Taiwan Alliance to Promote Civil Partnership Rights', available at tapcpr.org/english/about-us.

[63] Youth Point (n 61). Also, beginning in 1998, SGDP groups began to focus more on rights agenda in elections. See Shen (n 60) 82–86.

until 2016, when Audrey Tang, the iconic and the first open transgender person, was appointed as Digital Minister, that the leading figure of SGDP occupied a key political office in the Government.[64]

C. TCC's Judicial Review and Rights Protection

Taiwan's successful democratic transition and constitutional reforms have also strengthened judicial power, particularly TCC's power in reviewing and invalidating unconstitutional statutes and government acts.[65] TCC has 15 justices with a non-renewable term of eight years, appointed by the President with the consent of the Legislative Yuan. The first female justice was appointed in August 1967, and since then, TCC has always had at least one female justice in any cohort. At present, TCC has four female justices out of 15, the record number in history.

Similar to other constitutional courts, TCC exercises powers of abstract and concrete review, receives individual complaints, dissolves unconstitutional political parties, and decides on presidential impeachment.[66] In abstract review, members of the Legislative Yuan or a central or local agency may petition to TCC regarding constitutionality of statutes. In concrete review, judges may petition to TCC if they believe the laws they are to apply conflict with the Constitution. Last but not the least, individuals may petition to TCC when they have exhausted all available judicial remedies and believe that the laws applied in their cases are in violation of the Constitution and their constitutionally protected rights infringed. In individual complaints, what TCC used to review was the constitutionality of the law that was challenged, but beginning in January 2022, as a result of a new Constitutional Court Procedure Act, not only the law itself but also how the law was applied in the judgment can be reviewed and invalidated.

While TCC was created on the Chinese Mainland in 1948, and resumed office in Taiwan in 1952, it did not effectively function until the late 1980s when the Martial Law Decree was lifted and democratic transitions set in motion. Most renowned was one TCC decision, JY Interpretation No 261, made in 1990, in which TCC ordered national representatives who had not faced re-election since 1948 to retire before a specific date and mandated a second election to be held accordingly.[67] Also noteworthy was TCC's invalidation of a constitutional

[64] Wikipedia, 'Audrey Tang', available at en.wikipedia.org/wiki/Audrey_Tang.

[65] Yeh (n 16) 167–74; see also WC Chang, 'Constitutional Court of Taiwan (Judicial Yuan)' in Max Planck Encyclopedia of Comparative Constitutional Law [MPECCoL], Oxford Constitutional Law Online (2018), available at oxcon.ouplaw.com/view/10.1093/law-mpeccol/law-mpeccol-e538.

[66] Yeh (n 16) 162–65; Chang (n 65).

[67] JY Interpretation No 261 (1990).

revision in 1999, finding both the amending procedure and substance exceeded constitutional limits.[68] Since then, TCC has become a pivotal institution in ensuring constitutional rule of law and fundamental rights guarantees. As TCC allows individuals, who find legal provisions applied in their final judgments violating their constitutionally protected rights and in conflict with the Constitution, to lodge constitutional petitions, significant attention of civic and social groups including women and SGDP groups has consequently shifted from the constitutional reform and electoral competition discussed above to strategic constitutional litigation before TCC.[69]

In 1994, when a new cohort of TCC justices faced nomination and confirmation, women's groups waited no time to seize the opportunity for advancing the women's agenda. They first demanded a sizable proportion of female justices to be appointed and then prepared a list of questionnaires to inquire about nominated justices' understandings of sex and gender equality.[70] In response to women's groups, two female candidates, one from the Supreme Court and the other from academia, were nominated. Yet, only the one from the Supreme Court was confirmed. The other was rejected due to her husband's close relationship with the opposition.[71] Disappointed, women's groups continued to pressure TCC for women's agenda. And their victory quickly came in with JY Interpretation No 365, adopted in 1994 in which TCC ruled in favour of women's equal right in the family for the first time.[72] This first success in women's strategic constitutional litigation will be discussed in more detail in the flagship development below.

Unlike women's groups, SGDP groups did not turn to TCC until later. One activist, Chi, Chia-Wei, began to seek legal registry of his same-sex marriage via lawsuits in the late 1990s. His first petition to TCC was rejected in 2000, followed by repeated rejections until 2017, when TCC affirmed same-sex couples equal rights to marriage in JY Interpretation No 748.[73] Further details are discussed below in the flagship development.

D. Domestic Incorporation of International Human Rights

Women's groups have played key roles in advocating for the domestic incorporation of international human rights, particularly CEDAW.[74] They were drawn to CEDAW when helping draft the Act of the Equal Treatment of Both Sexes

[68] JY Interpretation No 499 (2000).
[69] Chang (n 15).
[70] Chen (n 24) 70–71.
[71] ibid 71.
[72] JY Interpretation No 365 (1994).
[73] JY Interpretation No 748 (2017).
[74] Chang (n 18).

at Work in the late 1980s.[75] Through researching foreign legal materials, the staffs and affiliated lawyers at the Awakening Foundation came to know about CEDAW. At the time, there was no discussion about incorporation.

In the early 2000s, when the Government undertook restructuring reforms, women's groups began referring to the concept of gender mainstreaming in advocating for establishing an independent commission of gender equality as well as for ensuring a gender parity governing structure.[76] In the course of advocacy, women's groups learned further about CEDAW and had the opportunity to meet with renowned women's activists who served as members to the CEDAW committee or the UN Commission on the Status of Women (CSW). In April 2004, women's groups held a workshop to call for participation in CSW meetings and to advocate CEDAW's incorporation into Taiwan. Soon after, the National Alliance of Taiwan Women Associations (NATWA), a primary network of women's groups, took the lead, and by the end of August 2004, the Taiwan Civil League for promoting CEDAW (the League for CEDAW) was formed.[77]

The League for CEDAW successfully put the CEDAW accession into the Government's agenda. Several key activists in the League were advisors for women's rights to the Government. As mentioned earlier, between 2000 and 2008, the DPP-led Government had a special focus on the protection of human rights. As part of that policy, a wide array of human rights organisations and activists were given consultative status and invited to policy discussions in the Government. This made the advocacy for CEDAW accession much easier.[78] On 5 January 2007, the Legislative Yuan passed the accession. On 27 February, the Government submitted the accession to the UN Secretary-General for deposition, which was nevertheless returned.[79] Notwithstanding the rejection, the League for CEDAW continued to press the Government to issue the initial state report, which was released in March 2009, followed by the independent review of international experts, who were sitting or retired CEDAW Committee members.[80] Also in 2009, the Government ratified ICCPR and ICESCR. An implementation act was passed to give legal effect for the rights enshrined in the two Covenants.[81] The Initial State Report of the two Covenants was released in 2012, followed by an international review in 2013.[82] Meanwhile, an implementation act to

[75] ibid 224.

[76] ibid 224–25.

[77] The groups included NATWA, the Awakening Foundation, the Taipei Chapter of the Awakening Foundation, Chang Fo-Chuan Center for the Study of Human Rights, Human Rights Program Center at Soochow University, Women's Research Program Center at National Taiwan University, ECPAT Taiwan, Taiwan Women's Film Association, the Garden of Hope Foundation, and the Taiwanese Feminist Scholars Association.

[78] Chang (n 18) 225.

[79] ibid 226.

[80] ibid.

[81] Chang (n 21).

[82] More details regarding the state reports of the two Covenants and their international reviews are available at Human Rights in Taiwan: www.humanrights.moj.gov.tw/17998.

enforce CEDAW was passed and became effective in 2012.[83] The second review of Taiwan's CEDAW state report was in 2014, the third in 2018, and the fourth in 2022.[84]

Following CEDAW and the two Covenants, a few other core international human rights conventions including the Convention on the Rights of the Child and the Convention on the Rights of Persons with Disabilities were also incorporated via their respective implementation acts and provided with the domestic legal effects.[85] The release and preparation of periodic state reports and more importantly, independent review by international experts, in which meetings are open to all NGOs, have provided an exceptional opportunity for women and SGDP groups to advance equal rights.[86] One most important achievement, as will be discussed in the section on constitutional framing below, was to channel SGDP's equal rights, which were not included in the Constitution, into legal and subsequently, constitutional terrain.

III. CONSTITUTIONAL FRAMING OF SEX, GENDER AND SEXUALITY

Taiwan's constitutional framing of equality is not at all elaborate, entailing equality between men and women but not equality for SGDP. The extension from sex, to gender, and to a sexuality framing of equality has initially been done through TCC's constitutional interpretations, and later, more substantially, through ICCPR, CEDAW and other domestically incorporated human rights conventions.

A. Limited Constitutional Framing

Taiwan's Constitution does not entail elaborate provisions on sex or gender equality. In Article 7, the Constitution recognises sex equality by affirming that citizens, whether *Nan* (men) or *Niu* (women), should be equal before the law.[87] As previously discussed, owing to the women's movement on the Chinese Mainland and their participation in the making of the Constitution, women's quota in political representation of all levels were secured by the Constitution promulgated in 1947. Nevertheless, the understandings of women's equality at the time were rather protectionist, which could be seen in the two provisions

[83] Chang (n 21).

[84] The fourth state report was released in early 2022, whose review was undertaken in the second half of 2022. For all state reports and international reviews, see Gender Equality Committee of the Executive Yuan (n 20).

[85] Chang (n 21).

[86] ibid.

[87] The ROC Constitution, Art 7.

under the section of policy directives. For example, in Article 153, women and children engaged in labour are to be provided with special protection according to their age and physical condition, and in Article 156, the state is obligated to protect motherhood and carry out the policy of promoting the welfare of women and children.

Women's participation in the constitutional reforms of the 1990s and 2000s has not made much significant advancement. As discussed above, the proposals for adding new rights to the Constitution, including the proposed Women Charter by women's groups, were rejected. The provisions that were eventually included was in the form of policy directives. Article 10(6) of the Additional Articles to the Constitution obligates the Government to 'protect the dignity of women, safeguard women's personal safety, eliminate sex and gender discrimination, and further substantive equality between men and women.'[88]

As such, the constitutional framing of equality remained with the equality between men and women, but not extended to equality for SGDP. As will be discussed below, extending the framing of equality from sex and gender to sexuality was not made until 2013, when the international experts reviewed Taiwan's Initial State Reports on the two Covenants and suggested such extended framing in their Concluding Observations.[89]

B. From Sex to Gender, and to Sexuality: CEDAW and the Two Covenants

The first-ever international review of Taiwan's State Report on international human rights conventions was in 2009 when the Initial State Report on CEDAW was reviewed by an independent panel of three international experts, Schöpp-Schilling from Germany, Heisoo Shin from South Korea and Anamah Tan from Singapore.[90] While the three experts were invited by the Government, they were

[88] Additional Articles to the ROC Constitution, Art 10(6). To this day, this clause is the only provision in the Constitution where the word 'dignity' appears. Yet, it remains unclear why the word was added in the 1992 constitutional amendment and what connection it had with women's equality. In 1995, when TCC upheld a judicial precedent on domestic violence in JY Interpretation No 371, it referred to the dignity of woman protected in this clause. In an opinion that concurs in part and dissents in part, Justice Su, Jyun-Hsiung, with a doctorate from Germany, discusses the concept of human dignity on the basis of Art 1 of the German Basic Law and Art 13 of Japan's post-WWII Constitution. For further discussion on human dignity and its judicial usage, see JCS Hsu, 'Human Dignity in the Taiwan Constitutional Court' in JCS Hsu (ed), *Human Dignity in Asia: Dialogue between Law and Culture* (Cambridge University Press, 2022).

[89] Concluding Observations and Recommendations Adopted by the International Group of Independent Experts in Review of the Initial Reports of the Government of Taiwan on the Implementation of the International Human Rights Covenants (1 March 2013), available at www.humanrights.moj.gov.tw/media/14391/5415171652675.pdf?mediaDL=true [hereinafter Concluding Observations and Recommendations for the Initial Reports of the International Human Rights Covenants].

[90] Gender Equality Committee of the Executive Yuan (n 20).

accorded full independence in completing the reviewing task.[91] The concluding observations and recommendations issued for the first review was rather informal, but those for the second and the following reviews were done in accordance with the standard format used by the UN CEDAW Committee. Starting from the second review, the panel was also expanded from the initial three members to five members.[92]

In the first CEDAW review, infrastructural issues such as gender statistics were the focus. The committee made inquiries on how the Government understood sex and gender differences and whether they were aware of intersectional discriminations between sex, gender and other attributes.[93] In the second review, the five-member committee raised a serious concern that

> despite the guarantee of equality for all people in Article 7 of Taiwan's Constitution, there is no legal definition of discrimination against women, and no law addresses multiple and intersecting forms of discrimination against women, including indigenous women, rural women, migrant women, women with disabilities, and lesbians, bisexuals, transsexuals and intersex persons.[94]

Further, the committee was also concerned with the lack of progress in the development of teaching materials at all levels on sexual orientation and gender identities, and recommended the Government to 'develop more awareness campaigns and teaching materials on gender diversity for all levels in consultation with gender equality experts in government, academia and civil society groups as well as with the LBTI community.'[95] The concern with 'the lack of legal recognition of the diversity of families in the country and that only heterosexual marriages are recognised but not same sex unions or cohabiting partnerships' was also raised.[96] The committee's concerns and suggestions may seem bold, but it was not alone in raising these concerns and making similar suggestions. A year before, in 2013, the international committee in reviewing Taiwan's Initial Report on the two Covenants had also made similar observations and recommendations.[97] More importantly, in both CEDAW and the two Covenant review meetings, as they were open for NGO participation, more than hundreds of NGOs including women and

[91] Chang (n 21).
[92] Gender Equality Committee of the Executive Yuan (n 20).
[93] ibid.
[94] Conclusions and Recommendations in Review of Taiwan's Second Report on Implementation of CEDAW (2014) para 6. [hereinafter Conclusions and Recommendations for the Second Report on CEDAW].
[95] ibid para 22.
[96] ibid para 31.
[97] Concluding Observations and Recommendations for the Initial Reports of the International Human Rights Covenants (n 89).

SGDP groups joined the meetings and strongly advocated for extending equal protection to SGDP.[98]

In 2013, the international review of Taiwan's Initial State Reports on the two Covenants was undertaken. A group of independent experts, from 10 different countries, were invited, including Philip Alston, Nisuke Ando, Virginia Bonoan-Dandan, Theodoor van Boven, Jerome Cohen, Shanthi Dairiam, Asma Jahangir, Manfred Nowak, Eibe Riedel and Heisoo Shin.[99] In their concluding observations and recommendations, they commended Taiwan for having ratified CEDAW and making it domestically applicable, noting that it is generally accepted that the provisions of the Covenants relating to gender issues need to be interpreted in line with the jurisprudence under CEDAW.[100] They also noted that 'transgender persons are widely considered to suffer from a form of mental illness and that persons with gender identities different from their biological sex, suffer many forms of discrimination, including bullying in schools.'[101] They also expressed concerns with 'the lack of legal recognition of the diversity of families in the country and that only heterosexual marriages are recognised but not same-sex marriages or cohabiting partnerships',[102] unequivocally finding it discriminatory.[103]

More importantly, noting that it is unclear to what extent the domestic courts have the power to give precedence to the two Covenants in case of a conflict with either pre-existing or subsequent legislation, the two Covenants review committee further recommends the Covenants be deemed part of the Constitution of Taiwan.[104] As such, the extension of equality framing from sex and gender to greater diversity including sexuality, sexual orientation and gender identities would be elevated to the level of the Constitution but not just that of law. This certainly was a much-welcome transformation in the legal and

[98] Conclusions and Recommendations for the Second Report on CEDAW (n 94) para 4; Concluding Observations and Recommendations for the Initial Reports of the International Human Rights Covenants (n 89) para 5.

[99] Concluding Observations and Recommendations for the Initial Reports of the International Human Rights Covenants (n 89) para 2.

[100] ibid para 26.

[101] ibid para 28.

[102] ibid para 78.

[103] ibid.

[104] Concluding Observations and Recommendations Adopted by the International Group of Independent Experts in Review of the Second Reports of the Government of Taiwan on the Implementation of the International Human Rights Covenants (20 January 2017) para 12, available at www.humanrights.moj.gov.tw/media/12296/327200414160793f3e.pdf?mediaDL=true [hereinafter Concluding Observations and Recommendations for the Second Reports of the International Human Rights Covenants]; Concluding Observations and Recommendations Adopted by the International Group of Independent Experts in Review of the Third Reports of the Government of Taiwan on the Implementation of the International Human Rights Covenants (13 May 2022) para 16, available at www.humanrights.moj.gov.tw/media/20212005/concluding-observations-and-recommendations_taiwan-international-review-%E8%8B%B1%E6%96%87%E5%AE%9A%E7%A8%BF%E7%89%88.pdf?mediaDL=true [hereinafter Concluding Observations and Recommendations for the Third Reports of the International Human Rights Covenants].

constitutional discourse of sex and gender equality. Although the Government has yet to acknowledge such a position, TCC's decision on same-sex marriage, JY Interpretation No 748, made in May 2017, was clearly influenced by the two international committees of CEDAW and the two Covenants. And, both committees commended TCC's progressive decision in their respective reviews in 2018 and 2022.[105]

IV. CONSTITUTIONAL JURISPRUDENCE

Before the 1980s, Taiwan was under strict social and political controls sanctioned by the imposition of the Martial Law Decree. The early 1990s saw the burgeoning of civil organisations and human rights groups seeking all available opportunities to push forward reforms. One of the major movements was made by women's groups in utilising strategic constitutional litigation to advance women's rights as the progressive exercise of judicial review power by TCC has offered an opportunity structure for rights advocacy. The earliest achievement was made in the equal protection of family-related rights, followed by equal right to work and anti-discrimination, and more recently, same-sex marriage. To better understand jurisprudential evolution of the case laws involving equal rights of women and SGDP, it is useful to first have a general understanding of TCC's doctrinal approach to the principle of equality.

A. General Jurisprudence of Equality Principle: From Reasonableness to Three-tier Standards of Review

TCC's doctrinal approach to the principle of equality has been rather formal until recently. In TCC's interpretation, Article 7 of the Constitution guaranteeing all individuals equal before the law does not mean that the law cannot treat people differently. Instead, if legislative purposes behind the differential treatments are legitimate, and the differential treatments are made reasonably to achieve such legislative purposes, the laws are not in violation of the principle of equality guaranteed in Article 7.[106] As reasonableness is a rather low threshold,

[105] Conclusions and Recommendations of the International Review Committee, Review of the Taiwan's Third Report on the Implementation of CEDAW (20 July 2018) para 71; Concluding Observations and Recommendations for the Third Reports of the International Human Rights Covenants (n 104) para 89.

[106] The first case in which TCC made clear this doctrinal interpretation in relation to the principle of equality was JY Interpretation No 485 (1999). In this case, TCC upheld a law giving the families residing in original housing a priority to buy a new residence unit in old village reconstruction for military personnel.

TCC has seldom struck down laws on the ground of equality violation, and such a doctrinal approach was criticised as toothless.[107]

In recent years, however, TCC began to apply a stringent standard of review if classifications by which differential treatments are made in the law involve biological defects beyond one's own control, or immutable traits. In such cases, legislative purposes behind the differential treatments must be met with important public interests, and the differential treatments much be substantially related to achieving such legislative purposes. TCC has since applied such a heightened standard of review in cases of colour-blind people who were denied the opportunity to take entrance exams for the Central Police Academy,[108] and vision-impaired individuals who were given the monopoly to engage in the practice of massage business.[109] In the former case, TCC upheld the Central Police Academy's policy not admitting colour-blind applicants. In the latter case, TCC found the law contravening the principle of equality 'since there is hardly a substantial nexus between the objectives and the means', because the law was 'excessively restrictive to non-vision impaired individuals' and led the Government to 'overlook the fact that the talents of the vision-impaired are not limited to the massage business alone'.[110]

Notably, in 2022, when reviewing the Indigenous Peoples' Status Act, TCC developed the most stringent standard of review for the classification involving race, requiring that legislative purposes be met with particularly important public interests, and that differential treatments be absolutely necessary and without any alternatives to achieve legislative purposes.[111] In this judgment, TCC struck down the disputed provision in which children of intermarriages between indigenous and non-indigenous peoples could obtain indigenous peoples status when taking the surname of the indigenous father or mother, or using the indigenous peoples traditional name.[112] For TCC, differential treatments in having an additional surname-taking requirement for children of intermarriages between indigenous and non-indigenous peoples, whereas no such additional requirement was for children of marriages between indigenous peoples, were not absolutely necessary to achieve legislative purposes in strengthening indigenous peoples identity.[113]

[107] For example, see JY Hwang, 'Choosing the Standards of Scrutiny for the Equality Right Cases: Questioning the Applicability of the Proportionality Principle' (2008) 37 *National Taiwan University Law Journal* 253.
[108] JY Interpretation No 626 (2007).
[109] JY Interpretation No 649 (2008).
[110] ibid reasoning, para 3.
[111] TCC Judgment No 111-Hsien-Pan-4 (2022).
[112] ibid reasoning, paras 42–43.
[113] ibid.

TCC's recent doctrinal approach to equality is heavily influenced by, if not identical with, the American constitutional jurisprudence in equality.[114] This is no surprise as TCC's borrowing of foreign jurisprudence and explicit or implicit references to foreign case laws have been reflective of scholarly or professional backgrounds of TCC justices.[115] When justices with doctorates from the United States are appointed, TCC's doctrinal approaches to free speech or principle of equality have shown the American jurisprudential influences,[116] whereas justices with doctorates from Germany have brought with them German jurisprudential influences on principle of proportionality, human dignity, statutory preservation or occupational freedom, among others.[117] Compared to the scholarly backgrounds of justices that have evidential influences on TCC's jurisprudential developments, TCC's sex and gender composition has not shown significance. Since the late 1960s, TCC has had at least one or two female justices in each term of the Court, and the present Court has four female justices among 15 justices. Yet, as most female justices are appointed from judicial practice, and those few appointees from scholarly backgrounds have doctorates from Germany, female justices have not really made observable influences on the development of equality jurisprudence.

B. Case Laws Relating to Equal Rights of Women and SGDP

TCC's case laws in affirming women's and SGDP's equal rights have reflected the general jurisprudence of the equality principle discussed above. A doctrinal turn from a rather formal understanding of equality, to occasionally embracing substantive equality, and more recently, to the adoption of a more stringent standard of review has been witnessed.

i. Family-related Rights

The first breakthrough in TCC's ruling of women's equal rights was JY Interpretation No 365 decided in 1994.[118] In this case, TCC found Article 1089 of the Civil Code unconstitutional as the disputed provision granted the final

[114] DS Law and WC Chang, 'The Limits of Global Judicial Dialogue' (2011) 86 *Washington Law Review* 523; WC Chang and JR Yeh, 'Judges as Discursive Agent: The Use of Foreign Precedents by the Constitutional Court of Taiwan' in T Groppi and MC Ponthoreau (eds), *The Use of Foreign Precedents by Constitutional Judges* (Hart Publishing, 2013).

[115] Chang and Yeh (n 114) 383, 391.

[116] As previously mentioned, the scholar critical of TCC's jurisprudence in equality had a doctorate from Harvard Law School, and was appointed to TCC in 2016. Since his joining, TCC has developed three-tier standards of review.

[117] Chang and Yeh (n 114) 391.

[118] JY Interpretation No 365 (1994).

decision-making authority to the father in parental disagreements over the child. Most important is the doctrine that TCC developed to review differential treatments on the basis of sex or gender. For TCC, 'different treatment in law based on sex is only allowed by the Constitution in exceptional situations where it is grounded on biological differences between sexes or differences in the social function of gender roles resulting therefrom.'[119] Given widespread education and more equal access to education between men and women as well as more equal opportunities for women in employment, TCC held the disputed provision violating the principle of equal protection between men and women and incompatible with the actual status of women in current family life.[120]

Although the doctrine that TCC developed in JY Interpretation No 365 was rather formal in the understanding of equality, it continued to be applied to cases involving women's equal rights and occasionally used to invalidate the disputed laws. For example, in JY Interpretation No 452, Article 1002 of the Civil Code requiring wives to take the residence of their husbands was struck down on the ground of violating the principle of equality.[121] In JY Interpretation No 457, a disputed provision was struck down because it treated married sons and daughters differently when determining whether the Government could reclaim the farmland leased to their deceased father, a veteran. In case of married sons, the lease continued, whereas in case of married daughters, the lease terminated.[122]

ii. Right to Work and Anti-discrimination

This rather formal doctrine TCC developed to review differential treatments on the basis of sex and gender has not been without criticism, particularly when TCC relied on it to uphold protective legislation without much reasoning or justification.[123] For example, in JY Interpretation No 490, when TCC upheld the constitutionality of compulsory military service which was challenged by Jehovah's Witnesses on religious grounds, it mentioned in passing that 'given the physical differences between males and females and the derived role differentiation in their respective social functions', it was within legislative discretion to require only eligible male citizens to perform military service.[124] Also, in JY Interpretation No 494, TCC upheld the provisions relating to overtime wage payment in the Labor Standards Act to protect the workers' rights and interests, without acknowledging that female workers were not permitted to work

[119] ibid reasoning, para 1.
[120] ibid reasoning, para 4.
[121] JY Interpretation No 452 (1998).
[122] JY Interpretation No 457 (1998).
[123] Hwang (n 107); WC Chang, 'Conceptualizing and Locating Gender Equality: ICCPR, ICESCR, and the Constitution in Comparison' (2014) 43 *National Taiwan University Law Journal* 771, 795.
[124] JY Interpretation No 490 (1999), holding and reasoning, para 1.

overnight and usually could not work on weekends, and thus overtime wage payments were mostly for male workers.[125]

Notably, in 2021, TCC decided to make a shift from its rather formal understanding of differential treatments based on sex and gender. In JY Interpretation No 807, when reviewing the ban on females working overnight in the Labor Standards Act, TCC decided to apply an intermediate standard of review, requiring that legislative purposes behind the differential treatments be met with important public interests, and the differential treatments be substantially related to achieving such legislative purposes.[126] Rather than explicitly rejecting its formal doctrine established in JY Interpretation No 365, TCC still referred to the interpretation but explained that differential treatments based on sex and gender are suspect classifications that are based on immutable traits of individuals or on historical and systematic stigmatisation and hence, it is necessary to apply an intermediate standard for review.[127] In the reasoning, TCC agreed that protecting female labour and particularly their health for child-bearing and rearing was met with important public interests, but the ban on females working overnight was not substantially related to achieving such important purposes because there were still alternatives, such as providing dormitories or transportation, or making other arrangements, and increasingly in many families, housework is shared by both the male and female, not to mention that a female worker who is single or without family burdens can choose to work overnight shifts. Finding the ban violating sex and gender equality guaranteed in Article 7 of the Constitution, TCC invalidated the ban.[128]

JY Interpretation No 807 represents the first case that TCC applies an intermediate standard of review to differential treatments based on sex and gender to strike down protective legislation for women. Because TCC has not rejected the previous doctrine established in JY Interpretation No 365, it remains to be seen if the intermediate standard of review for differential treatments based on sex and gender becomes stable.

iii. Women's Bodies

Prostitution has been outlawed despite the underground sex industry. The main legal basis was Article 80 of the Social Order Maintenance Act, penalising only those engaging in sexual transactions for financial gains, but not those purchasing for sex.[129] This became challenged before TCC in JY Interpretation

[125] JY Interpretation No 494 (1999).
[126] JY Interpretation No 807 (2021), reasoning, para 7.
[127] ibid reasoning, para 6.
[128] ibid holding and reasoning, para 12.
[129] Art 80(1)(1) of the Social Order Maintenance Act provides that the action of any individual who engages in sexual transactions or cohabitation with intent for financial gain is punishable by detention for no more than three days or by a fine up to TWD 30,000. JY Interpretation No 666 (2009) reasoning, para. 2.

No 666.[130] While many were expecting TCC to decide on legalisation (or not) of prostitution, TCC made a surprising turn to focus its constitutional ruling on substantive equality of women engaging in prostitution. In this case, TCC for the first time read a facially neutral law into a de facto discrimination. While those engaging in sexual transaction for profit could be both men and women, and those purchasing sex could also be men and women, for TCC it was evident that those engaging in sexual transaction for profit were predominantly women who were socially and economically disadvantaged.[131] Even if protecting public morals was a legitimate government purpose, there were still alternatives for the Government to consider, especially to provide education or works for those socially and economically disadvantageous women.[132]

Finding the provision violating substantive equality for those socially and economically disadvantageous women engaging in prostitution, TCC gave the legislature a two-year period for revision, and the impugned provision would lose effect immediately after two years.[133] Notably, TCC did not decide to legalise (or not) prostitution, but instead, left it entirely to the legislature provided that the equality violation of socially and economically disadvantageous women engaging in sex transactions should be resolved. This was certainly a strategic move for TCC to shift this heatedly debated issue back to the political branches.

After a heated debate, Article 80 was revised in 2011, permitting only sexual transactions in the special zones drawn by the local governments but continuing to penalise both parties engaging in sexual transactions outside those special zones.[134] Yet, perhaps wary of public criticisms, till this day, no local government has ever drawn any special zones for legal sexual transactions.

iv. Cultural/Religious Issues

A rather controversial decision on women's rights was JY Interpretation No 728, made in 2015.[135] In this case, a constitutional challenge was brought to the statute governing ancestor worship guilds[136] permitting a worship guild's internal regulation to decide whether a person would be a qualified successor to a worship guild. The petitioner was a married daughter who was not permitted to be a successor, arguing that the impugned provision posed a de facto discrimination against women as most guilds assigned only men as successors.

[130] ibid.
[131] ibid reasoning, para 3.
[132] ibid reasoning, para 4.
[133] ibid.
[134] Social Order Maintenance Act, Art 80(1)(1).
[135] JY Interpretation No 728 (2015).
[136] According to Art 3 of the Act for Ancestor Worship Guild, an ancestor worship guild is a group of people aiming at providing services for ancestor worship or other worships based on the properties donated by the initiators. The group of people usually belong to a large, extended family or under the same surname.

Unlike in the above-mentioned JY Interpretation No 666, TCC failed to find the de facto discrimination as a violation of sex equality. Instead, the Court sustained the impugned provision on the grounds of the freedom of association, property rights and freedom of contract held by the founders and their descendants as 'an ancestor worship guild is an association formed by the properties donated by the founders for the purpose of providing services for ancestor worship or other forms of worship.'[137] Thus, for the Court,

> even though such a disputed provision may constitute differential treatment in substance, since it is not arbitrary, it is not in conflict with the principle of sex equality embodied in article 7 of the Constitution nor does it infringe women's right to property.[138]

Perhaps aware of the criticism the decision would provoke, TCC in the last part of the interpretation urged the Government to 'conduct a timely review and modification of the related law to ensure that they are keeping pace with time, especially taking into consideration the State's positive duty to protect women' under Articles 2 and 5 of CEDAW, which were domestically incorporated as well as other constitutional provisions.[139] The reference to CEDAW provisions, however, has not diminished the anger of the women's group, which contends that the Court has yielded too much to tradition and religion.

In January 2023, TCC was requested to review another provision in the statute governing ancestor worship guilds that assigned the male offspring of the family, including the adopted children, to be the qualified successor if the ancestor worship guilds had no internal regulations for such matters.[140] Applying the recently developed intermediate standard of review, TCC unequivocally found the provision violating sex and gender equality as the legislative purpose was out of stigma and could not serve important public interests, and the differential treatment was not legitimate.[141] While this decision earned applause for TCC, it also drew criticism against it.[142] To the dismay of women's and SGDP's groups that filed *amici curiae* opinions in this case,[143] TCC failed to revisit the earlier decision, JY Interpretation No 728, in which the internal regulations of the ancestor worship guilds for qualified successors were respected despite the de facto discriminations again women. Women's and SGDP's groups then decided to turn to the Ministry of Interior and Legislative Yuan to demand

[137] JY Interpretation No 728 (2015) reasoning, para 2.
[138] ibid.
[139] ibid.
[140] The Act for Ancestor Worship Guild, Art 4.
[141] TCC Judgment No 112-Hsien-Pan-1 (2023).
[142] The Awakening Foundation made a critical statement after TCC released the judgment, see Awakening Foundation, available at www.awakening.org.tw/news/5861.
[143] For the *amici curiae* opinions by the Awakening Foundation and the TAPCPR, see Constitutional Court, ROC (Taiwan), available at cons.judicial.gov.tw/docdata.aspx?fid=38&id=309875.

a comprehensive revision of the statute governing ancestor worship guilds to reflect the changing dynamics of sex and gender.[144]

v. Citizenship-related Issues

Unlike its counterpart in Japan or South Korea, TCC has not directly touched upon equal citizenship issues. One indirectly related decision was JY Interpretation No 618, made in 2006. In that decision, TCC sustained a discriminatory provision in the Act Governing Relations between People of the Taiwan Area and Mainland Area in which no person from the Mainland Area permitted to enter into the Taiwan Area could serve as a civil servant unless he or she has had a household registration in the Taiwan Area for at least 10 years. The applicant of this case was a woman who married a Taiwanese man and since their marriage had resided in Taiwan. Like the applicant, those who came to Taiwan from Mainland China mostly did so through marriage and were mostly women. The provision entailed a de facto discrimination against women married to a Taiwanese husband from China. Yet, this indirect discrimination received no attention from TCC, which upheld it on the basis that differential treatments between those from Mainland and those originally from Taiwan were reasonable given the separation and even hostility between China and Taiwan, with fundamental differences in political, economic and social systems.[145]

V. FLAGSHIP DEVELOPMENTS

The three TCC decisions, JY Interpretation Nos 365, 748 and 791, all serve as flagship developments as they have presented an intricate relationship between the propositions of women's and SGDP's movements, constitutional discourse and the domestic incorporation of human rights.

A. JY Interpretation No 365 on Equal Right in Family

As previously mentioned, JY Interpretation No 365 was the first successful constitutional litigation for women's rights, initiated in 1994.[146] At the time, the Awakening Foundation and many women activists, lawyers and professors were working on a proposed revision of the Civil Code concerning equal rights of women within the family. Lawyer Lo, Ying-Hsueh was one collaborator among

[144] The Awakening Foundation made a critical statement after TCC released the judgment, see n 142.

[145] JY Interpretation No 618 (2006) reasoning, para 3.

[146] JY Interpretation No 365 (1994).

many. Their project began in 1990 with the financial sponsorship from Asia Foundation. After three years, in May 1993, the women's groups released their first draft of the amended Code and held many public hearings and workshops in the hope of generating public support. They also lobbied the legislators who had recently been elected in the first national legislative election held in 1992.

In the midst of public advocacy and legislative lobbying, two women clients coincidentally walked into Ms Lo's office with almost identical cases. Both women were separated from their husbands but sought to have their children live with them. However, according to the then-Article 1089 of the Civil Code, in case of parental disagreements, the father was given the right to decide matters concerning the children. As a result, both women lost their cases in the lower court proceedings. Having heard their cases, Ms Lo thought they presented a powerful test case and the timing was perhaps right to petition TCC for an interpretation regarding the Civil Code. Meanwhile, about 150 legislators from various political parties signed a proposal to request the Legislative Yuan to bring a constitutional petition to TCC. The proposal was quickly passed and submitted on 15 July 1994.

These petitions came to TCC at a rather critical time. The nine-year tenure of the justices (the fifth term) who had served since 1985 was about to expire at the end of September 1994. The confirmation hearing of new appointees took place in late August and early September. As previously mentioned, women's groups held a number of news conferences and made public inquiries into those appointees regarding their position on women's equal rights in the family.

On September 23, one week before leaving the bench, TCC made JY Interpretation No 365, holding that the then Article 1089 of the Civil Code was in violation of equality guaranteed by Article 7 of the Constitution.[147] TCC demanded the impugned provision to be amended and granted a grace period of two years before the provision would become null and void. Following this ruling, the Ministry of Justice quickly drafted a revision of Article 1089 and other similar provisions and sent the bill to the Legislative Yuan for discussion in March 1995. The revised provisions came into force in September 1996, just before the deadline.

JY Interpretation No 365 and subsequent successful legislative revisions energised women's groups and encouraged them to use constitutional litigation as part of their legal mobilisation strategies. Under the leadership of the Awakening Foundation, women lawyers decided to solicit test cases to challenge major provisions in the Civil Code they sought to amend.[148] They published advertisements in their magazines, newsletters, and websites while continuing

[147] ibid holding and reasoning, para 3.
[148] Chang (n 15) 143.

legislative lobbying on further revisions of the Civil Code and enactments of other bills concerning women's equal rights at work and in schools.

B. JY Interpretation No 748 on Same-sex Marriage

In line with the rising demands for equal rights of minorities, the demand for recognition of same-sex marriage also caught TCC's attention.[149] One gay man, Chi, Chia-Wei, had sought to register his gay marriage for years. With the legal assistance by the TAPCPR[150] and their leading gay rights lawyers, he lodged his case once again before TCC. Meanwhile, facing repeated requests for same-sex marriage registration, the Taipei city Government also petitioned to TCC for clarification. TCC consolidated these two cases, and held, rather exceptionally, an oral hearing on 24 March 2017. Both pro- and anti-gay marriage groups rallied before the Court's building, and a few anti-gay marriage activists came every morning to vocalise their positions.

On May 24, two months after the oral hearing, TCC issued JY Interpretation No 748, unequivocally holding that the provisions in the Marriage Chapter of the Civil Code that 'do not permit two persons of the same sex to create a permanent union of intimate and exclusive nature for the committed purpose of managing a life together' were 'in violation of both the people's freedom of marriage as protected by article 22 and the people's right to equality as guaranteed by article 7 of the Constitution.'[151] To remedy such a legislative failure, the Court demanded that 'the authorities concerned shall amend or enact relevant laws within two years', and unprecedentedly, the Court added that 'if relevant laws are not amended or enacted within the said two years, two persons of the same sex who intend to create the said permanent union shall be allowed to have their marriage registration effectuated at the authorities in charge of household registration, by submitting a written document signed by two or more witnesses' in accordance with the Marriage Chapter of the Civil Code.[152]

This was the first time that TCC provided a direct and specific remedy for legislative omission. So as not to overstep it authority, TCC struck a balance by yielding to the legislative authority 'to determine the formality for achieving the equal protection of the freedom of marriage.'[153] In other words, while affirming that the equal right to marriage of gay couples was a constitutional right and must be ensured, the Court left it open for the legislature to decide what

[149] JY Interpretation No 748 (2017). An English official press release of a short summary of this case, is available at Press Release on the Same-Sex Marriage Case: irs.judicial.gov.tw/GNNWS/NNWSS002.asp?id=267570&flag=1&regi=1&key=&MuchInfo=&courti.

[150] The organisation's mission statement and recent activities are available at Taiwan Alliance to Promote Civil Partnership Rights: tapcpr.org.

[151] JY Interpretation No 748 (2017). For the official translation of the holding, see n 149.

[152] ibid.

[153] ibid.

format – marriage, union, partnership, among others – of that equal protection would be and through what legislative measures – amending the Marriage Chapter of the Civil Code, adding a special chapter to the Civil Code or to enact a special law, among others – would be implemented. Only if the legislature failed to deliver would the direct remedy provided by the Court – a form of marriage for gay couples in accordance with the present Marriage Chapter of the Civil Code would be effectuated. This balanced judicial strategy proved to be successful as pro-gay marriage groups obtained the constitutional recognition of equal right of marriage for gay couples, and anti-gay marriage groups – although disappointed – felt that they could continue to fight for their position in the future legislative deliberations.

Consequently, on 24 May 2019, Taiwan became the first Asian country to legally recognise same-sex marriage. Same-sex marriage has since been legalised, and same-sex couples can now adopt children and enjoy the rights and benefits opposite-sex marriage couples have long held.

C. JY Interpretation No 791 on Adultery

The issue of JY Interpretation No 791 was whether adultery was unconstitutional. The case concerned two Articles. The first was Article 239 of Criminal Code of the Republic of China, which providing adultery was a crime. The other was Article 239 of Code of Criminal Procedure, providing that 'if the offense is one specified in Article 239 of the Criminal Code, the withdrawal of a complaint against a spouse shall not be considered to be a withdrawal of a complaint against the other adulterer.'

TCC held both Articles were unconstitutional. First, the Court reasoned that the Government should not intervene in a marriage by criminal law, because whether a marriage can run well depended on husband and wife and this was a private affair rather than a public interest concern. Punishing adultery by criminal law violated the freedom of sexual behaviour and the right to privacy. Therefore, Article 239 of Criminal Code was unconstitutional.

Second, TCC held that Article 239 of Code of Criminal Procedure was unconstitutional because it violated the right of equality. In general, 'in a case chargeable only upon complaint, the filing or withdrawal of a complaint against one of several co-offenders has the same effect as a filing or withdrawal of the complaint against all such co-offenders.' When a claimer withdrew a complaint against his or her spouse, it usually meant the claimer forgave the spouse. Therefore, maintaining the accusation against the other adulterer was only for the effect of revenge. For these reasons, TCC held that Article 239 treated an adulterer differently from other co-offenders without any reasonable cause, violating the right of equality.

Moreover, TCC stressed that the statistics of adultery represented more female offenders than male offenders, but, in theory, the number should have been equal. It meant that even though Article 239 of the Criminal Code and Article 239 of the Code of Criminal Procedure were facially neutral, they were unequal in practice, disproportionately punishing women. TCC pointed out that this circumstance would be terminated after these Articles were announced unconstitutional. It is clear that since JY Interpretation No 666, in which TCC looked into disparate impacts on women engaging in sexual transactions, TCC has embraced the concept of substantive equality and developed a way to look beyond facially neutral laws by addressing their structural conditions for equal rights.

VI. CONCLUSION

Women's groups and their advocacy strategies have been pivotal to the advancement of sex and gender equality in Taiwan. The strategies are not limited to litigation with TCC, but further extended to changing the legal framework and discourse altogether. The recent incorporation of CEDAW, the two Covenants, and its further implementation clearly saw such bottom-up efforts in changing legal and institutional frameworks under which sex and gender equality are to be pursued.

The pursuit of women and SGDP groups for sex/gender equality has been undertaken, and channelled through, contextual dynamics in the 1990s and 2000s, including four main aspects – constitutional reform, democratic transition, judicial review and domestic incorporation of international human rights. These contextual dynamics have offered, to varying degrees, opportunity structures in which women and SGDP groups' advocacy could utilise and equal rights could be realised. The making of the ROC Constitution in 1946, and the constitutional reforms undertaken in the 1990s have led to the adoption of a women's quota and gender parity in proportional representation. The democratic transition made the political space open for women and SGDP to compete in elections and serve in high offices, putting Taiwan first in Asia in terms of the percentage of women in representative institutions.

Moreover, TCC, with its extensive powers and standing rules, has been a pivotal venue for strategic litigation by women and SGDP groups. Not only has TCC recently adopted a more stringent standard of review in examining differential treatment based on sex, gender and sexuality, but it has also explicitly endorsed substantive equality by looking beyond facially neutral laws against underlying structural conditions for sex and gender equality. Although the recent doctrinal shift in equality doctrine has shown strong American influences through appointed justices with American doctorates, TCC's strategy in working with political branches by giving the legislature a period of time to forge consensus and review laws has been rather orthotonus and adaptive to Taiwan's democratic transitions. Those periods of time also gave women and SGDP groups a further opportunity structure in which they could engage in dialogue with the Government, the legislature and the general public. Without such dialogues, women's equal rights in the family, and more recently, equal right to same-sex marriage, could not be possibly be realised or gain social acceptance.

International human rights instruments including CEDAW and the two Covenants have also regenerated vital public discourse on sex and gender equality, particularly since the 2000s. The international reviews in which sitting or previous committee members of CEDAW and the two Covenants came to examine Taiwan's state reports and have discussions with government officials on how these international human rights instruments may assist Taiwan to better enhance sex and gender equality have evidently offered an additional opportunity structure. Given Taiwan's difficulty in participating with the UN and related international organisations, domestic incorporation of these international human rights instruments is particularly relevant to Taiwan, including the Government and the non-governmental sectors.

4

Gender, Sexuality and Constitutionalism in Hong Kong

KELLEY LOPER*

I. INTRODUCTION

CONSTITUTIONAL LAW HAS played a critical, though insufficient, role in advancing the rights of women and sexual and gender diverse people (SGDP) in Hong Kong, a Special Administrative Region (SAR) of China. An overview of salient developments illustrates the strengths and weaknesses of available opportunity structures, identifies gaps in the jurisprudence, and suggests untapped potential. The Hong Kong courts have adopted a 'generous and purposive' approach to the interpretation of fundamental rights, grounded in international human rights norms. Most notably, they have elaborated elements of a nascent substantive equality doctrine when construing the right to equality and non-discrimination. These tools, however, have been under-utilised and applied inconsistently, and have therefore failed to identify gender-related disadvantage in a broader range of domains. At the same time, a persistent democracy deficit and recent changes to the legal and political landscape – including the introduction of a National Security Law (NSL)[1] in 2020 and regressive reforms to the electoral system in 2021 – have limited possibilities through political channels and raised questions about the future of constitutional review as an avenue for pursing transformative remedies.

Hong Kong's British colonial legacy and its status as a SAR with a high degree of autonomy under Chinese sovereignty since 1997 have shaped competing conceptions of Hong Kong's constitutional identity. The 1984 Sino-British Joint Declaration and the Basic Law (BL),[2] Hong Kong's regional constitutional

* Portions of the research for this chapter were supported by a grant awarded by the Hong Kong Research Grants Council (Project code: 17613117).

[1] The Law of the People's Republic of China on Safeguarding National Security in Hong Kong [hereinafter NSL], available at www.elegislation.gov.hk/doc/hk/a406/eng_translation_(a406)_en.pdf.

[2] The Basic Law of the Hong Kong [SAR] of the People's Republic of China [hereinafter BL].

instrument, express the terms of a political compromise. Certain guarantees, including the continuation of a separate common law legal system, judicial independence and the incorporation of the International Covenant on Civil and Political Rights (ICCPR), have supported the judiciary's role as the primary protector of human rights.[3] The Bill of Rights Ordinance (BOR)[4] has attained constitutional status and duplicates most of the ICCPR's provisions, allowing the courts to frequently reference international human rights materials. Indeed, they have considered several landmark cases involving the rights of women and SGDP, and applied a proportionality test to scrutinise justifications for any breaches.[5] Judges have assessed the constitutionality of policies related to rural elections;[6] a system for allocating school places;[7] grooming requirements for prisoners;[8] criminal offenses;[9] same-sex couples' rights;[10] gender recognition;[11] transgender marriage;[12] human trafficking;[13] and sex work;[14] among other issues.

In certain areas, however, advocates and judges have not fully embraced the potential of available rights and constitutional tools. Indeed, some judicial decisions reinforce, rather than remedy, disadvantage based on gender. For example, the courts have upheld customary laws which directly discriminate against rural women.[15] They have also overlooked the implications of substantive equality when reviewing policies that disproportionately impact other groups of women

[3] BL, Arts 2, 4, 19, 39, 85.

[4] Cap 383, s 8.

[5] *Hysan Development Co Ltd v Town Planning Board* [2016] 19 HKCFAR 372 [hereinafter *Hysan*]; *Leung Chun Kwong v Secretary for the Civil Service* [2019] HKCFA 19 [hereinafter *Leung Chun Kwong*]; R Abeyratne, 'More Structure, More Deference: Proportionality in Hong Kong' in PJ Yap (ed), *Proportionality in Asia* (Cambridge University Press, 2020).

[6] *Secretary for Justice and Others v Chan Wah and Others* [2000] 3 HKLRD 641 [hereinafter *Chan Wah*].

[7] *EOC v Director of Education* [2001] 2 HKLRD 690 [hereinafter *EOC*].

[8] *Leung Kwok Hung (Long Hair) v Commissioner of Correctional Services* [2020] HKCFA 37 [hereinafter *Leung Kwok Hung*].

[9] *Leung v Secretary for Justice* [2006] 4 HKLRD 211; *Secretary for Justice v Yau Yuk Lung* [2007] 3 HKLRD 903 [hereinafter *Yau Yuk Lung*]; *Yeung Chu Wing v Secretary for Justice* [2019] 3 HKLRD 238 [hereinafter *Yeung Chu Wing*].

[10] *QT v Director of Immigration* [2018] HKCFA 28 [hereinafter *QT*]; *Leung Chun Kwong* (n 5); *Infinger v The Hong Kong Housing Authority* [2020] 1 HKLRD 1188 [hereinafter *Infinger*]; *Ng Hon Lam Edgar v Secretary for Justice* [2020] 4 HKLRD 908 [hereinafter *Ng Hon Lam*]; *Ng Hon Lam Edgar v Hong Kong Housing Authority* [2021] 3 HKLRD 427; *Cho Man Kit v Broadcasting Authority* [2008] HKEC 783.

[11] *Q v Commissioner of Registration* [2023] HKCFA 4.

[12] *W v Registrar of Marriages* [2013] 3 HKLRD 90 [hereinafter *W*].

[13] *ZN v Secretary for Justice* [2020] 23 HKCFAR 15 [hereinafter *ZN*]; *AM v Director of Immigration, Commissioner of Police, and Secretary for Justice and CB v Commissioner of Police, Secretary for Justice, and Secretary for Security* [2022] HKEC 1472 [hereinafter *AM and CB*].

[14] *SW v Secretary for Justice* [2019] HKCFI 63 [hereinafter *SW*].

[15] *Kwok Cheuk Kin v Director of Lands (No 2)* [2021] 24 HKCFAR 349 [hereinafter *Kwok Cheuk Kin*].

on intersectional grounds, such as migrant domestic workers (mainly women from the Philippines and Indonesia).[16]

Statistics on the status of women illustrate remaining gender gaps in education, employment, and other areas, although women now constitute the majority of the population.[17] In 2020, 79.4 per cent of women and girls (85.5 per cent of men and boys) over the age of 15 had received at least a secondary education.[18] At the same time, 52.3 per cent of students in publicly funded higher education programmes were female,[19] though men outnumbered women in science (62.3 per cent) and engineering and technology programmes (71.1 per cent).[20] The number of women joining the workforce has increased, partly due to large numbers of migrant domestic workers.[21] Overall, however, fewer women (49.6 per cent) than men (66.2 per cent) participate, a relatively low rate compared with other developed economies. Women's median monthly employment earnings were 85 per cent of men's,[22] and women directors of Hong Kong listed companies constituted 14.2 per cent of the total.[23]

Against this backdrop, this chapter elaborates on the array of constitutional and other factors influencing gender constitutionalism in Hong Kong. Section II provides background on Hong Kong's constitutional history before and since 1997, the role of social movements, the structure and jurisdiction of the courts, the political system and recent reforms. Section III sets out the framing of constitutional rights related to gender and sexuality, especially equality. Section IV considers salient constitutional jurisprudence in several domains. Section V details a notable flagship development: the emergence of a substantive equality doctrine in cases concerning sexual orientation discrimination. Section VI concludes.

[16] In 2020, 98.5% of 373,884 migrant domestic workers were women. Census and Statistics Department, HKSAR, 'Women and Men in Hong Kong Key Statistics, 2021 Edition', Tables 1.14, 4.41, available at www.censtatd.gov.hk/en/data/stat_report/product/B1130303/att/B11303032021AN21B0100.pdf; *Vallejos v Commissioner of Registration* [2013] 2 HKLRD 533 [hereinafter *Vallejos*].

[17] HKSAR Government, 'Women and Men in Hong Kong – Key Statistics – Demographic Characteristics', available at www.censtatd.gov.hk/en/EIndexbySubject.html?scode=180&pcode=D5600610; The World Bank, 'Population, Female (% of Total Population) – Hong Kong SAR, China', available at data.worldbank.org/indicator/SP.POP.TOTL.FE.ZS?locations=HK.

[18] Hong Kong Equal Opportunities Commission (EOC), 'Gender Equality in Hong Kong', available at www.eoc.org.hk/EOC/Upload/DiscriminationLaws/OtherResources/Gender%20Equality-Eng%20%28Aug%202021%29.pdf.

[19] ibid.

[20] ibid.

[21] G He and X Wu, 'Foreign Domestic Helpers Hiring and Women's Labor Supply in Hong Kong' (2019) 51 *Chinese Sociological Review* 397.

[22] ibid; Census and Statistics Department (n 16) xxiii.

[23] *EOC* (n 18).

II. BACKGROUND

A. Developments Pre-1997

The history of constitution-making in Hong Kong and the principle of 'One Country, Two Systems' have shaped the constitution's capacity to transform structural inequalities. Developments during the British colonial era significantly impacted the framework introduced on 1 July 1997. The colonial Government preserved some traditional cultural norms which discriminate against women while also importing patriarchal European values related to marriage and sexuality.[24] As in most of its colonies, the British introduced prohibitions against the 'abominable crime of buggery' in 1865.[25] At the same time, the Government's alliance with conservative business interests and commitment to neoliberal ideology reinforced resistance to change, including the introduction of antidiscrimination legislation and other measures perceived as inimical to free markets.[26]

During the last decade of colonial rule, however, negotiations over the arrangements for Hong Kong and increasing anxiety about human rights after 1997, generated progressive policy initiatives. In 1984, China and Britain concluded the Sino-British Joint Declaration setting out the terms of the eventual transfer based on 'One Country, Two Systems', a practical compromise promising Hong Kong a high degree of autonomy.[27] These assurances were incorporated in the BL, adopted by the National People's Congress on 4 April 1990. Despite China's vastly different system, the BL guaranteed no change to Hong Kong's way of life and capitalist system for 50 years; a continuation of the previous laws in force; and the domestication of the ICCPR, which China itself has not ratified.[28]

[24] MS Dairiam, 'CEDAW, Gender and Culture' in R Baksh and W Harcourt (eds), *Oxford Handbook of Transnational Feminist Movements* (Oxford University Press, 2015) 380–81.

[25] Offences Against the Person Ordinance (Cap 212) s 49; Human Rights Watch, 'This Alien Legacy: the Origins of "Sodomy" Laws in British Colonialism' (17 December 2008), available at www.hrw.org/report/2008/12/17/alien-legacy/origins-sodomy-laws-british-colonialism.

[26] CJ Petersen, 'Equality as a Human Right: The Development of Anti-Discrimination Law in Hong Kong' (1996) 34 *Columbia Journal of Transnational Law* 335; CJ Petersen, 'Hong Kong's First Anti-Discrimination Laws and their Potential Impact on the Employment Market' (1997) 27 *Hong Kong Law Journal* 324; CJ Petersen and K Loper, 'Equal Opportunities Law Reform in Hong Kong: The Impact of International Norms and Civil Society Advocacy' in M Tilbury, SNM Young, and L Ng (eds), *Reforming Law Reform: Perspectives on Law Reform Processes in Hong Kong and Beyond* (HKU Press, 2014) 173.

[27] AHY Chen, 'The Autonomy of Hong Kong under "One Country, Two Systems"' in TL Lui, SWK Chui and R Yep (eds), *Routledge Handbook of Contemporary Hong Kong* (Routledge, 2020); M Hau, 'The Official Mind of British Post-Imperialism: Influencing Parliamentary Opinions during the Anglo-Chinese Negotiations over the Future of Hong Kong, 1982–84' (2021) 43 *The International History Review* 1198.

[28] BL, Arts 5, 8, 39.

The colonial Government introduced the BOR in 1991 and the last British governor, Chris Patten, increased democratic representation in the 1995 elections.[29] Until 1991, there had been no directly elected seats. These changes created space for dynamic political debate and civil society advocacy, inspiring the growth of women's and SGDP's rights movements. The colonial Government had largely failed to address the concerns of these groups in the 1970s and 1980s and had denied that discrimination was a problem.[30] The relative openness of the 1990s encouraged other policy changes.[31] For example, the Government dismantled inheritance laws which directly discriminated against women in indigenous villages.[32] Women's rights organisations and sympathetic legislators also successfully advocated for anti-discrimination legislation.[33] The Sex Discrimination Ordinance (SDO)[34] prohibits sexual harassment and direct and indirect discrimination based on sex, marital status, pregnancy and breastfeeding in several fields and established the Equal Opportunities Commission (EOC). After years of lobbying, and in the wake of the 1995 World Conference on Women in Beijing, the British extended the Convention on the Elimination of All Forms of Discrimination Against Women (CEDAW) to Hong Kong in 1996. This momentum contributed to the establishment of a Women's Commission in 2001 in response to a CEDAW Committee recommendation.[35] The Women's Commission has had limited influence, however, and the Committee has expressed concerns about its weak mandate and insufficient resources.[36]

Progressive developments in the run-up to 1997 also influenced the SGDP rights movement. At the Governor's prompting, the Law Reform Commission recommended the removal of anti-sodomy offences in 1983. These were finally

[29] E Liu and SY Yue, *Political Development in Hong Kong since the 1980s* (Legislative Council Secretariat, 1996).

[30] FM Cheung, 'Introduction' in FM Cheung (ed), *EnGendering Hong Kong Society: A Gender Perspective of Women's Status* (CUHK Press, 1997) 1–2; CJ Petersen, 'Engendering a Legal System: The Unique Challenge of Postcolonial Hong Kong' in EWY Lee (ed), *Gender and Change in Hong Kong: Globalization, Postcolonialism, and Chinese Patriarchy* (HKU Press, 2003) 23–29.

[31] A Barrow, 'Hong Kong's Sex Discrimination Ordinance at Twenty-Five: Achievements, Legislative Change and Continuing Challenges' (2022) 22 *International Journal of Discrimination and the Law* 107.

[32] RE Stern, 'Unpacking Adaptation: The Female Inheritance Movement in Hong Kong' (2005) 10 *Mobilization: An International Quarterly* 421; SE Merry and RE Stern, 'The Female Inheritance Movement in Hong Kong: Theorizing the Local/Global Interface' (2005) 46 *Current Anthropology* 387.

[33] Petersen, 'Equality as a Human Right' (n 26).

[34] Cap 480. The term 'ordinance' indicates an ordinary statute in Hong Kong law.

[35] Committee on the Elimination of Discrimination Against Women [hereinafter CEDAW Committee] (1999) A/54/38/Rev.1 [32]; Hong Kong Legislative Council, 'Official Record of Proceedings' (1 June 2000) 7091–146, available at www.legco.gov.hk/yr99-00/english/counmtg/hansard/000601fe.pdf; PL Kwok, G Chow, CK Lee and R Wu, 'Women and the State in Hong Kong' in Cheung (n 30) 263; BLL Lai, KC Au and FM Cheung, 'Women's Concern Groups in Hong Kong' in Cheung (n 30) 287, 290, 291.

[36] CEDAW Committee (14 November 2014) CEDAW/C/CHN/CO/7-8 [50].

implemented in 1991 after sustained campaigns by activists[37] and set the stage for later strategic litigation.

B. The Constitutional Framework after 1997

Since 1 July 1997, The BL has maintained many of the protections introduced during the colonial era and strengthened the courts' powers of constitutional review.[38] Chapter III sets out a list of fundamental rights and Article 39 confirms the continued application of the ICCPR and the International Covenant on Economic, Social and Cultural Rights (ICESCR). Hong Kong reports on its own to the UN Human Rights Committee, and civil society organisations have participated by submitting shadow reports and utilising treaty body materials to support local advocacy.[39] In addition to the ICCPR, ICESCR and CEDAW, Hong Kong is bound by four other core human rights treaties. At the same time, BL Article 40 has preserved some colonial policies that discriminate against rural women by protecting the 'lawful traditional rights and interests of the indigenous inhabitants of the "New Territories"', a group comprising the descendants – through the male line – of residents of recognised villages in 1898,[40] the year Britain leased the 'New Territories' from China for 99 years.

C. The Judiciary

The constitutional framework described above underpins a robust, if sometimes inconsistent, approach to judicial review, and the judiciary has largely enjoyed public legitimacy since 1997.[41] Indeed, the courts have been the main drivers of change and produced a solid body of rights jurisprudence.[42] The legal aid

[37] Z Low, 'How Hong Kong Passed Homosexuality Law, Decriminalising Same-sex Acts, in 1991' *South China Morning Post* (12 July 2019), available at www.scmp.com/magazines/post-magazine/short-reads/article/3018139/how-hong-kong-passed-homosexuality-law.

[38] Y Ghai, 'Litigating the Basic Law: Jurisdiction, Interpretation and Procedure' in JMM Chan, HL Fu and Y Ghai (eds) *Hong Kong's Constitutional Debate: Conflict Over Interpretation* (HKU Press, 2000) 3.

[39] See, eg, Society for Community Organisation, Submission to the Human Rights Committee (May 2020), available at tbinternet.ohchr.org/_layouts/15/treatybodyexternal/Download.aspx?symbolno=INT%2FCCPR%2FICO%2FHKG%2F42252&Lang=en.

[40] SC Chan, 'Politicizing Tradition: The Identity of Indigenous Inhabitants in Hong Kong' (Winter 1998) 37 *Ethnology* 39.

[41] JMM Chan, 'A Shrinking Space: A Dynamic Relationship between the Judiciary in a Liberal Society of Hong Kong and a Socialist-Leninist Sovereign State' (2019) 72 *Current Legal Problems* 85; MYK Lee and YL Lo 'Contesting Visions of Hong Kong's Rule of Law and Young People's Political Discontent' (2020) 29 *Social & Legal Studies* 858, 874.

[42] JMM Chan, 'Civil Liberties, Rule of Law and Human Rights: The Hong Kong Special Administrative Region in its First Four Years' in SK Lau (ed), *The First Tung Chee-hwa Administration: The First Five Years of the Hong Kong Special Administrative Region* (CUHK Press, 2002);

system has allowed litigants without means to challenge constitutional rights violations[43] and the Government has generally implemented the courts' judgments. Hong Kong enjoys independent judicial power and the courts have jurisdiction over all cases in the region on issues falling within the scope of its autonomy.[44] The Court of Final Appeal (CFA), Hong Kong's apex court, has the power of final adjudication.[45] Although the power of interpreting the BL is vested in the National People's Congress Standing Committee in Beijing, Article 158 authorises Hong Kong courts to interpret, on their own, provisions within the limits of the SAR's autonomy.[46]

In exercising their powers of constitutional review, the courts have affirmed they have the jurisdiction – indeed, they are duty-bound – to review laws for compatibility with human rights and strike down any that fail to comply.[47] In performing this function, they have also established a doctrine of interpretation emphasising a generous approach to fundamental rights, in light of their purpose and context.[48] Despite Hong Kong's dualist legal system, judges frequently cite international materials as persuasive authority.[49] In one of the first BOR decisions, Justice Silke explained:

> In interpreting the [BOR] considerable assistance can be gained from the decisions of common law jurisdictions with a constitutionally entrenched Bill of Rights … from the general comments and decisions of the Human Rights Committee … and from the jurisprudence under the European Convention on Human Rights.[50]

This practice has enriched and grounded Hong Kong's constitutional rights doctrines in international developments. Activists and lawyers have participated by initiating litigation and crafting innovative arguments based on comparative experience. While applicants seeking judicial review must have 'sufficient

AHY Chen, 'International Human Rights Law and Domestic Constitutional Law: Internationalisation of Constitutional Law in Hong Kong' (2009) 4 *National Taiwan University Law Review* 237. Hong Kong judgments are freely available at www.hklii.hk/eng and www.judiciary.hk/en/judgments_legal_reference/index.html.

[43] SHC Lo, KK Cheng and WH Chui, *The Hong Kong Legal System* (Cambridge University Press, 2020) 310–17. Recent changes, however, make it more difficult for applicants to choose their own lawyer, impeding strategic litigation. S Cheng, 'Barring Legal Aid Recipients from Choosing Own Lawyer Could Breach Hong Kong's Basic Law and Bill of Rights, Barristers Say' *Hong Kong Free Press* (8 December 2021).

[44] BL, Arts 2, 19, 82, 85.

[45] BL, Arts 19, 82.

[46] BL, Art 158; JMM Chan, 'Reconciliation of the NPCSC's Power of Interpretation of the Basic Law with the Common Law in Hong Kong' (2020) 50 *Hong Kong Law Journal* 657.

[47] *Ng Ka Ling v the Director of Immigration* [1999] HKCFA [72] [hereinafter *Ng Ka Ling*].

[48] ibid [77]; *Director of Immigration v Chong Fung Yuen* [2001] 4 HKCFAR 211.

[49] BL, Art 84; A Mason, 'The Place of Comparative Law in the Developing Jurisprudence on the Rule of Law and Human Rights in Hong Kong' (2007) 37 *Hong Kong Law Journal* 299; SNM Young, 'Constitutional Rights in Hong Kong's Court of Final Appeal' (2011) 27 *Chinese (Taiwan) Yearbook of International Law & Affairs* 67, 81–82; DS Law, 'Judicial Comparativism and Judicial Diplomacy' (2015) 163 *University of Pennsylvania Law Review* 927.

[50] *R v Sin Yau Ming* [1992] 1 HKCLR 127, 141.

interest in the matter to which the application relates',[51] the CFA has explained the rules of standing may be broader when the aim is 'to vindicate the rule of law by raising a general legal or constitutional issue'. In that case, such 'An issue … may be said to affect everyone equally'[52] and 'The critical question … is … whether the purpose of judicial review, and in particular the rule of law, will be best served by allowing the applicant to proceed'.[53]

The structure of the courts is hierarchical. The High Court (the Court of First Instance (CFI) and the Court of Appeal (CA)) and the CFA hear constitutional cases.[54] Five judges sit during CFA hearings, including the Chief Justice, three permanent judges, and one non-permanent judge chosen from a panel of local and overseas judges. The inclusion of foreign, non-permanent judges is another feature of Hong Kong's autonomy intended to safeguard the independent legal system and enhance the prestige of the judiciary.[55] The Chief Executive appoints judges on the recommendation of a committee chaired by the Chief Justice.[56]

In practice, the courts have adjudicated only a handful of cases involving the rights of women.[57] Litigation is expensive, unless an applicant qualifies for legal aid, and the EOC does not have the jurisdiction to deal with sex discrimination claims based on the constitutional right to equality. Enforcement models oriented toward assigning individual fault and providing individual remedies – like the SDO – are often less able to achieve transformative results than constitutional adjudication, which can be more effective in challenging structural patterns of disadvantage.[58] The introduction of the National Security Law (NSL) in 2020 could further reduce strategic litigation going forward, although at the time of writing it was too early to fully assess its impact.[59] The law contains vague offences and institutions with powers not subject to judicial review.[60] The unelected Chief Executive is tasked with designating judges to handle national security cases.[61] Since the NSL's enactment, several civil society organisations

[51] High Court Ordinance (Cap 4A) s 21K(3).

[52] *Kwok Cheuk Kin* (n 15) [58].

[53] ibid [62].

[54] BL, Art 81; Hong Kong Judiciary, 'Structure of the Courts', available at www.judiciary.hk/en/about_us/courtchart.html.

[55] BL, Art 82; SNM Young and A Da Roza, 'The Judges' in SNM Young and Y Ghai (eds), *Hong Kong's Court of Final Appeal: The Development of the Law in China's Hong Kong* (Cambridge University Press, 2013) 259; A Dziedzic, 'Foreign Judges and Hong Kong's New National Security Law' (5 October 2020), available at papers.ssrn.com/sol3/papers.cfm?abstract_id=3705123.

[56] BL, Art 88.

[57] Sex Discrimination Ordinance [hereinafter SDO] ss 84–85; Hong Kong EOC 'Significant Court Cases', available at www.eoc.org.hk/en/legal-services/significant-court-cases/hong-kong; CJ Petersen, 'Investigation and Conciliation of Employment Discrimination Claims in the Context of Hong Kong' (2001) 5 *Employee Rights and Employment Policy Journal* 627.

[58] S Fredman, *Discrimination Law* (Oxford University Press, 2011) 4.

[59] JMM Chan, 'National Security Law 2020 in Hong Kong: One Year On' (2022 Special Issue) *Academia Sinica Law Journal* 39.

[60] NSL, Art 14.

[61] NSL, Art 44.

have disbanded,[62] which also limits access to justice. Less politically sensitive issues, such as gender discrimination, however, are likely to continue to be contested through an independent judicial process.[63]

D. The Political Sphere and Law Reform

Since 1997, the lack of democratic accountability has damaged the effectiveness of the political realm for achieving progressive change. Although Articles 45 and 68 of the BL provide that universal suffrage is the ultimate aim for electing Hong Kong's leader, the Chief Executive, and members of its legislative body, the Legislative Council (LegCo), these goals have not been realised. This democracy deficit has hampered legislative initiatives for the advancement of the rights of women and SGDP. Patten's electoral reforms were dismantled in 1997 and only one-third of legislators in the 1998 elections were directly elected. Although the proportion of directly elected seats in subsequent elections gradually increased, these legislators have had less influence than those elected by 'functional constituencies' (FCs), groups comprised of a relatively small number of voters from certain professions and industries.[64] With some exceptions, FCs have tended to elect candidates who are pro-business, pro-government, and resistant to human rights policies.[65] They have also helped solidify a conservative government-business alliance and undermined women's participation in politics.[66] Unpaid domestic workers ('housewives'), usually women, are not represented as an FC group and the majority of voters are men with relatively high socio-economic status.[67] A constitutional challenge against the FCs failed (the gender dimension was not raised)[68] and the Government has also ignored the CEDAW Committee's calls for a review.[69] The exclusion of certain groups

[62] Chan (n 59) 50; R Kwan, 'Explainer: Over 50 Groups Disband – How Hong Kong's Pro-democracy Forces Crumbled' *Hong Kong Free Press* (28 November 2021), available at hongkongfp.com/2021/11/28/explainer-over-50-groups-gone-in-11-months-how-hong-kongs-pro-democracy-forces-crumbled.

[63] K Loper, 'Intersecting Crises and Exponential Inequalities: The View from Hong Kong' in S Atrey and S Fredman (eds), *Exponential Inequalities: Equality Law in Times of Crisis* (Oxford University Press, 2023).

[64] BL, Annex II.

[65] M Sing, 'Hong Kong's Democrats Hold Their Own' (2009) 20 *Journal of Democracy* 98.

[66] C Loh (ed), *Functional Constituencies: A Unique Feature of the Hong Kong Legislative Council* (HKU Press, 2006); M Ngok, 'The Making of a Corporatist State in Hong Kong: The Road to Sectoral Intervention' (2016) 46 *Journal of Contemporary Asia* 247.

[67] 'Report of the Hong Kong Association of Business and Professional Women on the Initial Report on the Hong Kong [SAR] under [CEDAW]' (November 1998) CB(2)797/98-99(03), available at www.legco.gov.hk/yr98-99/english/panels/ha/papers/p797e03.pdf; CJ Petersen, 'Stuck on Formalities? A Critique of Hong Kong's Legal Framework for Gender Equality' in FM Cheung and E Holroyd (eds), *Mainstreaming Gender in Hong Kong Society* (CUHK Press, 2009) 414.

[68] *Chan Yu Nam v Secretary for Justice* [2012] HKC 38.

[69] CEDAW Committee (n 36) [58]–[59].

altogether, such as refugees and migrant domestic workers, who cannot vote, further exacerbates the democracy deficit.[70]

Although the pace of law reform has been slow, some incremental progress includes: paternity leave in 2014; increased paid maternity leave in 2020 (possibly in response to CEDAW Committee comments);[71] the Domestic and Cohabitation Relationships Violence Ordinance,[72] protecting partners in co-habiting same-sex and different-sex relationships;[73] the Race Discrimination Ordinance;[74] and a small number of amendments recommended by the EOC.[75] Despite local advocacy and repeated recommendations by human rights bodies, however, the Government has refrained from legislating to address discrimination on sexual orientation or gender identity grounds in the private sector.[76]

Resistance to law reform continues in other areas affecting women and SGDPs. Several reservations to CEDAW continue to apply and have been incorporated as exceptions in the SDO.[77] These include the preservation of the Small House Policy which grants the male descendants of indigenous villagers the right to build a three-story house on village land,[78] despite the CEDAW Committee's recommendation to 'ensure that indigenous women have the same rights and access to property.'[79] Other issues include an outdated definition of rape, although the CEDAW Committee and the Hong Kong Law Reform Commission have urged reform,[80] and the lack of specific anti-trafficking legislation.[81] While

[70] PJ Yap, '*Vallejos Evangeline B v Commissioner of Registration*: Why Foreign Domestic Helpers Do Not Have the Right of Abode' (2011) 41 *Hong Kong Law Journal* 611; N Constable, 'Tales of Two Cities: Legislating Pregnancy and Marriage among Foreign Domestic Workers in Singapore and Hong Kong' (2020) 46 *Journal of Ethnic and Migration Studies* 3491.

[71] Employment Ordinance (Cap 57) s 12(2), Pt IIIA; CEDAW Committee (n 36) [62]–[63].

[72] Cap 189.

[73] G Cross, 'Time to Get Serious about Domestic Violence in Hong Kong by Strengthening the Law' *South China Morning Post* (2 March 2015), available at www.scmp.com/comment/article/1727605/time-get-serious-about-domestic-violence-hong-kong-strengthening-law.

[74] Cap 602.

[75] EOC, 'Discrimination Law Review: Submissions to the Government' (March 2016), available at www.eoc.org.hk/eoc/upload/DLR/2016330179502227490.pdf; Discrimination Legislation (Miscellaneous Amendments) Ordinance 2020; Petersen and Loper (n 26).

[76] Human Rights Committee (26 August 2020) CCPR/C/CHN-HKG/Q/4 [8]; CJ Petersen, 'Sexual Orientation and Gender Identity in Hong Kong: A Case for the Strategic Use of Human Rights Treaties and the International Reporting Process' (2013) 14 *Asian-Pacific Law & Policy Journal* 28; A Barrow, 'Sexual Orientation, Gender Identity, and Equality in Hong Kong: Rights, Resistance, and Possibilities for Reform' (2020) 15 *Australian Journal of Comparative Law* 126.

[77] SDO s 22 and Sch V.

[78] *Kwok Cheuk Kin* (n 15).

[79] CEDAW Committee, Concluding Comments on China, CEDAW/C/CHN/CO/6 (25 August 2006).

[80] CEDAW Committee (n 36) [54]–[55]; The Law Reform Commission of Hong Kong, 'Review of Substantive Sexual Offences' (December 2019), available at www.hkreform.gov.hk/en/docs/rsubstantive_sexual_offences_e.pdf; E Chao, 'Why are Hong Kong's Rape Laws Still Rooted in the Past, Given all the Progress Elsewhere?' *South China Morning Post* (27 October 2021), available at www.scmp.com/comment/opinion/hong-kong/article/3153613/why-are-hong-kongs-rape-laws-still-rooted-past-given-all.

[81] CEDAW Committee (n 36) [56]–[57].

the 1971 Marriage Reform Ordinance[82] abolished polygamous marriages, previously allowed by Chinese customary law, the subsequent definition of marriage continues to exclude same-sex couples.[83] The CEDAW Committee has also expressed concern that the legal minimum marriage age is only 16.[84]

Attempts to legislate to expand the rights of transgender persons have also failed. In a 2013 CFA decision granting a transgender woman the right to marry in her acquired gender,[85] the court called on the legislature to respond, suggesting, in obiter, a comprehensive review, citing the UK Gender Recognition Act (2004) as a favourable model.[86] Although LegCo debated a Marriage (Amendment) Bill[87] in 2014, its scope was limited to marriage and post-operative transgender persons. The Bill ultimately failed since conservative politicians opposed legislation granting transgender rights and progressive legislators felt the Bill did not go far enough.[88]

LegCo election reforms in 2021 have further diminished the political sphere's capacity to advance the rights of women and SGDP.[89] The number of directly elected legislators was reduced to 20 of 90 seats; 30 were returned by FCs and 40 by an unrepresentative Election Committee, which also selects the Chief Executive.[90] The number of eligible voters for members of the Election Committee decreased by 97 per cent in 2021.[91] After the introduction of the NSL, most pro-democracy politicians – who were more likely to support progressive gender policies – were barred from running in 2021 or resigned.[92]

[82] Cap 178.

[83] K Loper, 'Human Rights and Substantive Equality: Prospects for Same-sex Relationship Recognition in Hong Kong' (2019) 44 *North Carolina Journal of International Law* 273; M Wan, 'The Invention of Tradition: Same-sex Marriage and its Discontents in Hong Kong' (2020) 18 *International Journal of Constitutional Law* 539; JMM Chan, 'From Eliminating Discrimination on the Ground of Sexual Orientation to Same-sex Marriage: the Hong Kong Experience' (2022) 27 *Australian Journal of Human Rights* 442.

[84] CEDAW Committee (n 36) [66]–[67].

[85] *W* (n 12).

[86] ibid [138]–[146].

[87] A Bill to Amend the Marriage Ordinance, available at www.legco.gov.hk/yr13-14/english/bills/b201402282.pdf.

[88] T Cheung and P Siu, 'Transgender Marriage Law Vetoed by Legco' *South China Morning Post* (23 October 2014), available at www.scmp.com/news/hong-kong/article/1622339/legco-vetoes-transgender-marriage-law-minister-accused-not-lobbying.

[89] BL, Annex I and Annex II (30 March 2021), available at www.basiclaw.gov.hk/en/basiclaw/annex1.html; www.basiclaw.gov.hk/en/basiclaw/annex2.html; SNM Young, 'The Decision of the National People's Congress on Improving the Election System of The Hong Kong Special Administrative Region' (2021) 60 *International Legal Materials* 1163; Loper (n 63).

[90] HKSAR: Improve Electoral System, 'Method of Selection of the Election Committee', available at www.cmab.gov.hk/improvement/en/ceo-ele-committee/index.html; G Cheung and KC Ng, 'Hong Kong Now Has a Powerful Election Committee' *South China Morning Post* (20 September 2021), available at www.scmp.com/news/hong-kong/politics/article/3149350/hong-kong-now-has-powerful-election-committee-will-it-be.

[91] In 2021, 8,000 voters were eligible compared with 246,440 in 2016. HKSAR, 'Voter Registration Statistics', available at www.voterregistration.gov.hk/eng/statistic20211.html#1.

[92] J Lam et al, 'Hong Kong Opposition Lawmakers to Resign En Masse over Beijing Resolution Empowering Local Government to Bypass Courts and Unseat Politicians' *South China Morning*

E. Participation

The low rate of women's participation in the judiciary, the legal profession, and the political and executive branches of government is striking. Few women were involved in the original constitution-making process. Only four of the 59-member committee, appointed by the National People's Congress in 1985 to draft the BL, were women.[93] The CFA has never had a woman permanent justice, although two women non-permanent foreign judges were appointed in 2018. The number of senior women lawyers is also relatively small. Although 60 per cent of junior barristers are women, they account for only 11 per cent of Senior Counsel.[94] Similarly, 65 per cent of trainee solicitors are women but only 30 per cent are partners.[95] Some suggest these disparities are due to persistent assumptions about gender roles, male-oriented workplace norms, and male dominated 'cultural capital'.[96] A recent survey revealed common experiences of women lawyers including: unsolicited advice to change their careers due to their gender; presumed notions about caregiving responsibilities; a 'boys' club' culture; and unwanted comments about their appearance, among other issues.[97]

In the political sphere, 30.3 per cent of 'non-official members serving on public sector advisory and statutory bodies' were women in 2020.[98] Although the Chief Executive from 2017 to 2022 was a woman, only five of 32 members of the Executive Council, the de facto cabinet, two of 16 policy secretaries, and 16.5 per cent of the Election Committee were women.[99] After the 2021 LegCo elections, 17 of its 90 members were women. Despite these low rates, the Government has not introduced quotas or other policies to increase women's participation. In 2014, the CEDAW Committee expressed concerns 'that temporary special measures are not used … to accelerate the achievement of substantive

Post (11 November 2020), available at www.scmp.com/news/hong-kong/politics/article/3109330/top-beijing-body-makes-patriotism-mandatory-hong-kong; B Wong, 'National Security Law: 47 Hong Kong Opposition Figures Charged with Subversion Facing Potential Life Sentences after Trial Moved to High Court' *South China Morning Post* (31 May 2021), available at www.scmp.com/news/hong-kong/law-and-crime/article/3135525/national-security-law-47-hong-kong-opposition-figures.

[93] HKSAR Basic Law Drafting Committee, Webb-Site Who's Who, available at webb-site.com/dbpub/officers.asp?p=32891&sort=resup&d=2022-02-27&u=0.

[94] The Secretariat, 'Gender Issues' *Hong Kong Lawyer* (February 2013); A Lum, 'Gender Bias a Problem in Hong Kong's Legal Profession, Justice Minister Teresa Cheng Says on International Women's Day' *South China Morning Post* (8 March 2019), available at www.scmp.com/news/hong-kong/law-and-crime/article/2189275/gender-bias-problem-hong-kongs-legal-profession-justice.

[95] Mayer Brown and Women in Law in Hong Kong, 'Understanding Everyday Behaviour and Gender Equality Issues in Hong Kong's Legal Sector' (January 2023), available at www.mayerbrown.com/-/media/files/perspectives-events/publications/2023/01/ebp_project.pdf.

[96] EWY Lee, 'Individualism and Patriarchy: The Identity of Entrepreneurial Women Lawyers in Hong Kong' in Lee (n 30) 78; S Liu and A Au, 'The Gateway to Global China: Hong Kong and the Future of Chinese Law Firms' (2020) 37 *Wisconsin International Law Journal* 308, 331.

[97] Mayer Brown and Women in Law in Hong Kong (n 95).

[98] *EOC* (n 18).

[99] ibid.

or de facto equality of women and men.'[100] This may reflect a lack of political support by both government and opposition political parties and a failure to acknowledge the problem.[101] The SDO allows (but does not require) special measures reasonably intended to ensure equal opportunities, but employers and others have not generally relied on this exception in practice.[102]

III. CONSTITUTIONAL FRAMING OF SEX, GENDER AND SEXUALITY

Since 1997, Hong Kong courts have applied a number of constitutional provisions when adjudicating claims involving the rights of women and SGDP. Of these, the right to equality has special significance. Although the BL does not expressly mention sex or gender as prohibited grounds of discrimination, it sets out a general guarantee in Article 25 that all Hong Kong residents shall be equal before the law. Article 41 extends this to persons in Hong Kong other than residents.

The courts have construed Article 25 in conjunction with Articles 1(1) and 22 of the BOR, which duplicate Articles 2(1), 3 and 26 of the ICCPR. BOR Article 1(1) provides that the other rights 'shall be enjoyed without distinction of any kind, such as race, colour, sex, language, religion, political or other opinion, national or social origin, property, birth or other status'. Article 22 demands equality before the law, equal protection of the law and the prohibition of discrimination on the same grounds. The courts have affirmed that unjustified sex, gender and sexual orientation discrimination, including indirect discrimination, is unconstitutional.[103] In doing so, they have developed an equality doctrine with certain elements that could support substantive equality, although, as discussed, the courts have not fully explored its contours.[104] Substantive equality goes beyond formal equal treatment to ameliorate de facto disadvantage, including intersectional realities reflecting the complexity of identity, and may require special measures to remedy structural inequalities.[105] Values such as human dignity help diagnose the consequences of stigma and prejudice.[106]

[100] CEDAW Committee (n 36) [52]–[53].

[101] PW Wong and EWY Lee, 'Gender and Political Participation in Hong Kong: Colonial Legacies and Postcolonial Development' in Cheung and Holroyd (n 67) 123.

[102] SDO, s 48; Petersen (n 67) 419–20.

[103] See, eg, *EOC* (n 7) [84]; *QT* (n 10) [106]; *Leung Chun Kwong* (n 5).

[104] Loper (n 83).

[105] CEDAW Committee, General Recommendation No 25 on Temporary Special Measures (2004) [8], [14].

[106] K Loper, 'Dignity as a Constitutional Value in Hong Kong: Toward a Contextual Approach?' in JCH Hsu (ed), *Human Dignity in Asia: Dialogue between Law and Culture* (Cambridge University Press, 2022).

In *Leung Chun Kwong*,[107] the CFA noted that discrimination not only includes: 'direct discrimination where like cases are not treated alike', but also 'indirect discrimination where an ostensibly neutral criterion is applied which operates to the significant prejudice of a particular group'.[108] In making out a claim, the applicant must first demonstrate she 'has been treated differently to a person in a comparable position and that the reason for this difference … can be identified as a prohibited ground'.[109] If so, the Government must justify such treatment[110] by demonstrating that it: 'pursues a legitimate aim'; 'is rationally connected to the aim'; 'is no more than is necessary to accomplish the aim'; and that 'a reasonable balance has been struck between the societal benefits arising from the application of differential treatment and the interference with the individual's equality rights'.[111]

The CA articulated a justification test in one of the first BOR decisions, citing the UN Human Rights Committee's view that 'not every differentiation of treatment will constitute discrimination, if the criteria for such differentiation are reasonable and objective and if the aim is to achieve a purpose which is legitimate.'[112] This distinction between justifiable 'differential treatment' and 'discrimination' is a hallmark of substantive equality and could support the constitutionality of special measures. The CFA later elaborated that the justification test for equality does indeed differ from the test as applied to other constitutional rights:

> Where the difference in treatment satisfies the justification test, the correct approach is to regard the difference in treatment as not constituting discrimination and not infringing the constitutional right to equality. Unlike some other constitutional rights … it is not a question of infringement of the right which may be constitutionally justified.[113]

This suggests that different but *favourable* treatment could be justified to ameliorate inequalities affecting marginalised groups disproportionately. In other words, formally unequal treatment promoting substantive equality is not discrimination in the first place.

The degree of judicial scrutiny depends partly on the nature of the prohibited grounds. When differential treatment implicates 'core values' which are 'especially pernicious' as 'personal characteristics … which an individual cannot change … and which, if used as a ground for discrimination, are recognised as

[107] *Leung Chun Kwong* (n 5).
[108] ibid [18] citing *QT* (n 10) [31]–[33].
[109] ibid [20].
[110] ibid.
[111] ibid [22] citing *QT* (n 10).
[112] *R v Man Wai Keung (No 2)* [1992] 2 HKCLR 207 citing Human Rights Committee, 'General Comment 18: Non-discrimination' HRI/GEN/1/Rev.9 (10 November 1989).
[113] *Yau Yuk Lung* (n 9) [22].

particularly demeaning for the victim ... the court will subject the impugned measure to "particularly severe scrutiny"'.[114] In such cases, the authorities must provide '"particularly convincing and weighty reasons" to justify the challenged difference in treatment ...'[115] This is true even when the treatment involves socio-economic policy.[116]

The courts have considered several additional constitutional provisions in cases involving the rights of women and SGDP, including, for example, the rights to privacy and family life,[117] freedom to marry,[118] freedom of expression,[119] dignity in detention,[120] freedom from cruel, inhuman or degrading treatment,[121] liberty and security of the person,[122] and freedom from slavery and forced labour.[123]

IV. CONSTITUTIONAL JURISPRUDENCE

This constitutional framework provides a useful set of tools for advancing the rights of women and SGDP through the courts. As mentioned, partly due to limited political representation, these groups have pursued a deliberate litigation strategy. The following, however, suggests these tools could be more consistently applied to identify and remedy a broader range of direct, indirect and intersectional disadvantage. Indeed, the courts' failure to recognise the existence of gender issues in some of the cases discussed below, illustrates the perpetuation of substantive inequalities.

The cases considered fall within six domains including: 1) citizenship; 2) bodies; 3) violence; 4) family; 5) cultural communities; and 6) the market. These cannot be strictly delineated, however, and several overlap. For example, cases involving migrant domestic workers might be classified within citizenship, violence, family, participation and the market; elections in indigenous villages implicate culture and participation; and the Small House Policy affects cultural communities and the market. This analysis illustrates both the possibilities of the constitution as an avenue for change and the absence of a gender lens that might have provided a sharper focus.

[114] *QT* (n 10) [107]–[108] citing *R (Carson) v Secretary of State for Work and Pensions* [2006] 1 AC 173 [55]; *Fok Chun Wa v Hospital Authority* [2012] 15 HKCFAR 409 [hereinafter *Fok Chun Wa*]; *Hysan* (n 5).

[115] ibid.

[116] ibid [105] citing *Fok Chun Wa* (n 114).

[117] Bill of Rights Ordinance [hereinafter BOR], Art 14.

[118] BOR, Art 19; BL, Art 37.

[119] BOR, Art 16; BL, Art 27.

[120] BOR, Art 6.

[121] BOR, Art 3.

[122] BOR, Art 5.

[123] BOR, Art 4.

A. Citizenship

Citizenship laws in Hong Kong do not formally discriminate on the basis of gender. However, the denial of citizenship to groups predominantly made up of women arguably amounts to indirect discrimination, often on intersectional grounds. The notion of citizenship in Hong Kong is complex. Chinese 'nationality' is governed by the Chinese Nationality Law.[124] 'Permanent residency', however, is more relevant for accessing constitutional rights locally. Hong Kong permanent residents of any nationality have the right of abode in Hong Kong without any condition of stay imposed.[125] While Article 41 of the BL extends rights to 'persons in Hong Kong other than Hong Kong residents', only permanent residents are granted the rights to vote, stand for election and participate in public affairs.[126] Article 24 clarifies the categories of permanent residents. Chinese citizens from other parts of China must meet certain conditions: being born in Hong Kong, having ordinarily resided in Hong Kong for seven years, or, if born outside of Hong Kong, having a Chinese permanent resident parent.[127] In this sense, the border with mainland China functions much like an international border. Non-Chinese citizens who have ordinarily resided in Hong Kong for seven years and have taken Hong Kong as their permanent home also qualify.[128]

In *Ng Ka Ling and Others v Director of Immigration*,[129] the CFA explained the importance of equality when construing Article 24. Among other issues, the court considered whether a child born out of wedlock in the mainland qualifies for the right of abode. The child's mother had passed away and her father was a Hong Kong permanent resident. The Chief Justice explained that 'the principle of equality, the antithesis of any discrimination', as enshrined in 'both the [BL] and the ICCPR' forms part of the context that must be considered when interpreting a 'provision defining the class of permanent residents'.[130] Differentiating between children based on their parents' marital status was unjustifiable discrimination and thus unconstitutional.[131]

The CFA did not apply equality, however, in *Vallejos v Commissioner of Registration*,[132] a case involving migrant domestic workers who had worked in Hong Kong for more than 20 years but could not become permanent residents due to an exception in the Immigration Ordinance.[133] The Court upheld

[124] BL, Annex III.
[125] Immigration Ordinance (Cap 115) s 2A(1).
[126] BL, Arts 21, 26.
[127] BL, Arts 24(1)–(3).
[128] BL, Art 24(4); see also, Arts 24(5)–24(6).
[129] *Ng Ka Ling* (n 47).
[130] ibid 41.
[131] ibid.
[132] *Vallejos* (n 16).
[133] Immigration Ordinance (Cap 115), s 2(4)(a)(vi).

the restriction, reasoning that their time in Hong Kong on a series of two-year contracts did not amount to 'ordinary residence' as recognised by Article 24(4). Although the CFI and CA had briefly mentioned the applicants' alternative argument that the policy was discriminatory since it did not apply to other categories of imported workers,[134] this was summarily dismissed by both courts. Indeed, the CA noted without further explanation that 'this is not a case about discrimination and article 25 is simply not engaged',[135] adding, 'it must be up to the sovereign authority to decide the extent to which the status of permanent resident should be conceded to foreign nationals'.[136] While international law allows states discretion when determining citizenship, international human rights bodies have clarified the criteria must not discriminate on the grounds of race, gender, etc.[137]

This case was a missed opportunity for a fuller exploration of substantive equality. While the exclusion appeared neutral on gender grounds, the Court might have noted the majority of migrant domestic workers are women from certain national origins. A substantive equality analysis might have revealed de facto discrimination on 'core' grounds such as sex, gender or race, or the intersection of two or more characteristics. If such differential treatment had been identified, the Government would have needed to provide 'weighty reasons' for these distinctions. International and comparative human rights materials might have supported such an interpretation.[138]

B. Bodies

Unlike many other jurisdictions, Hong Kong courts have not considered constitutional issues related to abortion, which was legalised in 1976 and is generally available in practice, despite some problems with the legal framework.[139] Other issues related to women's (and men's) bodies, however, have been adjudicated and reflect the continuing influence of traditional gender roles and binary understandings of gender in Hong Kong.

[134] *Vallejos v Commissioner of Registration* [2011] HKEC 1289 (CFI); *Vallejos v Commissioner of Registration* [2012] HKEC 433 (CA).

[135] ibid (CA) [132].

[136] ibid.

[137] Committee on the Elimination of Racial Discrimination, 'General Recommendation XXX' (2005) [13]–[15].

[138] See, eg, Committee on the Elimination of Racial Discrimination 'General Recommendation XXV' (2000) [2]; *Mahlangu and Another v Minister of Labour and Others* (CCT306/19) [2020] ZACC 24 (South Africa).

[139] CEDAW Committee (n 36) [54]–[55]; PL Kwok et al, 'Women and the State in Hong Kong' in Cheung (n 30) 243–44; L Siu, 'Reproductive Rights: Laws and Access to Abortion – Interview with Ruby Lai' *Heinrich-Böll-Stiftung* (11 March 2021), available at hk.boell.org/en/2021/03/11/reproductive-rights-laws-and-access-abortion-interview-ruby-lai.

In *Fok Chun Wa v Hospital Authority*,[140] the CFA considered whether higher obstetric charges for non-resident, pregnant women violated the right to equality. The applicant in this case was a pregnant mainland woman, married to a Hong Kong permanent resident, and waiting to settle in Hong Kong. The mainland spouses (predominantly women)[141] of Hong Kong residents must apply for a 'one-way permit' to join their families, which can take up to six or seven years.[142] In the meantime, most are granted 'two-way permits' which allow temporary visits but without access to the same benefits as residents.[143]

In rejecting the claim, the court accorded a wide 'margin of appreciation' to the executive since the policy involved the allocation of scarce resources.[144] In considering equality, the court reasoned that the applicant was not similarly situated to resident women, and should therefore be treated as any other non-resident. In practice, most of the women affected, including the claimant, were married to Hong Kong permanent resident men. The Court did not consider, however, whether the policy indirectly discriminated on the basis of sex (a 'core value' ground) or place of origin (or both), and thus required a more rigorous review.[145] In cases involving 'residence status', the Court explained it would 'hesitate much more before interfering.'[146] The judgment also does not mention the impact on male permanent resident fathers or the gender norms implicit in assuming pregnancy only involves the mother. As with *Vallejos*, greater attention to substantive equality might have given rise to a richer reflection on the implications of intersectional disadvantage experienced by women immigrants. Instead, the CFA retreated to a more formal analysis of the prohibited grounds and deference to the authorities.

Legal recognition of gender identity – especially if different from one's assigned gender at birth – is another body-related issue with important implications for privacy as well as participation in public life. Hong Kong still lacks a general legal framework for recognition of a transgender person's acquired gender. The CEDAW Committee has noted ongoing intersectional discrimination against transgender women[147] and the UN Committee against Torture has

[140] *Fok Chun Wa* (n 114).

[141] In 2020, 64% of one-way permit holders over 25 were women, Census and Statistics Department (n 16).

[142] J Ng and R Yeo, 'Hong Kong's Housing Crisis: Soaring Prices Put Flats Beyond Reach, While Queue to Rent Keeps Growing Longer' *South China Morning Post* (11 August 2021), available at www.scmp.com/news/hong-kong/society/article/3144514/hong-kongs-housing-crisis-soaring-prices-put-flats-beyond.

[143] ibid; F Sun, 'Insulted, Humiliated, Shunned: Hong Kong's Mainland Chinese Immigrants Face Unending Discrimination in Struggle to Feel at Home, Survey Shows' *South China Morning Post* (2 October 2021), available at www.scmp.com/news/hong-kong/society/article/3150851/insulted-humiliated-shunned-hong-kongs-mainland-chinese.

[144] *Fok Chun Wa* (n 114) [61]–[77].

[145] ibid [77].

[146] ibid.

[147] CEDAW Committee (n 36) [68]–[69].

called on Hong Kong to 'remove abusive preconditions' for legal recognition, including sterilisation.[148]

In *Q v Commissioner of Registration*,[149] the CFA recognised that such a requirement is unconstitutional, albeit in limited circumstances. The case involved two transgender men who were unable to change their gender markers on their identity cards because they had not undergone full 'sex reassignment surgery', including the removal and construction of sex organs. The CFA held the policy breached the right to privacy under BOR Article 14.[150] Significantly, in reaching this conclusion, the court noted that 'privacy is a concept inherently linked to a person's dignity' and that 'The refusal to allow an amendment to the gender marker involves … humiliation, distress and loss of dignity in routine activities.'[151] The Court rejected the Government's arguments that the policy was the 'only workable, objective and verifiable criterion', that other criteria would give rise to 'practical administrative problems', and other forms of treatment are not irreversible.[152]

An earlier case, *Luigi Recasa Navarro v Commissioner of Correctional Services*,[153] involved a transgender woman prisoner who also had not undergone sex reassignment surgery (so was considered biologically male). The applicant claimed her isolation within a male prison facility violated her constitutional right to non-discrimination on the basis of 'gender identity', among other rights.[154] In applying the right to equality, the Court[155] determined that since the claimant 'retained all the male genitalia' she was in 'materially different circumstances compared with either non-transsexual female' or male prisoners.[156] In this context, therefore, her acquired gender was not recognised and her isolation was deemed necessary to protect her and the other inmates.[157] Here the Court took a formal approach to identifying a comparator and, unlike the CFA in *Q*, did not identify the impact the lack of recognition of the applicant's acquired gender might have on her dignity.

In another case related to 'bodies' and associated gender norms, an opposition politician – well-known for his signature long hair style – challenged the requirement that male, but not female, prisoners keep their hair short.[158]

148 UN Committee against Torture, Concluding observations on the fifth periodic report of China with respect to the Hong Kong Special Administrative Region, CAT/C/CHN-HKG/CO/5 (3 February 2016).
149 *Q* (n 11).
150 ibid, overturning *Q v Commissioner of Registration* [2022] 1 HKLRD 803 (CA).
151 ibid (CFA) [46].
152 ibid [63].
153 *Navarro Luigi Recasa v Commissioner of Correctional Services* [2018] 4 HKLRD 38 [hereinafter *Navarro*].
154 Cap 487.
155 *Navarro* (n 153) [78] citing Ma CJ in *Fok Chun Wa* (n 114).
156 ibid (*Navarro*) [84].
157 ibid [87].
158 *Leung Kwok Hung* (n 8).

The CFA held this amounted to direct sex discrimination and dismissed the Government's attempt to justify the rule as necessary to impose 'reasonable uniformity and conformity in appearance among inmates' in order to foster 'custodial discipline' 'by reference to the underlying conventional standards of appearance in society for men and women'.[159] Although the case was decided solely based on the SDO, the lower courts had considered the policy's constitutionality[160] and the CFA explained, 'on the facts of the present case, the outcome would not be different under [Article] 25 of the [BL].'[161]

While agreeing custodial discipline was a legitimate aim, the Court did not accept that 'a difference in treatment regarding the length of hair between male and female prisoners based on asserted conventional standards has any reasonable connection with custodial discipline'.[162] It added that the Government had not supported the 'premise that there exist conventional standards of appearance for men and women in society in relation to the length of hair',[163] and this amounted to unproven gender stereotyping.[164] As noted by Holning Lau, this reasoning is relatively progressive compared with other jurisdictions, and might inform future constitutional claims related to gender expression and gender stereotypes.[165]

C. Family

The courts have also considered constitutional issues related to the 'family', including transgender marriage, same-sex marriage and the separation of permanent resident children from their non-resident mothers.[166] Like many of the cases discussed in this chapter, these decisions reveal, and sometimes reinforce, patriarchal and heteronormative hierarchies. As in other domains, these cases also illustrate the courts' tendency to side-step the full implications of substantive equality.

In *W v Registrar of Marriages*,[167] the CFA upheld the right of a transgender woman who had completed sex-reassignment surgery to marry in her acquired

[159] ibid [44], [46].

[160] *Leung Kwok Hung and Commissioner of Correctional Services* [2017] 1 HKLRD 1041(CFI); *Leung Kwok Hung (Long Hair) and Commissioner of Correctional Services* [2018] HKCA 225 (CA).

[161] *Leung Kwok Hung* (n 8) [56].

[162] ibid [49].

[163] ibid [51]–[52].

[164] ibid [53].

[165] H Lau, 'Expansive Conceptualizations of Sex Discrimination in Asia' (Law and Society Association Annual Meeting, Chicago, May 2021).

[166] The courts have also adopted principles of gender equality when allocating assets upon divorce, see *LKW v DD* (2010) 13 HKCFAR 53.

[167] *W* (n 12).

gender based on Article 19(2) of the BOR and Article 37 of the BL. It explained that excluding a post-operative 'male-female transsexual' when construing Hong Kong marriage laws is unconstitutional.[168] The constitution rejects 'any unduly restrictive or exclusionary approach to the right to marry'[169] and the 'legal rules governing [this right] must be compatible with' the constitution 'and must not impair the essence of the right'.[170] The CFA also dismissed societal consensus as a relevant consideration when reviewing policies affecting marginalised minorities,[171] explaining that although Hong Kong's constitutional documents are 'living instruments intended to meet changing needs and circumstances',[172]

> it is one thing to have regard to such changes as a basis for accepting a more *generous* interpretation of a fundamental right and quite another to point to the absence of a majority consensus as a reason for *denying* recognition of minority rights.[173]

While 'expanding the reach of the right … may be warranted … in line with present-day conditions', 'Reliance on the absence of a majority consensus as a reason for rejecting a minority's claim is inimical in principle to fundamental rights'.[174] The implications of the case were limited, however, to gender recognition in relation to marriage and only after sex reassignment surgery.

Despite recognising a right to transgender marriage and determining that same-sex couples must enjoy certain rights associated with marriage, as discussed in section V, the courts have thus far rejected constitutional claims for same-sex marriage or civil partnerships. In *Sham Tsz Kit v Secretary for Justice*,[175] the CA upheld the CFI's earlier decision[176] that the freedom to marry is limited to heterosexual marriage. In reaching this conclusion, the CA explained that a generous interpretation of fundamental rights in light of the 'context and purpose', required that rights 'be read together … as a coherent, internally consistent whole'.[177] It added: 'In so reading, if there is a specific provision on a particular subject matter constituting a *lex specialis*, it will prevail over some other general provisions'.[178] In other words, the more specific right to marry superseded the broader rights to equality and privacy. The Court also considered the legal and historical aspects of context including 'the state of the domestic

[168] ibid [123].
[169] ibid [63].
[170] ibid [68].
[171] ibid [90], [114], [115]; K Loper, 'The Courts, Public Opinion and the Rights of Lesbian, Gay, Bisexual and Transgender Persons: A Hong Kong Perspective' (2019) 20 *Australian Journal of Asian Law* 39.
[172] ibid (W) [84] citing *Tyrer v UK* (1979-80) 2 EHRR 1 [31], among other cases.
[173] ibid (W) [115].
[174] ibid [115]–[116].
[175] *Sham Tsz Kit v Secretary for Justice* [2022] 4 HKLRD 368 (CA) [hereinafter *Sham Tsz Kit*]. The CFA heard the appeal in June 2023. The judgment was still pending at the time of writing.
[176] *MK v The Government of the Hong Kong SAR* [2019] HKC 92 (CFI).
[177] *Sham Tsz Kit* (n 175) [24], [35], [36].
[178] ibid [36].

law on marriage in April 1990, when the [BL] was promulgated' and the traditional understanding of marriage as between partners of a different sex.[179] This approach essentially froze the meaning of marriage in time, avoided application of the proportionality test, and once again neglected consideration of the implications of substantive equality.[180]

In another case involving family rights, *Comilang Milagros Tecson v Director of Immigration*,[181] the CFA took a similar approach when rejecting claims by two foreign national mothers (former migrant domestic workers) who did not have the right of abode in Hong Kong and were therefore unable to care for their permanent resident children. The applicants based their arguments on several grounds including the right to freely raise a family in BL Article 37. Without exploring the substance of these provisions, the court dismissed the claim based on section 11 of the BOR which excludes 'any immigration legislation governing entry into, stay in and departure from Hong Kong' with regard to 'persons not having the right to enter and remain in Hong Kong'.[182] As with the other cases involving migrant domestic workers, this decision illustrates the limits of the constitution as an avenue for advancing the rights of particular groups of women who experience intersectional disadvantage. The court's privileging of the more specific exception in section 11 was cited as a precedent for the similar *lex specialis* approach in *Sham Tsz Kit*,[183] as discussed above, and in preserving the Small House Policy, as discussed below.

D. Cultural Communities

This section considers two cases involving conflicts between the rights of indigenous villagers, protected by BL Article 40, and gender equality, which illustrate the intersectional divide between rural and urban women in Hong Kong and the residual gendered effects of the colonial legacy. They also exemplify the courts' mixed, but generally cautious approach to dismantling discriminatory policies that challenge vested interests.[184]

In *Secretary for Justice v Chan Wah*,[185] the CFA determined that the exclusion of non-indigenous villagers from voting in village representative elections was unconstitutional. The electoral arrangements granted the right to vote to non-indigenous women married to indigenous men, but not non-indigenous

[179] ibid [24], [30], [31]; Wan (n 83).

[180] K Loper, 'Equality, Dignity and Same-sex Marriage: Reflections on Developments in Hong Kong' (2023) 53 *Hong Kong Law Journal* 37.

[181] *Comilang v Director of Immigration* [2019] HKCFA 10.

[182] ibid [24]–[35].

[183] *Sham Tsz Kit* (n 175) [37].

[184] I Ng, *Hong Kong Rural Women under Chinese Rule: Gender Politics, Reunification and Globalisation in Post-colonial Hong Kong* (Routledge, 2019). The Heung Yee Kuk, a conservative, patriarchal statutory advisory body to the Government on New Territories affairs, has been an outspoken, powerful opponent of gender equality.

[185] *Chan Wah* (n 6).

men married to indigenous women. The CFA held that the right to vote and stand for election in Article 21(a) of the BOR does not fall within the meaning of 'traditional rights' protected by Article 40.[186] The Court also held that the system unlawfully discriminated under the SDO. The lower courts had affirmed that the right to political participation in the BOR must be enjoyed without discrimination of any kind.[187] Although the applicants in *Chan Wah* were men, their exclusion reflected traditional expectations that a woman leave her home to join her husband's family upon marriage, a cultural norm that perpetuates other forms of disadvantage affecting rural women in particular.[188]

In *Kwok Cheuk Kin v Director of Lands*,[189] however, the CFA rejected a challenge to the constitutionality of the Small House Policy.[190] The applicants had argued that the policy directly discriminated on the grounds of sex and/or non-indigenous status based on the SDO and the constitutional right to equality. Although the Court determined that the differential treatment could not be justified, the policy was nevertheless saved by Article 40. As in *Comilang* and later in *Sham Tsz Kit*, the CFA reasoned that as a rule of statutory construction, 'the specific [Article 40] prevails over the general [Articles 25 and 22]. This is simply one aspect of the more general principle that legislative instruments must be read as a coherent whole'.[191] In other words, this approach essentially shielded a directly discriminatory policy from scrutiny.

E. The Market

Hong Kong courts have also dealt with constitutional cases involving women and the market, a notion including employment, education and social security. Again, many of these expose the courts' failure to fully explore the implications of substantive equality and the value of human dignity to the detriment of the most marginalised communities in Hong Kong, including migrant domestic workers and victims of trafficking. Other cases, however, demonstrate – or at least hint at – the potential of constitutional rights to remedy some gendered harms and the relevance of international human rights law as persuasive authority.

i. Employment

While most sexual harassment and sex discrimination cases in employment fall within the scope of the SDO, the courts have constitutionally reviewed

[186] ibid [657 B-F].
[187] *Tse Kwan Sang v Pat Heung Rural Committee & Another* [1999] 3 HKLRD 267; Ng (n 184).
[188] Ng (n 184).
[189] *Kwok Cheuk Kin* (n 15).
[190] See section II.D of this chapter.
[191] *Kwok Cheuk Kin* (n 15) [44(2)].

employment policies affecting migrant domestic workers, sex workers, and victims of human trafficking.

In *Lubiano Nancy Almorin v Director of Immigration*,[192] the CA upheld a lower court decision dismissing a challenge to the requirement that migrant domestic workers live with their employers. Before the CFI,[193] counsel for the claimant argued the policy violated her constitutional right to equality because other imported workers were not subject to the same restrictions. The judge decided, however, that these groups were not in analogous situations.[194] Although it was therefore unnecessary to apply the justification test, the judgment explained, in obiter, that the rule was justifiable since it pursued the 'legitimate aim of meeting the demand of Hong Kong families for live-in domestic service which could not be filled by local domestic helpers'.[195] It was also rationally connected to the aim, no more than necessary to achieve it, and met the balancing requirement since workers could freely choose whether to accept the conditions of their contracts.[196] This emphasis on the comparator also illustrates the lack of a full understanding of substantive equality's requirements. Indeed, substantive equality recognises that a comparator is not always necessary and often reinforces formalistic reasoning and dominant societal norms.[197] Furthermore, the Court did not raise issues of possible indirect, intersectional discrimination on 'core values' grounds such as sex, gender, ethnic origin and socio-economic status.[198]

ii. Sex Work and Human Trafficking

Sex work is a legal grey area in Hong Kong. Prostitution itself is legal but anyone knowingly living 'wholly or in part on the earnings of prostitution of another' commits an offence.[199] As a result, most sex workers in Hong Kong operate out of 'one-woman brothels', increasing the risk of abuse.[200]

[192] *Lubiano Nancy Almorin v Director of Immigration* [2020] 5 HKLRD 107. See also *Fernandez Yvette Dingle v Commissioner of Labour* [2021] HKCFI 307 and *Julita F Raza & Others v Chief Executive in Council & Others* [2006] HKEC 1339.

[193] *Lubiano Nancy Almorin v Director of Immigration* [2018] 1 HKLRD 1141.

[194] ibid [103].

[195] ibid [107]–[109].

[196] ibid.

[197] S Fredman, 'Substantive Equality Revisited' (2016) 14 *International Journal of Constitutional Law* 712, 719.

[198] Some migrant domestic workers are also asylum seekers and decision-makers have not fully considered the gendered aspects of certain types of protection claims (author's interviews with refugee lawyers, 2020–21).

[199] Crimes Ordinance (Cap 200), s 137(1)–(2).

[200] JCM Li, 'Violence Against Chinese Female Sex Workers in Hong Kong: From Understanding to Prevention' (2013) 57 *International Journal of Offender Therapy and Comparative Criminology* 613.

In *SW v Secretary for Justice*,[201] a sex worker challenged these restrictions,[202] arguing the isolation increased her risk of experiencing violence and breached her right to liberty and security of the person in Article 5(1) of the BOR.[203] The judgment reviewed a range of international jurisprudence and academic debate but ultimately concluded the Court was bound by a textual and rather formal CA decision that: 'the language and structure of [the right] only provided for the fair operation of the law in relation to the arrest and detention of a person'.[204]

The courts have also reviewed challenges to the absence of specific legislation addressing human trafficking. *ZN v Secretary for Justice*[205] involved a Pakistani national who had been subjected to abuse, violence and restriction of movement when working as a migrant domestic worker in Hong Kong. He argued he was a victim of human trafficking in violation of Article 4 of the BOR which prohibits slavery, servitude, and forced or compulsory labour. Although the claimant was male, the case has broader implications for the rights of migrant domestic workers generally. As Fok PJ noted: 'With a total of approximately 370,000 foreign domestic helpers working in Hong Kong, there is potentially a sizeable number of persons at risk of exploitative practices that might constitute either forced or compulsory labour or human trafficking'.[206]

The CFI had initially ruled the Government failed to fulfil its obligation to introduce a specific criminal offence against human trafficking.[207] The CA reversed this decision, however, holding that Article 4 does not include human trafficking nor impose such a positive obligation.[208] The CFA agreed, explaining Article 4(1) might prohibit trafficking for the purposes of slavery, but not generally or for the distinct purposes of servitude or compulsory or forced labour in Article 4(3).[209] It also held that the Government has a 'wide margin of discretion', and while the authorities must 'take steps to afford practical and effective protection of those rights', determining such effectiveness depends on the specific context.[210] In this case, the claimant failed to establish a causal connection between the treatment and the lack of a specific offence.[211] The court noted, however, that this did not preclude a different outcome in a future case with distinct facts.

[201] *SW* (n 14).
[202] Crimes Ordinance (Cap 200), ss 137, 139, 143, 144, 145, 151.
[203] *SW* (n 14) [8].
[204] ibid [29] citing Keith JA in *HKSAR v Coady* [2000] 2 HKLRD 195 [86].
[205] *ZN* (n 13).
[206] ibid [8].
[207] *ZN v Secretary for Justice (No 2)* [2017] 1 HKLRD 559.
[208] *ZN v Secretary for Justice* [2018] 3 HKLRD 778.
[209] ibid [80]; [31]–[33].
[210] ibid [88]–[92].
[211] ibid [92].

Indeed, two years later, in *AM v Director of Immigration*, Coleman J noted: 'the [CFA] left a door ajar' and 'The Applicants in the present case invite me to open the door wide and to step through'.[212] Like *ZN*, two migrant domestic workers challenged the lack of specific legislation on forced or compulsory labour or human trafficking, despite the existence of 'a variety (or patchwork) of criminal offences'.[213] The employer of the second applicant (CB), had subjected her to sexual abuse and the police officer who first interviewed her also suspected she was a victim of human trafficking, referring her case to a recently established Trafficking in Persons Investigation Team. The new officer, however, reversed the initial assessment and CB argued the investigation was not effective due to 'the absence of a bespoke offence criminalising forced labour' and thus breached Article 4.[214] The CFI held in CB's favour, deciding the police had not met their 'relevant investigative duties' which arise 'once the Government is aware or ought to be aware that there is a credible suspicion of [forced or compulsory labour or human trafficking]'.[215] They had prematurely terminated the investigation and the court declared the 'failures … were causally connected to the absence of specific legislation'.[216] As Coleman J had explained, 'The nature and scope of the investigation required must be informed by the ultimate duty imposed by [article 4], namely to put in place measurements to provide practical and effective protection against forced labour'.[217] The court did not, however, indicate the specifics of such legislation.[218]

iii. Education

In *EOC v Director of Education*,[219] the CFI held that a system for allocating secondary school places discriminated directly on the basis of sex and breached the constitutional right to equality and the SDO. In operating the system, the Government had boosted scores for boys and applied a gender quota which, in practice, tended to favour individual boys over individual girls. The Government argued the policy sought to address temporary developmental differences between boys and girls and it was justified as a 'special measure' for boys based on section 48 of the SDO which exempts acts 'reasonably intended to ensure that persons of a particular sex … have equal opportunities'.[220] The CFI determined that although the system pursued a legitimate aim, the Director did not show 'convincing and weighty reasons that her use of the mechanisms' was rationally

[212] *AM and CB* (n 13) [1].
[213] ibid [38].
[214] ibid [144].
[215] ibid [5].
[216] ibid [270].
[217] ibid [254].
[218] ibid [265].
[219] *EOC* (n 7) [19].
[220] ibid.

connected to that objective.[221] The Court also noted the 'late bloomer' effect for boys was not established by evidence.[222]

The case is particularly notable since the Court relied on CEDAW for interpretive guidance.[223] It referred to Article 10, which 'makes it plain that stereotyped concepts of both men and women are in themselves, if not discriminatory, at least the wellspring from which discrimination flows'[224] to reject the Government's 'broad assumptions' about developmental differences. The judgment also noted that special measures for 'accelerating de facto equality' in CEDAW must be 'temporary' but the Hong Kong system was a 'settled' regime.[225] While the decision dismantled institutional discrimination against girls, the Court's dismissal of special measures merely on the basis they were 'temporary' belied an opportunity for a richer analysis.[226] The Court might have elaborated on the substantive aims of special measures and that CEDAW is asymmetrical and targets de facto discrimination against women and girls. Had it done so, such reasoning might have supported future efforts to increase women's participation through positive measures.

iv. Social Security

Non-discriminatory access to social security also impacts women's participation in 'the market'. As discussed, women immigrants from mainland China disproportionately experience poverty and other disadvantage based on intersectional identities. The applicant in *Kong Yunming v Director of Social Welfare*,[227] was an elderly woman from the mainland who was married to a Hong Kong permanent resident. Her husband died shortly after she arrived on a one-way permit. Although destitute, she was denied social security because recipients must have been resident in Hong Kong for seven years. The CFA's decision that the requirement violated her constitutional right to social welfare in Article 36 of the BL clarified, for the first time, that courts must apply a proportionality test for restrictions on socio-economic rights.[228] The lower courts had also considered whether this exclusion constitutes discrimination under 'other status' in Article 22 of the BOR.[229] As in the other cases involving women migrants, however, the

[221] ibid [121], [127].
[222] ibid [132]–[133].
[223] ibid [90].
[224] ibid [88].
[225] ibid [111].
[226] K Loper, 'Constitutional Adjudication and Substantive Gender Equality in Hong Kong' in B Baines, D Barak-Erez and T Kahana (eds), *Feminist Constitutionalism: Global Perspectives* (Cambridge University Press, 2012) 149, 159.
[227] *Kong Yunming v Director of Social Welfare* (2013) 16 HKCFAR 950.
[228] C Chan, 'Focus: Kong Yunming v Director of Social Welfare, "Introduction"' (2014) 44 *Hong Kong Law Journal* 1.
[229] *Kong Yunming v Director of Social Welfare* [2009] 4 HKLRD 382 (CFI); *Kong Yunming v Director of Social Welfare* [2012] HKEC 229 (CA).

courts did not explore whether the policy had intersectional effects (eg on older women immigrants living in poverty).

V. FLAGSHIP CONSTITUTIONAL DEVELOPMENTS

Despite failing to fully view disadvantage through a gender-focused lens, the Hong Kong courts have made significant progress in a series of constitutional cases which have successfully challenged sexual orientation discrimination. These decisions clarify the elements of a constitutional equality doctrine with potential to promote substantive equality. They also illustrate the ongoing influence of the colonial legacy, the growth of strategic litigation, and the impact of international human rights law. This area has provided richer constitutional jurisprudence than cases involving the rights of women and gender diverse persons. This may be due to government inaction on sexual orientation discrimination legislation, which has spurred advocates to leverage constitutional review.[230] The forms of exclusion experienced by lesbian, gay and bisexual people may also be more apparent than discrimination against women, and thus provide a straightforward target, more amenable to constitutional review.

A. Discriminatory Criminal Provisions

The first set of cases challenged discriminatory criminal offences on 'buggery', retained even after the decriminalisation of sodomy in 1991. In *Leung v Secretary for Justice*,[231] the CA held that differing ages of consent (16 for vaginal intercourse and 21 for 'buggery' between a man and a man or a woman and a man) violated the right to equality. The court observed that although the age of consent for 'buggery' was formally 'equal' on sex or sexual orientation grounds,

> Denying persons of a minority class the right to sexual expression in the only way available to them, even if that way is denied to all, remains discriminatory when persons of a majority class are permitted the right to sexual expression in a way natural to them.'[232]

This was the first time a Hong Kong court affirmed that indirect discrimination is unconstitutional, although the judgment used the term 'disguised' discrimination.

[230] Wan (n 83) 543; S Lau, 'Lawyer Michael Vidler: Rights Hero Pushing Waves of Change' *South China Morning Post* (20 May 2013), available at www.scmp.com/news/hong-kong/article/1241387/rights-hero-pushing-waves-change.
[231] *Leung v Secretary for Justice* (n 9).
[232] ibid [141].

In *Yau Yuk Lung*,[233] the CFA held the offence of 'homosexual buggery committed otherwise than in private' amounted to direct sexual orientation discrimination and was therefore unconstitutional.[234] In the judgment, Li CJ set out key elements of the constitutional equality doctrine: 'equality is a fundamental human right' and 'the antithesis of discrimination';[235] 'discriminatory law is unfair and violates the human dignity of those discriminated against';[236] 'It generates ill-will and a sense of grievance … [and] breeds tension and discord in society'.[237] This emphasis on unfair discrimination and human dignity also provides a substantive underpinning to the equality doctrine. The judgment also articulates the distinct justification test for equality, as discussed above, that supports substantive equality's recognition that differential treatment is not always discrimination and could take the form of justifiable 'special measures'.[238]

B. The Rights of Same-sex Couples

Cases concerning the rights of same-sex couples have further contributed to the development of the nascent equality doctrine described in section III. These cases more clearly establish that indirect discrimination is unconstitutional and requires the same intensity of review. They also further elaborate on the relevance of human dignity to the stringent proportionality test required in equality cases involving 'core values'.

In *QT v Director of Immigration*,[239] the CFA held that a policy denying dependant visas to the same-sex partners of expatriates working in Hong Kong amounts to indirect sexual orientation discrimination. The Director of Immigration had argued the policy was necessary to: provide administrative convenience; strike a balance between attracting talent and immigration control; and not undermine the 'special status of marriage'.[240] The Court rejected this reasoning as circular (differential treatment based on marital status cannot be justified on the same ground) and noted the lack of a rational connection between the treatment and the aims. Indeed, the policy was actually counterproductive. The judgment also emphasised the importance of dignity, citing Lord Walker of Gestingthorpe who observed: 'discrimination is regarded as particularly objectionable because it disregards fundamental notions of human dignity and equality before the law'[241] and *Law v Canada*: 'Human dignity is harmed by

[233] *Yau Yuk Lung* (n 9).
[234] Crimes Ordinance (Cap 200), s 118F.
[235] *Yau Yuk Lung* (n 9) [1].
[236] ibid [2].
[237] ibid.
[238] See also *Yeung Chu Wing* (n 9), declaring several remaining provisions unconstitutional.
[239] *QT* (n 10).
[240] ibid [88]–[89].
[241] ibid [49] citing *R (Carson) v Secretary of State for Work and Pensions* [2006] 1 AC 173.

unfair treatment premised upon personal traits or circumstances which do not relate to individual needs, capacities, or merits.'[242]

The courts have applied similar reasoning when reviewing other policies excluding same-sex couples. *Leung Chun Kwong v Secretary for the Civil Service*[243] involved a civil servant who married his same-sex partner abroad but was denied spousal benefits and was unable to file joint tax returns. Applying *QT*, the CFA held these policies amounted to unjustifiable, indirect differential treatment on the grounds of sexual orientation. In *Infinger, Nick v The Hong Kong Housing Authority*,[244] the CA upheld the CFI's decision that same-sex couples must have access to public housing on an equal basis with different-sex couples. In *Ng Hon Lam Edgar v Secretary for Justice*,[245] the CFI determined that the exclusion of same-sex partners married overseas from survivor benefits in Hong Kong discriminated indirectly on the basis of sexual orientation.

At the time of writing, the CFA had not yet rendered its decision on the appeal on same-sex marriage, discussed above. Therefore, it is too early to tell whether the court will apply the more robust equality analysis based on this body of jurisprudence and contribute to these flagship developments or reinforce the lower courts' restrictive, formal approach.

VI. CONCLUSION

This overview examines the complex set of factors shaping the Constitution and its role in advancing the rights of women and SGDPs. Overall, the 'generous and purposive approach' to construing constitutional rights and reliance on international and comparative materials suggest potential. In particular, the emerging substantive equality doctrine, if applied consistently, could help identify a greater range of disadvantage experienced by marginalised groups. Thus far, however, the judiciary has taken a largely formal approach, without recognising the full implications of their own equality jurisprudence. For example, they have not accounted for intersectional inequalities on the grounds of race, gender and socio-economic status, especially in cases involving migrant domestic workers, and frequently grant the legislature broad discretion. The courts have also applied other tools limiting the scope of substantive equality – such as *lex specialis* – to preserve formally discriminatory policies. Furthermore, while embracing international human rights norms in some cases, the courts have dismissed other international provisions, citing Hong Kong's dualist system.

[242] ibid [note 137] citing *Law v Canada (Minister of Employment and Immigration)* [1999] SCR 497.

[243] *Leung Chun Kwong* (n 5).

[244] *Infinger* (n 10).

[245] *Ng Hon Lam* (n 10).

The rapidly changing legal and political landscape may also impact the courts' ability to enhance gender justice going forward. While likely to remain a more promising opportunity structure than the political sphere, the judiciary is facing its own challenges. Hong Kong's democracy deficit makes it especially difficult for excluded groups to access remedies through constitutional – as well as political – channels and reveals the interdependence of different opportunity structures. The courts play an important democratic role and, as Sandra Fredman has observed, participation is a critical feature of substantive equality, requiring the inclusion of groups lacking political and social voice.[246]

[246] S Fredman, 'From Deference to Democracy: The Role of Equality Under the Human Rights Act 1998' (2006) 122 *Law Quarterly Review* 53; Fredman (n 197) 727.

5

Gender Equality, Individual Empowerment and Constitutional Rights Review: South Korea's Dynamic Development

YOON JIN SHIN

I. INTRODUCTION

THE CONSTITUTIONAL COURT of Korea was established by the Ninth Amendment of the Constitution of the Republic of Korea (the Constitution of South Korea) in 1987.[1] The 1987 Amendment ended three decades of military dictatorship in the country and began the era of democracy. The creation of the Constitutional Court, which empowers individuals to bring a direct constitutional challenge against domestic law and government actions, highlighted the constitutional moment in South Korea, one that promised to reform the society on the basis of human rights, democracy and the rule of law.

Since its commencement of operation in September 1988, the Constitutional Court of Korea has been one of the most active constitutional courts in Asia and around the world, holding the power of strong judicial review and enlivened by vibrant rights mobilisations from civil society and individuals.[2] In particular, gender-related issues have been extensively litigated at the Court, and have led to numerous groundbreaking decisions. Active gender-related constitutional litigation is relevant to the fact that modern domestic law in South Korea, while largely

[1] The First Constitution of South Korea was promulgated in 1948. Since then, the Constitution has been amended nine times, and the current Constitution of South Korea is the result of the Ninth Amendment in 1987.

[2] As of 8 September 2022, the Court has received 46,433 cases and decided on 44,781 cases, delivering 1,936 verdicts of unconstitutionality. During the last five years, the Court has received an average of 233 cases and decided on 220 cases per month. The latest data is available at Constitutional Court of Korea,'한눈에 보는 사건통계' www.ccourt.go.kr/site/kor/stats/newEventStaticBoard1.do.

influenced by the Japanese legal system due to the history of occupation between 1910 and 1945, also reflected a long-standing and deeply embedded patriarchal tradition in Korea rooted in Confucianism for several centuries. In contrast with the country's rapid economic growth and democratic development over the last few decades, the level of gender equality in South Korea, an area closely connected to culture and established social structures, has improved much more slowly. According to the Global Gender Gap Index 2020 published by the World Economic Forum, South Korea, the 12th largest economy in the world and a country ranked 23rd in the Democracy Index 2019 by the Economist Intelligence Unit,[3] ranked 108th out of 153 countries in terms of gender equality.[4] This rating is in fact an improvement as it ranked 115th out of 149 in 2018, 118th out of 144 in 2017, and 116th out of 144 in 2016.[5] While women's educational equality has been notably improved in recent years, political underrepresentation, disparities in economic sectors, including average salaries, job security and managerial-level gender ratio, prevalent sexual and domestic violence against women, and an underlying patriarchal and misogynistic culture and social mindset keep the country in the bottom tier of the gender equality rankings.

Since the democratisation of the country in the late 1980s, grassroots women's rights groups and human rights lawyers have continued earnest efforts for gender equality and women's empowerment.[6] While continuing legislative campaigns in various domains, women's rights groups, in close cooperation with human rights lawyers, have actively pursued constitutional litigation, which the newly created constitutional court system systematically enabled for individuals.[7] In cases where gender discrimination or rights violations were deemed to have

[3] Data available at International Monetary Fund, available at www.imf.org/external/pubs/ft/weo/2019/02/weodata/index.aspx; Economist Intelligence, 'Democracy Index 2020: In sickness and in health?', available at www.eiu.com/topic/democracy-index.

[4] World Economic Forum, 'Global Gender Gap Report 2020', available at www3.weforum.org/docs/WEF_GGGR_2020.pdf.

[5] The yearly reports can be found at World Economic Forum, 'Reports', available at www.weforum.org/reports?utf8=%E2%9C%93&query=gender+gap.

[6] The history of women's social movement in Korea dates back to the late 19th century and the years of the independence movement against Japanese occupation. Most of the representative women's rights NGOs currently active in South Korea were founded alongside the democratisation of the country in 1987, including (by sector): Womenlink (founded in 1987, leading diverse initiatives for women's empowerment), Korean Women Workers Association (founded in 1987, focusing on gender discrimination in employment), Korea Women's Hot Line (founded in 1983, supporting victims of gender violence, especially domestic violence), Korea Sexual Violence Relief Center (founded in 1991, expertise in supporting victims of sexual violence), Women Migrant Human Rights Center of Korea (founded in 2005, focusing on supporting migrant women in Korea), and Korea Women's Association United (KWAU), founded in 1987 as an umbrella organisation of these groups and 23 other women's rights NGOs in South Korea. MINBYUN (Lawyers for a Democratic Society), a human rights lawyers' association founded in 1988 (comparable to the ACLU in the United States), and their member lawyers have been constant expert supporters for human rights movements in South Korea, including advocacy for gender equality.

[7] NGOs do not have standing to bring a constitutional claim to the Constitutional Court on behalf of individuals they represent.

been caused or aggravated by law or a government action, as opposed to being purely a result of social conventions or culture, constitutional litigation has been considered a primary platform for civil society. Constitutional-level mobilisation has often been considered more effective than campaigning that targets only the legislature, a branch that has been filled predominantly by men and greatly influenced by majoritarian preferences among constituents in a society with lingering patriarchal ideology.[8] Constitutional rights review has been regarded as a unique empowering mechanism for socially marginalised and disadvantaged groups and individuals such as women, because the success of their claims does not chiefly depend on public opinion but can be achieved by rights-based constitutionalism and judicial independence. As examined in sections III and IV, the Constitutional Court has frequently found a good cause to deliver transformative decisions in gender-related cases because, in spite of the newly democratised political system and constitutional framework, statutory-level laws in those areas have been reformed relatively slowly by the legislature. While it is true that South Korea's ratification of the Convention on the Elimination of All Forms of Discrimination Against Women (CEDAW) in 1984 provided momentum for lawmakers to amend patriarchal domestic laws without constitutional adjudication, the Government also made a number of reservations upon ratification, which could not be withdrawn for several years.[9]

In recent years there has been further growth in women's rights movements, with ordinary women citizens in South Korea beginning to speak more openly about their sexuality rights. Specifically, more women gained courage to join the Me Too movement of 2018 and anti-abortion-ban campaigns, both examples of women's bottom-up empowerment movements in the country. The human rights and equality issues of gender and sexual minorities have much more recently begun to be publicly spoken about in South Korea, and accordingly there have been fewer relevant cases argued before the Constitutional Court than women's rights cases.

[8] While female citizens in South Korea have enjoyed universal suffrage since the first general election held in 1948, women have been significantly underrepresented in the legislature. As of 2020, women occupy only 19% of the seats at the National Assembly of Korea (57 out of 300 seats), which is in fact an increase from 17% in 2016, 15.7% in 2012 and 13% in 2008. There was only one female member out of 200 in the First National Assembly (1948–1950), only one or two females until the 6th Assembly (until 1967), and less than 10 members until the 14th Assembly (until 1996). The 15th Assembly (1996–2000) had 12 members, and in the 16th (2000–2004), the number of female legislators increased to 16 (5.9%), then 39 (13%) in the 17th Assembly (2004–2008), mainly due to the effect of the quota system for female candidates, which was first adopted in 2002 and further expanded in 2005. The quota system mandates that each political party must appoint women for 50% of its candidates for the proportional representative seats in the National Assembly. With regard to National Assembly seats directly elected by local constituencies, each party is *recommended* to appoint 30% of its candidates from among women.

[9] Upon ratification of the Convention on the Elimination of All Forms of Discrimination Against Women (CEDAW), South Korea made reservations with regard to Art 9 and Art 16(1)(c), (d), (f) and (g) of the Convention. In 1991, the reservations to Art 16(1)(c), (d) and (f) were withdrawn. The reservation to Art 9 was withdrawn in 1999.

After providing background information about the Court and the relevant constitutional framework in South Korea (section II), this chapter provides an overview of a series of decisions by the Constitutional Court delivered in various areas of gender equality and women's rights, and also sheds light on cases concerning gender and sexual minorities (section III). Two of the Court's landmark cases – *Household Head System* and *Abortion* – are examined in greater depth for their social background, detailed reasoning and further implications (section IV). The research concludes by evaluating South Korean practice in terms of *bottom-up constitutionalism*, which is based on and also facilitates the empowerment of individuals who have been disadvantaged by gender bias and discriminatory social norms and conventions, and discussing remaining challenges (section V).

II. CONSTITUTIONAL FRAMING AND BACKGROUNDS

The Constitutional Court of Korea is a constitutional organ in South Korea which has the sole authority of constitutional review.[10] The Constitutional Court is composed of nine justices, most of whom have been appointed from among senior judges at ordinary courts. Reflecting the principle of separation of powers, three justices are nominated by the National Assembly, three by the President, and three by the Chief Justice of the Supreme Court. The term of their service is six years and, while reappointment is legally possible, it has been a customary rule that justices serve only one term. The bench of 2019 included three female justices for the first time in the Constitutional Court's history. The first female justice was appointed in 2003 and served until 2006. After five years without a woman at the bench, the second female justice was appointed in 2011 (serving until 2017). The latest four members were appointed in 2017, 2018, 2019 and 2023 respectively.[11]

The Constitutional Court has jurisdiction over five different types of constitutional adjudication: constitutional complaints; constitutionality of statutes; impeachment; dissolution of a political party; and competence disputes.[12] The most accessible route for ordinary individuals to request constitutional rights review is the first type, constitutional complaints, which predominantly occupies the Court's docket. Anyone can file a constitutional complaint if she believes her constitutional rights are violated by law or government actions, and

[10] South Korea also has the Supreme Court, which is the highest among ordinary courts and does not hold a power of constitutional review over statutes or government actions.

[11] To date, a total of 57 justices have been appointed at the Court, of whom six are women.

[12] For the relevant information in English, see the Court's English website information page, Constitutional Court of Korea, 'Adjudication on the Constitutionality of Statutes', available at english.ccourt.go.kr/site/eng/03/10301010000002020081101.jsp.

can also request a court-appointed counsel if suffering economic difficulties.[13] The system thus empowers individuals marginalised in the earlier lawmaking process to initiate and participate in a subsequent constitutional norm-making. The second type of constitutional rights adjudication, constitutionality of statutes, is triggered when an individual whose case is pending at an ordinary court asserts the unconstitutionality of the applicable statute and the relevant court agrees to send the case to the Constitutional Court for constitutionality review. Many of the landmark decisions of the Constitutional Court in gender areas took this path. In rights adjudication, the Constitutional Court conducts an ex post facto concrete review with the power to order immediate invalidation of the law or government actions if found in violation of the Constitution (six votes out of nine justices are required to invalidate a statute or government action as unconstitutional). However, as a compromise rooted in a tension with the Supreme Court of Korea, the highest among ordinary courts, the Constitutional Court does not hold the power to conduct constitutional review against decisions of ordinary courts. In most cases, decisions by the Constitutional Court are strictly observed and efficiently enforced by the legislature and other branches of government. The Constitutional Court is generally received by the public with higher respect and trust than other government branches for its relatively stronger independence from political factors and their expertise in constitutional interpretation. Justices are free to write dissenting opinions. Occasions are not rare in gender-related cases where a dissenting opinion that upheld the claimant's rights in a previous decision became a majority opinion in a later case on the same subject, as the dissent brought about further debates and deliberations in society and among justices.

Basic constitutional provisions for gender equality and special consideration of women have existed since the First Constitution of South Korea proclaimed in 1948.[14] The current Constitution also contains several provisions that specifically mention women and gender. Article 11, a general equality provision, explicitly lists 'sex' as one of the prohibited grounds of discrimination.[15] A provision on work-related rights mandates special protection of working women

[13] If there are specific remedial procedures provided by the relevant law, one should first exhaust such procedures before filing a constitutional complaint. As of August 2020, a total of 39,496 constitutional complaint applications have been submitted to the Court, which occupies 97.2% of the Court's docket.

[14] First Constitution of the Republic of Korea (proclaimed 17 July 1948) [hereinafter First Constitution], Art 8 (general prohibition of gender discrimination), Art 17 (special protection of women and minors at work) and Art 20 (mandating marriage to be based on equal rights between women and men). During the drafting stage of the First Constitution, the Constitution of the United States and of several democratic states in Europe, in particular the Weimar Constitution of 1919, were referenced by the Constitutional Assembly.

[15] The Constitution of the Republic of Korea (amended 29 October 1987) [hereinafter Constitution], Art 11(1): 'All citizens shall be equal before the law, and there shall be no discrimination in political, economic, social or cultural life on account of sex, religion or social status'. This provision is almost identical to Art 8 of the First Constitution.

and prohibits discrimination against them,[16] and it is a constitutional duty of the state to promote women's rights, welfare and motherhood.[17] Another significant gender-sensitive provision stands in the context of marriage and family life. Article 36(1) provides: 'Marriage and family life shall be entered into and sustained on the basis of individual dignity and equality of the sexes, and the State shall do everything in its power to achieve that goal'.[18] These provisions are placed in the fundamental rights section of the Constitution, titled, 'Rights and Duties of Citizens' (Articles 10–39), and all the individual rights, including social and economic rights (such as the rights to work, health, education, and social security), principles and state duties therein are acknowledged by practice and scholarship as judicially enforceable.[19] For example, as discussed in the following sections, Article 36(1) has played a crucial role in challenging the patriarchal family law system in South Korea. Article 10, stipulating human dignity and the right to pursue happiness, has been invoked as an important foundational provision from which more concrete and unwritten constitutional rights can be derived, such as the right to self-determination in abortion cases.[20]

Although many of these provisions already existed in similar forms in the First Constitution and in the subsequent amendments, those constitutional provisions did not play a lively role before the Ninth Amendment in 1987 due to the absence of a functioning constitutional adjudication system and the political circumstances shaped by military dictatorship and the male-dominant legislature. Because the current Constitution of South Korea has not been amended since 1987, and also because its textual framework does provide an expansive list of constitutional rights as well as general provisions on equality and dignity, the focus of advocacy for civil society and human rights lawyers has been the actual utilisation and concretisation of those provisions. This has been pursued through constitutional litigation and mobilisation to persuade justices to produce progressive constitutional interpretation.

With regard to *international law*, Article 6(1) of the Constitution provides, 'Treaties duly concluded and promulgated under the Constitution and the generally recognised rules of international law shall have the same effect as

[16] Constitution, Art 32(4): 'Special protection shall be accorded to working women, and they shall not be subject to unjust discrimination in terms of employment, wages and working conditions'. This provision has its root in Art 17 of the First Constitution ('Special protection shall be accorded to working women and children').

[17] Constitution, Art 34(3): 'The State shall endeavor to promote the welfare and rights of women'; Art 36(2): 'The State shall endeavor to protect mothers'. These provisions were newly introduced by the Ninth Amendment.

[18] An earlier version of this provision was first introduced by the Eighth Amendment in 1980.

[19] See 김복기 [B Kim], '사회적 기본권의 법적 성격 [The Legal Nature of Social Basic Rights]' (2014) 3 사회보장법연구111.

[20] Constitution, Art 10: 'All citizens shall be assured of human worth and dignity and have the right to pursuit of happiness. It shall be the duty of the State to confirm and guarantee the fundamental and inviolable human rights of individuals'. The provision on human dignity and worth was first introduced by the Fifth Amendment in 1963.

the *domestic laws* of the Republic of Korea' (emphasis added), and indicates a monist approach to international law.[21] Taking a step further, the Constitutional Court interprets this provision as embodying the *constitutional principle of respecting international law*. If a domestic law or state action runs counter to the mandates of international human rights law, it constitutes not only a violation of international law, but also a violation of the *constitutional* principle of respecting international law. The Constitutional Court, through this interpretation, adopts international human rights law as a substantive standard of rights review, while maintaining the framework of constitutional adjudication.[22] However, there has been no case yet where the Constitutional Court explicitly held that the challenged statute had indeed violated relevant international human rights law and thus Article 6(1) of the Constitution. CEDAW has been cited by the Constitutional Court in a few cases, not as a direct standard of review, but as a reference point in its reasoning to find that domestic law violated relevant constitutional rights and principles.[23] This indirect appearance of CEDAW in constitutional decisions seems partly due to the Constitutional Court's tendency not to directly apply international law when it is already obvious that the challenged domestic law is in violation of constitutional provisions, a situation frequently found in gender areas. Another factor is that South Korea made reservations to several provisions when ratifying CEDAW, thus the claimant could not invoke those provisions when filing constitutional claims to the Constitutional Court.[24]

In fact, the Constitutional Court consults *foreign law* and legal practices more frequently than international law, especially when adjudicating high-profile human rights cases. In its earlier years of operation, the Constitutional Court showed heavy dependence on a small number of role-model countries – predominantly Germany follow by the United States. As the Court's own jurisprudence has grown, it has developed the practice of conducting comparative surveys to comprehend the global trends and practices of foreign counterparts in important human rights and constitutional issues.[25] As such, foreign law and legal practices have often been cited as weighty references in gender and women's rights cases.

[21] See YJ Shin, 'Cosmopolitanising Rights Practice: The Case of South Korea' in T Suami, A Peters, D Vanoverbeke and M Kumm (eds), *Global Constitutionalism from European and East Asian Perspectives* (Cambridge University Press, 2018).

[22] ibid 253.

[23] Constitutional Court of Korea, 98Hun-Ma363 (23 December 1999); 97Hun-Ka12 (31 August 2000); 2013Hun-Ka2 (31 March 2016) (in dissenting opinions).

[24] See n 9.

[25] Shin (n 21) 255–60. However, a geographic imbalance remains among referenced jurisdictions. Legal practices in Western countries are much more frequently cited in Constitutional Court decisions than cases of Asian jurisdictions. See YJ Shin, 'Transnational Constitutional Engagement: A Contextualization of Global Constitutionalism by the Constitutional Court of South Korea' (2021) 10 *Global Constitutionalism* 256.

III. CONSTITUTIONAL JURISPRUDENCE: OVERVIEW BY DOMAIN

A. Citizenship

Until 1997, the Nationality Act in South Korea squarely codified a patrilineal ideology in granting Korean citizenship to children born in Korea. Only a child whose father was a Korean citizen was given Korean citizenship at birth, regardless of the citizenship of the mother. A child whose mother was Korean but whose father was not Korean could not attain citizenship. This law reflected a traditional family order that counted only male lineage, which, combined with a nationalist citizenship policy, formed a *patriarchal jus sanguinis* nationality scheme. For this reason, the South Korean Government made a reservation to Article 9 of CEDAW upon ratification in 1984. In response to the expressed concerns and recommendations of the Committee on the Elimination of Discrimination against Women (the CEDAW Committee) with regard to South Korea's reservation and the discriminatory domestic law on nationality, the South Korean Government amended the Nationality Act in 1997 to take a gender-neutral approach in granting citizenship (for a child to attain citizenship at birth if either parent is Korean).[26] However, this new amendment provided for a retroactive application only for the previous 10 years, excluding numerous individuals from the possibility to attain citizenship. An individual who was thus still recognised as a foreigner and was facing deportation, even though his mother was a Korean citizen, filed a constitutional challenge against the Nationality Act (before the 1997 amendment) that applied to him. The Constitutional Court held the Act unconstitutional as it violated gender equality under Article 11 and Article 36(1), as well as the right to equality of the child (Article 11) who would, as a legal foreigner, experience various restrictions in constitutional rights such as the right to an occupation, political rights, the right to public service and the right to property and movement.[27] Pursuant to this decision, a subsequent amendment to the Act was made to apply the new provision to every person under the age of 20 at the time of the amendment.

B. Bodily Integrity and Sexual Self-Determination

Criminal law premised on patriarchal conceptions of women's bodies and sexuality is among the areas where constitutional review has been frequently

[26] Committee on the Elimination of Discrimination against Women [hereinafter CEDAW Committee], 'Report of the Committee on the Elimination of Discrimination against Women (Sixth session)' (1987) A/42/38, para 157; CEDAW Committee, 'Concluding Observations of the Committee on the Elimination of Discrimination Against Women' (25 February 1994) A/48/38(SUPP), para 448.

[27] Constitutional Court of Korea, 97Hun-Ka12, 12-2 KCCR [Korean Constitutional Court Report] 167 (31 August 2000).

conducted in South Korea. One of the significant cases recently decided by the Constitutional Court concerns the abortion ban. In April 2019, overruling its earlier decision, the Constitutional Court held that the blanket ban on abortion under the Criminal Act infringes on women's right to self-determination in violation of the proportionality principle.[28] Further details on the background and reasoning of this decision will be discussed in section IV of this chapter.

Criminal law in South Korea has visibly reflected a traditional conception of women's sexuality in multiple aspects. For example, until 2009 the Criminal Act penalised 'a person who induces *a woman who is not prone to an obscene act* into sexual intercourse under pretence of marriage' (emphasis added).[29] This provision was adopted to criminally punish a man who induced a woman to have sexual intercourse with a false promise of marriage, and to protect the 'innocent' woman 'who was deceived and lost her chastity', as indicated in the italicised phrase above. Applying the four-step proportionality review, the Constitutional Court invalidated this provision as it excessively restricted the right to sexual self-determination (derived from Article 10 of the Constitution providing for dignity, personal worth and the right to pursue happiness) and the right to privacy of men (Article 17 of the Constitution).[30] While the Court examined whether the law violated constitutional rights of *men* because it was men on whom the law imposed criminal punishment, the Court, in the course of its reasoning, provided important remarks on women's sexual autonomy and the patriarchal orientation underlying the criminal law. Notably, the majority opinion by six justices held that the provision did not pass even the *first* step of proportionality review (the legitimacy of the legislative purpose). The Constitutional Court noted that this criminal provision targeted consensual sexual intercourse, not sexual assault, between a man and a woman before marriage. Consensual sexual intercourse constitutes one's sexual freedom and an essential part of one's dignity and pursuit of happiness.[31] The justices pointed out that the law that aims to protect, ex post facto, women's betrayed trust in 'marriage' as a condition of sexual intercourse unjustly treats women like 'infants', who lack capacity to autonomously exercise sexual self-determination.[32] In the Court's view, this provision was based on a patriarchal ideology conceptualising women's sexuality only in terms of 'chastity' (the premise that women should have sex only in the context of marriage), as evidenced by the conditional phrase 'a woman who is not prone to an obscene act' (excluding a

[28] Constitutional Court of Korea, 2017Hun-Ba127, 31-1 KCCR 404 (11 April 2019).

[29] Criminal Act (before amendment on 18 December 2012) Art 304.

[30] Constitutional Court of Korea, 2008Hun-Ba58, 21-2 KCCR 520 (26 November 2009). The Court with this decision reversed its earlier decision issued in 2002 that, in an 8:1 split, upheld this provision under the proportionality review, emphasising the need to protect women's sexual self-determination, their weaker social status, and the social reality that perceives differently the sexuality of men and women. Constitutional Court of Korea, 99Hun-Ba40 (31 October 2002).

[31] Constitutional Court of Korea, 2008Hun-Ba58, 21-2 KCCR 520, 528-29 (26 November 2009).

[32] ibid 529.

so-called 'fallen woman').[33] The Court held that this criminal provision pursued a purpose that was not justifiable under contemporary constitutional standards.[34] In reaching this conclusion, the Constitutional Court referred to legal practices of other countries which do not have comparable criminal law provisions, including the United States, Germany, France and Japan. The Court also pointed out that it is a global trend to decriminalise a private and consensual act, noting that a provision like that in South Korean criminal law either does not exist or was abolished before the 1970s in most states except for a few countries such as Turkey, Cuba and Romania.[35]

Another criminal regulation rooted in traditional sexual morality was that concerned with adultery. The Criminal Act had for decades penalised, with a sentence of imprisonment, women as well as men who committed adultery. In 2015, the Constitutional Court invalidated this provision as it excessively restricted one's rights to privacy and sexual self-determination.[36] In its reasoning, the Court pointed out recent changes in the public conception of family, sexual life and relevant ethics, and opined that it is not justified to regulate individuals' sexual acts based on mutual consent with criminal punishment, unless there is a clear danger to a significant public interest.[37] The Court also referred to the global trend of decriminalising adultery, citing the examples of Denmark, Sweden, Germany, France, Spain, Switzerland, Austria, Japan and Argentina.[38]

In the areas of sexual violence, South Korean criminal law has increased the severity of punishment against offenders and also imposed additional security measures, including the attachment of a GPS device to offenders upon their return to society, a registration and disclosure of offenders' personal information on a designated website, employment restrictions in certain sectors and the ordering of pharmacologic treatment in certain cases. In a series of decisions, the Constitutional Court upheld the majority of these special measures and aggravated punishments as proportional, considering the public interest in suppressing sexual violence.[39] However, there are also several cases where the Court found the scope and applications of the measures concerned too broad and indiscriminate and thus unconstitutional.[40] Concerns have also been raised,

[33] ibid 529–30.

[34] ibid 530.

[35] ibid 526, 532–33.

[36] Constitutional Court of Korea, 2009Hun-Ba17, 27-1 KCCR 20 (26 February 2015). This decision reversed the Court's earlier decisions on the same provision. Constitutional Court of Korea, 2007Hun-Ka17 (30 October 2008) (a 4:5 decision), 89Hun-Ma82 (10 September 1990) (a 6:3 decision).

[37] ibid 27.

[38] ibid 25.

[39] See, for instance, Constitutional Court of Korea, 2015Hun-Ba196 (29 December 2016); 2013Hun-Ma423 (24 July 2014); 2012Hun-Ba144 (26 July 2012); 2010Hun-Ba401 (31 May 2012). For other relevant cases and their aftermath, see The Constitutional Court of Korea, *Thirty Years of the Constitutional Court of Korea:1988–2018* (Constitutional Court 2018) 613–20.

[40] See, eg, Constitutional Court of Korea, 2013Hun-Ka9 (23 December 2015) (finding unconstitutional a lack of procedure to appeal pharmacologic treatment at time of release from prison);

even among women's rights groups, that the policy of strengthening penalties and regulatory sanctions are not so effective in deterring sexual violence, because violence against women mostly originates from structural gender inequality and misogynistic culture prevalent in society. Critiques argue that treating criminals only as abnormal deviants improperly drives attention away from pervasive gender injustices and the violent culture that women have to face on a daily basis, which require general social education and awareness-raising rather than focusing on expanding exceptional criminal countermeasures.[41]

In the '*Comfort Women*' case decided in 2011, the Constitutional Court held unconstitutional the *inaction* of the South Korean Government for not taking any meaningful action to resolve legal disputes with Japan.[42] The disputes turned on the issue of the responsibility of Japan with regard to 'Comfort Women', the victims of sexual slavery by the Japanese military during World War II, which inflicted significant harm on their dignity and fundamental rights. The Constitutional Court concluded that the South Korean Government has a constitutional obligation to pursue a dispute resolution process against Japan. The Court found that this duty to take actions is derived from Article 10 of the Constitution, which provides human dignity and worth and mandates the state to ensure the fundamental rights of the individual. In reaching the conclusion, the Constitutional Court cited a report by the Special Rapporteur on violence against women Radhika Coomaraswamy ('Report on the mission to the Democratic People's Republic of Korea, the Republic of Korea and Japan on the issue of military sexual slavery in wartime', adopted by the UN Commission on Human Rights in 1996) and a 1998 report by Gay J McDougall, Special Rapporteur on systematic rape, sexual slavery and slavery-like practices during armed conflict (on the issue of 'comfort women' in Korea and Japan); a relevant resolution by the UN Human Rights Council in 2008; a recommendation by the Human Rights Committee against Japan in 2008, as well as a series of resolutions made by the legislative branches of the United States, the Netherlands, Canada and the European Parliament, urging the Japanese Government to take appropriate actions regarding the issue.[43] After the decision by the Constitutional Court, the South Korean Government initiated a talk for settlement with Japan through a diplomatic channel, but without any consultation

Constitutional Court of Korea, 2013Hun-Ma585 (31 March 2016) (finding unconstitutional a blanket employment restriction in medical institutions for ten years against any type of sexual crime offenders).

[41] See, eg, 변혜정[H Byeon], '진정! 화학적 거세가 성폭력 방지에 적합한가?: 일상에서 성폭력을 예방할 수 있는 방법[Is 'Chemical Castration' Really Appropriate to Prevent Sexual Violence?: Sexual Violence Preventive Measures in Everyday Life]' (2010) 2010.7 월간 한국노총 32; Korea Sexual Violence Relief Center, *1122*성폭력 법 개정의 성과와 과제: 반성폭력 운동의 미래를 묻다 [*1122 Sexual Violence Legal Reform Achievements and Challenges: The Future of the Anti-Sexual Violence Movement*] (Korea Sexual Violence Relief Center 2013).

[42] Constitutional Court of Korea, 2006Hun-Ma788, 23-2 KCCR 366 (30 August 2011).

[43] ibid 379–80.

with the victims. The results of the talk were delivered in December 2015 by the foreign ministers of the two Governments in the form of a press announcement. In 2016, the 'Comfort Women' survivors brought a constitutional challenge against this announcement, which was made without the victims' participation and did not acknowledge the legal responsibility of Japan nor the victims' legal right to remedies.[44] However, the Constitutional Court dismissed this claim at the procedural stage, providing the reason that the 2015 announcement was not made in the form of a treaty or a legal agreement and thus did not have any legal effect concerning the victims' rights.[45] Official recognition of legal responsibility toward the victims and any legal remedies have yet to be made by the Japanese Government.

With regard to prostitution, South Korean criminal law penalises not only sex buyers but also women who 'voluntarily' become involved with commercial sex acts, while those who have been 'coerced' into prostitution are protected as victims.[46] A woman who was prosecuted under this law challenged its constitutionality, and the criminal court in charge of her case agreed to request constitutionality review by the Constitutional Court. In its decision, the Constitutional Court admitted that this criminal provision indeed restricts the right to sexual self-determination and the right to privacy of those involved in prostitution (both sellers and buyers) and the right of sex workers to choose their occupation.[47] However, the Court held that this criminal law did not violate the proportionality principle, considering prostitution's harmful effect on society in light of the following aspects: that even voluntary sex work can undermine sex workers' personal autonomy by commercialising sex acts; that sex work is by nature inhumane and exploitative, given the inequality between buyers and sex workers, most of whom are in economically disadvantaged positions; that commercialising sex harms sexual culture and morality in society and is likely to contribute to increasing crimes of sexual violence; that the sex industry can distort the regular flow of money and the labour force in society; that punishing women in prostitution is necessary for suppressing the expansion of the commercial sex industry and the new inducement of young women or migrant women from less developed countries into the sex industry; and that there can be an extent of voluntariness criminally attributable to individual women, even though they might engage in prostitution because of economic hardship.[48] Three justices dissented: one justice expressed an opinion that the

[44] The announcement stated that the two governments had agreed to settle the issue by establishing a charity fund for the victims, and that the issue is considered to be resolved 'permanently and irreversibly' by this arrangement. This announcement was heavily criticized by civil society in South Korea and by the survivors.

[45] Constitutional Court of Korea, 2016Hun-Ma253, 31-2 KCCR 212 (27 December 2019).

[46] Act on the Punishment of Arrangement of Commercial Sex Acts, etc, No 12349 (amended 28 January 2014) Art 21(1).

[47] Constitutional Court of Korea, 2013Hun-Ka2, 28-1 KCCR 259, 271 (31 March 2016).

[48] ibid 272–76. This was a 6:3 decision and the only female justice then on the bench joined the majority opinion.

whole provision was unconstitutional, while the other two opined that punishing sex-buyers is constitutional, but penalising women in prostitution is not. They argued that the criminal law punishing those women ignores structural gender injustices in society that led them into the sex industry and indeed violates the proportionality principle by imposing criminal measures on those women, who in fact need protection and support.[49] Importantly, these justices referred to the recommendation by the CEDAW Committee for the South Korean Government to decriminalise women's engagement in commercial sex acts, as well as the European Parliament resolution of 26 February 2014 titled 'Sexual exploitation and prostitution and its impact on gender equality'.[50] In the CEDAW monitoring session held after this Constitutional Court decision, the Committee again expressed its concern about the South Korean legal system's subjection of women in prostitution to criminal punishment.[51]

C. Family

While South Korean family law has, until recently, straightforwardly reflected deep-rooted patriarchal norms, decades of grassroots movements for legal reform have not been answered effectively by the legislature. Of the cases raised against family law and adjudicated by the Constitutional Court, *Household Head System* counts among the most significant.[52] A more detailed analysis of this case is conducted in section IV.

One of the earlier decisions of the Constitutional Court which brought about meaningful transformation of family law relates to a prohibition of marriage between citizens who share the same family roots (eg marriage between those with the common surname 'Kim' of an identical regional origin dating back to at least several centuries ago). In 1997, the Constitutional Court held that this provision unconstitutionally violated individuals' human dignity and the right to pursue happiness under Article 10 of the Constitution, as well as the gender equality principle under Article 11 and Article 36(1).[53] The justices found the provision discriminatory on the basis of gender because it prohibited marriage based only on the male lineage without justified reasons.[54] The Court emphasised that tradition and social ethics change over time and that preserving an outdated social order that had lost reasonableness under contemporary moral standards could not be a legitimate legislative purpose in restricting constitutional rights.[55]

[49] ibid 280, 282, 285.
[50] ibid 281.
[51] CEDAW Committee, 'Concluding Observations on the Eighth Periodic Report of the Republic of Korea' (14 March 2018) CEDAW/C/KOR/CO/8, para 24(d).
[52] Constitutional Court of Korea, 2001Hun-Ka9, 17-1 KCCR 1 (3 February 2005).
[53] Constitutional Court of Korea, 95Hun-Ka6, 9-2 KCCR 1 (16 July 1997).
[54] ibid 16–17.
[55] ibid 17–19.

South Korean family law has for a long time adopted, and still maintains, a paternal family name system. In 2005, the Constitutional Court, in another historic decision, held unconstitutional the Civil Act provision mandating that a child's surname must follow that of the father.[56] The Constitutional Court viewed the state's unilateral and unconditional assignment of the paternal family name to each newborn baby as a violation of individual dignity and gender equality in the family, as prescribed in Article 36(1) of the Constitution. Following this decision, adopting the Constitutional Court's mandate only partially, the National Assembly amended the Civil Act provision in such a way as to preserve the paternal family name principle but to allow couples to give their child the mother's surname if both partners agree to do so at the time of their marriage registration.[57] Such agreements are thus treated as the only exception to the patrilineal principle, and are hardly put into practice. The current provision needs further amendment in order for South Korea to withdraw its last remaining reservation to CEDAW, with respect to Article 16(1)(g).[58] The CEDAW Committee has repeatedly expressed its concern regarding this patrilineal principle in South Korean family law, which was sustained even after the Constitutional Court decision.[59]

D. Public Service

While the South Korean Constitution stipulates 'the duty to national defence' of all citizens, a mandatory military service (for 18 to 21 months), enforced under the current conscription system, has been imposed only on male citizens by the Military Service Act. Over the years, a series of constitutional challenges have been raised by conscripted male citizens against this male-only military service system. From among the two different review standards that the Constitutional Court applies in equality cases – a weaker rationality test and a stricter proportionality test – the Constitutional Court chose to apply the rationality test

[56] Constitutional Court of Korea, 2003Hun-Ka5, 17-2 KCCR 544 (22 December 2005). Civil Act (before amendment in 2005) Art 781(1): 'A child shall succeed his or her father's surname and origin of surname and shall have the name entered into his or her father's family register: Provided, that when the father is a foreigner, the child may succeed the mother's surname and origin of surname'.

[57] Civil Act (as amended in 2005) Art 781(1): 'A child shall succeed his or her father's surname and origin of surname: Provided, that when the parents agree to have the child assume his or her mother's surname and origin of surname at the time of filing a report on their marriage, he or she shall succeed the mother's surname and origin of surname'.

[58] CEDAW Art 16 relates to equality and elimination of discrimination 'in all matters relating to marriage and family relations'. Para 1(g) provides that states shall ensure to men and women: 'The same personal rights as husband and wife, including the right to choose a family name, a profession and an occupation'.

[59] See, eg, CEDAW Committee (n 51) para 46; CEDAW Committee, 'Concluding Observations: Republic of Korea' (1 August 2011) CEDAW/C/KOR/CO/7, para 10.

in these cases. The reasons for this choice provided by the Court include the following: that military service is not an area where the Constitution *specifically* mandates gender equality, as it does regarding labour (Article 32(4)) or marriage and family life (Article 36(1));[60] that it further cannot be regarded as a case which involves a significant burden on constitutional rights, because military service is a constitutional *duty* of citizens; and that operation of the conscription system is an area where wider legislative discretion is allowed, as it is closely related to national security and needs to accommodate diverse policy considerations.[61] The Constitutional Court held that there is a rational basis for mandating only male citizens to serve in the military, citing general differences in physical characteristics between women and men, including women's menstruation and possibilities of pregnancy, childbirth and childrearing, and concerns about sexual crimes or affairs.[62] The Court also mentioned comparative practices, pointing out that among about 70 countries that adopt a conscription system, only a few states, such as Israel, impose military duties on women.[63] This decision has been criticised for weaknesses in its reasoning, including the premise that men are inherently more suitable than women for military duties and ignoring the changing features of contemporary military service.[64]

As part of the assistance policy for male citizens who completed mandatory military service, the public service employment exam system in South Korea for many years granted extra points to male applicants who had fulfilled their military duty. These applicants automatically received three to five additional points out of 100, even when the average qualification score of the exam was as high as 95.5. This point system made it extremely hard, if not almost impossible, to pass the exam for all women and for men who did not serve in the military because of physical conditions or other justified reasons. Four female university students and one man with a physical disability who were preparing for government employment exams brought a constitutional challenge against this system. In 1999, the Constitutional Court delivered a landmark decision holding the system unconstitutional as it violated the claimants' right to equality and the right to access public service under conditions of equality.[65] The Court first clarified that the equality upheld by the Constitution is *substantive* equality (as opposed to formal equality) and adopted the concept of indirect discrimination by articulating the view that it constitutes gender discrimination if the

[60] The *general* equality provision, Art 11, is not considered by the Court as the provision in which the Constitution 'specifically' mandates gender equality.

[61] Constitutional Court of Korea, 2010Hun-Ma460, 23-1 KCCR 519, 524–25 (30 June 2011). The same reasoning appears in Constitutional Court of Korea, 2011Hun-Ma825 (27 February 2014) and 2006Hun-Ma328, 22-2 KCCR 446 (25 November 2010).

[62] Constitutional Court of Korea, 2010Hun-Ma460, 23-1 KCCR 519, 525–26 (30 June 2011).

[63] ibid 526.

[64] See, eg 김현지 [H Kim], '판례평석: 남성중심의 병역의무 관념의 해체 [Case Commentary: Deconstructing the Exclusivity of Men's Involuntary Conscription]' (2011) 9 공익과 인권 463.

[65] Constitutional Court of Korea, 98Hun-Ma363, 11-2 KCCR 770 (23 December 1999).

actual consequence of a certain treatment predominantly affects individuals of a particular gender. In this case, under the male-only national conscription system, few women can belong to the law's superficially neutral categorisation, 'discharged soldiers', the group entitled to receive extra points.[66] This is also the first case where the Constitutional Court applied a *proportionality* test in equality cases. In conducting the review, as it normally does, the Court incorporated an impact-based analysis of discrimination. The Court pointed to the fact that, out of 99 persons who passed the recent public service exam, only three applicants managed to pass without the help of the extra points.[67] The automatic awarding of extra points was a decisive factor in the outcome, thereby depriving those who did not serve in the military – including all women as well as men with disabilities – almost entirely of opportunities to serve in the public sector.[68] The Constitutional Court held this system constitutionally unacceptable, as it generated a severe imbalance between the relevant interests. The Court noted that assisting those who served in the military by smoothing their reintegration into society is only a policy-level interest.[69] Following this decision, the extra point system was abolished and the rate of women passing the public service exam has since dramatically increased.

E. Gender Binary and Heteronormativity

i. Military Sodomy Law

Compared to the above-discussed cases concerning women's rights and equality, the Constitutional Court has taken a more conservative stance towards the rights of sexual minorities. The Court has yet to explicitly recognise sexual orientation or gender identity as generally prohibited grounds of discrimination under the Constitution. However, constitutional challenges claiming the rights and equality of gender and sexual minorities have more frequently been brought to the Court in recent years. In particular, the so-called military sodomy law has been challenged multiple times. The Military Criminal Act in South Korea punishes, with up to two years' imprisonment, soldiers who have consensual intercourse or other types of physical sexual contact with someone of the same sex.[70] The Military Criminal Act has been constitutionally challenged multiple

[66] ibid 784–85, 789.
[67] ibid 791.
[68] ibid 792.
[69] ibid 793.
[70] Military Criminal Act, Art 92-5 (Disgraceful Conduct): 'A person who commits sodomy or other disgraceful conduct shall be punished by imprisonment with prison labour for not more than two years'. This provision has been amended in 2013 as follows, Military Criminal Act, Art 92-6 (Indecent Act): 'A person who commits anal intercourse with any person prescribed in Article 1 (1) through (3) [soldiers and military personnel] or any other indecent act shall be punished by imprisonment with labour for not more than two years'.

times by soldiers convicted under this provision. In its latest decision in 2016, the Constitutional Court again upheld this law, applying the proportionality test as it has done in previous decisions.[71] It held that the provision does not excessively restrict the right to sexual self-determination, privacy, bodily freedom, or equality of the soldiers subject to criminal punishment.[72] The five-justice majority opinion first stated that the legislative purpose of this military criminal law is to 'establish sound life of military community and military discipline'.[73] Then it found that 'prohibiting acts of sexual gratification between same-sex soldiers' and 'imposing imprisonment with prison labour' are appropriate means for achieving this legislative purpose, and that the provision also meets the principle of the least restrictive means.[74] At the last step of the proportionality review, the Court stated that the extent of rights restriction on soldiers is not greater than the public interest achieved, ie, 'sound life of military community and military discipline', and ultimately, 'national security, the premise of the nation's existence and the basis of all freedoms'.[75]

Four justices dissented in this case. However, they viewed the provision as unconstitutional not because it violated the claimants' constitutional rights, but because the phrase 'sodomy or other disgraceful conduct' does not satisfy the principle of clarity, the basic requirement for any criminal provisions.[76] Criticisms have been raised by lawyers and scholars against this law and the series of Court decisions that have upheld it.[77] Although the Constitutional Court applied a proportionality test, the reasoning was too brief and rather superficial, lacking a serious examination of the causal relationship between consensual same-sex relationship and a detrimental impact on national security.[78] The decision is also criticised for confirming the homophobia underlying the military law, instead of scrutinising it.[79] Expressing concern about the overall human rights situation of gender and sexual minorities and widespread discrimination against those minorities in South Korea, the UN Human Rights Committee in 2015 urged the South Korean Government to repeal this provision.[80] Several subsequent constitutional challenges against this provision were brought by multiple

[71] Constitutional Court of Korea, 2012Hun-Ba258, 28-2 KCCR 1 (28 July 2016).

[72] ibid 11.

[73] ibid 9–10.

[74] ibid 10.

[75] ibid. See also Constitutional Court of Korea, 2001Hun-Ba70, 14-1 KCCR 601 (27 June 2002); 2008Hun-Ka21, 23-1 KCCR 178 (31 March 2011).

[76] Constitutional Court of Korea, 2012Hun-Ba258, 28-2 KCCR 1, 12-17 (28 July 2016).

[77] eg 이호중 [H Lee], '군형법 제92조의5 추행죄의 위헌성과 폐지론 [The Unconstitutionality of the Crime of Sodomy in Military Criminal Law]' (2011) 23 형사법연구 229; 한가람 [G Han], '군형법상 "추행"죄와 제도화된 동성애 혐오/공포 ['Disgraceful Conduct' of the Military Criminal Act and Institutionalized Homophobia]' (2017) 17 공익과 인권 397.

[78] Lee (n 77).

[79] Han (n 77).

[80] Human Rights Committee, 'Concluding Observations on the Fourth Periodic Report of the Republic of Korea' (3 December 2015) CCPR/C/KOR/CO/4, paras 14 and 15.

other soldiers prosecuted under the provision. The cases are currently pending at the Constitutional Court.[81] Remarkably, on April 2022, the Supreme Court of Korea delivered a landmark judgment overturning, for the first time, a lower court decision which convicted a soldier under this provision.[82] In the reasoning, the Supreme Court articulated that consensual same-sex sexual conduct should not be considered an 'indecent act' prosecutable under the provision, and that punishing such an act would violate constitutionally protected equality, dignity and the right to sexual self-determination of the defendant soldier. It now remains to be seen whether the Constitutional Court will change its position in its next decision on this Military Criminal Act provision.

ii. Resident/Family Registration and Gender Binary

Every South Korean citizen upon her birth is assigned a Resident Registration Number, which serves as a permanent, 12-digit individual identification number. The first six digits of this number indicate one's birth date, and the seventh digit reveals one's gender. Male citizens are given the number '1', female citizens the number '2' (recently born males are being allocated the number '3', and females '4'). In 2016, a group of human rights activists for the rights of women and gender and sexual minorities brought a petition to the National Human Rights Commission challenging this number system, which categorically puts men prior to women and allows no option other than to choose between male and female.[83] This ID number system unnecessarily exposes one's biological sex to anyone at all times and also has discriminatory effects on transgender persons and persons with non-binary gender identities. Persons whose gender identification number on their ID cards is different from their present identity are suffering various difficulties in life, including with finding jobs, seeing a doctor as well as in exercising voting rights.[84] The Commission has yet to give an answer to this petition.

The national Family Relationship Registration System that registers every South Korean citizen in the government database for various purposes also adopts the binary approach to gender. One's registered gender is usually decided at birth by parents or doctors based on one's physical characteristics, and it has been extremely difficult in South Korea for transgender persons to attain court approval to modify their officially registered genders. The Supreme Court of Korea, through its decision and official guidelines for lower courts, has required

[81] See, eg, Constitutional Court of Korea, 2020Hun-Ka3 (submitted 18 February 2020).

[82] Supreme Court of Korea, 2019Do3047 (21 April 2022).

[83] See 김형규, '숫자 1과 2 사이에 걸친 사연들 '주민번호 성별 표시는 성차별입니다'', 경향신문 (27 January 2016), available at news.khan.co.kr/kh_news/khan_art_view.html?artid=20160127173 6551&code=940100.

[84] See CEDAW Committee (n 51) paras 14–15.

full sex-reassignment surgery in order to issue court approval, a surgery which entails significant social and economic burdens and health risks to applicants.[85] Lately, a few lower courts began to issue decisions allowing modification of the registered gender of a person who did not undergo a full physical operation.[86] In response to consistent criticisms by human rights groups as well as the UN Human Rights Committee's recommendation to the South Korean government to 'facilitate access to the legal recognition of gender reassignment',[87] in March 2020 the Supreme Court partially amended the guidelines. Now a medical document that verifies the completion of sex-reassignment surgery is one of the 'reference' materials that can be submitted by an applicant, not a 'required' document for application. Human rights groups still find this revision insufficient, as such a provision allows discretion by individual courts. Owing to the lack of a Constitutional Court power to review the decisions and internal rules of ordinary courts, it is not easy for individuals to challenge the decision at the constitutional level if their application for gender correction is denied by a local court.

iii. Same-sex Marriage

South Korean family law as interpreted by the administration and the judiciary does not recognise same-sex marriage or any other forms of legal partnership between same-sex couples. In 2014, a well-known movie director and his male partner brought a lawsuit against a local government's refusal to accept their marriage register application. A district court dismissed this case without judgment on the merits, stating, 'The reason our society recognises marriage between a man and a woman and gives them legal status and privileges is because they will reproduce and raise children … and form a platform to sustain and develop our society'.[88] A constitutional claim concerning same-sex marriage has yet to be brought to the Constitutional Court. Human rights lawyers and activists in South Korea may perceive that it is too soon to expect the Court's progressiveness in this regard and that a negative pronouncement by the Constitutional Court could aggravate the disadvantaged situations of sexual minorities in society.

Rights advocacy for gender and sexual minorities in legal and constitutional contexts has emerged later than women's rights movements in the country. The groups are politically less empowered and represented, although expert human rights lawyers and NGOs have been their consistent supporters. Conservative Christian church groups are the most aggressive objectors to gender and sexual

[85] Supreme Court of Korea, 2004Seu42 (22 June 2006). 성전환자의 성별정정허가신청사건등 사무처리지침 [Guidelines for the Work Process with Applications for the Correction of Gender] Arts 3 and 6.

[86] See, eg, Seoul Western District Court, 2013HoPa1406 (19 November 2013).

[87] Human Rights Committee (n 80) para 15.

[88] Seoul Western District Court, 2014HoPa1842 (25 May 2016).

minorities' equality and mobilising efforts. Over the last 15 years, their systematic anti-LGBTIQ public campaigns and vigorous lobbying activities have posed the biggest hurdles to adopting a general anti-discrimination law in South Korea.[89] The bill is currently in the hands of the National Assembly and the proposed inclusion of gender identity and sexual orientation among prohibited grounds of discrimination has been a main target of attack by the opposition groups.[90]

IV. CASE STUDY: HOUSEHOLD HEAD SYSTEM AND ABORTION

This section focuses on two landmark decisions by the Constitutional Court of Korea as example case studies – *Household Head System* decided in 2005, and the *Abortion* case delivered in 2019.

A. Household Head System (2005)

While South Korea is generally classified as a continental law country, its family law, which constitutes part of the Civil Act, also reflected an older patriarchal culture and ideology in society, originating in the Confucian tradition that has been adopted and localised in Korea for several centuries. The law established an explicit version of male supremacy across most areas of family life, including family structure, authority over children, inheritance, divorce, custody and family lineage. Many of the most obviously discriminatory provisions were amended when the South Korean Government decided to join CEDAW. However, the Household Head System, *Hojuje*, one of the core patriarchal components of South Korean family law remained until as late as 2005. Under this system, a 'household' comprised a 'house head', the eldest male in a family, and his subordinate family members. If, for example, a two-year old boy were the only male in the family, he would become the head of the family, while his elder sister, mother and grandmother would be his subordinates. This family law made a female citizen belong to her father when she was born, to her husband when married, and then to her son when her husband died, which directly reflected the Virtue of Threefold Obedience, the traditional Confucian norm imposed on women.[91]

[89] See South Korean Coalition for Anti-Discrimination Legislation, available at equalityact.kr/%ec%b0%a8%eb%b3%84%ea%b8%88%ec%a7%80%eb%b2%95%ec%a0%9c%ec%a0%95%ec%97%b0%eb%8c%80.

[90] See CEDAW Committee (n 51) paras 12–13; Human Rights Committee (n 80) paras 12–13 (both Committees urging the South Korean Government to adopt a comprehensive anti-discrimination law, expressing special concern about the situations of gender and sexual minorities in South Korea).

[91] See K Knapp, 'Sancong Side 三从四德 (Threefold Obedience and Four Virtues)' in XZ Yao (ed), *Encyclopedia of Confucianism* (Routledge 2015); 김미영[M Kim], '유교 가족 윤리와 "여성 정체성": 삼종지도(三從之道)를 중심으로 [Confucian Family Ethics and Womanly Virtue: Centering on the Way of Three Obediences]' (2007) 33 철학연구 47.

For the five decades following the adoption of *Hojuje*, numerous women's rights NGOs and their coalitions made arduous efforts to abolish this family system that openly codified an ideology of male supremacy.[92] The earlier movement for abolishing *Hojuje* and reforming family law was led by Lee Tai-young (1914–1998), the first female lawyer in South Korea (and also the first female law student at Seoul National University). After she attained a lawyer's licence in 1952, and when then South Korean President Rhee Syngman rejected her appointment as a judge mainly because of her being a woman, Lee started a family law reform movement through various channels and established the Korea Legal Aid Center for Family Relations in 1956. Her legacy was succeeded by the Citizens Alliance for Abolishing *Hojuje*, organised in 1998, a nationwide coalition of 137 human rights and women's NGOs in South Korea. While continuing lobbying efforts toward the Government and the legislature, the Alliance decided to bring a case before the Constitutional Court. A team of human rights lawyers began strategic litigation in 2000 and supported dozens of women citizens in submitting applications to government offices requesting to register them as a head of their respective household, or to change their household currently with a male head to one without any house head. After receiving expected rejections from the Government, these women brought their cases to family courts to challenge them, arguing that *Hojuje* is unconstitutional and thus should not be applied in their cases. Beginning around 2001, many of the local family courts that received these arguments suspended the court proceedings and relayed the cases to the Constitutional Court, requesting a constitutional review of *Hojuje*. A total of eight cases from local courts were brought to the Constitutional Court and were combined for a unified review.

In recognition of the graveness of the case, the Constitutional Court held five open-hearing sessions from November 2003 to December 2004, which is not so common a practice for the Court, and invited expert witnesses for each side.[93] The claimants' counsels submitted written and video-recorded statements of numerous women citizens testifying about the various negative impact of *Hojuje* on their lives and their daughters, including legal discrimination caused by the system. The women also testified about the social and psychological harms of reproducing misogyny already prevalent in society and imposing low self-esteem on women and young girls, making them regard themselves as inferior to men. On the other hand, conservative groups invoked Article 9 of the Constitution,

[92] As early as 1953, a women's group, *Daehanbuyinhoei* (meaning the Korean Wives Association), announced '15 million women's declaration of being human', arguing for the reformation of the family law that devalued women. For the history of family law reform movements by women in South Korea, see, eg 김영정 [Y Kim], 여성가족정책사 현장 재조명: 호주제 폐지 운동을 중심으로 본 가족 이슈 변화와 방향 [*Revisiting the History of Women and Family Policy: Changes and Directions in Family Issues Based on the Movement to Abolish the Household Head System*] (Seoul Foundation of Women & Family 2018).

[93] The Constitutional Court has discretion on whether to hold open hearings. It usually holds hearings open to the public in high-profile cases such as *Hojuje* and *Abortion*.

which states, 'The State shall strive to sustain and develop the cultural heritage and to enhance national culture', insisting that *Hojuje* embodied an important national culture and tradition that the Constitution mandates the state to preserve. The claimant side instead pointed to Article 36(1) of the Constitution, which states, 'Marriage and family life shall be entered into and sustained on the basis of individual dignity and equality of the sexes, and the State shall do everything in its power to achieve that goal'.

In February 2005, in a 7:2 decision, the Constitutional Court held *Hojuje* unconstitutional as it violated individuals' dignity and gender equality within the family, as prescribed in Article 36(1).[94] In reaching this conclusion, the majority opinion conducted an in-depth analysis of normative relations between tradition and constitutional rights. While recognising the importance of producing a harmonised interpretation of different constitutional provisions, the Court articulated that tradition and culture, as protected by Article 9, possess both historical and contemporary aspects, and should thus be valid according to today's moral standards.[95] The Constitutional Court found that Article 36(1) indicates a constitutional resolution of modern Korea, as proclaimed by the adoption of the First Constitution of 1948, to no longer acknowledge a long-standing patriarchal family order in society.[96] If a traditional order goes against these constitutional values and principles (individual dignity and gender equality), it cannot be justified in the name of Article 9.[97] In other words, a tradition or culture that violates the constitutional rights of individuals is not the kind that Article 9 mandates the state to preserve. The Constitutional Court therefore held that sustaining the patriarchal family order cannot serve as a legitimate purpose for restricting constitutional rights of individuals in a family, and thus failed to meet even the first step of the four-step proportionality review.[98] On the other hand, the two dissenting justices exhibited an opposite understanding of the relationship between rights and tradition.[99] They asserted that the constitutional rights of individuals are guaranteed only within the scope of tradition and that the patriarchal family tradition is valuable for preserving the uniqueness and morality of society.[100]

Following this decision, the National Assembly, in March 2005, adopted a bill to abolish *Hojuje*. An entirely new, digitalised and individualised citizen registration system was developed and began to operate in South Korea from 2007. Every South Korean citizen is now registered as an equal and independent individual, neither as a household head nor as a subordinated member to a head.

[94] Constitutional Court of Korea, 2001Hun-Ka9, 17-1 KCCR 1 (3 February 2005).
[95] ibid 17.
[96] ibid 16.
[97] ibid 16–17.
[98] ibid 18, 22–25.
[99] ibid 25–38.
[100] ibid 30–32, 36.

The *Household Head System* decision made groundbreaking progress for gender equality in South Korea, a country where the legal system had long normalised and reproduced a patriarchal social order. The case is particularly remarkable in that the achievement came about through the relentless self-liberating efforts by women, who had been legally relegated as inferior members of the family and society. The decades-long abolition movement is a vivid example of value-oriented solidarity among ordinary citizens, NGOs, human rights lawyers and scholars, one that was finally answered by the Constitutional Court through the constitutional review mechanism. The Court's decision evidences the emancipatory strength of constitutionalism for disadvantaged groups whose rights and equality have been denied in the name of tradition and national culture.[101] The constitutional rights contestation process deconsecrates tradition and demands its justification in constitutional terms. The Constitutional Court's reasoning made it clear that preserving tradition for tradition's sake does not constitute a legitimate purpose for restricting constitutional rights and principles. The constitutional doctrine developed through this case provides an effective normative framework for enhancing gender equality in a society embedded with a patriarchal culture and tradition, and for eventually transforming that very culture and tradition.

B. Abortion (2019)

The year 2019 was another historic year for the advancement of gender equality and women's human rights in South Korea. The Constitutional Court held that the 66-year-old criminal law punishing women who undergo abortion is unconstitutional, reversing the Court's earlier 2012 decision.[102] Under South Korean criminal law, abortion was criminalised in principle, allowing only a small number of exceptions, as in the case of rape or incest, when there is a serious risk to a pregnant woman's health, or when a parent has a certain type of genetic disorder or infectious disease stipulated under law. The 2019 *Abortion* case is remarkable not only in terms of its normative importance, but also with regard to women's rights movements behind this historic development. The momentum was built up alongside the Me Too movement that erupted in South Korea in early 2018, when women across society finally gained enough confidence and social support to speak out about their past or current experiences of sexual violence, especially the prolonged suffering they had to endure due to the hierarchal relationship with offenders and the lack of support systems. The changed social environment encouraged ordinary women to speak up against

[101] Shin (n 21) 268.
[102] Constitutional Court of Korea, 2017Hun-Ba127, 31-1 KCCR 404 (11 April 2019). The earlier decision is Constitutional Court of Korea, 2010Hun-Ba402, 24-2 KCCR 471 (23 August 2012).

various other cases of social and legal oppression and discrimination against women's sexuality and autonomy, including the criminalisation of abortion.[103]

A widespread movement against the abortion law was triggered by a government decree announced in September 2016 to suspend the medical licences of doctors who perform an abortion procedure, classifying it as an 'immoral medical act'. Opposition to this scheme started in October 2016 with thousands of ordinary women citizens, who were communicating online, along with a number of women's rights NGOs, and organised Black Sunday Korea protests (demonstrating solidarity with the Black Protest in Poland, which was organised at around the same period) in multiple major cities around the country. These protests are considered to be the first large-scale protests held in public against the abortion ban in South Korea. As the protest developed, two distinct streams emerged from within the movement.[104] One stream was led by ordinary women citizens who joined an online campaign alliance called BWAVE (meaning Black Wave). Up until the decision of the Constitutional Court, BWAVE initiated various offline activities, including raising funds and posting anti-abortion-ban advertisements at subway stations, submitting signed petitions to the Government and presidential candidates, organising protests in front of the Constitutional Court and writing letters to its justices.[105] Another stream of the movement was led by Joint Action of Abolishing Abortion Ban for Everyone (*Mo-nak-pe* in the Korean abbreviation), an association officially launched in September 2017, composed of dozens of organisations, including numerous women's rights NGOs, young feminist groups, progressive doctors' associations, labour unions, student groups, individual lawyers and researchers, and political parties such as the Labor Party and the Green Party.[106] Supporters of the abortion ban have mostly been religious groups, including Catholics and Protestants.[107] These groups tend to define childbirth as a sacred and unique joy that women should appreciate, and assert that legalising abortion would inflict harm not only on potential life but also on women.[108] The CEDAW Committee repeatedly expressed its concern about the South Korean criminal law against abortion and urged the removal of punitive measures imposed on women.[109]

[103] The recent feminist movement is highlighted by the series of 'Hyehwa Station Protest' held in 2018, where more than ten thousand women, mostly in their 20s or 30s, protested against various types of violence and discrimination against women. See eg, for foreign media coverage, L Bicker, '#MeToo movement takes hold in South Korea' *BBC* (Seoul, 26 March 2018), available at www.bbc.com/news/world-asia-43534074.

[104] See E Lee, 'Abortion Law and Reproductive Equality' (Master's thesis, Seoul National University School of Law 2020).

[105] ibid 37–38.

[106] ibid 45–46.

[107] According to a survey by Statistics Korea in 2015, Christians constitute about 28% of the Korean population, see Statistics Korea (2015), available at kosis.kr/statHtml/statHtml.do?orgId=101&tblId=DT_1PM1502&vw_cd=&list_id=&scrId=&seqNo=&lang_mode=ko&obj_var_id=&itm_id=&conn_path=E1.

[108] Lee (n 104) 26–30.

[109] CEDAW Committee (n 51) paras 42–43; CEDAW Committee (n 59) para 35.

In response to the accumulated criticisms and requests, the Constitutional Court of Korea delivered a historic decision on women's rights in April 2019. In a 7:2 decision, the Court held that the Criminal Act penalising virtually all abortions (with only a few statutory exceptions) is unconstitutional, as it violates women's right to self-determination.[110] The Court articulated that Article 10 of the Constitution, which provides for human dignity and worth and the right to pursue happiness, guarantees the right to personhood, and the right to self-determination at its core.[111] One has the right to self-determination to freely and autonomously make fundamental decisions in one's life, and an individual person, as a bearer of human dignity, should be treated as an ultimate and supreme worth and not as a means for other legal interests.[112] The justices emphasised that the right to self-determination should be applied equally to men and women and, for women, the right to self-determination importantly includes the right to decide autonomously about childbirth.[113] In its reasoning, the Constitutional Court applied the four-step proportionality test in reviewing whether the legal restriction on women's self-determination, by criminalising abortion, is constitutionally justified. The justices acknowledged that the state has a legitimate interest in protecting the life of a foetus.[114] In conducting the third and last steps of proportionality review, the Court discussed various normative as well as social factors, including the following: That the Criminal Act, through a threat of criminal punishment, compels a woman to continue her pregnancy and give birth to a child, subjecting her to radical changes to her body and psychology, including the pain of delivery, risks to her health and even her life, and the burden of childrearing;[115] that nurturing a child requires continuous devotion over an extended period of time, imposing significant pressures on women's social, educational and economic life;[116] that the choice of whether to continue with pregnancy and childbirth is a holistic decision that fundamentally impacts a woman's life and is central to her dignity and autonomy;[117] that it is possible to assign different legal effects to periods before and after the 22nd week of pregnancy when a foetus becomes viable.[118]

[110] Constitutional Court of Korea, 2017Hun-Ba127, 31-1 KCCR 404 (11 April 2019).
[111] ibid 415.
[112] ibid 415–16.
[113] ibid 416.
[114] With regard to the life of the foetus, four of the seven justices who joined the unconstitutionality decision explicitly acknowledged the constitutional right to life that a foetus holds, while the other three justices avoided such an outward recognition of foetuses' constitutional rights, but recognised the public interest in protecting the life of the foetus. All these seven justices agreed the challenged criminal law provision did not satisfy the proportionality principle.
[115] Constitutional Court of Korea, 2017Hun-Ba127, 31-1 KCCR 404, 418 (11 April 2019).
[116] ibid 419, 424–25.
[117] ibid 419.
[118] ibid 419–20.

The Constitutional Court also emphasised the special relationship between a pregnant woman and a foetus and that the Government did not implement enough measures to protect the life of a foetus effectively rather than simply imposing penal sanctions on women:

> The relationship between a pregnant woman and a foetus is special, not simply adversarial. A foetus is closely connected to the woman's body and is entirely relied on her for its life and growth. … the wellbeing of the pregnant woman is therefore the wellbeing of the foetus. … This special bond persists in abortion situations. Pregnant women often proceed with abortion considering their socio-economic situations and the expected future of the unborn baby. … A fair solution for the protection of the life of a foetus cannot be drawn from the fixed offender vs. victim premise regarding the relationship between the two. … The state is required to substantively harmonize constitutional rights of the two in a way to optimize both. Considering their special relationship, the duty of the state to protect the life of foetuses can be realized only when the measures taken include the protection of pregnant women in both physical and social senses. Improving social and legal conditions that will prevent unwanted pregnancy and reduce abortions …, assisting pregnant women with making a deliberative decision based on sufficient information and support from experts, and removing socioeconomic barriers to pregnancy, childbirth and childrearing will be more effective ways for the state to protect the life of foetuses.[119]

The justices also referred to comparative practices around the globe. In its reasoning, the Constitutional Court opinion designated a separate section, 'Law of Other States', within a chapter titled 'Grounds for Judgment'.[120] The section discussed various legislative approaches to abortion across different jurisdictions, including those adopted by European countries that belong to the continental law family, the United Kingdom and the United States. The 'viability' standard provided in *Roe v Wade* and the UN global surveys of abortion practices were importantly mentioned.

Based on this examination, the Constitutional Court held that the Criminal Act provision which uniformly forbids and criminalises abortions infringes on women's right to self-determination while having limited effect in enhancing the public interest of protecting the life of foetuses.[121] Two justices dissented, as they viewed the public interest to protect foetuses' right to life as outweighing women's right to self-determination.[122] Through this decision, the Constitutional Court reversed its previous decision of 2012. In the 2012 case, the majority opinion of five justices held that the criminal law punishing abortion satisfied the proportionality principle, having stressed the importance of the dignity of human life and concluding that pregnant women's right to self-determination is 'never as

[119] ibid 421–22.
[120] ibid 417.
[121] ibid 425–26.
[122] ibid 438–50.

important as the public interest of protecting the right to life of the foetus'.[123] The dissenting opinion by the other four justices in that case became the majority opinion by seven justices seven years later.

While the seven justices agreed on the unconstitutionality of the provision in the 2019 decision, the majority (four) of them decided to grant the legislature a period of time for drafting an amendment, instead of invalidating the law immediately. As a new bill was not adopted by the end of 2020, the current provision lost its effect at the beginning of 2021. According to the majority opinion, the legislature has discretion in deciding procedural and time-wise conditions for abortions, but the new law should be consistent with the Constitutional Court's key interpretation.

V. CONCLUSION

Since its birth, the Constitutional Court of Korea has been one of the most actively functioning constitutional courts in Asia and around the globe. Multiple constitutional actors and their dynamic interactions have played key roles in its vibrancy. These constitutional actors include the Constitutional Court, which has identified itself as the last defender of human rights and democracy in the newly democratised country, and mobilised individuals, supported by vigilant human rights NGOs and dedicated lawyers, empowered as norm-makers through the constitutional rights review system. Gender equality and women's rights are among the areas where energetic and progressive interactions between these actors have been most prominent. Through constitutional rights contestations, women, who faced centuries of discrimination and marginalisation in a deeply patriarchal society, have empowered themselves to challenge the oppressive laws that have been imposed on them, but in the initial making of which they had little input. Their persistent and constantly growing mobilisations have in turn empowered the Constitutional Court to deliver numerous transformative decisions with confidence and out of a sense of responsibility for facilitating a substantive progress of society in a constitutionally principled and normatively sound manner. The story of South Korea demonstrates the emancipatory function that rights-based constitutionalism and its adjudication system can play for traditionally disempowered groups and individuals. Its rich list of cases for the last three decades illustrates the ongoing history of a society that has gradually overcome its patriarchal traditions through individuals' earnest constitutional mobilisation and the Constitutional Court's effective, if not immediate, responses. South Korea's dynamic constitutional development in gender equality and women's rights exemplifies the practice of *bottom-up constitutionalism* based on individual empowerment. Mobilisation and empowerment of ordinary

[123] Constitutional Court of Korea, 2010Hun-Ba402, 24-2 KCCR 471 (23 August 2012).

women citizens in South Korea who redefined themselves as active rights-holders and constitutional norm-makers provide an inspirational example for other disadvantaged groups in South Korea and for other parts of the world, especially where a democratic constitutional system and oppressive culture and tradition coexist.

There are remaining challenges. As examined, the Constitutional Court of Korea has shown a more conservative stance when it comes to gender and sexual minorities' rights. At least several more years may be expected before there is a plausible chance to see same-sex marriage legalised, as in Taiwan. However, the Constitutional Court will soon have to face more difficult challenges to take seriously the rights of individuals who receive less public support and attention, such as gender and sexual minorities. Non-citizens' constitutional rights are another underdeveloped area in South Korea, with growing significance in recent years. Migrant and non-citizen women, denied the opportunity to be heard in the legislature, may achieve this instead through the constitutional justice system, as the Constitutional Court has acknowledged constitutional standing of non-citizens in multiple cases.[124] Constitutional rights adjudication equally accessible to these individuals can advance democracy towards a more inclusive and cosmopolitan one.[125] Another challenge is gender conflict among the younger generation in South Korea, which seems to have been aggravated in recent years. The Constitutional Court is expected by civil society to play a more effective and independent role in realising principled rights-based constitutionalism. As constitutional practices in South Korea become more transnationally open and engaging, the Constitutional Court will have to seek to concretise the meaning of human rights and equality in a way that can be justified for more diverse and broader audiences. The rich and dynamically developing constitutional jurisprudence in South Korea in gender contexts illuminates the strength of rights-based constitutional review as well as its expected roles and further challenges in a world of increasing diversity, mobility and connectivity.

[124] YJ Shin, 'Non-Citizens' Rights, Constitutional Review and an Inclusive Democracy: A Case Study of South Korea' (2020) 19 *Journal of Korean Law* 81.
[125] ibid 115–18.

6

Gender and Constitutionalism in Malaysia

DIAN AH SHAH

I. INTRODUCTION

SCHOLARS AND ANALYSTS studying the interrelationship between gender, equality and constitutionalism in Malaysia are bound to be confronted with a variety of contradictions.[1] In looking for positive developments, one finds state policies and commitments that seek to actively uplift the socio-economic conditions of women. In 1995, for instance, Malaysia ratified the Convention on the Elimination of All Forms of Discrimination Against Women (CEDAW). As a result, in 2001, the Federal Parliament amended Article 8(2) of the Federal Constitution to include gender in the list of prohibited grounds of discrimination, and this provision came into force on 28 September 2001. A series of policy initiatives favourable to women preceded and followed the constitutional amendment: in January 2001, for the first time, the Government established a ministry dedicated to pursuing policies for women's development (the Ministry of Women, Family, and Community Development). Pursuant to its CEDAW obligations, under the Ninth Malaysia Plan tabled in 2005 (a blueprint of the Government's five-year development plan for the nation), the Government announced that it will seek to increase women's participation in the nation's labour force and to review existing laws that discriminate

[1] From the state's perspective, in the realms of lawmaking and policy-making, the term 'gender' or the concept of 'gender equality' is understood and used in terms of established, binary ideas about male and female identities. This is, for instance, apparent from the state's annual population census – the gender ratio of the population is defined in terms of ratio of males to females. See Department of Statistics Malaysia [hereinafter DOSM], 'Demographic Statistics First Quarter 2020, Malaysia' (12 May 2020), available at www.dosm.gov.my/v1/index.php?r=column/cthemeByCat&cat=430&bul_id=aFYzVjJ3anNyQytHZGxzcUZxTG9Ydz09&menu_id=L0pheU43NWJwRWVSZklWdzQ4TlhUUT09.

against women.[2] It also introduced a new policy – that there should be 30 per cent participation by women at decision-making levels in Malaysia.[3]

Following these changes, the Government made several amendments to existing legislation, with the aim of improving the status and protection of women. For instance, in 2012, amendments to the Employment Act 1955 incorporated – for the first time – provisions to criminalise sexual harassment at the workplace. Prior to that, in 1999, the Ministry of Human Resource had already introduced a Code of Practice on the Prevention and Eradication of Sexual Harassment in the Workplace, but these were merely guidelines for employers on the meaning and forms of sexual harassment, and any disciplinary or remedial rules that employers ought to pursue. In short, the Code did not provide a basis for any legal action against the perpetrator. Another significant legal milestone came in the form of amendments to the Domestic Violence Act 1994, which came into force in 2012. Crucially, the amendment broadened the scope of 'domestic violence' to include mental, emotional, and psychological abuse.[4] It also introduced provisions to allow victims to seek an ex parte interim protection order from the court.[5] In addition, data from the International Labour Organization suggests that there was an exponential increase in the female labour force participation rate between 2010 and 2014 (averaging 46.9 per cent in that period).[6] Official government statistics show that in 2019, almost 25 per cent of legislators, senior officials and managers were women.[7]

Despite these positive developments, gender discrimination and inequality remain pressing issues that challenge the very idea and practice of constitutionalism in Malaysia. The Federal Constitution itself contains contradictions. Consider the issue of citizenship – despite the amendment to Article 8, under current laws and arrangements, Malaysian women who are married to foreign citizens are unable to automatically register their overseas-born children as Malaysians; by contrast, if a child is born overseas to a Malaysian father, the child would automatically be granted citizenship.[8] While a Malaysian mother

[2] Ninth Malaysia Plan, 32–33, available at www.epu.gov.my/sites/default/files/2021-05/Ninth%20Malaysia%20Plan%20Document.pdf.

[3] Government of Malaysia, 'Towards Achieving at least 30 Percent Participation of Women at Decision Making Levels in Malaysia' (United Nations Development Programme Project Document, November 2006), available at www.undp.org/content/dam/malaysia/docs/WomenE/GenderProDocs/Towards%20Achieving%20At%20Least%2030%20Per%20Cent%20Participation%20of%20Women%20at%20Decision%20Making%20Levels%20in%20Malaysia.pdf.

[4] See The Domestic Violence (Amendment) Act 2012, s 2(a)(iv).

[5] ibid s 12.

[6] International Labour Organization (ILO), 'Labor Force Participation Rate, Female (Modeled ILO Estimate) – Malaysia', available at data.worldbank.org/indicator/SL.TLF.CACT.FE.ZS?locations=MY.

[7] DOSM, 'Statistics on Women Empowerment in Selected Domains, Malaysia, 2019' (25 November 2019), available at www.dosm.gov.my/v1/index.php/index.php?r=column/cthemeByCat&cat=444&bul_id=U2UvVllQQlJsbzkwclQrdVlnMzJTdz09&menu_id=L0pheU43NWJwRWVSZklWdzQ4TlhUUT09.

[8] Federal Constitution of Malaysia 1957, Second Schedule, Pt II.

may apply for citizenship for her child, there is no guarantee that it will be granted. In one case, for instance, a Malaysian woman (married to an American spouse) whose child was born in the United States applied for citizenship, but after four years of waiting her application was rejected without reason.[9] As with many of the cases that are highlighted in this chapter, such discriminatory laws and structural barriers have grave implications for substantive gender equality – they not only affect the status of women in the country; discrimination also affects the rights, freedoms, and entitlements for women in personal and professional domains.

This chapter seeks to illustrate how – despite the ratification of CEDAW and various positive legal and policy initiatives – securing gender equality in Malaysia remains fraught with challenges, and it is therefore best described as a work-in-progress. Crucially, it will demonstrate the extent to which gender justice and discrimination may be shaped by local politics that are defined and informed by existing patriarchal and religious structures and culture. This chapter will proceed as follows. In section II, I provide a brief background to Malaysia's constitutional structure and relatively recent political developments in order to contextualise subsequent discussions about constitutional norms and jurisprudence on gender. Section III then discusses – in greater detail – aspects of the Malaysian constitutional history and constitution-making debates in the pre-independence era that inform, directly and indirectly the constitutional protection of gender equality. As we shall see, gender discrimination was only addressed explicitly in the Federal Constitution 44 years after independence, and gender issues did not figure prominently in the constitution-making debates. I also explain the relevant constitutional provisions that are important in understanding the parameters of gender rights and equality in Malaysia. This serves as a segue to section IV, where I discuss several cases that have defined Malaysia's evolving constitutional jurisprudence especially over the past decade, including a flagship constitutional development in an issue that lies at the intersection of family law, child conversion and religion. Given the salience of religion in the legal and political spheres, I will demonstrate the ways in which religious laws and imperatives also figure into these cases. All in all, these cases have contributed to the rich body of case laws implicating gender equality, but perhaps more importantly, they shape the broader constitutional and political battles that I explain in my concluding reflections.

II. BACKGROUND AND CONSTITUTIONAL STRUCTURES: RELIGION, CONSTITUTIONAL RIGHTS AND FEDERALISM

Malaysia is an ethnically, religiously and culturally diverse state. According to the latest data in 2020, the estimated population stood at 32.73 million,

[9] Personal conversation (September 2020).

of which 16.9 million are male and 15.84 million are female.[10] In terms of the ethnic composition, 69.6 per cent are *Bumiputra*,[11] 23.4 per cent are Chinese, and seven per cent are Indians, but there are 179 officially defined ethnic groups that include native tribes from the East Malaysia states of Sabah and Sarawak. Religion is also a politically salient social marker – Islam is the dominant religion (about 61 per cent of the population), followed by Buddhism (19 per cent) and Christianity (nine per cent) – and there are overlapping cleavages across territorial, linguistic and cultural lines. These national-level statistics largely reflect the religious demography in Peninsula and Sabah,[12] but the demography in Sarawak is significantly different. There, the Christians comprise about 44 per cent of the population, while Muslims make up 30 per cent of the population.

In many ways, this diverse social fabric has defined Malaysia's constitutional arrangements and structure. The system of government is derived from the Westminster model of parliamentary democracy, owing to over eight centuries of British colonial governance. In addition, as in Britain, Malaysia is a constitutional monarchy with the *Yang di-Pertuan Agong* (the King, who is a federal constitutional monarch) as a Head of State, whose formal duties – be they ceremonial or executive – are explicitly spelled out in the Constitution. It is also worth noting that there are state monarchs (Malay rulers or sultans) in nine states, and a hallmark of Malaysia's autochthonous constitution rests in the fact that the federal monarch position is rotated amongst the nine state monarchs through an internal election mechanism within the Malay Conference of Rulers.[13] Succession to the throne is patrilineal, and in line with centuries-held governing customs and traditions, the Sultan must be a Muslim and serves as the Head of Islam in his state. Even during the British colonial period, the British Residential System provided a British resident whose advice 'must be asked and acted upon' by the Sultan on all matters, but the Sultan retained control over matters pertaining to Islam and Malay customs.[14]

The sultanate and aspects of Islamic governance in the individual states are thus significant as far as the traditional identity of the polity is concerned. Islam has had a long presence in Malaya (ie, what is now West Malaysia or Peninsula Malaysia), dating back to the fourteenth century establishment of the Malacca

[10] DOSM (n 1).

[11] The term *Bumiputra* (literally translated as 'the sons of the soil') typically encompasses those from the Malay ethnic group (about 60% of the population), the *Orang Asal* (original inhabitants) and the native tribes from Sabah and Sarawak.

[12] Christianity is the next biggest religion in Sabah after Islam. Christians comprise 26% of the population in Sabah, while Buddhists comprise 6% of the population.

[13] The King reigns for a term of five years. The Malay Conference of Rulers is an institution comprising non-hereditary Malay rulers from nine states in the Federation of Malaysia.

[14] KYL Tan, 'The Creation of Greater Malaysia: Law, Politics, Ethnicity, and Religion' in A Harding and DAH Shah (eds), *Law and Society in Malaysia: Pluralism, Ethnicity and Religion* (Routledge, 2018) 3. See also A Harding, *Law, Government and the Constitution in Malaysia* (Kluwer Law International, 1996) 13.

sultanate. The Constitution recognises Islam as the 'religion of the Federation', but it also guarantees that other religions 'may be practiced in peace and harmony' (Article 3(1)). This provision is the product of a significant process of inter-ethnic bargaining during the pre-independence constitution-making exercise.[15] To be sure, despite the historical significance of Islam in Malaya, the constitutional drafters were deeply divided on establishing a state religion. There were demands from the Malay grassroots for a special constitutional position for Islam, but the non-Malays were concerned that such a provision would legitimise religious discrimination in the soon-to-be independent country. This was complicated by objections from the Malay sultans (who are the constitutional heads of Islam in their respective states), who feared that such a constitutional recognition of Islam would allow the Federal Government to control matters on Islam, thereby encroaching upon their centuries-held power over Islamic matters. In the end, it was the assurances from the then-ruling Government that paved the way for the inclusion of Article 3(1). The then-Prime Minister emphasised that the provision *would not* create a theocratic state, that Malaya would retain its secular character, and that the arrangement was to model the British constitutional scheme where, despite the establishment of the Anglican Church, religious freedom is nevertheless guaranteed.[16] To reflect this, Article 3(4) provides that the constitutional position of Islam does not 'derogate[] from other provisions in the Constitution'. This provision is crucial because it is clear that the establishment of Islam cannot be the basis for abolishing or restricting rights that are guaranteed by the Constitution.

Gender and constitutionalism in Malaysia must be considered alongside two other important facets of the constitutional structure: the federal-state division of power, particularly in matters implicating Islam, and the separation of the civil and *Syariah* jurisdictions, which was secured through a constitutional amendment in 1988. Under Malaysia's federalised arrangement in matters involving Islam, individual states in the Federation retain a degree of autonomy in legislating, regulating and administering Islamic law. This was the constitution-makers' solution to placate the Malay rulers' concerns about the constitutional recognition of Islam and the federal–state power dynamics relating to Islam.[17] Yet, the power of the states in this respect is not all-encompassing and unlimited. There are broad public and private dimensions to *Syariah*, but in the context of Malaysia's constitutional scheme, the states could only legislate on specific issues pertaining to Islamic law. Under the Constitution's Ninth Schedule, List II, these include personal and family laws of 'persons professing the religion of Islam', the constitution, organisation and procedure of *Syariah* courts, and Islamic charitable and religious trusts. State legislatures are also

[15] DAH Shah, *Constitutions, Religion, and Politics in Asia: Indonesia, Malaysia and Sri Lanka* (Cambridge University Press, 2017) 45–46.

[16] ibid 46.

[17] ibid 45–46.

entitled to create and punish 'offences against precepts of Islam'. However, there are explicit constitutional limitations on this power: laws punishing offences against the precepts of Islam apply only to Muslims and, in theory, state legislatures cannot legislate on matters that are exclusively within the federal jurisdiction.[18]

All this brings to the fore the role of the *Syariah* courts in Malaysia's constitutional order. Until the late 1980s, the state-level *Syariah* courts lacked a clear sphere of jurisdictional autonomy. Notably, they were subordinate to civil (secular) courts in the sense that the High Courts possessed overriding jurisdiction over the religious courts. As a result, the country was often confronted with the situation where civil courts and religious courts issued conflicting decisions. In fact, years later, the case of *Sukma Darmawan* highlighted the fact that the High Court 'quite regularly reviewed' the decisions of the *Syariah* court.[19] This problem of civil–*Syariah* conflict drove the constitutional amendment in 1988 that sought to clearly demarcate the jurisdictional boundaries between the civil and *Syariah* branches.[20] In addition, it was thought that addressing specific questions involving *Syariah* law required the expertise of those trained in Islamic jurisprudence.[21] Thus, the 1988 amendment introduced Article 121(1A), which stripped the civil courts of jurisdiction in matters that are exclusively within the *Syariah* jurisdiction. This amendment does not completely oust the civil court's supervisory powers over the *Syariah* courts (particularly in matters involving constitutional interpretation), nor does it elevate the *Syariah* courts to a status parallel to that of the civil courts.[22] This is because *Syariah* courts remain creatures of state legislation with limited jurisdiction, and therefore, subordinate to the civil courts that derive their authority from the Constitution.[23] On the other hand, there is the view that the amendment elevated the position of the *Syariah* courts, making them equal in status (and thus not subordinate) to the civil court.

[18] Federal Constitution of Malaysia, Arts 74 and 75. In other words, crimes that are considered to be 'against the precepts of Islam' but are nonetheless under the federal list of legislative power, such as murder, theft, robbery, rape and incest, are beyond state legislative power.

[19] For a comprehensive explanation of the rationale behind Art 121(1A), see LA Thio, 'Jurisdictional Imbroglio: Civil and Religious Courts, Turf Wars and Article 121(1A) of the Federal Constitution' in A Harding and HP Lee (eds), *Constitutional Landmarks in Malaysia: The First 50 Years 1957–2007* (Lexis, 2007) 202–03.

[20] A Ibrahim, 'The Amendment of Article 121 of the Federal Constitution: Its Effect on the Administration of Islamic Law' (1989) 2 *Malayan Law Journal* xvii.

[21] SS Faruqi, 'Freedom of Religion under the Constitution' *The Sun* (18 May 2006), available at www.sun2surf.com/article.cfm?id=14147.

[22] S Kanesalingam, 'Article 121(1A) – What Does it Really Mean?' *The Malaysian Bar* (11 December 2006), available at www.malaysianbar.org.my/members_opinions_and_comments/article_1211a_what_does_it_really_mean_.html; SS Faruqi, *Document of Destiny: The Constitution of the Federation of Malaysia* (Star Publications, 2008) 131.

[23] See *Indira Gandhi a/p Mutho v Pengarah Jabatan Agama Islam Perak & Ors and Other Appeals* [2018] 3 *Malayan Law Journal* 545 (Federal Court).

These competing positions are important because as we shall see below, they shape the trajectory of Malaysia's constitutional jurisprudence and discourse on fundamental rights, including issues implicating gender and equality. At a broader level, it is worth noting the often complex and uneasy relationship between constitutional recognition of Islam, *Syariah*'s limited jurisdictional autonomy, and the 'secular' issue of fundamental rights, including gender equality. More specifically, Malaysia is confronted with several competing, evolving norms: safeguarding religious harmony and public order in a divided society; protecting equality; and even upholding Islam as the state religion.

Due to the political salience of ethnicity and religion, and the growing religious conservatism and politicisation of religion since the 1980s (in part spurred by the Iranian revolution), there has been an increasing tendency for the outcomes of these conflicts to gravitate towards privileging the dominant religion and majoritarian religious sensitivities. For instance, the notion that state legislatures do not possess the authority to enact just *any* laws concerning Islam (ie, that their legislative power is limited to matters specified in List II of the Ninth Schedule of the Constitution) has been strongly contested.[24] In religious conversion cases (which implicate fundamental rights questions), civil courts have shown some reluctance to adjudicate conversions out of Islam as these are seen as matters under the authority of *Syariah* courts. In various state-level *Syariah* criminal enactments, same-sex relations and blasphemy are criminalised, even though the Penal Code – which, unlike *Syariah* law, applies to everyone regardless of their religious identity – contains provisions dealing with these offences. In the north-eastern states of Kelantan and Terengganu, the *Syariah* criminal codes cover theft, homicide and robbery, even though these crimes are under federal jurisdiction. It also used to be the case that the jurisdiction of *Syariah* courts to adjudicate a matter falling within List II must be explicitly conferred by a statute.[25] However, there has been an inclination towards a different approach – one that grants jurisdiction to the *Syariah* courts by *implication*, even in the absence of any explicit statute conferring jurisdiction on the *Syariah* courts.[26]

III. CONSTITUTIONAL FRAMING OF GENDER

Since the first elections administered before independence, women have always had a role to play in the political process. Aside from universal and equal suffrage,

[24] Faruqi (n 22) 134.

[25] *Dalip Kaur v Pegawai Polis Daerah, Balai Polis Daerah, Bukit Mertajam & Another* [1992] 1 *Malayan Law Journal* 1.

[26] *Md Hakim Lee v Majlis Agama Islam Wilayah Persekutuan, Kuala Lumpur* [1998] 1 *Malayan Law Journal* 681; *Soon Singh v Pertubuhan Kebajikan Islam Malaysia (PERKIM) Kedah* [1999] 1 *Malayan Law Journal* 489; and *Lina Joy v. Majlis Agama Islam Wilayah & Another* [2007] 4 *Malayan Law Journal* 585.

women were part of the political and election machinery in the political coalition led by the United Malays National Organisation (UMNO) party. Women were also fielded as candidates in pre-independence elections (in the 1955 federal legislative elections, one woman was elected) and the women's wing in UMNO (then known as *Kaum Ibu*) had been very vocal in campaigning for increased female representation.[27] However, when the Constitution was promulgated before independence in 1957, race, religion, descent and place of birth were the only identity markers specified for the purposes of the anti-discrimination provision. The constitution-making process was led by a five-man British-appointed commission (the Reid Commission), and it was very much a top-down exercise. Gender issues did not feature prominently in the constitution-making debates, as the most pressing social and political issues revolved around ethnic and religious cleavages. Indeed, race and religion have always been the most politically salient identity markers, with the potential to trigger violent conflict. In addition, the local political actors involved in the constitution-making process were deeply sceptical about the incorporation of the bill of rights in the Constitution. One concern was on how a bill of rights would affect the rights and interests of different ethnic groups in the community: the Malays, for example, were anxious to protect the special privileges and interests enjoyed during the British colonial period, which would contradict the right to equality sought by the non-Malays. Those special privileges included preferential promotion in the civil service, free education, and an 'inalienable right to the most fertile land in the state'.[28] Others, however, were worried that a poorly drafted bill of rights could hamper expediency in government policy- and decision-making. Nevertheless, a 'thin' bill of rights was eventually adopted (largely on the insistence of Sir Ivor Jennings, the chief architect of the constitution), and it was drafted in a way that provided the Government with a lot of latitude to restrict rights.

Therefore, although 'gender' is a welcome addition to the anti-discriminatory provision in Article 8(2), its subsequent operation and implementation may be understood within this seemingly 'deferential' framework and conception of constitutional rights guarantees. The clause provides that:

> [T]here shall be no discrimination against citizens on the ground only of religion, race, descent, place of birth or *gender* in any law or in the appointment to any office or employment under a public authority or in the administration of any law relating to the acquisition, holding or disposition of property or the establishing or carrying on of any trade, business, profession, vocation or employment.[29]

In addition, due to salience of religion (chiefly, Islam) in the social and political order and the operation of (religious) personal law, there are exceptions

[27] D Martin, 'Women's Vote in Malaysia' *New Mandala* (5 May 2013), available at www.newmandala.org/womens-vote-in-malaysia.

[28] COH Parkinson, *Bills of Rights and Decolonization: The Emergence of Domestic Human Rights Instruments in Britain's Overseas Territories* (Oxford University Press, 2007) 74.

[29] Federal Constitution of Malaysia 1957 (emphasis added), Art 8(2).

carved out in Article 8(5). Article 8(5) provides that the equality clause does not invalidate or prohibit 'any provision regulating personal law' (Article 8(5)(a)), and provisions or practices that restrict employment in connection with the affairs of any religion or religious institutions (Article 8(5)(b)). These exceptions reflect – to some extent – the scope of Malaysia's ratification of the CEDAW several years earlier.

The ratification of CEDAW in 1995 was a momentous occasion for Malaysia because it was one of the two international treaties that the country ratified for the first time.[30] However, in the context of the Southeast Asian region, at the time, Malaysia was one of the last five (of 11) remaining countries that had not ratified the Convention.[31] The exact reasons behind the ratification of these treaties are unclear – under Malaysia's Westminster model of government, such decisions are made internally within the Cabinet and they do not require parliamentary debate and approval. However, it is conceivable that the government responded to advocacy by women's rights organisations and the Human Rights Commission of Malaysia (SUHAKAM). In fact, these organisations, along with the Ministry of Women, Family and Community Development (established in 2001) later lobbied for the amendment to Article 8(2) of the Constitution.[32]

When the Government tabled the bill to amend the Constitution, the Minister for Legal Affairs explained that in light of the substantial contributions of women toward Malaysia's development, it was time the Constitution provided stronger recognition of equality between 'female citizens' and 'male citizens'.[33] This is a clear indication that Malaysia adopts a binary view of gender, which is rooted in traditional conceptions of sexual orientation. In addition, it was thought that, given Malaysia's ratification of CEDAW, the proposed constitutional amendment would come closest to 'clarifying and perfecting' the country's obligations under CEDAW.[34] This recognition of the role of women in nation-building, alongside discussions on 'gender budgeting' and 'gender consciousness',[35] stood in stark contrast to the pre-independence

[30] The CEDAW was ratified in August 1995, while the Convention on the Rights of the Child (CRC) was ratified several months earlier, on 17 February 1995.

[31] The other four countries are: Myanmar, Timor Leste, Brunei and Singapore.

[32] SUHAKAM, *SUHAKAM's Report on the Status of Women's Rights in Malaysia* (Human Rights Commission of Malaysia, 2010) 3.

[33] Parliamentary Debates, Tenth Parliament, Third Session, Second Meeting, 31 July 2001 (Datuk Seri Utama Dr Rais bin Yatim) 34–35.

[34] Parliamentary Debates, Tenth Parliament, Third Session, Second Meeting, 1 August 2001 (Datuk Seri Utama Dr Rais bin Yatim) 76.

[35] See, eg, Parliamentary Debates, Tenth Parliament, Third Session, Second Meeting, 1 August 2001, 52–53, 60, 90. Gender budgeting involves adopting a gender-conscious or gender-responsive budget, by taking into account the impact of various parts of the national budget and allocation of resources on women and men. See Ministry of Women, Family and Community Development, 'Gender Budgeting in Malaysia' (2005), available at my.undp.org/content/malaysia/en/home/library/womens_empowerment/GBMalaysia.html.

constitution-making debates in 1957, where issues regarding the rights and protection of women received virtually no attention.

Nonetheless, it is important to recognise that there are limitations to implementing and enforcing the commitment to CEDAW norms. There are several aspects to these limitations. The first is that as a dualist state, Malaysia has yet to enact a statute to enforce and incorporate the obligations under CEDAW into national law. This is unlike its commitment to the Convention on the Rights of the Child (CRC) as in 2001, the Government enacted the Child Act pursuant to its obligations under the CRC. Second, when Malaysia ratified CEDAW, the Government declared a number of reservations, including to Articles 9(2) and 16(1)(a), (c), (f) and (g), on the basis that these provisions contradicted the Federal Constitution and the operation of *Syariah* law. In addition, the ratification was subject to the understanding that CEDAW's provisions do not contradict the Federal Constitution and *Syariah* law in the country. In July 2010, the Government withdrew reservations to Article 5(a) on social and cultural patterns and prejudices relating to male and female conduct, Article 7(b) on participation in government and public offices, and Article 16(c) on rights and responsibilities during marriage and the dissolution of marriage.

These reservations were removed owing – in part – to SUHAKAM's persistent recommendations. In particular, SUHAKAM took the position that while Islam recognises the rights and roles of both men and women in familial relationships and views a man as the protector of his wife and children, these do not necessarily establish male superiority over female.[36] It also emphasised – in relation to the reservation on Article 7(b) – that the *Quran* does not exclude or prohibit women from taking on a leadership position. Following this, there has been some progress in a variety of public positions, including political representation. In 1999, women Members of Parliament comprised 10.36 per cent of the federal legislature. By contrast, following the elections in May 2018, there were 33 women MPs (14.9 per cent) and during the short-lived tenure of the *Pakatan Harapan* (PH) Government from May 2018 to February 2020 there were nine women in the Cabinet (out of a total of 55 ministers and deputy ministers).[37] This still fell short of the 30 per cent quota for female policymakers pledged in the PH Government's election manifesto. In the judiciary, the promotion of three women justices in 2019 meant that 50 per cent of the Federal Court (the highest court in the country) comprise women, and both the Chief Justice and the President of the Court of Appeal are women. There have been developments in the *Syariah* courts too. Organisations such as Sisters in Islam (SIS) have campaigned since 1999 for the appointment of female *Syariah* judges. In 2010,

[36] SUHAKAM (n 32) 9.

[37] WAW Ismail, 'Women in Politics: Reflections from Malaysia' in International IDEA (ed), *Perempuan Bukan Sekadar Jumlah* (International IDEA, 2002) 192; A Izharuddin, 'Securing the Electoral Success of Women in Malaysia Baharu' *New Mandala* (19 November 2019), available at www.newmandala.org/securing-the-electoral-success-of-women-in-malaysia-baharu.

the Government finally appointed – for the first time in the country's history – two female *Syariah* court judges in the Federal Territories in a bid to enhance justice in cases implicating women's rights and the family.[38] However, even then, the Government admitted that there were regulations and practices at state level that limit the kinds of cases that female judges could hear (primarily, divorce and marriage cases), and that it was working with state religious bodies to lift such restrictions.[39] This highlights another layer of consideration in thinking about constitutionalising gender equality in Malaysia: the federal–state politics in matter implicating religion (Islam).

Despite these developments, Malaysia has endured a thorny journey in implementing gender equality and strengthening women's development throughout the two decades after the ratification of CEDAW. In February 2018, the CEDAW Committee raised concerns, among others, about the effects of Malaysia's dual (ie, civil and *Syariah*) jurisdiction system on Muslim women's rights, the guardianship of children, and the discrimination against sexual and gender diverse people (SGDP).[40] These concerns were not unfounded, and indeed, a consideration of this civil–*Syariah* conundrum in the constitutional framework cannot be separated from any discussions on gender equality in Malaysia. For example, for many years, divorced women faced an uphill battle to secure custody of their children and, in other cases, non-Muslim women were unable to challenge the secret conversion of their underage children to Islam. In the second half of 2018, reports of child marriage – an issue that cuts across the ethnic and religious divide – and the enforcement of the *Syariah* Criminal Code against women alleged to have engaged in prostitution and homosexual activities in the state of Terengganu raised many eyebrows. While child marriage is technically illegal for non-Muslims who are governed by the Law Reform (Marriage and Divorce) Act 1976 (LRA 1976) (which stipulates that the minimum age for marriage is 18 years), statistics from 2005 to 2015 show that there were 5,215 reported cases of child marriage among non-Muslim girls.[41] For Muslims, however, marriage below the age of 18 is permissible with *Syariah* court approval. Statistics from the Malaysian Department of *Syariah* Judiciary revealed that there were 10,240 child marriage applications from 2005 to 2015.[42]

[38] L Gooch, 'Uncertain Role for Female Shariah Judges in Malaysia' *New York Times* (14 July 2010), available at www.nytimes.com/2010/07/15/world/asia/15iht-malay.html. There were subsequent appointments after 2010: in 2016, two female judges were appointed to the Selangor *Syariah* High Court, and in 2017, eight female judges were appointed to the *Syariah* lower court.

[39] Parliamentary Debates, Twelfth Parliament, Third Session, Third Meeting, 8 December 2010, 11–12.

[40] Committee on the Elimination of Discrimination against Women [hereinafter CEDAW Committee], 'Concluding observations on the combined third to fifth periodic reports of Malaysia' (14 March 2018) CEDAW/C/MYS/CO3-5.

[41] Statistics from the National Population and Family Development Board, as presented in NAM Awal and MAA Samuri, 'Child Marriage in Malaysia' (2018) Working Paper for UNICEF Malaysia, 20, available at www.unicef.org/malaysia/media/711/file/Child%20marriage%20in%20Malaysia.pdf.

[42] ibid 19.

These examples, and several others which I shall highlight below, have raised important questions about the rights of women and their constitutional status, and more importantly, in the Malaysian context, about how the state navigates the boundaries between civil law and religious (*Syariah*) law. Pursuant to the constitutional provisions explained above (especially Article 121(1A)), states across the Federation have enacted statutes on Islamic family law, which deal with questions on marriage, the dissolution of marriage, maintenance and custody for Muslims. Non-Muslims are governed by the LRA 1976, which was largely based on the English Matrimonial Causes Act 1973, but subsequently amended to afford stronger protections for women in matters regarding marriage and the family. When the Act came into force in March 1982, it abolished and criminalised polygamy.[43] In 1986, the Act was amended to prohibit polygamous marriages contracted outside of Malaysia.[44] The LRA 1976 also imposes a minimum age of 18 for marriage, although a female who has reached the age of 16 may marry if she had obtained authorisation from the Chief Minister.[45] In addition, the LRA 1976 affords equal rights for both men and women to enter into marriage and to seek dissolution of a marriage.[46] For instance, either party in a marriage may apply to the court to annul the marriage if it is void or voidable as per the terms of the statute.[47]

The situation is different for Muslims, who are bound by the Islamic family law enactments of the states in which they are domiciled. Given the federalised arrangement on matters implicating Islam, in theory, all 14 states in the Federation could enact very different laws regulating personal and family matters for Muslims. However, in practice, in light of the Federal Government's efforts to achieve uniformity for Islamic laws across the country, most states now follow the 'Federal model'. This refers to the Islamic Family Law (Federal Territories) Act 1984, which was prepared by the Attorney-General's Chambers and enacted by the Federal Parliament for the Federal Territories. It was part of the Federal Government's key initiatives in the 1980s to reform Islamic laws and institutions. Despite the emergent Muslim conservatism triggered and spurred by the Iranian revolution at that time, the Government sought to ensure that reform did not only entail reformulating the content of Islamic laws; it also meant efforts to modernise,[48] standardise and expand the corpus of laws applicable to Muslims. To be sure, the states that follow the Federal model did not

[43] Under s 7 of the Law Reform (Marriage and Divorce) Act 1976 [hereinafter LRA 1976], those who engage in polygamous marriages are liable to imprisonment of up to seven years.

[44] See Law Reform (Marriage and Divorce) (Amendment) Act 1986.

[45] LRA 1976, s 10.

[46] See 'Joint Report on Muslim Family Law and Muslim Women's Rights in Malaysia' (Musawah and Sisters in Islam, 69th CEDAW Session, Geneva, February 2018) 5 [hereinafter Joint Report].

[47] Conditions under which a marriage can be declared void are set out in s 69 of the LRA 1976, while circumstances that render the marriage voidable are provided in s 70.

[48] DL Horowitz, 'The Qur'an and the Common Law: Islamic Law Reform and the Theory of Legal Change' (1994) 42 *American Journal of Comparative Law* 233, 253.

adopt the principles and provisions of the statute in its entirety. State legislatures modified their enactments according to the recommendations of the state religious affairs departments, but these divergences are largely insignificant.[49] The competing model is one that was drafted in the conservative, 'strongly Shafi'i state of Kelantan'.[50] The states of Kelantan, Kedah and Malacca preferred the Kelantan model.[51] The Federal model is more progressive in the sense that it contains principles and rules that were borrowed from Muslim laws in countries such as India and Pakistan and from the less dominant schools of Sunni Islam (Malaysia widely follows the *Shafi'i* school of thought).[52] In fact, it was considered one of the most progressive Islamic family law statutes in the Muslim world.[53]

This divergence is important, because there are differences in the rights and interests of women in matters relating to marriage, polygamy and divorce. Consider, for example, the grounds for divorce. Both the Kelantan and the Federal models provide several forms of divorce, namely, *talaq* (pronouncement of divorce by men); *khul* (divorce by payment or redemption, through mutual consent); *taqliq* (divorce based on the husband's breach of a condition in the marriage contract); and *fasakh* (dissolution of marriage via judicial proceedings). The latter gives women the right to obtain an order for dissolution from the court if particular grounds for *fasakh* are fulfilled. However, in the original Kelantan model,[54] the grounds for *fasakh* are narrow compared to a wider range of grounds in the Federal model.[55] For instance, the 1984 Federal model entitles a woman to obtain a dissolution order on the ground that she is treated with cruelty (such as assault). After amendments in 2002, the provisions of the Kelantan enactment were brought much closer to the 1984 Federal model. In addition, the 1984 Federal model also required pronouncements of divorce by men (*talaq*) to be made before a judge, and stringent conditions were imposed for polygamy. For example, men intending to engage in polygamy are required to seek court approval and the permission of their existing wives. In addition, they must show, among other conditions, that the polygamous marriage was just *and* necessary, and it would not 'lower the standard of living' of any existing wife and dependents.[56]

It is worth noting that when the Federal model was tabled for debate in Parliament, there was no indication that the reforms were advanced as a matter of constitutional concern or urgency. In fact, they even preceded the Government's

[49] M Siraj, 'Women and the Law: Significant Developments in Malaysia' (1994) 28 *Law & Society Review* 561, 565.
[50] Horowitz (n 48) 271.
[51] Joint Report (n 46).
[52] Horowitz (n 48) 264.
[53] Joint Report (n 46) 6.
[54] This refers to the Islamic Family Law Enactment (Kelantan) 1983.
[55] Islamic Family Law (Federal Territories) Act 1984, s 52.
[56] ibid s 23.

ratification of CEDAW, and the minister who tabled the bill merely explained that the proposed reforms were necessary to streamline the provisions concerning Muslim family law.[57] Given the social and political dynamics at the time, where the Government faced strong pressures from Muslim revivalist movements to demonstrate a stronger commitment to Islamic principles, the motivations behind the reform could therefore be said to be political.[58] The irony is that those pressures created circumstances 'favourable for marriage law reforms', as the Government sought to ensure that the provisions on polygamy and divorce conformed to modernist views of the *Quranic* principles of justice.[59] However, these reforms were later scaled back by amendments in the 1990s and in the early 2000s, as conservative religious leaders opined that the then-existing provision did not reflect traditional *Syariah*.[60]

IV. EVOLVING CONSTITUTIONAL JURISPRUDENCE ON GENDER

The complex legal and constitutional framework that governs the protection of gender equality and gender justice in Malaysia has generated an interesting, though limited, body of constitutional jurisprudence implicating gender. Before delving into these cases in greater detail, it is pertinent to recognise that Malaysia's superior courts (ie, the High Court, the Court of Appeal and the Federal Court) possess judicial review powers, and strategic litigation has been an important means of enforcing and securing constitutional rights guarantees. It is also worth noting again that in practice, constitutional contests on fundamental rights in Malaysia often implicate broader considerations about the constitutional position of Islam, the federalised arrangement in administering Islam, and the civil–*Syariah* jurisdictional separation.

In resolving these tensions and competing claims, after the 1988 amendments in particular, the civil courts have demonstrated the tendency to avoid adjudicating issues that raise important constitutional rights questions when such issues are deemed to be overlapping with Islamic law questions. For instance, in *Lina Joy*, a woman who had converted to Christianity sought to remove the word 'Islam' from her national identity card. However, her application to the National Registry Department (NRD) was denied on the ground that there was no clear documentary evidence that she had renounced Islam. Put simply, she failed to show a certificate of apostasy from the *Syariah* court. When Lina Joy challenged the NRD's decision at the Federal Court, the court technically did not deny

[57] Parliamentary Debates, Sixth Parliament, Second Session, 24 April 1984 (Dato Shahrir bin Abdul Samad) 1403–04.

[58] Shah (n 15) 76, 87, 213.

[59] MH Kamali, 'Islamic Law in Malaysia: Issues and Developments' (1997) 4 *Yearbook of Islamic and Middle Eastern Law* 153, 153–54.

[60] ibid 154.

that Joy had no right to convert. Instead, the majority opinion provided that Lina Joy had to follow the right *procedures* to do so (ie, by presenting herself before the *Syariah* court to obtain the court's approval for the conversion), even though there was no *Syariah* legislation in the Federal Territories dealing with the question of conversion or granting the *Syariah* courts jurisdiction over conversion matters. In any case, by deciding the way it did, the court declined to rule that the constitutional protection of religious freedom commands the right to change one's religion; instead, it left the issue to be decided by the religious courts.[61] Notions of public order (and what it means to protect public order) have also figured into the Court's assessment of the boundaries of religious freedom. In the current case, there was a concern that allowing complete, unrestrained freedom to convert would cause 'chaos' in the Muslim community.[62] The Federal Court did not explain this further, but based on the submissions to the Court, one way to surmise this concern over 'chaos' is to understand it in terms of the prevailing anxieties about proselytisation of Muslims and the cohesion of the Muslim community. In any case, although *Lina Joy* did not involve the question of gender equality, these constitutional norms and practices surrounding the relative priority between fundamental rights and the constitutional position of Islam, as well as the civil–*Syariah* jurisdictional relationship, have continued to determine the contours of gender rights in Malaysia.

In explaining the development of Malaysia's constitutional jurisprudence on gender, I will pay special attention to several cases involving sexual and gender diverse people and the participation and representation of women, particularly in the employment market. These categories of cases are particularly significant as there have been important milestones in the protection of gender equality, despite earlier setbacks.

As I mentioned earlier, when the word 'gender' was included in the anti-discrimination clause in the Federal Constitution, it was conceived as embodying the traditional, binary idea of sexual identity and orientation (ie, male–female dichotomy and heterosexual relationships). However, there has been some progress in Malaysia's constitutional jurisprudence implicating sexually and gender-diverse people. In *Tan Pooi Yee*,[63] an individual who identified himself as a male was born as a female, and he had subsequently undergone gender

[61] Harding argues, in reference to the *Lina Joy* case, that where crucial fundamental rights questions are at stake, express statutory authorization is required. See A Harding, *The Constitution of Malaysia: A Contextual Analysis* (Hart Publishing, 2012) 243. See also the case of *Latifah bte Mat Zin v Rosmawati bte Sharibun & Another* [2007] 5 *Malayan Law Journal* 101, where Justice Abdul Hamid Mohamed, who delivered the Federal Court's judgment, argued that as courts (including the *Syariah* courts) are creatures of statutes (that is, state legislation in the case of *Syariah* courts), and therefore, *Syariah* courts should look to 'the relevant State laws' to determine whether they have jurisdiction over a particular matter (116–17).

[62] *Lina Joy v Majlis Agama Islam Wilayah & Another* [2007] 4 *Malayan Law Journal* 585, 612.

[63] *Tan Pooi Yee v Ketua Pengarah Jabatan Pendaftaran Negara* [2016] 12 *Malayan Law Journal* 370.

reassignment surgery. He applied to the National Registration Department (NRD) to change the gender particulars in his national identity card. The NRD, however, rejected his application on the technical ground that there was no legal authority or statutory procedure allowing any amendments to the identity card for individuals who had undergone gender reassignment surgery.[64] In addition, it was thought that the mere fact that a person had undergone gender reassignment surgery was not enough to effect a change in a person's gender particulars or gender identity.[65] For the NRD, the surgery 'did not affect the status of the plaintiff's gender at the time of birth' and the plaintiff should proffer medical evidence in the form of chromosomal, gonadal and genital tests.[66] The High Court rejected the NRD's narrow position, and determined instead that the plaintiff had shown sufficient medical evidence attesting to his gender. What is interesting is that while the plaintiff in this case did not raise a constitutional argument, the Court nevertheless opined that the protection of his right to life under Article 5(1) of the Constitution hinged on the plaintiff being accorded judicial recognition as a male.[67]

Another significant case involved three Muslim men who were arrested, detained and prosecuted by religious authorities in the state of Negeri Sembilan for cross-dressing. This was done pursuant to section 66 of the Syariah Criminal Enactment 1992 (*Negeri Sembilan*), which imposes criminal sanctions on males who dress and pose as women in public. The three men in this case were medically diagnosed with Gender Identity Disorder. The Court of Appeal declared section 66 was unconstitutional for infringing the constitutional guarantee of the right to life (in this case, the right to life was given a broad interpretation that includes the right to live with dignity and the right to livelihood)[68] and Article 8(2)'s anti-discrimination clause. In particular, with respect to the anti-discrimination clause, the court opined that discrimination on the basis of gender is rooted in the fact that section 66 only prohibits male Muslims from cross-dressing; there were no comparable provisions prohibiting or criminalizing females who dress or pose as males.[69]

[64] ibid 389.

[65] ibid 385. The Senior Federal Counsel acting for the NRD argued that 'the fact that a gender reassignment surgical procedure was conducted should not be and is not the criteria for such a declaration [for a change in the gender particulars on the ID card] as the aim of such surgical gender reassignment intervention is *just to make a person feel more comfortable with his or her own body*' (emphasis added).

[66] The NRD relied on the requirements laid down in the English cases of *Corbett v Corbett* and *Bellinger v Bellinger*.

[67] *Tan Pooi Yee v Ketua Pengarah Jabatan Pendaftaran Negara* (n 63) 396. A similar position was taken by the High Court in a similar case in 2005: *Re JG, JG v Pengarah Jabatan Pendaftaran Negara* [2006] 1 *Malayan Law Journal* 90.

[68] *Muhammad Juzaili Bin Mohd Khamis & Ors v State Government of Negeri Sembilan & Ors* [2014] *Malayan Law Journal* Unreported 1063, [35]–[43].

[69] ibid [50]–[51].

In the broader scheme of things, this judgment was a watershed moment in the history of Malaysian constitutional law, as it was the first time that a civil court had declared a provision of state *Syariah* law as unconstitutional. As the following section on custody battles will show (and as I have explained previously in reference to the *Lina Joy* case), civil courts have not been willing to question the constitutionality or legality of laws or actions that implicate Islam, fearing that they would 'trespass' into the *Syariah* jurisdiction. Unfortunately, the significance of the cross-dressing decision was short-lived as just under a year later, the Federal Court overturned the decision on technical (procedural) grounds.[70]

The Federal Court's approach in the cross-dressing case (*Juzaili*) reflects the long-standing avoidance or abrogation approach of civil courts when they are confronted with cases implicating religion (more specifically Islam). As I have explained in the preceding sections, this approach is underlined by the belief that the 1988 Amendment has taken away the jurisdiction of the civil courts in adjudicating any matter involving Islam, and it is adhered to even where crucial constitutional rights questions arise and where the outcomes have led to injustice, particularly against women.

In spite of this, given the constitutional and political contexts of the country, there is still something significant about an appellate court (Court of Appeal) demonstrating its willingness to declare a provision of a *Syariah* law as unconstitutional in *Juzaili*. The decision signals that religious laws or indeed, as we shall see, the exercise of powers by religious authorities are subject to the Federal Constitution. This does not just cover substantive constitutional rights guarantees, but also other key constitutional arrangements such as the federal–state division of powers, as well as the (intended) meaning and effect of the constitutional recognition of Islam as the religion of the Federation. Indeed, five years after the *Juzaili* case, an individual who was charged under the Syariah Criminal Offences (Selangor) Enactment 1995 for an attempt to commit sexual intercourse against the order of nature with other males (in short, an attempt to engage in homosexual intercourse), sought to challenge the validity of section 28 of the Selangor Enactment as against the Federal Constitution.[71] It is important to note, however, that he did so not on the basis that the law violated the Constitution's guarantee against gender discrimination. Instead, he argued that the Selangor State Legislative Assembly did not have the jurisdiction and power over such sexual offences, as this has already been regulated under the Penal Code and thus is within the purview of the federal legislature. In May 2020, the Federal Court granted leave to challenge the impugned provision in the Selangor

[70] According to the Federal Court, the three men should have challenged the constitutionality of s 66 through the procedure set out in Art 4 of the Constitution, which requires leave from the Federal Court and Federal Government.

[71] *Iki Putra bin Mubarak v Kerajaan Negeri Selangor* [2020] 4 *Malayan Law Journal* 213 (Federal Court).

Enactment. In February 2021, the Federal Court determined that section 28 was unconstitutional, as state legislatures do not have the power to regulate matters that are explicitly under the federal legislature's jurisdiction.

Another area in which the constitutional jurisprudence on gender has been rapidly evolving concerns the participation of women in the employment market and democracy. With regard to the former, a series of cases concerning pregnancy discrimination has brought to light the Malaysian courts' attitudes toward the country's obligations under CEDAW and the Constitution's promise of non-discrimination on the basis of gender. The landmark case in this respect was *Noorfadilla* – a case involving a woman whose contract as an untrained relief teacher was revoked when her employer (a local school) discovered that she was pregnant.[72] This was based on a policy of the government education office – that pregnant women could not be employed because of the long period of absence due to maternity leave (two months), the possibility that she may not be able to attend to her job due to her health during the pregnancy, and the practicality of replacing her with a new teacher when she gives birth.[73]

Noorfadilla challenged the decision of the education office on the ground that it amounted to gender discrimination under Article 8(2) of the Constitution. Thus the crux of the case hinged on the interpretation of 'gender discrimination' and 'equality' for the purposes of Article 8(2). In this regard, it is worth recalling that Malaysia has not enacted an implementing legislation for its obligations under CEDAW. Yet, in delivering its decision, the High Court acknowledged that the word 'gender' was included in Article 8(2) pursuant to Malaysia's CEDAW obligations,[74] which demonstrates the Government's intention to comply with its CEDAW obligations. And, in absence of implementing legislation, the Court declared that it had the 'duty' to take into account the Government's international obligations in interpreting the boundaries of the constitutional guarantees in Article 8(2).[75] Thus, referring to Article 1 of CEDAW on the definition of 'discrimination against women' and Article 11 on the obligation of state parties to take all appropriate measures to eliminate discrimination against women, the Court held that the education office's actions were a form of gender discrimination. In particular, pregnancy discrimination constituted gender discrimination because biologically, only women have the capacity to become pregnant.[76]

The declaration in *Noorfadilla* that an administrative action was unconstitutional vis-à-vis Article 8(2) was the first decision of its kind. The strategy of 'interpretive incorporation'[77] that the Court adopted allows unincorporated

[72] *Noorfadilla binti Ahmad Saikin v Chayed Basirun and Ors* [2012] 1 *Malayan Law Journal* 832.
[73] ibid 838.
[74] ibid 839.
[75] ibid 843.
[76] ibid 845.
[77] See JL Neo, 'Calibrating Interpretive Incorporation: Constitutional Interpretation and Pregnancy Discrimination under CEDAW' (2013) 35 *Human Rights Quarterly* 910.

international human rights treaties to find relevance in, and be enforced through, domestic adjudication.[78] Yet, as Neo argues, while this use of CEDAW as persuasive authority (ie, soft law) to supplement the meaning of Article 8(2) was useful in the context of Noorfadilla's case (ie, an action against a public authority), the absence of incorporating domestic legislation diminishes the force of CEDAW where discrimination in the private sector is involved.[79] To be sure, taking into consideration CEDAW's entire scheme, private individuals or organisations are not exempt from the principles in CEDAW. However, the lack of implementing domestic legislation to prohibit gender discrimination (in both the public and private sectors) has meant that there are no directly enforceable rights and interests for individuals, particularly as against private corporations.

This problem was reflected in a later pregnancy discrimination case in 2014. A woman, Rafizah Shima, had signed an employment agreement with an airline company (Air Asia) containing a clause that forbade her from getting pregnant during her four-year training programme.[80] The clause also explicitly provided that the agreement would be repudiated if she became pregnant during the programme. Rafizah did in fact become pregnant and informed Air Asia four months before the final year of her training programme was to end. When Air Asia terminated her employment, the company successfully filed a civil suit against her for breach of agreement. Rafizah then appealed at the High Court, arguing that the agreement discriminated against her as a married woman and violated Article 8 of the Constitution and CEDAW.

The question in this case, therefore, turned on whether Rafizah could rely on the Constitution and CEDAW to nullify the provision in the employment agreement that prohibited her from (and sanctioned her for) getting pregnant. The facts of the case and the question it raised were similar to *Beatrice Fernandez*, where a woman was also terminated from her employment with an airline company after she became pregnant.[81] The Court of Appeal in the *Air Asia* case followed the path of the Federal Court in *Beatrice Fernandez*, holding that Article 8 protection does not extend to private agreements and that treaties such as CEDAW have no effect domestically without express incorporation by an Act of Parliament.[82] Curiously, the Court concluded – after focusing mainly on a detailed assessment of the legal doctrines concerning the application of international law obligations in the domestic setting – that the employment agreement 'does not discriminate against the rights of women'.[83] Even if the

[78] ibid 916.

[79] ibid 925.

[80] *Air Asia v Rafizah Shima bt Mohamed Aris* [2014] 5 *Malayan Law Journal* 318.

[81] *Beatrice AT Fernandez v Sistem Penerbangan Malaysia & Anor* [2004] 4 *Malayan Law Journal* 466.

[82] *Air Asia v Rafizah Shima bt Mohamed Aris* (n 80) [49].

[83] ibid [55].

Court was correct in its assessment of the applicability and enforceability of treaty obligations in a dualist country like Malaysia, it reached the conclusion without considering (as the High Court did in *Noorfadilla*) the ways in which such agreements could be discriminatory and the fact that CEDAW does not make a public–private distinction. In particular, Article 2(e) of CEDAW obligates a state party to 'take all appropriate measures to eliminate discrimination against women by any person, organization or enterprise'. Fundamentally, this means that states are also responsible if they fail to take 'appropriate measures' against the discriminatory acts or omissions of non-state actors, including corporations.[84]

The *Air Asia* case illustrates that despite the constitutional provision against gender discrimination and Malaysia's commitment to CEDAW, there is still much to be done to advance gender equality and non-discrimination. Implicit in the Court's conclusion in *Air Asia* was that Rafizah knew what she was getting into by signing the employment contract, and therefore she is presumed to have consented to the terms, even if they were discriminatory. This raises the broader question about how existing practices and standards in the employment market may deter women's participation and thus perpetuate their under-representation in the labour force. The Women's Action Organisation reported that the labour force participation rate for women has remained consistently low for many years – in 2016, the rate stood at 54.3 per cent,[85] compared to 54.1 per cent and 54.7 per cent in 2015 and 2017, respectively.[86] There remains a clear wage gap between male and female employees, and there is no definitive Anti-Sexual Harassment legislation, aside from a *voluntary* Code of Practice on the Prevention and Eradication of Sexual Harassment in the Workplace and amendments made to employment legislation to include provisions on sexual harassment. Non-governmental organisations such as the Joint Action Group for Gender Equality (JAG) have campaigned for comprehensive sexual harassment legislation through meetings and consultations with various ministries, and in fact in 2001, it submitted a draft law to the Government. However, there has been no further action on the part of the Government for many years. Under the Government that took power following the political change in May 2018, there was some hope for improvement as the governing coalition campaigned for strengthening gender equality and laws against sexual harassment. There was clear political will in this respect, as an Anti-Sexual Harassment Bill was in the works and was initially planned for tabling in March 2019. However, this was

[84] The obligations of the state vis-à-vis non-state actors have been explained in detail in the CEDAW Committee's General Recommendation No 35.

[85] Women's Aid Organisation (WAO), *The Status of Women's Human Rights: 24 years of CEDAW in Malaysia* (Valley Printers, 2019) 47.

[86] See Department of Statistics of Malaysia, 'Labour Force Survey Report, Malaysia, 2017' (27 April 2018), available at www.dosm.gov.my/v1/index.php?r=column/cthemeByCat&cat=126&bul_id=aEdIelhlVTBtOHhjOUxqcXhyc2pCUT09&menu_id=U3VPMldoYUxzVzFaYmNkWXZteGduZz09.

halted by the sudden change of government in February 2020, and later it was passed in August 2022 by the new *Barisan Nasional* (BN)-led Government that took over in August 2021.

V. FLAGSHIP DEVELOPMENT(S)

In addition to the cases discussed above, one crucial development in the protection of women's rights has emerged in the area of family law. What I have in mind here are cases concerning inter-religious custody battles that have long plagued the legal and political arena. These cases are important because they sit at the intersection of fundamental rights and the demarcation of civil–*Syariah* jurisdictions in personal law matters. There is a distinctive and almost identical storyline to these cases, but it is the case of *Indira Gandhi*[87] that has propelled the issues of child conversion and inter-religious custody battles to the forefront of the Malaysian debates on constitutional politics. The three women at the centre of the *Subashini*,[88] *Deepa*,[89] and *Indira Gandhi* cases were previously married to their respective spouses under a civil marriage governed by the Law Reform (Marriage & Divorce) Act 1976. At some point in the marriages, their spouses decided to convert to Islam and unilaterally convert the children in the marriage without the knowledge of the wives.

For the purposes of this chapter, my focus is not on the issue of religious conversion but on how these cases trigger equally important battles on child custody and the rights of non-Muslim women in the face of powerful Islamic institutions. This is because when the marriage finally dissolved (whether 'officially' by court order or due to the husband leaving the non-Muslim spouse), the Muslim husbands applied for and was granted custody of the children at the *Syariah* courts. Custody was granted without the knowledge of the three women, and the proceedings were carried out despite the fact that the women could never challenge the custody before the *Syariah* courts because such courts have no jurisdiction over non-Muslims. Subashini, Indira Gandhi and Deepa were left with no other legal recourse but to go to the civil courts to obtain a custody order for their children. In all three cases, the High Court granted custody to the three women based on the provisions of the Law Reform (Marriage and Divorce) Act 1976 that govern non-Muslims' family law issues. Thus, parties were left with two conflicting decisions: one from the religious courts; and one from the civil (secular) courts.

Stories like these have been quite common in Malaysia, and they raise important constitutional questions about the rights of non-Muslim spouses

[87] *Pathmanathan Krishnan v Indira Gandhi Mutho and Other Appeals* [2016] 1 *Current Law Journal* 911.
[88] *Subashini a/p Rajasingham v Saravanan a/l Thangathoray* [2008] 2 *Malayan Law Journal* 147.
[89] *Viran Nagapan v Deepa Subramaniam and Other Appeals* [2016] 3 *Current Law Journal* 505.

and the civil–*Syariah* jurisdictional conflict. Can one parent convert a child or children without the consent and/or knowledge of the other parent? Do such conversions violate a non-consenting parent's right to equality? If such conversions are effected anyway, in what ways can non-consenting parents challenge them? These questions are magnified by the fact that typically, such cases involve women seeking remedy against the actions of their husbands. Typically, by the time the High Court grants custody to the mother, the children would have already been in the custody of their fathers. In some cases, such as in *Indira Gandhi*, the father had absconded with the children with no trace.

The mothers in *Subashini* and *Indira Gandhi* foregrounded their grievances as constitutional rights claims.[90] From Subashini and Indira's perspectives, the secret conversions of their children were invalid because, as mothers, they should have an equal say in crucial decisions relating to the upbringing of their children. They argued, therefore, that a minor's conversion required the consent of *both* parents, pursuant to Article 12(3)–(4) of the Constitution, which prohibits requiring a person to receive religious instruction or to participate in religious ceremony other than his or her own and provides that a minor's parent or guardian (in singular) shall decide his or her religion. They also asserted that these provisions must be read together with Article 8's equal protection and non-discrimination clause. This is important because conversion of the child would deprive the non-converting parent's guardianship rights, as well as the parent's ability to challenge the child's conversion and to be heard in custody matters in the *Syariah* court. In addition, the Eleventh Schedule of the Constitution stipulates that 'words in the singular include the plural'. For the husbands, however, the consent of one parent is sufficient to convert a child to a different religion, and the wives had no right, after the fact, to challenge the conversion.

The Federal Court in *Subashini* took a very literal approach to the question of parental consent, deciding that the term 'parent' is used in the singular and that Article 8 is *not violated* where a child is converted – without the knowledge or permission of the non-converting (ie, non-Muslim) parent – to Islam.[91] Accordingly, this case laid down the rule that the conversion of a child by a single parent is valid and not unconstitutional. The upshot is that in Malaysia exists a situation where either parent could potentially convert his or her children at will without informing the other spouse. Recognising, perhaps, that this is unsatisfactory given the prevailing societal divisions on religion, the minority opinion in *Subashini* attempted to soften the impact of the majority decision by arguing that the other parent may object to or prevent his or her child from being converted.[92] There are two problems with this suggestion, particularly in cases

[90] In *Deepa*, the non-Muslim mother did not raise any constitutional rights question before the courts.

[91] *Subashini a/p Rajasingham v Saravanan a/l Thangathoray* (n 88) 172.

[92] ibid 225.

of conversion to Islam. The first is that this 'solution' was suggested according to the specific circumstances of Subashini's case, that is, where the child in question (Subashini's youngest son) had *not* yet been converted to Islam. Subashini's older son had already been converted, but she was seeking an injunction from the court to prevent the conversion of her youngest son in the event that her husband was planning to do so. The majority judgment dismissed her appeal. In any case, the next question is this: if the non-consenting spouse decides to challenge the conversion of a child who had already been validly converted according to the *Syariah* system, how would he or she do so? Thus the second problem, which arises from the realities of the *Syariah* jurisprudence, is that if the child is converted to Islam, he or she is under the jurisdiction of the *Syariah* courts but a non-Muslim parent cannot challenge the conversion in the *Syariah* courts. The non-Muslim parent would also then immediately lose custodial rights over his or her children because Muslim children would be placed under the custody of the Muslim parent.

These problems and concerns, in fact, materialised in *Indira Gandhi*. Upon learning that her children had been converted to Islam and that the *Syariah* Court had granted custody to her husband, Indira sought to invalidate the conversion. By the time Indira commenced the proceedings, only two of her three children remained under her custody. The third, Indira's youngest child, was nine months old when taken away by her ex-husband. The High Court was more sympathetic with Indira. Although the judge conceded that he was bound by the Federal Court's judgment in *Subashini* regarding the constitutionality of the children's conversion vis-à-vis Articles 12 and 8, he – at some length – explained the ways in which unilateral conversion violated Article 8's equal protection guarantee and highlighted the inequalities that arise because the non-Muslim parent could not contest the validity of the conversion in the *Syariah* court.[93] The judge ultimately decided that the unilateral conversion violated the Constitution's religious freedom guarantee. He went further by referring to Article 3's provision on Islam and stressed that the establishment of Islam as the state religion would not affect the rights of non-Muslims. The High Court judge also considered the principles in the CRC and CEDAW to be 'highly persuasive in interpreting the fundamental liberties guarantees in the Constitution.[94] In particular, citing Article 8(1)–(2) of the CRC – provisions that concern the preservation and deprivation of the child's identity – the Court posited that unilateral conversions 'would fundamentally negate the requirements of the CRC'.[95] With regard to CEDAW, as in *Noorfadila*, the High Court took the position that the ratification of CEDAW meant that Malaysia is now legally obliged to give effect to the rights contained

[93] *Indira Gandhi a/p Mutho v Pengarah Jabatan Agama Islam Perak & Ors* [2013] *Malayan Law Journal* 552, 576–78.

[94] ibid 587.

[95] ibid 588.

in the convention.[96] Hence, in determining whether the consent of one or both parents is required for the religious conversion of a minor, the Court argued that an interpretation consistent with international principles (ie, equal rights of the mother and father in guardianship matters) would be adopted.[97] Upon appeal, however, the Court of Appeal overruled the High Court's decision. The majority judgment ruled that the conversion was lawful and decided just as the Federal Court did in *Subashini*: that the consent of a single parent is enough to convert a child to another religion.

An analysis of these two cases alone is enough to demonstrate the deeply divided opinions and conceptions on matters implicating religion and gender rights, not just within the society but also within the judiciary. The appellants' (one of whom was the Perak Islamic Religious Affairs Department) memorandum of appeal suggested that they did not believe the challenge against the children's conversion was a constitutional question nor a matter driven by a sense of injustice to the mother whose children were converted without her knowledge or consent.[98] Rather, they saw it as a question of process and status determination – one that hinged on the *Syariah* Court's exercise of power. The fact that the non-Muslim parent is legally disadvantaged in such situations was ignored. It is also telling that the appellants argued that the High Court judge's reasoning based on international human rights law was problematic for Muslims in Malaysia.[99] All this appears to suggest that in cases involving Muslims and Islam, human rights norms could not apply and that because Islam is given a special position in the Constitution, the interests of Islam and Muslims must trump the interests of others.

These cases have exposed a grave lacuna in the Malaysian legal system that not only affects dispute resolution in divorce and custody matters, but also the protection of gender equality in general. Consider the case of *Shamala* – another conversion-and-custody battle between the *Syariah* and civil jurisdictions. In *Shamala* the High Court actually acknowledged that the Hindu mother could not challenge her children's conversion in the *Syariah* court, which also meant that she could not challenge the custody awarded by the *Syariah* court. Its solution was that Shamala should seek 'assistance' from the Islamic Council of the Federal Territories.[100] Whether this solution is well-thought-out is dubious, especially since even the *Syariah* authorities have been criticised for their inefficiency in dealing with cases concerning the renunciation of Islam.[101] In addition, if the solution lies in seeking extra-legal 'assistance' from a religious

[96] ibid 591.

[97] ibid 592.

[98] *Pathmanathan Krishnan v Indira Gandhi Mutho and Other Appeals* (n 87) 944.

[99] ibid.

[100] *Shamala Sathiyaseelan v Dr Jeyaganesh C Mogarajah & Anor* (2004) 2 *Malayan Law Journal* 648, 658.

[101] Faruqi (n 22) 134.

body whose advisory role on matters implicating Islamic law and persons professing the religion of Islam, then this speaks volumes of the legal system's inability to provide relief in cases where a non-Muslim's rights and interests are at stake.

Leaving these problems aside, in the past three years, there has been positive progress from the Federal Court. The Federal Court has displayed greater willingness to guard their jurisdiction in divorce and custody cases arising from the breakdown of a civil marriage where one spouse has converted to Islam (as opposed to religious conversion cases). In *Deepa*, the Federal Court affirmed that the *Syariah* courts do not possess jurisdiction over a case if one party is a non-Muslim, even if the subject matter of the case is within its jurisdiction and that the civil courts would continue to have exclusive jurisdiction over divorce and custody matters of a civil marriage, despite the conversion of one spouse.[102] With regard to conflicting orders, the *Deepa* decision also addressed this, as the case involved two contradictory custody orders from the *Syariah* and civil courts. Although technically the *Syariah* court had no jurisdiction to make the custody order (and this was indeed recognised by the Federal Court), the Federal Court nevertheless took the view that the *Syariah* order was a valid order 'until it is set aside'.[103] From a practical perspective, the Federal Court's approach is unhelpful for law enforcement officers and contesting parties who have had to face two conflicting orders.[104] More worryingly, by affirming the validity of the *Syariah* court's custodial order in favour of the husband (which preceded the civil court's custodial order in favour of the mother) and by ruling that a civil court cannot make a recovery order to execute a civil court's judgment while a conflicting *Syariah* judgment remains in force, the Federal Court appears to have implicitly encouraged unscrupulous parties to abuse the *Syariah* system by rushing to a *Syariah* court to obtain a favourable judgment before the civil courts could hear the application for custody.

The evolution in Malaysia's constitutional jurisprudence has continued with the recent Federal Court decision in *Indira Gandhi*.[105] Although the decision did not specifically address gender equality or the constitutional protection of the right to non-discrimination (Article 8), it nevertheless bore implications on a mother's custody rights over her children and her quest for an equal say in crucial decisions relating to the upbringing of her children. Two aspects of the decision are relevant in light of the foregoing discussions on gender equality. First, the Federal Court held that the Constitution mandates that the conversion

[102] *Viran Nagapan v. Deepa Subramaniam and Other Appeals* (n 89) 506.

[103] ibid 508.

[104] In fact, the Court recognised that both the civil and *Syariah* orders were equally valid and would bind law enforcement officers.

[105] *Indira Gandhi a/p Mutho v Pengarah Jabatan Agama Islam Perak* [2018] 1 *Malayan Law Journal* 545 (Federal Court).

of minors requires the consent of *both* parents.[106] This reverses the long-held position that the word 'parent' in Article 12(4) of the Federal Constitution is to be construed in the singular – a position that has proven to be problematic as it neglects the right of the other parent (who typically, in cases of unilateral conversion of minors, tends to be the mother) to determine the child's religion.[107] Second, on the protracted and thorny battle about the scope of the civil courts' judicial power, the Federal Court opined that notwithstanding the religious implications of the case, it remains empowered to review the legality and constitutionality of a public authority's administrative action. In this case, the religious authority's decision to issue the Certificates of Conversion for Indira's children.[108] This, therefore, provides a greater degree of certainty for non-Muslim parents: they could now be sure that they could challenge the legality of their children's conversion before the civil courts, instead of being told that only *Syariah* courts have jurisdiction to adjudicate such matters.

Despite significant progress, the civil–*Syariah* jurisdictional battle is far from over, with continuing implications for gender justice and fundamental rights. Consider, as another example, cases of harassment and persecution of women's rights NGOs by religious authorities. The specific case I have in mind here is Sisters in Islam (SIS), a civil society organisation set up to promote the fundamental rights of women (Muslim and non-Muslim alike). SIS's work has strengthened women's participation in the democratic discourse by empowering women and challenging policies and practices in Muslim Family Law including issues such as child marriage and polygamy, religious conversion, violence against women, moral policing and the female dress codes. Aside from advocacy, it also provides legal advice and support for women in family law matters. Due to its progressive interpretation of Islamic principles underlined by the Quran and its commitment to universal human rights norms, SIS has consistently been the subject of harassment by religious authorities. In 2014, the Religious Council of Selangor issued a *fatwa* (religious edict or legal opinion) declaring SIS as a deviant organisation for advancing 'liberalism and pluralism'. The motive is clear: to silence and suppress SIS's influence and activities, which have challenged the state's more conservative and dogmatic approach to Islam. SIS contested the *fatwa* on the grounds that it contradicted various fundamental guarantees of the Constitution, namely the freedom of expression and equality. However, these grounds were not considered by the High Court, which decided instead that it had no jurisdiction to rule on such matters because contests on

[106] ibid 603. The Court held that conversion is 'a momentous decision affecting the life of a child' and under such circumstances, it is 'undoubtedly in the best interests of the child that the consent of both parents must be sought'.

[107] See, eg, *Subashini a/p Rajasingam v Saravanan a/l Thangathoray* (n 88) (Federal Court); *Pathmanathan Krishnan v Indira Gandhi Mutho and Other Appeals* (n 87) (Court of Appeal).

[108] *Indira Gandhi a/p Mutho v Pengarah Jabatan Agama Islam Perak* (n 105) 588.

the substance and validity of a *fatwa* (which, according to the Religious Council, amounts to 'Islamic law') remain under the jurisdiction of the *Syariah* courts.[109] This decision therefore brings us back to the problematic situation – which was thought to have been resolved by the Federal Court in *Indira Gandhi* in 2018 – where civil courts would decline jurisdiction over issues that implicate Islam, even if fundamental constitutional rights and constitutional interpretation questions arise.

VI. CONCLUSION

After 18 years since the inclusion of the word 'gender' in the Constitution's anti-discrimination clause, Malaysia's constitutional discourse and jurisprudence on gender equality can be best described as a work-in-progress. As this chapter has illustrated, despite the constitutional amendment and commitment to CEDAW, further legal reforms – such as the enactment of an implementing statute for CEDAW or an anti-sexual harassment statute – have been slow. In 2016, there were talks of drafting a law to promote gender equality, and this was echoed by the Government elected into office in May 2018, but there has been no further development since then. Where concrete progress has been made, it has been by way of amending existing legislation to provide stronger protection for women. For instance, in 2011, the Government amended the Domestic Violence Act 1994 to broaden the definition of domestic violence beyond physical violence, and in 2012 it amended the Employment Act 1955 to prohibit sexual harassment in the workplace. In many of these developments, the role of civil society in advocating and lobbying for reforms has been significant.

One way to understand this piecemeal development is by considering the time-consuming and rigorous nature of researching, discussing, drafting and enacting new laws. In addition, gender issues – though vigorously championed by several lawmakers – have probably not been seen as legislative priorities, compared to bread-and-butter issues and other issues such as national security or inter-ethnic relations. It has been far easier and more common for governments – both old and new – to announce specific policies to advance gender equality, such as the National Action Plan for the Advancement of Women (formulated in 1997), the gender-sensitive budget project (launched in 2003), the 30 per cent target for women as members of board of directors in government-linked companies (announced in 2018), and most recently, in 2019, the development of a gender

[109] See *SIS Forum (Malaysia) & Ors v Jawatankuasa Fatwa Negeri Selangor & Ors* [2016] 1 LNS 1364. This case has gone back and forth between the High Court, Court of Appeal and Federal Court. In September 2018, the Federal Court remitted the case back to the High Court for examination of issues of merit and jurisdiction. In August 2019, the High Court took the same position as the 2016 decision – that civil courts have no jurisdiction over matters involving Islam (such as the issuance of a *fatwa*) and that such matters should be adjudicated by the *Syariah* courts.

mainstreaming framework for government sectors. However, although these policies are easier to craft than drafting and enacting legislation, their implementation has been inconsistent and inefficient.

At the same time, as we have seen, the constitutional amendment and CEDAW obligations have opened avenues for challenging decisions of public authorities that directly or indirectly affect gender rights. In particular, cases such as *Noorfadilla* (High Court), *Juzaili* (Court of Appeal) and *Indira Gandhi* (Federal Court) illustrate the potential that constitutional review affords in improving gender equality. Yet, there are two striking challenges. First, it appears that courts are still grappling with defining 'gender discrimination' and its parameters and scope of application. Although the interpretive approach in *Noorfadilla* is welcomed, it remains a High Court decision susceptible to overruling by higher courts. The Court of Appeal in *Air Asia* was adamant that CEDAW lacked legal effect until an implementing statute is passed by Parliament, but it did not examine in any detail the contours of gender discrimination in private sector employment.

The second challenge is rooted in other provisions of the Malaysian Constitution, more specifically, the demarcation of jurisdiction between the civil and *Syariah* branches in personal law matters. In addition, Article 8(5) provides that the guarantees in Article 8 do not prohibit any constitutional provision regulating personal law. This of course refers to the Ninth Schedule, List II, which specifies the areas in which Islamic law (as enacted by state legislatures) may govern the life of Muslims. However, due to the perception that any matters on Islam are under the exclusive purview of the states (and state religious authorities such as the *Syariah* courts), efforts to scrutinise and reform personal and family laws so that they do not discriminate against women have proven to be difficult. The fact that a constitutional supremacy scheme requires that state (religious) laws conform to constitutional limits (including fundamental rights guarantees) has often been ignored or dismissed on the ground that Islam is a 'state matter'. This is complicated by identity politics, and the growing tendency to amend Islamic personal and family laws in ways that reflect the more conservative varieties of Islamic interpretation and practice.

In a society that has been conditioned and defined by patriarchy, public sensitivity and awareness on gender issues remain wanting. Therefore, moving forward, the role of women's rights groups in advocacy, grassroots education, legal aid and government lobbying will be important in improving gender equality in Malaysia.

7

Gender Equality in Singapore: Whither the Constitution?

DARYL WJ YANG AND JACLYN L NEO

I. INTRODUCTION

ARTICLE 12(1) OF the Constitution of the Republic of Singapore (the 'Constitution') guarantees that 'All persons are equal before the law and entitled to the equal protection of the law.' Article 12(2) explicitly identifies religion, race, descent and place of birth as prohibited grounds of discrimination. Gender, however, is not protected under the Constitution. In fact, until 2004, Article 122 discriminated against Singaporean women by granting citizenship to children born overseas only through patrilineal descent. This clearly discriminatory Article required the Government to enter a reservation to Article 9(2) of the Convention on the Elimination of All Forms of Discrimination Against Women (CEDAW),[1] which requires states to grant women equal rights with respect to the nationality of their children. In its initial report to the CEDAW Committee, the Singapore Government defended the discriminatory provision as necessary to ensure that the country's immigration policy 'remains in line with our Asian tradition where husbands are the heads of households'.[2]

In 2004, the Constitution was amended to give Singaporean women equal right to pass down citizenship to their foreign-born children and resulted largely from the efforts of the Association of Women for Action and Research (AWARE), the main organisation campaigning for gender equality in Singapore. Specifically, AWARE successfully lobbied the Government-constituted Remaking Singapore Committee (RSC), an ad hoc committee set up by the Government to receive feedback and look into reshaping the political, social and cultural norms

[1] Convention on the Elimination of All Forms of Discrimination Against Women, New York, 18 December 1979, in force 3 September 1981, 1249 UNTS 13; (1980) 19 ILM 33.

[2] UNCHR, 'Singapore's Initial Report to the UN Committee for the Convention on the Elimination of All Forms of Discrimination Against Women' (1 December 1999) CEDAW/C/SGP/1, para 2.3. [hereinafter Singapore's Initial CEDAW Periodic Report].

of Singapore, to include a proposal for change in their recommendations.[3] The Government's move to reform was driven by both intrinsic and instrumental aims. While the amendment vindicates the principle of gender equality, it also served to counter population and economic concerns arising from dwindling birth rates. As Singaporean women 'progressed in education and earning power' and became 'more mobile', the amendment was seen as necessary to ensure that they and their children are able to have 'a sense of belonging in the country'.[4] As the then Deputy Prime Minister put it, 'we are doing it for the right reason but there is a purpose'.[5]

This process of change highlights two critical features by which gender equality reform takes root in Singapore. The first is the intertwining of gender equality with economic pragmatism and the second is the preference to stimulate change through advocacy, cooperation and consultation, rather than through constitutional litigation. On the first feature, a consistent thread in political discourse has been the need to support and encourage female labour. Gender equality is recognised as important not only for its inherent value but also because it serves the country's economic interests. The People's Action Party (PAP), which won the 1959 General Election by a landslide (and every other general election in Singapore since), included gender equality reform in its 1959 election manifesto:

> Women who form nearly half of our population have an important part to play in our national construction. In the first instance in order to emancipate them from the binds of feudalism and conservatism a monogamous marriage law will be passed … We shall foster the principle, if necessary by legislation, that there shall be equality of women with men in all spheres and we shall encourage them to come forward to play a leading role in politics, administration, business and industry, education and in other spheres.[6]

This focus on equality of women may have helped the PAP gain female voters.[7] Among the PAP's achievements was the delivery of its promise of legal reform, with the enactment of the Women's Charter[8] shortly after the elections in 1961.

[3] PM Chuang and K Lim, 'Push for Rights of S'pore Women's Foreign-Born' *The Business Times* (12 June 2003).

[4] ibid.

[5] 'Singapore Parliamentary Debates, Official Report' (19 April 2004) vol 77 at col 280 'Constitution of the Republic of Singapore (Amendment) Bill' (Lee Hsien Loong, Deputy Prime Minister); see also EKB Tan, 'A Union of Gender Equality and Pragmatic Patriarchy: International Marriages and Citizenship Laws in Singapore' (2008) 12 *Citizenship Studies* 73.

[6] People's Action Party (Singapore), *The Tasks Ahead: PAP's Five-Year Plan, 1959–1964: Part 1* (Petir, 1959) 7–8 and 11; see also WK Leong, 'Fifty Years and More of the Women's Charter of Singapore' (2008) *Singapore Journal of Legal Studies* 1.

[7] N Tan, 'Why Are Gender Reforms Adopted in Singapore? Party Pragmatism and Electoral Incentives' (2016) 89 *Pacific Affairs* 369, 376 citing KY Lee, *The Singapore Story: Memoirs of Lee Kuan Yew* (Marshall Cavendish, 2012) 325. See also PGL Chew, 'No Fire in the Belly: Women's Political Role in Singapore' in W Lundström-Burghoorn, C Milwertz and K Iwanaga (eds), *Gender Politics in Asia: Women Manoeuvring Within Dominant Gender Orders* (NIAS Press, 2008) 191.

[8] Cap 353 (Rev Ed 2009).

As observed in Parliament, the Charter 'marks a complete break from the past' and 'is a big step forward.'[9]

The second feature of gender equality reform in Singapore is the preference for a non-confrontational, constructive and cooperative approach. Leading up to the 2004 constitutional amendment on citizenship by descent, AWARE had pointed out in its submissions to the RSC that the patrilinear idea of citizenship and descent 'discriminates against Singaporean women [and] may well have the effect of keeping Singapore women with foreign husbands and children away from Singapore'.[10] As the leading advocacy group for gender equality in Singapore, AWARE's strategy is instructive and indicative of the parameters for civil society engagement. Lyons points out that AWARE's members were consciously aware that their continued existence was conditional on their 'acceptance of the government's own ground rules of "consensus" ahead of "confrontation"'.[11] Other women's advocacy groups, like the Singapore Council of Women (now defunct) and the Singapore Muslim Women's Association (*Persatuan Pemudi Islam Singapura*), also adopt mainly behind-the-scenes engagement with government leaders and agencies that foster relationships of trust and collaboration with the state.[12] Constitutional litigation is generally avoided as it amounts to a public confrontation with the Government.[13]

Accordingly, while gender equality is perhaps the most active focal point for Singapore's limited civil society, much of this advocacy work occurs on a sub-constitutional level. Most recently, the Government released the White Paper on Singapore Women's Development (the 'White Paper') after completing a year-long, nationwide engagement on women's development in 2021 which was declared the Year of Celebrating SG Women.[14] The White Paper recommended a slew of measures, including a new legislation against workplace discrimination, greater support for caregivers who are predominantly women, and increased penalties for sexual offences.

However, beyond the 2004 amendment to Article 122, there has yet to be a major push for a constitutional struggle for gender equality. The reason for this is partly historical. Women in Singapore did not have to demand the right to vote but were granted suffrage alongside men when Singapore became

[9] State of Singapore, 'Legislative Assembly Debates, Official Report' (6 April 1960) vol 12, No 1 at col 480; see also Leong (n 6) 5.

[10] AWARE, 'Remaking Singapore: Views of Half the Nation' (2001) 2, available at http://www.aware.org.sg/wp-content/uploads/Remaking_Singapore.pdf.

[11] LT Lyons, 'The Limits of Feminist Political Intervention in Singapore' (2000) 30 *Journal of Contemporary Asia* 67, 71.

[12] E Shaddick, LS Goh and I Oh, 'Against a Teleological Reading of the Advancement of Women's Rights in Singapore' in J Song (ed), *A History of Human Rights Society in Singapore* (Taylor & Francis Group, 2017) 134–35.

[13] C Lim, 'Keep Calm and Play the Long Game' in C Singam and M Thomas (eds), *The Art of Advocacy in Singapore* (Ethos Books, 2017) 314.

[14] Reach Singapore, 'White Paper on Singapore's Women's Development' (March 2022), available at https://www.reach.gov.sg/Participate/conversations-on-singapore-womens-development.

self-governing and then independent.[15] Women were also not 'written into'[16] the Constitution but were presumably considered to enjoy fundamental rights as citizens. Compared to religious, ethnic and linguistic divisions, gender was not seen as a particularly pressing issue for constitutional consideration.[17] The Constitutional Commission convened shortly after Singapore's independence in 1965 was tasked to focus on safeguarding the rights and interests of racial, linguistic and religious minorities in the Constitution. Gender was not raised as a constitutional issue then. Today, despite AWARE's lobbying for the inclusion of gender as an explicitly prohibited basis for discrimination in Article 12(2) of the Constitution, this remains a largely marginal issue that receives scant public attention. These developments are consistent with Singapore's nascent constitutional litigation culture and the generally low levels of constitutional consciousness among the Singapore public.[18] Other limitations such as narrow standing requirements in applying for judicial review,[19] judicial preference for textualist or limited purposive interpretation of constitutional provisions,[20] as well as an extremely modest philosophy on the judicial role,[21] have generally discouraged an activist constitutional culture of litigation. In addition, there is no specific definition of discrimination against women in Singapore's constitutional and legislative framework; consequently, lesbian, bisexual and transgender women, intersex persons, women migrant domestic workers, and foreign wives remain susceptible to intersecting forms of discrimination.[22] So far, there have only been two (unsuccessful) attempts to employ the equality clause in the Constitution to vindicate gender equality. Both concerned the right of men to equality, rather than women, and were initiated by one particular human rights lawyer independent of existing grassroots advocacy efforts.[23]

[15] 'Politics' *Women's Action*, available at www.womensaction.sg/article/politics; 'Wooing Women Voters' *Singapore Women's Hall of Fame*, available at www.swhf.sg/tlow-i-am-woman-hear-me-roar.

[16] R Rubio-Marín and WC Chang, 'Sites of Constitutional Struggle for Women's Equality' in M Tushnet, T Fleiner and C Saunders (eds), *Routledge Handbook of Constitutional Law* (Routledge, 2013) 301.

[17] Williams made this observation about constitutional structure generally. See SH Williams, 'Introduction: Comparative Constitutional Law, Gender Equality, and Constitutional Design' in SH Williams (ed), *Constituting Equality: Gender Equality and Comparative Constitutional Law* (Cambridge University Press, 2009) 5.

[18] LA Thio, 'In Search of the Singapore Constitution: Retrospect and Prospect' in LA Thio and KYL Tan (eds), *Evolution of a Revolution: Forty Years of the Singapore Constitution* (Routledge-Cavendish, 2014) 358–59.

[19] Generally, JTT Lee, 'A Place to Stand to Move the Earth: Standing and the Rule of Law' (2020) *Singapore Journal of Legal Studies* 367.

[20] M Teo, 'Interpreting Frequently Amended Constitutions: Singapore's Dual Approach' (2021) 42 *Statute Law Review* 364.

[21] JL Neo, 'Autonomy, Deference and Control: Judicial Doctrine and Facets of Separation of Powers in Singapore' (2018) 5 *Journal of International and Comparative Law* 461, 465.

[22] UNCHR 'CEDAW Committee's Concluding Observations on the Fifth Periodic Report of Singapore' (21 November 2017) CEDAW/C/SGP/CO/5, paras 34, 36 and 40.

[23] LJ Chua, 'Collective Litigation and the Constitutional Challenges to Decriminalizing Homosexuality in Singapore' (2017) 44 *Journal of Law and Society* 433.

This is in line with advocacy groups' preference for consultative change rather than direct confrontation that could threaten their long-term viability and political goodwill for future reform efforts.[24]

These two features, in turn, point to a sometimes-paradoxical relationship between gender and constitutionalism in Singapore. On the one hand, gender equality is one of the major social issues prioritised by the Government. In fact, CEDAW is one of only four international human rights treaties that Singapore has ratified, to which it has repeatedly reiterated its commitment.[25] The impact of CEDAW is significant, as the Government is obliged to justify any law or policy that treats women differently from men.[26] On the other hand, there is, to date, rather limited structural reform to counter patriarchal ideas associated with the supposed 'Asian family structure', which suggests clear gender roles within a heterosexual family.[27] Many of the reform initiatives are constrained by a facile commitment to the principle of meritocracy.[28] This resistance to structural reform stems from the emphasis on the heterosexual nuclear family as the basic building block of Singapore society, which, in turn, risks perpetuating a hierarchical relationship between genders where the male is considered the 'provider and protector of the family' while the female is responsible for 'reproducing the nation'.[29] For instance, Singapore's male-only conscription policy, known as National Service (NS), has been described as an 'exclusively masculine expression of citizenship',[30] which sustains the inequalities of the existing patriarchal hierarchy.[31] Other laws such as post-divorce maintenance rules that are available only to women and not men, except in the narrow circumstances of incapacitation, also reflect outdated patriarchal view on gender roles in marriage.[32]

The 'non-constitutionalisation' of gender equality must also be seen as an outcome and constitutive element of 'strategic egalitarianism', where equality is contingent on the achievement of specific political and

[24] Lyons (n 11) 71.

[25] UNCHR 'Singapore's Fifth Report to the UN Committee for the Convention on the Elimination of All Forms of Discrimination Against Women' (6 November 2015) CEDAW/C/SGP/5, 2.

[26] LA Thio, 'The Impact of Internationalisation on Domestic Governance: Gender Egalitarianism & the Transformative Potential of CEDAW' (1997) 1 *Singapore Journal of International & Comparative Law* 278.

[27] S Lawson, 'Patriarchy and Resistance in Singapore' in M Mikula (ed), *Women, Activism and Social Change: Stretching Boundaries* (Routledge, 2008).

[28] See Tan (n 7) 378.

[29] KPASS Tan, 'Civic Society and the New Economy in Patriarchal Singapore: Emasculating the Political, Feminizing the Public' (2001) 15 *Crossroads: An interdisciplinary journal of Southeast Asian studies* 95.

[30] ibid 98.

[31] ibid 100. See also S Obendorf, 'Both Contagion and Cure: Queer Politics in the Global City-State' in A Yue and J Zubillaga-Pow (eds), *Queer Singapore: Illiberal Citizenship and Mediated Cultures* (HKU Press, 2012) 99; C Tan, 'Pink Dot: Cultural and Sexual Citizenship in Gay Singapore' (2015) 88 *Anthropological Quarterly* 969, 978.

[32] The Women's Charter, s 69.

economic goals.[33] Strategic egalitarianism explains why different policies separately advance and inhibit gender equality. For instance, the Woman's Charter enshrines equality in marriage and the Employment Act prohibits pregnancy discrimination. Yet, a quota on female medical students was imposed until 2004 and up until 2005, female civil servants could not claim medical benefits for their male dependents. As in most countries, there remains a gender wage gap in Singapore; a 2019 study shows that the median monthly salary of a woman working fulltime was 16.3 per cent less than a man in the same position.[34] Outliers aside,[35] the persistent under-representation of women in corporate[36] and political leadership[37] suggests that ad hoc gender reform may have limited efficacy in advancing gender equality.

This chapter examines the confluence of constitutional, political and social factors to show why the Constitution has, so far, taken a backseat in gender equality reforms. Section II provides a background to Singapore's constitutional history to explain the absence of sex/gender as legal category in the Constitution. It points to the role of international human rights law as a crucial impetus for change. Social movement networks have also played a significant role in changing gender norms at social and sub-constitutional levels. Section III examines important legislative changes that have improved gender norms in Singapore. This discussion will further demonstrate how gender equality is primarily addressed outside of the judicial arena, often without direct reference to the constitution, though there may be constitutional implications. It will also highlight the reasons why activists have avoided constitutional litigation to advance gender equality. Section IV surveys the two constitutional cases that touched on issues of gender and sexuality, demonstrating yet again the limits of constitutional litigation in Singapore, particularly in the absence of an express prohibition against gender discrimination in the constitutional text. It also examines several issues that had potential constitutional implications but where

[33] MM Lazar, 'For the Good of the Nation: 'Strategic Egalitarianism' in the Singapore Context' (2001) 7 *Nations and Nationalism* 59.

[34] J Seow, 'Singapore Women Earn 6% Less Than Men, but Gap Has Narrowed: Study' *The Straits Times* (9 January 2020), available at www.straitstimes.com/singapore/manpower/singapore-women-earn-6-less-than-men-but-gap-has-narrowed-study.

[35] L Lam, 'Halimah Yacob Set to Be Singapore's First Female President: A Timeline of Her Career' *The Straits Times* (Singapore, 11 September 2017), available at www.straitstimes.com/singapore/halimah-yacob-set-to-be-singapores-first-female-president-a-timeline-of-her-career.

[36] J Woo, 'Singapore Must Appoint 130 New Female Directors Each Year to Reach 2020 Board Diversity Goal: Grace Fu' *The Business Times* (27 January 2018), available at www.businesstimes.com.sg/government-economy/singapore-must-appoint-130-new-female-directors-each-year-to-reach-2020-board; N Khong, 'Singapore's Gender Wage Gap Widens in 2018' *TodayOnline* (28 February 2019), available at www.todayonline.com/singapore/singapore-gender-wage-gap-widens-2018.

[37] There are currently 27 (29%) elected female parliamentarians out of a total of 93 elected members. See N Tan, 'Party quotas and rising women politicians in Singapore' (2015) 11 *Politics and Gender* 196; C Agarwal, 'We Need More Women in Singapore Politics' *TodayOnline* (8 March 2018), available at www.todayonline.com/commentary/we-need-more-women-singapore-politics.

constitutional arguments were not raised or discussed. Section V examines two reform initiatives to demonstrate the contextual dynamics of advancing gender equality through strategic engagement rather than through constitutional litigation.

II. BACKGROUND: SINGAPORE'S CONSTITUTIONAL LANDSCAPE

Singapore is a democratic state with a dominant party; the PAP has formed the Government after every general election since Singapore's independence in 1965. Within such a political context, policy and legal reform depends very much on the political will of the ruling party. Though the Constitution reigns supreme by virtue of Article 4 and the courts may strike down any law that is inconsistent with the Constitution,[38] civil society advocates tend to regard strategic engagement with the Government as much more effective than constitutional litigation, which is seen as confrontational and risky.[39]

This is compounded by the fact that Singapore is largely a conservative society where laws and policies tend to be underpinned by traditionalist views of family and sexual morality. A 2015 survey found that about 40 per cent of women believe that a woman's primary role is to care for her husband and 30 per cent disagree that men and women are equal.[40] In addition, national surveys repeatedly show that most Singaporeans remain uncomfortable or opposed to same-sex marriage and to the decriminalisation of homosexuality. In a 2019 survey, slightly more than half (50.4 per cent) of the respondents said that gay sex was 'always wrong' while 48.5 per cent said that gay marriage was 'always wrong'.[41] Accordingly, attempts to advance gender equality or gay rights are sometimes met with resistance and hostility. In recent times, confrontations between gay rights activists and conservative religious groups have been particularly intense. For instance, after gay activists began to organise Pink Dot, an annual gathering to demonstrate public support for the decriminalisation of section 377A of the Penal Code, Christian and Muslim groups mobilised

[38] The Singapore Constitution, Art 4, states that the Constitution is 'the supreme law of the Republic of Singapore and any law enacted by the Legislature after the commencement of this Constitution which is inconsistent with this Constitution shall, to the extent of the inconsistency, be void.'

[39] LJ Chua, *Mobilizing Gay Singapore: Rights and Resistance in an Authoritarian State* (NUS Press, 2014) 144.

[40] C Wong, 'Singapore Ranked 12th in Attitudes on Gender Equality, After China and Hong Kong: YouGov' *TodayOnline* (14 November 2015), available at www.todayonline.com/singapore/singapore-ranked-12th-attitudes-gender-equality-after-china-and-hong-kong-yougov.

[41] M Mathews, L Lim and S Selvarajan, 'Religion, Morality and Conservatism in Singapore' (2019) IPS Working Papers no 34, available at lkyspp.nus.edu.sg/ips/news/details/ips-working-paper-no.-34-religion-morality-and-conservatism-in-singapore.

their communities to sign petitions, write letters to elected representatives, and participate in religious events to express their disagreement and opposition.[42]

That constitutional litigation is not often seen as an effective mode to induce social change[43] is not limited to gender and sexuality issues, but is symptomatic of the general constitutional landscape in the country, which tends to favour cooperative methods of change over confrontational litigation. Until recently, constitutional litigation in Singapore was rarely pursued. There was only a total of 153 reported constitutional law cases in Singapore between 1963 and 2013.[44] This averages to around three cases each year,[45] a small number compared to other common law jurisdictions,[46] even accounting for differences in size. There has been an increase in constitutional litigation in more recent years, notwithstanding a 'lower success rate of constitutional claims'.[47] So far, there have only been four cases where the courts have directly rejected the Government's interpretation of constitutional provisions.[48] The reticence towards constitutional review in Singapore has been noted even by the former Chief Justice, who, in 2010, pointed to the 'sense of unease about the dormant state of judicial review in Singapore' and sought to dispel 'the notion that the courts might have something to do with it'.[49] Clarifying the rightful place of judicial review, he argued that 'the rule of law requires the court to determine whether any public authority has crossed the line of legality'[50] and that 'judicial review is the means by which legal rights are protected and good governance enforced'.[51]

Nonetheless, constitutional litigation to advance social change will likely continue to be limited in Singapore for several reasons. First, narrow standing rules, which require an applicant to have 'sufficient interest' or 'real interest' in the subject matter,[52] severely limit the possibility of public interest litigation, which has been crucial in many countries for constitutional advocacy through the courts.[53] Interested parties such as civil society organisations do not have

[42] See for instance, S Han, 'Wear White: The Mediatized Politics of Religious Anti-LGBT Activism in Singapore' (2018) 31 *Nordic Journal of Religion and Society* 41.

[43] See generally, T Ginsburg, *Judicial Review in New Democracies: Constitutional Courts in Asian Cases* (Cambridge University Press, 2003).

[44] JTT Lee, 'Foreign Precedents in Constitutional Adjudication by the Supreme Court of Singapore, 1963–2013' (2015) 24 *Washington International Law Journal* 249, 253 and 260.

[45] ibid.

[46] ibid.

[47] ibid.

[48] *Chng Suan Tze v Minister for Home Affairs and others and other appeals* [1988] 2 SLR(R) 525, [1988] SGCA 16; *Taw Cheng Kong v Public Prosecutor* [1998] 1 SLR(R) 78, [1998] SGHC 10; *Vellama d/o Marie Muthu v Attorney-General* [2013] 4 SLR 1, [2013] SGCA 39; *Tan Seet Eng v Attorney-General and another matter* [2015] 2 SLR 453, [2015] SGCA 59.

[49] SK Chan, 'Judicial Review – From Angst to Empathy: A Lecture to Singapore Management University Second Year Law Students' (2010) 22 *Singapore Academy of Law Journal* 469, [2].

[50] ibid.

[51] ibid [6]–[7].

[52] *Jeyaretnam Kenneth Andrew v Attorney-General* [2014] 1 SLR 345, [2013] SGCA 56.

[53] Lee (n 19); S Jhaveri, 'Advancing Constitutional Justice in Singapore: Enhancing Access and Standing in Judicial Review Cases' (2017) *Singapore Journal of Legal Studies* 53.

standing to file a constitutional challenge unless they are directly affected. Secondly, the Singapore courts have generally taken a textualist or limited purposive approach to constitutional interpretation, which tends not to support a more expansive interpretation of rights. This approach includes the development of doctrines such as the presumption of constitutionality, which requires applicants to show that a law or executive action is unconstitutional rather than for the Government to show why its actions are constitutional.[54] Thirdly, the Singapore judiciary has cautioned against using the courts to advance social policy,[55] arguing in at least one case that courts are not 'mini-legislatures'.[56] This means that courts could be less willing to scrutinise the Government's reasons for gender discrimination on the basis of public policy.[57]

Fourthly, constitutional provisions in Singapore only provide vertical rights, not horizontal rights. There is also no anti-discrimination legislation.[58] Attempts to constitutionalise private discriminatory practices have not been successful. In 2013, a homosexual man unsuccessfully applied for a declaration that Article 12(1) of the Singapore Constitution prohibited workplace discrimination on the basis of sexual orientation. He alleged that he was harassed by his employer into resigning because of his homosexuality.[59] The suit was struck out as an abuse of process on the basis that his 'real grievance of alleged discrimination is against his former employer, and not the Government'.[60] Accordingly, the Court held that the applicant did not have standing to seek the declaration since there was no Government action to challenge.[61] As the jurisprudence stands in Singapore, constitutional rights do not give rise to positive obligations on the part of the Government to protect individuals from

[54] JTT Lee, 'Rethinking the Presumption of Constitutionality' in JL Neo (ed), *Constitutional Interpretation in Singapore: Theory and Practice* (Routledge, 2017); RZX Choo, 'Reconsidering the Presumption of Constitutionality and Pre-Constitutional Legislation' (*Law Gazette*, May 2019), available at lawgazette.com.sg/feature/reconsidering-the-presumption-of-constitutionality.

[55] S Menon, 'Executive Power: Rethinking the Modalities of Control' (2019) 29 *Duke Journal of Comparative & International Law* 277.

[56] *Lim Meng Suang and another v Attorney-General and another appeal and another matter* [2015] 1 SLR 26, [2014] SGCA 53 [38] [hereinafter *Lim Meng Suang*].

[57] Choo (n 54).

[58] At the time of writing, the Singapore Government has indicated its intention to enact a new workplace discrimination legislation which would prohibit discrimination on the basis of sex, marital status, pregnancy status and caregiving responsibilities. A Ng, 'Tripartite committee recommends protection against age, sex and race biases as part of workplace fairness law' *Channel NewsAsia* (13 February 2023), available at www.channelnewsasia.com/singapore/anti-discrimination-workplace-law-fairness-3273846.

[59] 'High Court Rejects Anti-Discrimination Bid by Gay Man' *The Straits Times* (26 November 2013), available at www.straitstimes.com/singapore/high-court-rejects-anti-discrimination-bid-by-gay-man.

[60] ibid.

[61] Attorney-General's Chambers, 'Media Statement: Appeal and Intervention Applications Withdrawn Wee Kim San Lawrence Bernard v Attorney-General Originating Summons No 763 of 2013 (Registrar's Appeal No 402 of 2013)' (22 April 2014), available at www.agc.gov.sg/docs/default-source/newsroom-doucments/media-releases/2014/agc-media-statement_lawrence-wee-v-ag_withdrawal-of-appeal-and-intervention-applications_22-april-2014.pdf.

discrimination by other private actors. Neither is there a positive obligation to enact non-discrimination legislation to prevent harm to those who suffer discrimination.

Finally, courts have emphasised that the equal protection clause under the Constitution only requires a threshold review of constitutionality. Under the reasonable classification test, the Government only has to show that the criterion for differentiation is intelligible and that there is a rational nexus between that criterion and the legislative object. There is no scope for reviewing the legitimacy of the legislative object.[62] Gender discrimination litigation is likely to be rather limited to extreme cases under Article 12(1)'s general equal protection clause. There would be greater prospect for gender discrimination litigation if gender was explicitly included as a prohibited basis for discrimination under Article 12(2) of the Constitution. The impact of such an inclusion is uncertain since there has not been any litigation surrounding this provision in Singapore. By way of comparison, after Malaysia included gender as a prohibited basis for discrimination in its equivalent provision of the Constitution in 2001 to comply with its CEDAW obligations, the Malaysian equivalent of Singapore's Article 12(2) has opened up scope for challenging gender discrimination. One development there is the use of the doctrine of interpretive incorporation to use the constitutional provision to bring about domestic compliance with CEDAW standards.[63] While this suggests that the constitutionalisation of gender equality could lead to more constitutional litigation, it also bears noting that there is a more active rights litigation scene in Malaysia than in Singapore.[64]

At present, gender equality reform is primarily justified around the need to fulfil CEDAW obligations with the state responding to consultative advocacy by civil society groups. Although Singapore adopts a dualist approach towards international law, the ratification of CEDAW has opened up a new space for activists to raise issues affecting women at an international level. The CEDAW reporting requirements have been described as a 'precious site for Governmental accountability and exchange between the state and civil society'.[65] State obligations imposed by CEDAW also equip activists with additional moral resources when engaging with the state by providing a set of international standards against which to monitor and evaluate the state's performance.[66] CEDAW therefore forms a focal point for gender equality reform in Singapore, serving as a platform for dialogue between the Government and civil society organisations, as moderated by the CEDAW Committee. For instance, the Government's

[62] *Lim Meng Suang* (n 56).

[63] JL Neo, 'Calibrating Interpretive Incorporation: Constitutional Interpretation and Pregnancy Discrimination Under CEDAW' (2013) 35 *Human Rights Quarterly* 910.

[64] GKY Chan, 'The Right of Access to Justice: Judicial Discourse in Singapore and Malaysia' (2007) 2 *Asian Journal of Comparative Law* 1, 4.

[65] Shaddick et al (n 12) 146.

[66] ibid 143.

reliance on formal equality under Article 12(1) is often faced with rebuttals from civil society organisations as well as the CEDAW Committee regarding 'prevalent and systematic discrimination against women based on sexual orientation and gender identity'.[67]

Another important feature of Singapore's legal landscape that has implications for gender equality is its legally pluralistic system which accommodates Muslim personal law. The administration of Muslim personal law is constitutionally provided for in Article 153, supported by Article 152(2) of the Constitution. State-funded institutions like the Islamic Religious Council (*Majlis Ugama Islam Singapura*, or MUIS) and the *Syariah* Court of Singapore administer these laws, which require certain exemptions from general laws (eg, the registration of marriage and monogamy) under the Women's Charter.[68] Polygamy is only allowed in Muslim marriages and is banned for all other types of customary and religious marriages.[69] Writing in 1960, Huang strongly criticised this position:

> The aim of the charter is to abolish polygamy and its attendant social defects. It is meant to protect all women, and as such the exclusion of Muslim women from the operation of the charter can only be justified if they are not in need of such protection. But this is not borne out by the facts as is seen in the frequent abuses arising from the practice of polygamy. The exception so made militates against Muslim women and is irrational and unjust ... One might justifiably suspect that this discrimination is motivated by *political rather than social considerations*.[70]

Noor Aisha has criticised the duality of Singapore's Constitution for perpetuating discriminatory attitudes against the Malay-Muslim community while essentialising Malay-Muslims.[71] Indeed, the administration of Muslim family law is one manifestation of a potential conflict between protecting the autonomy of a minority religious group, on the one hand, and ensuring gender equality, on the other. This arrangement of legal pluralism resulted in reservations to Articles 2, 11 and 16 of CEDAW on the basis that 'Singapore is a multi-racial and multi-religious society' and that the reservations are necessary to respect 'the

[67] UNCHR, 'List of Issues and Questions in Relation to the Fourth Periodic Report of Singapore' (4 November 2010) CEDAW/C/SGP/Q/4, para 31.

[68] The Women's Charter, s 3(4) specifies that it does not apply to 'marriage[s] between persons who are Muslims'.

[69] All customary systems of marriage then existing in Singapore permitted polygamy, which in fact was still then a reasonably widespread practice, especially among the ethnic Chinese majority: WK Leong, 'Common Law and Chinese Marriage Custom in Singapore' in AJ Harding (ed), *The Common Law in Singapore and Malaysia* (Butterworths, 1985); State of Singapore, 'Legislative Assembly Debates, Official Report' (22 March 1961), vol 14 at col 1214 (Dr Goh Keng Swee (Minister for Finance)).

[70] SM Huang, 'The Women's Charter' (1960) 2 *University of Malaya Law Journal* 147. It should be noted that the fact that this strongest critique of a progressive legislation is found in the footnote probably buttresses the very criticism that Muslim marriages was then a highly politicised matter.

[71] NAA Rahman, 'Muslim Personal Laws and Citizens' Rights: The Case of Singapore' (2012) 7 *Asian Journal of Comparative Law* 1.

freedom of minorities to practise their religious or personal laws'.[72] Notably, the Constitution carves out an exception for Muslim personal law: Article 12(3)(a) states that the equal protection clause would not invalidate or prohibit any provision regulating personal law. The need to grant exceptional status to Muslims is partly historical, as Singapore was part of a Malay sultanate and later became a constituent state of Malaysia before becoming independent in 1965. Granting the Malays special protection was seen as necessary to ensure social stability and to avoid kin-state interference.[73]

Constitutional protection of gender equality, however, does not only depend on rights protection. Williams argues that there is a need to look beyond rights to the broader range of constitutional provisions and mechanisms to better understand the intersection of constitutional law and gender equality.[74] At least one structural feature in the Constitution has led to increased political participation of women: the Nominated Members of Parliament (NMP) scheme.[75] The scheme was put in place to enhance viewpoint plurality in parliamentary debates through the appointment of non-partisan representatives of different sectors, such as the arts, disability and sports, by a Special Select Committee of elected parliamentarians.[76] One of the positive side outcomes has been an increase in female participation in Parliament. This has given some feminist activists a national platform to advocate for gender equality. For instance, as NMP, Kanwaljit Soin, a well-known women's rights advocate, played a key role in advocating for legislative reform to protect women from family violence under the Women's Charter.[77] NMPs have also raised issues affecting LGBT Singaporeans such as school bullying and LGBT censorship,[78] topics which elected politicians may find uncomfortable (or politically costly) to bring up.[79] It was also an NMP who submitted a parliamentary petition in 2007 urging

[72] Singapore's Initial CEDAW Periodic Report (n 2) para 2.2.

[73] JL Neo, 'The Constitution and the Protection of Minorities: A Judicious Balance?' in LA Thio and KYL Tan (eds), *Evolution of a Revolution: Forty Years of the Singapore Constitution* (Routledge-Cavendish, 2009).

[74] Williams (n 17) 5.

[75] The Singapore Constitution, Art 39(1)(c).

[76] See generally, WJ Abdullah, 'Electoral innovation in competitive authoritarian states: a case for the Nominated Member of Parliament (NMP) in Singapore' (2016) 17 *Japanese Journal of Political Science* 190.

[77] Shaddick et al (n 12) 142.

[78] Singapore Parliamentary Debates, Official Report (10 September 2018) vol 94 'Complaints over Library Books with Homosexual Content' (Kok Heng Luen), available at sprs.parl.gov.sg/search/sprs3topic?reportid=oral-answer-65; *Singapore Parliamentary Debates, Official Report* (4 September 2019) vol 94 'Measures at Educational Institutions to Detect, Minimise and Combat Bullying Based on Gender Expression' (Assoc Prof Walter Theseira), available at sprs.parl.gov.sg/search/sprs3topic?reportid=oral-answer-2064.

[79] HM Ang and R Phua, 'For Nominated Members of Parliament, It's Not Just About Talking in Parliament' *Channel NewsAsia* (23 February 2020), available at www.channelnewsasia.com/news/singapore/singapore-nominated-members-of-parliament-sessions-questions-12430120.

the Government to repeal section 377A of the Penal Code, a colonial-era law criminalising male homosexual conduct.[80]

III. CONSTITUTIONAL FRAMING OF SEX, GENDER AND SEXUALITY

A. Non-Inclusion of Gender as Prohibited Ground of Discrimination in the Constitution

Constitution drafters in Singapore were primarily concerned with racial, ethnic and religious divisions rather than gender equality. Indeed, the first Constitutional Commission appointed in 1966 to formulate the newly independent nation's Constitution was tasked to examine how best to safeguard 'rights of the racial, linguistic and religious minorities',[81] without any consideration of gender. The Commission took a strongly individualistic approach, concluding that 'the best and most appropriate way' to safeguard minorities was to adopt an equality approach whereby fundamental rights of individuals were entrenched.[82] Equality was framed primarily through racial and religious lenses, rather than in gender terms. The non-inclusion of gender in Article 12(2) followed its Malaysian predecessor. There was no discussion of gender during the drafting of the Federal Constitution, though Hickling suggests that the exclusion of the word 'sex' was deliberate to 'keep the male sex dominant in the Federation, at least in the field of civil service'.[83]

The Singapore Government periodically maintains that Article 12(1), which 'enshrines the principle of equality of all persons before the law', is available to address gender discrimination,[84] and that 'a woman aggrieved by any legal provision may also apply to the courts to seek a judicial review of that particular legislation on the grounds that it is ultra vires Article 12 of the Constitution on equality'.[85] AWARE continues to advocate for constitutional change in its

[80] Chua, *Mobilizing Gay Singapore* (n 39) 110–11.
[81] *Report of Constitutional Commission 1966*, para 11, reproduced in KYL Tan and LA Thio, *Constitutional Law in Malaysia and Singapore* (2nd edn, Lexis Nexis, 1997) 1021.
[82] ibid.
[83] RH Hickling, 'Some Aspects of Fundamental Liberties under the Constitution of the Federation of Malaysia' (1963) 29 *MLJ* xliv, xlix, cited in JTT Lee, 'Equal Protection and Sexual Orientation' (1995) 16 *Singapore Law Review* 228.
[84] UNCHR, 'Singapore's Third Report to the UN Committee for the Convention on the Elimination of All Forms of Discrimination Against Women' (1 November 2004) CEDAW/C/SGP/3, para 1.1.
[85] ibid para 2.7. See also UNCHR, 'Singapore's Fourth Report to the UN Committee for the Convention on the Elimination of All Forms of Discrimination Against Women' (2 April 2009) CEDAW/C/SGP/4, para 2.4; UNCHR,'Singapore's Fifth Report to the UN Committee for the Convention on the Elimination of All Forms of Discrimination Against Women' (6 November 2015) CEDAW/C/SGP/5, para 2.1.

reports to the CEDAW Committee,[86] and argued (unsuccessfully) in its RSC submissions that the failure to enshrine gender as a constitutionally prohibited ground of discrimination 'breaches the social contract made more than 40 years ago [by] the PAP'.[87] The absence of gender from Article 12(2) appears to be another instance of strategic egalitarianism: in March 2021, the Minister for Law & Home Affairs acknowledged that while there should be something 'aspirational' in the Constitution that that recognises the equal rights of men and women, it should be weighed against the potential economic impact of increased litigation.[88]

B. Statutory Entrenchment of Women's Rights

One reason for the lack of a strong movement to enshrine gender equality in the Constitution is that many of these rights have already been statutorily provided for. The 1961 Women's Charter and the 1974 Termination of Pregnancy Act (TPA)[89] provide (mostly) equal rights in marriage and reproductive rights, despite the absence of any binding constitutional requirement.

i. Equal Rights in Marriage

The Women's Charter was enacted by the PAP Government to expressly accord women the same rights as their husbands in the domestic sphere, and was transformative of gender norms during a time described as 'feudalistic'.[90] Leong characterises the Women's Charter as 'a beacon in promulgating the idea of marriage as an equal co-operative partnership of different efforts'.[91] Indeed, section 46 of the Women's Charter, which was modelled after a Swiss provision, exhorts husband and wife to cooperate for their mutual benefit as well as to care for their children.[92]

[86] AWARE, 'CEDAW Shadow Report for the 39th CEDAW Session (July–August 2007)' (May 2007), available at aware.org.sg/downloads/CEDAW_2007-Report.pdf; AWARE, 'CEDAW Shadow Report 2011' (May 2011), available at aware.org.sg/wp-content/uploads/AWARE-CEDAW-Shadow-Report-2011.pdf; NGO Coalition, '"Many Voices, One Movement" Coalition Report of National NGOs' (October 2017), available at sgcedawcoalition.files.wordpress.com/2017/10/many-voices-one-movement-coalition-report-of-national-ngos-on-singapore.pdf.

[87] AWARE (n 10).

[88] SA Tan, 'More to be done to ensure equal rights for women: Panel' *The Straits Times* (9 March 2021), available at www.straitstimes.com/singapore/community/more-to-be-done-to-ensure-equal-rights-for-women-panel.

[89] Cap 324 (Rev Ed 1985).

[90] State of Singapore, 'Legislative Assembly Debates, Official Report' (6 April 1960) vol 12 at col 443, 'First Reading of the Bill for the Women's Charter' (Chan Choy Siong (Delta)).

[91] Leong (n 6) 24.

[92] ibid 12–14.

Though the Women's Charter 'rejected local customs and religious laws on marriage and the family' and was informed principally by Catholic norms and English law,[93] its enactment faced little public opposition. This successful imposition of monogamous marriage for non-Muslims was attributed to the 'happy confluence of the economic pragmatism that was the driving motivation of the ruling party [and] the influence of Westernisation and modernisation'.[94] Notably, the prohibition on polygamy was also supported by many Chinese-educated Chinese population who were influenced by the reformed Marriage Law in communist China and the anti-yellow culture struggles there against concubinage and prostitution.[95] The Women's Charter was seen as a key step towards increasing female education and participation in the workforce.[96] This pragmatic and utilitarian approach towards gender equality did not go unnoticed; a woman scholar wrote in 1975 that the Government policy to encourage female participation in the economy was 'by no means clear … a commitment (to the) principle of belief in emancipation, that women are entitled to the equal right as men to work'.[97] Because it focused mainly on the status of women within the context of the family, the Women's Charter has also been described as 'more like a Family Law Act than a charter of rights' and a 'highly overrated document' in terms of its impact on gender equality.[98]

Presently, Muslim family law still encompasses some inegalitarian practices, such as the requirement for the consent of a *wali* (male guardian) to a woman's marriage, polygamy (up to four wives), and double portions for male beneficiaries in inheritance rules.[99] Critics have proposed that Muslim family law be made optional rather than compulsory.[100] However, gender equality reform in Muslim family law is complicated by racial/religious sensitivities in Singapore's social context and concerns that the Malay-Muslim minority would resent strong state intervention in their internal religious affairs. Civil society groups also tread a fine line. For instance, AWARE has deliberately avoided advocacy on these issues on behalf of Muslim women to avoid antagonising the wider Muslim community or disturbing the fragile state of religious harmony in Singapore.[101]

[93] WK Leong, *Family Law in Singapore: Cases and Commentary on the Women's Charter and Family Law* (Malayan Law Journal, 1990) 15.

[94] Leong (n 6) 9 citing ABL Phang, *The Development of Singapore Law: Historical and Socio-Legal Perspectives* (Butterworths, 1990) 276.

[95] A Wee, 'The Women's Charter, 1961: Where We Were Coming From and How We Got There' in TW Devasahayam (ed) *Singapore Women's Charter: roles, responsibilities, and rights in marriage* (Institute of Southeast Asian Studies, 2011) 70.

[96] Leong (n 6) 9.

[97] HC Chan quoted in N Purushotam, 'Women and Knowledge/Power: Notes on the Singapore Dilemma' in KC Ban et al (eds), *Imagining Singapore* (Times Academic Press, 1992) 326.

[98] Lawson (n 27) 11; Purushotam (n 97) 323.

[99] Cap 3 (Rev Ed 2009), Pt VII.

[100] Rahman (n 71).

[101] Lyons (n 11) 74.

Therefore, much gender equality reform is addressed internally, by the Islamic Religious Council and the *Syariah* Court. Some such steps include the *Syariah* Court requiring husbands to obtain its permission to marry more than one woman and imposing certain requirements (such as financial viability) and the ability to ensure parity in treatment. Today, polygamy has become quite rare in Singapore. Other progressive steps to promote gender equality include the appointment of women to the *Syariah* Court and the Fatwa Committee.[102]

ii. Reproductive Rights

Reproductive rights have never been strongly contested in Singapore, which has one of the most liberal abortion laws in the world.[103] The Abortion Act of 1969, renamed the Termination of Pregnancy Act in 1974, allowed abortions for pregnancies up to 24 weeks.[104] Abortion can still be performed for pregnancies of more than 24 weeks if it is immediately necessary to save the life or to prevent grave permanent injury to the physical or mental health of the pregnant woman. There is no minimum age requirement for the procedure, nor is it legally required for minors to seek parental consent if they are under 21 years of age. However, subsidiary legislation – namely, the Termination of Pregnancy Regulations[105] – requires women seeking an abortion to undergo personal counselling and a 48-hour cooling-off period before proceeding with the procedure.[106] Unmarried girls under the age of 16 are also required to attend pre-abortion counselling when they seek to terminate their pregnancies.[107]

Economic pragmatism, rather than rights or moral considerations, motivated these fairly permissive abortion laws. During the second reading of the Abortion Bill, the Minister of Health suggested that a more liberal approach towards abortion would be in the interest of the 'greater good for our society'[108] because 'it is mainly from the ranks of the unwanted children, the illegitimate and broken homes where most of the delinquents, the criminals and the

[102] R Rashith, '1st Female Syariah Court Registrar Steps Down' *The Straits Times* (13 January 2018), available at www.straitstimes.com/singapore/1st-female-syariah-court-registrar-steps-down; 'First Woman in Fatwa Committee as Full Member' *The Straits Times* (27 September 2019), available at www.straitstimes.com/singapore/first-woman-in-fatwa-committee-as-full-member. See also Z Mir-Hosseini, 'The Construction of Gender in Islamic Legal Thought and Strategies for Reform' (Muis occasional papers series 3, paper no 8, 2009).

[103] See generally, SH Tan, 'Religion and Abortion in Singapore' in DKS Koh and KK Kwa (eds), *Issues of Law and Justice in Singapore: Some Christian Reflections* (Armour Publishing, 2009) 87.

[104] Cap 324 (Rev Ed 1987).

[105] Termination of Pregnancy Act, s 11.

[106] Reg 5(1) read with reg 5(3), Termination of Pregnancy Regulations; see also Ministry of Health, 'Guidelines on Termination of Pregnancy' (1 April 2004) para 5.2, available at www.moh.gov.sg/docs/librariesprovider4/default-document-library/(2)_guidelines-on-termination-of-pregnancy.pdf.

[107] Reg 5(2), Termination of Pregnancy Regulations; Ministry of Health (n 106) para 5.3.

[108] 'Singapore Parliamentary Debates, Official Report' (8 April 1969) vol 28 at col 890 'Abortion Bill' (Chua Sian Chin (Minister for Health)).

antisocial elements are derived.' He thus concludes: 'Our society in Singapore cannot afford to breed such people.'[109]

IV. CONSTITUTIONAL JURISPRUDENCE

Gender and constitutional law has attracted increased attention as feminist advocates around the world employ constitutional litigation and constitution-making to advance their cause.[110] Chang points out that, in contrast to Anglo-European states, constitutional litigation occurred more recently in Asia only as legal and judicial strategies became available after social and political reforms in the 1980s and 1990s.[111] Singapore stands apart from this global and regional phenomenon as constitutional litigation is regarded as an undesirable strategy to achieve egalitarian and rights-based objectives in the context of a dominant party regime.[112] To date, there have only been two constitutional cases where gender equality was raised as an issue, albeit to advocate for the equal treatment of men rather than women. This raises important questions as to how gender equality reforms serve both to protect men and women. The question of the intersection between gender and sexuality also arises in one of the cases as gender equality claims were raised to advocate for the equal treatment of homosexual men.

In this section, we first discuss the two constitutional cases and the limited engagement by the courts with the issues raised therein. We then examine several cases with potential constitutional implications but where constitutional arguments were not raised or discussed. This examination will support our argument that gender equality is primarily addressed outside of the judicial arena, and often without direct reference to the Constitution even if there may be constitutional implications.

A. Challenge to the Criminalisation of Male Homosexual Conduct under Section 377A of the Penal Code

Lim Meng Suang was a combined constitutional challenge against section 377A of the Penal Code, which criminalises 'gross indecency' between men. Among the constitutional bases for the challenge was the equality clause under Article 12(1).

[109] ibid at col 873.

[110] B Baines and R Rubio-Marín, 'Introduction: Towards a Feminist Constitutional Agenda' in B Baines and R Rubio-Marín (eds), *The Gender of Constitutional Jurisprudence* (Cambridge University Press, 2005).

[111] WC Chang, 'Public Interest Litigation in Taiwan: Strategy for Law and Policy Changes in the Course of Democratization' in PJ Yap and H Lau (eds), *Public Interest Litigation in Asia* (Routledge, 2011).

[112] Chua, *Mobilizing Gay Singapore* (n 39).

The applicants unsuccessfully argued that the law was discriminatory on the basis of gender or sexual orientation as it only applied to homosexual men, thus discriminating against them vis-à-vis homosexual women and heterosexual men. On the equality argument, the Court adopted a rational basis review encapsulated in what is known as the reasonable classification test.

Described as a 'threshold test', the reasonable classification test only requires that the statute employ an 'intelligible differentia' and that the classification bears a rational relation to the statutory objective. The Court acknowledged that since all that is necessary is an identifiable differentiation between two classes of persons, the differentia would 'very seldom' fail to pass legal muster.[113] This would happen only if the differentia is 'so unreasonable as to be illogical and/or incoherent', which must be of an 'extreme' nature where there can be 'no reasonable dispute (let alone controversy) as to that fact from a moral, political and/or ethical point of view'.[114] Furthermore, the Court noted that 'the requisite rational relation will – more often than not – be found' because there is no need for a perfect relation or complete coincidence.[115] A law would fail at this stage only if there is a 'clear disconnect' between the statutory objective and the differentia used.[116]

On the facts, the Court held that the classification prescribed by section 377A was intelligible and bore a rational relation to the purpose of section 377A, which was to criminalise male homosexual conduct because such conduct was not acceptable or desirable in Singapore society.[117] It showed discomfort with being asked to address what was considered a morally controversial issue concerning homosexual conduct. Repeatedly, the Court cautioned against considerations of 'substantive moral, political and/or ethical issues',[118] and declared that the Court should not be treated as a 'mini-legislature'.[119]

The severe limits of rational review under the reasonable classification test were acknowledged by the Court, which sees it as lacking the 'requisite (or complete) normative as well as analytical impetus' to realise the guarantee of equal protection.[120] In contrast, one may argue that Article 12(2), with its explicit reference to prohibited bases of discrimination, provides more specific and concrete legal criteria. However, the Court in *Lim Meng Suang* declined specifically to extend Article 12(2) to include gender, sexual orientation or gender identity since these were 'noticeably absent' from the provision.[121]

[113] *Lim Meng Suang* (n 56) [67].
[114] ibid [67].
[115] ibid [68].
[116] ibid [68].
[117] ibid [153]. These findings have recently been criticised by the former Chief Justice Chan Sek Keong. See SK Chan, 'Equal Justice under the Constitution and Section 377A of the Penal Code' (2019) 31 *Singapore Academy of Law Journal* 773.
[118] *Lim Meng Suang* (n 56) [65].
[119] ibid [70].
[120] ibid [61].
[121] ibid [92] and [182].

The Court's interpretation of Article 12(2) and its relationship with Article 12(1) raises important considerations for future advocacy efforts in Singapore. The Court of Appeal's judgment suggests that only discrimination on the grounds specified in Article 12(2) is prohibited under the Constitution:

> Article 12(2) prohibits specific grounds of discrimination, which are the *only grounds of discrimination* that are proscribed under the Singapore Constitution. Any discrimination (albeit only) on any of the grounds stated in Article 12(2) will render the statute concerned void pursuant to Article 4 to the extent of the inconsistency with Article 12(2).[122]

Insofar as this passage suggests that even a challenge under Article 12(1) is limited to the explicit grounds of race, religion, descent and place of birth as stated in Article 12(2), and nothing else, this is a seriously restrictive and curious reading of both provisions. It would mean that any basis for discrimination other than those specified in Article 12(2) could not be challenged under Article 12(1). This raises the question of what separate purpose Article 12(1) serves in the first place. One suggestion in the judgment is that Article 12(2) applies only to citizens of Singapore, while non-citizens are accorded protection under Article 12(1) pursuant to the reasonable classification test. This seems like a possible, but overly formalistic, distinction. An alternative interpretation is that Article 12(1) is a general aspirational provision open to judicial development in appropriate cases of discrimination not directly covered by Article 12(2). This interpretation was proposed but not accepted by the Court of Appeal.

However, at the same time, the Court showed openness to considering gender discrimination under Article 12(1) in its response to a hypothetical puzzle posed by counsel as to whether a law banning all women from driving would violate Article 12(1). The Court gallantly held that such a law, which it considers 'extreme', would arguably be unconstitutional. However, the Court explained that it would fail the reasonable classification test's first prong because gender here would arguably be an 'illogical and/or incoherent' differentia.[123] This part of the judgment leaves open the possibility that challenges under Article 12(1) may include gender discrimination. However, bearing in mind the low standard of rational review, such challenges are only likely to prevail if the discrimination cannot be justified on any rational grounds, ie is capricious or arbitrary.[124]

[122] ibid [102(d)].

[123] ibid [114]. In *Tan Seng Kee v Attorney-General* [2022] 1 SLR 1347 [hereinafter *Tan Seng Kee (CA)*], the Court of Appeal further clarified (at [319]) that such a law may also fail the second limb of the reasonable classification test on the basis that the differentia bears no rational relation to any conceivable object. Specifically, the Court observed that it is 'impermissible to frame the object of a law banning all women from driving as precisely that', ie to ban all women from driving. This is because the object of the law would be to introduce the differentia that it embodies, which would be circular in reasoning and renders the reasonable classification test 'purely formalistic' (at [320]).

[124] JL Neo, 'Equal Protection and the Reasonable Classification Test in Singapore: After Lim Meng Suang v Attorney-General' (2016) *Singapore Journal of Legal Studies* 95.

As even the Court recognised, the current Parliament is very unlikely to pass an arbitrary or capricious law that it cannot justify on rational grounds. Rational review, *aka* the reasonable classification test, as it currently stands, is unlikely to be very conducive for advancing gender equality through constitutional litigation.[125]

The foregoing discussion suggests that advocating for a constitutional amendment to include gender/sex in Article 12(2) may be critical to the future of gender equality. After all, the Court's reading of Article 12(2) (with potential impact on Article 12(1)) reflects a judicial philosophy that sees its constitutional role as more limited, where constitutional change ought to come through legislative avenues instead. This is reflected in the Court's statement that:

> Although only specific grounds of discrimination are prohibited under Article 12(2), the necessary flexibility to include additional prohibited grounds of discrimination exists inasmuch as Article 12(2) can be amended by the Singapore Parliament (pursuant to Article 5 of the Singapore Constitution) in order to reflect the prevailing social mores as well as aspirations of Singapore society at any given point in time.[126]

Returning to the challenge to section 377A, the Court's judgment here means that the criminalisation of male homosexual conduct was not unconstitutional in Singapore. In rejecting proposals to repeal the law in 2007, the Prime Minister even gave an assurance in Parliament that the provision would not be used to prosecute consensual homosexual intercourse between adult men.[127] However, in a more recent statement, the Attorney-General has clarified that the Government has not removed or restricted prosecutorial discretion for the provision.[128] This position accords with the need to ensure separation of powers and prosecutorial independence.

In a development that demonstrates the power of network movements and cross-border dialogues, three more constitutional challenges were filed in 2019,[129] to challenge section 377A in Singapore by gay men inspired by the

[125] In *Tan Seng Kee (CA)*, the Court of Appeal explored an alternative, more stringent approach to the reasonable classification test as set out in *Syed Suhail bin Syed Zin v Attorney-General* [2021] 1 SLR 809 (hereinafter *Syed Suhail*), which is a case concerning administrative review of an executive action rather than a constitutional review of a statutory provision. However, as the Court did not conclusively decide whether the *Lim Meng Suang* or *Syed Suhail* approach to the reasonable classification test should be preferred (at [329]), it remains to be seen how this area of law will develop.

[126] *Lim Meng Suang* (n 56) [102].

[127] 'Singapore Parliamentary Debates, Official Report' (23 October 2007) vol 83 at cols 2396–407 'Penal Code (Amendment) Act' (Lee Hsien Loong, Prime Minister).

[128] J Wong, 'A-G: Prosecutor's Discretion on Section 377A Not Curbed' *The Straits Times* (3 October 2018), available at www.straitstimes.com/singapore/courts-crime/a-g-prosecutors-discretion-on-section-377a-not-curbed.

[129] R Kurohi, 'Three court challenges against Section 377A to be heard in November' *The Straits Times* (9 October 2019), available at www.straitstimes.com/singapore/courts-crime/three-court-challenges-against-section-377a-to-be-heard-in-november.

success of *Navtej Singh Johar v Union of India*.[130] In March 2020, the High Court issued its decision in *Ong Ming Johnson v Attorney-General*,[131] following the *Lim Meng Suang* precedent and dismissing the applications. This was followed by the Court of Appeal's dismissal of the appeals in February 2022 on the technical ground that the appellants lacked standing because of the Attorney General's prior representation that he would not actively prosecute section 377A gave rise to a substantive legitimate expectation against all prosecutions under that law.[132]

Days after the Court of Appeal issued its decision, the Singapore Government announced that it was studying the ruling and would consult with different segments on society on the law. The Prime Minister subsequently announced that his Government would repeal the law after it was advised that there was a 'significant risk of section 377A being struck down, on the grounds that it breaches [Article 12]'.[133] In this regard, the Court of Appeal had reconsidered the constitutionality of section 377A in obiter and left the question open based on what its legislative object was. Specifically, it noted that the law could fall foul of the reasonable classification test if the statutory purpose of section 377A was 'targeted specifically at male prostitution only' since the law would be over-inclusive by applying generally to all men who had sex with other men.[134]

In addition to repealing section 377A, presumably in order to balance the competing interests on the matter, the Prime Minister announced that his Government would also table a constitutional amendment to 'protect the definition of marriage from being challenged constitutionally in the courts' on the basis that 'judges and courts have neither the expertise nor the mandate to settle political questions, nor to rule on social norms and values'.[135] A new Article 156 of the Constitution, titled 'Institution of marriage', came into effect in January 2023 and states that nothing in Part 4 of the Constitution – which sets out constitutional guarantees of fundamental liberties – would invalidate laws or exercises of executive authority by reason that such laws or executive actions define or are based on the definition of marriage as a union between a man and a woman.

[130] WP (Crl) No 76 of 2016.
[131] [2020] SGHC 63.
[132] *Tan Seng Kee (CA)* (n 123).
[133] HL Lee, 'National Day Rally 2022' *Prime Minister's Office* (21 August 2022), available at www.pmo.gov.sg/Newsroom/National-Day-Rally-2022-English; see also YC Tham, 'Real risk of courts striking down Section 377A in future if law is not repealed: Panellists' *The Straits Times* (26 September 2022), available at www.straitstimes.com/singapore/politics/real-risk-of-courts-striking-down-section-377a-in-future-if-law-is-not-repealed-panel.
[134] *Tan Seng Kee (CA)* (n 123) at [324].
[135] Lee (n 133).

B. Challenge to the Exemption of Women from the Punishment of Caning

In *Yong Vui Kong v Public Prosecutor*,[136] the Court of Appeal had to consider the constitutionality of a law that exempts women (as well as men above the age of 50) from the punishment of caning.[137] The appellant argued, inter alia, that this violated the guarantee of equal protection under Article 12(1) of the Constitution. He submitted that there is 'no valid justification' for such differential treatment of males and females and that it would be 'patronising and outdated to regard females as the more delicate sex in need of protection'.[138]

To be clear, the appellant was not arguing that women (and men over 50) should be liable to caning as a form of punishment, but that there is no rational basis to distinguish men under 50 from these groups and therefore the punishment should be declared unconstitutional. This argument based on equality was rejected by the Court. Again, applying the reasonable classification test, the Court upheld the law on the basis that there was a rational relation between this exclusion and the objective of ensuring that only those who are physically fit to be caned are subject to caning.[139]

Two reasons were identified for the exclusion of women. First, the Court suggested that the rationale for the law exempting women was to vindicate 'the moral sense of the community'.[140] It conceded that it was not clear what this 'moral sense' entails but referred to legislative debates from 1886 on the drafting of the original enactment by the colonial Government.[141] Though not directly acknowledged by the Court, this suggests that the differential treatment of women under Singapore law remains drawn from Victorian era sensibilities: the exclusion of women reflects 'the moral sense that it is barbaric to inflict violence upon women' and for the concern that 'their decency would be violated'.[142] The Court's references to the need to protect decency and modesty[143] point to the colonial-inherited practice of caning (which entails the use of a rattan cane on bare buttocks),[144] which may be considered inappropriate for women.

The second reason the Court accepted was the 'differences in male and female physiology', which meant that women are, in general, 'less able to withstand caning'.[145]

[136] *Yong Vui Kong v Public Prosecutor* [2015] 2 SLR 1129, [2015] SGCA 11 [hereinafter *Yong Vui Kong*].
[137] Criminal Procedure Code (Cap 68, Rev Ed 2012), s 325(1).
[138] *Yong Vui Kong* (n 136) [109].
[139] ibid [110].
[140] ibid [109].
[141] ibid [108].
[142] ibid [111].
[143] ibid [109].
[144] P James, 'Letters: Always Caning in Singapore' *The Daily Telegraph* (29 September 1994).
[145] *Yong Vui Kong* (n 136) [109]–[110].

According to the Court, there is a rational nexus because Parliament is legitimately entitled to consider these 'obvious physiological differences'.[146] The Court conceded that 'these differences might not always obtain in individual cases' and that 'there may be cases where a given female is as physically robust if not even more so than a given male'.[147] However, the reasonable classification test only requires that the law is not completely arbitrary or capricious. Accordingly, while the Court, for the first time, acknowledged the 'gendered social attitudes' reflected in the law, it nonetheless reiterated that it is not the role of the judiciary to pass judgment on the soundness or rationality of such attitudes, or the legitimacy of the object of the law unless it is manifestly discriminatory that no reasonable person would consider the differentia adopted by the law to be a valid means of differentiation.[148]

C. Non-Constitutional Litigation Involving Gender and Sexuality Rights

As mentioned, constitutional litigation is seen as confrontational and as embarrassing the Government. Sub-constitutional litigation, focused on statutory interpretation, however, appears less confrontational. Accordingly, gender issues have been raised in several more cases which did not address constitutional rights.[149] Here, we discuss two such cases.

i. Transgender Rights and Marriage

In 2017, the Registry of Marriage voided a marriage between a transgender woman and her wife. They had married as man and woman before the husband underwent gender reassignment surgery.[150] Singapore allows transgender persons to change their legal gender after completing gender reassignment surgery.[151] Section 12(2) of the Women's Charter permits a valid marriage 'between a person who has undergone a sex re-assignment procedure and any person of the opposite sex'.[152] Comparatively, section 12(1) of the Women's Charter does not permit same-sex marriage, stating that 'a marriage solemnised in Singapore or elsewhere between persons who, at the date of the marriage, are not respectively male and female shall be void'. The couple initially filed for judicial review

[146] ibid [110].
[147] ibid [110].
[148] ibid [111].
[149] On sub-constitutional litigation, see generally PJ Yap, *Constitutional Dialogue in Common Law Asia* (Oxford University Press, 2015).
[150] XH Kok, 'ROM Voids Marriage between Same-Sex Couple' *The Straits Times* (18 July 2017), available at www.straitstimes.com/singapore/rom-voids-marriage-between-same-sex-couple.
[151] Note however that there has not been any official recognition of a third gender identity or intersexuality.
[152] Cap 353 (Rev Ed 2009).

to challenge the Registry's decision. It is not clear what the legal basis was for voiding the marriage since the law only requires that a couple be respectively male and female *at the date of marriage*.[153] It does not explicitly require that the couple remain respectively male and female after the date of marriage. No doubt, part of the consideration in this administrative decision by the Registry is that same-sex marriage is not recognised in Singapore and there appears to be a strong resistance towards legalisation. The legal issues, however, were not fully canvassed in court as the couple later dropped the case, purportedly due to privacy reasons as the court had not granted the couple's application to anonymise their names in the suit.[154]

ii. Adoption by Homosexual Persons

Another case involves the question of whether a homosexual person can adopt, specifically a child born through surrogacy. Under the Adoption of Children Act 1939 (ACA),[155] both married couples and singles can adopt a child. However, a single male is not allowed to adopt a female child unless permitted under special circumstances. The provision of surrogacy services is prohibited in Singapore, though Singaporeans have sought such services overseas. Children born through surrogacy arrangements have been brought back and passed off as their fully biological child.[156]

The permissibility of surrogacy arrangements was thrown into question when the gay father of a child born through surrogacy sought to adopt his American-born biological son in Singapore. His application was initially denied but later allowed on appeal on the basis that the adoption would be in the best interest of the child.[157] The Government has, in response, made statements that this ruling did not signal an acceptance of same-sex families, and that it would relook its policies on adoption.[158] Interestingly, though the applicant could have

[153] The Women's Charter, s 12(1) provides that 'a marriage solemnized in Singapore or elsewhere between persons who, at the date of the marriage, are not respectively male and female shall be void.'

[154] KC Vijayan, 'Same-Sex Couple Drops Case against ROM for Voiding Their Marriage' *The Straits Times* (17 May 2018), available at www.straitstimes.com/singapore/courts-crime/same-sex-couple-drop-case-against-rom; K Han, 'About that ROM/Same-Sex Couple Case' *Medium* (17 May 2018), available at medium.com/@kixes/about-that-rom-same-sex-couple-case-8e26a98ca941.

[155] Cap 4 (Rev Ed 2012).

[156] SA Tan and TF Tay, 'More Singapore Couples Seeking Surrogacy Services' *The Straits Times* (31 December 2017), available at www.straitstimes.com/singapore/more-spore-couples-seeking-surrogacy-services.

[157] *UKM v Attorney-General* [2018] SGHCF 18; see also KC Vijayan, 'Landmark High Court Case Allows Singaporean Gay Dad to Adopt Surrogate Son' *The Straits Times* (17 December 2018), available at www.straitstimes.com/singapore/courts-crime/landmark-high-court-case-allows-gay-dad-to-adopt-surrogate-son.

[158] R Au-Yong, 'Parliament: Authorities looking at adoption laws and surrogacy, do not support gay families, says Minister Desmond Lee' *The Strait Times* (January 2019), available at https://www.straitstimes.com/singapore/parliament-authorities-looking-at-adoption-laws-and-surrogacy-does-not-support-gay. The Adoption of Children Act was subsequently passed in 2022, which makes it practically impossible for same-sex couples to adopt.

challenged the discriminatory effect of the interplay between adoption, family and citizenship law in Singapore, there was no constitutional challenge in the application. Instead, the main constitutional issue the court addressed was in relation to its role and function within the constitutional framework of the separation of powers and how public policy should be taken into account in judicial adjudication.[159]

V. STRATEGIC ENGAGEMENT AND LITIGATION AVERSION

Instead of constitutional litigation, social and policy change have often been achieved through constructive collaborations where the state worked in tandem with advocates to reverse discrimination in state policy and in addressing problems women faced such as domestic violence, sexual harassment[160] and marital rape.[161] Many policy reversals have also been brought about after strong challenges by women politicians in the parliamentary arena. For instance, following sustained criticism by female parliamentarians as well as feminist activists,[162] a policy was reformed to confer on female civil servants the same medical benefits for their dependents 'in support of the Government's efforts to promote a more pro-family work environment'.[163]

A key policy reversal that was achieved through strategic engagement, rather than constitutional litigation, was the removal of a gender quota in Singapore's (then) only medical school. The quota, which was put in place in 1979, capped female enrolment to just one-third, and has been identified as a major contributing factor to a continuing imbalance in female representation in leadership positions in the profession today.[164] The Government justified the introduction of the quota on the basis that it was costly to train doctors and that more female doctors were leaving the profession or working part-time to raise families.[165]

[159] *UKM* (n 157) [124]–[126].

[160] Cap 256A (Rev Ed 2015). See also Shaddick et al (n 12) 142.

[161] 'AWARE Welcomes Repeal of Marital Rape and Suicide Decriminalisation, Recommends Clear Definition of Consent and Comprehensive Public Education' (*AWARE*, 2 October 2018), available at www.aware.org.sg/2018/10/aware-welcomes-repeal-of-marital-rape-and-suicide-decriminalisation-recommends-clear-definition-of-consent-and-comprehensive-public-education.

[162] 'Equal Medical Benefits for Women Needed: Call Made by Women MPs to Make "Overdue" Change to the Policy' *The Straits Times* (13 May 2002); AWARE (n 10); LA Thio, 'Recent Constitutional Developments: Of Shadows and Whips, Race, Rifts and Rights, Terror and "Tudungs", Women and Wrongs' (2002) *Singapore Journal of Legal Studies* 328, 348–49.

[163] Ministry of Information, Communications and the Arts, 'Press Release: Civil Service Moves Ahead with Changes to Promote a Pro-Family Environment and Better Work-Life Balance for Civil Servants' (*National Archives of Singapore*, 25 August 2004), available at www.nas.gov.sg/archivesonline/data/pdfdoc/2004082596.htm.

[164] YH Gan and S Archuleta, 'Holding Up Half the Sky – Women in Singapore Medicine' (*MediCine*, May 2020), available at medicine.nus.edu.sg/newsletters/issue34/insights/holding-up-half-the-sky-women-in-singapore-medicine.

[165] T Tan, 'More Women Studying Medicine after Lifting of Quota' *The Straits Times* (14 July 2017), available at www.straitstimes.com/singapore/more-women-studying-medicine-after-lifting-of-quota.

Notably, there were no women in Parliament at the time the quota was introduced. The only female Member of Parliament then had retired in 1970 and there was no female representation in Parliament until 1984.[166] Parliamentary debate on the quota was revived in 1994, not by an elected member of parliament but by an NMP, Kanwaljit Soin. A former President of AWARE, Soin argued in Parliament that this quota 'not only … offend[s] the letter and spirit of our Constitution, but it is also against our ethos of building a society based on justice and meritocracy'.[167] In response, the Minister for Education said that the university had consulted its lawyers, who advised that the quota was not unconstitutional. He added that if she disagreed, she could 'put this to a test in a court of law'.[168]

Significantly, neither Soin nor any other activist or lawyer took up the Minister's suggestion and the quota remained operative for another decade before the Government abolished it in 2003. The way in which change came about highlights another key plank in effective advocacy, and that is the reliance on evidence-based advocacy. In January 2002, before the Ministry of Health announced that it was willing to review the quota, the Association of Women Doctors (Singapore) had released survey results demonstrating only a one per cent difference in the attrition rate between male and female doctors.[169] This was a turning point, accelerated by further advocacy and supporters coming on board the reform agenda. In its submissions to the RSC in July 2002, AWARE reiterated that the quota was 'an outrageous act of outright discrimination' and urged the Government to abolish it.[170] An RSC sub-committee focusing on women's issues agreed, with the chairperson highlighting that admission into the medical faculty should be based only on merit.[171] In September 2002, the Government Parliamentary Committee for Community Development and Sports similarly announced its support for the removal of the quota. By February 2003, a Government minister announced at a speech to the Association of Women Doctors that the quota had been abolished given that there was 'no significant problem in deploying female doctors nowadays'.[172] Notably, the Government's decision to abolish the quota did not

[166] N Tan, 'Elected Women Politicians in Singapore's Parliament: An Analysis of Socio-Demographic Profile' in M Najafizadeh and L Lindsey (eds), *Women of Asia: Globalization, Development, and Gender Equity* (Routledge, 2018) 199.

[167] 'Singapore Parliamentary Debates, Official Report' (25 August 1994) vol 63 at col 486 'Quota on Female Medical Students' (NMP Kanwaljit Soin).

[168] 'Singapore Parliamentary Debates, Official Report' (25 August 1994) vol 63 at col 487 'Quota on Female Medical Students' (Lee Yock Suan (Minister for Education)).

[169] HT Liang, 'Ministry to Relook Quota for Women Doctors' *The Straits Times* (19 January 2001).

[170] AWARE (n 10) 5.

[171] SA Chia, 'Women's Panel Pushes to End Discrimination' *The Straits Times* (24 August 2002).

[172] PA Tambyah, 'Selection of Medical Students in Singapore: A Historical Perspective' (2005) 34 *Annals of the Academy of Medicine Singapore* 147C, 149C.

reference its international obligations under CEDAW or the constitutional principle of equality.[173] Instead, economic pragmatism was a strong factor in the move to abolish. The principle of meritocracy was also repeatedly invoked in justifying the removal of the quota.

Another major reform initiative came in the form of the repeal of marital rape immunity in the Penal Code. In 2019, the Government announced that it would repeal marital immunity for rape following years of advocacy by various constituents, including AWARE.[174] Absolute marital immunity for rape persisted until 2007, when it was reduced to partial immunity except where the couple lived apart under a judgment for divorce or a written separation agreement, or if divorce proceedings had begun, or if the wife had obtained a personal protection order against the husband.[175] Though AWARE had argued that marital immunity to rape 'breaches the principle of equal protection before the law' as guaranteed by the Constitution,[176] there was no impetus to file a constitutional challenge. Instead, in 2009, a group of volunteers launched the 'No To Rape' campaign, with the support of AWARE and MARUAH, another Singaporean human rights organisation. This campaign launched an online petition to the Prime Minister to fully repeal marital rape immunity, which garnered about 3,600 signatures. Besides working on the international front through participation in CEDAW reviews and the Universal Periodic Report exercise, AWARE and MARUAH also worked with the 'No To Rape' campaign to influence public opinion by organising public seminars and galvanising debate in public newspaper forums.[177] These efforts gained traction and, in 2019, the Penal Code Review Committee recommended the absolute removal of martial rape immunity, which came into effect in a wide-ranging Criminal Law Reform Act.[178]

VI. CONCLUSION

As this chapter demonstrates, the equal protection provisions – and other provisions guaranteeing individual liberties under Part 4 of the Constitution – remain untapped resources that could be invoked should future governments become less protective of gender equality. Thio has argued that constitutionalising gender as

[173] Thio, *Of Shadows and Whips* (n 162) 351.

[174] R Rashith, 'Penal Code review committee: Husbands may soon have no more marital immunity for rape' *The Straits Times* (9 September 2018), available at www.straitstimes.com/singapore/penal-code-review-committee-husbands-may-soon-have-no-more-marital-immunity-for-rape.

[175] The Penal Code (repealed 2020), s 375(4).

[176] PC Wong, P Ray, V Wee and N Samsudin, 'The Right to Protection from Marital Rape' (*AWARE*, 10 December 2012), available at www.aware.org.sg/2012/12/the-right-to-protection-from-marital-rape.

[177] J Tan, 'What Took Us So Long to Move against Marital Immunity for Rape?' *Channel NewsAsia* (13 September 2018), available at www.channelnewsasia.com/news/commentary/penal-code-review-rape-marital-immunity-sexual-assault-violence-10706304.

[178] Criminal Law Reform Act (No. 15 of 2019).

a prohibited basis for discrimination under Article 12(2) will 'contribute towards the development of a constitutional jurisprudence which gives appropriate effect to the principle of gender equality' and reflects the seriousness of Singapore's commitment to CEDAW.[179] The absence of a binding constitutional norm of gender equality in Singapore may prove problematic in the future and may well have to be resolved as Singapore matures as a constitutional democracy and its citizenry turns more to constitutional litigation to advance their claims.

The evolution of constitutional jurisprudence on gender equality would also raise interesting questions as to how clashes between gender equality and other constitutional rights would be addressed. So far, there has been one case which involves a potential conflict between freedom of religion and gender-protective law where a pregnant employee successfully challenged her dismissal by a church organisation for pregnancy discrimination, which is prohibited under statute.[180] The Church brought a constitutional challenge against the Commissioner for Labour's decision, claiming that its constitutional right to manage its own religious affairs and to religious freedom had been violated. Unfortunately, the Church later withdrew the suit, issuing a statement that it had 'come to understand and recognise the rationale/basis for the Minister's decision'.[181] Had the case proceeded to trial, this would have been the first case involving the clash between religious freedom and women's equal rights in employment.

On the whole, the Singapore experience demonstrates how gender equality may be achieved even when constitutional litigation is limited in a litigation-averse political culture, where national identity, including gender, is closely constructed by the dominant party government. It points to the importance of sub-constitutional litigation and strategic engagement by advocacy groups but also to the limits to this strategic navigation in accelerating social change. A pragmatic strategy of engagement may well reach its limits, and may require the pursuit of a constitutionalised protection for gender equality in the long run. At the very least, the Singapore example helpfully points to a broader and important question for the 'feminist constitutional agenda'[182] as to when, whether, and in what instances constitutional law and adjudication could be the most effective means by which to achieve gender equality. There simply cannot be a one-size-fits-all agenda; every reform agenda has to be localised to meet the social and political conditions of each country.

[179] Thio, *The transformative potential of CEDAW* (n 26) 324–25.

[180] YC Toh, 'Faith Community Baptist Church Drops High Court Review over Sacking of Pregnant Church Worker' *The Straits Times* (18 May 2015), available at www.straitstimes.com/singapore/courts-crime/faith-community-baptist-church-drops-high-court-review-over-sacking-of.

[181] Y Lim, 'Church Drops Bid for Judicial Review of Compensating Sacked Pregnant Worker', *TodayOnline* (18 May 2015), available at www.todayonline.com/singapore/fcbc-withdraws-bid-judicial-review-moms-order-compensate-ex-employee.

[182] Generally, Baines and Rubio-Marín (n 110).

8

*Gender, Sexuality and Democratic Constitutionalism in the Philippines**

BRYAN DENNIS G TIOJANCO**

I. INTRODUCTION

LEGISLATION HAS PAVED the path to gender justice in the Philippines. This fact reflects two longstanding Filipino traditions: widespread acceptance of the ballot as the fount of political legitimacy,[1] and mobilised participation in politics of women and, more recently, LGBTs.[2] The Supreme Court (SC) reinforces the democracy principle (the very first principle the 1987 Philippine Constitution ('Constitution') declares[3]) in its decisions on gender equality and justice in two ways: by giving Congress great leeway to resolve these issues, and by upholding and enforcing gender justice legislation.

This institutionalised faith in the democratic process has paid off. Since its first Gender Gap Index in 2006 the World Economic Forum has always ranked the Philippines first in Asia, and up until 2018 the only Asian country among the top 10 most gender equal in the world.[4] The country slipped to 16th place

* I thank Rebecka Koziomtzis for her expert assistance in my research for this chapter.

** Philippine laws, including the 1987 Philippine Constitution [hereinafter 'Constitution'], are available online at the *Official Gazette*: www.officialgazette.gov.ph; decisions of the Philippine Supreme Court from 1996 onwards and the Record of the 1986 Constitutional Commission [hereinafter RCC] are available online at the SC E-Library: elibrary.judiciary.gov.ph/.

[1] RE Agpalo, 'Legitimacy and the Political Elite in the Philippines' (1975) 2 *Philippine Political Science Journal* 1.

[2] M Hega, V Alporha and M Evangelista, *Feminism and the Women's Movement in the Philippines: Struggles, Advances, and Challenges* (Friedrich-Ebert-Stiftung, 2018); United Nations Development Programme [hereinafter UNDP] and United States Agency for International Development [hereinafter USAID], 'Being LGBT in Asia: The Philippines Country Report' (2014) 8–9, 15–20.

[3] Constitution, Art II, s 1.

[4] World Economic Forum [hereinafter WEF], 'The Global Gender Gap Report' (2018) 8, available at www3.weforum.org/docs/WEF_GGGR_2018.pdf; WEF, 'The Global Gender Gap Report' (2006) 9, available at www3.weforum.org/docs/WEF_GenderGap_Report_2006.pdf; P Pasion, 'PH Slides to 10th Spot of Global Gender Gap Report for 2017' *Rappler* (2 November 2017), available at www.rappler.com/nation/187075-philippine-ranking-2017-global-gender-gap-report; *cf* Organization for

worldwide in the 2020 index and again to 19th in 2022, but still 'boasts the smallest gender gap of the Asian continent by far.'[5] Filipino women are the second most politically empowered in Asia.[6] They hold 53 per cent of managerial positions in workplaces. On average female household heads earn and save nearly 10 per cent more than male ones.[7] And since 1971 there have been 10–20 per cent more women than men enrolled in higher education.[8] This affirms the 'common observation that Filipino women are the most liberated in Asia and one of the most empowered.'[9]

The Philippines is also considered Asia's 'most gay-friendly nation' – with public acceptance of lesbians, gays, bisexuals and transgenders (LGBTs) at around 73 per cent in 2013 (compared to nine per cent in Malaysia and three per cent in Indonesia).[10] Unlike in Singapore, Malaysia and Myanmar, in the Philippines homosexual acts are not crimes.[11] In 2016 a transgender won a congressional district seat.[12] And while the *Ang Ladlad LGBT Party* has yet to win a congressional party-list seat, it has helped build an LGBT community.[13]

Yet there is still much to improve. Less than half of Filipino women are part of the country's labour force (compared to 75 per cent of men).[14] In 2022 the percentage of women in senior management roles dropped from 48 per cent to

Economic Co-operation and Development, 'Social Institutions and Gender Index' (2019), available at www.genderindex.org/wp-content/uploads/files/datasheets/2019/PH.pdf (gender discrimination in the Philippines is 'very high').

[5] WEF, 'The Global Gender Gap Report' (2020) 9 and 32, available at www3.weforum.org/docs/WEF_GGGR_2020.pdf (second best is Lao PDR at 43rd); WEF, 'Global Gender Gap Report' (2022) 10, available at www3.weforum.org/docs/WEF_GGGR_2022.pdf (second best is Singapore at 49th).

[6] India ranked first in the 2020 index, Bangladesh ranked first in the 2022 index.

[7] 'Factsheet on Women and Men in the Philippines' (Philippine Statistics Authority [hereinafter PSA], 5 March 2020), available at psa.gov.ph/gender-stat/wmf.

[8] 'Philippines: Female to Male Ratio, Students at Tertiary Level Education' *TheGlobal Economy.com*, available at www.theglobaleconomy.com/Philippines/Female_to_male_ratio_students_tertiary_level_educa; T Quismundo, 'CHEd: There's Gender Gap in College, Work' *Philippine Daily Inquirer* (31 May 2012), available at newsinfo.inquirer.net/204499/ched-theres-gender-gap-in-college-work#:~:text=The%20CHEd%20chairperson%20was%20asked,44%20percent%20of%20the%20total.

[9] ME Atienza and RL Rico, 'Women and Politics in the Philippines' in TE Tadem and N Morada (eds), *Philippine Politics and Governance: Challenges to Democratization and Development* (University of the Philippines, 2006) 205, 210.

[10] R Turner, 'The Philippines: Make Way for the Baklas' (2017) 24 *The Gay & Lesbian Review Worldwide* 28; 'The Global Divide on Homosexuality' (Pew Research Center, 4 June 2013), available at www.pewresearch.org/global/2013/06/04/the-global-divide-on-homosexuality.

[11] R Kwatra, 'LGBTIQ Rights in Southeast Asia – Where We Stand and Pathway Forward' (*Huffpost*, 20 June 2017), available at www.huffpost.com/entry/lgbtiq-rights-in-southeast-asia-where-we-stand-pathway_b_5948115fe4b0f7875b83e4a6.

[12] E Izadi, 'The First Transgender Politician Was Just Elected to Congress in the Philippines' *The Washington Post* (11 May 2016), available at www.washingtonpost.com/news/worldviews/wp/2016/05/10/hatred-and-discrimination-did-not-triumph-philippines-elects-first-transgender-congress-member.

[13] J Cornelio and RC Dagle, 'Weaponising Religious Freedom: Same-Sex Marriage and Gender Equality in the Philippines' (2019) 14 *Religion & Human Rights* 65, 66–67.

[14] 'Philippines: Female Labor Force Participation' (*TheGlobalEconomy.com*), available at www.theglobaleconomy.com/Philippines/Female_labor_force_participation; PSA (n 7).

39 per cent (despite this, the Philippines still boasts the third-highest percentage of women leaders in mid-sized firms among the 29 countries ranked).[15] Women also presently occupy only 23 per cent of elective governmental positions.[16] In agriculture, where one in four Filipinos make their living, male farmworkers are paid around 10 per cent more than female ones.[17] On average one woman or child is raped every hour – and each year sees a rise in reported women victims of rape, physical, economic, sexual or emotional abuse, prostitution and trafficking.[18] Thirteen of every 100 women report that they cannot refuse their husband's sexual demands.[19] The Philippines is the only state other than the Vatican City where divorce is not generally allowed (only spouses married to either a Muslim husband or a foreigner can have their divorce legally recognised).[20] Indigenous women 'face triple discrimination based on gender, ethnicity, and socioeconomic status' and so suffer from abject poverty, insufficient education if not illiteracy, low employment, deprivation of basic, health and sanitation facilities, political disempowerment, and a high risk of domestic and sexual violence.[21]

Public acceptance of LGBTs is conditional on their conformity with fixed expectations and performance of allotted roles at home, school and the workplace.[22] The Roman Catholic Church, to which eight of 10 Filipinos belong, considers same-sex relationships and unions unacceptable. Some Protestant churches condemn homosexuality. And many Muslims interpret Islam, the country's largest non-Christian faith, as abhorring homosexuality.[23]

[15] 'Women in Business Report' *The Philippine Star* (7 March 2022), available at https://www.philstar.com/business/2022/03/07/2165355/women-business-report.

[16] PSA (n 7).

[17] LM Simeon, 'Gender Pay Inequality Rampant in Agriculture Sector' *The Philippine Star* (1 September 2020), available at www.philstar.com/business/2020/09/01/2039161/gender-pay-inequality-rampant-agriculture-sector; IN Cigaral, 'Agriculture Output Slightly Grew in 2019' *The Philippine Star* (22 January 2020), available at www.philstar.com/business/2020/01/22/1986895/agriculture-output-slightly-grew-2019.

[18] Y Morales, 'One Person Raped Per Hour in PH – Report' *CNN Philippines* (8 March 2017), available at cnnphilippines.com/news/2017/03/07/One-person-raped-per-hour-in-PH.html; C Ordinario, 'More Women Raped, Physically Abused Last Year–Govt Data' *Business Mirror* (9 March 2020), available at businessmirror.com.ph/2020/03/09/more-women-raped-physically-abused-last-year-govt-data.

[19] PSA (n 7) 4.

[20] Family Code of the Phils (Family Code), Exec Order No 209 (1987) Art 26, para 2; *Republic v Manalo*, GR No 221029 (24 April 2018); Code of Muslim Personal Laws of the Philippines, Pres Dec No 1083, Title II (1977); *Sumagka v Sumagka*, GR No 200697 (10 June 2019); *Zamoranos v People*, GR No 193902, 665 Phil 447 (1 June 2011).

[21] Commission on Human Rights of the Philippines, 'Written Statement for the Virtual Day of General Discussion on the Rights of Indigenous Women and Girls' (7 July 2021) para.12, available at chr.gov.ph/written-statement-for-the-virtual-day-of-general-discussion-on-the-rights-of-indigenous-women-and-girls.

[22] AC Presto, 'Revisiting Intersectional Identities: Voices of Poor Bakla Youth in Rural Philippines' (2020) 29 *Review of Women's Studies* 113, 119, 129–34, 140.

[23] UNDP and USAID (n 2) 25–28.

As such, LGBTs are considered abnormal and often bullied or discriminated.[24] And although there have been various reports of LGBT-related crimes (including killings) within the country, the Philippines refused to support either the 2011 joint statement at the UN Human Rights Council (UNHRC) or the 2016 UNHRC resolution which condemned violence and discrimination based on sexual orientation, gender identity and gender expression (SOGIE).[25]

Section II of this chapter discusses the three structural principles of Philippine democracy which shape the gendered landscape of Philippine law: the separation of powers; the People Power Principle; and the separation of church and state. Section III discusses the framing of gender and sexuality in the drafting of the Constitution, its general guarantees of civil, political and socioeconomic rights, and its specific clauses on gender equality and justice. Section IV discusses the relevant constitutional jurisprudence, which traditionally has followed legislative policy on gender equality and justice and recently has been updating old rules in ways that promote gender justice. Section V muddles our picture with two stories of the SC serving as a roadblock to addressing persistent women's rights concerns. Section VI concludes by noting that democratic constitutionalism has been the motor of gender justice in the country.

II. BACKGROUND INFORMATION

Three structural principles of Philippine government shape the gendered landscape of Philippine law: the separation of powers, the People Power Principle, and the separation of church and state. These principles enforce the country's commitment to democracy.

The separation of powers and of church and state have a long pedigree in the country. Historically both can be traced to the abortive 1899 Malolos Constitution. Doctrinally the separation of church and state is traced to United States President William McKinley's Instructions to the Second Philippine Commission of April 7, 1900, the first of three principal organic acts by which the United States governed the archipelago (at that time one of its unincorporated territories);[26] the separation of powers is traced to the Philippine Bill of 1902, the second of the three organic acts.[27] The People Power Principle, on the other hand, is relatively new. It is a legacy of the 1986 People Power

[24] 'Just Let Us Be: Discrimination Against LGBT Students in the Philippines' (Human Rights Watch [hereinafter HRW], 21 June 2017), available at www.hrw.org/report/2017/06/21/just-let-us-be/discrimination-against-lgbt-students-philippines; Presto (n 22) 115.

[25] UN General Assembly, 'Resolution Adopted by the Human Rights Council on 30 June 2016', available at documents-dds-ny.un.org/doc/UNDOC/GEN/G16/154/15/PDF/G1615415.pdf?OpenElement; UNDP and USAID (n 2) 21.

[26] *Estrada v Escritor*, AM No P-02-1651 (4 August 2003).

[27] *United States v Bull*, GR No L-5270, 15 Phil 7, 27 (15 January 1910).

Revolution which overthrew the Marcos dictatorship and restored Philippine democracy.[28]

The separation-of-powers principle is inferred from the Constitution's separate clauses vesting the legislative power mainly in Congress, the executive power in the President, and the judicial power in both the SC and statutory law courts.[29] In theory the legislative, executive and judicial departments are coordinate and coequal. In practice, however, the President has historically dominated Philippine government.[30] Both the President and Vice-President are directly elected nationwide for six-year terms.[31] Two of the seven Presidents and three of the eight Vice-Presidents under the Constitution, including the incumbent Vice-President, have been women.[32]

Congress consists of a Senate and a House of Representatives ('House').[33] The Senate is composed of 24 senators elected nationwide, 12 at a time, every three years.[34] A Senator's term of office is six years.[35] 29 per cent (seven) of incumbent senators are women.[36] The House is presently composed of 311 house members.[37] 251 of them are district representatives,[38] which are apportioned demographically among localities every three years.[39] 28 per cent (70) of incumbent district representatives are women. The remaining 60 members of the House[40] (19 per cent of its total membership) are elected though a party-list system of national, regional and sectoral parties.[41] 25 per cent (15) of incumbent party-list representatives are women. Members of the House are elected for three-year terms.[42]

[28] M Thompson, *The Anti-Marcos Struggle: Personalistic Rule and Democratic Transition in the Philippines* (Yale University Press, 1995).

[29] Constitution, Art VI, ss 1 and 32, Art VII, s 1 and Art VIII, s 1.

[30] VV Mendoza, From McKinley's Instructions to the New Constitution: Documents on the Philippine Constitutional System (Central Lawbook Pub Co, 1978).

[31] Constitution, Art VII, s 4.

[32] The Editors of Encyclopaedia Britannica, 'Corazon Aquino: president of the Philippines', (Britannica, 21 January 2023), available at www.britannica.com/biography/Corazon-Aquino; The Editors of Encyclopaedia Britannica, 'Gloria Macapagal Arroyo: president of the Philippines', (Britannica, 1 April 2023), available at www.britannica.com/biography/Gloria-Macapagal-Arroyo; Republic of the Philippines Office of the Vice President, 'Biography', available at www.ovp.gov.ph/biography; Republic of the Philippines Office of the Vice President, 'Previous Vice Presidents', available at www.ovp.gov.ph/previous-vps.

[33] Constitution, Art VI, s 1.

[34] Constitution, At VI, s 2 and Art XVIII, s 2.

[35] Constitution, Art VI, s 4.

[36] '19th Congress Senators' (Senate of the Philippines – 19th Congress), available at legacy.senate.gov.ph/senators/sen19th.asp.

[37] 'House Members' (House of Representatives – 19th Congress), available at congress.gov.ph/members.

[38] 'District Representatives' (House of Representatives – 19th Congress), available at congress.gov.ph/members/?v=district.

[39] Constitution, Art VI, s 5.

[40] 'Party List Representatives' (*House of Representatives* – 19th Congress), available at congress.gov.ph/members/?v=pl.

[41] Constitution, Art VI, s 5(1).

[42] Constitution, Art VI, s 7.

Judicial power in the Philippines has since 1902 included judicial review, viz, the power to determine the legal validity of official actions.[43] The Constitution expands judicial power to include 'the duty … to determine whether or not there has been a grave abuse of discretion amounting to lack or excess of jurisdiction on the part of any branch or instrumentality of the Government.'[44] The SC can exercise original jurisdiction to determine grave abuse of discretion,[45] but even without such abuse it can correct unconstitutional official actions.[46] All exercises of judicial review by other courts can also be appealed to it.[47]

The SC is composed of a Chief Justice and 14 Associate Justices who, like all judges and Justices, enjoy security of tenure until they are 70. It currently sits in three five-member divisions but must sit *en banc* in certain cases such as when exercising judicial review.[48] Of the 15 Justices presently sitting, 87 per cent (13) are men and only 13 per cent (two) are women.[49]

The President appoints all SC Justices from a list prepared by the Judicial and Bar Council (JBC), a constitutional body composed of the Chief Justice, the Justice Secretary, a member of Congress, a lawyer, a law professor, a retired SC Justice, and a representative of the private sector.[50] Presently only one incumbent member of the JBC is a woman – and she sits only on a half-the-year timeshare arrangement.[51] During its first 20 years the JBC nominated 65 men and 15 women to the SC.[52] In its latest shortlist for the position of SC Justice, four of the six nominees were women;[53] the President appointed one of them to the post.[54]

[43] See AL Castañeda, 'The Origins of Philippine Judicial Review, 1900–1935' (2001) 46 *Ateneo Law Journal* 121, 134–37.

[44] Constitution, Art VIII, s 1.

[45] Constitution, Art VIII, s 5(1); The 1997 Rules of Civil Procedure, r 65.

[46] eg, *Atong Paglaum v Commission on Elections* (Comelec), GR No 203766 (2 April 2013).

[47] Constitution, Art VIII, s 5(2)(a).

[48] Constitution, Art VIII, ss 2, 4(1), 11.

[49] Supreme Court of the Philippines, 'Incumbent Justices', available at sc.judiciary.gov.ph/incumbent-justices.

[50] Constitution, Art VIII, ss 8–9.

[51] Judicial and Bar Council (JBC), 'The Council', available at jbc.judiciary.gov.ph/index.php/about-us/the-organization/the-council. Both Houses of Congress have agreed on a six-month rotational representation in the JBC; a House Representative represents Congress from January to June, a Senator from July to December: see *Umali v Judicial and Bar Council*, GR No 228628 (25 July 2017).

[52] D Gatmaytan and C Magno, 'Averting Diversity: A Review of Nominations and Appointments to the Philippine Supreme Court (1988-2008)' in D Gatmaytan (ed), *More Equal than Others: Constitutional Law and Politics* (University of the Philippines, 2017) 53, 62–65.

[53] JBC, 'Nominations for the position of Associate Justice of the Supreme Court of the Philippines' (12 April 2022), available at jbc.judiciary.gov.ph/pdffolder/shortlist/2022/Shortlist_SC-AJ_4-12-22.pdf.

[54] R Panaligan, 'Duterte names CA Justice Filomena Singh 15th Supreme Court member' *Manila Bulletin* (18 May 2022), available at mb.com.ph/2022/05/18/duterte-names-ca-justice-filomena-singh-15th-supreme-court-member.

The gender ratio in the lower courts is better. In the Court of Appeals, the country's second highest court, 30 of the 66 (45 per cent) Justices are women.[55] In the Sandiganbayan eight of the 20 (40 per cent) Justices are women (one seat is vacant), as are eight of the nine (89 per cent) Justices in the Court of Tax Appeals.[56] 1,106 of the country's 2,026 (55 per cent) trial court judges are women.[57] This is a remarkable improvement from 2001, when only about one in five judges were women.[58] In 2011 only 597 of the 1,637 lower court judges were women.[59] Since then more than half of the judges appointed have been women.[60]

The People Power Principle implements the constitutional 'right of the people and their organizations to effective and reasonable participation at all levels of social, political, and economic decision-making'.[61] Thus the Constitution enables direct citizen participation in policy-making through initiative, referendum and recall.[62] It politically empowers different kinds of citizen groups: workers, farmers, the urban and rural poor, people's organisations, non-governmental, community-based, or sectoral organizations, etc.[63] In various degrees the Constitution enables them to participate in public decision-making as a 'part of due process in the pursuit of social justice.'[64]

Philippine civil society has used these people power provisions to pursue gender justice. An all-women political party fielded candidates in the 1987 elections but failed to win a seat either nationally or locally. In 1998 women's groups participated in the party-list elections and succeeded in electing a women's sector representative. In 2004 another women's party, GABRIELA, also won a party-list seat;[65] since then it has continuously held one to two

[55] Court of Appeals, 'Incumbent Justices', available at ca.judiciary.gov.ph/faces/page/core/Main.xhtml.

[56] 'Sandiganbayan Incumbent Justices', available at sb.judiciary.gov.ph/justices.html; Court of Tax Appeals, 'Organizational Structure', available at cta.judiciary.gov.ph/org_struc.

[57] R Panaligan, 'More female than male members in judiciary' *Manila Bulletin* (10 March 2022), available at mb.com.ph/2022/03/10/more-female-than-male-members-in-judiciary.

[58] Justice AM Herrera, 'Selected Speeches and Writings' (2009) 11 *Philippine Judicial Academy (PHILJA) Judicial Journal* 1, 312.

[59] Supreme Court, 'Number of Male and Female Judges in the Lower Courts for 2019 (as of December 31, 2019)', available at sc.judiciary.gov.ph/gender-data/oca-oas.

[60] Supreme Court, 'Sex-Disaggregated Date of Seminars for Judges and Lawyers', available at sc.judiciary.gov.ph/gender-data. I base this estimate on the reported number of participants (983 total; 543 women = 55%) in the yearly orientation seminar-workshop for newly appointed judges. Data for the years 2013–14 are unavailable.

[61] Constitution, Art XIII, s 16.

[62] Constitution, Art VI, s 32, Art X, s 3, Art XVII, s 2.

[63] Constitution, Art II, ss 18 and 23, Art VI, ss 5(1)–(2), Art XIII, ss 3–7, 9–10, 15–16.

[64] C Monsod, 'The Relevance of the 1986 EDSA People Power Today' (*School of Economics Auditorium, University of the Philippines-Diliman, Quezon City*, 24 February 2017), available at www.rappler.com/nation/162426-relevance-edsa-people-power-today.

[65] Atienza and Rico (n 9) 224.

party-list seats.[66] One senator who staunchly supports gender justice, Risa Hontiveros, started her legislative career as a party-list representative.[67] Their successes include several gender justice statutes. The Anti-Violence Against Women and Their Children Act of 2004 (Anti-VAWC Act),[68] for example, was enacted following almost a decade of advocacy by sexual-violence survivors, women's groups and mostly female legislators.[69] These efforts are bolstered by The Magna Carta of Women's mandate that government 'take steps to review and, when necessary, amend and/or repeal existing laws that are discriminatory to women.'[70] Following this mandate, the Philippine Commission on Women (PCW), the Government's official policy-making, coordinating and monitoring agency on women and gender equality concerns,[71] has launched a Women's Priority Legislative Agenda (WPLA) aimed at the amendment or repeal of discriminatory laws and the enactment of legislation promoting women's rights and empowerment.[72] In the last decade at least four items in the WPLA were enacted into law.[73]

The Ang Ladlad LGBT Party has run for a party-list seat on several occasions although has yet to win one.[74] The Commission on Elections (Comelec) had refused to accredit it as a political party 'on moral grounds', but the SC overruled it, explaining that 'moral disapproval of an unpopular minority – is not a legitimate state interest that is sufficient to satisfy rational basis review under the equal protection clause.'[75] Since 1999 LGBT groups have been successful in placing SOGIE equality on the congressional agenda.[76] At least 10 such bills in the House and four in the Senate are now pending.[77] These efforts are led by an

[66] C Salazar, '"Red-tagged" Gabriela, Kabataan win party-list seats amid dwindling gov't opposition' *Philippine Center for Investigative Journalism* (Quezon City, 26 May 2022), available at pcij.org/blog/3359/red-tagged-gabriela-kabataan-win-party-list-seats-amid-dwindling-govt-opposition; S Tomacruz, 'Comelec Proclaims 51 Winning Groups in 2019 Party-List Elections' *Rappler* (22 May 2019), available at www.rappler.com/nation/politics/elections/2019/230843-party-list-groups-proclaimed-winners-2019; '46 Groups Proclaimed as Party List Winners' *Rappler* (20 May 2016), available at www.rappler.com/nation/politics/elections/2016/133630-groups-proclaimed-party-list; R Chua, '38 Party-List Winners Proclaimed' *ABS-CBN News* (28 May 2013), available at news.abs-cbn.com/nation/05/28/13/comelec-proclaims-24-more-party-list-winners.

[67] Senate of the Philippines, 'Biography: Senator Risa Hontiveros', available at ldr.senate.gov.ph/senator/hontiveros-risa.

[68] Rep Act No 9262 (2004).

[69] MR Guanzon, 'Legal and Conceptual Framework of Battered Woman Syndrome as a Defense' (2012) 86 *Philippine Law Journal* 124, 125.

[70] Rep Act No 9710 (2009) s 12.

[71] The Magna Carta of Women, ss 39–40; Philippine Commission on Women (PCW) Resolution No 1, s 2019, 1st Whereas Clause. The PCW was formerly known as the National Commission on the Role of Filipino Women.

[72] PCW, 'Herstory', available at pcw.gov.ph/herstory.

[73] PCW, 'Beijing Declaration and Platform for Action 2014–2019 Philippine Progress Report' (2020) 6 [hereinafter BPfA +25 Progress Report 2014–2019].

[74] Cornelio and Dagle (n 13) 66.

[75] *Ang Ladlad LGBT Party v Comelec*, GR No 190582, 632 Phil 32 (8 April 2010).

[76] See Cornelio and Dagle (n 13) 76–87.

[77] See *Falcis v Civil Registrar General*, GR No 217910 (3 September 2019).

advocacy network dedicated to the passage of a SOGIE equality law.[78] LGBTs are already specifically protected in various laws. The Implementing Rules and Regulations of the Anti-Bullying Act of 2013 defines 'any act that humiliates or excludes a person on the basis of perceived or actual sexual orientation and gender identity' as a prohibited instance of 'Gender-based bullying'.[79] The Philippine HIV and AIDS Policy Act implements a policy of nondiscrimination 'on the basis of perceived or actual HIV status, sex, gender, sexual orientation, gender identity and expression', among others.[80] The Safe Spaces Act criminalises gender-based sexual harassment – including 'misogynistic, transphobic, homophobic, and sexist slurs' – in streets and public spaces, workplaces and online.[81]

The enactment of the country's gender justice laws has been motivated in part by its treaty obligations. The Philippines has ratified nearly all United Nations (UN) human rights treaties, including the International Covenant on Economic, Social and Cultural Rights (ICESCR) in 1974, the Convention on the Elimination of All Forms of Discrimination Against Women (CEDAW) in 1981, the International Covenant on Civil and Political Rights (ICCPR) in 1986 and the Convention on the Rights of the Child (CRC) in 1990.[82] Since the country follows the doctrine of incorporation, under the principle of *pacta sunt servanda* it is bound to align its laws with these treaties.[83] The Anti-Rape Law of 1997,[84] for example, was enacted promptly after the Senate in 1996 began inquiring into how the country must implement the Platform for Action of the 1995 Beijing Conference on Women.[85] Also, as the SC notes, 'Corrective labor and social laws on gender inequality have emerged with more frequency [since 1980], largely due to our country's commitment as a signatory to the … CEDAW'.[86] The Magna

[78] XJ Bilon and CD Leon, 'With No National Law, Can We Rely on Local Ordinances to Protect LGBTQs against Discrimination?' *CNN Philippines* (25 June 2018), available at cnnphilippines.com/life/culture/2018/06/25/antidiscrimination-bill-lgbtq.html.

[79] Implementing Rules & Regulations of Rep Act No 10627 (2013) ss 3.b.1.2 and 5.

[80] Rep Act No 11166 (2018) s 2 (2018).

[81] Rep Act No 11313 (2019) ss 3(a), 4, 12 and 16.

[82] See United Nations (UN) Office of the High Commissioner of Human Rights, 'Ratification Status for the Philippines', available at tbinternet.ohchr.org/_layouts/15/TreatyBodyExternal/Treaty.aspx?CountryID=137&Lang=EN. The Philippines has not signed the International Convention for the Protection of All Persons from Enforced Disappearances. UN Treaty Collection, available at treaties.un.org/pages/ViewDetails.aspx?src=IND&mtdsg_no=IV-16&chapter=4&clang=_en. The SC has also interpreted the Universal Declaration of Human Rights, to which the country is a signatory, to be 'part of the generally accepted principles of international law and binding on the State': *Republic v Ramas*, GR No 104768 (21 July 2003) ('The Interregnum Decision').

[83] *Tañada v Angara*, 338 Phil 546 (1997). M Magallona, 'Theses on the Impact of International Legal Relation on the Constitutional System' (2011) 1 *Philippines Law & Society Review* 6. Compare *Abbas v Comelec*, GR No 89651 (10 November 1989) (a treaty can be amended by a subsequent statute).

[84] Rep Act No 8353 (1997).

[85] V Lique, 'The Anti-Rape Law and The Changing Times: Nature, Issues and Incidents' (1998) 43 *Ateneo Law Journal* 141, 147–48.

[86] *Phil Telegraph & Telephone Co v National Labor Relations Commission (NLRC)*, GR No 118978, 338 Phil 1093 (23 May 1997).

Carta for Women, for example, refers to international human rights of women as well as the CEDAW.[87] The PCW also regularly monitors and evaluates the country's compliance with the 1995 Beijing Declaration and Platform for Action and the 2000 Beijing+5, a global agenda for women empowerment, as well as the UN Sustainable Development Goals, which aims for gender equality and women empowerment – all of which the Philippines has formally adopted.[88] The SC has also stated that the Philippines adheres to the international law principle of non-discrimination 'regardless of sexual orientation', and that it 'stands willing to assume the responsibility of giving effect to the Philippines' international law obligations.'[89]

While the women's and LGBT movements have gained good ground for gender justice, its advance has been slowed by the Roman Catholic Church's legal and political entrenchments. The Constitution declares that 'The separation of Church and State shall be inviolable' and that 'No law shall be made respecting an establishment of religion'.[90] The SC explains this to mean not only that 'none of our laws should be based on any religious law, doctrine, or teaching', but also that 'religious sects … can neither cause the government to adopt their particular doctrines as policy for everyone, nor can they cause the government to restrict other groups.'[91] In reality, however, Philippine family, civil and criminal law are immersed in Catholic doctrines.[92] Both the Civil Code of the Philippines (Civil Code),[93] which borrows heavily from the Spanish Civil Code of 1889, and the Family Code of the Philippines (Family Code), which draws from the 1983 Roman Catholic Code of Canon Law,[94] codify Roman Catholic morality, including the *Aquinian* variant of natural law.[95] Perhaps the most litigated ground for declaring a marriage void *ab initio*, ie, that one's spouse was 'psychologically incapacitated to comply with the essential marital

[87] Rep Act No 9710 (2009) ss 2–3.

[88] PCW, 'Monitoring and Evaluation of Gender Equality and Women's Empowerment in the Philippines: A Compendium of Indicators' (2019), available at www.bfar.da.gov.ph/wp-content/uploads/2021/12/ME_of_GEWEVol1.pdf.

[89] *Ang Ladlad LGBT Party v Comelec* (n 75).

[90] Constitution, Art II, s 6 and Art III, s 5.

[91] *Republic v Manalo* (n 20).

[92] CR Austria, 'The Church, the State and Women's Bodies in the Context of Religious Fundamentalism in the Philippines' (2004) 12 *Reproductive Health Matters* 96, 96.

[93] Rep Act No 386 (1949) (Civil Code).

[94] *Mallilin v Jamesolamin*, GR No 192718, 754 Phil 158 (18 February 2015); *Antonio v Reyes*, GR No 155800, 519 Phil 337 (10 March 2006); *Republic of the Philippines v Molina*, GR No 108763, 335 Phil. 664 (13 February 1997); *Santos v Bedia-Santos*, GR No 112019 (4 January 1995); MA Dizon, 'Psychological Incapacity and the Canon Law on Marriage: An Exegesis on the Psychological Element of Matrimonial Consent' (2000) 75 *Philippine Law Journal* 365; GW Healy, 'Marriage: The 1983 Code of Canon Law, and the 1987 Family Code of the Philippines' (1988) 2 *Landas: Journal of Loyola School of Theology* 104.

[95] P Agabin, 'The Philosophy of the Civil Code' (1991) 66 *Philippine Law Journal* 1; R Balane, 'The Spanish Antecedents of the Philippine Civil Code' (1979) 54 *Philippine Law Journal* 1.

obligations', was lifted from Roman Catholic Canon Law.[96] Hence trial courts tend to declare marriages 'civilly void' if a church tribunal had already decreed them 'canonically invalid',[97] and find guidance in 'decisions of church tribunals which, although not binding on the civil courts, may be given persuasive effect'.[98] They also give 'great respect' and 'great persuasive weight' to decisions of the National Appellate Matrimonial Tribunal of the Catholic Church in the Philippines.[99] Relatedly, natural rights legal theory remains the predominant constitutional philosophy in the country,[100] and it is uncontroversial for courts to refer to natural law and rights in their decisions.[101]

In the Philippines the separation of church and state does not mean the *exclusion* of religion from politics, but the equal *inclusion* of all religious denominations within the political system. The Church's active participation in Philippine politics is justifiable in this regard.[102] The problem is that church–state separation envisions the non-domination of any one or more religious denominations in political decision-making, and domination of crucial aspects of public policy is precisely what the Catholic Church has historically accomplished.[103] The country's population policy, for example, features 'a Catholic moral teaching-centred stance'.[104] Former president Gloria Macapagal-Arroyo 'made it a point to personally meet the bishops whenever' distance permitted, and regularly 'gave them money – purportedly for social services.'[105] During elections the Church actively campaigns for and against candidates.[106]

The Code of Muslim Personal Laws of the Philippines governs the family relations of Muslim Filipinos.[107] It also governs marriages solemnised in accordance with it or with Muslim Law even if only the groom is Muslim.[108]

[96] Family Code, Art 36; Dizon (n 94).
[97] *Republic v Molina* (n 94).
[98] *Salita v Magtolis*, GR No 106429 (13 June 1994), quoting A Sempio-Diy, *Handbook on the Family Code of the Philippines* (Joer Printing Services, 1988) 37.
[99] *Republic v Molina* (n 94).
[100] E Fernando, 'Natural Rights Legal Theory' (1999) 74 *Philippine Law Journal* 1.
[101] See, eg, The Interregnum Decision (Puno, Justice, *separate opinion*). The SC has declared certain rights as 'grounded on natural law', RH Law Decision (the right to life), and hence 'need not even be written in the Constitution for they are assumed to exist from the inception of humankind', *Oposa v Factoran*, GR No 101083 (30 July 1993) (the right to a balanced and healthful ecology).
[102] ML Rebullida, 'Religion, Church, and Politics in the Philippines' in Tadem and Morada (eds) (n 9) 63–88.
[103] A Rufo, *Altar of Secrets: Sex, Politics, and Money in the Philippine Catholic Church* (Journalism for Nation Building Foundation, 2013) 137.
[104] Cornelio and Dagle (n 13) 65 and 89.
[105] Rufo (n 103) 123.
[106] eg, ibid 140–41 and 144; M Dañguilan, *The RH Bill Story: Contentions and Compromises* (Ateneo De Manila University Press, 2018) 225–28.
[107] Pres Dec No 1083 (1977); *Sumagka v Sumagka* (n 20).
[108] Pres Dec No 1083, Title II, ch 1, Art 13; *Zamoranos v People*, GR No 193902, 665 Phil. 447 (1 June 2011).

Women and men have unequal rights and obligations under it; for example, women are characteristically entitled to less shares in an inheritance (eg, a childless surviving husband inherits half of the estate, a childless surviving wife only a fourth);[109] men can have more than one wife, but women cannot have more than one husband;[110] it is much easier for a husband to divorce his wife than the other way around;[111] and only men can exercise guardianship over the property of minors.[112] The Code was decreed the year after the 1976 Tripoli Agreement between the Philippine Government and Muslim rebels, which guarantees that in Muslim Mindanao, 'Muslims shall have the right to set up their own Courts which implement the Islamic Shari'ah laws.'[113] The Organic Law for the Bangsamoro Autonomous Region in Muslim Mindanao, implementing the Constitution, gives the Bangsamoro Parliament the power to enact laws on personal, family and property law jurisdiction.[114]

Religious leaders remain vocal against the passage of laws promoting LGBT rights and SOGIE equality. The Catholic clergy has given the acronym 'DEATH' to proposals to legalise *d*ivorce, *e*uthanasia, *a*bortion, *t*otal population control, and *h*omosexual marriage.[115] To counter the Church's national clout, social movements have sometimes turned to local governments.[116] Implementing the constitutional principle of local autonomy, the Local Government Code of 1991 grants every local government wide-ranging power to promote the general welfare.[117] With it some local governments have enacted ordinances prohibiting discrimination on the basis of SOGIE.[118] Examples include the Gender and Development Code of Quezon City and Manila's Sexual Harassment in Public Spaces ordinance.[119] Women, however, remain underrepresented in local governments: only 12 of 81 Governors, 13 of 80 Vice-Governors, 415 of 1,634 Mayors, 316 of 1,633 Vice-Mayors, and 3,148 of 13,544 members of local legislative bodies are women.[120]

[109] Pres Dec No 1083, Title III, ch 1.
[110] Pres Dec No 1083, Title II, ch 2, Art 27.
[111] Pres Dec No 1083, Title II, ch 3.
[112] Pres Dec No 1083, Title V, ch 2, Art 80.
[113] Agreement Between the Government of the Republic of the Philippines and Moro National Liberation Front with the Participation of the Quadripartite Ministerial Commission Members of the Islamic Conference and the Secretary General of the Organization of Islamic Conference, City of Tripoli, 23 December 1976, para 3(3).
[114] Rep Act No 11054 (2018) Art X, s 4. Constitution, Art X, s 20(4).
[115] HRW (n 24); Cornelio and Dagle (n 13) 77–87.
[116] Bilon and Leon (n 78).
[117] Rep Act No 7160 (1991) bk 1, title I, ch 1, s 16; Constitution, Art X, s 2.
[118] HRW (n 24).
[119] BPfA +25 Progress Report 2014–2019 (n 73) 77.
[120] PSA (n 7); 'Party List Representatives' (House of Representatives): congress.gov.ph/members/?v=pl; 'Camarines Sur Rep. Marissa Andaya dies of cancer' *Philippine Daily Inquirer* (6 July 2020), available at newsinfo.inquirer.net/1302300/camarines-sur-rep-marissa-andaya-dies-of-cancer.

III. CONSTITUTIONAL FRAMING OF SEX/GENDER/SEXUALITY

A. The 1986 Constitutional Commission

The Commission that drafted the Constitution (ConCom) had 48 members. Forty of them were Catholic, including two priests and the lay leader who founded Opus Dei in the Philippines. One commissioner was a Protestant minister.[121] Their religious views influenced the Constitution's clauses related to gender issues. Only six commissioners were women,[122] and three of them were devout Catholics: one was a nun;[123] the second, elected president of the ConCom, was a church organist;[124] and the third a religious leader.[125] President Corazon 'Cory' Aquino, who appointed the members of the ConCom, was also a devout Catholic.[126]

Women's groups were active in writing to the ConCom and attending its sessions.[127] One female commissioner, Felicitas Aquino, was a feminist legal activist.[128] She coauthored a provision on working women's rights.[129]

The commissioners were guided by Cory's opening address to the ConCom requesting them 'not to do that legislature's work for it' and 'not be distracted by political debates and matters of policy that do not belong within your constitution-making exercise'.[130] As we have seen, it has been through statutes that the Constitution's broad promises of gender justice have been fleshed out.

[121] MV Paez-Hidalgo, D Saaguil and G Israel, 'Socio-Demographic Profile of the Members of the 1986 Constitutional Commission' (1987) XXXI *Philippine Journal of Public Administration* 36, 54–55; R Pangalangan, 'Religion and the Secular State: National Report for the Philippines' in J Martinez-Torrón and WC Durham, Jr (eds), *Religion and the Secular State: National Reports* (The International Center for Law and Religion Studies, Brigham Young University, 2010) 559, 560.

[122] See Paez-Hidalgo, Saaguil and Israel (n 121) 48–49.

[123] Christine Tan: *Official Directory of the Constitutional Commission 1986* (Manila, Constitutional Commission, 1986) 115 [hereinafter Official Directory].

[124] LC Anastacio, *The Foundations of the Modern Philippine State: Imperial Rule and the American Constitutional Tradition in the Philippine Islands, 1898–1935* (Cambridge University Press, 2016) 1; Cecilia Muñoz Palma: Official Directory (n 123) 87.

[125] Maria Teresa Nieva: Official Directory (n 123) 79.

[126] Law Governing the Constitutional Commission of 1986 (1986), s 2(1).

[127] Dañguilan (n 106) 29–35; eg, Communication No 458 – Constitutional Commission of 1986: Communication from the Women's Health Care Foundation, Inc, 1589 Quezon Avenue, Quezon City, signed by its Executive Director, Florence M Tadiar, submitting, for the consideration of the Constitutional Commission, a 'Statement on Women's Rights.', in III RCC 49 (6 August 1986).

[128] Official Directory (n 123) 115; M Fineman, '"Filipina Females are … Running This Country Today": In New Philippines, Best Man for Job Is Often Woman' *Los Angeles Times* (28 August 1986), available at www.latimes.com/archives/la-xpm-1986-08-28-mn-13831-story.html.

[129] Constitution, Art XIII, s 14; II RCC 46 (2 August 1986); III RCC 51 (8 August 1986).

[130] Corazon Aquino, 'Address of the President' in 1 RCC 1 (2 June 1986).

B. The 1987 Constitution

The Constitution guarantees to every person, regardless of gender, the 'equal protection of the laws.'[131] All adult Filipino citizens have the right to vote[132] (this has been the norm since the country overwhelmingly voted yes to woman suffrage in 1937).[133] Both women and men transmit their Filipino citizenship to their children, and unless they renounce it both retain their citizenship when they marry foreigners (this has been the norm since the 1973 Constitution; previously women automatically lost their Filipino citizenship when they married foreigners and hence could not then transmit such citizenship to their legitimate children).[134] All citizens, regardless of gender, have the constitutional right to 'quality education at all levels'.[135] The state is also constitutionally mandated to 'promote … equality of employment opportunities for all', regardless of sex.[136]

The Constitution explicitly mentions women In various clauses. First, it undertakes to 'equally protect the life of the mother and the life of the unborn from conception.'[137] The 'whole purpose' of the right to life of the unborn, explained ConCom Commissioner Joaquin Bernas, a Jesuit priest, is 'to stop the Philippine Supreme Court from adopting the American doctrine on abortion'[138] that a woman's right to abortion can be defeated only by a compelling state interest, hence only during the third trimester of pregnancy.[139] Thus abortion remains a crime in the Philippines; it is illegal under any and all circumstances, even when the life of either the pregnant woman or the foetus is in danger.[140]

Second, the Constitution 'recognizes the role of women in nation-building' and undertakes to 'ensure the fundamental equality before the law of women and men.'[141] The original proposed text was 'a self-implementing provision that would itself repeal all discriminatory and antifeminist laws in the Civil Code and the Revised Penal Code.'[142] After some male commissioners protested that the proposal would 'precipitate massive dislocations in family life' and

[131] Constitution, Art III, s 1.

[132] Constitution, Art V, ss 1–2.

[133] The returns were: 447,681 affirmative votes to 44,307 negative votes. 2nd Annual Report of the U.S. High Commissioner to the Phil. Islands to the President & Congress of the U.S. – Covering the Calendar Year 1937 with a Review of Government Finances for the Years 1935, 1936, & 1937 (1939) 48–49.

[134] Constitution, Art IV, ss 1 and 4; *Tecson v Comelec*, GR No 161434 (3 March 2004).

[135] Constitution, Art XIV, s 1.

[136] Constitution, Art XIII, s 3.

[137] Constitution, Art II, s 12.

[138] I RCC 32 (17 July 1986).

[139] *Roe v Wade*, 410 US 113 (1973).

[140] Act No 3815, Revised Penal Code, Arts 256–59 (1930).

[141] Constitution, Art II, s 14.

[142] IV RCC 85 (17 September 1986).

inappropriately 'chang[e] the customs and traditions of the Filipino people by constitutional mandate',[143] however, it was reworded so that it would instead 'establish[] the principle of nonsexism' but 'not amend the Civil Code'; thus 'the process of transition to a new set of laws on the rights of women would require the amendatory process in the legislature.'[144] Nevertheless, the understanding was that 'even without a statutory implementation, the courts can evolve' doctrine in light of the non-sexism principle, with the Civil Code 'hav[ing] to yield' to it.[145]

Implementing this principle, Cory in 1987 promulgated the Family Code which amended many discriminatory rules of the Civil Code on family relations and thereby equalised the sphere of family life.[146] Three examples: first, while before only the husband could object to his wife's exercise of a profession or occupation or engagement in business, now both spouses may object;[147] second, while before the default rule (ie, absent marriage settlements) was that only the husband could administer the absolute community property or conjugal partnership of gains (as the case may be), now the default is that both spouses jointly administer the community property or conjugal partnership;[148] third, before the husband alone decides where the family resides, now both the husband and wife decide.[149]

Third, the Constitution introduced the closed-list, party-list system in the House, where voters, in addition to electing a district representative, can also vote for their preferred party-list group. While legislative district elections are local and first-past-the post, party-list elections are national and proportional. Party-list representatives constitute one-fifth of the seats in the House; district representatives fill the remaining four-fifths.[150] The party-list system was designed to 'democratize political power' by giving seats in the House to national, regional and sectoral parties or organisations that 'cannot win in legislative district elections' but which 'can garner, in nationwide elections, at least the same number of votes that winning candidates can garner in legislative district elections.'[151] For the first three terms following ratification the Constitution reserved party-list seats to certain marginalised and underrepresented sectors, including women (but not LGBTs).[152] The women sector was a late addition proposed by commissioner Maria Teresa Nieva, who said women 'have been marginalized for too long as far as the political life of the country

[143] ibid.
[144] IV RCC 89 (22 September 1986).
[145] ibid.
[146] Family Code, Art 254.
[147] Compare Family Code, Art 73 with Civil Code, Art 117.
[148] Compare Family Code, Art 96 with Civil Code, Art 112.
[149] Compare Family Code, Art 69 with Civil Code, Art 110.
[150] Constitution, Art VI, s 5(2).
[151] *Atong Paglaum v Comelec* (n 46).
[152] Constitution, Art VI, s 5(2).

is concerned.'[153] There was no explicit intention to exclude LGBTs; they were simply not named.

Fourth, the Constitution 'priorit[ises] the needs of the underprivileged sick, elderly, disabled, women, and children' in its mandated healthcare programme.[154] The SC has declared this provision 'self-executory': 'There is no need for legislation to implement' it.[155] Nevertheless, under the 2019 Universal Health Care Act, the risk, 'in the case of a pregnant woman', of 'permanent injury or loss of her unborn child, or a non-institutional delivery' is considered an emergency for which every Filipino is entitled to health-service access.[156]

Fifth, the Constitution undertakes to 'protect working women by providing safe and healthful working conditions, taking into account their maternal functions, and such facilities and opportunities that will enhance their welfare and enable them to realise their full potential in the service of the nation.'[157] The Labor Code of the Philippines ('Labor Code') requires the establishment of 'standards that will ensure the safety and health of women employees', including, when appropriate, 'separate toilet rooms and lavatories for men and women', 'a dressing room for women' and 'a nursery'.[158] Recently the 105-Day Expanded Maternity Leave Law[159] was also enacted. There is now a pending House Bill introduced by GABRIELA Women's Party Representative Arlene Brosas seeking to grant a fully paid monthly menstrual leave of up to two days to all female workers.[160]

IV. CONSTITUTIONAL JURISPRUDENCE

Courts have tracked legislative policy in their decisions on gender equality and justice. This interpretive approach has had mixed results. While courts have both readily enforced recent progressive legislation and reliably upheld these statutes against constitutional challenges, they have also refused to align antiquated, even century-old laws with existing constitutional guarantees. Fortunately the SC has recently been interpreting old statutory rules in light of the non-sexism principle and the CEDAW in ways which promote gender justice.

Courts have readily enforced statutes implementing the Constitution's gender justice promises. The Labor Code, for example, promises to 'ensure equal work opportunities regardless of sex, race or creed', and makes it 'unlawful for any employer to discriminate against any woman employee

[153] II RCC 45 (1 August 1986).
[154] Constitution, Art XIII, s 11.
[155] RH Law Decision.
[156] Rep Act No 11223 (2019), ss 4(g) and 6.
[157] Constitution, Art XIII, s 14.
[158] Pres Dec No 442 (1974), as amended, Art 130 (Labor Code).
[159] Rep Act No 11210 (2019).
[160] House of Representatives, Nineteenth Congress, House Bill No 7758 (2023).

with respect to terms and conditions of employment solely on account of her sex'.[161] Implementing the Labor Code prohibition of work stipulations against marriage, the SC has declared that an employment 'policy of not accepting or considering as disqualified from work any woman worker who contracts marriage' violates not only this prohibition, but also 'good morals and public policy, tending as it does to deprive a woman of the freedom to choose her status, a privilege that by all accounts inheres in the individual as an intangible and inalienable right.'[162] The SC has also ruled that an employee cannot be suspended from work for getting pregnant out of wedlock 'until such time that she marries her boyfriend' because the Magna Carta of Women 'protects women against discrimination in all matters relating to marriage and family relations, including the right to choose freely a spouse and to enter into marriage only with their free and full consent' (unless the employer can prove that marriage is 'reasonably related to the essential operation of the job involved' such that the employee would otherwise likely be 'unable to properly perform the duties of the job').[163]

Courts have also reliably upheld gender justice legislation against constitutional challenges. One way the SC does this is through its interpretive 'principle that laws should be construed in a manner that its constitutionality is sustained'.[164] In its 2014 *RH Law Decision*, for example, the SC determined that since human life begins 'upon fertilization', only 'contraceptives that kill or destroy the fertilised ovum should be deemed an abortive and thus prohibited' by the constitutional right to life of the unborn; hence the RH Law is valid insofar as it allows access only to non-abortive contraceptives, which 'take action prior to fertilization'.[165]

Another way the SC upholds gender justice statutes is by assessing them under a deferential judicial standard. The SC generally uses two tiers of review: strict scrutiny and rational basis. In concurrences and dissents a middle tier, viz, intermediate (or heightened) scrutiny, has been proposed.

The rational basis test demands merely that the means employed by government 'reasonably relates to the legislative purpose'.[166] It is generally used to assess the constitutionality of economic legislation and in equal protection challenges.[167] The great deference given to policy-making bodies at this level

[161] Labor Code, Arts 3 and 135.

[162] *Philippine Telegraph & Telephone Co v NLRC*, GR No 118978 (23 May 1997); Labor Code, Art 134.

[163] *Capin-Cadiz v Brent Hospital and Colleges*, GR No 187417, 781 Phil 610 (24 February 2016) (emphasis omitted).

[164] *Imbong v Ochoa*, GR No 204819, 732 Phil 1 (8 April 2014).

[165] ibid (emphasis omitted).

[166] *Central Bank* (now Bangko Sentral ng Pilipinas) *Employees Association v Bangko Sentral ng Pilipinas*, 487 Phil 531, 583–84 (2004).

[167] *White Light Corp v City of Manila*, GR No 122846 (20 January 2009); *Ang Ladlad LGBT Party v Comelec* (n 75).

of scrutiny often saves the statute, executive order, ordinance or other issuance involved.[168]

Strict scrutiny requires that the government measure is (1) necessary to achieve a compelling state interest, and (2) the least restrictive means to protect such interest, or narrowly tailored to accomplish the interest.[169] The Government has the burden to prove these two requirements.[170] The SC has used this test in cases challenging express fundamental rights such as the right to travel[171] and religious freedom.[172] The right of procreation and to marry are also considered fundamental rights.[173]

Intermediate scrutiny requires that 'the statute serves an important purpose and that the discriminatory means employed is substantially related to the achievement of those objectives.'[174] A concurrence to the SC's 2010 decision in *Ang Ladlad LGBT Party v Comelec* urged its application to equal protection cases where the contested classification is based on a 'quasi-suspect classification' such as gender or sexual orientation;[175] the main opinion, however, instead used rational basis review to overturn the Comelec's refusal to accredit an LGBT party for the party-list elections on moral grounds. In its 2019 same-sex marriage decision, the SC again refused to apply the intermediate scrutiny test proposed in the *Ang Ladlad* concurrence, explaining that while it 'may adopt in a subsequent case the views in a separate opinion', it is up to the party invoking it to persuade the Court 'that the discussion there is the correct legal analysis that must govern.'[176]

The SC used the rational basis test in its 2013 decision proclaiming that the Anti-VAWC Act 'did not violate the equal protection clause by favoring women over men as victims of violence and abuse to whom the State extends its protection.'[177] Thus it upheld the strong judicial remedies against spousal and child abuse which the law afforded women but not men. The Court pronounced that the 'unequal power relationship between women and men; the fact that women are more likely than men to be victims of violence; and the widespread gender bias and prejudice against women all make for real differences' which justify granting women protective legal measures unavailable to men.[178]

[168] See, eg, *Ermita-Malate Hotel and Motel Operators v City of Manila*, GR No L-24693 (31 July 1967); *British American Tobacco v Camacho*, GR No 163583 (20 August 2008).

[169] *SPARK v Quezon City*, GR No 225442 (8 August 2017); *White Light Corp v City of Manila* (n 167).

[170] *Republic v Manalo* (n 20).

[171] ibid.

[172] RH Law Decision.

[173] *Republic v Manalo* (n 20).

[174] *Central Bank* (now Bangko Sentral ng Pilipinas) *Employees Association v Bangko Sentral ng Pilipinas* (n 166) (Carpio Morales, Justice, dissenting).

[175] *Ang Ladlad LGBT Party v Comelec* (n 75) (separate concurring opinion of Puno, CJ) (emphases omitted).

[176] *Falcis v Civil Registrar General* (n 77).

[177] *Garcia v Drilon*, GR No 179267, 712 Phil. 44 (25 June 2013).

[178] ibid (emphasis omitted).

These real differences can be cited to justify the various other gender justice laws favouring women, such as The Magna Carta of Women's establishment of 'affirmative action mechanisms' promoting 'the participation and equitable representation of women in all spheres of society', including a gender-balancing hiring policy in favour of women in the lower bureaucracy, reserving 40 per cent of seats in local developmental councils to women, and offering incentives to encourage women leadership in the workplace.[179]

The democracy principle is a strong undertow in equal protection cases. The SC has been more willing to strike down a contested classification when it is (1) made by an appointive body, such as the Comelec;[180] (2) made in a city ordinance;[181] or (3) the unintended result of a (presumably) badly drafted statute and hence would be contrary to the legislative intent.[182] Otherwise the SC practices 'deference and constitutional avoidance' in order 'To remain true to its democratic moorings' – explaining that gender justice issues involve 'an overlapping process of articulation, deliberation, and consensus' which are 'better left to Congress.'[183] The SC also worries that judicial resolution of these issues 'may unwittingly diminish the LGBTQI+ community's capacity to create a strong movement that ensures lasting recognition, as well as public understanding, of SOGIESC.'[184]

This democratic undertow explains why in the law of persons and family relations the SC seems to reject a task that other peak courts have assumed: aligning longstanding personal and family laws with constitutional norms.[185] The SC dismissed the same-sex marriage petition despite pronouncing that 'To continue to ground the family … on the concept of the complementarity of the sexes is to perpetuate the discrimination faced by couples, whether opposite-sex or same-sex, who do not fit that mold'.[186] The SC explained that if it legalised same-sex marriage it would 'impliedly amend' 'the entirety of laws relating to marriage', and thereby would 'arrogat[e] legislative power unto itself and violat[e] the principle of separation of powers.'[187]

Similarly, in *Silverio v Republic of the Philippines* (which begins with a Biblical quote[188]), the SC refused to change the entries for first name and sex in the birth certificate of a male transexual who had undergone sex reassignment surgery partly because 'there is no law legally recognizing sex reassignment', and judicially recognising it would have 'serious and wide-ranging legal and

[179] Magna Carta of Women, s 11.
[180] *Ang Ladlad LGBT Party v Comelec* (n 75).
[181] *City of Manila v Laguio*, GR No 118127, 495 Phil 289 (12 April 2005).
[182] *Republic v Manalo* (n 20).
[183] *Falcis v Civil Registrar General* (n 77).
[184] ibid.
[185] See the chapters on South Korea and Taiwan of this volume.
[186] *Falcis v Civil Registrar General* (n 77).
[187] ibid.
[188] 'When God created man, He made him in the likeness of God; He created them male and female': Genesis 5:1–2.

public policy consequences'.[189] Despite noting that 'the Civil Register Law was enacted in the early 1900s and remains unchanged', the SC refused to rely on Article 9 of the Civil Code mandating that 'No judge or court shall decline to render judgment by reason of the silence, obscurity or insufficiency of the laws' because, it said, the proper guidelines that would govern the recognition of the effects of sex reassignment 'involve questions of public policy to be addressed solely by the legislature, not by the courts.'[190]

In a later decision the SC allowed an intersex individual (who had female chromosomes but high levels of male hormones) to change the entries in his birth certificate for name (from Jennifer to Jeff) and gender (from female to male).[191] The SC found that since with intersex individuals 'gender classification at birth [is] inconclusive', it is only 'at maturity that the gender of such persons … is fixed.'[192] Thus it ruled that with intersex individuals 'the determining factor in his[/her] gender classification would be what the individual … having reached the age of majority, with good reason thinks of his/her sex.'[193] In contrast to its refusal to apply Article 9 of the Civil Code in its *Silverio* decision, the SC this time explained that 'In the absence of a law on the matter, the Court will not dictate on … a matter so innately private as one's sexuality and lifestyle preferences' considering 'the human right to the pursuit of happiness and of health', which includes 'the primordial choice of what courses of action to take along the path of his sexual development and maturation.'[194] This contradictory position might have sprung from the implicit normative weight the SC placed on its observation that the intersex individual had 'simply let nature take its course and ha[d] not taken unnatural steps [eg, sex reassignment surgery] to arrest or interfere with what he was born with.'

In two recent rulings the SC interpreted the non-sexism principle as requiring 'a more active application than the passive orientation' of the equal protection clause.[195] In the first ruling, the SC also relied on the mandates of the CEDAW ('to modify or abolish existing laws, regulations, customs and practices which constitution discrimination against women') and of The Magna Carta of Women (to 'take all appropriate measures to eliminate discrimination against women in all matters relating to marriage and family relations') to liberally interpret the Family Code rule that:

> Where a marriage between a Filipino citizen and a foreigner is validly celebrated and a divorce is thereafter validly obtained abroad by the alien spouse capacitating

[189] *Rommel Jacinto Dantes Silverio v Republic of the Philippines*, GR No 174689, 562 Phil 953 (19 October 2007).
[190] ibid.
[191] *Republic of the Philippines v Cagandahan*, GR No 166676, 586 Phil. 637 (12 September 2008).
[192] ibid.
[193] ibid.
[194] ibid.
[195] *Racho v Tanaka*, GR No 199515, 834 Phil 21 (25 June 2018).

> him or her to remarry, the Filipino spouse shall have capacity to remarry under Philippine law

to mean that 'it is irrelevant for courts to determine if it is the foreign spouse that procures the divorce abroad.'[196] Citing official data that 'Filipino *women* are more likely to enter into mixed marriages than Filipino *men*' (66.7 per cent of Filipino marriages abroad were between Filipino brides and foreign grooms, while only 1.8 per cent were between Filipino grooms and foreign brides), the SC explained that a narrow interpretation allowing only the foreign spouse to initiate divorce proceedings 'may be unconstitutional' as it not only would disproportionately burden Filipino women, but also 'contributes to the patriarchy' as it 'encourages unequal partnerships and perpetuates abuse in intimate relationships.'[197] As a nod to the democracy principle, the SC cited previous jurisprudence explaining why the liberal interpretation is more consistent with both the letter of the statute and the intent of the legislature than the narrow one.[198]

In the second ruling the SC additionally relied on the Women in Development and Nation Building Act's mandate (to 'ensure the fundamental equality before the law of women and men') to support the interpretive rule that 'where the text of a law allows for an interpretation that treats women and men more equally, that is the correct interpretation.'[199] Relying on this rule and on precedent, the SC interpreted the Civil Code rule that 'Legitimate and legitimated children shall principally use the surname of the father' as providing 'no legal obstacle if a legitimate or legitimated child should choose to use the surname of its mother to which it is equally entitled.'[200] Hence the SC allowed a legitimate child to discard his estranged father's surname and instead use the maiden name of his mother who had singlehandedly raised him and his siblings.[201]

V. FLAGSHIP CONSTITUTIONAL DEVELOPMENTS IN TERMS OF GENDER AND SEXUAL EQUALITY

The legislated path to gender justice in the country has not been smooth. This section discusses two case studies where the SC served as a speedbump, if not a roadblock, to addressing persistent women's rights concerns.

[196] ibid.
[197] ibid.
[198] ibid. quoting *Republic v Manalo* (n 20).
[199] *Alanis III v Court of Appeals*, GR No 216425 (11 November 2020).
[200] ibid quoting *Alfon v Republic*, GR No L-51201, 186 Phil 600 (29 May 1980).
[201] ibid. He was also allowed to change his first name.

A. The Reproductive Health Law

The first is the decades-long struggle between the Catholic Church and civil society groups that led to the RH Law, which was enacted to provide the citizenry access to and information about modern family planning methods, and promote the people's right to reproductive health.[202] The Catholic Bishops' Conference of the Philippines opposed these policies, arguing that 'Contraception corrupts the soul' and that the 'wide and free accessibility of contraceptives, even to the youth, will result in the destruction of family life and in greater violence against women.'[203] The idea for the RH Law started in 1999 in an international conference at The Hague, the ICPD+5, where Philippine government delegates and civic leaders discussed how the International Conference on Population and Development's Programme of Action could be realised in the country.[204] 2001 saw the filing of the first RH Bill, which the Catholic Church promptly denounced for 'claiming that unimpeded mastery over one's own body is a "human right."'[205] This sentiment was swiftly supported by a senator, who said he was 'not quite comfortable with the basic premise … that women have absolute discretion on what they want to do with their bodies.'[206] Thus started 11 years of pitched battle over the fate of the RH Law between civil society groups and the Church. Helping the push for its passage was the Reproductive Health Advocacy Network, a broad coalition of civil society groups which held rallies and marches, lobbied in Congress, assisted allied legislators, campaigned for sympathetic candidates, and advocated for reproductive health in newspapers, online and on air.[207] To oppose its passage the Church used the pulpit to discredit pro-RH legislators, calling them 'fornicators, murderers, and abortionists.'[208] The Church and Congress also formally created the Bishops-Legislators Caucus of the Philippines, which met every two months to discuss pending bills on 'life and the family'.[209] At the time there was also the Office of the Presidential Adviser for Ecclesiastical Affairs, which was dedicated to liaising with the Catholic Church.[210]

The RH Bill's first nine years coincided with the presidency of Macapagal-Arroyo, who depended upon the Church to prop up her embattled presidency, and whose policies followed Church doctrine.[211] In the Philippines the

[202] RH Law Decision.
[203] S Villegas, 'Contraception is Corruption! A CBCP Pastoral Letter on the latest decision on the Reproductive Health Bill' (15 December 2012), available at cbcponline.net/contraception-is-corruption-a-cbcp-pastoral-letter-on-the-latest-decision-on-the-reproductive-health-bill.
[204] Dañguilan (n 106) 108–09.
[205] Quoted in ibid 119.
[206] Quoted in ibid 149.
[207] ibid 121–32.
[208] ibid 140.
[209] ibid 160–61.
[210] ibid 97–98.
[211] ibid 97–107; Rufo (n 103) 114–27.

president's control over patronage pulls legislators towards his or her policies.[212] Hence in its first nine years the RH Bill was stranded at one or another House committee and was not scheduled for debates when it finally reached the plenary.[213] In 2010 the presidency passed to Benigno Aquino III, who publicly pushed for the passage of the RH Bill despite threats of excommunication.[214] He formally listed it as a priority bill and at crucial points met with legislators to speed up its passage.[215] The RH Bill was finally passed by Congress on December 19, 2012; two days later Aquino signed it into law.

A few weeks after the RH Law was enacted, Catholic Church groups petitioned the SC to suspend its implementation.[216] The SC's ensuing actions showed a judicial willingness to delay the implementation of the law amid a series of suits against it. While the case was pending, the Court suspended the law indefinitely. Thus it was suspended for more than a year, from 19 March 2013 to 8 April 2014, when the SC declared the RH Law and its implementing rules and regulations (RH IRR) as 'not unconstitutional', save for a few unconstitutional provisions, and lifted its suspension order.[217] The Court ruled that the law prohibits abortion, which it stated is consistent with what it identified as the '"principle of no abortion" embodied in the constitutional protection of life'.[218] It also upheld the statutory power of the Food and Drug Administration (FDA) to determine, after due process, if a certain drug induces abortion.[219]

Barely two months after one of the losing petitioners, Alliance for the Family Foundation Philippines (ALFI), wrote to the FDA asking how it was complying with the RH Law Decision. On November 2014 the FDA certified two contraceptives, Implanon and Implanon NXT, despite ALFI's protests, which it ignored. ALFI went to the SC, which issued a temporary restraining order (TRO) enjoining the FDA from 'granting any and all pending applications for reproductive products and supplies, including contraceptive drugs and devices' and 'procuring, selling, distributing, dispensing or administering, advertising, and promoting the hormonal contraceptives, "Implanon" and "Implanon NXT."'[220]

In 2016 the SC found that the FDA did not give proper notice and hearing before it certified, procured and administered Implanon and Implanon NXT. It thus ordered the FDA to afford ALFI and others 'the basic requirements of

[212] Y Kasuya, *Presidential Bandwagon: Parties and Party Systems in the Philippines* (Anvil, 2009).
[213] Dañguilan (n 106) 219–22.
[214] ibid 225–52.
[215] ibid 252–53, 285 and 337.
[216] ibid 487.
[217] RH Law Decision.
[218] ibid.
[219] ibid.
[220] *Alliance for the Family Foundation, Philippines, Inc (ALFI) v Garin*, GR No 217872, 793 Phil 831 (24 August 2016).

due process' in determining if contraceptives it plans to certify, procure and administer (including Implanon and Implanon NXT) are in fact prohibited abortifacients. It also refused to lift the TRO against the FDA.[221] In January 2017 President Rodrigo Duterte issued an executive order 'to intensify and accelerate the implementation' of the RH Law.[222] A news briefing at the presidential palace explained that the executive order was meant to 'pressure the Supreme Court to stop dillydallying on this TRO'.[223] The FDA, in the meantime, did not conduct the court-ordered summary hearing but instead asked the SC to reconsider. On April 2017 the Court ordered the FDA to properly consider and promptly decide upon ALFI's opposition, adding that the TRO will be deemed lifted only if afterwards it is found that the questioned contraceptives do not induce abortion.[224]

In July 2017, in his second State of the Nation Address, Duterte appealed to the SC 'to seriously consider the national interest and our development goals before issuing TROs', saying that the TRO against the FDA had 'caused a wastage of P350-million worth of taxpayers' money' (considering that 'The medicines will expire next month'), and had hence 'impaired the government's ability to fully implement responsible planning – family planning methods in the RH Law.'[225] The Chief Justice responded three days later, clarifying that the SC had not issued a TRO against the implementation of the RH Law but only 'against two specific contraceptives', adding that the 'TRO also has a sunset provision – as soon as the FDA certifies as provided by law that they are not abortifacient, the TRO is lifted'; thus 'The reason why the TRO has not been lifted yet is not with the Court but with the FDA.'[226]

Finally, on 10 November 2017, the FDA, after due process, certified 51 contraceptives, including Implanon and Implanon Nxt, as 'non-abortifacient'.[227] Thus it was only about five years after the RH Law was enacted that the SC allowed government to begin distributing contraceptives.[228]

[221] ibid.

[222] R Duterte, Executive Order No. 12 (9 January 2017).

[223] P Ranada, 'EO 12 to "Pressure" SC Ruling on Contraceptive Implants – Pernia' *Rappler* (11 January 2017), available at www.rappler.com/nation/158018-duterte-executive-order-family-planning-supreme-court-tro.

[224] *ALFI v Garin*, GR No 217872, 809 Phil. 897 (26 April 2017).

[225] R Duterte, 'State of the Nation Address' (Batasang Pambansa Complex, Quezon City, 24 July 2017), available at www.officialgazette.gov.ph/2017/07/24/rodrigo-roa-duterte-second-state-of-the-nation-address-july-24-2017.

[226] SC Public Information Office, 'The Chief Justice's Response to the President's Statement on the Issuance of a Temporary Restraining Order Against the Implementation of the RH Law and all Contraceptive Products' (27 July 2017).

[227] FDA, FDA Advisory No 2017-302 'Results of the Food and Drug Administration's (FDA) Re-evaluation of Contraceptive Products for Recertification' (10 November 2017), available at www.doh.gov.ph/sites/default/files/health_magazine/FDA%20Advisory%20No.%202017-302.pdf (emphasis omitted).

[228] Dañguilan (n 106) 519.

B. Persistent Rape Myths

The second case study is the SC's continued adherence to rape myths that violate women's rights. The CEDAW enjoins states parties to 'modify or abolish existing laws, regulations, customs and practices which constitute discrimination against women',[229] and to try to eliminate 'practices which are based on ... stereotyped roles for men and women'.[230] Both undertakings establish a 'due diligence obligation to banish gender stereotypes ... in the judicial handling' of rape cases.[231] The Magna Carta of Women implements the CEDAW in mandating the state, 'as the primary duty-bearer', to 'Refrain from discriminating against women and violating their rights', and in declaring 'rights recognised under international instruments duly signed and ratified by the Philippines' – which includes CEDAW – as part of 'rights of woman' within its scope.[232] The SC's insistence on rape myths that violate women's rights under CEDAW therefore also violates women's rights under the Magna Carta of Women. Considering that it is Congress which the framers envisioned would primarily elucidate the principle of non-sexism, this insistence contradicts the constitutional principle of democracy.[233]

Concededly, Congress itself has not been fully compliant. Time and again the Committee on the Elimination of Discrimination against Women (CEDAW Committee) has emphasised that rape's 'essential element' is lack of consent.[234] In 2011, noting that 'the lack of consent is not an essential element of the definition of rape in the Philippines', the Committee recommended the 'Review of the definition of rape in the legislation so as to place the lack of consent at its centre'.[235] In 2014 the Committee noted that its 'specific recommendation' to the Philippines to redefine rape in terms of 'lack of consent' has not been heeded.[236] It repeated this recommendation to the Philippines to place lack of consent at the center of its rape law, particularly by dropping 'any requirement that sexual assault be committed by force or violence'.[237]

The SC has interpreted The Anti-Rape Law of 1997 as having redefined rape in terms of lack of consent. In 2014, the same year the CEDAW Committee criticised the country's failure to redefine rape, the SC declared that 'A person commits rape when he sexually assaults another who does not consent or is

[229] CEDAW, Art 2(f).
[230] CEDAW, Art 5(a).
[231] *Vertido v Phils*, Communication No 18/2008 (16 July 2010) para 8.4.
[232] The Magna Carta of Women, ss 5 and 8.
[233] IV RCC 89 (22 September 1986).
[234] *Vertido v Phils* (n 231) para 8.7.
[235] ibid paras 8.7 and 8.9(b)(1).
[236] *RPB v The Philippines*, Committee on the Elimination of Discrimination against Women (CEDAW Committee), Communication No 34/2011 (21 February 2014) para 8.10.
[237] ibid para 9(b)(i).

incapable of giving consent to a sexual act.'[238] It cited its earlier landmark decision from that year, *People v Jumawan*,[239] declaring that 'Sexual intercourse, albeit within the realm of marriage, if not consensual, is rape. This is the clear State policy expressly legislated in … the Anti-Rape Law of 1997.' *Jumawan* based its consent-based definition of rape on both the text of The Anti-Rape Law of 1997 and the legislative intent behind it to align the Philippine law on rape with CEDAW and the 1993 UN Declaration on the Elimination of Violence Against Women.[240] Very recently, however, the SC seems to have backtracked by defining 'carnal knowledge' under The Anti-Rape Law of 1997 to mean 'the penis penetrating the cleft of the labia majora' of the vagina, so that 'a mere grazing by the penis of the fleshy portion, not the vulval cleft of the labia majora,' is considered 'only attempted rape and not consummated rape'.[241] Justice Marvic Leonen dissented to this, arguing that a consent-based definition of rape that includes 'not merely the penetration of a penis in a vagina' but also 'numerous other acts that may or may not require penetration' is more 'in line with our obligations under the … CEDAW' to criminalise the violation of a person's 'full autonomy to decide who to be intimate with and what acts may be shared through that intimacy.'[242]

The judiciary is also sometimes at fault even when legislation explicitly aligns itself with the CEDAW. Against the myth that only 'women who live the wrong way' are raped,[243] the Rape Victim Assistance and Protection Act of 1998 established a rape shield against evidence on a complainant's past sexual conduct, opinions or reputation 'unless, and only to the extent that the court finds, that such evidence is material and relevant to' a rape prosecution.[244] The shield thus places the burden of argument on the accused rapist to prove the pertinence of character evidence. But the SC swiftly lifted the burden of argument off the defence by presuming that generally 'the willingness of the woman is material' in rape prosecutions, hence 'the woman's character as to her chastity is admissible to show whether or not she consented to [the] man's act.'[245] In doing so the Court shrunk the scope of the statutory shield to rape prosecutions, where the law provides 'the woman's consent is immaterial and not in issue', such as when she is under 12 years old.[246] Years later the Court reinforced this rape myth that evidence against a woman's 'character for chastity' can show the unlikelihood of an alleged rape, citing a 1986 precedent where a rape conviction was overturned

[238] *People v Quintos*, GR No 199402, 746 Phil 809 (12 November 2014).
[239] *People v Jumawan*, GR No 187495, 733 Phil 102 (21 April 2014).
[240] United Nations General Assembly resolution 48/104 of 20 December 1993.
[241] *People v Añonuevo*, GR No 248049 (4 October 2022).
[242] ibid (dissenting and concurring opinion of Leonen, J).
[243] L Madigan and N Gamble, *The Second Rape: Society's Continued Betrayal of the Victim* (Lexington Books, 1991) 4.
[244] Rape Victim Assistance and Protection Act of 1998, s 6.
[245] *Naval v Panday*, AM No RTJ-95-1283, 378 Phil 924 (21 December 1999) (emphasis omitted).
[246] ibid.

upon proof that 'the alleged victim was morally loose and apparently uncaring about her chastity'.[247]

The SC's continued practice of acquitting accused rapists on the basis of rape myths led the CEDAW Committee, in its 2010 *Vertido v the Philippines* decision, to conclude that the Philippines does not comply with its obligations under the CEDAW.[248] The Committee recommended that the Philippines 'Ensure that all legal procedures in cases involving crimes of rape … are … not affected by prejudices or stereotypical gender notions', and to conduct 'Appropriate training for judges … in understanding crimes of rape … in a gender-sensitive manner.'[249] It 'stresse[d] that there should be no assumption in law or in practice that a woman gives her consent because she has not physically resisted the unwanted sexual conduct, regardless of whether the perpetrator threatened to use or used physical violence.'[250]

In 2011, barely six months after *Vertido*, a Philippine trial court acquitted an accused rapist on the basis of 'the myth that women must physically resist the sexual assault.'[251] This led the CEDAW Committee, in its 2014 *RPB v The Philippines* decision, to reiterate its recommendation that rape trials should be 'free from prejudices or stereotypical notions regarding the victim's gender', among others.[252] It stated that 'there should be no assumption in law or in practice that a woman gives her consent because she has not physically resisted the unwanted sexual conduct, regardless of whether the perpetrator threatened to use or used physical violence.'[253]

In 2013 the SC promulgated two decisions aligning its case law with the CEDAW Committee recommendation. In the first, the Court stated that 'failure of a rape victim to shout, fight back, or escape from the scoundrel is not tantamount to consent or approval because the law imposes no obligation to exhibit defiance or present proof of struggle.'[254] In the second, the Court upheld a rape conviction even though the complainant had been silent during the rape after the rapist 'threatened to kill her if she made any noise.'[255]

Puzzlingly, the SC has returned to acquitting accused rapists on the basis of the rape myth that nonresistance implies consent.[256] In *People v Mahinay*, the victim testified that she fell asleep from dizziness while drinking alcohol

[247] *Civil Service Commission v Belagan*, GR No 132164, 483 Phil 601 (19 October 2004), citing *People v Tempongko, Jr*, GR No 69668, 144 SCRA 583 (2 October 1986).
[248] *Vertido v Phils* (n 231).
[249] ibid 8.9.
[250] ibid 8.5.
[251] *RPB v The Philippines* (n 236).
[252] ibid para 9(b)(iii).
[253] ibid para 8.10.
[254] *People v Linsie*, GR No 199494, 722 Phil 374 (27 November 2013).
[255] *People v Manicat*, GR No 205413, 722 Phil 522 (2 December 2013).
[256] See BD Tiojanco and R Koziomtzis, 'Supreme Court Rape Myths Violate Women's Rights' *Phil Daily Inquirer* (19 May 2017), available at opinion.inquirer.net/104105/supreme-court-rape-myths-violate-womens-rights.

with the accused and another friend. She was roused from sleep when the other friend started having sex with her. She was afraid that a knife atop a nearby table 'would be used to kill her if she resisted', so she cried. She was still dizzy, frightened and shivering when the friend left and the accused approached her to ask if he could also have sex with her. She did not answer as she was still shivering, but the accused nevertheless raped her. Both the trial court and the Court of Appeals found the victim's testimony 'credible, natural, convincing and consistent with human nature and the normal course of things', and so held the accused guilty. But, in 2017, the SC acquitted the accused. It held that the victim gave the accused 'the impression thru her unexplainable silence of her tacit consent' because 'she did not, and chose not to utter a word or make any sign of rejection.'[257]

A few months later the SC repeated this reasoning in overturning another rape conviction. The medico-legal examination had reported 'abrasions on [the victim's] left breast and contusions on her right hand'. This bolstered the Court of Appeals' conclusion that 'the element of force was present', and that the victim 'was subjected to bodily harm before [the accused] succeeded in having carnal knowledge with her.' The SC, however, held that 'the mere presence of abrasions and contusions on her did not preclude the giving of her consent to the sexual intercourse, for abrasions and contusions *could also be suffered* during voluntary submission of the partners to each other's lust.' The Court acquitted the accused rapist, saying that there was no evidence that the victim 'resisted in that whole time,' and 'What she did not do was eloquent proof of her consent.'[258]

VI. CONCLUSION

Congress enacted the Anti-VAWC Act, which allows abused women to invoke battered woman syndrome as a defence from criminal and civil liability,[259] a few months after the SC promulgated a decision saying that 'While our hearts empathize with recurrently battered persons, we can only work within the limits of law … Neither can we amend the Revised Penal Code. Only Congress, in its wisdom, may do so.'[260] As the SC itself recognised, 'nine … years of spirited advocacy by women's groups' for an Anti-VAWC Act preceded its enactment.[261] It also recognised that the RH Law was enacted after years marked by 'television debates to sticker campaigns, from rallies by socio-political activists to

[257] *People v Tionloc*, GR No 212193, 805 Phil 907 (15 February 2017).
[258] *People v Mahinay*, GR No 199894, 808 Phil 455 (5 April 2017).
[259] Anti-VAWC Act, s 26.
[260] *People v Genosa*, GR No 135981 (15 January 2004).
[261] *Garcia v Drilon* (n 177).

mass gatherings organized by members of the clergy'.[262] While the country still awaits a divorce law, the SC has ruled that the Constitution's article on the family 'was not meant to be a general prohibition on divorce' and has noted not only that 'Through the years, there has been constant clamor from various sectors of the Philippine society to re-institute absolute divorce', but that there is a divorce bill pending in Congress.[263] As for same-sex marriage, the SC says it is an issue that 'should invite more public discussion in the halls of Congress', where 'the task of devising an arrangement where same-sex relations will earn state recognition is better left'.[264] These decisions recognise that gender justice in the Philippines has been a product of *democratic constitutionalism*: by the citizenry using the People Power Principle to flesh out and enforce the Constitution's various guarantees of gender justice through lawmaking, elections and other forms of political participation. The judiciary, although sometimes used to delay or derail this cause, has chosen a democratic constitutionalist role of enforcing the gender justice legislation that is an outcome of these politics.[265] More recently, the SC has also expressed a willingness to use the constitutional non-sexism principle to liberally interpret statutes in ways which promote gender justice and equality. But as the judicially delayed implementation of the RH Law and the persistence of rape myths in jurisprudence caution, the citizenry should not take this liberality from the courts for granted and must continually press for gender justice from the bench.

[262] RH Law Decision.
[263] *Republic v Manalo* (n 20).
[264] *Falcis v Civil Registrar General* (n 77).
[265] See R Post and R Siegel, 'Roe Rage: Democratic Constitutionalism and Backlash' (2007) 42 *Harvard Civil Rights-Civil Liberties Law Review* 373.

9

Gender and Constitutionalism in Indonesia

SIMON BUTT*

I. INTRODUCTION

IN 1999, INDONESIA embarked on a series of ambitious democratic reforms during a period known as *reformasi*. For almost four decades prior – under Presidents Soekarno (1959–1966) and Soeharto (1966–1998) – Indonesia had been a highly centralised authoritarian state. But within a few short years after the fall of Soeharto, the country transformed into a vibrant liberal democracy – at least on paper. The reforms achieved during this period included government decentralisation, free and fair elections, the creation of an anti-corruption commission, the depoliticisation of the military and a strengthening of judicial independence.[1]

Particularly important were amendments to Indonesia's Constitution, made in four rounds between 1999 and 2002.[2] These amendments were extensive, converting the original threadbare Constitution – promulgated on 18 August 1945, the day after the declaration of Indonesian independence from the Dutch – into a modern and extensive one. While imperfect, the amendment process yielded a 'thoroughly democratic document' and allowed for the preservation of institutions that protected pluralism.[3] One of the most important

* The author is indebted to Miftah Fadhli for his excellent research work for this chapter.

[1] N Hosen, *Human rights, politics and corruption in Indonesia: a critical reflection on the post Soeharto era* (Republic of Letters, 2010); H Crouch, *Political Reform in Indonesia after Soeharto* (ISEAS, 2010); DL Horowitz, *Constitutional Change and Democracy in Indonesia* (Cambridge University Press, 2013); S Butt, *Corruption and Law in Indonesia* (Routledge, 2012); T Lindsey (ed), *Indonesia: Law and Society*, 2nd edn (Federation Press, 2008); GF Bell, 'Indonesia: the Challenges of Legal Diversity and Law Reform' in EA Black and GF Bell (eds), *Law and Legal Institutions of Asia: Traditions, Adaptations and Innovations* (Cambridge University Press, 2011).

[2] D Indrayana, *Indonesian Constitutional Reform, 1999–2002: An Evaluation of Constitution-Making in Transition* (Kompas, 2008); S Butt, *The Constitutional Court and Democracy in Indonesia* (Brill, 2015).

[3] Horowitz (n 1) i.

amendments was the inclusion of several civil, political and economic rights based on international norms, including rights associated with gender equality. These rights were backed by the establishment of a Constitutional Court (*Mahkamah Konstitusi*) to ensure that, wherever possible, the national Parliament embodies these human rights in the statutes it enacts.[4] The Court can invalidate legislation that it declares to be unconstitutional.

Also relevant were statutory reforms aimed at improving the socio-economic position of women and, in particular, female participation in politics. Under these measures, Indonesia recognised for the first time the Convention on the Elimination of All Forms of Discrimination Against Women (CEDAW). Perhaps the most important of these statutory reforms is the 1999 Human Rights Law.

The effectiveness of these reforms on gender and sexual equality, however, has been mixed. For example, the Government has enacted new legislation directed at addressing gender-based violence (particularly in domestic contexts) and the President has appointed women to key ministerial positions.[5] But the lower socio-economic position of women – often explained as a product of conservative religious and cultural norms[6] – continues to be a matter of concern. Indonesia today ranks 104th on the United Nations Development Programme (UNDP)'s Gender Inequality Index, which measures the performance of 160 countries on education, health, economic and political participation.[7] Similarly, in the 2020 Global Gender Gap Index, produced by the World Economic Forum, Indonesia ranks 85th among 153 countries for performance according to economic participation and opportunity, educational attainment, health and political empowerment.[8] Although national parliamentary representation of women reached 20 per cent in 2020, it has been traditionally closer to 10 per cent.[9] And some post-Soeharto laws clearly undermine the movement towards gender equality, the most egregious of which include subnational regulations, particularly those issued in Aceh.

As this chapter discusses, the Constitutional Court has been at the forefront of interpreting and applying these new constitutional rights, including in cases that have gender dimensions. But decisions from that Court have likewise had mixed results for women. Some of these cases have undoubtedly helped improve the socio-economic position of women. For example, the Court has invalidated

[4] Hendrianto, 'Institutional Choice and the New Indonesian Constitutional Court' in A Harding and P Nicholson (eds), *New courts in Asia* (Routledge, 2009).

[5] R Diprose, 'Reducing Barriers to Gender Equality in Indonesia' *East Asia Forum* (25 March 2019), available at www.eastasiaforum.org/2019/03/25/reducing-barriers-to-gender-inequality-in-indonesia.

[6] R Diprose, K Setiawan and A Savirani. 'How Women Are Changing Indonesia' *Pursuit* (5 December 2019), available at pursuit.unimelb.edu.au/Arts/how-women-are-changing-indonesia.

[7] Diprose (n 5).

[8] D Heriyanto, 'More Indonesian Women in Labor Market, Fewer in Politics: Gender Gap Report' *The Jakarta Post* (2 January 2020), available at www.thejakartapost.com/news/2019/12/30/more-indonesian-women-in-labor-market-fewer-in-politics-gender-gap-report.html.

[9] The World Bank, 'Proportion of Seats Held by Women in National Parliaments (%) – Indonesia', available at data.worldbank.org/indicator/SG.GEN.PARL.ZS?locations=ID.

legislation that makes women solely financially responsible for any children they have outside a valid marriage. The Court has also been instrumental in raising the marriage age. While these decisions appear to promote autonomy for women, it bears noting that they are limited to family law, which seems to confine progress within the strictures of marriage. Cases involving political rights have been less positive for women, primarily because the Court has decided that the imperative of female political representation should give way to other democratic principles. It has, therefore, invalidated parliamentary gender quotas. Still, the Court has removed statutory limitations on women governing Indonesia's only provincial sultanate.

Beyond gender equality, these constitutional reforms and cases have brought no advances for LGBTQI groups. While homosexuality is not prohibited under Indonesian law, social persecution and even police raids – often justified by Indonesia's pornography law – have targeted so-called 'gay sex parties'.[10] The best that can be said about the country's Constitutional Court is that, in 2017, it deflected a constitutional claim to criminalise sexual intercourse outside of marriage, including between homosexuals. However, the decision was rendered by narrow majority of the Court, and some commentators have argued that it does not bode well for future constitutional developments in this area.[11]

Against this background, it bears noting aspects of the modern Indonesian state that present obstacles to greater constitutional protection of gender-related rights. As this chapter will explain, these obstacles include the Constitutional Court's limited jurisdiction and powers of enforcement and the reluctance of other Indonesian courts – including the general courts, religious courts and the Supreme Court – to directly apply the Constitution and to enforce the Human Rights Law. Also relevant is the propensity of some local governments, particularly in Aceh, to issue subnational by-laws that discriminate against women, and the reluctance of the Supreme Court to invalidate them, even if they are illegal. Also unclear is the status of international law within Indonesia's domestic legal system.

A particularly important factor that often hinders the pursuit of gender and sexual equality in Indonesia is the influence of conservative Muslims and the interpretations of Islamic law they propound. For example, the constitutional challenge aiming to prohibit extra-marital sexual intercourse noted above was brought by a conservative group. Constitutionally, Indonesia has always been a religious state. All of the constitutions previously adopted have declared that the 'State is based on Almighty God' (*Negara Berdasarkan Ketuhanan yang Maha Esa*). This is the first principle of Indonesia's constitutionally enshrined national philosophy, Pancasila (literally, 'the Five Principles'). But no particular religion

[10] Human Rights Watch, 'Indonesia: Investigate Police Raid on "Gay Party"' (7 September 2020), available at www.hrw.org/news/2020/09/07/indonesia-investigate-police-raid-gay-party.

[11] S Butt, 'Religious Conservatism, Islamic Criminal Law and the Judiciary in Indonesia: A Tale of Three Courts' (2018) 50 *Journal of Legal Pluralism and Unofficial Law* 402.

has been adopted as a state religion, and Indonesia has long been known for religious diversity, tolerance and pluralism.[12] Still, conservative Islamic groups have continually pushed for increased government support for Islam, a greater say in government policies, and for state law to better reflect Islamic principles. Although these aspirations were easily suppressed during the Soeharto period, they now have a more prominent voice through organisations such as the Indonesian Council of Islamic Scholars (*Majelis Ulama Indonesia*). Over the past decade or so in particular, Indonesian observers have identified a conservative turn within the nation's Islamic faith, a growing influence of conservatism in politics, and an increasing intolerance for liberalism and religious minorities.[13] Some of the gender-based reforms, whether constitutional and statutory, have met resistance from these groups, much to the chagrin of pluralists and other activists.

Indonesia has a National Commission on Human Rights (*Komnas HAM*) and National Commission on Violence Against Women (*Komnas Perempuan*) to help monitor the Government's performance in upholding these rights, to push for improvements, and to educate citizens about their rights.[14] Many other organisations work alongside these groups, including *Koalisi Perempuan Indonesia* (Indonesian Women's Coalition), *Kalyanamitra, Solidaritas Perempuan* (Women's Solidarity), The Asian Muslim Action Network, LBH APIK (Women's Legal Aid), *Kapal Perempuan* (Women's Vessel) and Rifka Annisa. However, despite some victories in some areas,[15] these organisations and commissions have generally had limited success.

[12] S Fenwick, *Blasphemy, Islam And the State: Pluralism And Liberalism in Indonesia* (Routledge, 2017); AH Johns, 'Indonesia: Islam And Cultural Pluralism' in JL Esposito (ed), *Islam in Asia: Religion, Politics, and Society* (Oxford University Press, 1987) 202–29; A Salim, *Contemporary Islamic Law in Indonesia: Sharia And Legal Pluralism* (Edinburgh University Press, 2015); A Salim, 'Dynamic Legal Pluralism in Indonesia: Contested Legal Orders in Contemporary Aceh' (2010) 42 *Journal of Legal Pluralism and Unofficial Law* 1.

[13] T Lindsey and H Pausacker (eds), *Religion, Law And Intolerance in Indonesia* (Routledge, 2016); J Menchik, *Islam And Democracy in Indonesia: Tolerance without Liberalism* (Cambridge University Press, 2016); M Crouch, 'Proselytization, Religious Diversity And the State in Indonesia: The Offense of Deceiving A Child to Change Religion' in J Finucane and RM Feener (eds), *Proselytizing And the Limits of Religious Pluralism in Contemporary Asia* (Springer, 2014); M van Bruinessen (ed), *Contemporary Developments in Indonesian Islam: Explaining the 'Conservative Turn'* (Institute of Southeast Asian Studies, 2013).

[14] K Setiawan, *Promoting Human Rights: National Human Rights Commissions in Indonesia and Malaysia* (Leiden University Press, 2013); *Komnas Perempuan* itself was established in the period immediately following the fall of Soeharto, in response to the rape of ethnic Chinese women that occurred during the May 1998 riots that precipitated Soeharto's resignation. *Komnas Perempuan* has a Plenary Council and an Operational Division (*Badan Pekerja*) (Art 5). The Plenary Council consists of a chairperson, and up to two vice chairs and 19 members (Arts 6, 8 and 9). It may establish sub-commissions as necessary (Art 11(1)), and, to date, had established sub-commissions on legal and policy reform, monitoring, rehabilitation, education and community participation. It had also established working groups on migrant workers, Papua, and women and the Constitution and national law.

[15] For example, a Domestic Violence Law was enacted in 2004 after a large coalition of 60 civil society organisations led a sustained campaign for legislation on violence against women, see

II. BACKGROUND INFORMATION

On paper, the opportunity structure for the pursuit of gender- and sexuality-related rights in Indonesia is relatively open. The constitutional system established that developed in the years after Soeharto's retirement provides many rights to pursue recognition, equality and non-discrimination. These rights are introduced in section III ('Constitutional Framing of Gender and Sexuality'). In this section, I examine the institutions in which those rights can be applied, the relatively open access to those institutions, and non-constitutional aspects of Indonesia's legal system which are considered in Indonesia to support the socio-economic and political interests of women.

A. The Constitutional Court (*Mahkamah Konstitusi*)

As mentioned, the institution charged with interpreting and applying these constitutional rights is the Constitutional Court. This Court, established in 2003, was the first Indonesian institution with power of constitutional review.[16] The executive, legislature, and judicial branches of government are each responsible for filling three seats on the Court. Although providing a detailed assessment of the Court's performance is beyond the scope of this chapter, it bears noting that the Constitutional Court is Indonesia's most professional judicial institution, having issued many landmark decisions since its establishment, in areas ranging from socio-economic rights to electoral systems and, as discussed below, gender-related issues.[17] The Court has adopted relatively open standing rules, providing access to individuals adversely affected by the legislation for which constitutional review is sought, and to non-government organisations who work in areas covered by that legislation.[18] Its judgments are generally considered to be authoritative in matters of constitutional law and are usually followed as a matter of course.[19]

P Venning, 'Marrying Contested Approaches: Empowerment And the Imposition of International Principles: Domestic Violence Case Resolution in Indonesia' (2010) 46 *Journal of Development Studies* 397.

[16] A power provided under Art 24C(1)–(2) of the 1945 Constitution and Art 10 of Law No 24 of 2003 on the Constitutional Court. The Court also has jurisdiction to resolve disputes about the relative jurisdiction of state institutions, the dissolution of political parties and general election results. It must also 'provide a decision' if the DPR suspects that the president or vice president has committed treason or corruption, another serious crime or form of misconduct, or otherwise no longer fulfils the constitutional requirements to hold office.

[17] S Butt, 'Indonesia's Constitutional Court – The Conservative Activist or Pragmatic Strategist?' in B Dressel (ed), *The Judicialization of Politics in Asia* (Routledge, 2012).

[18] Butt (n 2) 48–60.

[19] S Butt and T Lindsey, 'Economic Reform When the Constitution Matters: Indonesia's Constitutional Court and Article 33' (2008) 44 *Bulletin of Indonesian Economic Studies* 239.

Although two of its judges have been involved in corruption scandals, many of its other judges rank amongst Indonesia's brightest legal minds.[20] However, during its almost two-decade history, the Court has only had two women judges, out of 26 appointees. Both of these women had particularly distinguished careers as academics at top Indonesian law schools before joining the bench. The first, Maria Farida Indrati, who retired from the Court in 2018, is a well-respected public law professor at the University of Indonesia, with particular expertise in the lawmaking process.[21] She became known for her dissents, particularly in cases involving gender issues. Enny Nurbaningsih, the second female judge appointed to the Constitutional Court, is also a public law expert, and a professor at the University of Gadjah Mada Law Faculty.

Disappointingly, it is commonly said, even by the Constitutional Court itself, that Professor Nurbaningsih replaced Professor Indrati as 'the' female judge on the bench.[22] The implication here is that, from now on, if a female judge leaves the Court, she will be replaced by another female. Strangely, there is little discussion in legal or public policy circles about having more than one female judge on the Court at any given time.[23] There is certainly no shortage of well-respected female law graduates or lawyers, or any widespread perception that females are less qualified for judicial positions than men.[24] The reason appears to be discrimination, practised among all three arms of government which are responsible for appointing three judges each to the Court. It bears noting, however, that representation in this Court – 11 per cent– is low even by Indonesian standards. By comparison, 26 per cent of 3,760 district court judges[25] and 23 per cent of 3,042 religious court judges[26] are women. Only the Supreme Court's representation is

[20] S Hendrianto, *Law and Politics of Constitutional Courts: Indonesia and the Search for Judicial Heroes* (Routledge, 2018).

[21] The book for which she is best known is MF Indrati, *Ilmu Perundang-undangan: Jenis, Fungsi, dan Materi Muatan* (Kanisius, 2007).

[22] See Professor Nurbaningsih's profile on the Constitutional Court's website, Mahkamah Konstitusi Republik Indonesia, 'Profil Hakim Prof. Dr. Enny Nurbaningsih, SH.,M.Hum.', available at mkri.id/index.php?page=web.ProfilHakim&id=678&menu=3.

[23] NE Elnizar, 'Simon Butt: Seharusnya Lebih Banyak Perempuan Menjadi Hakim MK' (*Hukumonline*, 31 August 2018), available at www.hukumonline.com/berita/a/simon-butt--seharusnya-lebih-banyak-perempuan-menjadi-hakim-mk-lt5b892ecc3c8fa.

[24] Precise figures on current female representation in the legal profession are unavailable, but by one account, the number sat at just above 25% in 2010; see E Michelson, 'Women in the Legal Profession, 1970–2010: A Study of the Global Supply of Lawyers' (2013) 20 *Indiana Journal of Global Legal Studies* 1071, 1115.

[25] Badan Peradilan Umum, 'Laporan Pelaksanaan Kegiatan Direktorat Jenderal Badan Peradilan Umum Tahun 2019' (2020) 52, available at badilum.mahkamahagung.go.id/publik/laporan/laporan-tahunan/2945-laporan-tahunan-pelaksanaan-kegiatan-direktorat-jenderal-badan-peradilan-umum-tahun-2019.html.

[26] Look for more detail in Badan Peradilan Agama, 'Laporan Pelaksanaan Kegiatan Direktorat Jenderal Peradilan Agama Tahun 2019' (2020) 22, available at drive.google.com/file/d/1IcNMBI4deG5PH0vF6w8SH5D_ZDYdVGy4/view.

lower – with four of 47 judges.[27] Of course, greater representation by women would better reflect the gender composition of Indonesia.

It is important to note that the scope of the Constitutional Court's review powers is limited: the Court can only review *national statutes* for compliance with the *Constitution*. This is far from 'complete' jurisdiction, because the bulk of Indonesian law is contained in lower-level instruments, such as regulations issued by the Government, President and ministers, and subnational by-laws.[28] These laws are simply beyond the purview of the Court, which – despite its typically progressive decision-making – has rejected applications seeking their review. By contrast, the Supreme Court has jurisdiction to review some of these lower-level laws, but appears only to have power to review them for compliance with national legislation, not other lower-level instruments, much less the Constitution.[29] While the Supreme Court's jurisdiction is wider, its decision-making is arguably more conservative (it seems less willing to invalidate laws than the Constitutional Court), and it continues to suffer from widely held concerns about its integrity and competence.[30] The Constitutional Court also cannot review the constitutionality of government action and policy, as can constitutional courts in some other countries.[31] And the Court lacks the formal power to enforce its own decisions. For this, it must rely on political good will, which, in turn, seems to depend on public support.[32] In this regard, much appears to depend on the popularity of its judges rather than the content of its decisions.[33] In practice, then, this patchwork approach to judicial review, the reluctance of the Supreme Court to exercise it, and the Constitutional Court's lack of enforcement powers, have confined the open 'on paper' opportunity structure.

B. Statutory and Other Legal Reforms

Against this backdrop of constitutional developments sits the statutory framework. Before Soeharto's reign ended in 1998, Indonesia's human rights track

[27] AP Taher, 'Mahkamah Agung Ungkap Alasan Hakim Perempuan Masih Minim' (*Tirto.id*, 8 March 2019), available at tirto.id/mahkamah-agung-ungkap-alasan-hakim-perempuan-masih-minim-diSj.

[28] H Thoolen (ed), *Indonesia and the Rule of Law: Twenty Years of "New Order" Government: A Study* (Frances Pinter, 1987).

[29] S Butt, 'Judicial Reasoning and Review in the Indonesian Supreme Court' (2019) 6 *Asian Journal of Law and Society* 67.

[30] S Pompe, *The Indonesian Supreme Court: A Study of Institutional Collapse* (Cornell University Press, 2005).

[31] AS Sweet, 'Constitutional Courts' in M Rosenfeld and A Sajó (eds), *The Oxford Handbook of Comparative Constitutional Law* (Oxford University Press, 2012).

[32] For discussion about other limitations the Constitution, statute and the Court itself have imposed on the Court's jurisdiction, see Butt (n 2).

[33] The Court arguably reached its zenith of authority during the tenure of its first two Chief Justices, who were publicly well known and popular, and had political aspirations; see Hendrianto (n 20).

record was particularly poor.[34] His New Order Government referred to human rights as a Western construct often inconsistent with 'Asian values'.[35] However, contrary to this general avoidance of human rights, Indonesia – in an effort to attract more women to participate in the national economy and in response to international pressure – acceded to CEDAW during the Soeharto period,[36] ratifying it by Law 7 of 1984.[37] In 2000, during the early days of *Reformasi*, Indonesia also signed the CEDAW Optional Protocol that establishes a mechanism for complaints and allows the Committee on the Elimination of Discrimination Against Women to investigate grave or systemic violations of the Convention.[38] But Indonesia has not yet ratified it.[39]

The Indonesian Government has issued various laws intended to implement CEDAW or that otherwise reflect its principles. Many of these were enacted after the fall of Soeharto, in 1998. They include Presidential Decision 181 of 1998 on the Formation of the National Commission on Violence Against Women (*Komnas Perempuan*).[40] Presidential Instruction 9 of 2000 on Gender Mainstreaming in National Development requires politicians to consider gender when making policy and planning development, and when implementing, monitoring and evaluating those policies and development plans. Other relevant measures include Law 23 of 2003 on Child Protection, Law 21 of 2007 on the Elimination of Human Trafficking, Minister of Women's Empowerment Regulation 1 of 2008 on Guidelines for Improving Quality of Life for Women, and Law 23 of 2004 on Eradication of Domestic Violence. As discussed below, electoral statutes have been enacted to require parties to ensure that at least 30 per cent of their candidates are female.

One of the first items on the post-Soeharto reform agenda was improving Indonesia's legal framework for human rights protection. To that end, the national legislature enacted a Human Rights Law in 1999.[41] This Law,

[34] TM Lubis, *In Search of Human Rights: Legal-political Dilemmas of Indonesia's New Order, 1966–1990* (Gramedia Pustaka Utama, 1993).

[35] T Lindsey, 'Indonesia: Devaluing Asian Values, Rewriting Rule of Law' in RP Peerenboom (ed), *Asian Discourses of Rule of Law* (RoutledgeCurzon, 2004) 286.

[36] Indonesia also ratified the UN Convention on the Rights of the Child and the Convention on the Political Rights of Women by Law No 68 of 1956.

[37] See MT Lindsay, 'Daughters of Development: The State and Women in Indonesia' (thesis, University of British Columbia 1997), esp ch 5.

[38] United Nations Department of Public Information, 'Optional Protocol to Women's Convention Comes into Force' (21 December 2000) WOM/1242, available at www.un.org/womenwatch/daw/cedaw/protocol/wom1242.htm.

[39] It bears noting that the status of international law in Indonesia's legal system remains an issue of significant debate, though human rights treaties have supposedly been incorporated into domestic law, see S Butt, 'The Position of International Law within the Indonesian Legal System' (2014) 28 *Emory International Law Review* 1.

[40] This decision was subsequently replaced by Presidential Regulation No 65 of 2005 on *Komnas Perempuan*. For a discussion of the different types of legal instruments used in Indonesia and their relative authority, see S Butt and T Lindsey, *Indonesian Law* (Oxford University Press, 2018) ch 2.

[41] Law 39 of 1999 on Human Rights. The Human Rights Law was enacted pursuant to People's Consultative Assembly Decree XVII on Human Rights.

portions of which were subsequently codified in the Constitution, embodies the rights of all citizens to: receive special treatment and protection (Article 5(3)); form a family (Article 10); obtain justice without discrimination (Article 17); seek protection for themselves and their families, honour, dignity, and property (Article 29); own property (Article 36); earn equal pay for equal work regardless of gender (Article 38); vote and participate in general elections (Article 43(1)); and participate in government (Article 43(2)–(3)). The Law also specifies women's rights, including rights to representation in politics (Article 46), to education (Article 48), to work of their choosing (Article 49), to bring legal action (Article 50), and in marriage (Article 51).

The Human Rights Law also clarifies that every person in Indonesia must comply with Indonesian law (written and unwritten) and international human rights laws ratified by Indonesia (Article 67), which are deemed part of the national law (Article 7(2)). The Indonesian Parliament has also ratified many key international human rights instruments since 1998,[42] though most of the rights they contain were already in the 1999 Human Rights Law.

Also important was the enactment of the Human Rights Court Law in 2000,[43] which establishes a set of human rights courts in district capitals and municipalities (Article 3). These courts try gross human rights violations (Article 4), including cases of genocide and crimes against humanity, according to the Rome Statute of the International Criminal Court (Article 7 and its Elucidation). Critically, Article 40 prohibits as crimes against humanity rape, sexual enslavement, forced prostitution, forced pregnancy, forced sterilisation, or other similar forms of sexual assault; and persecution of a particular group or association based on political views, race, nationality, ethnic origin, culture, religion, sex or any other basis regarded universally as contravening international law. Contravention of Article 40 results in a prison sentence of 10–20 years.[44] These human rights courts now hear very few cases.[45]

The courts with primary responsibility to interpret and apply these statutes are the Supreme Court and the courts below it, particularly the general courts (which hear most types of civil and criminal cases) and the human rights courts (for gross human rights violations). The judges working in these courts tend to be quite conservative, particularly compared with Constitutional

[42] Including the Convention Against Torture and other Cruel, Inhuman or Degrading Treatments or Punishments (CAT) in 1998, the Convention on the Elimination of All Forms of Racial Discrimination (CERD) in July 1999, and the International Covenant on Civil and Political Rights (ICCPR) and International Covenant on Economic, Social and Cultural Rights (ICESCR) in 2005 and 2006.

[43] Law 26 of 2000 on the Human Rights Court.

[44] The human rights courts are now very rarely used, having served the main purpose of their establishment: trying human rights abuses from New Order period and the aftermath of the 1999 independence reference in East Timor (now Timor Leste), see Butt and Lindsey (n 40) 85–86.

[45] Indeed, it appears that the Supreme Court has even stopped reporting about their activities in some years. For example, they were the only branch of courts not mentioned in the Supreme Court's Annual Report for 2016, see Mahkamah Agung, *Laporan Tahunan 2016* (Mahkamah Agung, 2017).

Court judges.[46] Judges on these non-constitutional courts often appear reluctant to directly apply the rights contained in the Human Rights Law (including the international human rights it subsumes through Article 67) or even in the Constitution. Only rarely does one read or hear of cases where these courts have upheld these rights. Most non-constitutional judges are also generally averse to giving direct effect to international norms, amid significant controversy and debate about whether international law is binding on domestic courts, even after parliamentary ratification.[47] Only if these rights are adopted in more specific legislation – such as the Child Protection or Domestic Violence laws – are these courts likely to apply or enforce them.

These practices have continued, despite Indonesia being admonished during period reviews of its compliance with some of the human rights treaties it has signed.[48] One result of this reluctance is that the precise content of these rights has not been tested by Indonesia's general courts in non-constitutional cases.

C. Decentralisation and Regional Regulations[49]

The Supreme Court has power to review lower-level laws against national statutes, including the 1999 Human Rights Law. Research has identified thousands of lower-level laws that appear to violate the rights contained in this Law.[50] One might expect the Supreme Court to be busy invalidating these laws. The Court, however, appears keen to avoid engaging in judicial review whenever possible,[51] including in gender-related cases.

This avoidance is clear from an examination of the Supreme Court's judicial review of subnational laws. The post-Soeharto period witnessed significant decentralisation reforms, which sought to disperse the executive power of the central Government to various national and subnational individuals and institutions. Legislative and executive officials at the provincial, city and county levels were given responsibility to regulate a wide variety of matters, such as health, education, infrastructure, transportation, land and the environment. The laws enacted by these officials are called 'regional regulations' (*Peraturan Daerah*, or *Perda*), and they encompass regulations and decisions issued by these subnational parliaments and executives.

[46] Butt (n 11).
[47] Butt (n 39).
[48] ibid.
[49] This section draws from Butt (n 29); Butt (n 11); Butt and Lindsey (n 40).
[50] S Kamil and CS Bamualim (eds), *Syariah Islam Dan HAM: Dampak Perda Syariah Terhadap Kebebasan Sipil, Hak Perempuan, Dan Non-Muslim* (Center for the Study of Religion and Culture, State Islamic University Syarif Hidayatullah, 2007); S Butt and N Parsons, *Analytical paper: Perda review mechanisms* (Report prepared for AusAID, 2011), on file with the author.
[51] S Butt and N Parsons, 'Judicial Review and the Supreme Court in Indonesia: A New Space for Law?' (2014) 97 *Indonesia* 55.

Although many subnational lawmakers are undoubtedly well intentioned and professional, and while they have improved community standards in the areas of health, education and the environment,[52] many are suspected of incompetency and self-dealing.[53] A primary concern, voiced by politicians and scholars alike, is that many subnational lawmakers have used their powers to raise revenue, both legitimate and otherwise.[54] Another concern is that some subnational laws have been oppressive or discriminatory, or adopt Islamic norms at the expense of human rights protection.[55] These include laws imposing dress codes, requiring citizens to pray, banning gambling and alcohol, and prohibiting prostitution.[56] Many of these are said to unfairly target women.[57] For example, between 2009 and 2016, the National Commission on Violence Against Women (*Komnas Perempuan*) identified 421 bylaws that discriminated against women and minorities.[58]

The Supreme Court has been asked to review subnational laws for compliance with the Human Rights Law in numerous cases. However, the Court has generally been reluctant to exercise its review powers, and when it does, it often fails to consider the parties' arguments, it is reluctant to examine the merits of the case, it issues decisions inconsistent with previous decisions, and it often provides few if any reasons for its holdings.[59] This is true of the Court's

[52] BD Lewis, 'Decentralised Government: Greater Demand Needed to Raise Service Quality in Indonesia' (*East Asia Forum*, 22 March 2014), available at www.eastasiaforum.org/2014/03/22/decentralised-government-greater-demand-needed-to-raise-service-quality-in-indonesia; BD Lewis and D Pattinasarany, 'Determining Citizen Satisfaction with Local Public Education in Indonesia: The Significance of Actual Service Quality and Governance Conditions' (2009) 40 *Growth and Change* 85.

[53] Many appear to be corrupt: around 350 regional heads were involved in corruption scandals, and almost 80 were caught 'red-handed' by the Anti-corruption Commission, between 2004 and 2016; see K Setiawan, 'ICW: 350 Kepala Daerah Kena Korupsi, 78 Tertangkap Tangan' *Tempo.co* (2017), available at nasional.tempo.co/read/833691/icw-350-kepala-daerah-kena-korupsi-78-tertangkap-tangan.

[54] Governments need revenue to function, but many subnational governments in Indonesia have imposed user charges for non-identifiable government-provided services and taxes that duplicate those imposed by another tier of government. These laws are said to damage the investment climate, particularly in regional areas, because they create a 'high cost economy'; see Pratikno, 'Exercising Freedom: Local Autonomy And Democracy in Indonesia, 1999–2001' in P Sulistiyanto, M Erb and C Faucher (eds), *Regionalism in Post-Suharto Indonesia* (RoutledgeCurzon, 2005) 21; Ilyas Saad, 'Implementasi Otonomi Daerah Sudah Mengarah Pada Penciptaan Distorsi Dan High Cost Economy' in *Decentralization, Regulatory Reform, and the Business Climate* (Partnership for Economic Growth, 2003); B Brodjonegoro, 'Three Years of Fiscal Decentralization in Indonesia: Its Impacts on Regional Economic Development and Fiscal Sustainability' (International Symposium on Fiscal Decentralization in Asia Revisited, Hitotsubashi University, 20–21 February 2004); A Maryono, 'Thousands of Bylaws Halt Investment: BKPM' *Jakarta Post* (26 October 2009); OECD, OECD investment policy reviews (Organisation for Economic Co-operation and Development, 2010) 21.

[55] Kamil and Bamualim (n 50).

[56] I Ropi, *Religion and Regulation in Indonesia* (Palgrave Macmillan, 2017) 189–94.

[57] M Crouch, 'Regional Regulations in Indonesia: Failing Vulnerable Groups' (2009) 43 *Review of Indonesian and Malaysian Affairs* 53.

[58] 'Komnas Perempuan Finds 421 Discriminatory Policies' *Tempo.co* (19 August 2016), available at en.tempo.co/read/797156/komnas-perempuan-finds-421-discriminatory-policies.

[59] S Butt and N Parsons, 'Reining in Regional Governments? Local Taxes and Investment in Decentralised Indonesia' (2012) 34 *Sydney Law Review* 91; S Butt, 'Regional Autonomy and the Proliferation of Perda in Indonesia: An Assessment of Bureaucratic and Judicial Review Mechanisms'

decision-making in all types of cases, not just cases involving human rights with implications for gender or sexuality.

These shortcomings came into sharp relief when the Supreme Court was asked to review one of the most conservative and discriminatory subnational laws in Indonesia: Qanun Aceh 6 of 2014 on Islamic Criminal Law (*Hukum Jinayat*).[60] Aceh is the only province of Indonesia with power to issue laws based on Islamic norms.[61] This Qanun significantly expands the scope and application of Islamic criminal law in Aceh, including some of its punishments.[62] It prohibits consumption and distribution of alcohol, gambling, *khalwat* (being alone in an enclosed or private place with a member of the opposite sex who is not a spouse or relative) and *ikhtilath* (consensual intimate relations, such as flirting, touching, hugging and kissing, between an unmarried male and female in a private or public area). It also prohibits adultery, sodomy, lesbian sex, sexual abuse and rape. Punishments for these offences range from 10 strokes of the cane, a fine of 100 grams of gold or 10 months in prison for *khalwat* (Article 23(1)), to 150–200 strokes, 1,500–2,000 grams of gold or 150–200 months in prison for rape of a child or family member (Articles 49 and 50). The Qanun makes it particularly difficult for alleged victims to successfully pursue rape allegations, as alleged perpetrators can often escape a finding of guilt by declaring a willingness to face God's wrath if he or she is lying (Article 55). The Qanun also requires alleged victims to provide initial evidence of the rape and imposes punishments on them if the defendant is ultimately found not guilty. Article 72 stipulates that the Qanun Jinayat is the applicable law if an offence is regulated in both the Qanun Jinayat and the national Criminal Code (*Kitab Undang-undang Hukum Pidana*, or KUHP).

Unsurprisingly, the Qanun drew heavy criticism from gender and human rights activists in Indonesia and abroad,[63] prompting the Institute for Criminal Justice Reform and the Women's Solidarity Association to seek judicial review by the Supreme Court.[64] The Institute argued that the Qanun violated higher-level

(2010) 32 *Sydney Law Review* 177; M Effendi, *Kewenangan uji materil peraturan perundang-undangan dibawah undang-undang* (Mahkamah Agung, 2013).

[60] '*Qanun*' is an Arabic term for 'law', see John L Esposito, 'Qanun' The Oxford Dictionary of Islam, (Oxford Islamic Studies Online, 2017). In Aceh, it is synonymous with the term 'Perda' issued in other provinces.

[61] T Lindsey and K Steiner (eds), *Islam, Law and the State in Indonesia* vol 1 (IB Tauris, 2012).

[62] The Qanun applies primarily to Muslim individuals, but also to corporations conducting business in Aceh (Art 5) and, perhaps most controversially, to non-Muslims who commit offences proscribed in the Qanun Jinayat, but not national criminal law.

[63] See, eg, P Kine, 'Indonesia's Aceh Authorities Lash Hundreds Under Sharia Statutes' (*Human Rights Watch*, 8 February 2017), available at www.hrw.org/news/2017/02/08/indonesias-aceh-authorities-lash-hundreds-under-sharia-statutes.

[64] The Supreme Court's standing rules to bring judicial review applications appear to permit claims from a wide range of applicants. Art 1(4) of Supreme Court Regulation 1 of 2011 on Judicial Review defines 'applicant' as 'a group of the community or individuals who submit an application to the Supreme Court objecting to the enactment of a law below of a level lower than a statute'.

laws, including the KUHP (which does not include caning as a permissible form of punishment in an otherwise exhaustive list of punishments), the 1999 Human Rights Law and the International Covenant on Civil and Political Rights (ICCPR, which prohibits torture, including humiliating or inhumane punishments), and the Criminal Procedure Code (which requires police, not victims, to provide evidence of these crimes and does not include an oath before God as a valid form of evidence). The Institute also made relatively minor technical arguments about the terminology used in the Qanun and its drafting which, the Institute claimed, violated the 2011 Lawmaking Law.

The Supreme Court did not consider any of the applicant's arguments. This was because the Constitutional Court was examining the constitutionality of the 2011 Lawmaking Law in a separate case.[65] More specifically, the Constitutional Court was hearing a challenge to Article 7(1) of the Lawmaking Law, one of the provisions the applicants argued the Qanun violated. But there seemed to be no legal reason preventing the Supreme Court from severing that aspect of the case from the main human rights arguments.

The reasons for the Supreme Court's reluctance are unclear. Indonesian courts are said to be particularly sensitive to public opinion,[66] and it is possible to speculate that some Supreme Court judges believe that disturbing the regulatory status quo is more likely to draw criticism than simply doing nothing, even in the face of apparently egregious laws under review. It is possible, too, that some judges are simply uncomfortable with intervening in the highly fraught politics of regional government and lawmaking.

Having considered the national statutory and regional regulatory frameworks relating to gender issues, this chapter now to turns to the provisions of the Constitution covering gender and sexuality and their interpretation and application by the Constitutional Court.

III. CONSTITUTIONAL FRAMING OF GENDER AND SEXUALITY

In 2000, Indonesia's People's Consultative Assembly (*Majelis Permusyawaratan Rakyat* or MPR) deliberated and approved the addition of an extensive Charter of Rights into a new Chapter XA of the Constitution. Of these rights, the most relevant to the present discussion are:

- The right to life, and to sustain life and livelihood (Article 28A of the Constitution).

[65] Constitutional Court Decision No 59/PUU-XIII/2015.

[66] J Cochrane, 'Trouble with Facts Plagues Indonesian Courts' *Financial Review* (29 October 2017), available at www.afr.com/world/asia/trouble-with-facts-plagues-indonesian-courts-20171029-gzaj9k; A Woodhouse, *Village Justice in Indonesia: Case Studies on Access to Justice, Village Democracy and Governance* (World Bank Social Development Unit, 2004).

- The right to legal recognition, guarantees, protection and certainty, and to equal treatment before the law (Article 28D(1)). (Article 27(1) reiterates the right to equal treatment before the law.)
- The right to equal opportunity in government (Article 28D(3)).
- The right of every person to protect themselves and their families of their honour, dignity and property, and to a feeling of security and protection from threats (Article 28G(1)).
- The right to assistance and special treatment to obtain the same opportunities and benefits to achieve equality and justice (Article 28H(2)).
- The right to protection against discriminatory treatment (Article 28I(2)).

These rights are not absolute. While the Constitution requires the state to protect and enforce these rights (Articles 28I(4)–(5)), Article 28J(2) states: 'The rights set out above may be limited by legislation directed at protecting the rights and freedom of others, and which accords with moral considerations, religious values, security and public order in a democratic society.' Even though Article 28J(2) seems to invite a proportionality test, the Court has, in its decisions, provided little guidance about how it balances competing rights and interests.

Article 28I(1) lists a number of rights that 'cannot be limited under any circumstances'. These rights include the right to life, the right to freedom of thought and conscience, and the right to be recognised as an individual before the law. However, the Constitutional Court has, rather consistently, held that even these rights can be limited, using the criteria established in Article 28J(2).[67]

IV. CONSTITUTIONAL JURISPRUDENCE

Indonesia's Constitutional Court has decided only a limited number of gender- and sexuality-related cases.[68] For example, there have been no constitutional cases related to citizenship, bodies or violence. The constitutional cases relating to gender have focused on either politics or family law. This section begins with political cases in which gender quotas for parliamentary representation have been challenged. The discussion then turns to a case on the legality of excluding a female from heading a sultanate. The following section covers family law

[67] See, eg, Constitutional Court Decision No 140/PUU-VII/2009; Constitutional Court Decision No 2/PUU-V/2007; Constitutional Court Decision No 3/PUU-V/2007. For discussion, see S Butt and T Lindsey, *The Indonesian Constitution: A Contextual Analysis* (Hart Publishing, 2012).

[68] The Constitutional Court's decisions are available on its website, Mahkamah Konstitusi RI, available at www.mkri.id. A large (but incomplete) database of decisions of other courts is hosted by the Supreme Court, Mahkamah Agung RI, 'Direktori Putusan', available at putusan3.mahkamahagung.go.id.

cases, which, given their positive outcomes and positive impact, are perhaps better described as comprising the Court's flagship constitutional jurisprudence on matters of gender and sexual equality.

A. Gender Quotas

The most vexing issue raised in the Constitutional Court's gender-related political cases appears to be parliamentary quotas. Indonesia has a national Parliament (*Dewan Perwakilan Raykat*, or DPR), which has 556 members and is Indonesia's primary legislative institution. However, the decentralisation reforms of the *reformasi* period have given Indonesia a multi-layered system of government. The country is divided into 34 provinces (*propinsi*) and over 500 counties (*kabupaten*) and cities (*kota*), all of which have separate legislative and executive governments.[69]

Indonesia has traditionally employed a proportional system for legislative elections, both national and subnational. In the first post-Soeharto elections, held in 1999, a closed-list system was employed for these elections. Parties with enough votes to obtain seats could allocate those seats to the candidates they preferred, as ranked on a candidate list, regardless of how many votes the candidates received.[70] This system was widely criticised for motivating candidates to pay parties for placement high on candidate lists to increase their chances of election.[71] The system was changed to an 'open-list' system for the 2004 elections,[72] which allowed voters to choose a particular candidate from a party *or* to simply vote for a party. An individual candidate would automatically receive a seat if the number of votes he or she obtained met the 'seat quota' in a given electoral district – that is, the number of overall votes divided by the number of available seats.[73] The system was changed again for the 2009 election to allow voters to choose an individual candidate, a party, or both.[74] Critically, it was also made easier for party members to be elected as individual candidates: in order to obtain a seat, they needed only 30 per cent of the seat quota. Any

[69] The lawmaking powers granted to these subnational legislatures and executives are broad, including to enact regulations and issue binding decisions on virtually any matter, save those reserved by statute for the central Government (Art 18(5) of the Constitution): foreign affairs, defence and security, national monetary and fiscal matters and religion (Art 10(3) of the 2004 Regional Government Law).

[70] The 1999 General Election Law, Art 1(7).

[71] S Sherlock, *Indonesia's 2009 Elections: The New Electoral System and the Competing Parties* (Centre for Democratic Institutions, 2009) 5.

[72] The 2003 General Election Law, Art 6(1).

[73] See Art 107 of the 2003 General Election Law. The party could then use the votes obtained by individuals who did not meet this quota, along with the votes cast for the party, to allocate any remaining seats to its preferred candidates by reference to its party candidate list.

[74] The 2008 General Election Law, Art 214(a)–(e).

remaining seats would then be allocated to candidates based on their position on the candidate list.[75]

The Court made party lists obsolete in the *Open List Case* in 2008,[76] requiring parties to allocate seats to their candidates receiving the most votes, rather than according to their position on the list. The Court held that the list system violated the 'principle of people's sovereignty' established by Article 1(2) of the Constitution. For the majority, democracy was a fundamental and absolute principle. Candidates must, therefore, be elected based on the number of votes they receive, the Court concluded, not their position on the party list.[77]

The *Open List Case* also thwarted post-Soeharto reform efforts, pursued primarily through women's groups and civil society organisations, to increase the participation of women in politics, particularly as legislators.[78] Women comprised only eight per cent of members of the DPR following the 1999 elections.[79] An initial strategy to increase female representation was to require parties to include among their candidates a minimum percentage of females. The 2003 General Election Law first introduced these quotas, though the measure was aspirational rather than mandatory. Article 65 merely required parties to 'consider' (*mempertimbangkan*) having candidate lists containing at least 30 per cent women. This did little to improve female representation, with only around 11 per cent of DPR members elected in 2004 being women.[80]

The 2008 General Election Law appeared to make the 30 per cent quota mandatory, declaring that 'candidate lists … are to contain at least 30 per cent female representatives' (Article 53). It also required that for every three candidates on the list, at least one must be a woman (Article 55(2)). The proportion of females in the DPR increased to 18 per cent after the 2009 elections. Subsequent election laws contained similar provisions.[81] Of course, this quota system relied on the list system and, in particular, the ability of the parties to allocate at least one seat to each woman for every two men, regardless of how many votes their candidates obtained.

One of the applicants in the *Open List Case*, DPRD candidate Muhammad Sholeh, had directly attacked the quota system for discriminating against male candidates. The Court, by an eight-to-one majority, rejected this argument, upholding Article 55(2). According to the majority, the Indonesian Parliament had enacted Article 55 to fulfil Indonesia's various international gender-related

[75] Sherlock (n 71) 6.

[76] Constitutional Court Decision No 22-24/PUU-VI/2008.

[77] ibid 105.

[78] KI Parawansa, 'Obstacles to Women's Political Participation in Indonesia' (*International Idea*, 2002), available at www.idea.int/sites/default/files/publications/chapters/women-in-parliament/perempuan-di-parlemen-bukan-sekedar-jumlah-EN-case-study-indonesia-2.pdf.

[79] Sherlock (n 71) 14.

[80] See Komisi Pemilihan Umum, available at www.kpu.go.id.

[81] See Law 8 of 2012 on General Elections for Members of the DPR, DPD, and DPRD, Arts 55, 58(1)–(2) and 59(1)–(2).

obligations, including those under CEDAW. Article 28H(2) of the Constitution, the majority reasoned, also gave every person the right to 'facilitation' or 'special measures' (*perlakuan khusus*) to ensure that they have the same opportunities and benefits as others to obtain equality and justice. Other countries had enacted similar provisions, the majority noted. Thus, the decision concluded, even if affirmative action breached the constitutional rights of male candidates as alleged by the applicant, this would be permissible under Article 28J(2) of the limitations clause in the Constitution.[82]

Conveying what can only be described as outdated views, the all-male majority also declared that the 30 per cent quota struck an appropriate balance between increasing the chances of women being elected while 'allowing the public to evaluate the acceptability of women entering the political fray, not just because they are women, but from the perspective of their capacity and capability as legislators and their place in Indonesian culture'.[83]

Justice Indrati issued a strong dissent on this aspect of the case. Though she agreed that Article 55(2) was constitutional, she pointed out a flaw in the majority opinion. On the one hand, she observed, the majority found Article 55(2) to be discriminatory but not unconstitutional because it justifiably provided for affirmative action in furtherance of Article 28H(2) of the Constitution and CEDAW. Yet Justice Indrati noted that Article 4 of CEDAW specifies that affirmative action is not discrimination.[84]

Although the Constitutional Court's decision in the *Open List* case (2008) made the requirement that women comprise 30 per cent of party lists redundant, the requirement was maintained, with some adjustments, in the 2012 General Election Law. In the *Affirmative Action Case* (2013), 30 applicants, comprising mainly individuals, NGOs working on gender issues and some parliamentarians, challenged two provisions of the 2012 General Election Law. The first of these two provisions, Article 56(2) and its commentary, required that there be 'at least one female candidate for every three candidates on the candidate list'. The applicants sought clarification from the Court that there was nothing to prevent more than one woman appearing among the first three candidates. The Court agreed with this interpretation but pointed out that, since its decision in the *Open List* case, the relative position of candidates on the list had become meaningless. While parties still needed to ensure that 30 per cent of their candidates

[82] Constitutional Court Decision No 22-24/PUU-VI/2008, 98–99.

[83] ibid 98.

[84] To be fair, the majority's decision was perhaps more nuanced than Justice Indrati expressed. In an earlier part of its judgment, the majority appeared to have deliberately avoided declaring that affirmative action was discriminatory; but in its final holding, the Court said that 'even though it is viewed as reverse discrimination, it does not breach the Constitution', see Constitutional Court Decision No 22-24/PUU-VI/2008, para 4.1. The majority also mentioned that even though affirmative action had been 'received' by Indonesia through CEDAW, it had to prioritise the Constitution over CEDAW, see Constitutional Court Decision No 22-24/PUU-VI/2008, para 3.16.

were women, there was no absolute requirement that women occupy 30 per cent of the seats in Parliament. Whether this occurred was for voters to decide.[85]

Unsurprisingly, these decisions have not been well received by some women's organisations.[86] It bears noting that female representation in Indonesia's parliaments remains low. Indonesia ranks 102 of 193 countries for gender representation in its national Parliament,[87] with women comprising just 20 per cent of the national Parliament[88] and about 30 per cent of the national 'upper house'.[89] Of the 19,817 parliamentary seats spread across Indonesia's subnational parliaments,[90] approximately 16 per cent were occupied by women at the time this book went to publication.

B. The *Sultan* Case (2016)

Another Constitutional Court decision relating to politics and gender resulted from a 2016 case that drew significant controversy in Yogyakarta, one of Indonesia's 'special' provinces.[91] The primary difference between Yogyakarta and other provinces is the position of the Sultan, who also holds office as governor

[85] The quota appears to have had limited effect in any event. While the rule has increased the number of women candidates participating in elections – from around 32% in 2004 to around 40% in 2019 – this has not necessarily translated into seats, which has generally been between 11–18%, see B Hillman, 'The Limits of Gender Quotas: Women's Parliamentary Representation in Indonesia' (2018) 48 *Journal of Contemporary Asia* 322, 323, 326; B Bland, 'Indonesia: Look beyond Quotas for Gender Representation' (*The Interpreter*, 21 March 2019), available at www.lowyinstitute.org/the-interpreter/indonesia-look-beyond-quotas-gender-representation.

[86] 'Putusan MK Merugikan Caleg Perempuan' (*Koalisi Perempuan Indonesia*, 2 December 2011), available at www.koalisiperempuan.or.id/2011/12/02/putusan-mk-merugikan-caleg-perempuan; 'Kursi Perempuan di DPR Belum Capai Kuota' (*jpnn.com*, 15 December 2011), available at www.jpnn.com/news/kursi-perempuan-di-dpr-belum-capai-kuota.

[87] Inter-Parliamentary Union, 'Women in National Parliaments', available at archive.ipu.org/wmn-e/world.htm.

[88] S Gerintya, 'Bagaimana Keterwakilan Perempuan dan Anak Muda di DPR 2019–2024?' (*tirto.id*, 12 October 2019), available at tirto.id/bagaimana-keterwakilan-perempuan-dan-anak-muda-di-dpr-2019-2024-ejwt.

[89] A Djafar, 'Dari 136 Anggota DPD yang akan Dilantik, 42 Perempuan' (*GATRAcom*, 1 October 2019), available at www.gatra.com/detail/news/448130/politik/dari-136-anggota-dpd-yang-akan-dilantik-42-perempuan. This upper house is the Dewan Perwakilan Daerah, or Regional Representative Council, the main task of which is to represent the interests of Indonesia's regional areas in the national legislature. However, this council is relatively toothless – while it must be involved in deliberations relating to regional affairs, its views can be disregarded by the national legislature. Only around 17% of members of provincial parliaments are female. There are no female representatives in the DPD from eight provinces: Aceh, Bangka Belitung Islands, Riau Islands, Bali, South Kalimantan, Central Sulawesi, West Sulawesi, and West Papua; see R Setiawan, 'Isi Kursi DPR 2019–2024, Porsi Perempuan Meningkat' (*tirto.id*, 8 September 2019), available at tirto.id/isi-kursi-dpr-2019-2024-porsi-perempuan-meningkat-ehHG.

[90] DA Rachman, 'Pemilu 2019, Jumlah Kursi Anggota DPRD Berjumlah 19.817' *Kompas.com* (Jakarta, 18 April 2018), available at nasional.kompas.com/read/2018/04/18/13240581/pemilu-2019-jumlah-kursi-anggota-dprd-berjumlah-19817.

[91] Yogyakarta was formally granted special status as a province through Law No 3 of 1950 on the Establishment of the Special Region of Yogyakarta.

of the province, with Prince Paku Alam as Deputy. Some see this arrangement as inconsistent with post-Soeharto principles of democracy in Indonesia, where all other governors and regional heads are directly elected.

The sultanate is an inherited office, which follows male lineage. But the current Sultan, Sri Sultan Hamengkubuwono X, has five daughters and no sons. He wants one of his daughters to become heir to his throne. This preference conflicts with cultural traditions as well as Law No 13 of 2012 on the Special Region of Yogyakarta. Article 18(1) of that Law requires gubernatorial 'candidates' to provide various documents, including the names of their 'wife' and children. Given that Indonesia does not recognise same-sex marriage, the only implication from this requirement is that the governor (Sultan) and deputy governor (Prince Paku Alam) must be male.

Various women's organisations, business owners and even officials from the sultan's palace (*kraton*) applied to the Constitutional Court for review of Article 18(1). Among their arguments was that the provision was discriminatory. The Court agreed. In reaching this conclusion, the Court referred to Article 28I(2) of the Constitution (which prohibits discrimination), as well as ICCPR and CEDAW (which also prohibit discrimination), noting that, because Indonesia has ratified these conventions, it must adhere to them.[92] This decision was applauded by the Princess herself, as well as *Komnas Perempuan*.[93]

V. FLAGSHIP CONSTITUTIONAL DEVELOPMENTS

This section discusses important decisions in which the Constitutional Court has interpreted and applied constitutional rights to promote gender and sexual equality in matters of family law.

A. Child Marriage

In Indonesia and internationally, child marriage has long been considered deleterious for the younger party, who is almost inevitably female. Child marriage

[92] Constitutional Court Decision No 88/PUU-XIV/2016, 311. The Court set out Arts 2(1) and 3 of ICCPR and Arts 1–3 of CEDAW.

[93] F Chan, 'Sultan and governor of Yogyakarta breaks royal traditions and is a champion of women's rights' *The Strait Times* (15 October 2017), available at www.straitstimes.com/asia/se-asia/sultan-and-governor-of-yogyakarta-breaks-royal-traditions-and-is-a-champion-of-womens; Y Medistiara, 'Raja Perempuan Bisa Jadi Guvernur Yogya, Komnas Apresiasi MK' *detikNews* (4 September 2017), available at news.detik.com/berita/d-3627527/raja-perempuan-bisa-jadi-gubernur-yogya-komnas-apresiasi-mk. Although some groups argued that the decision constituted unjustifiable interference with the internal affairs of the Sultanate, see 'GKR Mangkubumi Bisa Bertakhta sebagai Sultan Hamengku Buwono' *Radar Jogja* (7 October 2017), available at radarjogja.jawapos.com/breaking-news/2017/10/07/gkr-mangkubumi-bisa-bertakhta-sebagai-sultan-hamengku-buwono.

is associated with increased mortality and domestic violence, and often leads to young mothers leaving school early and bearing children with health problems.[94]

Indonesia's 1974 Marriage Law had set the minimum marriage for females at 16 years and for males at 19 (Article 7(1)). But the Law allowed a party to seek 'dispensation' from a 'court or other official appointed by the parents of the couple' to avoid this age requirement, permitting couples to marry even younger (Article 7(2)).

The Constitutional Court has decided two cases about the constitutionality of the 16-year minimum age for females that Article 7(1) of the Marriage Law establishes. The first case, decided in 2015, was brought by several women's organisations.[95] These organisations wanted the minimum marriage age to 18 for females, and remain 19 for males (Article 7(1)). They argued that the provisions caused legal uncertainty, especially when viewed alongside other legislation that defined a child as being under the age of 18 or 21.[96] The applicants also pointed to the deleterious physical and mental health effects associated with early marriage. Most child brides, they noted, were forced to leave high school before graduation and often had trouble adjusting to their new families, leaving them socially and economically disadvantaged for life. For the applicants, Article 7(1) therefore violated the right to life under Article 28A of the Constitution; the right to continuation of life, growth and development under Article 28B(2); and the right to education and to increase the quality of one's life and welfare under Article 28C(1)).[97]

The Court heard the views of 'related parties',[98] including women's groups and several others supporting the applicants' views; and Hindu, Confucian and Christian representatives. Indonesia's three most prominent Islamic organisations likewise presented their views: the Council of Islamic Scholars (*Majelis Ulama Indonesia*, or MUI), Muhammadiyah and Nahdatul Ulama. In separate submissions, they urged the Court to leave Article 7(1) in force. All three groups agreed that Islam did not specify a minimum age for marriage, but that, under Islamic law, the general requirement was that both parties have reached puberty. There is some diversity between schools of Islamic law about what signs can be used to indicate puberty. But all three organisations mentioned that most of these schools consider a woman aged nine or above to have reached puberty if

[94] L Rumble, A Peterman, N Irdiana, M Triyana and E Minnick, 'An Empirical Exploration of Female Child Marriage Determinants in Indonesia' (2018) 18 *BMC Public Health* 1, 1–2.

[95] Constitutional Court Decision No 30-74/PUU-XII/2014. The Constitutional Court has established comparatively relaxed rules that grant standing to a variety of applicants, including groups with shared interests and public and private legal entities; see Butt and Linsey (n 40) 104.

[96] Constitutional Court Decision No 30-74/PUU-XII/2014, 220-22. Here the applicants pointed to many statutes, including labour, education and imprisonment.

[97] ibid 222.

[98] The Court also allows a broad range of 'related parties' (*pihak terkait*) to make submissions in cases that touch upon their interests: Butt (n 2) 48–49. For example, the National Commission on Violence Against Women, *Komnas Perempuan*, made submissions to support positive discrimination in the *Open List* case, discussed below.

she has begun menstruating, and a male is considered to have reached puberty if he has nocturnal emissions and reaches either the age of nine[99] or 12.[100] Some schools emphasise the development of pubic hair as an indicator.[101] However, according to most scholars, if either males or females reach the age of 15 they can be deemed to have reached puberty, even if these indicators are not present.[102]

All three Islamic organisations suggested that allowing child marriage was preferable to young couples engaging in pre-marital sex. As MUI put it:

> [I]f there is a gap between the state minimum age and Islamic teachings, then this causes damage to occur in the community, like adultery, free sex and pregnancy out of marriage which, in turn, leads to abortions. With a minimum marrying age of 16 for females, the negative excesses that occur in the community can be anticipated.[103]

In upholding the challenged legislation, the Court emphasised that the right to marry was fundamental, citing passages from the *Koran*, Hindu teachings, its previous decisions and Article 28B(1) of the Constitution, which states that 'Every person has the right to create a family and to have descendants through a valid marriage'.[104] While marriage needed to comply with the laws of the state, the Court accepted that marriage was closely associated with religious values and needed to be carried out in accordance with the religion of the parties. Here, the Court noted that different religions have different rules about marriage age. As for Islam in particular, the Court agreed that no rules about minimum marriage existed, reasoning that:

> [M]inimum age is not a component of marriage, so as to prevent greater harm (*kemudharatan*), particularly in light of developments nowadays … where the possibility of harm can spread more quickly, influenced by a variety of different situations, including food, the environment, social mixing, technology, the openness of information, amongst others, which increase the speed of sexual urges. These sexual urges should be channeled through a marriage in accordance with religious teachings, so that a child is not born out of wedlock …[105]

On the other hand, the Court also accepted that child marriage could lead to the social and economic problems that the applicants raised, and could lead to divorce and neglected children.[106] However, the Court acknowledged that the issues raised by the minimum marriage age were complex, which led the Court

[99] Constitutional Court Decision No 30-74/PUU-XII/2014, 168 (MUI statement), 187 (NU statement).
[100] ibid 185 (Muhammadiyah statement).
[101] ibid 185, 187.
[102] ibid 168, 185; see also Madekhan, 'The Social Construction of Child Marriage According to the Kiai in Lamongan, East Java' in M Grijns, H Horii, S Irianto and P Saptandari (eds), *Marrying Young in Indonesia: Voices, Laws and Practices* (Yayasan Pustaka Obor Indonesia, 2019).
[103] Constitutional Court Decision No 30-74/PUU-XII/2014, 169.
[104] ibid 226–27.
[105] ibid 229.
[106] ibid 229–30.

to conclude that any changes to the Law should be reserved for the legislature, not the judicial branch. The Court, therefore, dismissed the application.

Justice Indrati issued an impassioned sole dissent. She accepted that child marriage caused the various problems the applicants mentioned and many others.[107] She suggested that the Marriage Law, enacted over four decades earlier, required revision, given that Indonesian human rights law has developed significantly in the interim, particularly with the introduction of constitutional rights. Indrati also noted that Indonesia had 'bound itself to CEDAW' and that many other statutes now defined children as being 18 or younger. One such statute was the Child Protection Law which, under Article 26(1), requires parents to 'prevent child marriage of their children'. For Indrati, Article 26(1) was an 'implementing instrument' of Article 28B(2) of the Constitution, which meant that the minimum marriage age of 16 violated the Constitution.

However, a unanimous Court took the opposite view in 2017, when it was asked to reassess the constitutionality of Article 7(1).[108] The applicants in this case were three women who had been subjected to childhood marriage with older men, and who claimed that child marriage had caused serious harm to their health and economic prospects. While raising arguments similar to those made by the applicants in the 2014 case, they focused here on discrimination, insisting that Article 7(1) provides different minimum age for males and females, and that child marriages led to more disadvantages for females than males, including in the enjoyment of constitutional rights.

In rendering its decision, the Court accepted that Parliament had discretion to set a minimum marriage age, provided that the Parliament's policy choice did not 'exceed its jurisdiction, violate morality and rationality, cause intolerable injustice, and violate the 1945 Constitution'.[109] Here, Parliament had violated morality and rationality, the Court concluded, and caused intolerable injustice by discriminating on the basis of gender under Article 7(1), thereby breaching Article 28D(1) of the Constitution.[110]

As Dina Afrianty has observed,[111] this decision was somewhat controversial, given that the composition of the bench had changed little between 2015 and 2019. Indeed, Indrati, the only judge to dissent in 2014, was not even on the bench. Although it acknowledged departing from its previous decision,[112] the Court did not explain why, or expressly mention Indrati's dissent, even though

[107] ibid 236.

[108] Constitutional Court Decision No 22/PUU-XV/2017.

[109] ibid 46.

[110] ibid 47.

[111] D Afrianty, 'Child Marriage: Constitutional Court Finally Ditches Religious Arguments' (*Indonesia at Melbourne*, 24 January 2019), available at indonesiaatmelbourne.unimelb.edu.au/child-marriage-constitutional-court-finally-ditches-religious-arguments.

[112] As a civil law country, Indonesia does not have a formal system of precedent. However, it is recognised that following previous decisions strengthens consistency and predictability, and is, therefore, generally thought to be desirable by most judges, lawyers and scholars.

it seemed to adopt some of her reasoning. For example, the Court emphasised the development of Indonesia's human rights regime since the 1974 Marriage Law, and the enactment of the Child Protection Law. The Court also mentioned CEDAW and Indonesia's obligations under it.[113] The Court added that, once married, women would no longer be considered children, which would then exclude them from various constitutional rights. For example, Article 28B(2) states that 'Every child has the right to continuation of life, growth and development, and the right to protection from violence and discrimination'. The Court also held that child marriage contravened other constitutional rights, including rights to education, to live a healthy life and to grow.

The Court observed that child marriage in Indonesia was high – 10 per cent across all marriages in Indonesia, with over 25 per cent in 23 of Indonesia's 34 provinces – and warned of a 'Child Marriage Emergency'.[114] Nevertheless, the Court declined to stipulate a minimum marriage age. Instead, it gave the DPR a four-year deadline to change the policy, leaving Article 7(1) valid in the interim.[115] If the DPR did not act, then the Court held that the minimum marriage age would be 18, which corresponded with the Child Protection Law. As discussed below, the national parliament responded with an amendment to the Marriage Law in late 2019.

B. Responsibility for Children Born Out of Wedlock

According to Article 43(1) of Indonesia's 1974 Marriage Law,[116] children born out of wedlock only have a civil legal relationship with their mother and mother's family. A child could therefore only seek support and inheritance from its mother, and only its mother's name would be listed on its birth certificate. Unless the biological father voluntarily and formally recognised the child, the Law prevented the child from inheriting from the father or forcing the father to pay maintenance.[117]

Article 43(1) was challenged before the Constitutional Court by a well-known Indonesian celebrity dancer, Machica Mochtar in the *Wedlock case*.[118] She entered a polygamous marriage with a senior politician, Moerdiono, in 1993. However, under the Marriage Law, a polygamous marriage requires judicial approval, which Moerdiono did not obtain, and so the Religious Affairs Office refused to register the marriage. Nevertheless, it appears that Mochtar

[113] Constitutional Court Decision No 22/PUU-XV/2017, 57.
[114] ibid 55.
[115] Constitutional Court Decision No 22/PUU-XV/2017, 58.
[116] Law No 1 of 1974 on Marriage.
[117] See Art 282 of the Civil Code (*Kitab Undang-Undang Hukum Perdata*, known in its original Dutch as *Burgelijk Wetboek*)).
[118] Constitutional Court Decision No 46/PUU-VIII/2010.

and Moerdiono acknowledged each other as husband and wife, having a son, Muhammad Iqbal Ramadhan ('Iqbal'). The couple divorced in 2008, but Moerdiono refused to acknowledge Iqbal as his son and paid no maintenance. Mochtar promptly sued Moerdiono in a religious court., But while the Court recognised their marriage status under Islamic law, it declined to order Moerdiono to pay maintenance because the unregistered marriage was not recognised by the state.[119] Moerdiono died in late 2011 and Iqbal received no inheritance.

An eight-judge majority of the Court invalidated Article 43(1). The judges decided that the connection between a child and father is not entirely determined by marriage; it is unjust for only the mother to be responsible for the care of the child; and that children born out of wedlock should not be denied support from their biological fathers through no fault of their own.[120] However, rather than striking down Article 43(1) altogether, the Court declared it conditionally unconstitutional.[121] In other words, it decided that Article 43(1) would be invalid unless interpreted as follows:

> A child born out of marriage has a civil legal relationship with its mother and her family, and its father and his family [provided that paternity] can be proven by science and technology and/or another form of legally-recognised evidence that the father has a blood relationship with the child.[122] [my translation]

In a concurring opinion, Justice Indrati noted that many marriages are conducted in accordance with the couple's religious tenets but are not registered and that, under current practice, this is usually detrimental to the woman and any children born. (This is because, to formally obtain maintenance or to claim an inheritance – including before a religious court – marriage registration and birth certificates must usually be presented.) Indrati emphasised that children born out of wedlock are often subject to discrimination. She concluded that 'the fulfillment of the rights of children born from a marriage, regardless of whether the marriage accords with the law of the state, remains the responsibility of both biological parents'.[123]

Of course, it is difficult to argue with the result in this case: imposition of paternal responsibility. Unfortunately, however, the constitutional grounds on which the Court relied were not clear. The majority mentioned only vague concepts of justice, fairness, legal certainty and legal protection. Only Justice

[119] ASh, 'MK: Laki-Laki "Buaya Darat" Wajib Bertanggung Jawab' (*Hukumonline*, 17 February 2012), available at www.hukumonline.com/berita/a/mk-lakilaki-buaya-darat-wajib-bertanggung-jawab---lt4f3e288a2589c.

[120] Constitutional Court Decision No 46/PUU-VIII/2010, para 3.13.

[121] For a further discussion on the concepts of conditional constitutionality and conditional unconstitutionality in the Indonesian context, see S Butt, 'Conditional Constitutionality and Conditional Unconstitutionality in Indonesia' in PJ Yap (ed), *Constitutional Remedies in Asia* (Routledge, 2019).

[122] Constitutional Court Decision No 46/PUU-VIII/2010, para 3.13.

[123] ibid para 6.6.

Indrati seemed to settle on the right of children to be free from discrimination under Article 28B(2) of the Constitution.

Although the decision drew praise from some quarters, including the National Commission on Human Rights, for bringing an end to discrimination against children, the decision drew sharp criticism from the Indonesian Council of Islamic Scholars, which issued Fatwa 11 of 2012 on the Position of Children Born out of Wedlock and Their Treatment.[124] This criticism and Fatwa appeared to have misunderstood the decision to mean that children born out of wedlock can become the heirs of their fathers for the purpose of Islamic inheritance law. Soon after the Fatwa was issued, then Constitutional Court Chief Justice Mahfud MD responded, claiming that MUI 'did not understand the decision'. Rejecting the claim that the decision endorsed extramarital sex, Chief Justice Mahfud declared that the decision had a deterrent effect because it required biological fathers to financially provide for their illegitimate children.[125] Mahfud also denied that the decision breached Islamic law. A child born of unmarried parents was still not formally a 'descendant' of its father, at least for the purposes of Islamic law, so the child could not claim an inheritance or maintenance.[126] The decision merely allowed the child to seek compensation from the father under national law.[127]

As these cases demonstrate, the Indonesian Constitutional Court – since its establishment in 2003 – has issued a handful of important cases relating to gender-related rights. However, there is little to be gained from an 'on paper' decision that is largely ignored by the Government or citizens 'in practice'. As mentioned, the Constitutional Court has no formal powers of enforcement. It could not, for example, force the Government to make changes to the minimum marriage age within the three-year deadline it imposed. It also cannot force other courts to comply with its decisions, even though they are arguably bound by those decisions. This has been problematic in the aftermath of the *Wedlock* case. Initial indications are that Indonesia's religious courts, where most of the nation's paternity and inheritance disputes are decided, have applied the decision inconsistently, sometimes recognising it and other times not.[128] One

[124] Majelis Ulama Indonesia (MUI) Fatwa No 11 of 2012.

[125] 'Anak di Luar Nikah – Mahfud: MUI Salah Memahami Putusan' *Seputar Indonesia* (29 March 2012).

[126] 'Wawancara Ketua Mahkamah Konstitusi Mahfud MD – Ikuti Saja Fatwa MUI' *Seputar Indonesia* (25 March 2012).

[127] H Pramono (ed), 'Mahfud MD Jelaskan Putusan kepada Ulama se-Jatim' *Tribun News* (21 April 2012), available at surabaya.tribunnews.com/2012/04/21/mahfud-md-jelaskan-putusan-mk-kepada-ulama-se-jatim.

[128] Nurhadi, 'Implementasi Putusan Mahkamah Konstitusi Nomor 46/PUU-VIII/2010 Tentang Anak Di Luar Kawin' (2018) 11 *Jurnal Yudisial* 243; ZN Rosidah, 'Implementasi Putusan Mahkamah Konstitusi No. 46/PUU-VIII/2010 Tentang Hak Perdata Anak Luar Kawin Di Pengadilan Negeri Dan Pengadilan Agama Surakarta' (2017) 2 *Al-Ahkam: Jurnal Ilmu Syariah dan Hukum* 175.

explanation for this is that religious courts use a Compilation of Islamic Law,[129] enacted as Presidential Instruction No 1 of 1991, as their primary reference point when deciding cases. Article 100 of the Compilation virtually restates the original formulation of Article 43(1) of the Marriage Law, the provision struck down by the Constitutional Court in Mochtar's case. Religious courts may be continuing to follow the Compilation, even though the Marriage Law (including the Court's reformulation of Article 43(1)) is a national statute and formally prevails over it. Even the Supreme Court appears to have applied the *Wedlock* case differently in its own cases.[130] The Constitutional Court can do nothing about this, because it cannot review the validity of lower-order regulations such as presidential instructions, much less exercise how they are applied.

In October 2019, the national parliament appeared to comply with the Constitutional Court's decision in the minimum marriage age case and may even have gone beyond it, changing the minimum marriage age from 16 for girls and 18 for boys to 19 for both genders. However, the parliament made no changes to Article 43(1) of the Marriage Law to bring it into line with the Court's decision in the *Wedlock* case. The significance of leaving Article 43(1) alone is unclear. It may be that the Parliament thought that the Constitutional Court's decision was self-explanatory and required no legislative action. Alternatively, it could indicate that the Parliament rejects the Constitutional Court's decision and wants to revert Article 43(1) to its original, pre-*Wedlock* form.

In any event, the Court can do nothing to prevent citizens from ignoring its ruling and, indeed, the Marriage Law of the state. Forced child marriages are likely to continue, and fathers will likely continue denying responsibility for their children born out of wedlock by failing to register their marriage or by failing to voluntarily and formally recognise their child in a religious court. Here, the influence of conservative Islamic groups, such as MUI, is relevant, because their criticisms of the Court's decisions could encourage receptive Muslims to avoid contact with these institutions – and hence the reach of these decisions – in the interests of devotion to Islam. Soon after the Court issued its decision in the *Wedlock* case, for example, MUI condemned the decision for violating Islamic law, interpreting the decision to imply that children born out of wedlock would become the heirs of their biological fathers. Similarly, the Court's decision in the 2017 child marriage case did not, as discussed, accord with Islamic law and was not well received by conservative Islamic groups. It is possible that many Muslims who follow guidance from MUI and other conservatives will continue to see Islam as being more authoritative than the law of the state, at least in

[129] Lindsey and Steiner (n 61); E Nurlaelawati, *Modernization, Tradition and Identity: The Kompilasi Hukum Islam And Legal Practice in the Indonesian Religious Courts* (Amsterdam University Press, 2010).

[130] See Supreme Court Decision Number 329 K/AG/2014 and Supreme Court Number 597 K/AG/2015, discussed in Nurhadi, 'The Dualism of the Supreme Court's Decisions on the Position of Non-marital Child' (2019) 8 *Jurnal Hukum dan Peradilan* 228.

matters of family law. Where this happens, the potential of these constitutional rights, and the Constitutional Court's enforcement of them, to help improve gender equality in Indonesia will be greatly diminished.

VI. CONCLUSION

As the cases discussed in this chapter demonstrate, the Indonesian Constitutional Court – since its establishment in 2003 – has issued a handful of important cases relating to gender-related rights. However, there is little to be gained from an 'on paper' decision that is not followed by the government or citizens 'in practice'. As mentioned, the Constitutional Court has no formal powers of enforcement. It could not, for example, force the government to make changes to the minimum marriage age within the three-year deadline it imposed. It also cannot force other courts to comply with its decisions, even though they are arguably bound by those decisions. This has been problematical in the aftermath of the *Wedlock case*. Initial indications are that Indonesia's religious courts, where most of Indonesia's paternity and inheritance disputes are decided, have applied the decision inconsistently, sometimes recognising it, and other times not.[131] One explanation for this is that religious courts use a Compilation of Islamic Law,[132] enacted as Presidential Instruction No 1 of 1991, as their primary reference point when deciding cases. Article 100 of the Compilation virtually restates the original formulation of Article 43(1) of the Marriage Law, the provision struck down by the Constitutional Court in Mochtar's case. Religious courts may be continuing to follow the Compilation, even though the Marriage Law (including the Court's reformulation of Article 43(1)) is a national statute and formally prevails over it. Even the Supreme Court appears to have applied the *Wedlock case* differently in its own cases.[133] The Constitutional Court can do nothing about this, because it cannot review the validity of lower-order regulations such as presidential instructions, much less exercise how they are applied.

In October 2019, the national parliament appeared to comply with the Court's decision in the minimum marriage age case and may even have gone beyond it, changing the minimum marriage age from 16 for girls and 18 for boys to 19 for both genders. However, it made no changes to Article 43(1) of the Marriage Law to bring it into line with the Court's decision in the *Wedlock* case. The significance of leaving Article 43(1) alone is unclear. It may be that the parliament thought that the Constitutional Court's decision was self-explanatory and required no legislative action. Alternatively, it could indicate that the parliament

[131] Nurhadi (n 128); Rosidah (n 128).

[132] Lindsey and Steiner (n 61); Nurlaelawati (n 129).

[133] See Supreme Court Decision Number 329 K/AG/2014 and Supreme Court Number 597 K/AG/2015, discussed in Nurhadi (n 130).

rejects the Constitutional Court's decision and wants to revert Article 43(1) to its original, pre-*Wedlock* form.

In any event, the Court can do nothing to prevent citizens from ignoring its ruling and, indeed, the Marriage Law of the state altogether. Some children are likely to continue to be pushed into marriage, and fathers are likely to continue to deny responsibility for their children born out of wedlock, where they can avoid the reach of state institutions, such as by not seeking to register their child marriage, or by not formally seeking maintenance or an inheritance in a religious court. Here, the influence of conservative Islamic groups, such as MUI, is relevant, because their criticisms of the decisions could encourage receptive Muslims to avoid contact with these institutions – and hence the reach of these decisions – in the interests of devotion to Islam. Soon after the Court issued its decision in the *Wedlock case*, for example, MUI condemned the decision for violating Islamic law, interpreting the decision to imply that children born out of wedlock would become the heirs of their biological fathers. Similarly, the Court's decision in the 2017 child marriage case did not, as discussed, accord with Islamic law and was not well received by conservative Islamic groups. It is possible that many Muslims who follow guidance from MUI and other conservatives will continue to see Islam as being more authoritative than the law of the state, at least in matters of family law. Where this happens, the potential of these constitutional rights, and the Constitutional Court's enforcement of them, to help improve gender equality in Indonesia will be greatly diminished.

10

In Search of Principle: 70 Years of Gender Jurisprudence in India

GAUTAM BHATIA AND SHREYA ATREY

I. INTRODUCTION

THE LARGEST DEMOCRACY in the world – India – with over 1.3 billion people is home to about 660 million women and sexual minorities. Their lives are ridden with contradictions captured in dramatic, but nevertheless true, headlines which announce India as the world's most dangerous country for women[1] and at the same time affirm that India worships its women.[2] Similarly, while *hijras* are celebrated as a unique community enriching India's vibrant democracy, they remain severely discriminated against, facing exponential levels of violence on an everyday basis.[3] The wider community of LGBTQIA+ people too remains vulnerable, facing routine discrimination including stereotyping, exclusion and violence despite proclamations of their equal citizenship by the Supreme Court in 2018.[4]

In fact, every despairing statistic or fact can be matched against an equally progressive development in law. For example, 99 per cent of rape cases are going unreported, and of those which do get reported, only 25 per cent end up in convictions.[5] Yet, the constitutional discourse around

[1] 'Poll Ranks India the World's Most Dangerous Country for Women' (*The Guardian*, 28 June 2018), available at www.theguardian.com/global-development/2018/jun/28/poll-ranks-india-most-dangerous-country-for-women.

[2] 'Gods Reside in Places Where a Woman Is Worshipped' (*Zee News*, 8 October 2015), available at zeenews.india.com/node/6112.

[3] See this dichotomy explored in S Mal, 'The Hijras of India: A Marginal Community with Paradox Sexual Identity' (2018) 34 *Indian Journal of Social Psychiatry* 79; G Kalra, 'Hijras: The Unique Transgender Culture of India' (2011) 5 *International Journal of Culture and Mental Health* 121; V Lal, 'Not This, Not That: The Hijras of India and the Cultural Politics of Sexuality' (1999) 61 *Social Text* 119.

[4] *Navtej Johar v Union of India*, Writ Petition (Criminal) No. 76 of 2016 (Decided on 6 September 2018) [hereinafter *Navtej Johar*].

[5] S Bandyopadhyay, 'A Closer Look at Statistics on Sexual Violence in India' (*The Wire*, 8 May 2018), available at thewire.in/society/a-closer-look-at-statistics-on-sexual-violence-in-india.

sexual violence has thrived, and has even had an impact beyond India.[6] Parliamentary committees such as the Justice Verma Committee[7] and the Supreme Court's decision in *Vishaka v State of Rajasthan*[8] in particular, have been discussed around the world for their transformative thinking on addressing sexual violence. Since these developments seem to have had little impact on the actual incidence of sexual violence *in* India, the question remains: what makes them significant? In fact, what makes constitutional jurisprudence relevant at all to the rights of women and sexual minorities in India, given the bleak reality?

This chapter shows that the now 70-years-strong constitutional jurisprudence in postcolonial India reflects the unremitting struggle for the rights of women and sexual minorities. Constitutional adjudication in particular has served as a key site for challenging the norms and practices which impinge on the enjoyment of fundamental rights. The gender jurisprudence of the constitutional courts – the Supreme Court and the 28 High Courts – bears out the contradiction between avowed rights and their realisation in sharp relief.[9] It shows what Kalapana Kannabiran calls, in the context of sexual assault jurisprudence, 'the self-contradictory moves in the fields of law'[10] where often, neither the reasoning nor the rhetoric of the courts matches the outcomes of the cases. Thus, this chapter aims to exhume the contradictions inherent in the long trajectory of development of this jurisprudence where progressive or transformative outcomes have been celebrated with or without progressive reasoning. A careful perusal of the substantive reasoning behind outcomes in constitutional cases reveals that much of the Indian jurisprudence has been seeped in the very structures of disadvantage – of patriarchy, misogyny, protectionism, homophobia, transphobia, racism, casteism, ableism, classism, etc – which claimants sought to subvert. Only a small, and rather recent, cross-section of cases after the 1990s reveals anything different. Compared to the long and more complicated history of gender jurisprudence, the recent jurisprudence appears ambitious but not conclusive in having transformed the gender jurisprudence in India. Contradictions remain, not least because the condition of women and sexual minorities remains dismal, but because the doctrine itself is more complicated and diverse than assumed when seen simply through the lens of good or bad outcomes.

[6] See esp MC Nussbaum, 'Women's Progress and Women's Human Rights' (2016) 38 *Human Rights Quarterly* 589.

[7] JS Verma, L Seith and G Subramaniam, 'Report of the Committee on the Amendments to Criminal Law' (23 January 2013). The summary of the report is available at prsindia.org/policy/report-summaries/justice-verma-committee-report-summary.

[8] *Vishaka v State of Rajasthan*, 1997 AIR 3011 [hereinafter *Vishaka*].

[9] All cases are in English and available online on legal databases such as Manupatra or IndiaKanoon.

[10] K Kannabiran, *Tools of Justice: Non-Discrimination and the Indian Constitution* (Routledge, 2012) 303.

The above is the central argument of the chapter. Section II of this chapter provides the backdrop in which constitutionalism has become relevant to the women's movement in India. This is important in understanding the terms in which the Constitution came to incorporate or ignore issues concerning women (sexual minorities were not as much in the picture at the time the Constitution was being negotiated between 1947 and 1950[11]). Section III explains the understanding of 'gender' (used here as the shorthand for characteristics to do with sex, gender and sexuality[12]) embodied in the Constitution. It shows that even though 'sex' and 'women' were frequently referenced, a broader – substantive and intersectional – understanding of gender or gender equality remained absent. Section IV elaborates on how gender and gender equality have developed in constitutional jurisprudence especially in relation to rights claims. It argues that constitutional jurisprudence in India has always been a mixed bag. Women and sexual minorities have had occasional successes. Judicial rhetoric that matched the successes has been progressive in some respects but also deeply regressive in others. The overall tenor of rights jurisprudence in the last 70 years of postcolonial constitutionalism has been largely patriarchal. Section V shows that the recent jurisprudence seems to have disrupted this narrative in a fundamental way: the judicial outcome and rhetoric seemed to match the reasoning deployed by the Supreme Court. Along with some of the previous decisions such as *Anuj Garg v Hotel Association of India* (2007),[13] a slew of pronouncements since the seminal judgment in *Puttaswamy v Union of India*[14] has contributed to the development of gender jurisprudence with a substantive version of gender equality. It is not (only) the good outcomes or rhetoric, but the *explication of* good substantive ideas, and *reasoning with* those substantive ideas, that mattered in these cases. This exercise in interrogating substantive ideas is particularly relevant in the Indian context, where commentators frequently praise the jurisprudence for its good outcomes and rhetoric, but avoid judging it for the content and process of its reasoning. This praise has distorted the picture of what counts as good gender jurisprudence.[15] It is important to set this record straight and to scrutinise, ever so closely, constitutional jurisprudence for what it *is*, rather than what it says it is or purports to be. Section VI concludes with the idea that even though the recent jurisprudence is promising, the promise of that jurisprudence is not fully realised yet. There needs to be an open and continuous

[11] Though they were very much part of the broader social and cultural life. See A Dutta, 'An Epistemology of Collusion: Hijras, Kothis and the Historical (Dis)continuity of Gender/Sexual Identities in Eastern India' (2012) 24 *Gender & History* 825.

[12] 'Gender' is used as an inclusive shorthand in this chapter for categories of sex, pregnancy, sexual orientation, sexuality, transgender status, etc. See generally for an extended explanation J Conaghan, *Law and Gender* (Oxford University Press, 2013) 22–23.

[13] *Anuj Garg v Hotel Association of India* (2008) 3 SCC 1 [hereinafter *Anuj Garg*].

[14] *Puttaswamy v Union of India* 2017 (10) SCALE 1 [hereinafter *Puttaswamy*].

[15] See this argument developed in: S Atrey, 'Women's Human Rights: From Progress to Transformation, An Intersectional Response to Martha Nussbaum' (2018) 40 *Human Rights Quarterly* 859.

dialogue between social movements and gender equality on the firm terrain of the Constitution. This chapter hopes to contribute to that dialogue.

II. BACKGROUND INFORMATION

India is not only the largest democracy in the world, but is also governed by the longest Constitution in the world. With over 470 substantive provisions divided into 25 Parts and 12 Schedules, the Constitution is a formidable document. It is weighty not just because of its sheer volume, but also because it is the centrepiece of moral, social, political, economic and legal discourse in India.[16] It is considered unique in comparison with other significant constitutions of the world because of its overwhelming importance in the life of the postcolonial nation.[17] The Constitution, both in its letter and spirit, shapes the contours of major public debates and social struggles, including those relating to women and sexual minorities.[18] Women and sexual minorities have in turn shaped constitutionalism in India in a fundamental way. It is the dialectic relationship between the Constitution and feminism – or as is said in India, the women's movement[19] – which defines both.

The women's movement in India has spanned the course of modern history since the nineteenth century,[20] and perhaps even for over 2,000 years.[21] But the contemporary writing on gender post-independence (1947 onwards) has

[16] See esp G Austin, *Working a Democratic Constitution: A History of the Indian Experience* (Oxford University Press, 1999) (describing India's Constitution as a 'social revolution').

[17] R Bhargava (ed), *Politics and Ethics of the Indian Constitution* (Oxford University Press, 2008); Z Hasan, E Sridharan and R Sudarshan (eds), *India's Living Constitution: Ideas, Practices, Controversies* (Permanent Black, 2002).

[18] S Choudhry, M Khosla and PB Mehta (eds), *The Oxford Handbook of the Indian Constitution* (Oxford University Press, 2016) i ('a living constitution like India's has the extraordinary capacity to rearticulate – some would say domesticate – social struggles in the language of constitutionalism.'); Austin (n 16) 10 ('The Indian Constitution is a live document in a society rapidly changing and almost frenetically political. The touchstone for public and many private affairs, the Constitution is employed daily, if not hourly, by citizens in pursuit of their personal interests or in their desire to serve the public good').

[19] 'Women's movement', instead of 'feminist movement', is the preferred term in India. As Purkayastha et al explain: 'While much of the resistance to the label feminism has been interpreted in some feminist literature as cultural relativism and anti-Westernization, the theoretical controversy is more complex. For many of the scholars who reject a feminist epistemology, their unease arises from how the conceptualization of individuals is taken for granted … A sharp distinction is assumed to separate the individual from any collectivity, between "woman" as an identifiable, embodied individual and woman defined through multiple relationships. Like the reservations expressed by many of the race-gender scholars in the United States, such dichotomization is unacceptable to many Indian scholars.' B Purkayastha, M Subramaniam, M Desai and S Bose, 'The Study of Gender in India: A Partial Review' (2003) 17 *Gender and Society* 503, 506.

[20] M Kishwar, *A History of Doing: An Illustrated Account of Movements for Women's Rights and Feminism in India 1800–1990* (Verso, 1993).

[21] S Tharu and K Lalita (eds), *Women Writing in India: 600 BC to the Present* vols 1–2 (Feminist Press, 1993).

explicitly invoked the Constitution to articulate and ground the struggles of the movement. The Constitution has thus been more than simply a governance tool or a tool for claiming individual human rights, but a tool for renegotiating the conditions of women's lives completely. There is nothing self-evident about this, even though the Constitution does contain a bill of rights, equality provisions and such. As we show in the next section, the fact that the Constitution came to be negotiated with social movements in the background has had an indelible impact on the way women and minorities (Dalits, Muslims, etc) claimed a stake in the Constitution. This has only been reinforced in the last 70 years against the backdrop of a liberal Constitution, where demands exceed the express text of the Constitution. Thus, for example, the demand for the adoption of a Uniform Civil Code (UCC) to reform and standardise the personal and religious laws in India has been articulated by the women's movement as a distinctly feminist demand – about the well-being and equality of women – even though the Constitution does not articulate the aspiration for a UCC in these terms.[22] Similarly, the Constitution has been key in the perennial fight against gender-based violence and sexual harassment, even though the Constitution, on the face of it, contains no provision on gender-based violence or sexual harassment but only contains general provisions on equality and non-discrimination. For example, the protests ensuing after the decision in *Tukaram v State of Maharashtra*,[23] where the Supreme Court acquitted police officers of rape in custody, were framed centrally around the fate of Indian constitutionalism per se. A key moment in the fight against gender-based violence thus remains the influential open letter dated 16 September 1979, written as a response to *Tukaram*, by leading legal academics – Upendra Baxi, Vasudha Dhagamwar, Raghunath Kelkar and Lotika Sarkar – whose trenchant criticism of the Supreme Court's decision framed the issue for decades to come as a matter for women who were illiterate, Dalit, tribal and with little political power to not be 'condemned to their pre-constitutional Indian fate'.[24] The discourse on postcolonial constitutionalism, including on gender, has thus consistently been conceived as going beyond the formal limits of the text of the Constitution and constitutional law, and towards a broader discourse in constitutionalism which is in constant interaction with social movements like the women's movement.[25]

[22] See Art 44 of the Constitution couched in gender-less terms. *cf* N Menon, *Seeing Like a Feminist* (Zubaan, 2012) 151; L Arya, 'The Uniform Civil Code: The Politics of the Universal in Postcolonial India' (2006) 14 *Feminist Legal Studies* 293; F Agnes, *Law and Gender Inequality: The Politics of Women's Rights in India* (Oxford University Press, 2004) 71; M Kishwar, 'Codified Hindu Law: Myth and Reality' (1994) 29 *Economic and Political Weekly* 2145; A Parashar, *Women and Family Law Reform in India: Uniform Civil Code and Gender Equality* (Sage, 1992).

[23] (1979) 4 SCC (Jour) 17.

[24] U Baxi, V Dhagamwar, R Kelkar and L Sarkar, 'An Open Letter to the Chief Justice of India' (16 September 1979), available at aud.ac.in/uploads/1/admission/admissions2014/open%20letter.pdf.

[25] S Atrey, 'Feminist Constitutionalism: Mapping a Discourse in Contestation' (2022) 20 *International Journal of Constitutional Law* 611.

Furthermore, this broader discourse in constitutionalism has come to be embodied in one institution more than any other – the Supreme Court of India.[26] In fact, in the words of Sujit Choudhry, Madhav Khosla and Pratap Bhanu Mehta, 'the greatest success of constitutionalism in India is now the promiscuity of the language of constitutionalism … [wherein] a vast range of political, administrative, and judicial matters have become constitutional questions that are routinely brought to the [constitutional] courts.'[27] As the apex constitutional court in the country, the Supreme Court, has serviced this idea of constitutionalism being a site of resistance for key social struggles.[28] The Supreme Court is considered to have shown 'interpretational creativity' and 'receptiveness' to '[craft] thoughtful, contextual responses to women's inequality'.[29] Chief amongst these is *Vishaka*, a decision which has been praised far and wide for the Supreme Court's activism in judicially legislating sexual harassment guidelines in the absence of a domestic law on the subject.[30] The Supreme Court took its cue from the Convention on the Elimination of All Forms of Discrimination Against Women (CEDAW), which India had ratified but not implemented. The Court in *Vishaka* made CEDAW directly applicable when the legislature had failed to implement it through a law promoting sex equality or prohibiting sexual harassment. But equally, the Supreme Court is known to have blundered and has been called out for its less-than-progressive decisions. For example, it has viewed mothers as subordinate to fathers,[31] a bar on marriage of female employees as promoting the institution of marriage,[32] and the requirement to reveal reproductive history to employers as unconstitutional because it is embarrassing and humiliating but not because it was an invasion of privacy.[33]

Nonetheless, regardless of the actual results, the Supreme Court has remained an active site of engagement for the women's movement for litigating a range of issues including – personal or religious laws governing matters like marriage, property and maintenance; gender-based violence and sexual harassment; public employment; and sexual expression and reproductive justice. Part of the reason for this is the lack of opportunity structures for women elsewhere – either in the legislature or the Government. A relatively

[26] U Baxi, *The Indian Supreme Court and Politics* (Eastern Book Company, 1980); U Baxi, *Courage, Craft, and Contention: The Indian Supreme Court in the Eighties* (NM Tripathi, 1985).

[27] Choudhry, Khosla and Mehta (n 18).

[28] *cf* AK Thiruvengadam, 'Revisiting the Role of the Judiciary in Plural Societies' in S Khilnani, V Raghavan and AK Thiruvengadam (eds), *Comparative Constitutionalism in South Asia* (Oxford University Press, 2013).

[29] V Narain, 'Postcolonial Constitutionalism in India: Complexities and Contradictions' (2016) 25 *Southern California Interdisciplinary Law Journal* 107, 112–13.

[30] ibid.

[31] *Gita Hariharan v Reserve Bank of India*, AIR 1999 SC 1149.

[32] *Air India v Nargesh Meerza*, AIR 1981 SC 1829.

[33] *Neera Mathur v Life Insurance Corporation of India*, AIR 1992 SC 392.

underdeveloped and unsophisticated state infrastructure to deal with social justice issues has made the constitutional role of the courts urgent and perhaps inevitable.[34] The Supreme Court has even relaxed its standing requirements through its famed public interest litigation (PIL) system to allow direct access to dispossessed communities.[35] While enhanced access and openness to intervene cannot, in fact, have not, led to social change or been effective per se,[36] they have certainly contributed to the production of an enormous body of jurisprudence, including on gender and sexuality. This jurisprudence is also extremely diverse internally, given that the Supreme Court is rather different from its counterparts in South Africa or the United States. It is, like much else in India, a rather large court with 34 sitting judges. Benches are normally constituted of two or three, sometimes five, and rarely seven, nine or 13 judges. The Supreme Court never sits *en banc*. The turnover of judges is very high with appointments to the Supreme Court made close to the retirement age, which itself is rather low at 65 years.

These structural features make the Supreme Court unique in that it does not ever speak in one voice. On top of that, judgments are often lengthy, stretching several hundred pages. Concurring and dissenting opinions are common. All this makes it hard to decipher a clear and coherent line of constitutional jurisprudence, let alone precedent. These factors have thus led to a highly variegated gender jurisprudence straddling themes of protectionism, misogyny, formal equality, substantive equality and transformation, often all at the same time. It is in this context – of the close association between the women's movement and postcolonial constitutionalism, and in particular, the diverse history and context of constitutional adjudication – that the wide-ranging constitutional jurisprudence in sections IV and V will be discussed.

III. CONSTITUTIONAL FRAMING OF SEX/GENDER/SEXUALITY

The Constitution of India came into force on 26 January 1950. The preamble orientates the Constitution toward values of justice, liberty, equality and fraternity. Article 14 guarantees the right to equality. Article 15(1) prohibits discrimination against citizens 'on grounds only of religion, race, caste, sex,

[34] D Kapur and PB Mehta, 'Introduction' in D Kapur and PB Mehta (eds), *Public Institutions in India: Performance and Design* (Oxford University Press, 2005) 1.

[35] SP Sathe, *Judicial Activism in India: Transgressing Borders and Enforcing Limits* (Oxford University Press, 2002); W Vandenhole, 'Human Rights Law, Development and Social Action Litigation in India' (2002) 3 *Asia-Pacific Journal on Human Rights and Law* 136; U Baxi, 'Taking Suffering Seriously: Social Action Litigation in the Supreme Court of India' (1985) 4 *Third World Legal Studies* 107.

[36] A Bhuwania, *Courting the People: Public Interest Litigation in Post-Emergency India* (Cambridge University Press, 2016); AK Thiruvengadam, 'Swallowing a Bitter PIL? Reflections on Progressive Strategies for Public Interest Litigation in India' in O Vilhena, U Baxi and F Viljoen (eds), *Transformative Constitutionalism: Comparing the Apex Courts in Brazil, India and South Africa* (Pretoria University Law Press, 2013).

place of birth or any of them'. Article 15(3) allows the state to make special provisions for women and children. Article 16 guarantees equality of opportunity for all in public employment. Article 21 guarantees the right to life for everyone. Article 39 – which is part of the unenforceable 'Directive Principles of State Policy' – asks the state to direct its policies for securing, amongst other things, equal rights to livelihood and equal pay for equal work for men and women. Article 51A on fundamental duties directs the citizens to renounce practices derogatory to the dignity of women. Women are also mentioned specifically in Part IX on 'Panchayats' or the local self-governing units at the village level. Articles 243D and 243T secure at least one-third of the seats for women (including women belonging to 'Scheduled Castes' (ie, the group of castes most disadvantaged due to structural and institutional discrimination over the years) in panchayats and municipalities. These were added by the 73rd Amendment to the Constitution in 1992. The Constitution in Article 253 allows for international norms to be implemented in India in the classic dualist mode of being incorporated in domestic law by the Parliament, thus making way for implementing international treaties like CEDAW through domestic legislation like the Sexual Harassment of Women at Workplace (Prevention, Prohibition and Redressal) Act 2013. This is however not guaranteed, such that while signing up to international human rights treaties like CEDAW is rapid, their incorporation by passage of domestic legislation is a matter of chance. Thus, for example, India signed up to CEDAW in 1980 and since then has never passed a single comprehensive sex-equality legislation. So even though India signed up to CEDAW without much difficulty, the will to guarantee sex equality in domestic legislation has been lacking.

Given the historical context in which the Constitution came about, a broad understanding of gender is extant in constitutionalism in India.[37] Even though the word 'gender' itself is absent in the provisions identified above, its discourse can be traced to the text of the Constitution, where it refers to 'sex' or 'women' (Articles 14, 15, 16, 39, 51A, 243D and 243T), where the understanding of sex or women has always been infiltrated with gendered aspects of sex and women's lives, rather than being limited by the biological condition. As we will see in the following sections, constitutional jurisprudence has since come to interpret these terms broadly to include sexual orientation[38] and trans status[39] in the twenty-first century. At this stage, what is significant to note is that these developments have only been possible because of the historical context in which the Constitution was negotiated and drafted by the Constituent Assembly (1947–1950). Only 15 of the 299 members of the Constituent Assembly were women. However, the socio-political context in which the Constituent Assembly

[37] See for a reclamation of the historical archive of gender and sexuality: A Arondekar, *For the Record: On Sexuality and the Colonial Archive in India* (Duke University Press, 2009).

[38] *Navtej Johar* (n 4) (see esp Chandrachud and Malhotra JJ's concurring opinions).

[39] *National Legal Services Authority v Union of India* (2014) 5 SCC 438.

operated had come to be defined by women and women's issues. This context, and especially, the anti-colonial nationalist movement against the British rule and the social reform movement against social evils like *Sati* (burning widows on the funeral pyres of their husbands) and the *Devdasi* system (sacrificing lower-caste women to temples for sexual exploitation) in the late eighteenth and nineteen centuries placed women and women's issues at the forefront.[40] Women's participation in the anti-imperial struggle had ensured that they were perforce considered equal democratic citizens in independent India. There was no need to advocate for universal suffrage or the inclusion of sex equality in the Constitution – both of which they had already successfully negotiated with the imperial rulers.[41] Similarly, the ongoing concern with social and religious practices which subordinated women had ensured that the Constitution included not only a general prohibition on sex discrimination, but also gave the state the power to make special provisions for women and children (these have been interpreted as allowing affirmative action for women in various spheres, while also – occasionally – serving to justify patriarchal, 'protective' laws, such as the criminalisation of adultery). Against this backdrop, the importance of women and women's equality became the starting point for the Constitution and did not need to be especially established or fought for.

But perhaps because these were already a given, the Constitution did not specifically provide, for example, a women's quota or reservation in constitutional bodies, especially legislative and judicial bodies.[42] Nor did it provide for an overhaul or reform of personal and religious laws which governed women's private lives at home and in families in relation to matters of marriage, guardianship, adoption, inheritance, etc.[43] Further, women, under the Constitution, were considered a monolith, reflecting little of the fundamental differences between them based on their religion, caste, sexuality, disability, etc.[44] In fact, the strong presence of upper-caste middle-class urban women in the anti-colonial struggle may have overdetermined, even romanticised, women's equality and progress at the time. So while sex or gender equality was a given, it was only understood as formal equality. Substantive equality for women and sexual minorities in the

[40] R O'Hanlon, *A Comparison between Women and Men: Tarabai Shinde and the Critique of Gender Relations in Colonial India* (Oxford University Press, 1994).

[41] See for an historical account of women suffragettes in India in the early 20th century, S Mukherjee, *Indian Suffragettes: Female Identities and Transnational Networks* (Oxford University Press, 2018).

[42] ME John, 'Alternate Modernities? Reservations and Women's Movement in 20th Century India' (2000) 35 *Economic and Political Weekly* 3822.

[43] *cf* Art 44, a directive principle of state policy not an enforceable fundamental right, on the state to enact a uniform civil code.

[44] See for an intersectional understanding of gender in India: S Rege, 'Dalit Women Talk Differently: A Critique of "Difference" and towards a Dalit Feminist Standpoint Position' (1998) 33 *Economic and Political Weekly* WS39; G Omvedt, *Reinventing Revolution: New Social Movements and the Socialist Tradition in India* (Sharpe, 1993); G Dietrich, *Reflections on the Women's Movement in India* (Horizon Books, 1992).

context of 'the woman question', to do with their actual life conditions, was muted when the Constitution came into force in 1950.[45]

This discourse on gender in early constitutionalism confirms that: (i) the concern for women, women's issues and women's equality was recognised but only to a limited or instrumental extent, defined in the context of women's participation in the nationalist movement and the project of establishing the postcolonial nation state; but (ii) that a broader conversation around women, women's issues and women's equality – to do with the lived reality of women and sexual minorities as shaped by the social, economic, cultural and political norms – was absent in the run-up to and in the early days of Indian constitutionalism. The succeeding gender jurisprudence, discussed in the next section, confirms this. It reveals a slow and inconsistent march towards achieving substantive gender equality for women and sexual minorities in India.

IV. CONSTITUTIONAL JURISPRUDENCE

As indicated above, Article 14 of the Indian Constitution guarantees the equal protection of laws, and Article 15(1) specifically proscribes discrimination on the ground of sex. In the seven decades since the Constitution came into being, women and sexual minorities have invoked Articles 14 and 15 as springboards for making constitutional claims upon the state. These claims have ranged across discrimination, including but not limited to, in access to the labour market and government employment, criminal law, family and inheritance rules, personal and religious laws, sexual harassment, and the criminalisation or non-recognition of sexual minorities.

The existence of multiple constitutional courts (the Supreme Court of India, and the 28 High Courts), with huge dockets, means that an issue-based survey of jurisprudence would take up far more space than this chapter allows. The structure of this section, therefore, is chronological: it traces the development of ideas around the constitutional rights of women and sexual minorities, as articulated in the jurisprudence of the Indian courts, and their evolution over seven decades. This approach – we suggest – itself brings in a representative cross-section of cases from different domains.

Consistent with the argument in the previous sections, in this section we will argue that feminist jurisprudence in India is an evolving, and a very much unfinished project. For more than 50 out of 70 years, issues around sex discrimination were decided in the absence of any legal or constitutional *reasoning* that addressed – or incorporated – feminist concerns. While this has

[45] RS Rajan, *The Scandal of the State: Women, Law, and Citizenship in Postcolonial India* (Duke University Press, 2003). See also JW Scott, *Only Paradoxes to Offer: French Feminists and the Rights of Man* (Harvard University Press, 1996).

begun to change in the last decade and a half – along with litigation concerning the rights of sexual minorities, feminist reasoning in Indian constitutional jurisprudence is still only in its early stages, and its future directions remain unclear.

Let us begin with the constitutional text, in particular Article 15(1), which merely prohibits 'discrimination on grounds only of … sex', but provides no further guidance. From the outset, therefore, it was perhaps inevitable that the meaning of these words – and whether and to what extent they could map onto the lived experiences of discrimination and disadvantage experienced by women and sexual minorities – would have to be developed in judicial forums.

Opportunities for this development arose soon after independence. The Indian Constitution had a 'savings clause' (Article 372), which ensured that until affirmatively challenged and struck down by a court, pre-colonial laws would continue to operate as if they were presumptively valid. Effectively, this decision by the constitutional framers transposed the bulk of colonial law (along with its many patriarchal premises) into the postcolonial nation.

Initial constitutional challenges, therefore, focused upon 'colonial holdovers' that seemed starkly at odds with the constitutional guarantee against sex discrimination, as well as postcolonial laws, rules and regulations that were mechanically modelled upon their colonial antecedents. These ranged across civil law, criminal law and employment law (to name just a few legal domains), and included, for example, different rules to determine when plaintiffs in legal proceedings could be compelled to furnish securities, different rules governing the consequences of marriage for employment in the civil services, outright prohibitions upon certain forms of employment, such as a jail superintendent or a nurse, and different punishments for 'adultery'.

As indicated above, in terms of outcomes, courts came down on different sides. A closer look at the reasoning, however, reveals that whether or not specific discriminatory laws or regulations were struck down, judicial reasoning around issues of sex, gender and discrimination was severely constricted. In the first set of cases – where discriminatory rules were upheld – the Court resorted either to a formalistic analysis in order to argue that there was no discrimination at all, or invoked unreconstructed stereotypes about gender roles to hold that there was differential treatment, but that it did not amount to discrimination. An example of the former is *Mahadeb Jiew v BB Sen*.[46] The Code of Civil Procedure authorised courts to demand securities from male plaintiffs if they were living abroad *and* did not possess sufficient immovable property in India, while for female plaintiffs, regardless of where they lived, securities could be demanded where they did not have sufficient immovable property. The High Court of Calcutta upheld this rule on the basis that the distinction it drew mapped onto *both* sex and place of property, and therefore did not discriminate on grounds *only* of

[46] *Mahadeb Jiew v BB Sen*, AIR 1951 Cal 563.

sex. That the rule was based on assumptions about men and women's relative financial capacities was deemed irrelevant by the Court.

An example of the latter is *RS Singh v State of Punjab*,[47] where a host of assumptions about gender roles – from differing physical strength to the performance of 'maternal functions' – were invoked to uphold an order disqualifying women from being appointed as superintendents in men's jails. This line of judicial reasoning reached its apotheosis at the Supreme Court in the (in)famous *Nargesh Mirza* case, which concerned airline service regulations about the employment of (male) air flight pursers and (female) air hostesses. The former were required to retire at the age of 58, while the latter were compelled to do so at the age of 35 years, or upon their first pregnancy, or upon marriage (if they were married within four years of joining the service). During the litigation, the Court essentially entered into a form of 'negotiated settlement' between the parties, where the first pregnancy rule was altered to a third pregnancy, a number of intrusive physical examinations of women employees were introduced, and the amended rules were then upheld. Here again, the Supreme Court's rationale for upholding these Rules turned upon women's role as mothers and caregivers, and – almost bizarrely – the national imperative towards 'population control'.[48]

Even in decisions in which discriminatory rules and laws were found unconstitutional and were struck down, there was no analysis of the context in which they arose, or the patriarchal structures that they exemplified. In essence, these judgments were formalistic as well, only in a different direction. An early judgment concerned the constitutional validity of a state law that allowed the Government to declare certain individuals to be 'incapable of managing their property' (after which, the Government could essentially take over the property). If the individual was a man, this could only be done if a series of conditions existed (convictions for serious offences, unpaid debts, etc). If the individual was a woman, however, no such condition needed to be fulfilled. While the patriarchal assumptions underlying this law are evident (women were deemed to be less competent managers of property than men), the Supreme Court's reasoning was terse: the law treated men and women differently (it disadvantaged the latter), and therefore fell foul of the blanket, non-discrimination guarantee.[49] A different High Court's judgment striking down a rule that disqualified a woman from eligibility for civil service employment upon marriage was similarly formalistic and terse.[50]

Thus, even as the outcomes of these judgments were in favour of women litigants, and sex discriminatory laws were struck down, there was no engagement with the context of disadvantage that had given rise to such laws (and which, then, these laws served to reinforce), or – at a deeper level – with the question

[47] *RS Singh v State of Punjab*, AIR 1972 P&H 117.
[48] ibid [101].
[49] *Rani Raj Rajeshwari Devi v State of UP*, AIR 1954 All 608.
[50] *Radha Charan Patnaik v State of Orissa*, AIR 1969 Ori 237.

of *what*, precisely, the non-discrimination clause of the Constitution was meant to do. This absence of strong conceptual underpinnings ensured that, despite the existence of these judgments, other judges could – and, as we have seen, *did* – continue to hold that when discriminatory legislation tracked putatively *real* differences between men and women, it was not discriminatory in a legal or constitutional sense. It is of little surprise though that courts heavily dominated by upper-caste, upper-class cis-gendered heterosexual men (a situation that continues to date), appeared to read in their own prejudices into what was deemed to be 'natural'.[51]

Another fall-out of the absence of conceptual analysis was that the courts lacked a framework within which to analyse cases which did not fall neatly into any of the categories discussed above. A good example of this is the adultery law. Under the adultery law, a male adulterer stood to be criminally punished, while his female partner did not – and the prosecution could be brought only by the husband of the latter. This, then, was a law that was seen as benefiting women (by granting them immunity from criminal prosecution), though it was based on gendered assumptions of women's sexual passivity. In adjudicating an early challenge to the law, however, the Supreme Court limited itself to holding that Article 15(3) of the Constitution allowed the state to pass 'special provisions' for women and children, and that therefore, the adultery law had a safe harbour.[52] Of course, this is not enough; if the purpose of Article 15(3) was to provide a form of affirmative action in order to enable the overcoming of structural and systemic disadvantage, it is fairly clear that, far from falling within its scope, the adultery law ran counter to its basic premises because it reinforced women's disadvantage. On the other hand, if Article 15(3) was animated by a theory of state protectionism – where women and children were treated as devoid of agency and as 'wards' of the state – then, in that case, the adultery law would fit Article 15(3) like a glove. The Court's failure to even ask the question in those terms, however, meant that it was unable to frame, confront, and address the actual issues at stake in interpreting the constitutional prohibition on sex discrimination.

The judiciary's failure to articulate a coherent, conceptual account of equality and non-discrimination had other consequences too. One consequence was a straight-up *evasion* of judicial responsibility altogether, in cases where a finding of sex discrimination might have led to upsetting long-established social arrangements. This is evident, for example, in the judgment of a five-judge bench of the Supreme Court, which concerned the constitutionality of a provincial law that explicitly and directly discriminated against daughters when it came to inheritance. It would be difficult to imagine a *legally* simpler case of unconstitutional

[51] A critique of this discourse of judging is undertaken by the two feminist judgment rewriting projects underway in India.

[52] *Yusuf Abdul Aziz v State of Bombay*, 1954 SCR 930.

discrimination. The Court, however, ignored the issue by noting that the struggle 'for gender equality must be waged elsewhere'.[53] In essence, the Supreme Court created a constitutional black hole: a space where gender discrimination existed, but the laws that sanctioned it were, nonetheless, accorded immunity from constitutional scrutiny. Indeed, this approach exemplifies another feature of the Indian judiciary's long-held view: that uncodified 'personal laws' (ie, religious norms not formally codified by the state, and governing personal relations) were not subject to constitutional scrutiny.[54]

The second impact of this failure was that of *invisibilisation*. For example, over the years, Indian state legislatures have passed a number of laws restricting the ability of individuals to contest local government elections. One such law, passed by the State of Haryana, barred people with more than two children from contesting local elections, ostensibly as a part of the national project of population control.[55] The discriminatory impact of such a law is not hard to spot: in a country that remains riven with deeply unequal patriarchal social relations and class arrangements, whether, when and how many children to have is not always a straightforward question of 'individual choice', especially as far as women are concerned. The Supreme Court's analysis, however, did not even acknowledge that discriminatory impact existed, let alone asking whether it was justified or not.[56]

It was only in the late 2000s that we saw the first glimmers of a constitutional articulation of the scope and purpose of the constitutional right against discrimination. The beginnings were tentative: in *Anuj Garg*, for example, an 80-year-old prohibition upon the employment of women as bartenders was struck down by the Supreme Court. In doing so, the Court adopted the 'anti-stereotyping' approach, borrowed from American law: discriminatory legislation would be unconstitutional if it tracked unjustifiable 'stereotypes' about men and women, their relative capacities, or their social roles, or if it sought to 'generalise' about any of these aspects.[57]

Needless to say, the anti-stereotyping approach, while representing a beginning of sorts, is nonetheless an insufficient account of gender discrimination. Implicit within the approach is the assumption that *if* discriminatory legislation mapped on to real or 'actual' differences between men and women, it would be justified. Such an account – as has been well-documented – ignores the context in which those differences arise and the social and cultural norms that make

[53] *Ambika Prasad Mishra v State of UP*, AIR 1980 SC 1762.

[54] *State of Bombay v Narasu Appa Mali*, AIR 1952 Bom 84.

[55] *Javed v State of Haryana*, AIR 2003 SC 3057.

[56] The Supreme Court has since recognised indirect discrimination as a form of discrimination prohibited under Art 15(1) of the Constitution as recently as 2021 in the seminal judgment of *Nitisha v Union of India*, Writ Petition (Civil) No 1109 of 2020 (decided on 25 March 2021).

[57] *Anuj Garg* (n 13).

them salient.[58] In that sense, a strict adherence to the anti-stereotyping approach would severely limit the future development of gender discrimination doctrine.

That, however, has not been the case. Recent judgments of the Supreme Court have marked another potential beginning: the beginning of a more nuanced and context-sensitive approach to gender discrimination and equality. It is to this development that we turn in the next section.

V. FLAGSHIP CONSTITUTIONAL DEVELOPMENTS IN TERMS OF GENDER AND SEXUAL EQUALITY

In more than 70 years of Indian constitutional jurisprudence, it would perhaps be difficult to pick a specific flagship constitutional moment. Likely candidates would include, for example, the 1985 *Shah Bano* judgment where, notwithstanding the legal position that uncodified 'personal law' could not be made subject to the Constitution's fundamental rights chapter, the Supreme Court located a Muslim woman's right to maintenance within ordinary statutory law and extended to the Court's subsequent judgments that undermined legislative attempts to stymie that ruling;[59] the 1997 *Vishaka* judgment, that held that sexual harassment at the workplace constituted a violation of equality and non-discrimination, and passed legally enforceable guidelines until legislation was enacted 16 years later;[60] and the 2014 *NALSA* judgment, where the constitutional rights of the transgender community were recognised for the first time, along with a (yet unfulfilled) direction to the Government to bring the community within the ambit of affirmative action.[61]

All these rulings are no doubt extremely important, in terms of *outcome*, for advancing the rights of women and sexual minorities. Our selection of a 'flagship moment', however, is in keeping with our analysis in the previous section: Indian constitutionalism on gender has been constricted by a continuing judicial failure to engage with, and to articulate, a principled underlying basis to the Constitution's non-discrimination guarantee. In our flagship moment, we see the beginnings of an attempt – still embryonic, and with its future uncertain – on the part of the Supreme Court to address that failure.

Our 'flagship moment' covers a period of slightly more than a year: from 24 August 2017 to 27 September 2018, and spans four judgments of the Supreme Court. On 24 August 2017, a nine-judge bench of the Supreme Court (a rare bench strength) held that the Indian Constitution guaranteed a fundamental

[58] See, eg CA MacKinnon, 'Reflections on Sex Equality Under Law' (1991) 100 *Yale Law Journal* 1281, 1305–06.

[59] *Mohd Ahmed Khan v Shah Bano Begum* (1985) 2 SCC 556; *Danial Latifi v Union of India* (2001) 7 SCC 740.

[60] *Vishaka* (n 8).

[61] *NALSA v Union of India* (2014) 1 SCC 1.

right to privacy and went on to explain and conceptualise the scope and meaning of that right.[62] Within a year, that judgment – *Puttaswamy v Union of India* – or the principles flowing from it, were invoked by five-judge benches of the Court in three cases involving the rights of women and sexual minorities. These included judgments decriminalising same-sex relations,[63] striking down the adultery law,[64] and striking down a statutory rule that prohibited the entry of menstruating-age women into a South Indian temple.[65]

The starting point was the nine-judge privacy judgment, which came to the Supreme Court as a straightforward question: did the Indian Constitution guarantee the right to privacy (even though it did not find a place in the constitutional text)? The Court answered, unanimously, in the affirmative; and then proceeded to elaborate upon that in six concurring – but separate – opinions.

In the course of these concurring opinions the Court discussed many aspects of the right to privacy. Relevant to our purposes here is that by a clear majority, the Court rejected both the spatial and the institutional conceptions of privacy (ie, that privacy vested in spaces such as the home, or institutions such as the family) – conceptions that have historically been turned to anti-feminist ends, and to subordinate the rights of women and sexual minorities by leaving power relations within private spaces untouched.[66] Instead, the Court crafted a more nuanced, individualist but contextual idea of privacy, that – in the lead, plurality judgment – explicitly acknowledged feminist concerns,[67] and elsewhere, indicated that the Supreme Court's own prior judgments upholding the criminalisation of same-sex relations[68] and the restitution of conjugal rights,[69] might have to be reconsidered. Examples of this approach to privacy are scattered throughout the concurring opinions. They include, for example, locating the right to abortion and reproductive rights as a facet of the right to privacy;[70] bodily integrity as an aspect of privacy;[71] linking autonomy with the right to take 'intimate decisions'; and, as the lead plurality opinion specifically observed:

> Patriarchal notions still prevail in several societies including our own and are used as a shield to violate core constitutional rights of women based on gender and autonomy. As a result, gender violence is often treated as a matter of 'family honour' resulting in the victim of violence suffering twice over – the physical and mental trauma

[62] *Puttaswamy* (n 14).
[63] *Navtej Johar* (n 4).
[64] *Joseph Shine v Union of India* (2018) 2 SCC 189.
[65] *Indian Young Lawyers Association v Union of India*, 2018 SCC OnLine SC 690 [hereinafter *Sabarimala*].
[66] For a specific example of this observation in the context of Indian constitutional jurisprudence pre-*Puttaswamy*, see M Nussbaum, 'Is Privacy Bad for Women?' (*Boston Review*, 1 April 2000), available at www.bostonreview.net/articles/martha-c-nussbaum-privacy-bad-women.
[67] *Puttaswamy* (n 14) [140] (plurality opinion of Chandrachud J).
[68] ibid [128] (plurality opinion of Chandrachud J).
[69] ibid [40] (concurring opinion of Chelameswar J).
[70] ibid [38]–[40] (concurring opinion of Chelameswar J).
[71] ibid [81] (concurring opinion of Nariman J).

> of her dignity being violated and the perception that it has cause[d] an affront to 'honour'. *Privacy must not be utilised as a cover to conceal and assert patriarchal mindsets.* Catherine MacKinnon in a 1989 publication titled 'Towards a Feminist Theory of the State' adverts to the dangers of privacy when it is used to cover up physical harm done to women by perpetrating their subjection. *Yet, it must also be noticed that women have an inviolable interest in privacy. Privacy is the ultimate guarantee against violations caused by programmes not unknown to history, such as state imposed sterilization programmes or mandatory state imposed drug testing for women. The challenge in this area is to enable the state to take the violation of the dignity of women in the domestic sphere seriously while at the same time protecting the privacy entitlements of women grounded in the identity of gender and liberty.*[72]

Of course, in *Puttaswamy*, the Supreme Court was only answering an abstract question on the existence of the right to privacy under the Constitution. Its observations, therefore, were indicative at best, offering a gateway to a possible feminist jurisprudence. These observations were put into practice the year after, in a series of cases heard successively by a bench of five judges, and in which judgments were issued in quick succession – all in the month of September 2018.

In *Navtej Johar v Union of India*,[73] the Supreme Court reversed its own prior judgment in *Suresh Kumar Koushal v Naz Foundation*,[74] and decriminalised same-sex relations. As a prefatory point, it is important to note that unlike some of the other judgments discussed in this section, *Navtej Johar* was not primarily court-driven: it was the culmination of 16 years of litigation, which had already seen the Delhi High Court decriminalise same-sex relations in 2009,[75] which had then been initially overturned by the Supreme Court in *Koushal*. Both prior to, and during, the course of litigation, the case in court was supported and buttressed by a powerful community-led movement.[76] At all stages, testimonies of the community were placed before the various courts that heard the case. It was in this socio-political context that *Navtej Johar* finally came to be decided.

Section 377 of the Indian Penal Code – as it then stood – criminalised 'carnal intercourse against the order of nature'. *Suresh Kumar Koushal* had upheld the constitutionality of this section by applying a formalistic legal analysis, according to which the equality and non-discrimination provisions were not attracted at all, because the provision only criminalised 'acts' (ie, carnal intercourse against the order of nature), and not 'identities'. This specific finding was reversed by the Supreme Court in *Navtej Johar*, by paying close attention to the *context* in which a provision like section 377 operated, and the *impact* it had in entrenching the continued legal and social subordination of the LGBTQIA+ community. In this regard, the concurring judgment of Chandrachud J went even further,

[72] ibid [140] (concurring opinion of Chandrachud J) (emphasis supplied).
[73] *Navtej Johar* (n 4).
[74] *Suresh Kumar Koushal v Naz Foundation* (2014) 1 SCC 1.
[75] *Naz Foundation v NCT of Delhi*, 160 DLT 277.
[76] For documentation, see, eg, Orinam, 'A Community Effort: The Battle Against S377', available at orinam.net/377/background-of-sec-377/community-effort-battle-against-s377.

and directly addressed the overlap between discrimination on the basis of sexual orientation, and the underlying assumptions about 'correct' or 'normal' gender identity, upon which it was based.[77] In addition, Chandrachud J did two things in his concurring judgment. First, he acknowledged 'the intersectional nature of sex discrimination, which cannot be said to operate in isolation of other identities, especially from the socio-political and economic context.'[78] Secondly, he observed that 'any ground of discrimination, whether *direct or indirect*, is … prohibited by article 15.'[79] This marked the first time that the concepts of intersectionality and indirect discrimination were acknowledged, in those terms, in a judgment of the Supreme Court.

Chandrachud J's concurring opinion thus broke new ground, although in a limited way. He himself did not develop these concepts in greater detail, and the three other concurring opinions were premised on narrower, more limited reasoning: on the concept of individual choice;[80] on the arbitrariness of the phrase 'carnal intercourse against the order of nature';[81] and on the impermissibility of discriminating on the basis of 'immutable characteristics'.[82] Thus – as we have argued previously in this chapter – even though feminist jurisprudence found a voice in *Navtej Johar*, its constitutional standing remained fragile and tenuous.

The second judgment, *Joseph Shine v Union of India*,[83] also entailed a revisiting of the Supreme Court's own prior pronouncement, this time a far older one, the 1954 judgment where the adultery law was upheld on the basis that it was a 'special provision' that benefited women. In *Joseph Shine*, however, the Court examined the unarticulated premises of the adultery law and, unsurprisingly, concluded that even as it sought to confer a dubious 'benefit' upon women (by immunising them from criminal prosecution), it did so upon a set of premises (such as women's sexual passivity) that served to lock them into continued subordinate status. What also counted with the Court was a post-*Puttaswamy* scepticism of the use of criminal law and state power to control social relations within the framework of a dominant, patriarchal morality. Importantly, in the course of their analyses, the concurring opinions in the judgment united in affirming women's sexual autonomy, and consciously rejected the patriarchal approach that had characterised prior jurisprudence on sex discrimination. For example, Chandrachud J noted:

> Control over women's sexuality is the key patriarchal assumption that underlies family and marriage. In remedying injustices, the Court cannot shy away from delving

[77] *Navtej Johar* (n 4) [44] (concurring opinion of Chandrachud J).
[78] ibid [36].
[79] ibid.
[80] ibid (plurality opinion of Misra CJI).
[81] ibid (concurring opinion of Nariman J).
[82] ibid (concurring opinion of Malhotra J).
[83] *Joseph Shine v Union of India* (n 64).

> into the 'personal', and as a consequence, the 'public'. It becomes imperative for us to intervene when structures of injustice and persecution deeply entrenched in patriarchy are destructive of constitutional freedom. But, in adjudicating on the rights of women, the Court is not taking on a paternalistic role and 'granting' rights.[84]

On a similar note, Malhotra J found:

> Hence, the offence of adultery was treated as an injury to the husband, since it was considered to be a 'theft' of his property, for which he could proceed to prosecute the offender. The said classification is no longer relevant or valid, and cannot withstand the test of Article 14, and hence is liable to be struck down on this ground alone.[85]

A corollary of the substantive feminist reasoning employed by the judges in *Joseph Shine* was also that the purpose of Article 15(3) could be articulated with greater clarity. 'Special provisions' for women could no longer be justified under a protective-patriarchal logic; this left the alternative – also recognised by Malhotra J – that Article 15(3) was to be understood as an *affirmative action* provision, designed to allow the State to pass laws mitigating historical and structural disadvantages suffered by women.[86]

The final judgment – *Indian Young Lawyers' Association v Union of India*[87] – has proven to be the most controversial, and has faced a sustained backlash both from outside and within the Court, where it is presently being reviewed again. *Indian Young Lawyers' Association* – popularly known as 'the Sabarimala Case' – was a split 4–1 decision. The judges in the majority provided different reasons for why they believed the rule prohibiting the entry of menstruating-age women into the Sabarimala temple was invalid. Three judges out of four decided the case on somewhat narrow grounds: relying upon the doctrine of ultra vires, and the fact that, on evidence, it had not been demonstrated that the exclusion of women was a religiously mandated diktat. However, between the dissenting opinion of Malhotra J (the only woman judge on the bench) and the concurring opinion of Chandrachud J, there was substantive disagreement with respect to the intersection of religious norms and gender equality. Malhotra J argued that the exclusion of women from the temple did not amount to a 'pernicious practice', or a 'social evil', which warranted a secular court stepping in and overriding the internal autonomy of the religious group in question.[88] For Malhotra J, constitutional pluralism required respect for different internal norms, even when they might not strictly comport with constitutional commitments to gender equality.[89] Chandrachud J did not see the matter in this way. He referred to the social and structural role of menstruation in the subordination of

[84] ibid [51]–[52] (concurring opinion of Chandrachud J).
[85] ibid [12.2] (concurring opinion of Malhotra J).
[86] ibid [14] (concurring opinion of Malhotra J).
[87] *Sabarimala* (n 65).
[88] ibid [7.4] (dissenting opinion of Malhotra J).
[89] ibid [11] (dissenting opinion of Malhotra J).

women, and how its integration into a symbolic universe of purity and pollution had been historically used to exclude women from equal access to public spaces, as well as to justify discrimination (and even violence) upon them.[90] Thus, for Chandrachud J, the exclusion of women from the Temple was not simply a pure question of faith, to be left to the determination of the religious group or denomination. To Chandrachud J, its basis was integral to, and reinforced, the subordination and exclusion of women from broader social life.[91]

The difference of opinion between Malhotra and Chandrachud JJ thus revealed a fault line at the intersection of group autonomy and gender equality. While the correctness of the outcome of the judgment might be debated, Chandrachud J's reasoning is nonetheless important for its acknowledgment of crucial feminist insights – not least of which is an interrogation of the traditional public–private divide, and an acknowledgment that practices of oppression in the 'private' domain need not *automatically* be granted an immunity from constitutional scrutiny.

A combined reading of these four judgments, therefore, gives us what we may call a 'flagship constitutional development in terms of gender and sexual equality'. In short, these judgments reflect the following principles: (a) an acknowledgment that the focus of the Constitution's non-discrimination guarantee – as applied to women and sexual minorities – is to mitigate the structural and institutional disadvantage suffered by women and sexual minorities; (b) an understanding that disadvantage can be identified and remedied only through close attention to context – both historical and structural; (c) an understanding that the public–private divide is itself contingent (as opposed to 'natural'), has often served to entrench power relations, and must therefore be interrogated; (d) and an acknowledgment that discrimination can, therefore, be both direct and indirect, and that its impact is as important as legislative form or purpose.

We must be careful, however, not to overstate the case. These judgments represent a beginning – but only that. Some of the ideas *within* the judgments remain embryonic: as pointed out above. For example, in *Navtej Johar*, Justice Chandrachud cited the concept of intersectionality, but did not proceed to analyse it or apply it to the case at hand. The *Sabarimala* judgment – as also indicated above – is under review, and may yet be rolled back, as part of a forthcoming, overarching, nine-judge bench hearing that has been set up to decide the interplay between religious freedom and gender equality. The final scope that this case may take is as yet unclear, but an overarching judgment on whether and to what extent women have rights within and against their religious communities will certainly be momentous.

Furthermore, after its brief flourish in September of 2018, the Supreme Court has yet to take forward the jurisprudence that it began in those judgments. The

[90] ibid [57] (concurring opinion of Chandrachud J).
[91] ibid.

intervening two years have seen no further developments. That is not to say that opportunities have been lacking. For instance, the Transgender Act 2019 has been challenged by a number of transgender petitioners, on the basis that under the guise of securing their rights, it only perpetuates discrimination against sexual minorities (for example, by requiring magistrate-approved certificates as proof of trans status). These challenges have come upon the heels of extensive protests against the Act, itself a culmination of many years of campaigning and social movements, led by the transgender community.[92] When cases such as these are eventually heard, the endurance – and durability – of the 2017–18 'flagship moment' will be finally put to the test. Meanwhile, the social movement and struggle for gender justice continues.

VI. CONCLUSION

In this chapter, we set out to answer the question of whether constitutional law has provided a meaningful venue for the advancement of equal citizenship for women and sexual minorities in India. Our analysis in this chapter shows that the question admits of no straightforward answer. Over seven decades, Indian constitutional law has proven to be an uneven terrain when it comes to the claims of women and sexual minorities. In terms of the outcomes of court cases, there have been both victories and setbacks; however, not until very recently have the Indian courts begun to pay serious attention to the possibilities of substantive feminist *reasoning*, and the evolution of a sustainable constitutional doctrine around issues of the rights of women and sexual minorities.

The reasons for this have been explored in the previous sections. During the framing of the Constitution, a long history of women's participation in the public sphere (during the course of the nationalist movement), as well as an existing vocabulary of gender equality and women's rights going back many decades, directly influenced Constitutional provisions. Unlike in many other countries, women did not have to wage a long, post-Constitutional struggle for formal recognition as equal citizens, or for the right to vote. At the same time, however, the nature of the participants in the nationalist movement, as well as the subsumption of a distinct and identifiable women's movement into the broader struggle for political independence, meant that there was a certain *flattening* of issues. There was, thus, little to no discussion of how, precisely, the Constitution – and nascent Indian constitutionalism – would engage with the multiple and intersectional facets of disadvantage that constituted sex discrimination, in all its forms.

[92] For documentation, see 'The Transgender Persons (Protection of Rights Bill), Act 2019 and Rules 2020', available at orinam.net/resources-for/law-and-enforcement/the-transgender-persons-protection-of-rights-bill-2019.

This absence during the moment of constitutional framing spilt over into constitutional jurisprudence. Faced with constitutional claims made in the language of sex discrimination and gender equality, for the longest time, Indian judges (almost exclusively male) answered them either with a formalist reasoning (that did, admittedly, lead to positive outcomes for women at times), or within a patriarchal framework that the Constitution was (ostensibly) committed to dismantling. In these judgments, therefore, we see explicit articulations of paternalism (by framing discriminatory legislation as 'protective') and patriarchy (an endorsement of gender roles, and a dismissal of, or rendering invisible structural disadvantage).

The last decade or so, however, has seen the beginnings of what we may call a 'contrapuntal canon'. While feminist constitutional claims have always been advanced before courts, it is only in recent years that courts have begun to respond to them by framing the reasoning in response to such claims. In some cases this development has been the product of long-running social movements that first articulated their constitutional claims outside the courtroom, and then in it. A good example of this is the social movement and long-running litigation that was finally responsible for the decriminalisation of same-sex relations in 2018. Another is the movement of the transgender community, responsible for the 2014 *NALSA* judgment, and which continues to mobilise against the 2019 Transgender Act, which undermines the core principles of that judgment. In other cases, judicial doctrine appears to be court-driven, and – often – the product of one or two judges, writing disparate concurring judgments as part of larger benches.

For precisely this reason, the new jurisprudence is fragile, and its future remains uncertain within the Supreme Court – an institution that can have up to 34 judges – there is evidently no consensus around it. Outside the Court, there is no obvious overlap between the claims that women's movements consider to be urgent, and the decisions of the Court (for example, there was no widespread movement to decriminalise adultery, or for the entry of women into the Sabarimala Temple). This does not, of course, detract from the importance of these judgments, or from the reasoning in them, from a substantive feminist perspective. What it does indicate, however, is that if these green shoots are to blossom into something more long-lasting, there is a pressing need to deepen the dialogue between social movements and the courts, upon the terrain of the Constitution.

11

Gender, Sexuality and Constitutionalism in Nepal

MARA MALAGODI

I. INTRODUCTION

THIS CHAPTER ANALYSES the complex way in which Nepal's constitutional system frames sex, gender and sexuality. It adopts an inclusive, non-binary definition of gender that overlaps with sex on the basis that both sexual and gender identities are socially constructed in culturally contingent terms,[1] and that perceptions of the body are shaped by society.[2] Nepal's 2015 Constitution, and a number of recent, highly publicised decisions from the Supreme Court of Nepal, have recognised the rights of *both* women *and* sexual and gender diverse people (SGDP). However, the enforcement of these measures remains uneven and often problematic.

Nepal's recent strides in the domain of gender constitutionalism must be contextualised within the deep-seated structural inequalities and rigid hierarchies that have historically shaped its diverse society. Nepal is a land-locked country, situated between India and China, with a territory of about 150,000 square kilometres and a population of around 29 million. It is one of the poorest countries in the world, with a per capita income and GDP of approximately US$700. Roughly one-quarter of the population lives below the national poverty line.[3] Under the 2018 UNDP Gender Inequality Index, Nepal ranked 149 out of 189 countries.[4] Under the 2018 Global Gender Gap Index, Nepal ranked 105 out of 149 overall, 110 for economic opportunity and participation,

[1] M Malagodi and A Powell, 'A Rose by Any Other Names Would Smell as Sweet: Third Gender and Constitutional Identity in Nepal' Conference Presentation (8th Asian Constitutional Law Forum, Hanoi, 6–7 December 2019).

[2] L Nicholson, 'Interpreting Gender' (1994) 20 *Signs* 79, discussed in S Suteu, 'Gender in Comparative Constitutional Change' (2019) UCL Working Paper Series no 2.

[3] 'Basic Statistics: Poverty in Nepal' (Asian Development Bank, 2017), available at www.adb.org/countries/nepal/poverty.

[4] United Nations Development Programme, 'Human Development Report: The Gender Inequality Index' (2018), available at hdr.undp.org/en/composite/GII.

123 for educational attainment, 128 for health and survival, and 66 for political empowerment.[5] While Nepali women constitute more than half of the country's population (51.5 per cent) with a sex ratio of 94 (males per 100 females),[6] they continue to lag behind Nepali men socially, politically and economically, and face extensive forms of discrimination and oppression both in their private and public lives.

Similarly, Nepal's SGDP remain broadly discriminated against as individuals and as a group.[7] Following the 2007 landmark Supreme Court's decision in the *Sunil Babu Pant* case recognising the rights of SGDP, and in light of the inclusion of the 'third gender' (*tesro liñgi*) category in the 2011 Census – the first one in the world to do so – Nepal has been described as a 'rainbow paradise'.[8] However, the *Sunil Babu Pant* decision remains poorly implemented, Nepal has not legalised same-sex marriage, and the final count of the 2011 Census identified no 'third gender' Nepali citizens – due to the poor training of, and forms of discrimination by, census enumerators, along with the use of software that only allowed for a binary classification of gender.[9] Many queer activists have also criticised the 'third gender'/'other (gender)' category adopted across a number of post-2012 governmental policies to refer to SGDP on grounds that it erases most identities on the queer spectrum and entirely obscures questions of sexual orientation. These activists have instead called for the adoption of the term PoMSOGIESC (people of marginalised sexual orientation, gender identity and sex characteristics).[10]

The constitutional sphere is a crucial site to investigate the role of law in constructing, reconstructing, ossifying and potentially unhinging gender-based social hierarchies and forms of oppression and discrimination based on sexual conduct. In the context of Nepal, this chapter seeks to explain the contradiction in matters of gender equality that lies at the heart of the 2015 Constitution – the country's seventh – and the uneven actualisation of the constitutional promise of gender equality. On the one hand, the new Constitution contains an explicit commitment to ending all forms of discrimination, including gender discrimination (*laiñgik vibhed*), and the document features an impressive array of women's and SGDP rights, affirmative action measures, citizenship on the

[5] World Economic Forum, 'The Global Gender Gap Report' (2018), available at www3.weforum.org/docs/WEF_GGGR_2018.pdf.

[6] Government of Nepal Central Bureau of Statistics, 'Population Monograph of Nepal, Volume I' (2014), available at nepal.unfpa.org/sites/default/files/pub-pdf/PopulationMonograph2014Volume1.pdf.

[7] UNDP Williams Institute, 'Surveying Nepal's Sexual and Gender Minorities: An Inclusive Approach' (2014), available at williamsinstitute.law.ucla.edu/wp-content/uploads/Nepal-Survey-Oct-2014.pdf.

[8] *Sunil Babu Pant v HGM Nepal*, 2065, 50 *NKP* 485 (2007); Pahichan, 'Nepal: A Rainbow Paradise' (2017), available at pahichan.com/en/nepal-a-rainbow-paradise.

[9] K Knight, 'Zero in 26,620,809' *Kathmandu Post* (1 October 2011), available at kathmandupost.ekantipur.com/printedition/news/2011-10-01/zero-in-26620809.html.

[10] Queer Youth Group and Queer Rights Collective, 'The Reality of Transgender Rights in Nepal' *The Record* (25 September 2020), available at www.recordnepal.com/the-reality-of-transgender-rights-in-nepal.

basis of gender self-identification, and 'pink quotas' for women's political representation at different governance levels.[11] On the other hand, the new Constitution's provisions on citizenship feature explicit forms of gender-based discrimination against Nepali women in clear violation of Nepal's international legal obligations. These contradictions are also manifest in the lack of an intersectional approach to constitutional adjudication on women's and SGDP rights, and the deficient and discriminatory actualisation of these rights in both legislative and policy measures.

The central argument put forward in this chapter is that the advancement of gender constitutionalism in Nepal has been hampered by the path-dependent, gendered way in which the Nepali nation has been historically imagined, construed and crystallised into the country's constitutional framework and legal system over the years. Enduring forms of constitutional nationalism stand in tension with the nation's emerging cosmopolitan constitutionalism, resulting in profound contradictions in terms of gender equality. The expression 'constitutional nationalism' refers to the context-specific way in which the nation has been historically articulated at the constitutional level, privileging a particular group to the exclusion of others.[12] Constitutions are instruments for the self-reinforcing construction of a shared national identity, but the narratives underpinning the construction of the nation inevitably reflect the values, history and hierarchies of the dominant groups – and their historical hegemony.[13] These narratives are constructed on the basis of ethnicity, race, language, religion, region, gender and sexuality. Conversely the patterns of discrimination that result from this hegemonic articulation of the nation are inevitably intersectional.[14]

Nepal features a complex web of ethnic, linguistic, religious, regional, gender and sexuality-based differences, which have been historically ranked on a state-sanctioned Hindu caste hierarchy centred around the Shah monarchy since the nineteenth century. Hinduism is the religion of the majority of the population (81 per cent) with 125 caste and ethnic groups, but only the largest six account for more than five per cent of the total population. Moreover, none of these various groups constitutes an absolute majority in any region. The two biggest groups are the Chetri and the Bahun; together, these two *Pahari* ('hill') high-caste Hindu groups constitute the dominant *Khas-Arya* group

[11] The expression 'pink quotas' refers to positions and seats reserved for women in state institutions.

[12] M Masri, *The Dynamics of Exclusionary Constitutionalism: Israel as a Jewish and Democratic State* (Hart Publishing, 2017); M Malagodi, *Constitutional Nationalism and Legal Exclusion: Equality, Identity Politics, and Democracy in Nepal (1990–2007)* (Oxford University Press, 2013); S Suteu, 'The Multinational State That Wasn't: The Constitutional Definition of Romania as a National State' (2017) 11 *Vienna Online Journal on International Constitutional Law* 413; B Yack, 'Popular Sovereignty and Nationalism' (2001) 29 *Political Theory* 517.

[13] M Malagodi, 'Constitutional History and Constitutional Migration: Nepal' in DS Law (ed), *Constitutionalism in Context* (Cambridge University Press, 2022).

[14] S Atrey, *Intersectional Discrimination* (Oxford University Press, 2019).

(28.8 per cent) to which Nepal's royal family and most of the elites belong.[15] In terms of historically marginalised groups, *dalits* (lit. 'former untouchables') form about 14 per cent of Nepal's population. The 63 groups classified under the umbrella term *Adivasi Janajati* ('Indigenous people') account for 36 per cent of the total population. *Madhesi* groups (non-*Pahari* 'Terai plain dwellers', often erroneously described as 'of Indian origins') constitute slightly less than 20 per cent of the population.[16] In 2021 another Census was conducted, but at the time of writing the full data was not publicly available. Following the violence that accompanied the pro-federalism *Madhesi Andolan* ('movement') of 2007 and the protests in the Terai region for constitutional recognition in August and September 2015, the *Madhesi–Pahari* cleavage has emerged as the country's main political fault line.[17] The process of federalisation and the demands for equal citizenship remain the principal challenges in implementing Nepal's new constitution vis-à-vis the promotion of gender justice both in terms of redistribution and recognition.

In this respect, the chapter focuses on the intersectional role of gender and sexuality in the constitutionalisation of the nation in Nepal. The structural subordination of women to men has been pivotal to the historical construction of modern nation-states alongside the imposition of heteronormative and monogamous codes of sexual conduct.[18] However, as Helen Irving convincingly illustrates, gender – unlike ethnolinguistic and regional identities – is often overlooked as a salient difference in theories of constitutional and national identity because it is considered non-disruptive of the social compact. Instead, she invites 'an understanding of the gendered character of the whole organic constitution'.[19] I maintain that sexuality plays an equally important role and ought not to be unheeded. Ruth Rubio-Marín astutely observed that

> [M]odern constitutionalism simply drew from the … patriarchal differentiation between the public and the private spheres which emphasized the special, and biologically determined, role of women within the family. The principles of male dominance and hierarchy over married women in the family sphere went unchallenged'.[20]

[15] Government of Nepal, Central Bureau of Statistics, 2011 Census, available at cbs.gov.np/image/data/Population/Major%20Highlights/Major-Finding.pdf.

[16] Government of Nepal, Central Bureau of Statistics, 2011 Census, available at cbs.gov.np/image/data/Population/Population%20Monograph%20of%20Nepal%202014/Population%20Monograph%20V02.pdf.

[17] 'Like We Are Not Nepali: Protest and Police Crackdown in the Terai Region of Nepal' (Human Rights Watch, 16 October 2015), available at www.hrw.org/report/2015/10/16/we-are-not-nepali/protest-and-police-crackdown-terai-region-nepal.

[18] F Anthias and N Yuval-Davis, 'Introduction' in F Anthias and N Yuval-Davis (eds), *Woman-Nation-State* (Macmillan, 1989) 1–15.

[19] H Irving, 'Constitutional Identity Theory and Gender: The Missing Referent' (2017) Sydney Law School Legal Studies Research Paper 17/56.

[20] R Rubio-Marín, 'Gendered Nationalism and Constitutionalism' (2020) 18 *International Journal of Constitutional Law* 441, 442–43.

The policing of sexuality has also historically played a central role in processes of state-building through legal institutions, for instance through the punishment of non-reproductive sexual activities outside of marriage and the criminalisation of homosexuality. The gendered and heterosexist construction of the nation and its institutionalisation by legal means have acquired a degree of path-dependency making these narratives and institutions difficult to displace ideologically, politically and legally.

The advancement of gender-equality claims in recent years also has resulted from a global cross-pollination of constitutional models and the development of cosmopolitan constitutional forms steeped in international standards. David Law has characterised these recent constitutions as belonging to the 'universalist archetype', under which the ideological narratives that underpin the state's legitimacy also encompass international norms.[21] As a result, international instruments, the decisions of supranational courts, and best-practice examples from other jurisdictions have been increasingly deployed domestically to sustain the advancement of gender constitutionalism. Cosmopolitan constitutionalism harnesses the legitimacy that arises from the international constitutional order to promote gender equality, but often finds itself at odds with particularistic forms of constitutional nationalism, which are in turn sustained by historically specific forms of gendered hierarchies.

The focus on the gendered character of law is vital to explain the opportunities and challenges of gender constitutionalism, which hinge on factors internal *and* external to the Constitution. In Nepal, the women's and queer movements have concentrated their efforts first on strategic constitutional litigation anchored in international standards to unhinge deep-seated forms of legal discrimination. They have succeeded in building an impressive body of pro-women and pro-SGDP case law since the early 1990s.[22] These cases aimed primarily at having the Supreme Court declare unconstitutional various discriminatory legal provisions contained in the 1963 *Muluki Ain* ('Country Code')[23] and in legislation. This cosmopolitan approach has also been moderately successful in terms of constitution making, with a few glaring exceptions.

The constitutional promise of gender equality, however, has not been adequately translated into legislative and policy initiatives, which often ignore jurisprudential developments. An array of legislative reforms has been passed (eg. the partial legalisation of abortion and equal property rights for women in

[21] DS Law, 'Constitutional Archetypes' (2016) 95 *Texas Law Review* 153.

[22] M Malagodi, 'Challenges and Opportunities of Gender Equality Litigation in Nepal' (2018) 16 *International Journal of Constitutional Law* 527.

[23] The 'new' *Muluki Ain* ('Country Code') represented the backbone of Nepal's modern criminal and civil laws between 1963 and 2017–18.

2002 by amending the *Muluki Ain*), but they are often limited, if not outright problematic (as are many features of the 2017 Civil and Criminal Codes that replaced the 1963 *Muluki Ain* and came into force in August 2018). Moreover, many policies remain highly discriminatory; these are anchored in autochthonous, exclusionary and gendered social hierarchies – and ultimately in the nationalist discourse that sustains and legitimises them.

In this respect, the case of Nepal imparts an important lesson in terms of the opportunity structures to secure gender justice in the constitutional domain and beyond. Gender constitutionalism advances the furthest when a constitutional system in line with international standards is combined with culturally consonant forms of constitutional recognition of socio-cultural diversity and is underpinned by societal consensus built through extensive public and inclusive deliberations. Judge-led initiatives like those in Nepal, even when jurisprudentially innovative and inspiring in their combination of constitutional autochthony and cosmopolitan constitutionalism, often point to a failure of the political branches. Elected representatives often neglect to tackle issues surrounding the legal treatment of gender and sexuality, which they deem politically sensitive, either for fear of political reprisal or for ideological hostility. Legal reforms towards greater gender inclusion are often resisted by state authorities in the name of protecting the nation's autochthonous social values and religious traditions to legitimise patriarchal and heteronormative forms of exclusion. It is imperative, however, to secure the buy-in of the political branches, which translates into gender-sensitive legislation, policy-making and effective implementation of constitutional standards. If such buy-in is not secured, even the most significant advances of gender constitutionalism via the judicial route will remain precarious. While a solid pro-women and SGDP body of jurisprudence is of fundamental importance, for gender constitutionalism to take root, it must move beyond the courts. In short, the enduring success of gender constitutionalism is predicated on the cooperation of all the three branches of government in crafting a truly inclusive legal framework beyond a narratively construed hegemonic version of the nation.

The chapter begins with a section on Nepal's constitutional history and framework to embed the study of gender constitutionalism in its proper sociocultural context. It then analyses the constitutional framing of sex, gender and sexuality under the new 2015 Constitution. A section on the jurisprudential developments in matters of gender justice follows, highlighting the great contribution by the Supreme Court of Nepal in the advancement of gender constitutionalism while also explaining its limitations. The final section focuses on sexual and reproductive rights, one of the most innovative areas of gender constitutionalism in which Nepal has made enormous strides in a relatively short period, but where constitutional implementation remains extremely weak.

II. BACKGROUND

A. Constitutional History and Socio-cultural Context

Nepal was never colonised and is considered part of South Asia.[24] The most important constitutional and legal influences have entered the country from across its southern border since colonial times and India remains the biggest foreign jurisdictional influence.[25] Nepal features a long, uninterrupted history of autochthonous governance constructed around the authority of the Shah Hindu monarchy (1769–2008) and in opposition to India. The country's constitutional identity has been historically associated with a combination of Hinduism, monarchy and social hierarchy anchored in a specifically Nepali 'national' caste system created by law under the 1854 *Muluki Ain*.[26] Hinduism played a special role in legitimising the position of the monarchy and crafting a sense of national identity for Nepal as 'the world's last Hindu kingdom'.

The Shah Kings of Gorkha forged modern Nepal as the state entity we know today in the late eighteenth century. Firmly placed under different forms of authoritarian indigenous rule until 1951, the country briefly experimented with democracy in the 1950s, only to return to monarchical autocracy under the Panchayat regime (1960–1990).[27] The redemocratisation of 1990 opened up the political space for liberal constitutional reforms under the 1990 Constitution and through the accession to many international legal instruments.[28] The People's War launched by the Communist Party of Nepal (Maoist), however, plunged Nepal into a prolonged civil war (1996–2006). The resolution of the conflict ultimately hinged on the abrogation of the 1990 Constitution and the overthrowing of the again-turned-autocratic Shah monarchy. The 2006 People's Movement brought together the Maoist insurgents and the mainstream political parties, who succeeded in restoring parliamentary democracy. In January 2007 an interim constitution was promulgated. After a protracted and embattled peace process (2006–2015), the new permanent Constitution came into force on 20 September 2015 through the work of two Constituent Assemblies (CA)

[24] The expression 'South Asia' indicates here the eight countries that are the Member States of the South Asian Association for Regional Cooperation (SAARC): Afghanistan, Bangladesh, Bhutan, India, Maldives, Nepal, Pakistan and Sri Lanka.

[25] Malagodi (n 13).

[26] A Höfer, *The Caste Hierarchy and the State in Nepal* (Universitätsverlag Wagner, 1979).

[27] M Malagodi, 'Nepal' in DS Law, H Lau and A Schwartz (eds), *Oxford Handbook of Constitutional Law in Asia* (Oxford University Press (forthcoming 2023)).

[28] The main international legal instruments to which Nepal became party immediately after the return to democracy in 1990 are: the Convention on the Rights of the Child (14 September 1990); the Convention on the Elimination of All Forms of Discrimination Against Women (22 April 1991); the International Covenant on Economic, Social and Cultural Rights, the International Covenant on Civil and Political Rights, the Optional Protocol to the International Covenant on Civil and Political Rights, and the Convention Against Torture and Other Cruel, Inhuman or Degrading Treatment or Punishment (14 May 1991).

operating respectively in 2008–12 (CA1) and 2013–15 (CA2). The monarchy was abolished only in 2008 by CA1.

Nepal's post-conflict constitution-making context is pivotal to understanding the expectations surrounding the new Constitution and, ultimately, its mixed reception. The process of constitution-building began with the promise of delivering social inclusion through radical state restructuring. CA1 was the most representative body directly elected in Nepali history thanks to quotas for marginalised groups. CA1 received extensive international constitution-building assistance, which explains the many cosmopolitan features of the draft it produced. However, CA1 political fragmentation and lack of consensus over the thorniest issues (federalism, secularism, proportional representation, quotas, citizenship and judicial reform) led to its dissolution before the Constitution was finalised.[29] Notwithstanding four extensions of CA1 term by way of constitutional amendment (2010–12), protracted Supreme Court litigation on the constitutionality of these amendments brought CA1 to an end in 2012.[30] A political and legitimacy crisis ensued.

CA1 dissolution, combined with the victory of more conservative forces in CA2 elections in 2013, led to inordinate delays in constitution-making. The goal of constitutional inclusion effectively fell off the political agenda with increasing pushbacks against the politics of recognition. Moreover, the devastating earthquakes in 2015 and the unofficial Indian blockade of the open border with India created a climate of profound national vulnerability. In this context, Nepali political leaders fast-tracked the Constitution and chose to shore up national unity at the expense of inclusion.[31] This constitutional emphasis on national unity relied upon the divisive notion of *nepalipan*, the nineteenth-century nationalist construction of 'Nepali-ness' defined in opposition to Indians and Madhesi.[32] This ideological shift bore crucial repercussions on the formulation of the citizenship provisions whose gender-based discrimination can only be understood in intersectional terms.

B. Constitutional Structure

The 2015 Constitution establishes a federal democratic republic with a parliamentary system and an independent judiciary empowered to invalidate legislation

[29] M Malagodi, 'Constituent Assembly Failure in Pakistan and Nepal' in J Elster, R Gargarella, V Naresh and BE Rasch (eds), *Constituent Assemblies* (Cambridge University Press, 2018).

[30] M Malagodi, 'Limiting Constituent Power? Unconstitutional Constitutional Amendments and Time-Bound Constitution Making in Nepal' in R Abeyratne and NS Bui (eds), *The Law and Politics of Unconstitutional Constitutional Amendments in Asia* (Routledge, 2021) 133.

[31] M Malagodi, 'The Rejection of Constitutional Incrementalism in Nepal's Federalisation' (2018) 46 *Federal Law Review* 521.

[32] G Toffin and J Pfaff-Czarnecka, 'Introduction: Globalization and Belonging in the Himalayas and in Trans-Himalayan Social Spaces' in G Toffin and J Pfaff-Czarnecka (eds), *Facing Globalisation in the Himalayas: Belonging and the Politics of the Self* (Sage, 2014) 25–26.

on grounds of unconstitutionality. The Constitution is entrenched, difficult to amend, and contains an extensive section of justiciable fundamental rights. Nepal has adopted a parliamentary system since the early 1950s, and the 2015 Constitution retains this feature. At the central level, the bicameral Federal Parliament.[33] Executive power is shared between the President of the Republic, who is largely a ceremonial figure replacing the monarch as Head of State, and the Cabinet of Ministers as long as it retains the confidence of the House of Representatives.[34] The 2015 Constitution introduced a federal structure with three tiers of government: the federal Government at the centre, seven provinces and local government (divided between districts at the higher level and villages and municipalities at the lower level).[35]

C. Courts and Fundamental Rights

The 2015 Constitution continues Nepal's tradition of having an entrenched constitution with justiciable constitutional rights. The country has adopted a dualistic approach to the domestication of international law in light of constitutional supremacy and the requirements for enacting laws.[36] The Constitution is Nepal's fundamental law and all laws inconsistent with it are void.[37] The judiciary acts as the guardian of the Constitution through a three-tier court system (one Supreme Court, one High Court per province, and 75 first-instance District Courts) with jurisdiction in both civil and criminal matters.[38] The Supreme Court is the only institution authorised to provide the final and binding interpretation of the Constitution and it has extensive powers to review and invalidate primary legislation on constitutional grounds.

Since 1990, Nepal's Supreme Court has been empowered to issue prerogative writs (*habeas corpus*, *mandamus*, *certiorari*, prohibition and *quo warranto*) and employ the mechanism of public interest litigation (PIL) like in India.[39] This has allowed the Supreme Court to strengthen its position, as many public interest litigants have sought judicial review of legislation by the Supreme Court as their primary remedy. Under the new Constitution, only the newly established Constitutional Bench is allowed to invalidate legislation as unconstitutional. The reliance on this smaller Bench has considerably increased the Supreme Court's sizeable constitutional backlog.

[33] The 2015 Constitution of Nepal, Pt VIII, Arts 83–114.

[34] ibid Arts 61–73, 76.

[35] ibid Pts VII–X, Arts 74–125 (defining the federal government); Pts XIII–XVI, Arts 162–213 and Sch 4 (listing and defining the provinces); Pts XVII–XIX, Arts 214–30 (local government).

[36] Art 279 to be read in conjunction with s 9(2) of the Nepal Treaty Act 1990.

[37] The 2015 Constitution of Nepal, Art 1.

[38] ibid Pt XI, Arts 126–56.

[39] ibid Art 133.

Since 1990, the number and scope of fundamental rights contained in Nepal's Constitutions have steadily increased. On the basis of a quantitative analysis of linguistic patterns in the declaratory parts of the document and fundamental rights, David Law has characterised the 2015 Constitution as 'almost copied and pasted from United Nations documents', with the notable exception of gender-based discrimination in matters of citizenship, which 'in this day and age is comparable to a constitution of the likes of Saudi Arabia's'.[40] He argues that the 2015 Constitution belongs to the 'universalist archetype' harnessing the legitimacy of alignment with international standards.[41] However, the document also retains a divisive Hindu nationalist symbolism: a privileged position for a particularly conservative version of Hinduism (*sanātana*) carved out of the secularism clause,[42] a constitutional ban on religious conversion (implicitly to protect the dominant position of Hinduism) under the right to religious freedom,[43] affirmative action measure also for dominant upper caste *Khas-Arya* groups,[44] and the Hindu symbols of the cow as the national animal and saffron as the national colour.[45] Thus, the tension between cosmopolitan constitutionalism and constitutional nationalism remains at the heart of the 2015 constitutional text and shapes the constitutional battles for gender justice in Nepal.

In terms of constitutional adjudication, since 1990 Nepal's Supreme Court has played a pivotal role in advancing the rights of Nepali women and SGDP.[46] There remain, however, insurmountable issues of access to justice for women and SGDP from poor and historically marginalised backgrounds, a lack of diversity across the judiciary (still dominated by upper caste Hindu men),[47] and ideological reticence by both petitioners and judges to adopt an intersectional approach to gender-based claims with the potential to challenge traditional notions of Nepal's national identity and societal hierarchies. Moreover, constitutional implementation remains weak, even if Nepal features a vast body of groundbreaking gender equality jurisprudence. Similarly, the way in which the impressive array of constitutional rights has been actualised in ordinary legislation is often incomplete or even in direct contradiction with the text of the Constitution and Supreme Court decisions. This points to a tension between the judiciary and the political branches in the realisation of the constitutional promise of gender justice.

[40] DS Law, 'The Nepal Constitution of 2015: A Quantitative Perspective' (Conference on the 2015 Constitution of Nepal, Kathmandu, 11–13 August 2018).

[41] Law (n 21).

[42] The 2015 Constitution of Nepal, Art 4(1).

[43] ibid Art 26(3).

[44] ibid Arts 18, 42(1), 84(2), 176(6), 259(a) and 267(3).

[45] ibid Art 9(3).

[46] Malagodi (n 22).

[47] National Judicial Academy, 'Gender Equality and Social Inclusion in Nepal' (2013) 50–52.

III. CONSTITUTIONAL FRAMING OF SEX, GENDER AND SEXUALITY

Nepal's 2015 constitutional text is a fruitful site to explore the relationship between gender equality and constitutional identity. Nepal's approach to gender constitutionalism reflects a unique combination of provisions drawn from international law – especially the Convention on the Elimination of All Forms of Discrimination Against Women (CEDAW), the codification of the extensive pro-women and pro-SGDP decisions of Nepal's post-1990 Supreme Court, and the significant diversity of representation at the time of constitution-making. Looking back at Nepal's constitution-making process, female CA members constituted about 33 per cent of the total membership in both Assemblies. Moreover, the presence of Sunil Babu Pant, the first openly gay lawmaker in the country, and his membership to the CA1 Committee for Fundamental Rights and Directive Principles, were pivotal to the constitutional recognition of SGDP rights.[48] Similarly, the work of the CA1 Women's Caucus secured the coordinated efforts of female members beyond their respective party affiliations.

The CA2 Drafting Committee adopted the CA1 drafts almost in their entirety, leading to the inclusion of provisions on women's rights and representation in the promulgated Constitution.[49] However, gender-based discrimination in terms of citizenship endured due to broader political concerns of an intersectional nature concerning questions of national security and unity. This points to the limitations of pink quotas; as Silvia Suteu argues, the success in securing gender equality gains at the time of constitution-making is measured not just by percentages in women's representation, but also by the quality of popular deliberation and the impact of women's voices.[50]

The preamble contains an explicit commitment to ending all forms of discrimination, including 'gender discrimination' (*laiñgik vibhed*). In this respect, it is important to highlight that the way in which the constitutional text frames gender is ambiguous as to whether a binary or non-binary stance is adopted. Articles 18 and 42 refer to 'gender and sexual minorities' (*laiñgik tathā yaunik alpasañkyak*) respectively as groups that must not be discriminated against and that are entitled to affirmative action measures in public employment. It is unclear just by reading the constitutional texts whether self-identifying trans women are covered by the definition of 'women' (*mahilā*) in the Constitution, or under the term 'gender minorities' (*laiñgik alpasañkyak*) – or both.

[48] K Knight, 'Outliers: Sunil Babu Pant, the Blue Diamond Society, and Queer Organizing in Nepal' (2014) 19 *Studies in Nepali History and Society* 113, 162–63.

[49] Women's Caucus of the Constituent Assembly, 'Women's Rights and Agenda to Be Incorporated in the New Constitution' (International IDEA, 2010).

[50] S Suteu, 'Women and Participatory Constitution-making' in H Irving (ed), *Constitutions and Gender* (Edward Elgar, 2017) 41.

A. Women's and SGDP Rights

The 2015 constitutional commitment to ending all forms of discrimination, including 'gender discrimination', manifests itself through an impressive array of women's rights in the Parts on Fundamental Rights[51] and Directive Principles, Policies, and Responsibilities of the State.[52] Parts 3 and 4 of the Constitution are anchored in a cosmopolitan constitutional vision that places the courts in an ideal position to advance the cause of gender justice. Article 18 on the right to equality forbids discrimination on the basis of sex (*liñga*), marital status (*vaivāik sthiti*) and pregnancy (*garbhāvasthā*). In terms of positive obligations on the state, the Article also provides for affirmative action measures for socially and culturally backward women (*sāmājik vā sāñskritik dristile pichadiekā*).[53] Article 18 also prohibits discrimination against 'gender and sexual minorities', but these are not defined anywhere in the constitutional text.

Article 19 on the right to communication guarantees freedom from a priori censorship, but provides for extensive grounds upon which reasonable restrictions may be imposed by law, including the incitement of gender discrimination, but also on any act contrary to decent public behaviour and morality, and any act that may undermine the nationality, sovereignty and indivisibility of Nepal, or the good relations between federal units, or that jeopardises the harmonious relations among different caste groups tribes, or communities.[54] Again, threats to national unity are prioritised over inclusion.

The 2015 Constitution also features an entirely new set of women's rights under Article 38. This new provision guarantees equal rights to lineage (*vanshiya*); to safe motherhood (*surakshit mātritva*) and reproductive health (*prajanan svāsthya*);[55] to equal political participation in all state structures on the basis of proportional inclusion (*samānukpātik samāveshī siddhānta*); to affirmative action measures in education, health, employment and social security; and to equal rights to their spouse in property and family matters. Sub-clause (3) clearly prohibits any forms of violence and oppression against women.[56] Article 42 on the right to social justice grants 'socially backward women' and 'gender and sexual minority groups' the right to employment in state structures on the basis of inclusion in line with redistributive justice concerns,[57] while Article 43 identifies 'helpless single women' (*asahāya ekla mahilā*) as one of the groups entitled to the right to social security.[58]

[51] The 2015 Constitution of Nepal, Pt 3, Arts 16–48.

[52] ibid Arts 49–55.

[53] ibid Art 18.

[54] ibid Art 19.

[55] While abortion is not mentioned anywhere in the constitutional text, it has been construed to form part of these rights by the Supreme Court (see section V below).

[56] The 2015 Constitution of Nepal, Art 38.

[57] ibid Art 42.

[58] ibid Art 43.

Under the extensive Chapter on Directive Principles, Policies and Responsibilities of the State, Article 50(1) embraces gender equality (*laiṅgik samāntā*) as one of the principles.[59] Article 51(j) on social inclusion reiterates the importance of an intersectional approach to women's rights.[60] While Directives Principles are non-justiciable, drawing from the Indian experience, Nepali courts have treated them as helpful tools to interpret fundamental rights.

B. Quotas and Representation

The 2015 Constitution contains pink quotas for women's political representation at different governance levels – a tradition that began with the 1990 Constitution (which mandated a five per cent quota of women in the Lower House) and continued in expanded form under Article 63(5) of the 2007 interim Constitution (which mandated one-third of female candidates in the Constituent Assembly elections). At the central legislative level, Article 84(8) of the current constitution specifies that one-third of the total representation of each party in the Federal Parliament must be women.[61] Article 84(2) provides for closed lists of historically marginalised groups: 'women, *Dalit*, *Adivasi Janajati*, *Khas-Arya*, *Madhesi*, *Tharu*, Muslim, and backward regions'.[62] Significantly, the new Constitution added the controversial *Khas-Arya* to the list of protected categories entitled to benefit from affirmative action. Under Article 91, either the Speaker or Deputy Speaker of the House of Representatives must be a woman.[63] Similarly, Article 92 provides that either the Chairperson or Vice Chairperson of the House of Representatives must be a woman.[64] Article 86 also makes special provisions for women's representation in the Upper House.[65]

At the provincial legislative level, each Assembly features 40 per cent of the seats elected through proportional representation. Mirroring the identity-based quotas at the federal level, the election of minimum quotas of legislators from protected categories is guaranteed.[66] Article 176(6) makes provisions for closed lists of marginalised groups including women in the elections of the proportional seats in the Provincial Assemblies, while Article 176(9) mandates that one-third of the total representation of each party in the Provincial Assemblies must be women.[67] Article 182(2) provides that either the Speaker or Deputy Speaker of each Provincial Assembly must be a woman.[68] At the

[59] ibid Art 50.
[60] ibid Art 51.
[61] ibid Art 84.
[62] ibid Art 84(2).
[63] ibid Art 91.
[64] ibid Art 92.
[65] ibid Art 86.
[66] ibid Art 176(6).
[67] ibid Art 176.
[68] ibid Art 182.

local level, Articles 222(3) and 223(3) mandate that each Village Assembly and Municipal Assembly respectively have at least two women from every Ward.[69] The first local elections under the new Constitution took place in 2017 and returned 14,352 female elected representatives out of 35,041, ie 40.96 per cent.[70]

At the executive level, Article 70 prescribes that the President and Vice-President of Nepal must belong to different genders and communities,[71] making it mandatory that at least one is a woman. No provisions for pink quotas exist for the provincial executive.[72] Instead, women's representation is mandated at the local level in Village Executives (Article 215),[73] Municipal Executives (Article 216),[74] and District Executive Committees (Article 220).[75]

Nepal's recent developments in matters of pink quotas are in line with global trends.[76] This extensive set of constitutional provisions securing women's presence at all levels of governance explains why Nepal is ranked 66th in the 2018 Global Gender Gap Index in terms of political empowerment – much higher than any other indicators.[77] However, recent research by Seira Tamang on female political representation after the 2017 elections concludes that, while 'there is a certain level of success in the formal inclusion of women in political institutions, … the majority of elected women [in Nepal] remain powerless … The system gave women's representation, but there is no meaningful participation'.[78] In other words, the Constitution provided women with a seat at the table but not a voice, as deep-rooted patriarchal social structures remain hard to displace.

C. Citizenship

The legal treatment of citizenship represents the women's movement's biggest failure in Nepal and sits at odds with the otherwise progressive provisions on gender equality in the rest of the document. Cosmopolitan constitutionalism and constitutional nationalism clash most obviously in matters of citizenship.

[69] ibid Arts 222 and 223.

[70] The Asia Foundation, 'Nepal's Locally Elected Women Representatives', available at asiafoundation.org/wp-content/uploads/2018/07/Nepals-Locally-Elected-Women-Representatives-Exploratory-Study-of-Needs-and-Capacity-Assessment.pdf.

[71] The 2015 Constitution of Nepal, Art 70.

[72] ibid Pt 13, Arts 161–74.

[73] ibid Art 215.

[74] ibid Art 216.

[75] ibid Art 220.

[76] É Lépinard and R Rubio-Marín (eds), *Transforming Gender Citizenship: The Irresistible Rise of Gender Quotas in Europe* (Cambridge University Press, 2018).

[77] World Economic Forum (n 5).

[78] S Tamang, '"They've Given Us the Chair, but Bound Our Hands and Feet": Embedding Elected Female Representatives in Institutions in Nepal' (2018) 23 *Studies in Nepali History and Society* 309, 341.

While Nepal continues not to recognise dual citizenship, the 2015 Constitution also discriminates on the basis of gender in the way in which citizenship is passed on.[79] Nepali men married to foreign women can pass on citizenship by descent to their spouse and offspring, while Nepali women married to foreign men can only pass on naturalised citizenship.[80] The issue of unequal citizenship in Nepal is clearly of an intersectional nature, combining forms of oppression on the basis of both gender and regional identity. *Madhesi* women in the southern Terai region are the intended target of these provisions because of their marriage to Indian men, even if many other Nepali women married to foreigners have been equally affected. These restrictions have been a long-standing feature of Nepal's constitutional framework and are historically linked to the issue of *Madhesi* regionalism, which is complicated by the open border with India. The legal regulation of citizenship has been engineered with the goal of insulating the Nepali nation from India. The aim is to reduce cross-border marriages and prevent Indian men marrying Nepali women and their offspring from acquiring Nepali citizenship.[81]

The shift from gender-neutral language (person, citizen, individual, child) to gendered language (woman, wife, father, mother) in the Constitution's treatment of citizenship takes place when the word 'foreign' appears in the context of marital relationships. The change to gendered language also reveals that this *Panchayat*-style, hierarchical, and exclusionary version of Nepali identity is anchored in a gendered construction of the nation in which women's reproductive power must be cordoned off and patrolled against foreign penetration. Bizarrely, in the same Part, the 2015 Constitution also incorporates a provision for issuing citizenship documents on the basis of gender identity (*laiñgik pahicān*), ie gender self-identification, which can also be non-binary.[82] While this provision appears ground-breaking from an international comparative perspective, in practice, the issuance of citizenship ID cards as 'third gender' remains abysmally low,[83] and current policy prevents trans-women and trans-men from obtaining citizenship documents in their acquired gender.

IV. CONSTITUTIONAL JURISPRUDENCE

Nepal's Supreme Court has by and large greatly contributed to the advancement of gender constitutionalism in the country, even if in certain areas the lack of an intersectional approach in its reasoning has hampered the depth and

[79] The 2015 Constitution of Nepal, Pt 2, Arts 10–15.

[80] ibid Art 11.

[81] S Pudasaini, 'Writing Citizenship: Gender, Race and Tactical Alliances in Nepal's Constitution Drafting' (2017) 22 *Studies in Nepali History and Society* 85.

[82] The 2015 Constitution of Nepal, Art 12.

[83] M Bochenek and K Knight, 'Establishing a Third Gender Category in Nepal: Process and Prognosis' (2012) 26 *Emory International Law Review* 11, 31.

reach of its decisions. Moreover, in the most problematic areas pertaining to the position of women within the traditional bounds of the family, or even as a threat to national unity, the Court has been more deferential to the political branches and has failed to frame the role of women within society as individuals rather than a man's wife, daughter or sister.

A. Citizenship

Over a long string of cases since the early 1990s, the Supreme Court has consistently decided in favour of equal treatment of men and women in matters of citizenship. However, the Court has entirely sidestepped the intersectional root cause of this discrimination, especially with respect to cross-border marriages in the Terai. Moreover, there has been no systematic implementation of the many judicial orders by the executive. In citizenship cases, the petitioners are almost invariably individuals directly affected by the legal regime. In its post-2007 citizenship decisions, the Court has adopted an increasingly activist stance on women's citizenship rights,[84] culminating in the 2011 landmark *Sabina Damai* decision, in which it ordered the Government to issue citizenship documents to the petitioner on the basis of her mother's Nepali citizenship regardless of the fact that the identity of the father was unknown.[85]

In later cases, the Supreme Court repeatedly ordered the Government to implement its earlier decisions and introduce necessary legislative reforms.[86] But the problem persists as new individual cases continue to come to court. In fact, a recent study estimates that about 6.3 million Nepalis lack citizenship certificates.[87] The Government, however, has shown no intention of amending the Constitution to remove the discriminatory provisions and the new Citizenship Bill has been languishing for years. The entrenchment of gender-based discrimination in the 2015 Constitution provisions on citizenship constrains the role of the courts in aiding women in obtaining equal citizenship as the only route remains constitutional amendment.

B. Bodies, Gender and Sexuality

The Supreme Court has led the way in terms of recognition of SGDP rights, with the political branches either failing to implement the relevant judgments

[84] *Nakkali Maharjan v Office of the Prime Minister* 2065, 50 NKP 1340 (2008); *Ranjit Thapa v Office of the Prime Minister* 2066, 51 NKP 1014 (2009).

[85] *Sabina Damai v Government of Nepal* 2068, 53 NKP 247 (2011).

[86] *Nina Tamang v Government of Nepal* (2012); *Sita Devi Adhikari v Government of Nepal* (2013); *Bhola Nagarkoti v Government of Nepal* (2014); *Dipti Gurung v Government of Nepal* (2015).

[87] US State Department, '2020 Country Reports on Human Rights Practices: Nepal' (30 March 2021), available at www.state.gov/reports/2020-country-reports-on-human-rights-practices/nepal.

or distorting their core message. In 2007, the Supreme Court recognised in the landmark *Sunil Babu Pant* case that SGDP have faced unconstitutional discrimination on account of their identity, and it ordered the Government to introduce legislation respecting the fundamental rights of sexual and gender minorities, including third-gender individuals.[88] In support of its decision, the Court cited an extensive array of international human rights standards like CEDAW and foreign judgments. Significantly, the Court also referred to autochthonous South Asian culture and the accommodation of *Hijras* (a particular community of transgender individuals) throughout the Indian subcontinent under the 'third gender' category to establish an explicit link between international norms and local culture.

A number of decisions followed, seeking to recognise SGDP rights. In 2013, Sunil Babu Pant returned to the Supreme Court and in 2017 obtained another favourable decision in which the Court ordered the Government to develop a policy enabling transgender people to change their name.[89] In the *Dilu Buduja* case, the Supreme Court ordered that third gender persons be given a passport with the gender marker 'other'.[90] In the 2013 case of *Rajani Shah*, which dealt specifically with the question of sexual orientation, the Supreme Court held that 'individuals can decide as to choosing their ways of living either separately or in partnership together with homosexuals or heterosexuals – with or without solemnizing marriage' even if the current law only recognises heterosexual marriages.[91] Similarly, in the 2017 case of *Suman Panta*, the Supreme Court interpreted the language of the Immigration Rules to include a same-sex couple married abroad, even if Nepali law does not recognise same-sex marriages, and granted the foreign spouse a non-tourist dependant visa.[92]

The implementation of these decisions, however, has been abysmal. Nepal's new Civil Code, which came into force in 2018, expressly limits marriage to a union between a man and a woman (section 68), despite the fact that the 2015 Report by the court-mandated and government-appointed Same-Sex Marriage Committee had recommended the amendment of legislation to enshrine marriage equality. Moreover, since 2012 policy documents lump all queer communities together under the 'third gender' label, in a rather overt attempt to erase both sexual orientation and trans and non-binary identities from forms of queer

[88] *Sunil Babu Pant v HGM Nepal*, 2065, 50 *NKP* 485 (2007).

[89] *Sunil Babu Pant v Government of Nepal* (also known as *Anik Rana v Government of Nepal*), 2074, 9 *NKP* 9875 (2017). See also APTN and UNDP, 'Legal Gender Recognition: A Multi-Country Legal and Policy Review in Asia' (6 December 2017), available at www.undp.org/asia-pacific/publications/legal-gender-recognition-multi-country-legal-and-policy-review-asia.

[90] *Dilu Buduja v Ministry of Foreign Affairs*, 2070, 8 *NKP* 9048 (2013). See also National Judicial Academy, Nepal, 'Compendium of Landmark Judgments of the Supreme Court of Nepal on Gender Justice and Equality' 126 (2020), available at njanepal.org.np/public/reports/21040752654-landmark-decision-english.pdf.

[91] *Rajani Shah v National Women Commission et.al* (Writ No 069-WH-0030), decided on 11 April 2013.

[92] *Suman Panta v Ministry of Home Affairs et al* (Writ No 073-WO-1054), decided on 23 October 2017.

legal recognition. As such, the 'third gender' label is now fiercely opposed by new generations of queer activists. The pending case of a transgender woman, Rukshana Kapali, in the Constitutional Bench of the Supreme Court of Nepal seeks the recognition of her identity on government documents as 'female' not 'third gender' or 'other'.[93] In fact, the Supreme Court in obiter in its December 2023 decision in the case of *Adheep Pokhrel v Ministry of Home Affairs*, stated that the expression 'third gender' should be superseded and more inclusive terminology deployed in both legal and policy language.[94]

C. Gender-Based Violence

Nepal's Supreme Court has adjudicated several cases of gender-based violence since the 1990s. The Court has prioritised the protection of women regardless of their status and profession, treating cis women's freedom from violence as a gold standard of civilisation. This body of jurisprudence has adopted a universalist language and relied on international standards. Significantly there is no comparable body of case law on violence against SGDP in Nepal.

In an early example of jurisprudence on violence against women, the Court adjudicated on the constitutionality of a provision of the 1963 *Muluki Ain* excluding marital rape from the section on rape.[95] The Court ordered the Government to introduce appropriate legislation and declared marital rape a punishable criminal offence. When government lawyers argued that 'according to our Hindu traditions and values, a husband having sexual intercourse with his wife can never be considered rape', the Supreme Court rejected the argument and held that the *Dharmaśāstra* cannot condone marital rape because religion promotes love, not violence. It held that all women are entitled to the enjoyment of fundamental rights and protection from harm irrespective of their marital status. The Supreme Court subsequently invalidated part of the *Muluki Ain*'s chapter on rape discriminating against prostitutes.[96] It reaffirmed the principle that all women are equally entitled to protection from sexual violence, regardless of their role within the family or society. Similarly, the Court ordered the Government to enact legislation and interim directives guaranteeing a safe and healthy work environment for women employed in dance bars and massage parlours.[97]

[93] *Rukshana Kapali v Government of Nepal*, No 077-WO-0973 (2021), Petition to Supreme Court, 9. See also H Lau and M Malagodi 'Legal gender recognition in Nepal and comparative context' (forthcoming 2023) *University of Pennsylvania Journal of International Law*.

[94] *Adheep Pokhrel v Ministry of Home Affairs*, Mandamus Order No 079-WO-0198 (2022).

[95] *Mira Dhungana v Ministry of Law and Justice* (Writ No 55 of 2058), decided in 2059 BS (2002).

[96] *Sapana Pradhan Malla v Ministry of Law and Justice* (Writ No 56 of 2058), decided in 2059 BS (2002).

[97] *Prakash Mani Sharma v Office of the Prime Minister*, 2067, 52 *NKP* 1480 (2010).

The Supreme Court has also reviewed the procedures and institutions for investigating and trying cases of gender violence. In 2010, the Court ordered the Government to establish a fast-track court presided by female judges to hear cases on violence against women, especially domestic violence, and to safeguard the privacy of the victims.[98] In later cases, the Court ordered the government to implement a gender-friendly advertising policy,[99] and sought to protect human trafficking survivors by de-criminalising non-cooperation by the survivor.[100]

D. Gender and the Family

Nepal's Supreme Court adopted a pro-women approach in many cases in matters of property law, inheritance and family law. However, while the Court sought to achieve greater fairness in the distribution of material resources between men and women within the family, it did not challenge the binary gender roles within the family underpinning many forms of gender-based discrimination under Nepali private law. While the Supreme Court consistently ruled in favour of gender equality, it often stopped short of invalidating offending legislation and ordered the Government to introduce legal reforms. Moreover, the Court never recommended to the legislature the adoption of gender-neutral language in family law matters nor challenged the patriarchal assumptions behind the role of women within traditional familial structures.

Property law provisions under the 1963 *Muluki Ain* were largely based on the Hindu *Mitākṣarā* system,[101] which discriminated against women's inheritance and property rights by recognising only sons as coparceners. Activist lawyers used constitutional litigation to displace these provisions and relied extensively on international legal standards such as CEDAW. In the first case of this kind in 1995 – the famous *Mira Dhungana*, the Supreme Court acknowledged that Nepali law treated men and women differently in terms of property rights but justified this discrimination on the basis of the country's social and religious traditions.[102] As a result, the Court did not invalidate the offending legislation, but ordered the Government to initiate a comprehensive legislative revision. The same approach was adopted in *Canda Bajracharya* the following year, where the Court justified the country's traditional social structures underpinning the Hindu-derived property law regime on the basis of the constitutional definition of Nepal as a Hindu kingdom under the 1990 Constitution.[103]

[98] *Jyoti Poudel v Office of the Prime Minister*, 2067, 52 *NKP* 1903 (2010).
[99] *Raju Chapagai v Office of the Prime Minister*, 2065, 50 *NKP* 823 (2008).
[100] *Mira Dhungana v Ministry of Law and Justice* (Writ N. 2068-WS-0046 of year 2068), decided in 2069 BS (2012).
[101] The tenets of this property and inheritance system are contained in the *Mitākṣarā*, a legal commentary on the *Yājñavalkya-smṛti* from the 11th century AD.
[102] *Mira Dhungana v Ministry of Law and Justice*, 2052, 37 *NKP* 462 (1995).
[103] *Canda Bajracarya v Secretariat of Parliament*, 2053, 38 *NKP* 537 (1996).

These early cases played a crucial role in generating public debate over these issues. In 2002, Nepal's parliament passed the *Muluki Ain* (11th Amendment) Act to redress different forms of gender discrimination. In the post-2002 case law on women's property rights, the Supreme Court became progressively bolder, testing the effectiveness of the Amendment and invalidating discriminatory legislation.[104] After the promulgation of the 2007 interim constitution and the passing of the Gender Equality Act 2006, more cases on women's property rights reached the Supreme Court, with pro-women judicial activism increasing.[105] However, the 2011 Census revealed that women in only 19.71 per cent of Nepal's households enjoyed ownership over land and property.[106] The new 2017 Civil Code embraced equality between sons and daughters in matters of family property in line with the 2015 Constitution. In the end, the new Code did not adopt a will system as a result of women's rights activists' campaigns against it; they worried that deep-seated patriarchal notions of property and inheritance would continue to discriminate against women and exclude them from wills.[107]

In family law matters, Nepali legislation was also peppered with gender-based forms of discrimination. Since the 2002 reforms, activist lawyers succeeded at dislodging many of these provisions via constitutional litigation. These included different legal treatment for men and women in cases of bigamy,[108] in obtaining a dissolution of marriage on the basis of the spouse's infertility (only available to men),[109] in the minimum legal age to enter a marriage (higher for women),[110] and to remarry if the spouse was affected by an incurable venereal disease or serious mental disability (only available to men).[111] While the Supreme Court relied on international law to declare a violation of the constitutional right to equality in cases involving these issues, it has not challenged the cultural patriarchal norms underpinning the offending provisions and has largely deferred to the executive for further reform.

The legal treatment of dowry offers interesting insights into the status of women within the private sphere. A widespread yet criminalised social practice across South Asia, dowry reflects the inferior position of women in the family. As such, dowry echoes a gender-based structural social imbalance, requiring

[104] *Mira Dhungana v Office of the Prime Minister*, 2061, 46 *NKP* 377 (2004); *Sapana Pradhan Malla v Ministry of Law and Justice*, 2061, 46 *NKP* 387 (2004); *Prakash Mani Sharma v Office of the Prime Minister*, 2062, 47 *NKP* 931 (2005); *Lily Thapa v Office of the Prime Minister*, 2062, 47 *NKP* 1054 (2005); *Mira Dhungana v Ministry of Law and Justice*, 2063a, 48 *NKP* 979 (2006).

[105] See, for instance, *FWLD v Office of the Prime Minister*, 2069, 56 *NKP* 1534 (2012).

[106] International Organisation for Migration, 'Barriers to Women's Land and Property Access and Ownership in Nepal' (1 September 2016) ii.

[107] RK Kamat, 'New Civil Code Gives Women Reason to Rejoice' *The Himalayan Times* (26 August 2018), available at thehimalayantimes.com/kathmandu/new-civil-code-gives-women-reason-to-rejoice.

[108] *Chandra Kanta Gyawali v Office of the Prime Minister*, 2061, 46 *NKP* 1418 (2004).

[109] *Mira Dhungana v Office of the Prime Minister*, 2063b, 48 *NKP* 6 (2006).

[110] *Sapana Pradhan Malla v Office of the Prime Minister*, 2063, 48 *NKP* 289 (2006).

[111] *Sapana Pradhan Malla v Office of the Prime Minister*, 2065, 50 *NKP* 917 (2008).

extra 'material support' for women – a sort of insurance premium the bride's family must pay to secure the bride's future and a form of compensation to the groom's family for taking in the bride. Nepal's Supreme Court has invalidated the provision of the Social Behaviour and Reform Act 1976 discriminating between the bride's side and the groom's side in the punishment for giving and demanding dowry,[112] and ordered the Government to introduce legislative reforms on dowry regulation, increase the criminal sanctions for dowry-related offences, and ensure implementation both to deter and eradicate the practice.[113] The Court condemned the dowry as a social evil, but never addressed the root causes of the problem, ie the cultural taboo of the unmarried woman, and the social imperative of securing an appropriate matrimonial match *at all costs*.

E. Gender and Cultural and Religious Practices

The Supreme Court has approached Nepal's cultural practices harmful to women through the lenses of selective modernisation and development. It has ruled that the victimisation of women on the basis of allegations of witchcraft[114] and for *chaupadi* (ie the confinement of rural Hindu rural women to a cowshed or hut outside of the household after childbirth and during menstruation because they are considered ritually polluting, which exposes them to a severe risk of sexual violence and attacks by animals) are forms of superstition that must be eliminated.[115] The Court has unequivocally condemned these practices using the modern language of enlightenment and rights, and instructed the Government to introduce legislation to eradicate such practices, which nonetheless continue unabated.

With respect to the treatment of Hindu widows, who are traditionally shunned by society, the Court in an early decision justified the gender-based discrimination between a widow and a widower in light of religious traditions and the different status they hold within society.[116] Later judgments displayed a reformist approach and recognised the stigma attached to widows in Nepali society.[117] This culminated with the *Pro-Public* judgment, where the Supreme Court condemned the hardship and prejudice that widows face in Nepal, and ordered the Government to provide a monetary allowance to widows from the date of their husband's death.[118] While the Court sought to rectify this harm through redistributive measures, it did little in its reasoning to challenge

[112] *Mira Dhungana, v Office of the Prime Minister*, 2063c, 48 *NKP* 972 (2006).

[113] *Jyoti Lamsan Poudel v Office of the Prime Minister*, 2069, 54 *NKP* 1315 (2012).

[114] *Reshma Thapa v Office of the Prime Minister*, 2062, 47 *NKP* 205 (2005).

[115] *Dil Bahadur Bishwakarma v Office of the Prime Minister* (Writ No 3303 of year 2061), decided in 2062 BS (2005).

[116] *Tara Devi Poudel v Cabinet Secretariat*, 2058, 43 *NKP* 375 (2001).

[117] *Kavita Pandey v Government of Nepal*, 2067, 52 *NKP* 1128 (2010).

[118] *Pro-Public v Office of the Prime Minister*, 2069, 54 *NKP* 1534 (2012).

the religious roots of the practice and sidestepped the question of the harsh treatment of widows in many currents of Hinduism.

This selective approach is most evident in the 2008 Supreme Court decision on the rights of the Kumaris of the Kathmandu Valley – the child goddesses from the Newar community enthroned as a living incarnation of a deity until their first menstruation.[119] The most famous Kumari is the Royal Kumari of Kathmandu, who is considered an incarnation of Taleju, a manifestation of the Hindu goddess Durga. Traditionally the Royal Kumari has been associated with the protection of the monarchy and has become a crucial symbol of the Nepali nation. The petitioner alleged that the custom entails gross violations of these children's rights as the girls suffer from extreme restrictions of movement and receive very little funding from the Government. The Supreme Court, however, refused to label the practice as discriminatory and described it as essential to both Hindu and Buddhist worshippers, and to the social, cultural and religious life of the nation in line with long-standing forms of constitutional nationalism.[120]

F. Gender and the Market

Nepal's Supreme Court has adopted a modern and radically egalitarian approach to women's place in the market. An early example of this approach is the 2000 case of *Rina Bajracariya*, a petition alleging discrimination on the basis of gender in the retirement age of the employees of the Royal Nepal Airlines Corporation (RNAC).[121] The Court invalidated the offending legislation, holding that men and women are both entitled to fundamental rights in an equal manner and lambasting the Government for not removing legal barriers to gender equality. Here, the Court also espoused the modern capitalist logic of meritocracy in which discrimination is treated as an economic inefficiency to be corrected. Moreover, the judicial reasoning also reveals an association between gender equality and constitutional identity. Relying on international standards, the Court differentiated between the countries that adopt the principle of gender equality as civilised and humane and those that reject it as uncivilised and underdeveloped. The Court also explicitly associated the freedom of women with the dawn of democracy in Nepal, linking it to post-1990 developments and harnessing the legitimacy bestowed by cosmopolitan constitutionalism.

[119] *Pun Devi Maharjan v Government of Nepal* (Writ No 3581 of year 2062), decided in 2065 *BS* (2008).

[120] C Letizia, 'The Goddess Kumari at the Supreme Court: Divine Kinship and Secularism in Nepal' (2013) 67 *Focaal* 32.

[121] *Rina Bajracarya v HMG Council of Ministers*, 2057, 42 *NKP* 376 (2000).

In the end, Nepal's Supreme Court succeeded in promoting a more equal playing field for women in the workplace outside of the family by combining a strict approach to non-discrimination with a modicum of redistributive measures. This approach was also deployed in later discrimination cases. To support the advancement of women in the public sector, the Supreme Court ordered the Government to streamline the length of the probation period for female civil service employees.[122] Similarly, the Court struck down as violating the right to equality the rule of the Royal Nepal Army discontinuing the allowance to daughters of service men after their marriage.[123] On the same basis, the Supreme Court invalidated a Military and Police Regulation permitting only unmarried women to join the force – a rule with no counterpart for men.[124] The Court declared in unequivocal and consistent terms that once women step out of the family and into the labour market the constitutional right to equality mandates non-discrimination on the basis of gender and equal economic treatment between men and women. Gender equality in the labour market has been framed as a necessary precondition for economic development and modernisation among civilised nations.

V. FLAGSHIP CONSTITUTIONAL DEVELOPMENTS: SEXUAL AND REPRODUCTIVE RIGHTS

Sexual and reproductive rights constitute Nepal's flagship development in terms of gender constitutionalism, because while enormous strides have been made since 2002, constitutional implementation remains extremely weak due to the ethno-nationalist patriarchal ideology underpinning this legal framework. The umbrella term 'sexual and reproductive rights' denotes the constitutional and legal frameworks encompassing the issues of abortion, contraception, sexual health, maternal health, surrogacy, sterilisation, sex education and education supporting informed reproductive decisions. The nature of these rights, their extent and degree of implementation represent politically contested terrain. In practice, deeply patriarchal social mores have for centuries shaped the legal structures regulating reproduction and sexuality. These mores are couched in ethno-nationalist language where 'women are constructed as biological reproducers of "the nation"'.[125] Legal frameworks across the world have been designed to maintain control over women's bodies, preserve patriarchal social hierarchies, and reinforce the gender binary and monogamous heteronormative relationships. Over the last few decades, many social movements have

[122] *Pro-Public v Office of the Prime Minister*, 2063, 48 *NKP* 1 (2006).
[123] *Mira Dhungana v Office of the Prime Minister*, 2064, 49 *NKP* 972 (2007).
[124] *Sapana Pradhan Malla v Office of the Prime Minister*, 2066, 51 *NKP* 1089 (2009).
[125] N Yuval-David, 'Women and the Biological Reproduction of "the Nation"' (1996) 19 *Women's Studies International Forum* 17, 22.

campaigned for legal reforms emphasising individual well-being in matters of sexuality and reproduction. As a result, the constitutional arena has become a crucial battleground not just to safeguard individual autonomy, but also to change societal narratives about sexuality and reproduction, foreground the notion of dignity, and actualise this expanding set of rights.

In the context of Nepal, the focus on the constitutional treatment of sexual and reproductive rights illuminates *both* the issue of poor constitutional implementation of policy (ie the enduring gap between 'law in books' and 'law in action' within a generally progressive constitutional framework) *and* the overt clashes between the increasingly cosmopolitan constitutional vision of the higher judiciary and the political branches' translation of these rights into law (which has remained to a great extent wedded to deeply ethno-national patriarchal views of women's role in society and in the family). The tensions in the realisation of sexual and reproductive rights in Nepal are explained by the intimate yet fraught relationship between gender constitutionalism and nation-building narratives in two ways.

First, the articulation of sexual and reproductive rights in the constitutional domain and in ordinary laws sheds light on the gendered way of imagining the nation. In this context, women's subordination translates into the assumption that women's primary functions continue to be biological reproduction and care work. As such, these functions have been idealised, but also brutally patrolled through coercive legal means. Nepal is a case in point. Alongside an inadequate system of sexual and reproductive health services,[126] the country featured one of the world's most restrictive abortion regimes with pregnancy terminations criminalised under most circumstances.[127] In 2000, an estimated 20 per cent of the country's female inmates were incarcerated due to abortion and infanticide offences.[128] Moreover, before 2002, approximately half of all maternal deaths resulted from unsafe abortions, and women were consistently imprisoned for terminating their pregnancies.[129] The control by legal means of individuals' sexuality and women's reproductive choices is central to the ideological construction *and* the biological reproduction of the national community itself. In 2002, after sustained campaigning, the legislature finally amended the *Muluki Ain* to legalise abortion partially.[130] Constitutional change and legal

[126] PR Regmi, E van Teijlingen, P Simkhada and DR Acharya, 'Barriers to Sexual Health Services for Young People in Nepal' (2010) 28 *Journal of Health, Population and Nutrition* 619, 620.

[127] Abortion was criminalised under the 1963 *Muluki Ain*'s Chapter on Crimes against Human Life (ch 10, s 28).

[128] M Upreti, 'Towards Transformative Equality in Nepal: The *Lakshmi Dhikta* Decision' in RJ Cook, JN Erdman and BM Dickens (eds), *Abortion Law in Transnational Perspective* (University of Pennsylvania Press, 2014) 284.

[129] ibid 280.

[130] In 2002, the 11th Amendment of the *Muluki Ain* introduced s 28(b) providing several statutory exceptions to the criminalisation of abortion, such as abortion within 12 weeks of gestation with the consent of the pregnant woman, and where the life or the physical and mental health of the pregnant woman is at risk.

reforms in this area continue to face enormous obstacles as the long-standing campaign for reproductive rights in Nepal demonstrates. Reforms have been opposed as more or less direct assaults on the established social, moral and religious order – which are themselves constructed in a profoundly gendered way – and ultimately treated as an existential threat to the nation.

Second, more recent constitutions feature an increasing number of fundamental rights in line with international norms and standards – some of which expressly recognise sexual and reproductive rights. The promulgation of Nepal's 2007 interim Constitution marked a further shift towards reproductive justice by explicitly recognising sexual and reproductive rights, a feature retained by the current 2015 Constitution. The clear constitutional underpinning of reproductive rights in Nepal allowed for growing constitutional litigation in this area and the building of an impressive body of pro-women case law – now, at least on paper, one of the most progressive in the world. Moreover, Nepal's Supreme Court has increasingly relied on international instruments like CEDAW, the decisions of supranational courts, and best-practice examples from other jurisdictions to advance gender equality claims. Activists, in turn, have successfully deployed international standards to advance sexual and reproductive rights domestically. However, they have also been confronted repeatedly with strains of constitutional nationalism hindering such progress at all levels of governance. State actors often deploy the nationalist rhetoric of traditional culture and religion to legitimise deeply patriarchal and sexist attitudes. In fact, both the new 2017 Penal Code and 2018 Safe Motherhood and Reproductive Health Rights Act continue to criminalise abortion outside of the limited circumstances in which it is permitted. To make matters worse, access to medical care and services remains abysmal – a clear conflict with the many decisions by the Supreme Court.

A. Sexual and Reproductive Rights: Constitutional Framing and Litigation

Successful political lobbying brought significant legislative changes to sexual and reproductive rights in Nepal in 2002, opening the way to extensive constitutional litigation in this area. Since then, the Supreme Court has consistently prioritised the protection of women's bodily independence and reproductive decisions through an expansive interpretation of the constitutional rights to life and equality. In an early 2005 case, the Supreme Court tested the legislative reforms and directed the Government to amend sentencing laws for abortion-related crimes that distinguished between pregnant women and facilitators.[131] In 2008, an anti-abortion petitioner claimed that Nepal's abortion laws discriminate against Nepali men because the husband's consent to the procedure was not required.

[131] *Sapana Pradhan Malla v Office of the Prime Minister*, 2062, 47 NKP 10 (2005).

The Court, however, dismissed the petition, construing women's reproductive rights as part of women's right to life under the 1990 Constitution.[132]

The political pressure brought on the Government by these cases led to further legislative reforms. In 2006, the Gender Equality Act amended section 28 of the *Muluki Ain*, creating an exception to the criminalisation of abortion up to 18 weeks of gestation in cases of rape or incest. Another radical change took place in 2007 with the promulgation of the interim constitution, which specifically recognised as justiciable women's right to reproductive health under Article 20(2). This move gave the Supreme Court an even greater role in defining and patrolling both the extent and the implementation of these rights.

Activists immediately seized the opportunity for further strategic litigation. In 2008 the Supreme Court rendered the first comprehensive and groundbreaking decision on the remit of these new constitutional rights in *Prakash Mani Sharma*, a PIL case involving the issue of uterus prolapse. The Court placed positive obligations on the state to actualise these rights and issued an order of *mandamus* to the Government to secure medical treatment for women affected by uterus prolapse.[133] The Supreme Court grounded its decision in domestic constitutional provisions and read them in line with Nepal's international obligations by drawing on an array of comparative constitutional material. As a result, the Court construed reproductive and health rights broadly to encompass women's decisions regarding reproduction, abortion, voluntary marriage, child rearing and freedom from sexual violence. Adopting the same approach in later cases, the Supreme Court ordered the Government to protect the reproductive rights of female prisoners, furthering an intersectional understanding of these rights and highlighting the importance of securing access to these services across society.[134]

In 2010, the Supreme Court issued a landmark judgment in the case of *Lakshmi*, in which abortion rights were deemed to be at the core of sexual and reproductive rights and integral to the right against discrimination and the right to equality.[135] A poor woman from rural Far Western Nepal became pregnant for the sixth time. In agreement with her husband, she decided to terminate the pregnancy due to her poor health and financial constraints. She then approached a public hospital to obtain an abortion but could not afford the fee of NPR 1,130 (roughly US$14.5) for the procedure. As a result, Lakshmi was forced to continue her unwanted pregnancy. In 2007, a coalition of activist lawyers filed a PIL petition on her behalf in the Supreme Court. Three years later, the Court rendered one of the world's most comprehensive, thoughtful and groundbreaking judgments on sexual and reproductive rights and abortion.

[132] *Achyut Kharel v Office of the Prime Minister* (Writ No 3352 of year 2061), decided in 2065 BS (2008).

[133] *Prakash Mani Sharma v Office of the Prime Minister* (Writ No 064-WS-0230 of year 2064), decided in 2066 BS (2009).

[134] *Prakash Mani Sharma v Office of the Prime Minister*, 2065, 50 *NKP* 412 (2008); *Jang Bahadur Singh v Office of the Prime Minister*, 2068, 53 *NKP* 986 (2011).

[135] *Lakshmi v Office of the Prime Minister*, 2067, 52 *NKP* 1551 (2010).

Building on the explicit recognition of reproductive rights in the text of the 2007 interim Constitution, the Supreme Court interpreted these provisions broadly and placed a direct obligation on the state to provide access to safe and free abortion services. It held that abortion equates to the right to self-determination for women and as such it holds a special place within reproductive rights. It clearly stated that a woman is the master of her own body and must have the final word in deciding whether to have sexual relations, when to give birth to a child, and how to use her body. The Court also held that the criminalisation of abortion disproportionally impacts women, and that abortion should be entirely decriminalised. More specifically, it ruled that it was inappropriate to criminalise abortion, and especially to do so under the *Muluki Ain*'s Chapter on Crimes against Human Life since under Nepali law the foetus is not classified as human life. Thus, the foetus cannot be granted more importance than the protection of the physical and mental health of the mother. The Court concluded that a forced pregnancy and a forced continuation of pregnancy constitute violence against women. Upreti convincingly argued that the Supreme Court adopted here a radical notion of transformative equality.[136] The Court held that a constitutional right or a benefit provided by law must not be limited to a certain group of people or a particular class. In fact, gender interlocks not only with class, but also with other identity-based forms of social differentiation such as caste, ethnicity, language, religion, region, sexuality, age and disability. In *Lakshmi*, the Supreme Court veered towards an inclusive and substantive notion of gender equality anchored in an intersectional understanding of gender oppression.

Two decades of activism on the front of sexual and reproductive rights bore fruit also in the making of Nepal's permanent constitution. The 2015 Constitution followed the approach of the previous interim constitution and enshrined the right to safe motherhood and reproductive health under Article 38(2). The constitutional entrenchment of sexual and reproductive rights significantly gives the higher judiciary an explicit mandate to protect and enforce these rights. It also seeks to insulate and protect these rights from potential interference by the political branches, ultimately acknowledging the precarious and politically contingent nature of these advancements and the deep anxiety about their potential displacement. In line with the new Constitution and previous jurisprudence, the Supreme Court has so far maintained a coherent stance and prioritised a radical notion of equality in matters of sexual and reproductive rights geared to secure enforcement across different social groups. For instance, in 2017 the Court ruled that the Government is obliged to provide access to information about contraception and related services across the country, especially in remote areas and to marginalised groups.[137]

[136] Upreti (n 128) 287.

[137] *Manju Tamang v Government of Nepal* (Writ No 070-WO-0194 of year 2070), decided in 2074 *BS* (2017).

This expanding body of jurisprudence highlights the importance of acknowledging the economic, socio-cultural, political and geographic barriers that individuals face in accessing their sexual and reproductive rights in Nepal. First, the Supreme Court has become incredibly sensitive to the highly diverse and profoundly unequal socio-economic context in which these rights operate in Nepal. While grounding their reasoning in comparative jurisprudence, the Court has emphasised the crucial importance of focusing on domestic intersectional inequalities in terms of class, caste, ethnicity, religion and, of course, gender. More specifically, it has moved beyond the *Roe v Wade* approach that privileges autonomy over equality and adopted the notion of dignity combined with freedom and autonomy to realise substantive equality.

Second, Nepal's Supreme Court has underlined the crucial importance of placing positive obligations on the state to implement sexual and reproductive rights. The focus on removing the barriers of access to such services, especially for those of marginalised backgrounds, also entails an ideological shift. This body of case law no longer conceptualises the state as a neutral actor that must step aside to respect individual autonomy; the state must now fulfil an active role in the realisation of sexual and reproductive rights. In constitutional terms, this shift translates into a greater role of the higher judiciary in overseeing executive actions within the scope of these rights. However, the distinction between the courts' supervisory jurisdiction and outright policy intervention via judicial route now becomes ever more contested.[138]

B. Sexual and Reproductive Rights: Legislative Responses

Following the promulgation of the new Constitution in 2015, Nepal has undertaken extensive statutory reforms in the area of sexual and reproductive rights. The new legislative framework, however, retains an array of problematic features, especially in criminal matters that require further change to achieve true gender justice.

Nepal's Parliament did not follow the recommendations of the Supreme Court in the case of *Lakshmi* to decriminalise abortion entirely. With limited exceptions under section 15 of the Safe Motherhood and Reproductive Health Rights Act of 2018, abortion remains a criminal offence under section 188 of Nepal's new Penal Code.[139] Section 15 provides for lawful abortion under the following circumstance:

(a) Foetus (gestation) up to twelve weeks, with the consent of the pregnant woman;

[138] M Malagodi, 'Intersectional Inequalities and Reproductive Rights: An India-Nepal Comparison' (2020) 3 *University of Oxford Human Rights Hub Journal* 195.
[139] Country Penal (Code) Act 2017.

(b) Foetus (gestation) up to twenty-eight weeks, as per the consent of such woman, after the opinion of the licensed doctor that there may be danger upon the life of the pregnant woman or her physical or mental health may deteriorate or disabled infant may be born in case the abortion is not performed;
(c) Foetus (gestation) remained due to rape or incest, foetus (gestation) up to twenty-eight weeks with the consent of the pregnant woman;
(d) Foetus (gestation) up to twenty-eight weeks with the consent of the woman who is suffering from H.I.V. or other incurable disease of such nature;
(e) Foetus (gestation) up to twenty eight weeks with the consent of the woman, as per the opinion of the health worker involved in the treatment that damage may occur in the womb due to defects occurred in the foetus (gestation), or that there is such defect in the foetus of the womb that it cannot live even after the birth, that there is condition of disability in the foetus (gestation) due to genetic defect or any other cause.

Significantly, this new legislation goes against the Supreme Court's decision in *Lakshmi*, in which the court clearly stated that abortion should be entirely decriminalised. The text of the 2015 Constitution does not mention abortion anywhere and it will be up to the Supreme Court to construe the scope and extent of sexual and reproductive rights and the place of abortion within this framework. However, constitutional litigation demanding the complete decriminalisation of abortion both for pregnant women and service providers is already under way in the Constitutional Bench of the Supreme Court.[140] Moreover, Nepal has been urged to decriminalise abortion both by the CEDAW Committee in 2018 and during the Universal Periodic Review in 2021.[141]

In line with the Supreme Court's recommendation in *Lakshmi*, Nepal's Parliament enacted in 2018 the Safe Motherhood and Reproductive Health Rights Act to implement the constitutionally protected rights surrounding sexual and reproductive health.[142] The statute places extensive positive obligations on the state to provide citizens with: education, information, counselling and services relating to sexual and reproductive health under section 3(1); obstetric service and care under sections 5 and 6; newborn care under sections 7 and 8; family planning and contraception under sections 11 and 12; safe abortion under sections 15 and 16; and morbidity care under section 20. The aim of this legislation is to translate sexual and reproductive rights, framed as a social right in the constitutional text, into action on the ground. The effects of this legislation are yet to be seen, but access to services remains difficult, especially in more remote areas due to the COVID-19 pandemic.

[140] *Bandana Upreti and Samana Kafle v Government of Nepal* (Writ No 077 of year 2077 *BS*), petition filed on 7 March 2021.
[141] Centre for Reproductive Rights, 'Decriminalisation of Abortion in Nepal: Imperative to Uphold Women's Rights' (1 June 2021), available at reproductiverights.org/decriminalization-of-abortion-in-nepal-imperative-to-uphold-womens-rights.
[142] Safe Motherhood and Reproductive Health Rights Act 2018.

VI. CONCLUSION

The central argument put forward in this chapter is that the profound contradiction at the heart of Nepal's constitutional framework in matters of gender equality, the tensions in constitutional adjudication on women's and SGDP rights, and weak enforcement are explained by the patriarchal way in which the Nepali nation has been historically imagined, construed and institutionalised in legal terms over the years. However, the enduring gender-based discrimination in matters of citizenship ought not to be read simply as a stain on an otherwise progressive document to be explained away by the peculiarities of Nepal's geo-strategic position and justified by the fact that other countries feature similar discriminatory citizenship regimes. The provisions on citizenship in Nepal's new Constitution reflect a long-standing exclusionary view of the Nepali nation in which gender plays an integral role in its creation and upkeep. These enduring forms of constitutional nationalism explain why this framework proved impossible to remove even with the extensive international assistance Nepal received during the constitution-making process.

Perhaps the most accurate assessment of the country's most recent Constitution in terms of gender justice is one that situates it at the intersection of competing political claims reflected *both* in the ambiguities and contradictions of the constitutional text *and* the ideological opposition to prioritising women's and SGDP rights. The advancement of gender constitutionalism in Nepal has been hindered by the path-dependent, gendered way in which the Nepali nation has been historically imagined, construed and crystallised into the country's constitutional framework and legal system over the years. More specifically, enduring forms of constitutional nationalism and the tensions with forms of cosmopolitan constitutionalism explain the profound contradictions in terms of gender equality at the centre of Nepal's constitutional discourse. In particular, the treatment of sexual and reproductive rights reflects the political branches' selective approach to constitutional compliance and a patriarchal vision of the nation centred on biological reproduction. In this context, the courts have played a pivotal role in advancing gender constitutionalism as they embrace a more intersectional understanding of discrimination and a cosmopolitan approach to gender equality. A more inclusive Nepal can emerge in the constitutional sphere and beyond only if the political branches amend the provisions on citizenship to eliminate any form of discrimination and translate the broader constitutional commitments to gender justice into compliant legislation and policy to achieve substantive equality.

12

Constitutionalism and Gender in Pakistan: A Counter-patriarchal Struggle

SADAF AZIZ, ANGBEEN ATIF MIRZA AND CRISTÓBAL ALVEAR-GARIJO

I. INTRODUCTION: THE FOUNDATIONS OF A PATRIARCHAL MAJORITARIANISM IN THE PAKISTANI CONSTITUTIONALISM

THE STUDY OF gender and constitutionalism in Pakistan can yield far greater analysis about the erasure of substantial populations – women of religious and ethnic minority communities, sexually diverse people or people living in conditions of material impoverishment – than about the emergence of female citizen-subjects. The academic exercise done in this chapter by piecing together evidence of women's acknowledgment in the law is not to efface the denial of an equivalent recognition to other persons and populations. While patriarchal colonial and indigenous practices converted women into a minoritised group legally disregarded irrespective of being half of the population, post-independence political and social majoritarianism has progressively promoted the exclusion of all communities beyond Muslim males from the centre of the state. Women and minorities have partaken since then in a counter-majoritarian struggle for upholding their rights in a constitutional environment shaped by inconsistent jurisprudence and the slow reform of laws by the Centre and the provinces.

The patriarchal roots of the Pakistani legal system can be traced back to colonial and customary laws that were mostly detrimental to the position of women within family and society. Prominent Muslim women championed the idea in pre-independence times that a purer Islam, detached from customary interpretations, could effectively restore their rights,[1] lending their support first

[1] J Everett, '"All the Women Were Hindu and All the Muslims Were Men": State, Identity Politics and Gender, 1917–1951' (2001) 36 *Economic and Political Weekly* 2071, 2076.

to The Shariat Application Act 1937 and then to The Muslim Dissolution of Marriage Act 1939.[2] Nonetheless, colonial law gave little space for the advancement of rights from a gender and sexual perspective, particularly in the case of those communities shunned from within Victorian moral codes. Among them, *hijras* and *khawaja sira*,[3] present in the Indian subcontinent for centuries, were neither understood nor accepted by the British colonisers. This colonial rejection of the transgender community brought about an 'anti-*hijra* campaign' to complete their legal and social annihilation, making them suffer together with sexually diverse people by the criminalisation of the so-called unnatural offences under section 377 of The Indian Penal Code 1860 and later proscribing them under The Criminal Tribes Act 1871.[4]

Pakistani women, acknowledged as a rising force since pre-independence times, formed an initial coalition of interest with political and religious organisations and played a dynamic role in the early stages of state development. The mobilisation of women during the end of colonial times has been seen as a call for women to emerge from the observance of purdah – female seclusion – for the ends of engaging in political activity 'as symbols of a special Muslim identity'.[5] This participation, limited to economically privileged women who enjoyed elite accommodation within the apparatus of government and rule, led to certain developments in early independence times such as the progressive Muslim Family Laws Ordinance (MFLO) 1961 that safeguarded the protection of Muslim women within the Islamic family law system. The effects of women's demands for their rights and their attempts to access power gradually disengaged women both from the dominant governmental and religious actors. The mainly elite-oriented participation of women in the first decades turned into a more activist and feminist involvement concomitant with the anti-establishment, counter-majoritarian unrest witnessed in later times.

Despite the initial cross-sectional covenant under a nation-building agenda, Pakistan has witnessed a continuous tension between secular and religious dynamics in its constitution-making since its independence in 1947. The first constituent assembly, which was dissolved in 1954 without producing a

[2] S Ansari, 'Polygamy, Purdah and Political Representation: Engendering Citizenship in 1950s Pakistan' (2009) 43 *Modern Asian Studies* 1421, 1435.

[3] The Urdu term *khawaja sira* – as in the spelling followed by the Transgender Persons (Protection of Rights) Act, 2018 – was used to identify those transgender individuals that served as harem guards, state officials or military commanders during the Muslim Mughal court. Despite their legal status being equivalent to slavery, they played important roles in administrative matters and court affairs. See J Hinchy, 'The Sexual Politics of Imperial Expansion: Eunuchs and Indirect Colonial Rule in Mid-Nineteenth-Century North India' (2014) 26 *Gender & History* 414.

[4] J Hinchy, *Governing Gender and Sexuality in Colonial India: The Hijra, c.1850–1900* (Cambridge University Press, 2019) 93-109.

[5] A Jalal, 'The Convenience of Subservience: Women and the State of Pakistan' in D Kandiyoti (ed), *Women, Islam and the State* (Temple University Press, 1991) 84. See also K Mumtaz and F Shaheed, *Women of Pakistan: Two Steps Forward, One Step Back?* (Zed Books, 1987) 7 and 45; D Willmer, 'Women as Participants in the Pakistan Movement: Modernization and the Promise of a Moral State' (1996) 30 *Modern Asian Studies* 573, 577-79.

constitution, achieved the adoption of the Objectives Resolution in 1949 that situated Islam as a potential 'supraconstitutional source of legitimacy'.[6] The 1956 Constitution founded the Islamic Republic of Pakistan and the attempt of state secularism made by 1962 Constitution was just a year later rectified through its first amendment.[7] Although the 1973 Constitution also enshrined Islam as the state religion, Islamic provisions cohabitated with secular rights and existing liberal reforms, such as the MFLO, the latter intended to be protected from judicial review through the unchallenged position of laws included in the First Schedule[8] to the 1973 Constitution.[9]

The fragile Pakistani democracy, founded on a parliamentarian system, a broad federalism and the independence of the judiciary, continuously faced undemocratic usurpations by the military. The army-led establishment used religion in the late 1970s and during the 1980s as a legitimising force for curtailing democracy by luring the conservative sections of society with the restriction of the rights of women and minorities under a conservative interpretation of *Shariat*. This period of unstable constitutionalism, that allowed militant patriarchy to run rampant and placed women outside systems of recognition for some time, was not an easy field for furthering women's rights.

Couched in this religious legitimation, General Zia-ul-Haq passed a collection of Islamic laws, created a parallel judicial structure – comprised of the Federal Shariat Court and the Shariat Appellate Branch of the Supreme Court – and incorporated to the 1973 Constitution via Article 2-A the Objectives Resolution as the *grundnorm* 'to unequivocally redefine the ethos of the Constitution as non-secular',[10] although the Supreme Court has later stated that the principles of the Objectives Resolution cannot be invoked for striking down any other constitutional provision.[11] Within this Islamisation drive, the Hudood Ordinances were the most damaging laws, creating a terrain of impunity for those perpetrating sexual violence against women and a punitive environment for women survivors of such violence. The setback caused in the equality and non-discrimination system granted by the 1973 Constitution and the use of Islam made by courts to curtail women's rights at first was over time counterbalanced in certain areas with an Islamic human rights jurisprudence.[12]

[6] M Waseem, 'Constitutionalism and Extra-Constitutionalism in Pakistan' in M Tushnet and M Khosla (eds), *Unstable Constitutionalism: Law and Politics in South Asia* (Cambridge University Press, 2015) 148.

[7] The Constitution (First Amendment) Act (1963), Art 3.

[8] The First Schedule to the Constitution lists laws to be exempt from rights review under Art 8(1)–(2).

[9] MJ Nelson, 'Inheritance Unbound: The Politics of Personal Law Reform in Pakistan and India' in S Khilnani, V Raghavan and AK Thiruvengadam (eds), *Comparative Constitutionalism in South Asia* (Oxford University Press, 2016) 225-27.

[10] O Siddique, *Pakistan's Experience with Formal Law: An Alien Justice* (Cambridge University Press, 2014) 233.

[11] *Hakim Khan v Government of Pakistan*, PLD [1992] SC 595.

[12] M Lau, *The Role of Islam in the Legal System of Pakistan* (Martinus Nijhoff, 2006) 209-11.

The extreme erosions of fundamental rights experienced by women in Pakistan during Zia's rule had the consequence of fostering a commitment to a feminist internationalism, and this has had a profound impact on the landscape of Pakistani jurisprudence. Whereas Pakistan follows the doctrine of dualism as the implementation of international treaties falls under the domain of Parliament,[13] since Pakistan's accession in 1996 to the Convention on the Elimination of All Forms of Discrimination Against Women (CEDAW) some pieces of legislation have been aligned with both a jurisprudence promoting gender equality and a broad global gender justice agenda. The progress achieved by Pakistan on criminal law, equal access for women to voting registration or the protection for victims of acid and burn attacks have been recently saluted by the Committee on the Elimination of Discrimination Against Women (CEDAW Committee).[14]

Among these legal developments, some of the provinces[15] have adopted regulations on domestic violence and sexual harassment at the workplace[16] with the purpose of confronting the elevated level of violence against women within families and communities, of which honour killings are one of the most atrocious exemplifications. Far-reaching challenges, however, persist in the Pakistani legal system from a gender perspective. There is a lack of any comprehensive equality legislation, including a statutory regime of human rights for the protection of the private sphere. Furthermore, the insulation of family law as law of religious communities since colonial times has avoided the review of such laws against the touchstones of equality. While colonial and customary legislation with gender inequality provisions has partially endured, Islamic laws that were added to the criminal and civil procedures have been either statutorily amended or otherwise mediated by common law principles.

Recent years have also witnessed a debate between religious-based principles and the so-called Western rights. Conservative sections of society have supposedly seen international lobbying with an un-Islamic purpose behind the Aurat March (Women's March)[17] or The Transgender Persons (Protection of Rights) Act, 2018.[18] Interestingly, in the intersections of rights discourse and

[13] Constitution of the Islamic Republic of Pakistan (1973), Fourth Schedule: Legislative List, Part I: Federal Legislative List, 3: External affairs; the implementing of treaties and agreements (…).

[14] Committee on the Elimination of Discrimination against Women [hereinafter CEDAW Committee], 'Concluding observations on the fifth periodic report of Pakistan' (10–28 February 2020).

[15] Following the decentralisation of The Constitution (Eighteenth Amendment) Act, 2010, many of the areas related to equality and gender discrimination fall within the legislative purview of the provinces.

[16] For instance, in Balochistan: The Balochistan Domestic Violence (Prevention and Protection) Act (2014) and the Balochistan Protection Against Harassment of Women at the Workplace Act (2016).

[17] S Warraich, 'How dare they demand? *The News on Sunday* (8 March 2020), available at www.thenews.com.pk/tns/detail/624737-how-dare-they.

[18] N Iqbal, 'Transgender law not against Islamic code, Federal Shariat Court told' *Dawn* (4 March 2022), available at www.dawn.com/news/1678169.

through a rediscovery of *khawaja sira* as bearers of subcontinental heritage and Islamic values,[19] the transgender community has transitioned from invisibility and marginalisation to greater levels of recognition and protection despite the various forms of violence still suffered. However, this visibilisation has also situated them in a place of further contest wherein the postcolonial discourse of authentic *khawaja sira*, as distinct from the allegedly more Western constructed notion of gender and sexually diverse people, is being used to mediate and limit such protection.

Pakistani women have faced continuous challenges to own their place in a constitutional landscape shaped by patriarchy, religion, nationalism and class. The unstable Pakistani constitutionalism that has witnessed three constitutions and suffered four unlawful military regimes since independence has been a challenging environment for the full participation and equal treatment of women. Although principles of equality, non-discrimination, dignity and privacy were granted in the 1973 Constitution, jurisprudence was slow to elaborate fundamental rights from a gender perspective until recent times, and significant legal loopholes remain. Since then, key case law has fostered gender-centric legislation in domains where women were particularly legally mistreated, including adultery, rape and inheritance, and has positioned Pakistan at the forefront of countries around the world with certain legal milestones such as the right to a self-perceived gender identity.[20]

II. BACKGROUND: THE CONTESTED PARTICIPATION OF WOMEN IN THE NATION-BUILDING AND CONSTITUTION-MAKING

Women's activism in the anticolonial movements was broad-based but ultimately gave way to elite organisation amongst women who had a stronger tie to nation-building and statist consolidation. This women's movement, which found an initial understanding with political and religious powers within a broader nationalistic agenda, provided little room for a genuine women's rights agenda to develop. The emergence of international norms and transnational women's movements have recently infused intersectional and bottom-up dynamics, both in the awareness of women challenges and in the formation of stronger women's alliances, allowing women to find a reinvigorated place in the legal debate.

[19] A Jaffer, 'Spiritualising Marginality: Sufi Concepts and the Politics of Identity in Pakistan' (2017) 3 *Society and Culture in South Asia* 175, 182–83.

[20] Among the Council of Europe only nine Member States have a self-determination system while 38 states have a legal or administrative procedure to ensure legal gender recognition. See Steering Committee on Anti-Discrimination, Diversity and Inclusion (CDADI) of the Council of Europe, 'Thematic Report on Legal Gender Recognition in Europe: First thematic implementation review report on Recommendation CM/Rec(2010)5' (June 2022), available at rm.coe.int/thematic-report-on-legal-gender-recognition-in-europe-2022/1680a729b3.

In the early stage of the nation-building process, women's agency to collect, organise and operate in the spheres of welfare and social uplift was officially unfettered. The All Pakistan Women's Association (APWA) founded in 1949, a non-political organisation working for the social and educational progress of women, presented a charter for the economic rights of women to the first constituent assembly, a constituent body that included among the representatives who had been elected in the 1946 elections only two women.[21] The second constituent assembly, that finally enacted the short-lived 1956 Constitution, had no female representation at all.[22] Thereafter, not only did women's active participation in the political processes of the early state suffer reversal, but the conditions of statehood fostered a distinct orientation for the women's organisations that emerged in the post-independence era.[23]

The disclosing of Prime Minister Mohammad Ali Bogra's second marriage in 1955 led to widespread protests by many urban, educated women and the creation of the League for the Rights of Women as an offshoot of APWA, primarily to conduct an anti-polygamy campaign.[24] As a result of these protests, the Government was forced to appoint a Commission on Marriage and Family Laws comprised of four men and three women.[25] The report submitted by the commission in 1956, recommending laws relating to polygamy, divorce, maintenance and inheritance, was shelved due to the strong opposition of the *Ulema* (Islamic scholars). Following the suspension of the 1956 Constitution in 1958 and the appointment of General Ayub Khan as Chief Martial Law Administrator, the new regime was willing to counteract entrenched religious opposition in the service of enacting a modernising reformism.[26] This included the 1961 MFLO that passed some of the recommendations of the 1956 report made by the Commission on Marriage and Family Laws.[27]

The leadership amongst existing women's organisations at the time had deep filial associations with the Pakistani state and high office-holders in government, for whom concerns about national security were paramount. Historian Ayesha Jalal suggests that the restricted origins of this so-called feminist vanguard effectively provided a template for how women's issues came to

[21] S Khan, 'Women and State Laws and Policies in Pakistan: The Early Phase, 1947–77' (2013) 74 *Proceedings of the Indian History Congress* 726, 727.

[22] S Ansari, 'Winds of Change?: The Role of Women Activists in Lahore before and after Partition' (2008) 9 *Pakistan Vision* 1, 11.

[23] AA Malik, 'Gender and Nationalism: Political Awakening of Muslim Women of the Subcontinent in the 20th Century' (2017) 37 *Strategic Studies* 1, 8-12. See also Mumtaz and Shaheed (n 5) 47–48.

[24] Ansari (n 2) 1426-29.

[25] F Abbott, 'Pakistan's New Marriage Law: A Reflection of Qur'Anic Interpretation' (1962) 1 *Asian Survey* 26, 28.

[26] A Jalal, *The Struggle for Pakistan: A Muslim Homeland and Global Politics* (Harvard University Press, 2017) 111.

[27] R Saigol, *Feminism and the Women's Movement in Pakistan: Actors, Debates and Strategies* (Friedrich-Ebert-Stiftung, 2016) 11.

be articulated at the state level.[28] In other words, this is both a critique as well as a mere illustration of the seemingly endemic reversal to national liberation struggles and revolutionary nationalist movements, not only in Pakistan but also in other newly emergent countries. While female participation was often encouraged to build the movement, following the attainment of power, these governments sought to limit the independent women's organisations that 'might potentially challenge the authority of the state'.[29] Although airing demands on behalf of all women, these women belonging to the dominant classes generally avoided overstepping their class accommodations within the state.[30]

When Fatima Jinnah, the sister of Mohammed Ali Jinnah – pre-independence Muslim leader and founding father of Pakistan – consented to be the presidential candidate for the combined opposition in the 1965 elections, the dictator and incumbent President Ayub Khan used the *Ulema* to state that a woman could not be the head of state in a Muslim country, volleyed accusations on her being an agent of foreign powers and declared her an unfeminine and unmotherly figure.[31] In the ensuing showdown, Fatima Jinnah's steadfastness in facing down the gargantuan army machinery by referring to Ayub's regime as a dictatorship and citing the ways in which her brother's dream had been exploited propelled her beyond being a mere surrogate for her late brother to become the first female political leader in Pakistan, even though this army-controlled election was lost for Fatima Jinnah by a narrow margin.[32]

When in 1972 the Government of the Prime Minister Zulfiqar Ali Bhutto moved towards defining a new constitution, in the aftermath of the civil war that ended with the independence of East Pakistan (now Bangladesh) and the fall of Ayub's military successor, dictator Yahya Khan, in 1971, women's high political representation was ensured in the drafting committee that yielded an interim constitution in 1972. In this process, the bartering between religious parties, Bhutto's own progressive Pakistan People's Party and forces militating for greater regional representation in the Government dictated the blueprint for the coming 1973 Constitution.[33] As it turned out, both in the drafting and otherwise, Bhutto was unwilling to cede much space to the demands of women and in fact characterised such claims as 'peripheral' to the greater campaign of redressing class inequality and also, ultimately, retaining power.[34]

[28] Jalal (n 5) 79.
[29] Ansari (n 2) 1423.
[30] Jalal (n 5) 79.
[31] Saigol (n 27) 11. See also MR Pirbhai, *Fatima Jinnah: Mother of the Nation*, South Asia edn (Cambridge University Press, 2017) 226–27.
[32] L Ziring, 'Political Connections: Fatima Jinnah and Benazir Bhutto' (1994) 21 *Asian Affairs: An American Review* 67, 72.
[33] H Khan, *Constitutional and Political History of Pakistan* (3rd edn, Oxford University Press, 2017) 265-69.
[34] Khan (n 21) 730.

Dictator Zia-ul-Haq, who deposed Bhutto in 1977, used a legitimising rubric of Islamisation for his unlawful seizure of power.[35] Among the legislative measures taken, Zia introduced the Islamic laws of evidence – Qanun-e-Shahadat Order, 1984 – giving preponderant status to male testimony compared to female testimony in financial matters,[36] repealed sections of the MFLO on the age of marriage and on the second marriage of the husband being a ground for divorce[37] as well as the provision of the Code of Criminal Procedure 1898 on maintenance of wives and children.[38] Furthermore, in 1979 the offences of adultery and rape in the Pakistan Penal Code were repealed and punished since then through Hudood as *zina* (illicit sexual relations) and *zina bil-jabr* (illicit sexual relations made by force).[39]

The collective impact of these changes on the lives of women revived the women's movement, which, in spite of still being upper class and urban in composition, found itself directly at odds with the Government of the time. The most prominent of the organisations to emerge at this time was the Women's Action Forum (WAF), founded in 1981 to confront the Islamisation process. In February 1983, WAF held a public demonstration in Lahore decrying the discrimination against women by Zia's legal reforms which resulted in the participants being harassed and arrested by the authorities.[40] Since then, women lawyers and activists have played a key role in their advocacy of women's rights outside the establishment space through women-led non-profit organizations.[41]

After Zia's death in 1988 and in the context of a restoration of party-based democratic elections under the 1973 Constitution, Benazir Bhutto, the daughter of the late Zulfiqar Ali Bhutto, served twice as Pakistan's Prime Minister – from 1988 to 1990 and 1993 to 1996 – the first female premier in a Muslim-majority country. Benazir, who brought women's rights to the forefront of her campaign, was later criticised by the WAF for her inaction against the Hudood Ordinances.[42] The Hudood Ordinances were later reformed by dictator

[35] Jalal (n 5) 100–01.

[36] Qanun-e-Shahadat Order (1984), Art 17.

[37] The Muslim Family Laws Ordinance (1961), Arts 12 and 13.

[38] Code of Criminal Procedure (1898), Art 488. See also MZ Abbasi and SA Cheema, *Family Laws in Pakistan* (Oxford University Press, 2018) 12–13.

[39] The Offence of Zina (Enforcement of Hudood) Ordinance (1979). See also MH Cheema and AR Mustafa, 'From the Hudood Ordinances to the Protection of Women Act: Islamic Critiques of the Hudood Laws of Pakistan' (2008–09) 8 *UCLA Journal of Islamic and Near Eastern Law* 1, 10-13.

[40] S Khan, 'Challenges and Prospects for Women's Movements in Pakistan: A Case Study of Women Action Forum' (2011) 72 *Proceedings of the Indian History Congress* 1074, 1077-79.

[41] F Bari and SG Khattak, 'Power Configurations in Public and Private Arenas: The Women's Movement's Response' in AM Weiss and SZ Gilani (eds), *Power and Civil Society in Pakistan* (Oxford University Press, 2001) 237. See also F Critelli, 'A World Beyond the Veil: Pursuing Gender Equality in Pakistan' in Z Gross, L Davies and AK Diab (eds), *Gender, Religion and Education in a Chaotic Postmodern World* (Springer Dordrecht, 2013) 333–34.

[42] O Bennett-Jones, *The Bhutto Dynasty: The Struggle for Power in Pakistan* (Yale University Press, 2020) 162–63.

Pervez Musharraf, who in 1999 established a military regime in Pakistan for a fourth time.[43]

The emergence of lawyers as one of the main anti-establishment forces, following a nationwide lawyers' movement that ended with Musharraf's resignation in 2008 and the restoration of the suspended judiciary,[44] encouraged a greater participation of women in the legal world, fostering a feminist agenda aligned with international women movements and universalist norms as well as a more intersectionality-spirited activism together with minorities and the transgender community during recent years.[45] Collectivities of women successfully fought in 2010 to have a national law providing some redress against sexual harassment at the workplace.[46] Recently, the dominant group in the elections at the Pakistan Bar Council has been named under the halo of the lawyer and activist Asma Jahangir,[47] who successfully represented women and minorities in several landmark cases, and Justice Ayesha Malik, a justice behind key judgments on women's rights and gender justice, has been elevated in January 2022 as the first ever woman judge of the Supreme Court.[48]

III. CONSTITUTIONAL FRAMING OF SEX, GENDER AND SEXUALITY

In the constitutional landscape prior to the 1973 Constitution gender issues received less attention in a constitution-making mainly focused on addressing religious, ethnic and class-related challenges. Non-discrimination and equal protection guarantees were not explicit in naming gender or sex as a prohibited grounds for discrimination in either the 1956 or 1962 Constitutions. However, a history of petitioning for a rights charter through the independence movements influenced the nature of more specific guarantees in the 1956 Constitution including a gender-wise non-discrimination guarantee with regard to access to public places and for appointment in the service of Pakistan.[49] Furthermore, the 1956 Constitution granted women equal voting rights[50] with a far-reaching dual-voting franchise under which women were not only eligible to vote

[43] S Shafqat, 'Civil Society and the Lawyers' Movement of Pakistan' (2018) 43 *Law & Social Inquiry* 889, 900.

[44] H Khan, *A History of the Judiciary in Pakistan* (Oxford University Press, 2017) 523-28.

[45] L Zahid, 'Why do women march? A look at the Aurat March 2021 manifestos' *Images, Dawn* (15 March 2021), available at images.dawn.com/news/1186695.

[46] The Protection Against Harassment of Women at the Workplace Act (2010).

[47] H Malik, 'Asma Jahangir Group bags Pakistan Bar Council Elections' *The Express Tribune* (21 January 2021), available at tribune.com.pk/story/2280862/asma-jahangir-group-bags-pakistan-bar-council-elections.

[48] H Bhatti, 'Justice Ayesha Malik notified as country's first woman SC judge' *Dawn* (21 January 2022), available at www.dawn.com/news/1670724. See also www.supremecourt.gov.pk/judges/honorable-judge-details/?judgeName=Mrs.%20Justice%20Ayesha%20A.%20Malik.

[49] Constitution of the Islamic Republic of Pakistan (1956), Arts 14 and 17.

[50] ibid Art 143.

for a general seat but also in exclusivity for the 10 reserved seats for women candidates in Parliament, five per province,[51] designed as women's territorial constituencies inherited from the Government of India Act of 1935.[52] Although aimed at establishing a women-representative-of-women system, it was never implemented due to the absence of general elections during the short time that the 1956 Constitution was in force. The military-driven 1962 Constitution established indirect elections through an electoral college, reduced the reserved seats for women to six[53] and introduced fundamental rights as principles of policy, making them justiciable rights only after further amendments in the Constitution.[54]

With this discouraging 1962 constitutional precedent, the 1973 Constitution, although replete with expressions of formal equality for women and a promise for redressal of the socio-economic disadvantages, was inaugurated in a terrain that proved inauspicious for effecting real change. Chapter I of Part II recognises rights, freedoms, liberties, immunities or capacities as fundamental and protects them for either all persons or for all citizens of Pakistan. Amongst the fundamental rights elaborated in the Constitution, Article 25 on equality of citizens has been the foundation upon which women's rights have been expanded. Not only does it prohibit discrimination on the basis of sex, but it also provides special provisions for the protection of women and children. Thus, Article 25 contains a general clause on equality before the law and equal protection of law (Article 25(1)), a specific guarantee against discrimination on the grounds of sex (Article 25(2)) and a stand for affirmative actions (Article 25(3)).[55] Following the 1956 Constitution,[56] the 1973 Constitution also contains two other explicit non-discrimination guarantees that refer to sex, namely, in access to 'places of public entertainment or resort, not intended for religious purposes only' in Article 26(1), with an exception for any special provision for women and children in Article 26(2), and in the appointment to the civil service of Pakistan in Article 27(1).

[51] ibid Art 44(2): 'In addition to the seats for the members mentioned in clause (1), there shall, for a period of ten years from the Constitution Day, be ten seats reserved for women members only, of whom five shall be elected by constituencies in East Pakistan, and five by constituencies in West Pakistan; and constituencies shall accordingly be delimited as women's territorial constituencies for this purpose (…)'.

[52] V Dutoya, 'A representative claim made in the name of women?: Quotas and the political representation of women in India and Pakistan (1917–2010)' (2016) 66 *Revue Française de Science Politique (English Edition)* 49, 53.

[53] Constitution of the Republic of Pakistan (1962), Art 20(2).

[54] Khan (n 33) 149–50 and 157–58.

[55] Constitution of the Islamic Republic of Pakistan (1973), Art 25: '(1) All citizens are equal before law and are entitled to equal protection of law. (2) There shall be no discrimination on the basis of sex. (3) Nothing in this Article shall prevent the State from making any special provision for the protection of women and children'. Article 25(2) was initially enacted to say that there will be no discrimination on the basis of sex alone, but the word 'alone' was later removed by the Constitution (Eighteenth Amendment) Act 2010, Art 8.

[56] See Constitution of the Islamic Republic of Pakistan (1956), Arts 14 and 17.

However, the right to ensuring equality in access to education is pivoted explicitly to implement the guarantee of freedom of religion and conscience contained in Article 20.[57] In elaborating the safeguards against discrimination for admission to educational institutions, Article 22(3)(b), which specifically provides that 'no citizen shall be denied admission to any educational institution receiving aid from public revenues on the ground only of race, religion, caste or place of birth', makes no reference to sex. Despite these limitations, Article 25 has been read together with the educational rights to extend equality and affirmative treatment to the educational guarantees.[58] Furthermore, Article 9 on the right to life and liberty and Article 14(1) on the right to dignity and privacy have pivoted as key principles for enlarging rights to different fields of life, including the rights to access to justice or to a clean environment and water justice.[59]

Chapter II of Part II includes the unenforceable principles of policy used by courts as a prism for the interpretation of fundamental rights.[60] Besides women being mentioned in humane conditions of work and for maternity benefits as in the 1956 Constitution,[61] a sex parameter is now considered in the promotion of well-being and livelihood, along with caste, creed or race.[62] The constitutional system of Pakistan acknowledges for the first time a gender perspective in the formerly religious, ethnical and class-based public-policy lenses. Furthermore, Part II promotes the participation of women in national life in Article 34, includes a specific mention to encourage the participation of women in local government in Article 32 and protects the motherhood in Article 35.

Beyond fundamental rights and policy principles, women were also considered in the 1973 Constitution under the scope of their parliamentarian representation. The constitutional recognition of the historical under-representation of women within government fell short of an initial idea that was floated to ensure an exclusive female suffrage for reserved seats for women following the dual voting established in the 1956 Constitution, which was rejected both at the constitution-making committee and at the National Assembly.[63] Nonetheless, a total of 10 parliamentary seats were allocated to women for political parties to fill on a proportionate basis to their overall electoral performance,[64] which

[57] A brand-new Art 25A on the right to education was introduced by the Constitution (Eighteenth Amendment) Act (2010), interestingly in the same numeration given to the right to equality, but without reference to gender or sex despite the gender gap in education.

[58] See section IV.B of this chapter.

[59] *Government of Balochistan v Azizullah Memon*, PLD [1993] SC 341; *Asghar Leghari v Federation of Pakistan*, PLD [2018] Lahore 364.

[60] N Shah, *Women, the Koran and International Human Rights Law: The Experience of Pakistan* (Brill, 2006) 120–21.

[61] Constitution of the Islamic Republic of Pakistan (1956), Art 28(c); Constitution of the Islamic Republic of Pakistan (1973), Art 37(e).

[62] Constitution of the Islamic Republic of Pakistan (1973), Art 38(a) and (d).

[63] DH Saiyid, 'Women in Politics – Problems of Participation: A Case Study of Pakistan' (2001) 21 *Strategic Studies* 11, 14–15. See also Saigol (n 27) 12.

[64] Constitution of the Islamic Republic of Pakistan (1973), Art 51(4), as in the original text.

were progressively expanded up to the 60 reserved seats since 2002.[65] This gradual incorporation has been the logic of factoring in reserved seats, including in the provincial assemblies and the Senate, beyond the originally anticipated 10 years.

Hindered by both a lacklustre commitment to address women's issues through policy as well as a recalcitrant social sphere inclusive of conservative judges, the rights guaranteed in the 1973 Constitution were themselves of limited impact. Altogether, it is important to note that the 1973 Constitution was a particular kind of document which, although incorporating the broader expanse of what was being defined as universal human rights norms through international covenants and treaties, also provided room to derogate from those rights. Limitation clauses were built into the language of the rights listed and, while they vary to some extent, allowances for derogation from these rights are primarily in relation to national security and the sovereignty of Pakistan, public order and morality.[66] Therefore, the specific elaboration of social evils could readily be incorporated into the legitimising rubrics of public morality exemptions for the realisation of rights.

This constitutional design was also far from ensuring the full participation of women in national life as stated in Article 34. Measures for real equality found little place in the 1973 Constitution, including the lack of regulation on equal pay for equal work. Moreover, when these measures were established, a genuine equality agenda was missing. As an indicative example, the great majority of women parliamentarians[67] – those 60 holding reserved seats – are selected in an indirect system that, although allowing them to be presented as women's representatives, is implemented according to political parties' internal choices which certainly deprives them of their political legitimacy, jeopardises their constituency base, promotes nepotism and favouritism and, consequently, undermines their parliamentarian empowerment.[68] However, when it was enacted, women along with other progressive forces in the country paid little heed to the Constitution's apparent contradictions, instead celebrating it unreservedly as a liberatory document. As it would be apparent on the equality jurisprudence

[65] The Legal Framework Order (2002). The current distribution is as in the Constitution (Twenty-fifth Amendment) Act (2018), Art 3.

[66] As an illustrative example of these far-reaching limitation clauses, the freedom of speech, expression and press granted in Art 19 is 'subject to any reasonable restrictions imposed by law in the interest of the glory of Islam or the integrity, security or defence of Pakistan or any part thereof, friendly relations with foreign States, public order, decency or morality (…)'.

[67] In the 2018 elections to the National Assembly of Pakistan, only eight out of 183 female contestants secured seats, little more than 4%. See Fahad Chaudhry, 'Only 8 of 183 women candidates elected to NA in July 25 polls, ECP data shows' *Dawn* (7 September 2018), available at https://www.dawn.com/news/1431514.

[68] V Dutoya, 'From Women's Quota to 'Women's Politics': The Impact of Gender Quotas on Political Representations and Practices in the Pakistani National Parliament' (2013) 22 *Femina Politica* 17, 29–30. See also F Bari, *Bridging the Fault Lines? Rethinking the Gender Quota Approach in Pakistan* (Heinrich Böll Stiftung, 2015) 19.

generated from 1973 onwards, this Constitution did not precipitate a sea change in women's rights.

IV. CONSTITUTIONAL JURISPRUDENCE

The hierarchical Pakistani judicial system, inherited from colonial times, is composed of a subordinate court system, both civil and criminal, one High Court per province[69] and an apex Supreme Court. Besides jurisdictions of appellate court and constitutional arbiter,[70] the Supreme Court of Pakistan is also vested with special powers to grant fundamental rights. The power of judicial review of laws inconsistent with fundamental rights is vested in the superior judiciary through Article 8 even as it also provides for capacious exemptions such as for laws that govern members of the Armed Forces or the police and for those laws included in the First Schedule.[71] Extensive powers to try cases of 'public importance' pertaining to the enforcement of fundamental rights are also provided to the Supreme Court in Article 184(3)[72] under its original jurisdiction.

The Supreme Court had been reluctant to seise this power to entertain cases regarding fundamental rights until the commencement of a programme of public interest litigation in the 1990s following the footsteps of the Indian judiciary.[73] Beyond Constitution petitions being heard by the Supreme Court under Article 184(3), the enforcement of fundamental rights is also granted via *suo motu* actions[74] and lately as human rights cases.[75] Despite this diversity of remedies, challenges in access to justice for women as well as the lack of legal literacy and family-based reluctance[76] have meant that only a reduced number of equality cases have reached courts, mostly restricted to manifest and systematic violations reported by the victims themselves, making the enforcement of

[69] Lahore High Court in Lahore (Punjab), Sindh High Court in Karachi (Sindh), Peshawar High Court in Peshawar (Khyber Pakhtunkhwa), Balochistan High Court in Quetta (Balochistan) and Islamabad High Court in Islamabad (Islamabad Capital Territory). The autonomous northern territories of Gilgit-Baltistan and Azad Jammu and Kashmir are not constitutionally integrated in Pakistan and therefore they have their own judicial system and superior courts.

[70] Constitution of the Islamic Republic of Pakistan (1973), Arts 184(1), 185, 186 and 188.

[71] ibid Art 8(3)(a)(b).

[72] ibid Art 184(3), as part of the original jurisdiction of the Supreme Court. Under Art 199(1)(c), the High Courts can offer traditional remedies associated to writs for the enforcement of any of the fundamental rights but upon the petition of an aggrieved person.

[73] F Siddiqi, 'Public Interest Litigation: Predicable Continuities and Radical Departures' in MH Cheema and IS Gilani (eds) *The Politics and Jurisprudence of the Chaudhry Court 2005–2013* (Oxford University Press, 2015) 79–80. See also MS Khan, 'Genesis and Evolution of Public Interest Litigation in the Supreme Court of Pakistan: Toward a Dynamic Theory of Judicialization' (2014) 28 *Temple International & Comparative Law Journal* 285, 293-95.

[74] Action taken on matters of public importance by the Court's own accord.

[75] Since 2013 a Human Rights cell of the Supreme Court processes letters, applications and complaints on violations of Human Rights to provide a speedy relief to the common citizen.

[76] Improvements have been seen in the access to justice with the gradual establishment of gender-based violence courts since 2017.

rights a more complicated path to implement, and creating a gap between the law and its effectiveness. Efforts by activists, pro-bono advocates and public-spirited citizens have most recently helped cases to be heard by superior courts, notwithstanding the slow pace of justice and the overcrowded judiciary.

The Federal *Shariat* Court and the *Shariat* Appellate Branch – for the review of the Federal *Shariat* Court's judgments by the Supreme Court – were established *ex novo* by dictator Zia Ul-Haq in the early 1980s.[77] Article 203D gives extensive powers to the Federal *Shariat* Court to decide – on the petition of a citizen of Pakistan, the federal and provincial Governments or via *suo motu*[78] – whether any law or provision is repugnant to the Injunctions of Islam. These *Shariat* courts also became the appellate route for the enforcement of the Hudood Ordinances by any criminal court.[79] Despite no express or specific immunity being accorded to the Hudood Ordinances either against their amendment or repeal by a legislative procedure, or their judicial review under Article 8, the laws interestingly managed to attain an entrenched quasi-constitutional status, never having been challenged before a court of law for being discriminatory or violative of fair trial guarantees.

This parallel judicial structure brought the *Quran* and the *Sunnah* to the centre of the legal system not only as sources to ensure the conformity of the Pakistani legal system with Islam but also as fundamentals of the judicial reasoning. While the Federal *Shariat* Court initially pushed ahead with enlarging the scope of its review, it became somewhat more circumspect about such expansion in recent decades. Nonetheless, the Federal *Shariat* Court has progressively used Islam to expand the scope of fundamental rights[80] and interpreted as repugnant to Islam statutes inconsistent with the right to equality, declaring it as a principle 'enshrined in the Holy Quran'.[81]

The Supreme Court is formed by 17 justices,[82] headed by the Chief Justice of Pakistan as the most senior justice,[83] the Federal *Shariat* Court by eight Muslim judges,[84] including three *Ulema*,[85] and the *Shariat* Appellate Bench by three Muslim judges and two *Ulema*.[86] Although women were not excluded from being appointed in superior courts, the first female justice was not nominated in the Federal *Shariat* Court until 2013.[87] The appointment of judges, a power

[77] The Constitution (Amendment) Order (1980), Art 3 on new Ch 3A.

[78] The *suo moto* action was added by the Constitution (Second Amendment) Order (1982) Art 4 amending Art 203D.

[79] The Constitution (Second Amendment) Order (1982), Art 5 on new Art 203DD.

[80] Lau (n 12) 175–88 and 209–10.

[81] *Mukhtar Ahmad Sheikh v Government of Pakistan*, PLD [2009] FSC 65 [10].

[82] The Supreme Court (Number of Judges) Act (1997), Art 2.

[83] Constitution of the Islamic Republic of Pakistan (1973), Art 175A.3.

[84] ibid Art 203C.2.

[85] ibid Art 203C.3A.

[86] ibid Art 203F.3.

[87] L Holden, 'Women Judges and Women's Rights in Pakistan' (2017) 7 *Oñati Socio-legal Series* 752, 761.

previously conferred to the judiciary extensively,[88] is vested since 2010 to a cross-sectional Judicial Commission of Pakistan,[89] followed by the confirmation of the nominees by a Parliamentary Committee.[90] Nevertheless, the pre-eminence of judiciary in appointments to the bench under the broader principle of 'independence' for the judicial branch has been safeguarded by the Supreme Court against any alteration or abrogation by the amendatory powers of the Parliament as a salient feature of the Constitution.[91]

Equality cases were addressed by the Supreme Court, in an early stage, with a rational approach, using formalistic differentiations and paternalistic reasonings. This jurisprudence has later transitioned to a clearer substantive understanding of gender equality in line with the CEDAW to overcome the patriarchal-based discrimination of the Pakistani legal system but avoiding explicit anti-subordination formulas. The resilient Pakistani Supreme Court, although ploddingly and inconsistently, has eventually achieved to uphold a basic net of gender-aimed protections under the core principles of equality, non-discrimination, dignity and privacy.

A. Developments in the Protection of Gender Equality and Non-discrimination: Case Law on Citizenship and Employment

In the earliest legislative enactments by the state, a base of gender inequality was readily apparent. The citizenship law made no provision for the grant of citizenship to the foreign spouse of a Pakistani woman but it allowed, however, non-Pakistani wives of Pakistani men to apply for, and obtain, citizenship.[92] When challenged in the 1973 constitutional landscape by a Pakistani woman married to an Indian national, the Lahore High Court in 1997 upheld the law considering that, in cases of conflict, the application of Article 25 depended upon the facts and circumstances of each case.[93] The Court developed a stereotypical and paternalistic legal reasoning, stating first that a married woman 'has to follow the domicile of her husband' and that the challenged section was 'beneficial to women', but adding later that women were 'no longer to be treated

[88] *Al Jehad Trust v Federation of Pakistan*, PLD [1996] SC 324; followed by *Al Jehad Trust v Federation of Pakistan*, PLD [1997] SC 84.

[89] The Constitution (Eighteenth Amendment) Act (2010), Art 67 on the new Art 175A. In the case of appointment of judges of the Supreme Court, the JCP is composed of the two most senior justices, a former justice, a senior advocate of the Supreme Court, the Federal Minister for Law and Justice and the Attorney-General. With the Constitution (Nineteenth Amendment) Act, 2010, Art 4, the number of senior justices was changed from two to four.

[90] The role of the Parliamentary Committee was challenged before the Supreme Court in *Nadeem Ahmed v Federation of Pakistan*, PLD [2010] SC 1165. The rules for a better transparency were later included in the Constitution (Nineteenth Amendment) Act (2010), Art 4.

[91] *District Bar Association Rawalpindi v Federation of Pakistan*, PLD [2015] SC 401.

[92] The Pakistan Citizenship Act (1951), Art 10.

[93] *Sharifan v Federation of Pakistan*, PLD [1998] Lahore 59.

as a property of the male members of the society', even though the Court was noticeably endorsing that patriarchal behaviour.[94]

In 2007 the Federal *Shariat* Court, in a *suo moto* notice, held that the law was discriminatory and negated gender equality, and therefore was in violation not only of Article 25 and Pakistan's international commitments, but also of the Islamic injunctions of Article 2A and was consequently repugnant to the *Holy Quran* and the *Sunnah*.[95] The position of the Government stated by the Minister of Interior exemplified the patriarchal resistances to the advancement of women equality since 'foreign women marrying Pakistani husband[s] cannot be equated with foreign men married to Pakistani women in our society'.[96] In 2016, the Lahore High Court ordered to grant citizenship to the foreign husband of a Pakistani woman while declaring the law discriminatory and contrary to the CEDAW's commitments by which Pakistan is bound,[97] but a final verdict on the provision by the Supreme Court is still pending given the lack of action shown by the Government to overturn the law.

This slow articulation through case law of equality principles, which are cognisant of the history of gender equality as well as informed by international norms around positive discrimination and accommodation, is quite telling in the realm of employment. The Supreme Court heard together in 2005 a series of petitions filed by discriminated female employees against the requirement by Pakistan International Airlines (PIA) for women cabin stewards to retire from service at the age of 35 while men could continue until the age of 60.[98] The Court found PIA's practices to be discriminatory since the distinction was being made just on the basis of the employee's sex despite them performing the same duties; the Court also considered that this discrimination would not have happened if the female air hostesses were 'placed altogether in a different group', making an organisational differentiation sufficient to avoid formal equality.[99] Since then, a more meticulous approach has been taken regarding restrictions on women's access to positions based on occupational requirements where only men are deemed to be able to perform such duties. Courts have applied more thoroughgoing scrutiny to consider violative those practices restricting women access to positions previously restricted to men, not only in the business sector[100] but also in traditional occupations such as *lambardars* (village headmen).[101]

[94] ibid [8].
[95] *Suo Moto 1/K 2006*, PLD [2008] FSC 1.
[96] ibid [3].
[97] *Rukhsana Bibi v Government of Pakistan*, PLD [2016] Lahore 857.
[98] *Chairman PIAC v Samina Masood*, PLD [2005] SC 831.
[99] ibid [16].
[100] *Mrs Naseem Firdous v Punjab Small Industries Corporation*, PLD [1995] Lahore 584.
[101] *Mst Sarwari Bibi v Arshad Ali Khan*, YLR [2007] Lahore 702; a *lambardar* is a village officer appointed under the Land Revenue Act, 1967, to collect, or to supervise the collection of, the revenue of an estate. Land revenue collection has been of central importance to the maintenance of rural social orders and hierarchies.

Employment relations have also found a challenging discrimination ground in maternity benefits. Courts have had to step in to protect maternity from being used as a basis of discrimination against women, for instance by delaying regularisation of employment on account of maternity.[102] Furthermore, while ordering the reinstatement of a faculty member dismissed during her maternity leave, the Islamabad High Court declared in 2020 that maternity benefits fell under the equality and non-discrimination guarantee, along with the protection of motherhood granted in Article 35 and the obligations under CEDAW, the state being required to 'provide all circumstances conducive to a woman for exercise of her right to give birth to a child in a dignified manner, free from any threat that she could be thrown out from her job'.[103]

Courts have also considered positive discrimination where uniform criteria for men and women are alleged to be blind to the specific contextual features of women's participation in the Government workforce. In judgments on age cut-off for women in public employment – the age limit to apply for certain public posts being higher for women than for men – the Lahore High Court considered that this age relaxation was required 'to enable women to join professional career after marriage and child bearing'[104] and the Peshawar High Court found that the absence of age relaxation discriminates against divorced women who may want to enter the workforce at an older age.[105] The reasoning employed in these cases suggested that Article 25(3) was both a remedial power possessed by the state and a mandate to the state to take affirmative measures for the protection of women and children under it.

The evolution in judicial reasoning has allowed courts to move from a blanket acceptance that gender is a reasonable classification that can justifiably give rise to differential treatment in nearly all domains to either circumscribing or altogether abolishing differential treatment. These recent cases around Article 25 on citizenship and employment law show that differential treatment is progressively considered illegitimate in light of constitutional protections and demonstrate that courts have adopted a more contextual and purposeful approach to understand the non-discrimination guarantee and to promote substantive equality. Furthermore, affirmative measures for women open new windows for addressing any manner of constraint faced by women in situations created by gendered family roles.

[102] *Rupa Sayed v Pakistan International Airlines Corporation*, PLC (CS) [2009] Karachi 928.

[103] *Dr Aamna Saleem Khan v National University of Sciences and Technology (NUST)*, PLC (CS) [2021] Islamabad 212 [23].

[104] *Nazar Elahi v Government of Punjab*, CLC [2013] Lahore 1457 [9].

[105] *Mst Samina Naheed v The State*, [2010] PLC (CS) 364 Peshawar.

B. Overcoming a Stereotypical Approach for Safeguarding Reserved Posts for Women: Case Law on Quotas in Higher Education and Government Employment

Quotas for women in higher education and government employment have been challenged time and again on a discriminatory basis against men. The absence of an explicit constitutional guarantee for the protection of women and against discrimination in co-educational institutions has necessitated the forging of more ambitious interpretive practices by higher court judges than in other domains with the aim of upholding gender quotas established in admissions by colleges. The equality guarantee under the 1973 Constitution led in the first instance to a challenge to be heard at the Lahore High Court in 1975, which posed the specific question of whether quotas for women's admission to medical colleges, in a specific case where 100 seats were reserved to women by the Lahore Medical College, were discriminatory against male candidates.[106] Although the Court rejected the assertion that such reservations for women deny men their right to be considered solely on merit and offered a list of areas in which favoured rules for women could be allowed on the ground of Article 25(3), justices also provided that women as a class need protection, reinforcing gender stereotypes that discourage women's full and equal participation in social life rather than addressing women's historic under-representation and right to equality.[107]

The next challenge against affirmative action for women's access to higher education came in the form of testing the validity of limits placed on women's access to open merit seats in medical colleges in Punjab, given that women already had a number of reserved seats available. Article 25(2) was tested in light of Article 22, which guarantees safeguards as to educational institutions in respect of religion. The Lahore High Court saw Article 22 as limiting the freedom from discrimination provided in Article 25(2), since Article 22 did not contain gender as a protected category.[108] However, the Supreme Court in an appellate decision disagreed with this view and considered that no limitation can be placed to restrict girls from competing on merit with boys by suggesting that even in the specific conditions to which Article 22 safeguards are directed, the absence of a clear specific sex protection cannot take away from, or limit the application of the general protections accorded by Article 25(2).[109] The two provisions read together imply that a 'reasonable and intelligible classification' may militate for separate treatment, insofar as the provision of governmental resources may be concerned but that where they are pooled together, they must be treated equitably other than for the allowance of protective measures benefitting women and children.[110]

[106] *Ehsanul Haque v Federation of Pakistan*, PLD [1976] Lahore 501.
[107] ibid [4].
[108] *Government of Punjab v Naila Begum*, PLD [1987] Lahore 336.
[109] *Shirin Munir v Government of Punjab*, PLD [1990] SC 295.
[110] ibid [20].

A recent case has been raised after a 50 per cent quota for men and women was imposed by a variety of colleges, given women's achievement in securing up a majority of seats. This strict parity quota – half of the seats are reserved for girls and half for boys – was held to be contrary to the non-discrimination principle by the Balochistan High Court.[111] The Court went on to explain the initial framing of Article 25(3) as a landmark in 'the battle for gender justice' to undo the 'ugly face of the society' and, reading it together with the promotion of full participation of women stated in Article 34, suggested that 'an integral part' of Article 25(3) was to make special provisions for women.[112]

Quotas in favour of women have also been maintained by the Centre and provinces in the field of government employment in furtherance of the constitutional mandate of Articles 25(3) and 27(1). The quota regime varies insofar as the federal Government mandates appointment against 10 per cent of direct recruitment and amongst the Provinces, Punjab and Sindh have set it at 15 per cent.[113] The explicit inclusion of sex as a protected ground in Article 27 has meant that the jurisprudence developed in this area has had to consider their application to different stages of the employment relationship. In addition to providing for quotas, Article 27(1) includes a non-discrimination clause concerning the recruitment for positions in the service of Pakistan, which has led to slightly different outcomes vis-a-vis these protections being extended into the terms and conditions of employment. While the Lahore High Court has interpreted Article 27(1) to include protection from discrimination with respect to allowances and salaries for public employees,[114] the Supreme Court has rejected the attempt to expand the specific protections of Article 27(1) to promotions, as it is confined only to initial appointments.[115]

Given that the reference to reserved quotas in Article 27(1) is related to either sex for those posts where the performance of duties 'cannot be adequately performed by members of the other sex', public employment quotas for women have also faced challenges in certain job positions where the nature of the work involved practical risks. Justice Ayesha Malik, in a case where women's participation in the Counter Terrorism Department was reduced to their respective quotas without being able to participate on a merit basis, confirmed in appellation the overturning of those restrictions as she considered that another quota was de facto created for 'abled bodied Muslim men'.[116] The justice drew upon the CEDAW towards taking appropriate measures 'to modify social and cultural patterns of conduct for men and women with a view to achieve the

[111] *Talal Haleem v Principal Bolan Medical College, Quetta*, PLD [2015] Quetta 97.
[112] ibid [11].
[113] *OM 4/15/2006-R-2*, Government of Pakistan (22 May 2007); *SOR-IV(S&GAD)15-1/2012*, Government of the Punjab (21 May 2012); *SORI(SGA&CD)2-1/94*, Government of Sindh (8 March 2017).
[114] *Mrs Rehana Kausar v Pakistan Electric Power Company Limited*, PLJ [2015] Lahore 39.
[115] *Shahid Pervaiz v Ejaz Ahmad*, [2017] SCMR 206 [125].
[116] *Government of the Punjab v Qanoot Fatima*, PLJ [2018] Lahore 341 [11].

elimination of prejudices, customary and other practices which are based on the idea of inferiority of women or on stereotype roles'.[117]

The specific exception to the principle of non-discrimination provided for in Article 25(3) has been a potential opening to initiatives and programmes of affirmative action. While reading together these two protections, non-discrimination and preferential treatment, with specific fundamental rights on education and employment along with the principle of expanding women's participation in national life, the Supreme Court has established a robust jurisprudence not only in the legality but also in the necessity of promoting reserved posts for women to overcome the historical gender gap by the means of substantive equality. However, this equality jurisprudence is bounded insofar as constitutional protections are accorded only against state or state-like actors.

C. Upholding the Rights to Life, Dignity and Privacy beyond Patriarchal Resistances: Case Law on the Hudood Ordinances, Evidence Law and Transgender Rights

Although *Shariat* courts became the appellate forum for Hudood-related cases, non-*Shari*at courts were not completely shut out as writs were entertained where the Hudood laws were challenged on procedural grounds, such as the improper arrest, refusal of bail or the allegation that a police investigation was conducted inadequately.[118] Since early in the enforcement of Hudood offences, the privacy of home safeguarded by Article 14 has been built up as an effective mechanism for affording protections against forms of policing that constituted intrusions into privacy, the commission of *zina* – illicit sexual relations – being curtailed to public places. In 1997 the Lahore High Court held that the Ordinance 'was enacted to implement the Islamic provisions in this behalf and rightly does not provide for an intrusion into any one's house only to find out the commission of offence of *zina*', adding that the *Holy Quran* prohibits such invasions of home privacy.[119] In the following years, not only places of permanent residence but also hotel rooms and *baithaks* (drawing rooms where guests are entertained) were given the same kinds of protection against violations of privacy.[120]

Article 14, with regards to dignity, has recently been raised by courts to overturn certain practices of evidence such as questioning women survivors on their sexual history and chastity. A Lahore High Court ruling by Justice Ayesha Malik has imposed a ban on the conduct of vaginal tests with the purpose of determining the virginity of a rape victim, establishing that it offends the personal

[117] ibid [9].
[118] S Aziz, *The Constitution of Pakistan: A Contextual Analysis* (Hart Publishing, 2018) 233–34.
[119] *Riaz v Station House Officer, Jhang City*, PLD [1998] Lahore 35 [25].
[120] *Mst Rabia Bibi v The State*, PCrLJ [2004] Lahore 1451.

dignity of the female victim.[121] The very same day, Justice Mansoor Ali Shah[122] stated the inviolability of dignity as 'an absolute right and not subject to law', expanded the right to life of persons to include the right to 'live with dignity' and considered practices like reporting a victim's sexual life to be a form of discrediting a woman's 'independence, identity, autonomy and free choice thereby degrading her human worth and offending her right to dignity'.[123]

The advancement of transgender rights has also been rooted in the right to live with dignity. Following a constitutional petition filled on 6 February 2009, a series of decisions were taken by the Supreme Court on transgender rights.[124] At the end of 2009, an order by the Supreme Court granted the full range of constitutional rights to transgender persons, asking the Government to register them with their correct gender identification to avoid the denial of their access to rights and state services.[125] Nonetheless, these decisions are filled with stereotypical and patronising misunderstandings regarding their identity; naming them *unix*, establishing a gender disorder in their bodies and, therefore, comparing them with persons with disability.[126]

In a subsequent order of 2011, the Supreme Court entrenched their constitutional rights under the protection of life and dignity.[127] This recognition included not only the prohibition of discrimination but also the fact that the state was bound to provide the same substantial rights as to the rest of citizens, including the protection of their life and property and the secure of their dignity. Finally, in the disposal of the case in 2012, the court mandated for them 'to be respected by all the segments of society' and ordered the government 'to ensure their participation/jobs in all walk of life', paving the way to a future affirmative action system for the transgender community.[128]

V. FROM FLAGSHIP CASE LAW TOWARDS GENDER-CENTRIC LEGISLATION: JOINT DEVELOPMENTS IN ANTI-RAPE REGULATIONS, FAMILY LAW AND TRANSGENDER RIGHTS

Beyond the expansion of fundamental rights from a gender perspective through constitutional jurisprudence, case law by superior courts has also been the

[121] *Sadaf Aziz v Government of Punjab*, PCrLJ [2021] Lahore 205 [27].

[122] Justice Shah is a reformist judge whose judgments have been especially relevant in areas such as constitutional law, human rights or environmental law. See also www.supremecourt.gov.pk/judges/honorable-judge-details/?judgeName=Mr.%20Justice%20Syed%20Mansoor%20Ali%20Shah.

[123] *Atif Zareef v The State*, PLD [2021] SC 550 [11].

[124] JA Redding, 'Les droits des personnes transgenres au Pakistan (2009–2019)' (2020) 80 *Droit et Cultures* paras 6-9.

[125] *Muhammad Aslam Khaki v SSP (Operations) Rawalpindi*, order by the Supreme Court under Constitutional Petition 43/2009 (20 November 2009), available at www.icj.org/wp-content/uploads/2012/07/Khaki-v.-Rawalpindi-Supreme-Court-of-Pakistan.pdf.

[126] ibid [2]–[3].

[127] *Muhammad Aslam Khaki v SSP (Operations) Rawalpindi*, [2013] SCMR 187 [2].

[128] *Muhammad Aslam Khaki v SSP (Operations) Rawalpindi*, PLD [2013] SC 188 [1].

root of reformist legislation. In realms such as rape laws, and until women-centric pieces of legislation have been incrementally passed in response to progressive judgments, judges have covered legal loopholes with brand-new guidelines or redesigned legal tools. In other cases, such as in the family law field, the judiciary has not only triggered new regulations but has also been proved as the necessary, and sometimes unheard, watchdog for its implementation. Finally, landmark judgments have also paved the way to legislation that has shrined forward-looking rights including the milestone of a self-perceived gender identity.

The challenge of rape regulations exemplifies this *pas de deux* between the judiciary and the legislature led by case law. In earlier jurisprudence, complaints of *zina-bil-jabr* (illicit sexual relations made by force) could experience their rape allegations turned against them as charges of *zina* (illicit sexual relations).The fact that an 'unexplained pregnancy' was held to be sufficient proof for making unwedded women subject to punishment reflected the extreme vulnerability of women under the law and the need for court intervention.[129] Given the outcry over a case where the woman prosecuted was almost blind, the Federal Shariat Court took *suo moto* notice and reversed the conviction; the Court was able to provide more acute guidance on the principle that the burden of proof for an allegation of *zina* rests on the prosecution to show that both parties had in fact consented to sexual intercourse.[130] The first legislative amendment to the Hudood Ordinances made in 2006 included the removal of the offence of *zina bil jabr* liable to *hudd*, returning it to the Penal Code as rape, and the abolition of the exemption for marital rape.[131] It was also categorically prohibited to convert a claim of rape into an allegation of *zina*.[132]

While these changes were welcomed insofar as the structure of prohibition was more clearly oriented to penalising the violence of rape than before, the conduct of trials was still beset by the preoccupation with a woman's character. Specifically, the law of evidence provided that 'when a man is prosecuted for rape or an attempt to ravish, it may be shown that the prosecutrix was of generally immoral character'.[133] The possibility of impeaching women's character on the grounds of immorality was a deterrent to the filing of rape complaints, certainly inhibiting the possibility of a sex worker ever filing a rape allegation. When it was challenged before the Federal *Shariat* Court in 2009, the Court agreed that a woman's character was absolutely irrelevant to assessing

[129] *Mst Jehan Mina v The State*, PLD [1983] FSC 183.
[130] *Safia Bibi v The State* (1983), PLD [1985] FSC 120.
[131] The Protection of Women (Criminal Laws Amendment) (2006).
[132] The Protection of Women (Criminal Laws Amendment) (2006), Art 12A inserted as Art 5A of the Offence of Zina (Enforcement of Hudood) Ordinance (1979).
[133] Qanun-e-Shahadat Order (1984) Art 151(4), before amendment, as inherited from the Evidence Act (1872).

the commission of a rape.[134] This provision on the victim's alleged immorality was finally overruled in 2016[135] with an amendment instituting changes that have gone some way towards protecting the victim during the procedure and affirming the criminality of rape rather than allocating the blame. For instance, it mandates that rape cases should be conducted in camera,[136] allows for collection of DNA evidence from the accused in rape cases,[137] including from the victim with her consent,[138] and makes provisions for examination of a rape victim by a female medical practitioner.[139]

Courts have also been incisive in developing guidelines through case law, focusing on caring about victims of sexual violence. Rulings have provided directions that forensic practices must be aimed at ascertaining the act of sexual violence and adducing the culpability of the accused,[140] the DNA evidence has been typified as the 'gold standard' for identification purposes and the testimony of women victims of rape has been placed on a 'higher pedestal' than an injured witness since the rape victim also suffers psychologically and emotionally.[141] This approach aims to overcome the previous moralising about the relative worth or merit of a woman's experience of rape in Pakistan that has led to erosion of due process and equal treatment guarantees for women who do not meet the standard of being ideal victims.

A new step was taken in the form of an anti-rape law, providing for the establishment of special courts to deal with allegations of rape and anti-rape cells to act as the first responder to victims of rape, as well as medico-legal, police and investigation services under one roof.[142] The law provides a register of sex offenders[143] and, incorporating suggestions from case law, bars the use of regressive practices such as the two-finger test or the immoral-character-based analysis of the victim.[144] Despite being only an incremental reform, it reflects a newly evolving direction in terms of women's advocacy for greater protection against violence.

Statutory reform will still need to be brought about to ensure greater protection and official recourse for victims of sexual violence. At a slow pace of advance, it has been progressively acknowledged that the singular moral line drawn between licit and illicit sex, with the former taking place within heterosexual marriage bonds and the latter being all extramarital sex, cannot be

[134] *Mukhtar Ahmad Sheikh v Government of Pakistan*, PLD [2009] FSC 65 [7].
[135] The Criminal Law (Amendment) (Offences Relating to Rape) Act (2016), Art 16, removal of Art 151(4) Qanun-e-Shahadat Order (1984).
[136] ibid Art 13, amendment of Art 352, Code of Criminal Procedure (CCP) (1898).
[137] ibid Art 7, insertion of new Art 53A, CCP.
[138] ibid Art 11, insertion of new Art 164B, CCP.
[139] ibid Art 11, insertion of new Art 164A, CCP.
[140] *Sadaf Aziz v Government of Punjab* (n 121) [30] and [33].
[141] *Atif Zareef v The State* (n 123) [5].
[142] The Anti Rape (Investigation and Trial) Act (2021).
[143] ibid Art 24.
[144] ibid Arts 13(1) and 13(2).

easily mapped onto categories of legally permissible or barred. While this strict alignment seemed to inform the original thrust of criminal sanction within the Hudood Ordinances, legal categories are increasingly being defined as independent from moral ones. Therefore, illicit sex has progressively come coupled with non-consensual sex, definitions of consent have found their way into recent amendments of relevant laws, and protections for the dignity of the victim have been settled by courts.

Family law, governed by personal law and therefore regulated by different legal codes of which the ones of the religious minorities have remained mainly unchanged since colonial times, has been a challenging legal framework for the protection of women in Pakistan where superior courts have frequently been compelled to intervene for the actual enforcement of the law. Muslim regulations saw some reform, including the forward-looking Muslim Family Laws Ordinances that regulated the procedure of *talaq* (divorce) and *khula* (dissolution of marriage at the wife's request).[145] However, there remain instances where courts still need to elaborate on the intersections of *talaq* with other provisions of law, for example, irregular divorces being treated as an act of *zina* (illicit sexual relations).[146] Child marriages are also a good illustration of this combination of restraints, where colonial gender differences on the age of marriage persist in the legal system[147] and the idea of placing an age-of-majority limit on the age of marriage has been argued to be un-Islamic,[148] despite several efforts by the courts to issue orders for the sensitisation of Nikah registrars and to bring the attention of the Parliament on the contradictions under the law.[149]

Violation of women's rights have persisted in further areas such as forced marriages or inheritance rights. In an attempt to prevent this, a piece of legislation on anti-women practices was passed in 2011 with a series of measures to ensure the vesting of inheritance, considering a criminal offence to deprive a woman of her inheritance, and to prohibit forced marriages.[150] Despite these new regulations and the declaration made by courts on the right of an adult woman to select her spouse without any consent of her guardian[151] and on the

[145] The Muslim Family Laws Ordinance (1961), Arts 7 and 8.

[146] *Ameer Bakhsh v Additional Sessions Judge*, PCrLJ [2022] Lahore 1188.

[147] The Child Marriage Restraint Act (1929), differentiated in Art 2 the marital age for both genders, at 18 for boys and 16 for girls, previously 14 in the case of girls until amended in 1961 by the MFLO. Following the Eighteenth Amendment to the Constitution in 2010, provinces have adopted varying laws, with Sindh setting the age of marriage at 18 for both boys and girls, while Punjab retained the age of marriage at 16 for girls, and 18 for boys. The provinces of Khyber Pakhtunkhwa and Balochistan are in process of enacting their laws.

[148] A Wasim, 'Bill against child marriage divides parties in NA' *Dawn* (1 May 2019), available at www.dawn.com/news/1479444.

[149] *Mst Alishba Bibi v The State*, PLD [2020] Islamabad 28 [20]; *Mst Mumtaz Bibi v Qasim*, PLD [2022] Islamabad 228 [42].

[150] The Criminal Law (Third Amendment) Act (2011).

[151] *Hafiz Abdul Waheed v Asma Jehangir*, PLD [1997] Lahore 301; followed by the appeal decision *Hafiz Abdul Waheed v Asma Jehangir*, PLD [2004] SC 219.

unconstitutionality of any tribal custom in which women are given in forced marriage as compensation for reconciliation,[152] forced marriages often occur, especially against women from religious minorities that are abducted and forced to conversion.[153] In the domain of inheritance rights, courts have had to step in to uphold women's right to inherit[154] and justices such as Faez Isa[155] have repeatedly reminded the Government about its obligations to adopt measures for ensuring it.[156]

Case law has also been a strong point of departure for the recognition of rights through new pieces of legislation. Despite several orders having been made by the Supreme Court upholding transgender rights, courts had still to step in to protect gender identity rights as 'one of the most fundamental aspect(s) of life'.[157] In 2018 the Federal Parliament finally passed a piece of legislation which seeks to provide transgender persons with all fundamental rights, including the right to a self-perceived gender identity.[158] The Act provides an recognisable definition for transgender people from a sociocultural perspective – preceded by the names transgender man, transgender woman and *khawaja sira* – as 'any person whose gender identity or gender expression differs from the social norms and cultural expectations based on the sex they were assigned at the time of their birth'.[159] The law overcomes the derogatory *hijra* terminology with the Urdu term *khawaja sira*,[160] as a reappropriation by the Pakistani legal system of a community previously marginalised and only acknowledged from the perspective of health policy but nowadays reclaimed as a symbol of Pakistani diversity. Therefore, this third socio-cultural definition, read together with the given names, is a legal declaration for a self-perceived

[152] *Sakeena Bibi v Secretary Law, Government of Pakistan*, PLD [2022] FSC 57.

[153] See N Hussain and Z Rehman 'Interview to Kalpana Devi. Forced Marriage and Conversion and the Other Way Round: The Case of The Hindu Communities in Sindh' in N Hussain (ed) *Disputes Legacies: Pakistan Papers* (Simorgh Women's Resources and Publication Centre, 2019). See also the report 'Abductions, Forced Conversions, and Forced Marriages of Religious Minority Women and Girls in Pakistan' APPG for the Pakistani Minorities (September 2021), available at appgfreedomofreligionorbelief.org/media/APPG-Pakistan-Minorities-Report.pdf.

[154] *Muhammad Sajid Tareen v Government of Balochistan*, PLD [2021] Balochistan 172; *Farhan Aslam v Mst. Nuzba Shaheen*, [2021] SCMR 179.

[155] Justice Qazi Faez Isa, a judge that stood against the non-constitutional usurpation of 2007 when posted in the High Court of Balochistan, has been behind several cases of public importance. See also www.supremecourt.gov.pk/judges/honorable-judge-details/?judgeName=Mr.%20Justice%20Qazi%20Faez%20Isa.

[156] *Ghulam Qasim v Mst. Razia Begum*, PLD [2021] SC 812 [8]; *Atta Muhammad v Mst. Munir Sultan*, [2021] SCMR 73 [13].

[157] *Mian Asia v Federation of Pakistan*, PLD [2018] Lahore 54 [11].

[158] The Transgender Persons (Protection of Rights) Act (2018).

[159] ibid Art 2(1)(n). This definition also includes intersex persons and male-assigned-at-birth transgender persons that have followed reassignment surgery, what the law keeps naming as eunuchs with an unfortunate colonial reminiscence.

[160] S Khan, 'What is in a Name? Khwaja Sara, Hijra and Eunuchs in Pakistan' (2016) 23 *Indian Journal of Gender Studies* 218, 225-27.

gender identity, not only within but also beyond the binary gender assigned at birth, despite its challenging operability.[161]

The transgender community has advocated for a full implementation of this Act in intersectionality with women and minorities' rights, where advancements are beginning to show in rape law[162] and affirmative actions.[163] The law has been, however, challenged before the Federal *Shariat* Court as repugnant to the injunctions of Islam, allegedly providing legal recognition to homosexual rights.[164] While the Act is far from recognising the rights of sexually diverse people, what conservative sections label as 'Western rights', transgender history in Pakistan has shown how the criminalisation of communities creates a pervasive social stigma. Similarly, the criminalisation of homosexual sex under section 377 of the colonial Pakistan Penal Code still perpetuates the vulnerability of sexually diverse persons with no appearance of change due to the religious and social resistances.

VI. CONCLUSION: TOWARDS A COUNTER-PATRIARCHAL CONSTITUTIONALISM?

In a nation-building that was focused on resolving class, religious and ethnic dilemmas, a gender perspective had to await the advent of feminist internationalism into the constitutional landscape. The fight for access, safety, property, equality and the whole spectrum of women's rights has mostly been tethered to universalist norms and dictums about women's status and personhood. The emergence of women from different backgrounds into a counter-patriarchal struggle beyond the elite participation of the early days has been proved to be a powerful force to overturn the patterns that have jeopardised the agenda for women's rights in the last decades, including rampant Islamisation, dominant nationalism and the patriarchal foundations of society.

Despite recent advancements in case law and regulations, courts remain erratic in pursuing gender justice through jurisprudence. In 2020, the Lahore and Islamabad High Courts were spelling out the contours of freedom of

[161] JA Redding, 'The Pakistan Transgender Persons (Protection of Rights) Act of 2018 and its Impact on the Law of Gender in Pakistan' (2019) 20 *Australian Journal of Asian Law* 103, 104-06.

[162] The Criminal Law (Amendment) Ordinance (2020) Art 2. Transgender has been incorporated to the definition of 'person' in Art 375 of the Pakistan Penal Code (1860).

[163] The Pakistan Transgender Persons (Protection of Rights) Rules (2020) provides in Arts 17 and 18 a framework for the inclusion of transgender persons in educational institutions and government employment, being Sindh the first province to establish a 0.5% quota in government jobs for transgenders in the Sindh Civil Servants (Amendment) Act (2021), Art 2, although after the examination of the Standing Medical Board.

[164] Federal Shariat Court, Shariat Petitions 5 and 6/I/2020. See also JA Redding, 'Islamic challenges to Pakistan's transgender rights law' (2022) 10 *Melbourne Asia Review*, available at melbourneasiareview.edu.au/islamic-challenges-to-pakistans-transgender-rights-law.

speech and how it was to be exercised by women marching on International Women's Day in order to be able to walk down public streets.[165] Nonetheless, the Supreme Court seemed to have little hesitation about entering the political sphere.[166] In a public speech made in 2021, Justice Mansoor Ali Shah stated that the *suo moto* powers of the courts should be used for the protection of the rights of weaker segments of the society instead of dealing with political issues.[167] Thus, the development of this jurisdiction for women and minorities has still to be seised by a Supreme Court that has not yet been revealed as the expected counter-patriarchal ally in spite of certain landmark cases and the remarkable role of individual justices.

Case law, although unstable and sluggish, has reached the required base camp for a new momentum in the expansion of gender-based rights. Jurisprudence has established what can be considered as the three sides of a gender-justice cornerstone based on the right to equality and non-discrimination of Article 25, the right to life of Article 9 and the right to dignity and privacy of Article 14. Reading this cornerstone together with further constitutional regulations on education and employment as well as with the full participation of women stated in the principle of policy of Article 34, the Supreme Court has created a safety net for the protection of women in different spheres of life. While women's rights remain in the lead of this legal advancement, Pakistan has succeeded in being the first Muslim-majority country to enact a comprehensive piece of legislation recognising transgender rights. However, a robust development of individual rights against community rights and patriarchal morality, including the expansion of the rights to life, dignity and privacy, is still pending.

Patriarchy and majoritarianism remain at the core of the Pakistani legal system, politicising the judicial debate and monitoring the agenda. While this patriarchal game is performed, women's rights tend to be neglected and the judicial struggle for the enforcement of minorities' rights rests hopeless. Moreover, the confrontation of Islamic principles with the so-called Western agenda, in which feminism has been conveniently included by conservative sections of society, has created a challenging environment for the advancement of the rights of the segments of the population that are in the margins of a

[165] *Munir Ahmad v Federation of Pakistan*, PLD [2020] Lahore 528; *Imran Javed Aziz v Federation of Pakistan*, PLD [2020] Islamabad 302. While the Lahore High Court gave directions to the district administration for the issuance of an NOC to hold the 'Aurat March 2020' – a Women's March on the occasion of the International Women's Day – and the women were also directed to avoid slogans contrary to the law, the Islamabad High Court expected women to conduct it in consistency with the norms of decency.

[166] O Siddique, 'The Judicialization of Politics in Pakistan: The Supreme Court after the Lawyer's Movement' in M Tushnet and M Khosla (eds), *Unstable Constitutionalism: Law and Politics in South Asia* (Cambridge University Press, 2015) 189.

[167] J Kurshid, 'SC judge dispels impression of division in judiciary' *The News International* (21 November 2021), available at www.thenews.com.pk/print/910462-sc-judge-dispels-impression-of-division-in-judiciary.

Muslim-male-centred society. Colonial values and customary practices, from the lower value of women's testimony to the criminalisation of homosexual sex, have been resilient in the Pakistani legal system. Only when the narratives of the establishment meet women and minorities' needs, mainly as a consequence of popular outcry, are patriarchal forces prone to recognise, grant and enforce their demands. Even so, the advancement of women's and transgender person's rights in this joint counter-patriarchal struggle stand as a stronghold for other minorities.

13

Women, Gender and the Constitution in Sri Lanka

MARIO GOMEZ*

I. INTRODUCTION

SRI LANKA IS a paradox island in many ways. High social indicators for women in the areas of literacy, maternal mortality, and life expectancy coexist with poor labour-force participation rates. Years of universal suffrage, producing the world's first woman prime minister and electing a woman president, coexist with extremely poor representation for women at all levels of governance. The Constitution protects fundamental rights and provides for an enforceable remedy but continues to sanction past laws even when they conflict with fundamental rights.

In Sri Lanka, Hindu temples coexist with Buddhist shrines, multiple faiths worship at the same sacred spaces and share similar rituals, and historical monuments exhibit profound religious syncretism. And yet the nation has experienced egregious bouts of ethnic and religious violence in which women have played the role of both victim and victimiser. Between 1983 and 2009, the Liberation Tigers of Tamil Eelam (LTTE) periodically used women as suicide bombers in their campaign of armed violence.[1]

This chapter examines a few of these paradoxes insofar as they relate to women, gender, sexuality and the Constitution. It looks at how constitutional law, constitutional values and constitutional litigation have advanced or failed to advance women's rights and the rights of sexual minorities in Sri Lanka. It also looks briefly at how ordinary legislation and public policy have advanced constitutional values of gender equality and non-discrimination.

* My thanks to Ruth Rubio-Marín and Wen-Chen Chang, for comments on previous versions of this paper; to Raaya Gomez for help with some of the early research; and to the Centre for Asian Legal Studies, National University of Singapore, for institutional support.

[1] The LTTE was the dominant armed group in Sri Lanka's 26-year ethnic war against the state. For writing on the conflict, see SJ Tambiah, *Sri Lanka: Ethnic Fratricide and the Dismantling of Democracy* (Chicago University Press, 1986); N DeVotta, *Blowback: Linguistic Nationalism, Institutional Decay, and Ethnic Conflict in Sri Lanka* (Stanford University Press, 2004); M Gomez, 'Keeping Rights Alive: Reform and Reconciliation in Post-War Sri Lanka' (2011) 17 *Asian Yearbook of International Law* 117.

In recent years, the women's movement has emerged as one of the most vibrant social movements globally and succeeded in driving legislative, institutional and policy change at several levels.[2] Sri Lanka has been no different, and women's groups and advocates have steered through several important institutional and policy changes.[3] Sri Lanka ratified the Convention on the Elimination of All Forms of Discrimination Against Women (CEDAW) in 1981 and women obtained the right to vote in 1931, long before their South Asian counterparts. Yet, gender equality remains an aspiration.[4] This chapter examines some of these changes with a focus on how constitutional rights and values have driven legislative and policy change.

In 2022, the United Nations Development Programme (UNDP) Human Development Index ranked the country 73 out of 191 countries, with a score of 0.782;[5] in the Gender Inequality Index, the country was ranked 73 out of 191 countries, with a score of 0.383;[6] and in the Global Gender Gap Report of 2022 the country was ranked 110 out of 146, with a score of 0.670.[7]

Table 13.1 Socio-economic statistics[8]

	Male	Female
Literacy rate (10 years or more)	96.9%	94.6%
Mean age at marriage	27.2 years	23.4 years
Life expectancy at birth[9]	72.0 years	78.6 years
Maternal mortality rate[10]	N/A	36%
Labour Force participation rate[11]	71.1%	30.9%

[2] See K Jayawardena, *Feminism and Nationalism in the Third World* (Zed Books, 1986) for a discussion of the role of women in political struggles in Asia and the Middle East.

[3] See N de Mel, *Women & the Nation's Narrative: Gender and Nationalism in Twentieth Century Sri Lanka* (Social Scientists' Association, 2001) 233–78 for a discussion of the engagement of women and women's groups in some contemporary political issues.

[4] Committee on the Elimination of Discrimination against Women [hereinafter CEDAW Committee], 'Concluding Observations on the Eighth Periodic Report of Sri Lanka' (9 March 2017) CEDAW/C/LKA/CO/8.

[5] United Nations Development Programme [hereinafter UNDP], 'Human Development Report 2021–22', available at hdr.undp.org/content/human-development-report-2021-22.

[6] UNDP, 'Gender Inequality Index' (2022), available at hdr.undp.org/data-center/thematic-composite-indices/gender-inequality-index#/indicies/GII.

[7] WEF, 'Global Gender Gap Report 2022' (July 2022), available at www3.weforum.org/docs/WEF_GGGR_2022.pdf?_gl=1*14wr6r3*_up*MQ..&gclid=CjwKCAjwolqhBhAGEiwArXT7K9UMGw-MFW8mFTXQ0nZddT7IQfyU689yfHDzv9_lSL5CQPw7pai8GxoCl-UQAvD_BwE.

[8] Department of Census and Statistics, 'Census of Population and Housing 2012 – Final Report' (undated), available at www.statistics.gov.lk/Resource/en/Population/CPH_2011/CPH_2012_5Per_Rpt.pdf. In 2020 there were two female Court of Appeal judges out of 12 and one female judge out of 11 on the Supreme Court [hereinafter SC]. This changed with adoption of the 20th Amendment in October 2020 and the expansion of the number of judges in both courts.

[9] Department of Census and Statistics, 'Life Tables for Sri Lanka 2011–2013 by District and Sex' (18 October 2019), available at www.lifetable.de/File/GetDocument/data/LKA/LKA006020112013AU1.pdf.

[10] The World Bank, 'Maternal Mortality Ratio- Sri Lanka' (2017), available at data.worldbank.org/indicator/SH.STA.MMRT?locations=LK.

[11] Department of Census and Statistics, 'Sri Lanka Labour Force Survey Quarterly Report. 2nd Quarter – 2021' VII, available at www.statistics.gov.lk/LabourForce/StaticalInformation/QuarterlyReports/2ndQuarter2021.

During the 26 years of conflict between 1983 and 2009, many women were displaced, resulting in lost productive assets, livelihoods and income, and causing a breakdown of the traditional family system. Several women lost their spouses and sons to the conflict, resulting in a large number of women-led households.

Section II of this chapter provides background to Sri Lanka's Constitution. Section III, in turn, examines how the legal system approaches sexual orientation, how it relates to international norms, and how it applies fundamental rights to private actors. Section IV examines the relevant constitutional jurisprudence, including case law on gender-based violence. Section V discusses three flagship statutory developments that have advanced constitutional values: the amendment to the criminal law in 1995, the Domestic Violence Act, and the quota for women at the local government level. Section VI discusses two key proposed reforms to advance gender equality: the proposal to establish an independent commission for women, and the proposal to reform the Muslim personal law. In conclusion, section VII argues that constitutional litigation has had only a minimal transformative impact on gender relations in Sri Lanka and offers an explanation for this.

II. CONSTITUTIONAL CONTEXT AND FRAMEWORK

A. Overview

The Donoughmore Constitution, adopted in 1931, provided limited self-government to colonial Sri Lanka, known then as Ceylon. The first post-independence constitution of 1947 lasted 25 years, when it was replaced by the First Republican constitution of 1972. The 1972 Constitution was superseded just six years later by the Second Republican Constitution in 1978, which continues in effect today.

The 20 amendments to the current Constitution have transformed the original text in important ways. Over the years, three main constitutional questions have been at the forefront of constitutional politics: the place of Buddhism in the Constitution; presidentialism; and power-sharing, especially how power should be devolved to the Tamil-dominated North and the ethnically diverse Eastern province.[12] Since the end of the war in 2009, questions relating to accountability, truth, reparations and memorialisation have also figured in the country's constitutional debates.

[12] See M Gomez, 'Constitutional Struggle in Sri Lanka' (2022) 50 *Federal Law Review* 174.

B. Key Elements of the 1978 Constitution

The 1978 Constitution introduced a powerful Executive Presidency, an electoral system based on proportional representation, a justiciable bill of rights, and the mechanism of a referendum. However, the Constitution preserved inconsistent past laws and provided for pre-enactment review of legislative bills only, with no post-enactment judicial review.[13] The idea of the unitary state was retained from the 1972 Constitution. Buddhism was assigned the 'foremost place' in the nation's fundamental law. Mainly as a result of Indian intervention, a semi-federal framework was introduced by way of the Provincial Council system in 1987.[14]

C. The 19th Amendment to the Constitution

In January 2015, the country went through an unexpected political transition when former President Rajapaksa lost a presidential election to his onetime ally Maithripala Sirisena. At the parliamentary election of August 2015, the new President's National Unity coalition – consisting of traditional rivals, the United National Party (UNP) and the Sri Lanka Freedom Party – secured a parliamentary majority.

One of the first acts of the new Government, even before the parliamentary election was held, was to reform the Executive Presidency. Of the 225 members of Parliament, 215 voted in favour of the 19th Amendment, nine abstained, and one voted against the amendment.[15]

The 19th Amendment to the Constitution, passed by Parliament in May 2015, made some important changes. It reduced the President and Parliament's term from six years to five, restored the two-term limit on holding presidential office, and provided that the President could no longer dissolve Parliament before four and a half years of its term. The amendment also made the President's official acts subject to the Supreme Court (SC)'s fundamental-rights jurisdiction.

The 19th Amendment reintroduced the Constitutional Council (CC). The objective underlying the CC was to create an independent institution consisting of members of Parliament from different political parties along with eminent civil-society representatives who would participate in the appointment of persons to key public institutions, including the courts. The CC was given the authority to recommend to the President the appointment of

[13] A Welikala (ed), *Reforming Sri Lankan Presidentialism: Provenance, Problems and Prospects* (Centre for Policy Alternatives, 2015).

[14] Through the 13th Amendment to the Constitution (1987) and the Provincial Councils Act of 1987.

[15] A Welikala (ed), *The Nineteenth Amendment to the Constitution: Content and Context* (Centre for Policy Alternatives, 2016).

members of Independent Commissions, and to approve the President's nominees to the higher courts and other key offices, such as the Attorney-General, the Inspector-General of Police and the Auditor-General. A prominent woman from civil society was part of the CC between 2015 and 2018.

Weak political leadership and serious differences of opinion between the Prime Minister and the President caused the democratic transition of 2015 to collapse. It was also jolted by a serious security lapse, resulting in the Easter Sunday bombings of April 2019, which killed hundreds and damaged prominent churches and hotels. This created a public momentum for the return of a 'strongman', which in turn prompted the adoption of the 20th Amendment.

D. The 20th Amendment to the Constitution

The 20th Amendment, passed in October 2020, takes Sri Lanka once more into the fold of constitutional authoritarianism and rolled back many of the gains of the 19th Amendment by concentrating power once more in a strong elected President. The President may remove the Prime Minister at will, hold any Cabinet portfolio, and has the discretion to assign other ministerial portfolios among members of the Cabinet. The President may dissolve a democratically elected legislature after half its term (two and a half years) without any reason.

The CC, which acted as a check on the President's power to make appointments to the independent commissions and the higher courts has been abolished and replaced by an ineffective Parliamentary Council. As a result, appointments to the higher judiciary and to the independent commissions may be made by the president with no checks.

III. INTERNATIONAL NORMS AND CONSTITUTION

Sri Lanka has a dualist approach in its interaction with international law.[16] International conventions and treaties that Sri Lanka has ratified do not have domestic application unless local legislation has been passed for their incorporation.[17] The country, however, has a good record with regard to the ratification of international instruments, and has ratified all the core human rights treaties.[18] Despite this dualist approach, Sri Lankan judges have used

[16] N Rodley, 'The Singarasa Case: Quis Custodiet … ? A Test for the Bangalore Principles of Judicial Conduct' (2008) 41 *Israel Law Review* 500; *Leelawathie v Minister of Defence and External Affairs* 68 NLR 487.

[17] D Udagama, 'The Politics of Domestic Implementation of International Human Rights Law: A Case Study of Sri Lanka' (2015) 16 *Asia-Pacific Journal on Human Rights and the Law* 104.

[18] See *Sri Lanka: State of Human Rights 2016* (Law & Society Trust, 2016) for a list of international instruments ratified by Sri Lanka.

international treaties, and the jurisprudence of international and regional courts, in dealing with constitutional and other remedies. The *Singarasa* case, however, complicated matters when a five-judge panel held that the ratification of the First Optional protocol to the ICCPR by the Sri Lankan Government was unconstitutional.[19]

In a landmark decision for the rights of women and sexual minorities, the Committee on the Elimination of Discrimination against Women (CEDAW Committee), upheld the claim of a lesbian, gay, bisexual, transgender and intersex (LGBTI) activist who alleged discrimination on the basis of her sexual orientation. Rosanna Flamer-Caldera, in her complaint under the Optional Protocol, stated that she had been subjected to discrimination, harassment, stigmatisation, threats, high-profile attacks on her character, and threats of violence by state officials and members of the public, including on social media. She stated that the criminalisation of same-sex sexual activity has resulted in discrimination, violence and harassment faced by the LGBTI community. Members of the community are not protected against police harassment and the law has had an impact on how she lives and conducts herself in public and private. The CEDAW Committee, in its opinion, observed that the activist had been subjected to discrimination that emanated from the criminalisation of same-sex activity in the Penal Code. The CEDAW Committee noted that decriminalisation of consensual same-sex relations is essential to prevent and protect against violence, discrimination and harmful gender stereotypes. The CEDAW Committee found that Sri Lanka was in breach of several of the rights of the CEDAW by criminalising same-sex activity and failing to provide protection for the activist's LGBTI-related work.[20]

A. The Bill of Rights

The Bill of Rights has been one of the most important ways in which women have sought to advance gender equality. However, it was not until 1978 (30 years after independence) that the Constitution introduced a Bill if Rights with a remedy for its enforcement. The SC is made the first and final court for all cases alleging a violation of the Bill of Rights.[21] The Constitution permits the court to 'grant such relief or make such directions as it may deem just and equitable in the circumstance'.[22]

[19] *Singarasa v Attorney General* SC Spl No 182/99. See Rodley (n 16) and Udagama (n 17) for discussion of this case.

[20] *Rosanna Flamer-Caldera v Sri Lanka*. Views adopted by the CEDAW Committee, under the Optional Protocol, concerning CEDAW Communication No 134/2018 (21 February 2022).

[21] See generally J Wickramaratne, *Fundamental Rights in Sri Lanka*, 3rd edn (Stamford Lake, 2021).

[22] The Constitution of Sri Lanka, Art 126(4) [hereinafter the Constitution].

B. Gender and the Constitution

Fundamental rights are contained in Chapter III of the Constitution. Five provisions of the Constitution are of particular relevance to the rights of women and sexual minorities. They include: Article 11, which prohibits torture and cruel, inhuman or degrading treatment or punishment; Article 12(1), which contains equal protection; Article 12(2), which prohibits discrimination on various grounds including sex discrimination; Article 12(3), which goes against discriminative treatment in public space; and Article 12(4), which endorses affirmative action to minorities, including women.

Article 12(4), which permits 'special provision' being made for the advancement of women, indirectly recognises that women have been historically discriminated against. However, in at least two decisions, the SC has stated that Article 12(4) cannot be used to support affirmative action on behalf of women, children and disabled persons in the absence of 'proved inequality'. In *Ramupillai v Festus Perera*, one judge observed:

> Article 12(4) in particular does not authorize 'affirmative action' for women, children and disabled persons, but out of an abundance of caution, declares that nothing in Article 12 shall prevent affirmative action; apart from proved 'inequality', Article 12(4) would not permit, for example a quota of 60% being stipulated for women in any sphere.[23]

In *Ramupillai*, the Court struck down a scheme of ethnic quotas for recruitment and promotions within the public-service sector, citing the state's inability to establish inequality. However, in decisions unrelated to gender, the SC has recognised the notion of 'substantive equality' holding that Article 12 required substantive as well as formal equality. Not only must laws, rules, and procedures be fair, the Court explained, they must also be applied 'even handedly'.[24] In a previous case the Court observed that affirmative action was designed to ensure 'true equality', and a formal interpretation of the equality clause would overlook the substantive content of the equality clause in the Constitution.[25] In its brief determination on the constitutionality of a women's quota at provincial level, the SC held that a quota for women was not unconstitutional and the quota supported the equality provisions in Article 12(4) of the Constitution.[26]

[23] *Ramupillai v Festus Perera* [1991] 1 Sri LR 11 (Justice Mark Fernando), cited with approval by the SC in Special Determination on the 'Local Authorities (Special Provisions) Bill' and the 'Local Authorities Elections (Amendment) Bill'; SC Special Determination Nos 02/2010–11/2010, 29. However, in its determination on the constitutionality of the two bills, the Court upheld a quota for women and youth. See also M Gomez, 'The Supreme Court Vetoes Ethnic Quotas: An analysis of Ramupillai v Festus Perera' (1991) 20 *Law & Society Trust Review*.

[24] *Dayarathna v The Minister of Health and Indigenous Medicine* [1999] 1 Sri LR 393, 401 (Justice Amerasinghe).

[25] *Seneviratne v UGC* [1978-79-80] 1 Sri LR 182, 217–18.

[26] SC Special Determination No 19/2017 (9 August 2017), which upheld the validity of a bill to establish a quota for women at provincial level. See also SC Special Determination Nos 3 and 4 of 2016 on the constitutional validity of setting a quota for women at local government level.

Sexual orientation is not a prohibited ground of discrimination in the Constitution. Article 12(2) states that 'No citizen shall be discriminated against on the grounds of race, religion, language, caste, sex, political opinion, place of birth *or any one of such grounds*.' Discrimination on the basis of sexual orientation, then, would have to be 'read in' through a process of judicial interpretation.[27]

The common perception is that the Sri Lankan Penal Code, based largely on Macaulay's Indian Penal Code of 1862, criminalises the homosexual acts of men and women, even though the language in the Code is ambiguous.[28] There are few recorded cases of prosecutions under these two sections, even if gays, lesbians and trans persons face harassment by the police.[29]

In a recent appeal, a conviction under section 365A was challenged in the SC.[30] The case, *Galabada Payagalage Sanath Wimalasiri v OIC*, is illustrative of changing judicial attitudes to the rights of sexual minorities. The case also indicates possible approaches to judicial interpretation to circumvent unambiguous provisions found in outdated criminal law. In this case, two men who were engaged in oral sex inside a car were taken into custody. One of them was subsequently identified as a police sub-inspector. They were convicted under section 365A of committing an act of gross indecency, and the magistrate imposed a sentence and fine. The conviction was affirmed by the High Court and an appeal was made to the SC. One of the questions in appeal was whether the sentence was excessive. The SC, while affirming the conviction, suspended the operation of the sentence suggesting that where the act was between consenting adults and was consensual, it may be permissible to vary the sentence, even if the court is compelled to convict based on the evidence. Contemporary thinking was that consensual sex between adults should not be policed by the state nor should it be grounds for criminalisation. Since the

[27] CEDAW Committee's Concluding Observations of 2011 and 2017 recommended the repeal of provisions in the Penal Code criminalizing consensual relations between same-sex adults. These views were repeated in *Rosanna Flamer-Caldera v Sri Lanka* (n 20).

[28] According to s 365, 'Whoever voluntarily has carnal intercourse against the order of nature with any man, woman or animal shall be punished', and section 365A states that 'Any person who, in public or private, commits, or is a party to the commission of, or procures or attempts to procures the commission by any person of, any act of gross indecency with another person, shall be guilty of an offence, and shall be punished'. Section 365A initially criminalised acts of gross indecency only between males. However, the Penal Code Amendment Act of 1995 changed 'any male person' to 'any person', which brought women within its ambit. See A Wickramasinghe, 'Homosexuality and the Law' (2017) *Sri Lanka Law College Review* 115 (arguing that these sections of the Penal Code criminalise both homosexual and heterosexual conduct); see also Act No 16 of 2006 (making additional changes to the Penal Code).

[29] Thangarajah refers to two cases where s 365A was used: *King v Wickramasinghe* and *Amerasinghe v Daluwatta*. Court of Appeal CA128/98; see P Thangarajah, 'Strengthening of Legal Protection for LGBT in Sri Lanka: Road to Decriminalization: Situation Analysis' (*Equal Ground*, undated) 6, on file with the author.

[30] *Galabada Payagalage Sanath Wimalasiri v OIC*, SC Appeal No 32/11, SC Minutes of 30 November 2016.

conviction could not be overturned, the sentence was suspended on the basis that it was excessive.[31]

There is nothing in the Sri Lankan Constitution that confines fundamental rights only to state or governmental actors. According to the Constitution, fundamental rights are enjoyed by 'citizens' and 'persons' and should as a matter of principle be enforceable against both public and private actors.[32] However, the constitutional remedy for the enforcement of fundamental rights is restricted to entities allied with the state.[33] A judge of the Sri Lankan SC has taken the view that the non-discrimination principle in the Constitution is binding not only on the state but also on all institutions and individuals.[34] Citizens shall not be discriminated against 'by anyone', although the special remedy under Article 126 is only available for executive or administrative action.[35]

This interpretation is supported by the language of Sri Lankan constitutional provisions: the guarantee against non-discrimination is made available to all 'persons',[36] and to all 'citizens'.[37] The same judge has argued that it may be possible to hold a private actor responsible even where there is no nexus with the executive. In these instances, a common-law remedy would lie, and the correct forum would be the District Court.[38] Some of the constitutional provisions support the view that the Sri Lankan Bill of Rights was meant to apply to private actors.[39]

C. Gender and Constitutional Reform

Flowing from the political transition of 2015, Parliament initiated a process of constitutional reform and constituted a Public Representations Committee (PRC) in 2016 to engage in public consultations around constitutional reform. The 20-member committee included three women. This was the first time that there had been such widespread public engagement on constitutional reform. Several women's groups and LGBTI groups, mobilised across the country and

[31] ibid.

[32] See *Ramupillai Festus Perera* [1991] 1 Sri LR 11, *Saman v Leeladasa* [1989] 1 Sri LR 1 and *Dissanayake v Kaleel* [1993] 2 Sri LR 135.

[33] See Arts 17 and 126 of the Constitution, which refer to violations or imminent violations by 'executive or administrative action'.

[34] Former SC Justice Mark Fernando in the cases cited above.

[35] *Ramupillai v Festus Perera* [1991] 1 Sri LR 11, 70 (Justice Mark Fernando).

[36] The Constitution, Art 12(1).

[37] ibid Art 12(2).

[38] See *Saman v Leeladasa* [1989] 1 Sri LR 1, *Ramupillai v Festus Perera* [1991] 1 Sri LR 11 and *Dissanayake v Kaleel* [1993] 2 Sri LR 135. See also *Mohamed Faiz v Attorney-General* [1995] 1 Sri LR 372 where an order was made against a private actor who was the main perpetrator of the rights violation. The SC held that the act constituted executive and administrative action because an officer of state stood by and permitted the violation to occur.

[39] See the Constitution, Art 12(3).

made extensive representations, not only on questions relating to equality and non-discrimination, but also on reconciliation and the need for a democratic, plural, multi-religious and multi-ethnic country. Female-headed households, widows, victims of violence and relatives of the disappeared and tortured, went before the PRC to share their experiences and to propose mechanisms for a constitution that would prevent the occurrence of such incidents in the future.[40] LGBTI groups called for the recognition of the rights of the LGBTI community and the PRC recommended the inclusion of a prohibition against sexual orientation and sexual or gender identity in the Constitution.[41]

The process of constitutional reform that commenced in 2016, however, came to halt with the election of a new president in 2019 and a new government taking office in August 2020. The new regime instead passed the 20th amendment within two months of taking office and set up a committee of experts to draft a new constitution.

IV. CONSTITUTIONAL JURISPRUDENCE

A. Overview of Gender Equality Jurisprudence

Even though an enforceable Bill of Rights, which includes a prohibition on discrimination on the basis of sex, has formally been a part of the Constitution since 1978, constitutional jurisprudence on gender equality is sparse. The lack of constitutional litigation around gender equality suggests that advocates for gender and sexual equality have fought their battles in other forums, including the legislative and policy forums. Lacking also is a dedicated public-interest group to ensure consistent litigation around gender equality.

The Sri Lankan fundamental-rights jurisdiction has expanded monumentally in the past 40 years. From a trickle of cases in the late 1970s and early 1980s has emerged a flood of such applications pending before the SC.[42] The sparse jurisprudence on gender must be considered against developments in other areas of the law, where advocates have used the constitutional Bill of Rights frequently. For example, environmental-rights advocates have resorted to constitutional litigation, as have those religious advocates seeking interpretations of the constitutional clause on Buddhism.[43]

One reason for this growth in the fundamental-rights jurisdiction is because the remedy is a relatively quick one. Applications must be made to the SC within

[40] Public Representations Committee on Constitutional Reform, 'Report on Public Representations on Constitutional Reform' (May 2016) 91–95, available at constitutionnet.org/sites/default/files/sri_lanka_prc_report-english-final.pdf.

[41] ibid 95 and 112–14.

[42] Wickramaratne (n 21).

[43] The Constitution, Art 9.

one month of the alleged infringement and there is no appeal from the SC. In most cases, an application will be disposed of within two years (although in recent years, cases have remained pending for longer). This is faster compared to other areas of the law, where proceedings, including the appeal, take much longer to conclude. In recent years the SC has provided fresh interpretations to many constitutional rights. This is true of Article 12 (the right to equality before the law and equal protection of the law) and Article 13 (freedom from arbitrary arrest and detention). In the initial years after the adoption of the Bill of Rights, the SC was reluctant to issue orders against the state. However, as the Court became more familiar with the jurisdiction, this has changed, and the Court has developed a significant jurisprudence over the years, especially around Article 12. Individual judges have also had an impact on the interpretation of rights and the development of the jurisprudence. The willingness to deliver an order against the state where a violation has been established, and the expansion of the fundamental-rights jurisdiction through a process of interpretation, are other reasons why the court docket has grown.[44]

Three key provisions have been used in those cases where advocates for gender and sexual equality have sought constitutional remedies: the prohibition on torture, cruel, inhuman, or degrading treatment or punishment; the right to equality before the law and equal protection of the law; and the prohibition on discrimination on the basis of sex.

Equality before the law, equal protection of the law, and the right to non-discrimination were used in *Fischer v The Controller of Immigration and Emigration* to challenge the different standards that applied to a Sri Lankan men and woman for obtaining a resident visa for foreign spouses.[45]

Fischer, a German national, was married to a Sri Lankan woman and applied for a residency visa. The Controller asked Fischer to deposit a sum of US$25,000 and an inward remittance of US$9,000 before his application would be considered. Fischer challenged the decision on the ground that it violated Article 12 of the Constitution. After the case was filed, the Controller provided Fischer with a residency visa enabling him to work. In response, Fischer withdrew his petition. The Court observed that, '*prima facie*, this (practice) places Sri Lankan females at a disadvantage vis a vis males'.[46] Significantly, the SC issued a direction to the Controller to publish new guidelines for the grant of visas to foreign spouses,

[44] See M Gomez, 'Blending Rights with Writs: Sri Lankan Public Law's New Brew' (2006) *Acta Juridica (Supplement)*; M Gomez, 'The Modern Benchmarks of Sri Lankan Public Law' (2001) 118 *South African Law Journal* 581; M Gomez, 'Mixing Writs with Rights: The Implications for Public Law in Sri Lanka' (2023) 18 *Asian Journal of Comparative Law* 253 for a discussion of some of the jurisprudence around the right to equal protection of the law.

[45] *Bernard Maximilian Fischer v The Controller of Immigration and Emigration*, SC Application No 436/99, SC Minutes of 24 May 1999. See also *Unity Dow v Attorney General of Botswana* [1992] LRC (Const.) 623 (CA) and [1991] LRC (Const) 574 (HC).

[46] M Gomez and S Gomez, *Striking a Balance: Using International Human Rights to Achieve Gender Equality* (Shakti, 2004) 72.

which would conform with Article 12. The new guidelines were adopted almost two years later. These discriminatory regulations have been challenged in at least two previous cases, both of which were settled before judgment could be delivered.[47]

In *Manohari v Secretary, Ministry of Education*, the SC made strong statements on gender equality and sex discrimination, including statements on the need to comply with Sri Lanka's international obligations, suggesting a more responsive and evolving approach from the court to claims of sexual equality.[48] In that case, the SC held that sexual harassment at the workplace was a violation of the constitutional prohibition on sex-based discrimination. A schoolteacher of music alleged continuous sexual harassment by the school principal and a fellow teacher. Despite complaints, including to the police, no consequences ensued, forcing her to publicly air her grievances on television. In light of the constitutional framework and international obligations the country had taken on, the Court held that there was a violation of the schoolteacher's fundamental rights. The Court noted that Article 12(2) of the Constitution prohibited discrimination on the basis of sex, that Article 12(4) permitted special provisions being made by law, subordinate legislation or executive action for the advancement of women, and that the country was a signatory to CEDAW, which created a framework of rights that the court should enforce.[49] The Court, held that there was a continuous period of harassment and that the teacher's fundamental rights to equality before the law and equal protection of the law were violated, and that her right to free speech and expression were violated. The school principal and the fellow teacher were ordered to pay compensation to the victim.[50]

In an ongoing case, a group of women have challenged a notification issued by the state prohibiting women from purchasing alcohol and from participating in the manufacture, transportation or sale of alcohol. The women contend that this notification amounts to gender-based discrimination and infringes the rights to equality before the law, equal protection of the law, and the right to engage in a lawful profession, business, trade or vocation.[51] The petitioners question the constitutionality of a regulation, issued on 18 January 2018, that prohibited women from being 'engaged in and/or employed in the manufacture,

[47] ibid.

[48] *Manohari v Secretary, Ministry of Education*, SC/FR/No 76/2012, SC Minutes of 28 September 2016.

[49] Convention on the Elimination of All Forms of Discrimination Against Women (CEDAW) was ratified only in 1981. See also *Cokeman v Attorney General*, (FR) 136/2014, SC Minutes of 15 November 2017 [hereinafter the *Cokeman* case].

[50] The same facts gave rise to a criminal case under the Penal Code: *Officer in Charge, Kollupitiya Police Station, v Malagoda*, SC Appeal 76/2018, SC Minutes of 12 February 2019. The teacher concerned was charged under s 345 of the Penal Code for committing the offence of sexual harassment. The magistrate acquitted the accused and the victim appealed to the High Court which convicted the accused. The SC confirmed the decision of the High Court.

[51] Draft petition, on file with the author.

collection, bottling, sale and transportation of liquor, and to be sold or given liquor within the premises of a tavern'.[52] The regulation amended a previous regulation amending obsolete rules under the Excise Ordinance of 1912 that prohibited the sale of alcohol to women and prohibited their involvement in the manufacture, transportation or sale of alcohol. To date, the case has not been taken up for argument, as the new cabinet of ministers has sought time to file new objections.[53]

In *Rossana Flamer-Caldera v Inspector-General of Police*, another case that has yet to reach the argument stage, several petitioners representing the LGBTI community and civil society have filed a writ in the Court of Appeal against a counsellor who was involved in training programmes for the police. The counsellor had made several derogatory statements against the LGBTI community, and the petitioners have sought her exclusion from future police training programmes.[54]

In a case involving a land dispute between private parties, the SC, on appeal from an order of the District Court and Provincial High Court, noted that the Third Schedule of the Land Development Ordinance appeared to conflict with Article 12 of the Constitution. The Land Development Ordinance privileges male heirs over female heirs in the succession to land. The SC observed that 'the provision has to be reviewed by policy makers in the light of the realities of the day and in particular Article 12 of the Constitution'.[55]

B. The Constitution and Gender-based Violence

The Sri Lankan Constitution does not recognise a life free of gender-based violence as a distinct fundamental right.[56] However, the Bill of Rights offers protection for women who may be subject to gender-based violence from officers associated with the state.[57] The SC has, in a few decisions, held that certain kinds of violent acts directed at women constitute a violation of Article 11 of the Constitution.

[52] Notification No 04/2018 issued by the Minister of Finance and Mass Media, and published in the Government Gazette Extraordinary No 2054-42, dated 18 January 2018, further to a cabinet decision of 16 January 2018.

[53] Email communication with one of the petitioners, 8 March 2021 and 7 February 2022, on file with the author.

[54] *Rossana Flamer-Caldera v Inspector-General of Police*, petition on file with the author.

[55] SC Appeal No 125 of 2010, SC Minutes of 17 December 2014, 8–9. See also CEDAW Committee (n 4).

[56] Contrast the Constitution of South Africa which provides for the right to be free from all forms of violence from either public or private sources, Constitution of South Africa (1996), Art 12(1)(c).

[57] The right to life is absent from the Sri Lankan Bill of Rights. However, see *Sriyani Silva v Iddamalgoda* [2003] 2 Sri LR 63, which held that the right to life is implicit in the Constitution. The rights to security of the person and to dignity, which have implications for gender-based violence, are also absent from the Sri Lankan law.

In a case where a 16-year-old girl was slapped and threatened by a police constable who tried to seduce her, the Court observed that she had been subjected by the police to '*such severe physical and mental pain*' that amounted to cruel, inhuman, and degrading treatment and punishment. The SC found that the constable's acts violated Article 11 of the Constitution and awarded the girl Rs 25,000 in compensation.[58]

In another case the Court drew a distinction between 'cruel and inhuman treatment' and 'degrading treatment' by examining the severity of the offence. In *Kumarasena v Sub-inspector Sriyantha*, a young girl was detained at the police station for six hours. At the invitation of the arresting officer, several other officers touched her body, squeezed her breasts, pinched her buttocks, addressed her as a 'love bird', questioned her as to whether she was wearing any underwear and invited her to come out with them.[59] The judge observed,

> the suffering occasioned was of an aggravated kind and attained the level of severity to be taken cognizance of as a violation of Article 11 … I therefore, declare that Article 11 of the Constitution was violated by the subjection of the petitioner to degrading treatment.[60]

In *WMK de Silva v Chairman, Ceylon Fertilizer Corporation*, the Court was reluctant to find a violation of Article 11 where an employer's acts of unkindness and gross incivility allegedly caused distress to a female employee.[61] The Court stated that this type of treatment amounted to an unfair labour practice and expressed the view that 'the acts complained of are clearly not torture or punishment; they fall far short of the degree of mental or physical coercisiveness (sic) or viciousness required to constitute 'cruel, inhuman or degrading punishment'.[62]

Although the Court was of the view that Article 11 not only embraced physical violence but also applied to the 'sphere of the soul or mind',[63] the Court was unwilling to hold the mental anguish the applicant suffered resulted in a violation of Article 11. This case stands in contrast to *Manohari*, where the Court held that continuous sexual harassment at the workplace amounted to a violation of Article 12 of the Constitution.

In *Nalika Kalupahana v Nihal Mahinda*, a public-interest petition by a lawyer succeeded in establishing a violation of Article 11.[64] The petition and supporting affidavit were drafted after an organisation received a letter from the father of a 14-year-old girl allegedly tortured and detained by police. At an initial hearing, the SC directed that the girl be 'properly represented'.

[58] *Samanthilaka v Ernest Perera* [1990] 1 Sri LR 318.
[59] *Kumarasena v Sub-inspector Sriyantha*, SC Application No 257/93, SC Minutes of 23 May 1994.
[60] ibid (Justice Amerasinghe).
[61] *Mrs WMK de Silva v Chairman, Ceylon Fertilizer Corporation* [1989] 2 Sri LR 393.
[62] ibid 401.
[63] ibid 405.
[64] *Nalika Kalupahana v Nihal Mahinda* [1997] 3 Sri LR 331.

Subsequently, the girl and her parents sought to withdraw the application. The SC, however, denied permission, noting that there were serious allegations of torture and that the girl continued to receive medical treatment and had not attended school since the incident. The public-interest petitioner indicated to the Court that pressure was being exerted on the parents to withdraw the application.[65] Based on the affidavits submitted, the Court held that the girl had been tortured, unlawfully detained and subjected to cruel, inhuman and degrading treatment when the police attempted to extract a confession from her relating to the commission of a theft. The victim in this case committed suicide after the case was decided.

As noted, the SC is the first and last court for fundamental-rights violations. For a woman victim of violence, the SC's procedures have advantages over those followed by a criminal court. Proceedings before the SC take place by way of petition, written submissions and affidavits. Seldom is oral examination allowed and cross-examination is never permitted. A woman victim of violence would not be required to make a complaint to an insensitive police officer; she would not be required to tell her story in open court; and, more importantly, she would not be subjected to the trauma of cross-examination, all of which occur in a criminal trial. Instead, she would be represented by a lawyer or legal-aid group.

A specific constitutional right guaranteeing the right to be free from all forms of violence, either from public or private sources (as found in the constitution of South Africa), would enhance the remedies that women victims of violence could seek and would support the remedies available under the criminal law. That violence against women constitutes a human-rights violation has been recognised by international human-rights law. Domestic law now needs to follow suit. This may be done by incorporating a specific fundamental right and remedy in the Constitution, or by the adoption of specific legislation dealing with violence against women. As with the right to information law, ordinary legislation can also help advance constitutional rights and values in effective ways.[66]

C. Constitutional Jurisprudence from Three Other Areas

While gender-equality advocates have sought constitutional remedies only sporadically, other actors have used the Constitution and the Bill of Rights to press a variety of claims. This section looks at several illustrative cases from three areas: environmental law; religious rights; and the right to administrative justice.

[65] ibid 332.

[66] M Gomez, 'The Right to Information and Transformative Development Outcomes' (2019) 12 *Law and Development Review* 837.

In the area of environmental law, three cases demonstrate the judicial willingness to develop new rights through constitutional interpretation and to expand laws on standing to help access remedies. Prior to the enactment of the Right to Information (RTI) law and the inclusion of a right to information in the Constitution, the SC in *Environmental Foundation v UDA* held that the right to freedom of speech, expression and publication contained in Article 14 included an implied right to information.[67] The SC held that, in refusing to provide information about the lease to the petitioner, the Urban Development Authority, violated the petitioner's right to information. In the *Eppawela Case*, which involved a challenge to the development of a phosphate deposit, the SC broadened the concept of standing and referred extensively to international law and concepts on sustainable development.[68] Finally, in the *Chunnakam Case*, another public-interest case, the SC held that citizens have a fundamental right to be free from unlawful, arbitrary or unreasonable executive or administrative acts or omissions which result in environmental pollution or degradation, even though the right is not explicitly recognised in the constitution.[69]

Religious actors have also resorted to constitutional litigation in a bid to secure a privileged position for Buddhism.[70] In pursuit of greater autonomy, some religious actors have sought to curtail state involvement in monastic life.[71] The SC response has been mixed, with some judicial decisions advancing Sinhala–Buddhist interests, while others have adopted a more cautionary approach by holding that Sri Lanka is a secular state.

Constitutional litigation has also expanded in an area of law that might be labelled as the 'right to administrative justice'. In applications for a writ, Sri Lankan courts have taken the position that the exercise of discretionary power by the public authority must conform with the requirements of Article 12 (the right to equality and equal protection) as well as with the other traditional grounds of review such as excess of jurisdiction, unreasonableness, natural justice and legitimate expectation. The courts have held in a few cases that public power must also be exercised in accordance with other constitutional provisions. The courts have also used fundamental rights, especially Article 12, to develop new grounds of review, such as the right to receive reasons. At the same time, the courts have asserted that the constitutional right to equality and

[67] *Environmental Foundation v UDA* ('*Galle Face Case*') [2009] 1 Sri LR 123; see also ibid.

[68] *Bulankulama v Secretary, Ministry of Industrial Development (Eppawela Case)* [2000] 3 Sri LR 243.

[69] *Gunawardena v Central Environmental Authority*, SC Minutes of 4 April 2019, 52. The Court reached this conclusion by reading Art 12(1) of the Constitution, the right to equality and equal protection, together with Art 27(14) of the constitution, which declares that 'The State shall protect, preserve and improve the environment for the benefit of the community'. See also *Ashik v Bandula, OIC Weligama* [2007] 1 Sri LR 191, 193.

[70] See the Constitution, Art 9, and *cf* Arts 10 and 14(1).

[71] For a discussion of how the state intervenes in Buddhist monastic life, see B Schonthal, 'Securing the Sasana through Law: Buddhist Constitutionalism and Buddhist Interest-Litigation in Sri Lanka' (2016) 50 *Modern Asian Studies* 1966.

equal protection includes the right to natural justice, to reasons, to a recognition of legitimate expectations, and to the right against arbitrary and unfair treatment.[72]

While constitutional litigation has been used extensively to seek protection of environmental rights, religious rights and rights related to administrative justice, women advocates seem to prefer legislative and policy change instead. The lack of an organisation dedicated to litigating gender-equality rights may also explain the largely undeveloped jurisprudence in this area. The recent case on sexual harassment and the two pending cases discussed above, however, suggest that this may be changing, and that gender-equality advocates are now willing to seek constitutional remedies more frequently.

V. FLAGSHIP DEVELOPMENTS

Ordinary legislation has been used to advance constitutional values of gender equality and non-discrimination. This section discusses three of these developments: amendments to the criminal law responding to gender-based violence; the introduction of a domestic violence law; and the introduction of mandatory quotas for women at the local government level.

A. Responding to Gender-based Violence Through the Criminal Law

Sri Lankan scholars and activists have drawn on the momentum generated by the global movements around gender-based violence. Assisted by sensitive public officers within the Ministry of Justice and in the Legal Draftsman's Department, advocates for sexual equality generated changes in the criminal law that expanded on the constitutional rights of equality and non-discrimination.[73] These changes were prompted by a political transition in 1994, creating a culture in which legal reform became possible.[74] In addition to the legal changes,

[72] See Gomez, 'Mixing Writs with Rights' (n 44); M Gomez, 'The Supreme Court in the 1990s: Controlling Public Power through the Law' (2000) *Bar Association Law Journal* 54; M Gomez, 'Fundamental Rights and the Sri Lankan Supreme Court' (1995) 8 *Colombo Law Review* 73 for a detailed discussion of these developments.

[73] Penal Code Amendment Act No 22 of 1995.

[74] Chandrika Bandaranaike Kumaratunge was elected in 1994 as the first woman President. Her agenda of reform was influenced by human rights groups. One of the few prosecutions for conflict-related sexual violence occurred during her tenure: see the *Krishanthi Kumaraswamy* case, High Court Decision of 3 July 1998, discussed in M Gomez and S Gomez, *From Rights and Shame* (Shakti, 1999) 102–03; see also C Kodikara, 'An Interview with Prashanthi Mahindaratne: The Krishanthi Kumaraswamy Case' in K Jayawardena and K Pinto-Jayawardena (eds), *The Search for Justice: The Sri Lanka Papers* (Zubaan Publishers, 2016) 405. Prashanthi Mahindaratne, a former Trial Attorney at the ICT for the Former Yugoslavia, was the lead counsel in the *Krishanthi Kumaraswamy* case. See also R Vijeyarasa, *The Woman President: Leadership, law and legacy for women based on experiences from South and Southeast Asia* (Oxford University Press, 2022).

women's groups began to systematically document cases of violence and establish support centres to help survivors of violence. In 2000, women's groups began a campaign to enact a separate law on domestic violence.

The thrust of the 1995 changes to the criminal law was to strengthen the capacity of the criminal justice system to respond more effectively to gender-based violence. It did this by introducing a new offence of sexual harassment; increasing the punishments in cases of rape, grave sexual abuse, and custodial rape; changing how the law approached consent in cases of rape; and introducing other procedural changes.[75]

Despite these statutory reforms, real change at the ground level has been slow.[76] The main institutions charged with implementing the criminal law are the police, the judiciary and the Attorney-General's Department. While women's groups have engaged with these three institutions in past years, attitudes and approaches have changed only marginally, long delays occur in criminal cases, and significant obstacles prevent prosecuting gender-based violence quickly and effectively.[77] Among members of the bar, women's issues remain marginalised and few lawyers, including women lawyers, have shown the willingness to litigate these matters.[78]

B. The Domestic Violence Act of 2005

The Domestic Violence Act was the result of sustained activism by women's groups. The legislation was also facilitated by a tolerant political culture within the Government, with a former Secretary to the Ministry of Justice, playing a pivotal role in the drafting process. The law prohibiting and sanctioning domestic violence, then, extended the constitutional rights to equality

[75] Penal Code Amendment Act No 22 of 1995. Additional changes were made by Act No 16 of 2006. See also S Goonesekere, *Compendium on Law, Gender Based Violence and Reproductive Rights* (UNFPA, 2017); P Thangarajah, 'Rape and the Evidentiary Process in Sri Lanka' in K Jayawardena and K Pinto-Jayawardena (eds), *The Search for Justice: The Sri Lanka Papers* (Zubaan Publishers, 2016) 170, 171. The initial amendment contained a provision on marital rape which was amended during the Parliamentary debate. See also the Prohibition of Ragging and other Form of Violence in Educational Institutions Act No 20 of 1998, s 2(2) which sought to respond to ragging and other forms of violence in educational institutions.

[76] For a discussion of three encounters that women have had with the law outside of the constitution, see N de Mel and D Samararatne, 'The Law's Gender: Entanglements and Recursions – Three Stories from Sri Lanka' (2017) *On_Culture: The Open Journal for the Study of Culture* 3.

[77] Thangarajah observes that in 2014 the police registered 2,008 cases of rape, but charges were filed only in 249 cases. There was only one conviction of rape in 2014; see Thangarajah (n 75) 171. See also S de Silva, 'A Snapshot of the Criminal Justice System: Building a Picture through Sexual Violence Cases in the Court of Appeal' (Law and Society Trust, April 2018). See also the case of *Kathubdeen v Republic of Sri Lanka* [1998] 3 Sri LR 107 and *cf* this with the approach in *Somawathie v Baksons* (1973) 72 NLR 204.

[78] For a discussion on the role of women lawyers in the country's legal profession, see D Samararatne, 'Gendering the Legal Complex: Women in Sri Lanka's Legal Profession' (2020) 47 *Journal of Law and Society* 666.

and non-discrimination to cover acts that occur within the private sphere of family life.

While scholars and activists had discussed the need for a domestic violence law for years, the idea gathered momentum in 2000 when a prominent women's organisation, the Women & Media Collective (WMC), took concrete steps towards this goal. Discussions with multiple stakeholders were initiated and a consultant was tasked with drafting a law. The proposed legislation was then discussed with multiple actors, including medical professionals, the media, women's groups, lawyers, academics, prosecutors and the state. Awareness-raising workshops around the country on domestic violence were also conducted.[79]

About a year later, the Ministry of Justice presented a different draft law on domestic violence. The Justice Ministry draft contained no definition of domestic violence but, rather, linked the law to offences against the dignity of the person contained in the Penal Code. It was an amended version of the Justice Ministry draft that was adopted by Parliament in 2005. While some women's groups favoured the criminalisation of domestic violence and the provision of criminal remedies for victims of domestic violence, others advocated for a broader approach that would have combined civil and criminal remedies in a single piece of legislation.

The 'Prevention of Domestic Violence' law was passed by Parliament on 9 August 2005 without dissent.[80] The law's main purpose was to prevent violence or threatened violence between spouses, partners or members of the family, and to provide victims with a speedy and easily accessible remedy. It allows a victim, including a male victim, to request from a magistrate a protection order and to access the family home, bank accounts, and to children, where the court considers these remedies appropriate. The new law came 10 years after the Penal Code Amendment of 1995, a few years after the Maintenance Act, and three years before the Citizenship Amendment Act.

The law defines domestic violence by linking it to the offences in chapter 16 of the Penal Code and 'Emotional Abuse'. Chapter 16 offences include 'Grievous Hurt', 'Hurt', 'Wrongful Restraint', 'Wrongful Confinement', 'Criminal Force', 'Assault', 'Rape' and 'Murder'. Emotional Abuse is defined as a pattern of cruel, inhuman, degrading or humiliating conduct of a serious nature.[81] Under the law, a victim of domestic violence, or a person who fears that a family member may commit an act of violence against them, may apply to the Magistrate's Court for an Interim Order or a Protection Order, both of which prohibit a person from committing an act of domestic violence.

The Magistrate may also make other orders. This includes preventing the abuser from visiting the victim's place of employment or school. It also includes

[79] The civil society draft was reproduced in journal, see (2001) 163 *Law & Society Trust Review*. For a discussion see M Gomez, 'The Draft Domestic Violence Law: What Will It Do?' (2001) 7 *Pravada* 14.

[80] Prevention of Domestic Violence Act No 34 of 2005.

[81] ibid s 23.

the power to exclude the abuser from the family home or a part of it, or to prevent the sale of the family home. The Magistrate may also order that the victim be provided with monetary or other assistance to enable him or her to go on with their lives with the least possible disruption. Where the respondent breaches the terms of the Interim Order or the Protection Order, he or she could be convicted after a summary trial before a Magistrate.[82]

C. Women and Politics

The lack of women's representation in political institutions at national, provincial and local government levels is a glaring illustration of inequality. Despite constituting more than half of the Sri Lankan population, women never held more than six per cent of the seats at any level of government until 2018, when a quota was introduced at the local government level. 'No group defined with such precision can lay claim to such a monumental imbalance in representation'.[83] All South Asian countries have better levels of representation in their political institutions.

Quotas for women in politics operate in over 100 countries around the world. These include voluntary and mandatory quotas and vary in terms of the percentage of seats they seek to reserve for women. They are now widely seen as one way of ensuring greater representation of women in political decision-making, even if their effectiveness in generating a transformative policy agenda has been questioned. In its determination on the constitutionality of the local election amendment bill in 2010, the SC rejected the argument put forward by women's groups that Article 12(4) of the Constitution mandated the state to introduce a quota. Quotas are controversial because they seek fairness and fair outcomes through *unequal* treatment.[84]

The 1997 draft Constitution proposed a reservation of 25 per cent for women at the local government level.[85] Yet this provision was removed when the 2000

[82] A study published in 2012 stated that, even though 94,000 cases of domestic violence were reported to the police in 2009, only 55 cases had been initiated by the police under the law; see *Sri Lanka: State of Human Rights 2015* (Law & Society Trust, 2015) 153. For some recent writing on the operation of domestic violence law, see 'INSIDE JUSTICE: Ensuring Formal Justice Sector Responsibility and Accountability to Redress Sexual and Gender Based Violence (SGBV) against Women and Girls in Sri Lanka', Baseline Report by Udeni Thewarapperuma for the Asia Foundation's Inside Justice Project; Women in Need (WIN), 'Why Accessing Justice is challenging for Victims of Sexual and Gender Based Violence?' (Asia Foundation, 2019); Women and Media Collective, 'Inside Justice: Media Mapping' (Asia Foundation, 2019).

[83] M Gomez and S Gomez, *Preferring Women: Gender and Politics in Sri Lanka* (Shakti, 2001).

[84] One of the early human rights treaties was the Convention on the Political Rights of Women (1954) adopted by the United Nations in 1952, which set international benchmarks for the participation of women in public life. See CEDAW General Recommendation No 23 on 'Political and Public Life' (1997); Human Rights Committee, General Comment No 28 on Article 3 (The Equality of Rights Between Men and Women) (29 March 2000) para 29.

[85] The Government's Proposals for Constitutional Reform, October 1997 (Ministry of Justice, Constitutional Affairs, Ethnic Affairs and National Integration), Regional List in the Second Sch, para 42.

draft was released after opposition from certain political parties. That process of constitution-making collapsed and the 2000 draft Constitution was not adopted by Parliament.

The system of local government quotas adopted in Sri Lanka was a weak and complicated one.[86] Sri Lankan women received the right to vote and the right to stand for election in 1931, eight years after the United Kingdom.[87] And until 2018, women never held more than six per cent of the seats at any level of government.[88] Currently there are 12 members in the 225-member Parliament, elected at the August 2020 Parliamentary election. There were 13 members in the previous Parliament (dissolved in March 2020).[89] There have never been more than 13 women Members of Parliament since 1947.[90] Representation at the local and provincial levels has varied between two and three per cent.[91] Despite these low numbers, Sri Lanka gave the world the first woman Prime Minister in the early 1960s, and her daughter served as President of the country from 1994 to 2005.

Table 13.2 Parliamentary representation of women since independence (1947–2020)

Year	Total	Women	% of women
1947–1952	101	3	3.0
1952–1956	101	2	2.0
1956–1959	101	4	4.0
1960 (March–April)	157	3	1.9
1960 (July)–1964	157	3	1.9
1965–1970	157	6	3.8
1970–1977	157	6	3.8
1977–1989	168	11	6.5
1989–1994	225	13	5.8

(continued)

[86] See C Kodikara and K Samuel, 'The Significance of the 25% Quota for Women in Local Government' *Groundviews* (7 February 2018), available at groundviews.org/2018/02/07/the-significance-of-the-25-quota-for-women-in-local-government; Law & Society Trust, 'Women's Political Participation in Sri Lanka's 2020 Parliamentary Election' (6 March 2020), available at lstlanka.org/lst_media/womens-political-participation-in-sri-lankas-2020-parliamentary-election.

[87] M de Alwis and K Jayawardena, *Casting Pearls: The Women's Franchise Movement in Sri Lanka* (Social Scientists' Association, 2001).

[88] Sri Lankan women received the right to vote earlier than their South Asian counterparts. Women in India, Pakistan, Bangladesh and Nepal received the right to vote and the right to stand for election in 1952, 1948, 1972 and 1951 respectively; UNDP, *Human Development in South Asia 1999: The Crisis of Governance* (Oxford University Press, 1999) 187.

[89] Parliament of Sri Lanka, 'Member Appointments/Portfolios', available at www.parliament.lk/en/members-of-parliament/statistics.

[90] V Gunasekera, 'Barriers to Women's Political Participation in Sri Lanka: Literature Review' (International Centre for Ethnic Studies, unpublished, 2020) on file with the author.

[91] Provincial Councils were introduced through the 13th Amendment to the Constitution in 1987.

Table 13.2 *(Continued)*

Year	Total	Women	% of women
1994–2000	225	12	5.3
2000–2001	225	9	4.0
2001–2004	225	10	4.4
2004–2010	225	13	5.8
2010–2014	225	13	5.8
2015–2019	225	13	5.8
2020–	225	12	5.3
(12 women members were originally elected in 1994. The President resigned her seat when she was elected President)			

Source: *Parliamentary Handbook*, cited in www.statistics.gov.lk/GenderStatistics/StaticalInformation/Publications/TheSriLankanWoman-PartnerinProgress2014.

Sri Lankan women's groups were initially divided in their support for quotas. But in 2001, these groups coalesced in their support for a mandatory quota. Prior to the October 2000 election, 12 women's groups came together to release a Women's Manifesto that called for a reservation for women at local, provincial and parliamentary levels.[92] This call has been repeated in subsequent manifestos,[93] the most recent of which[94] recommended that the number of cabinet ministers not exceed 20; that at least 25 per cent of the Cabinet consist of women; that the Government establish a new electoral system based on a combination of first-past-the-post seats and proportional representation; that temporary special measures be taken to ensure a minimum of 25 per cent representation of women, including at the decision-making level, in Parliament, and in government agencies; and that provisions be made, under the 19th Amendment, to establish an independent National Commission on Women and to ensure a gender balance in appointments to all independent Commissions.

The quota for women was introduced through three legal changes made to the local government elections law – in 2012, 2016 and 2017.[95] The number of local government seats was increased by one-third to accommodate these changes. According to the system that was introduced, 60 per cent of the seats were to be elected through the first-past-the-post system, and 40 per cent through proportional representation. The law stipulated that, overall, not less

[92] Gomez and Gomez (n 83) 84.

[93] See the Women's Manifesto for 2019–20, which reiterates a call for a 25% reservation, on file with the author.

[94] ibid.

[95] Local Authorities Elections (Amendment) Act No 22 of 2012; Local Authorities Elections (Amendment) Act No 1 of 2016; Local Authorities Elections (Amendment) Act No 16 of 2017.

than 25 per cent of the members in each local authority should be women. Vijeyarasa notes:

> [W]hile often described as a '25 per cent quota' for women, the laws together created the potential for the total number of women representatives at the local level to surpass 25% … In any case, the law seemed to be clear about one thing: the final result must be that not less than 25% of elected members per ward are women, which is guaranteed if necessary through the reward quota.[96]

The quota was applied for the first time at the local government elections in February 2018, which saw approximately 23 per cent of women elected. While the number of women represented at that level increased, the impact of the quota on driving a transformative agenda around women's rights and gender equality is debatable. Vijeyarasa observes that the quota resulted in the overt selection of party members' relatives and has to date done little to challenge patronage politics whereby nominated women are relatives of existing politicians, a 'widows, daughters and wives syndrome'.[97]

D. Other Notable Laws

Other laws that advanced the constitutional values of sexual equality include the Citizenship Act (CA) and the Maintenance Act (MA) of 1999. The CA, before its amendment, provided that a child may acquire citizenship from their father, grandfather or great grandfather. This provision was amended in 2003 to allow either parent who is or was a citizen of Sri Lanka to convey nationality to their children.[98] The MA introduced a concept of joint responsibility between husband and wife for family support and maintenance – a departure from a previous system that placed the primary obligation on the husband.[99] Changes were also made to laws governing maternity benefits. Under the initial law, a female worker was entitled to 84 days or 12 weeks of leave only for the first two children. She was granted half that entitlement for any subsequent children. These provisions were amended in 2018 to ensure the same leave entitlement for all children.[100] In 2016, a circular issued by the Ministry of Health permits the

[96] R Vijeyarasa, 'Women's absence in Sri Lankan politics: Lessons on the effectiveness and limitations of Quotas to Address Under-representation' (2020) 81 *Women Studies International Forum* 102371, 5; see also Jakimow, Gomez, Gunasekera, Harahap, Siahaan, Vanniasinkam, Vijeyarasa and Yumasdaleni, 'Broken Pathways to Politics: Clearing a Path from Grassroots to Representative Politics' (2023) *Journal of Women, Politics & Policy*, DOI: 10.1080/1554477X.2023.217436.

[97] Vijeyarasa (n 96) 6–9.

[98] Citizenship Act No 18 of 1948, as amended by the Citizenship (Amendment) Act No 35 of 2003.

[99] Maintenance Act No 37 of 1999; see S Goonesekere, 'Family Support and Maintenance: Emerging Issues in Some Developing Countries with Mixed Jurisdictions' (2006) 44 *Family Court Review* 361, 363.

[100] Shop and Office Employees (Regulation of Employment and Remuneration) (Amendment) Act No 14 of 2018 and the Maternity Benefits (Amendment) Act No 15 of 2018. See also

amending of the sex in the birth certificate to reflect the sexual identity with which an individual relates.[101]

VI. PROPOSED REFORMS

A. A National Commission for Women

For over two decades, the women's movement has been advocating for the enactment of the Women's Charter into a legally binding instrument and for the transformation of the National Committee on Women into an independent women's commission. Since the Women's Charter in 1993, despite several drafts and multiple engagements by women advocates with state actors, the proposal has not been enacted into law.[102]

A proposal to create a women's commission was first floated in 1998.[103] The main function of the Commission in terms of that draft law was to be the 'the promotion, advancement and protection of the rights of women within the framework of the guidelines provided by the Women's Charter of Sri Lanka.'[104] That legislation was not passed by Parliament. Since then, other draft laws were released in 2002, 2004, 2007 and 2009.

Once again, in February 2017, the Cabinet approved a proposal to establish a National Commission and a further draft was developed in 2018.[105] However, with few champions of gender equality within the political establishment, this law has not been passed by Parliament. That a law to establish a Women's Commission was first floated in 1998 and remains unenacted 25 years later is illustrative of the larger patriarchal values and political interests that stymie law reform in this area.

B. Reforming the Muslim Personal Law

Reforming Muslim personal laws has proven difficult despite the efforts of many women, including many Muslim women. Resistance to reform has come mainly from groups within the Muslim community who oppose gender

SME Goonetilleke, 'Maternity Legislation in Sri Lanka: Are Women Equal, Special or Different?' (2016) 11 *OUSL Journal* 53, 62.

[101] Ministry of Health, General Circular 01–34 of 16 June 2016, on file with the author.

[102] The non-enforceable Women's Charter was adopted by the state in 1993. The Charter established a National Committee on Women to monitor the rights set out in the Charter.

[103] A Bill to provide for the establishment of a National Commission on Women for the promotion, advancement and protection of rights of women in Sri Lanka (14 September 1998) on file with the author; see also Gomez and Gomez (n 46) 111–22.

[104] A Bill to provide for the establishment of a National Commission on Women for the promotion, advancement and protection of rights of women in Sri Lanka, issued on 14 September 1998, s 13.

[105] National Commission on Women Bill (2 August 2018) on file with the author.

equality.[106] The constitution preserves the sanctity of past law even if it conflicts with fundamental rights.[107] The clause was introduced to preserve the operation and applicability of Muslim and other personal laws, even in cases where there was a constitutional conflict.[108] Reform of the Muslim Marriage and Divorce Act of 1951 (MMDA) has been resisted by Muslim hardliners for many years.

Currently Muslims are not allowed to opt out of the MMDA and marry under the General Marriages Registration Ordinance. Muslim and other women have advocated for five key reforms to advance the rights of the married Muslim woman: raising the minimum age of marriage to 18, in line with the general law, with the proviso that marriages of girls over 16 can take place with the permission of the *quazi*;[109] the representation of women as *quazis* and on the Board of *Quazis*; the first forum of appeal under the MMDA; the mandatory consent of the woman, to marriage, as evidenced by her signature or thumb print; conditional polygamy; and that lawyers appointed as *quazis* should have a sound knowledge of Muslim law.[110] A proposal permitting Muslims to opt out of the Muslim law and to marry under the general marriage law is also being contemplated.[111]

VII. CONCLUSION: TRANSFORMING UNEQUAL GENDER RELATIONS AND HIERARCHIES

Constitutional law and litigation have not had a transformative impact on gender relations in Sri Lanka. The constitutional forum has been used only sporadically by gender-equality advocates and the jurisprudence on gender relations has been sparse. While there has been some important jurisprudence

[106] A Faaiz, 'Muslim Marriage and Divorce Act: The Struggle for Reform' in SA Saroor (ed), *Muslims in Post-War Sri Lanka: Repression, Resistance and Reform* (Perera Hussein, 2021) 136.

[107] The Constitution, Art 16.

[108] Three main personal laws apply in the country: the Kandyan Law, the Muslim Law and Thesavalamai (applicable to Tamils with a domicile in the Northern Province). These personal laws operate in limited circumstances, mainly in relation to marriage, divorce, inheritance and the adoption of children. See generally, L Marasinghe and S Scharenguivel (eds), *Compilation of Selected Aspects of The Special Laws of Sri Lanka* (Vijitha Yapa, 2015); S Goonesekere, *The Legal Status of the Female in Family Relations in Sri Lanka* (Gunasena, 1980); S Goonesekere, *Muslim Personal Laws in Sri Lanka* (Muslim Women's Research and Action Forum, 2000); C Kodikara, *Muslim Family Law in Sri Lanka: Theory, Practice and Issues of Concern to Women* (Muslim Women's Research and Action Forum, 1999); K Nagendra, *Matrimonial Property and Gender Inequality: A Study of Thesawalamai* (Stamford Lake, 2008).

[109] *Quazis*, sometimes spelt *Qadis*, are judges administering the Muslim Personal Law.

[110] See the position papers on the 'Muslim Personal Law Action Reforms Group (MPLRAG)', available at www.mplreforms.com; 'MMDA Reform: Where are we now?' *Daily Mirror* (24 August 2020).

[111] Interview with Muslim women's activist, on file with the author. In 2021, a Private Members' Bill was presented in Parliament to permit Muslims to opt out of the Muslim law, and to set the minimum age of marriage for *all* at 18. Parliament was prorogued before the bill could be debated.

that has advanced the rights of women and sexual minorities,[112] it would be hard to describe these developments as transformative. However, some of the decisions discussed above indicate that this may be changing.

In other areas of the law, which include environmental law, religious rights and administrative justice, constitutional review – whether rights-based or related to bills prior to enactment – constitutional litigation has had a bigger impact.[113] This, however, has not occurred in the area of gender equality and non-discrimination or with regard to rights of sexual minorities, despite Sri Lanka having had a vibrant legal culture and an independent judiciary even if it has occasionally gone through periods of constitutional authoritarianism and democratic backsliding.[114]

Many battles around gender inequality have been fought in other forums, including judicial and legislative forums. Women advocates have relied on constitutional rights and international norms to drive the law-reform process, to propel gender-sensitive laws, and to modify existing legislation.[115] Progressive legal reform advancing equality and women's rights has occurred when three factors have come together: sustained activism and advocacy by women's and other groups, a tolerant political culture that has enabled civil society to engage with policy-makers, and sensitive public officers and 'champions of equality' within government who have facilitated reform.

Law reform, however, does not always result in tangible outcomes on the ground. The outcomes that law reform generates would depend on multiple factors, including the effectiveness of civil society in raising public awareness and mobilising public opinion around the change; the acts of judges, lawyers, prosecutors and others involved with implementing new or modified legislation; the frequency of the legal challenges mounted under the new laws; the support provided to those who litigate under new laws; and the imagination of the bench and the bar in developing new legal arguments. Public attitudes grounded in patriarchal values remains one of the biggest obstacles to gender equality, and even progressive constitutional jurisprudence and legal reform may have a limited impact on transforming these public attitudes.

In politics, advocates for equality have had less success, due largely to the intense competition for political power among different parties. Male political actors have shown a strong resistance to giving up their power. The new

[112] For example, the cases on sexual harassment, and the criminal appeal on consensual homosexual relations, discussed above.

[113] Gomez, 'Mixing Writs with Rights' (n 44); B Schonthal, 'Litigating Vinaya: Buddhist Law and Public Law in Contemporary Sri Lanka' (2018) 3 *Buddhism Law & Society* 1. Schonthal in this piece argues that the Buddhist right has often resorted to litigation to advance their interests and points of view.

[114] See Gomez (n 12).

[115] This includes the laws on domestic violence, the amendments to the Penal Code in 1995, the amendments to the Maintenance Act and Citizenship Act discussed above, and the introduction of the women's quota at local government level.

local government quota, despite its complicated nature and despite its minimal impact, is a small step forward. But its impact will be limited until male political actors concede to their female counterparts and quotas are introduced at the national and provincial level as well.

However, some of the cases discussed in this chapter suggest that judicial attitudes may be changing to accommodate the perspectives and rights of women and sexual minorities. The cases on consensual same-sex relations, on sexual harassment at the workplace, on religious rights and free expression,[116] and on the Land Development Ordinance, discussed above, illustrate a change in judicial approach. This will encourage equality advocates to resort to constitutional norms and litigation more frequently. Favourable judicial decisions can catalyse further litigation around women's rights and the rights of sexual minorities and help build a robust jurisprudence in this area.

Currently, Sri Lanka is in the midst of its worst economic crisis. Inflation, a depreciating currency, shortages of fuel, power, medical supplies, and other essential goods, generated unprecedented street protests calling for reform of the country's political culture and political institutions. It resulted in the resignation of a Prime Minister and President. Women and the LGBTI community have been important players in this ongoing struggle for economic and political reform. It is not clear if this spontaneous people's movement will result in tangible outcomes, the creation of robust and democratic institutions, and a more democratic culture. Should this struggle result in positive democratic outcomes, then gender equality and equality for sexual minorities should be a pivotal part of this change. In other Asian societies, advocates and lawyers continue to struggle against patriarchal structures and intransigent attitudes. A popular people's movement opens the possibility of creating a different and transformative path towards real gender equality.

[116] The *Cokeman* case (n 49).

Index

References to tables are indicated by the page number followed by an *italic t*.

Printed in the USA
CPSIA information can be obtained
at www.ICGtesting.com
LVHW012055220124
769580LV00004B/58

9 781509 941919